The Diaries of a Cabinet Minister

RICHARD CROSSMAN

THE DIARIES
OF A
CABINET MINISTER

Volume I
1964–1966

Holt, Rinehart and Winston
New York

LIBRARY OF CONGRESS CATALOG CARD NUMBER: 75-37128
ISBN: 0–03–017466–X

FIRST PUBLISHED IN THE UNITED STATES IN 1976

PRINTED IN GREAT BRITAIN
10 9 8 7 6 5 4 3 2 1

Contents

Illustrations

Editorial Note

Short biographies of front-benchers and those who are mentioned frequently in the text will be found in the Biographical Notes. Those mentioned less frequently are given a footnote on the page on which they first appear. The notes do not take account of events after polling day, February 28th, 1974.

Introduction

This book is part of a diary which I kept from 1952 to the end of 1970. When I started it the Bevanite controversy was tearing the Labour Party to pieces, and I was one of the most active participants on the National Executive Committee. I felt that if no one kept a chronicle of it, in twenty years' time it would be impossible for a historian to get any coherent and continuous picture of what went on among the Bevanites.

This worried me, for though I had been an Oxford City councillor in the 1930s and was duly elected M.P. for a Coventry constituency in 1945, I was not only a politician. Unlike most of my colleagues in the council chamber and in Parliament I was an observer as well as a doer, a political scientist as well as a journalist M.P. And though I earned my living and served Bevan's cause by writing for the *Sunday Pictorial* and the *New Statesman*, my ambition was to write a book which fulfilled for our generation the functions of Bagehot's *English Constitution*[1] a hundred years ago by disclosing the secret operations of government, which are concealed by the thick masses of foliage which we call the myth of democracy. I knew that no academic could write this book. It could only be done by someone who knew party politics from inside, and that must include council politics, parliamentary politics and if possible the politics of Whitehall and No. 10.

By 1961 I had collected enough firm information to write a book on the working of the two-party system inside and outside Westminster, but my knowledge of government was all gathered from academic textbooks and the gossip of the smoking-room. Even worse, my chance of being offered a place in the Cabinet (the only job I would by then accept) was small. By organizing the opposition to Bevin's Palestine policy I had got myself excluded from any post under Attlee, and indeed from any role on the Opposition front bench for the next twelve years. When Gaitskell replaced Attlee I reckoned my chances were not substantially improved. I decided to find some academic post where I could write my books and resume the teaching which I enjoyed better than anything else.

But as Harold Laski used to remind us, in British politics while there is death there is hope. Gaitskell died and Harold Wilson succeeded him. My

[1] London: Fontana, 1963.

prospects were transformed. In the inner circle of the Bevanite group he and I had formed ourselves into a left-of-centre sub-group, well to the right of the devotees. As such, we had gone through some very unpleasant experiences together without our friendship being destroyed—partly because we had both learnt that, if they are to last, friendships in politics are best kept cool and detached. After I had helped to get Harold elected leader, and had accepted what seemed a modest place in his shadow administration (I was shadow Minister of Higher Education and Science) I was fairly sure that I would be one of Harold's own choices for Cabinet, as contrasted with the majority which he was committed by circumstances to accept.

We had not long to wait. The election came in the autumn, and when I went to No. 10 on October 17th I was told there had been a sudden change of plan; I was not to be Secretary of State for Education but Minister of Housing.

About this job I knew virtually nothing. Indeed, the only preparations I had made which were of any use were those that concerned my diary. Jennie Hall, my secretary, agreed to become my archivist and to look after the tapes on which the diary would be dictated each weekend at my home in North Oxfordshire. Transcription of the tapes, for obvious security reasons, would not be attempted till later in the life of the Government. I was aware when I made these arrangements that if I could achieve a continuous record of my whole Ministerial life, dictated while the memory was still hot and uncorrupted by 'improvements', this part of the diary would become of quite special historical value. At first I was thinking of it mainly as raw material to be used in my own book. But it was not very long before I realized the interest of a diary which gave a daily picture of how a Minister of the Wilson Government spent his time, exactly what he did in his Department, in Cabinet Committee and in Cabinet itself, and how much official time he spent outside his office visiting authorities under his control, and finally what he had left for his family at the weekend.

Memory is a terrible improver—even with a diary to check the tendency. And it is this which makes a politician's autobiography (even when he claims his rights and uses the official Cabinet papers) so wildly unreliable. Had I, for example, left this section of my diary unpublished for fifteen years and then based the relevant chapters of my memoirs on it, the best I could have hoped for was a book as reliable as the memoirs of Hugh Dalton[1] or of Harold Macmillan.[2] But if I could publish a diary of my years as a Minister without any editorial improvements, as a true record of how one Minister thought and felt, I would have done something towards lighting up the secret places of British politics and enabling any intelligent elector to have a picture of what went on behind the scenes between 1964 and 1970.

Of course the record is not complete, it never could be. But it is vastly fuller

[1] 3 volumes (London: Frederick Muller, 1953, 1956, 1962).
[2] 6 volumes (London: Macmillan, 1966, 1967, 1969, 1971, 1972, 1973).

than the kind of jottings on which most politicians base their memoirs. In writing it (the task to which I devoted most of Saturday evening and Sunday morning each week), I had before me a careful selection of all the relevant Cabinet and departmental papers—a task to which one member of my Private Office was always assigned. I also had a detailed record of my life each day—so far as my Private Office knew it. But this of course excluded my Party work, and as far as possible my private meetings with other Ministers and activities outside Westminster.

Of course the picture which this diary provides is neither objective nor fair—although as a lifelong political scientist I have tried to discipline myself to objectivity. In particular I have tried to avoid self-deception, especially about my own motives; the tendency to attribute to others my own worst failings; and the temptation to omit what might make me look silly in print. I have been urged by many to remove all the wounding passages about colleagues or officials. I have not done so because it would make the book untrue, and I hope that when some of them find me intolerably unfair, they will recall the follies and illusions I faithfully record about myself. A day-by-day account of a Government at work, as seen by one participant, is bound to be one-sided and immensely partisan. If it isn't, it too would fail to be true to life.

But why publish this record so soon, when many of the participants are still active in Government? To this question, over which I have pondered long, there are two replies. In the first place, there is now a ten-year gap between the date on which the diary begins and the date of publication. Reading the manuscript I found that most of it sounded like ancient history, much more remote than the Suez fiasco was when Lord Avon, with the help of all the State Papers, published his personal apologia a year or two after the event—indeed about as remote as the Profumo incident was when Harold Macmillan gave his fascinating version of it in his sixth volume. From Churchill downwards there are endless precedents for disregarding the thirty-year rule which is such a burden to professional English historians.

Since ex-Cabinet Ministers are entitled to access to secret documents when they publish their memoirs, and rely for their accounts of Cabinet proceedings mainly on memory, how much to publish is not a matter of Government ruling, far less of the Official Secrets Act, but a concern of personal taste and personal conscience. All my colleagues knew of the diary I was keeping and of my determination to publish it as soon as possible. Apart from the lawyers, who feather their nests in other ways, none of them had any moral objection. Indeed, Mr Wilson and Lord George-Brown have already gone into print, the first in a personal history which includes many controversial passages,[1] the second in a jolly book of memoirs[2] which seemed to me superior to those

[1] Harold Wilson, *The Labour Government 1964–70, A Personal Record* (London: Weidenfeld & Nicolson and Michael Joseph, 1971), hereafter cited as *Wilson*.
[2] Lord George-Brown, *In My Way* (London: Gollancz, 1971).

of Lord Wigg.[1] I have plenty of precedent therefore for making my own decision about publication.

But since these diaries provide so much new information, both trivial and important, I felt bound to consult my colleagues—in particular Mr Wilson and Mr Callaghan. Both begged me to promise them that I would not publish 'before the next election'. The surprise Heath election of 1974 removed an inhibition which I would have taken very seriously if it had imposed on me any further delay.

There is a second reason why the time interval should not be too long. In our own country these diaries are the first of their kind to appear in print, and the publication of the later volumes is unlikely to be completed until at least a year after the first volume. Since many passages will be vigorously challenged, it is best both for the personalities involved and for the historian that the controversy should take place while memories are green. Moreover, it is not only factual points which come under fire. In writing this book I assumed a theory of modern British democracy for which I am greatly indebted to Professor John Mackintosh. This theory has been challenged and to a considerable extent clarified in academic debate. I believe these diaries will provide our political scientists with a considerable mass of material on the basis of which the controversy can be carried further.

One final objection remains to be met before I close this introduction. Volume I, I shall be told, is already far too long. Why not cut out all the trivial descriptions of visitations to local authorities, all the accounts of detailed discussions at Cabinet Committees, all the records of how my Bills fared in Parliament, in order to concentrate on the political secrets of Cabinet government—what really happened in Cabinet—as well as the personal intrigues behind the scenes?

My answer is that though this kind of selection from these diaries might provide some sensational material for serialization in the Sunday press, they would cease to be a true account of the life of the Minister of Housing between 1964 and 1966. When I dictated my stint each weekend I included all that had impressed me in the previous week's activities and the remarks or conversations that stuck in my memory. One of the interests in reading it is to observe how obsessed I became only too often with minor departmental matters, so that I was scarcely aware of the great issues which were being decided in Cabinet while my mind was wandering or even while I snoozed in my chair.

It was the fact that the diaries faithfully reflected the total impression that I thought might give them special value. That is why after consultation with Mr Graham C. Greene I decided that there should be no expurgation and no excision except when passages were trivial, libellous or inaccurate. I have, however, included a fairly rich selection of my own generalizations and predictions, which sometimes provide an exercise in self-punishment since some of them read very foolishly today.

[1] Lord Wigg, *George Wigg* (London: Michael Joseph, 1972), hereafter cited as *Wigg*.

The reader can be assured, therefore, that this volume is a slightly shortened but completely unexpurgated version of the diary I kept during my twenty-two months at the Ministry of Housing.

Since the original, however, was not written or typed but dictated very much ad lib and often for two or three hours on end, I found that when transcribed it was hardly readable. It was full of passages which were mere repetitions of the previous week, sentences where, while I was fumbling for the right phrase, I repeated what I had just said, and finally there were paragraphs when I got tired but kept on dictating, producing tracts of windy verbosity devoid of grammar as well as of sense.

I decided therefore to re-dictate this whole first transcript in plain intelligible English. And in order to make sure that I didn't introduce any 'improvements' into the text, I persuaded Dr Janet Morgan of Nuffield College to be my historian, with the special task of comparing the text I proposed to publish with the original transcript, and making sure that the second version was faithful to the first. Dr Morgan is also entirely responsible for the link passages, the numbered notes and the biographical notes. Only the starred notes are by me. For students who are interested in textual problems the full text of the transcript will be permanently available in Warwick University.

FEBRUARY 1974   R.H.S.C.

1964

Thirteen years of Conservative government came to an end when Labour won the general election in 1964. In the late 1950s and early 1960s Conservative rule seemed to have brought Britain prosperity at home and, abroad, smooth disengagement from empire together with a policy of strong alliance with America and with NATO. But 1963 was an unhappy year for the Tories. Britain was excluded from the European Economic Community by General de Gaulle's veto, there were complications over the NATO alliance and even the deft leadership of Harold Macmillan could not camouflage the Conservatives' embarrassment over the security scandals of the summer. Macmillan staunchly hoped to lead the Party until the next general election but in October, on the crest of his success with the Test Ban Treaty, sudden illness obliged him to resign. This precipitated acrimonious quarrels within the Party and in public which continued until eventually Sir Alec Douglas-Home emerged as his successor.

Comparison with the Opposition made the Government front bench appear all the more weary and disheartened. Harold Wilson had become Leader of the Labour Party after Gaitskell's death in 1963 and he and his team offered a programme of effective socialist policies with scientific and technological development at their core. Mr Wilson had been an economic adviser himself at the Board of Trade, and he was younger than Sir Alec by thirteen years. He had an enthusiasm for new men and new policies similar to that with which President Kennedy had so impressed the American electorate in 1960.

Sir Alec and his advisers decided not to call an election until the autumn of 1964, at the very end of the 1959 Parliament's statutory life. Although Labour had won an overwhelming number of seats in the spring elections for the new Greater London Council and had had some notable victories in the other county council elections and some borough elections, evidence from by-elections and polls nevertheless showed a fairly even balance between Labour and Conservative support. The Conservatives, unlike Labour, had sufficient funds to maintain an advertising campaign throughout the summer and by October their leader hoped to have pulled his party together.

The international situation was far from calm; but both front benches were broadly agreed on Britain's policy and the role of her troops in the trouble-spots of Borneo, Aden and Cyprus. Of special anxiety to the Conservatives was Southern Rhodesia's demand for independence before her black population was fully enfranchised: black Commonwealth countries expected Britain to insist that independence be deferred; while Tory voters at home were likely to sympathize with the case of the white settlers in Rhodesia, with whom they felt ties of kinship. Sir Alec was able to smooth the issue through the Commonwealth Conference that met in London in the summer, and bargained with the Rhodesian Prime Minister for an official referendum on the matter, but some observers felt that a confrontation had only been postponed.

The general public, however, were more immediately concerned with the state of the economy at home rather than with affairs abroad. The spring budget had been designed to maintain expansion without inflation, and there had been little that was novel. Confidence rose on the Stock Exchange, unemployment fell during the summer and, until June, the reserves rose. But in that month gold reserves fell by £20 million, the trade gap widened and export figures fell away; and in July and August the situation continued to be worrying. Moreover, industrial production had been stagnant throughout 1964. But it was not until September, in the midst of the election campaign, that the Opposition leader attacked the Government's economic record. Mr Wilson did not wish to be blamed for accelerating a crisis of confidence in sterling and, certainly during the earlier part of the year, the Labour leadership suspected that the electorate would attach some responsibility for Britain's poor industrial performance to the strikes and strike threats that the unions had provoked. A strike of steel craftsmen was followed by that of manual workers in the electricity-supply industry and, later, by a strike of television technicians; and there was trouble at a Birmingham motor-components works only three weeks before the election. The opinion polls showed little difference in support for the two main parties in the first week of October. The Conservatives had a very slight lead, but perhaps Labour's morale was higher.

The election took place on Thursday, October 15th. Turn-out was 77 per cent, lower than at the previous general election. Labour had an overall majority of four seats and thus dislodged the Conservatives at last. Labour took 317 seats (44·1 per cent of the poll), the Conservatives 303 (43·4 per cent), and the Liberals 9 (11·2 per cent), and the election was therefore dubbed one not that Labour won but that the Conservatives lost. To have run so close, however, was seen as a personal vindication for Sir Alec; and there was some speculation that had the electorate known, as they knew on October 16th, of the fall of Khrushchev and the explosion in China of a nuclear weapon, the Conservatives, with their proclaimed support for an independent deterrent, might have won after all. The economic crisis was most urgent. A memorandum which the Treasury presented to the incoming Prime Minister showed an £800 million deficit on overseas payments in 1964, with little prospect of improvement. The Prime Minister, the First Secretary and the Chancellor advised the Cabinet of their decision to impose a 15 per cent surcharge on all imports, except foodstuffs and raw materials, for a temporary period of some six months. This aroused angry complaints from the E.E.C. and EFTA.

Labour's election manifesto had promised to re-nationalize steel and to extend the powers of the national British Road Services Company. They would repeal the Rent Act and establish a Parliamentary Commissioner to investigate complaints against Government Departments. Secondary education was to be reorganized on comprehensive lines, regional planning boards set up and enterprise stimulated by tax changes. Employees would be given a charter of rights, trade-union law would be revised and new social security schemes introduced. The Cabinet reviewed these promises when they met to discuss the Queen's Speech for the opening of Parliament on November 3rd.

The poor state of the economy was to bedevil the Labour Government through-out its terms of office. Without resources, the Government could not afford their brave programmes and they had to make hard choices. The promised increases in old-age pensions were among the first.

In their manifesto Labour had promised to set up four new ministries: for economic planning, technology, overseas development, and for Wales. The Cabinet list that Mr Wilson published, with twenty-three members, was as cumbersome as that of Sir Alec, and older, with an average age of fifty-six.[1] There were some surprises. George Brown became First Secretary of State in charge of the new Department of Economic Affairs, and James Callaghan went to the Treasury. Despite his defeat in the election, Patrick Gordon Walker became Foreign Secretary and waited for a seat to be found for him. Denis Healey was the new Minister of Defence, and Herbert Bowden Leader of the House. Barbara Castle was given responsibility for the new Ministry of Overseas Development and Frank Cousins for the Ministry of Technology. This last appointment was a surprise, and so was the switch Mr Wilson made between his shadow Ministers of Housing and of Education. Michael Stewart went to Education and Richard Crossman to Housing. His diary begins there.

Thursday, October 22nd

I was appointed Minister of Housing on Saturday, October 17th, 1964. Now it is only the 22nd but, oh dear, it seems a long, long time. It also seems as though I had really transferred myself completely to this new life as a Cabinet Minister. In a way it's just the same as I had expected and predicted. The room in which I sit is the same in which I saw Nye Bevan for almost the first time when he was Minister of Health,[2] and already I realize the tremendous effort it requires not to be taken over by the Civil Service. My Minister's room is like a padded cell, and in certain ways I am like a person who is suddenly certified a lunatic and put safely into this great, vast room, cut off from real life and surrounded by male and female trained nurses and attendants. When I am in a good mood they occasionally allow an ordinary human being to come and visit me; but they make sure that I behave right, and that the other person behaves right; and they know how to handle me. Of course, they don't behave *quite* like nurses because the Civil Service is profoundly deferential—'Yes, Minister! No, Minister! If you wish it, Minister!'—and combined with this there is a constant preoccupation to ensure that the Minister does what is correct. The Private Secretary's job is to make sure that when the Minister comes into Whitehall he doesn't let the side or himself down and behaves in accordance with the requirements of the institution.

It's also profoundly true that one has only to do absolutely nothing whatsoever in order to be floated forward on the stream. I have forgotten

[1] See p. 633 for full Cabinet list.
[2] Between 1945 and 1951 under the first Labour Government.

what day it was—indeed, the whole of my life in the last four days has merged into one, curious, single day—when I turned to my Private Secretary, George Moseley, and said, 'Now, you must teach me how to handle all this correspondence.' And he sat opposite me with his owlish eyes and said to me, 'Well, Minister, you see there are three ways of handling it. A letter can either be answered by you personally, in your own handwriting; or we can draft a personal reply for you to sign; or, if the letter is not worth your answering personally, we can draft an official answer.' 'What's an official answer?' I asked. 'Well, it says the Minister has received your letter and then the Department replies. Anyway, we'll draft all three variants,' said Mr Moseley, 'and if you just tell us which you want ... ' 'How do I do that?' I asked. 'Well, you put all your in-tray into your out-tray,' he said, 'and if you put it in without a mark on it then we deal with it and you need never see it again.'

I think I've recorded that literally. I've only to transfer everything that's in my in-tray to my out-tray without a single mark on it to ensure it will be dealt with—all my Private Office is concerned with is to see that the routine runs on, that the Minister's life is conducted in the right way.

What about that inner office? There are my two girls, dressed very neatly. Of course they aren't typists or stenographers, in fact they can't type. They are a higher grade of civil servant, personal assistants. Sitting round the great table with these two girls is young Mr Ponsford, the Assistant Principal. Somewhere in the background is an elderly lady. She is the shorthand-typist. I have tried to use her once so far this week and she was flurried and flustered because she just couldn't handle me in an ordinary way as I was a Minister. She sits in some distant cubicle, while the real Private Office consists of the two girls, one doing my Cabinet papers, one doing my engagements, Mr Ponsford and then, in a room nearer to me, George Moseley, whom I may possibly persuade to be a real human being. At present, oh dear, he blinks, he doesn't know what to do. He is extremely efficient and pertinacious to the last degree and is desperately anxious to prevent me from doing things wrong. If ever I write a note in my own handwriting—as I did the other day—suggesting somebody should come and see me, I find a note at the bottom of my red box that night saying, 'Of course, it's perfectly all right for you to do this. But we would like you to do it like this, rather than like that.'* There he is, in the room next door to me, watching, covering me all the time, seeing that what I do is correct. I sit in my own huge room all by myself. It hasn't of course a lavatory or wash-room.† On the mantelpiece there is a clock and over

* These red boxes, which chase the Minister around, became an important part of my life. Into them were shoved all the material, all the letters I had to sign, all the briefs I had to read—just thrown together in a heap with a lot of tiny little bits of paper as well, odd things and messages from my Private Secretary. This was my night-work, and it was not too exhausting since I did it in the early morning.

† There was a little wash-room on the other side of the room but I didn't discover it for days and no one showed it to me.

it a copy of a Holbein. In the other extreme corner is a dim little print. Nothing else on these ugly, modern, panelled walls, in this vast, dreary room with the roar of Whitehall outside if I open the window.[1] There I sit, insulated from the world, with things and people presented to me in the way the Ministry of Housing and Local Government wishes to present them.

Now, how have I spent my time in this first week? It's been almost entirely spent in seeing, in series, the top officials. First came the Deputy Secretaries, Mr Jones, a clever, keen Welshman in charge of planning, and a close friend of Dame Evelyn Sharp, the Permanent Secretary, and Mr Waddell, who is in charge of housing. Next I saw the Assistant Secretaries, in charge of the various divisions under them. I also had a special separate meeting with the Chief Architect; and with the Establishments Officer who the Dame told me used to run first the housing and then the planning sides of the Ministry—a rather pleasant buffer, he has now retired into Establishments. Then there was one other session, rather a surprise to me, about water, which was entirely laid on because the Ministry wanted to make sure that as a Party we were opposed to the nationalization of water, which we are not. We've still got New Towns to come, and that will complete the main sections of the Ministry.*

At each of these meetings, which have taken about one-and-a-half to two hours, I have been able to use the seminar techniques I'm used to: I ask questions to drive them on, to find out what's on in the Department. Of course, all through I've had an underlying anxiety caused by my complete lack of contact (thank God they can't quite realize it) with the subjects I'm dealing with. It's amazing how in politics one concentrates on a few subjects. For years I've been a specialist on social security and I know enough about it. Science and education I had picked up in the months when I was Shadow Minister.[2] But I've always left out of account this field of town and country planning, how it's organized, what it does, how planning permissions are given—all this is utterly remote to me and it's all unlike what I expected. And every now and then I wake up early in the morning and I think how can I possibly cope? Won't I be detected in my first speech? And all the time at the back of my mind I am getting ready for that first time in Parliament when I have to make a speech. I suppose it will be on housing policy in the debate on the Queen's Speech.

The person who dominates all the proceedings is, of course, Dame Evelyn She's been Permanent Secretary now for ten years,[3] she is aged sixty-one,

---

* In fact there were quite a number more—local government boundaries, finance, etc.

[1] The Ministry was then situated in that end of the New Treasury Building that faces Whitehall.

[2] Until 1963, when Harold Wilson became Leader of the Labour Party, Crossman had never held front-bench office; but after Gaitskell's death he became Shadow Minister of Education and Science and fully expected to be offered this Department when Labour won the 1964 election.

[3] From 1955.

one year past retirement age, and she is only in the Department now because she can't bear to leave. She is a biggish woman, about five feet ten inches, with tremendous blue eyes which look right through you, a pale, unmade-up face, uncoloured lips. She is dressed as middle- or upper-class professional women do dress, quite expensively but rather uglily. She is really a tremendous and dominating character. She has worked with a great many Ministers before me.[1] She was under the 1945–51 Labour Government in the Silkin Ministry of Town and Country Planning and in the Reith Town and Country Planning Ministry. She comes from the planning side of things. She is rather like Beatrice Webb[2] in her attitude to life, to the Left in the sense of wanting improvement and social justice quite passionately and yet a tremendous patrician and utterly contemptuous and arrogant, regarding local authorities as children which she has to examine and rebuke for their failures. She sees the ordinary human being as incapable of making a sensible decision. Practically everybody I ask her about, when I hear of somebody who is some good, she dismisses as utterly worthless. For example, I was told by Richard Titmuss that Professor David Donnison would be a good person to help on a Rent Act, and that Peter Self of the Town and Country Planning Association was worth considering.[3] I asked Dame Evelyn about them both and she told me that the Town and Country Planning Association was a mere cypher and that Donnison is a dangerous doctrinaire. So I had them both to dinner last night and, though I found Self a little boring, they are undoubtedly extremely competent people, and Donnison, I reckon, is outstandingly intelligent and lively. But she dismisses everybody in this way. Of course she is devoted to her Department and has the Civil Service's deference to her Minister. What will she make of me? Well, the truth about Dame Evelyn is that in one sense I am lucky: the first moment she met me was a moment of crisis when her Department was in danger.

Last Saturday, when I was appointed, she drove back from her country cottage at Lavenham and told me the moment she got to London that, largely owing to me, the Department had been sold down the river by Harold Wilson's decision that Fred Willey should be in charge of planning and that I should do housing.[4] When Harold told me of this decision my main feeling was one of relief that if Fred Willey took on planning I shouldn't be respon-

[1] Including Macmillan, Sandys, Brooke, Hill and Joseph.

[2] Beatrice Webb and her husband Sidney were early Fabians, and had helped to establish the *New Statesman* and the London School of Economics. See Beatrice Webb, *Diaries*, ed. Margaret Cole (London: Longman, 1952), and Ruth Adam and Kitty Muggeridge, *Beatrice Webb* (London: Secker & Warburg, 1967).

[3] Professor of Public Administration, University of London, since 1963 and a member of the South-East Regional Economic Council since 1966. He was chairman of the Executive of the Town and Country Planning Association 1961–9.

[4] The Prime Minister's original intention after the election had been to give the planning functions of the Ministry of Housing and Local Government to a separate Ministry of Land and Natural Resources. Fred Willey served as Minister until August 1967. See *Wilson*, p. 9.

sible for the appallingly complicated Bill on the Land Commission.[1] However, the Dame explained to me that what I had unconsciously done was to demolish the whole basis of her Department, because in her view—which I now suspect is correct—it's quite impossible to give physical planning, the land policy, to a new Ministry without giving it all control of housing. If I was to accept what Harold told me, Fred Willey would run all the land policy, Charlie Pannell, as Minister of Works, would run all the materials and labour side of housing, and I would be left titularly in charge.

As soon as she realized this Dame Evelyn got down to a Whitehall battle to save her Department from my stupidity and ignorance. That battle was waged through Saturday, Sunday, Monday and Tuesday, and was really only finally decided this morning. I had imagined that the final decision had been taken after a personal talk I had with Harold on Sunday morning by telephone, when I explained what Dame Evelyn had told me. He assured me that I was to lead the housing drive and that everything was perfectly all right. On Monday morning I talked to him again and he again assured me all was O.K. On both occasions he rebuked me and Dame Evelyn for the way she had been waging her Whitehall war; and he said, 'You don't know what she is like, going behind my back to the civil servants.' I knew quite well what she was like and I knew she had gone to the head of the Civil Service, Helsby, and to Eric Roll, head of George Brown's new D.E.A. Regardless of anything that Harold had said, she continued the war, capturing Fred Willey and putting him in a room by himself in our Ministry while she got hold of his new Permanent Secretary, Mr Bishop, and lectured him.[2] Yes, she fought and fought. When on Wednesday afternoon at a meeting I turned to her and said, 'Well, Dame Evelyn, you've won,' she replied, 'It's been the worst two days of my whole life.' 'Yes,' I said, 'but you have saved physical planning for us.' And she said, 'Of course, I always win. But it was exhausting.'

Meanwhile she has been looking after me, grooming me ... well, grooming is the wrong word because she is too tough and granite-like, but she has been watching, measuring, lecturing. Her mind is entirely intellectual and I suppose she has reckoned that she has met in me, I don't say her match, but quite a formidable character. Because I am also a hard intellectual, though I seem to argue rather less than she does and sometimes I realize that argument is no good and one has to hold one's peace.

Well, I think I am getting on with her pretty well and certainly I want her on my side; and she is delighted she has won this battle. Now I think she will go ahead and enjoy running the Department with me as my number one. She asked me the other day whether I wanted to keep George Moseley and I said

[1] This body would purchase land for local authority use. The Government also intended that it should exact 'Betterment Levy', a tax on the profits from land sold for development.

[2] Frederick Bishop served as Deputy Secretary to the Cabinet 1959–61 and at the Ministry of Agriculture, Fisheries and Food 1961–4. He served as Permanent Secretary at the Ministry of Land and Natural Resources from 1964 to 1965, when he resigned. In 1971 he became Director-General of the National Trust.

I would like to think it over. But next morning on my desk I found two little message-slips written in Mr Moseley's discreet hand: 'Will you please sign these if you want me and Ponsford?' Well, I signed them! I would much rather have had a livelier, more vital young man, in whom I could confide, but I may bring George Moseley out. Maybe Jennie Hall, my secretary, was as dim and quiet as that when she first came; but Jennie is a vital, rich creature, a wonderful, full-blooded person compared with this Moseley. I hope I'll get Moseley round, because now I have signed on the dotted line I've got him for keeps along with Ponsford, who I don't much like either.

So there he is, next door to me, dim, correct, quiet, official, gradually teaching me the technique of being a Minister. One of my troubles is that I don't meet anyone but a few of these top officials. Apart from them I see the porters, who come in and carry my bag out, and I see Molly, my driver, a nice respectable woman with spectacles and red hair. But of the rest of the Ministry I only see the officials Dame Evelyn wants me to see. I can't help realizing one has to be pretty strong-minded and curious not to be got down by this astonishing Whitehall hierarchy, by the way the establishment takes you into itself and folds you into its bosom. So far I think I've held out fairly successfully, mainly through the interrogatory seminar attitude I've adopted, but also by having a group of people outside who I talk to when I get away from the Ministry. I've got Arnold Goodman, who is introducing me on Monday night to a director of Wimpey who might possibly be added to my staff as director of the housing drive. Then there's Donnison—I've fixed a meeting with him and other experts on housing whom I hope to bring in to run an appraisal unit, because I'm quite certain that one of our troubles in the Department is that the Department doesn't know really what is going on. I'm trying to keep these two practical things as my short-term aims, first to bring in a progress-chaser, a builder or developer, possibly Hyams,[1] and second to build up an appraisal unit, a mixture of technologists and economists who will provide me with eyes and ears and enable me to preside over the Ministry in the way that I need to.

During this period—Monday to Thursday—of my first week there have been two Cabinet meetings. The first was a mere formality only concerned with the economic crisis and, honestly, we were told as little about it as the National Executive of the Party is ever told. It really was an absolute farce to have George Brown saying, 'Naturally you won't want to be told, for fear of the information leaking, how serious the situation is. You won't want to be told what methods we shall take but we shall take them.'

The main interest in this Cabinet meeting was arriving in Downing Street, pushing through the herd of photographers and entering No. 10, where I have only been once or twice before, and walking down that passage with the busts standing on the left-hand side and looking along to the left to a little room

---

[1] A successful property developer, whose enormous empty office buildings, including Centre Point, later became something of a scandal.

inside which were Marcia Williams and Brenda, Harold's other secretary, and George Wigg and Tommy Balogh, all looking rather blue now because they feel they are being squeezed out and contracted by the Civil Service.

The second Cabinet meeting, which took place this morning, was much more serious. The agenda was first of all the crisis in Rhodesia, then steel, then the Queen's Speech, and then the economic crisis. On the first of these the threat that the Rhodesians would declare themselves independent was the main thing we had to deal with.[1] We received the minute describing it last night from the Defence Committee. And in my red box I found a draft by Arthur Bottomley, written before he flew out to Zambia, in which he tried to browbeat the Rhodesian Government for threatening revolt, saying that this would be a terrible thing. I was able to ask why it was that he talked of rebellion and revolt whereas in the minutes of the Defence Committee this was called a unilateral declaration of independence. That was my first intervention in Cabinet and I made this very simple point: that it surely was unwise for us to use language which implied we would take action that we couldn't and never would take, i.e. to treat them as rebels. As I say, this was my first actual Cabinet intervention and I was commended by Harold and I think the point was taken.

Then we moved on to Fred Lee's paper on steel, in which he urged that for various technical reasons nationalization should be postponed to the second Session. The moment I heard the proposal I knew it was hopeless. George Brown weighed in, saying this was absolutely fatal. Steel must be taken early in the first Session. This view of George Brown's was reflected in speech after speech, everybody realizing (a) that it was impossible to drop steel, and (b) that if we had to keep it in the programme we ought to get it through as early as possible so that when we do go to the country or when we are defeated it will be on the Land Commission or rent control or pensions, on anything except steel. This was our first real Cabinet discussion. Most people took part. Harold sits there in the middle, facing out towards the Horseguards, and on the extreme left of the long thin oval table there is Barbara and at the extreme right-wing end there is myself and Fred Lee. We are the junior members of the Cabinet; the senior members of the Cabinet are towards the middle of the table. There is Harold in the middle on the near side and there is George Brown opposite him, flanked by Gerald Gardiner, the Lord Chancellor. I notice that Harold, who sits chewing his pipe, is very careful, like Attlee; says nothing at first and lets us all make the decision. There wasn't anybody really, except Douglas Houghton, who gave the faintest sympathy to Fred Lee. When he had been absolutely trounced and defeated Fred turned to me and said, 'I got the best of that.'

---

[1] Before granting independence the British Government insisted on certain guarantees; the principle of unimpeded progress towards majority rule and the end of the discriminatory system of land apportionment were two of the most important. The Rhodesian Cabinet threatened to declare independence unilaterally.

After that we turned to the Queen's Speech. This has been my chief pre-occupation in the Department in the last four days. I've been aware from the start that my main job in the first instance in the legislative programme, and that is what the Queen's Speech is about, would be to introduce a big measure for reasserting rent control. Characteristically enough, I find that though the Labour Party has been committed for five years to the repeal of the Enoch Powell Rent Act,[1] there is only one slim series of notes by Michael Stewart[2] on the kind of way to do it in the files at Transport House. That's all there is. Everything else has to be thought up on the spot. Now, the Dame felt very strongly that that was quite enough for us in the first Session. She had been glad to get rid of the Land Commission Bill to Fred Willey. She had briefed me to go to Cabinet to say that the third inordinately complicated measure, leasehold enfranchisement,[3] should be postponed to the next Session; and it was my job in Cabinet at all costs to resist the effort to suggest that this leasehold enfranchisement (which still remains the job of our Department) should come in this Session. But it is of great interest to Welsh M.P.s and to a lesser extent to Birmingham M.P.s, and in Cabinet I found myself under enormous pressure to agree that leasehold reform should be added to the Queen's Speech. It was only thanks to the previous decision to take steel this Session that I was able to ensure that we didn't have to do this.

The formal tone of Cabinet proceedings surprised me. It is really determined by a very simple thing. We don't call each other Dick and Harold and George as we do in in the National Executive. We address each other as 'Minister of Housing' or 'First Secretary' or 'Prime Minister', and this, corresponding to the House of Commons technique, does have a curiously flattening effect and helps us to behave civilly to each other.

As for Cabinet as a decision-taking body, my first impression is that it's a much more genuine forum of opinion than I had been led to expect or than I had described in my Introduction to Bagehot.[4] On the other hand it's quite clear that the preparations for dealing with the economic crisis, the item which followed the Queen's Speech, had been entirely done by Harold Wilson himself with the help of James Callaghan, George Brown and – I imagine – Douglas Jay at the Board of Trade. The crisis programme was just imposed on the rest of us. I didn't much like that. We were given the draft of the Statement due next Monday on the crisis and the measures to meet it. Personally, I didn't think very highly of the draft but Cabinet as a whole had no advance notice so we simply had to accept the *fait accompli* or resign.

[1] Which freed from rent control over half the houses in Great Britain previously affected by rent-restriction legislation; it also raised the rent limits on most of those remaining subject to controls.

[2] He had been Shadow Minister of Housing when Labour was in Opposition.

[3] This measure would give tenants on long leases the right to eventual purchase. It had originally been a Private Members' Bill sponsored by Denis Howell, Labour M.P. for Small Heath, Birmingham. The issue was especially vital in Birmingham and South Wales.

[4] Crossman's Introduction to W. Bagehot, *The English Constitution* (London: Fontana, 1963), sets out a description of Cabinet Government.

To judge from this first meeting the Prime Minister can consult whoever he likes in a crisis and once he has consulted, Cabinet must really go along. The contrast between this and the way Harold handled the steel issue was interesting. There is, I think, more possibility of decision in Cabinet than I realized as well as more possibility of Prime Ministerial dictatorship.

I continue to have this curious sense of fiction, the feeling that I am living in a Maurice Edelman novel. All this business of being a Cabinet Minister is still unreal to me. And this feeling has been particularly strengthened by the fact that every time we left Downing Street or moved along Whitehall there was always a crowd of people watching, cheering, clapping as we went in and out—it's as if we are taking part not in real life but in a piece of reportage on the British constitutional system.

Undoubtedly the most fantastic episode in this novel was the kissing hands and the rehearsal. It took place last Monday when we new Ministers were summoned to the Privy Council offices to rehearse the ceremony of becoming a Privy Councillor. I don't suppose anything more dull, pretentious, or plain silly has ever been invented. There we were, sixteen grown men. For over an hour we were taught how to stand up, how to kneel on one knee on a cushion, how to raise the right hand with the Bible in it, how to advance three paces towards the Queen, how to take the hand and kiss it, how to move back ten paces without falling over the stools—which had been carefully arranged so that you did fall over them. Oh dear! We did this from 11.10 to 12.15. At 12.15 all of us went out, each to his own car, and we drove to the Palace and there stood about until we entered a great drawing-room. At the other end there was this little woman with a beautiful waist, and she had to stand with her hand on the table for forty minutes while we went through this rigmarole. We were uneasy, she was uneasy. Then at the end informality broke out and she said, 'You all moved backwards very nicely,' and we all laughed. And then she pressed a bell and we all left her. We were Privy Councillors: we had kissed hands.

It was two-dimensional, so thin, so like a coloured illustration in *The Sphere*, not a piece of real life. It's the thinness of it that astonishes me still; and this is true not only of kissing hands but of Cabinet meetings.

In my own Ministry I am gradually moving out of the two-dimensional into the three-dimensional stage. Dame Evelyn is emerging more and more as a sharp character and we are gradually working towards something like solid co-operation. Perhaps the most successful meeting I've had was the one to discuss the Rent Bill. We sat down at tea-time in my room and discussed the notes she had had prepared. I was in the chair—I'm always in the chair, my voice is always listened to—and I had to conduct the meeting. I must say it went very well because when it came to the point I just took out of my pocket a text of Harold's speech on the subject and said, 'Our job as politicians is to give you a clear directive, so I'll read this aloud. Let's see whether there are any holes in it or ambiguities and spaces to fill out.'

Of course, the wonderful thing for me is that I've only got to air an idea and the civil servants, once they have understood it, say 'That's enough, Minister' and go away for a week and work on it—all the detailed work I am used to having to do myself is done for me.

Well, there is the first week. I've hardly mentioned the great issues, the economic crisis and the Government's reactions to it, because I wanted to get down this impression of the life of the departmental Minister, the sense of being insulated from the world. Every time I walk down those great steps into the open air outside the Ministry I breathe in and I feel I've entered real life again. I say to myself that I mustn't let myself be cut off in there and yet the moment I enter my bag is taken out of my hand, I'm pushed in, shepherded, nursed and above all cut off, alone. I can't bring my wife in, I can't bring Jennie Hall in, any friend of mine is only there on sufferance, Whitehall envelops me. Already I've given up any other kind of life. I come back to Vincent Square[1] in the evening for a little supper. Anne[2] is up for two days this week and she is beside me, eating with me. Yet I am somehow alone when I am with her, even at home, because they have begun to insulate me from real life with the papers and the red boxes that I bring home with me.

Monday, October 26th

This evening I went to dinner with Arnold Goodman to meet Hyams, the millionaire director of Wimpey and a property magnate, who Arnold thought was a possible adviser on housing or director of the housing drive. He turned out to be a man of thirty-six or so with a dapper black beard and a nice, solid, tough wife, crude in his intellect, smooth and professional in his appearance. By the end of the evening he was trying to suggest socialist sympathies with me. It was clear after we had discussed things for a long time that he was prepared with his million pounds in the bank, his house full of Rembrandts and Picassos, to try Labour politics as an extra. I am still reflecting whether I should appoint him.

Tuesday, October 27th

We had a dinner-party here for Dame Evelyn, Richard and Patricia Llewelyn-Davies and Lord Bowden,[3] who is now ensconced as Minister of State in the Department of Education and Science with special responsibility for higher education and the research councils. I had arranged this dinner in order to discuss the absence of research and information on which to base a solid and reliable appraisal. I had suspected this before I entered the Department; everything I had seen since then confirmed it. One morning I got Thomas Balogh and we interviewed our Chief Statistician in the

---

[1] The Crossmans' house was in Vincent Square, 15 minutes' easy walk from Westminster.

[2] Mrs Crossman.

[3] Principal of the University of Manchester Institute of Science and Technology since 1964. He was Minister of State at the Department of Education and Science, October 1964–October 1965. See page 42.

Department. He has been there nine months and his division was only established two years ago and is not fully manned. Just imagine, the Ministry of Housing and Local Government didn't have a statistician before! I managed to get some fascinating facts out of this man about the shortage of staff, not only in the Ministry but in the Registrar-General's Department which is also under me, and about how vital figures from the census, which we need for our housing policy, won't be available four years from now because *my* Ministry comes at the bottom of the list for borrowing the War Office's computer. Every time the War Office wants to compute its wages, our programme has to be taken out. So I am determined to insist on a central appraisal unit, on contracts with universities for research, and on organization with the universities of refresher courses for tired civil servants. And that was the point of our dinner.

Fortunately Dame Evelyn and Richard Llewelyn-Davies got on wonderfully. But I was aware throughout that her relations with me will be difficult. They will be all right but there will always be a tension between us because of another feature of ministerial life. At first I felt like someone in a padded cell, but I must now modify this. In fact, I feel like somebody floating on the most comfortable support. The whole Department is there to support the Minister. Into his in-tray come hour by hour notes with suggestions as to what he should do. Everything is done to sustain him in the line which officials think he should take. But if one is very careful and conscious one is aware that this supporting soft framework of recommendations is the result of a great deal of secret discussion between the civil servants below. There is a constant debate as to how the Minister should be advised or, shall we say, directed and pushed and cajoled into the line required by the Ministry. There is a tremendous *esprit de corps* in the Ministry and the whole hierarchy is determined to preserve its own policy. Each Ministry has its own departmental policy, and this policy goes on while Ministers come and go. And in this world, though the civil servants have a respect for the Minister, they have a much stronger loyalty to the Ministry. Were the Minister to challenge and direct the Ministry policy there would be no formal tension at first, only quiet resistance — but a great deal of it. I am therefore always on the look-out to see how far my own ideas are getting across, how far they are merely tolerated by the Ministry, and how far the Ministry policies are being imposed on my own mind.

Wednesday, October 28th
One of the most curious features in this new ministerial life is that one can't distinguish day from day or even day from night. Life seems to go on in a curious, new, abstracted, unbroken continuity, cutting one off from normal human relations. This week, for example, the children[1] had their mid-term holiday and after I had come up on Sunday night by train to avoid the crush

[1] Virginia, aged five, and Patrick, aged seven.

of the Motor Show traffic Anne brought the children up by car and they stayed at Vincent Square on Monday and Tuesday. Patrick was sharing the top flat with Tam Dalyell and Virginia was in my dressing-room on the ground floor. They behaved really very well indeed. They did their usual rounds, a day at the Science Museum with their mother, a day at St Paul's with Jennie, and they shopped and they were about the house, in the passages, playing games in the sitting-room, dashing, booming round. They had their life and curiously enough they knew I had my life and the two lives went on parallel in the house so they didn't even want me to read to them much when I came in. This was the kind of atmosphere we had. They were there coexisting with me but in a different dimension.

Yesterday, Tuesday morning, I brought them into the Ministry with my driver Molly in the great black Ministry Super-Snipe, and I allowed them to go up to my room before they went back across the park. They quite enjoyed it, seeing this great room in which Pop lives but they knew that they were in Pop's sad world and they were strangers from another planet.

I woke up with a terrible cold today and after breakfast I went off to Transport House for the first meeting of the N.E.C. since the general election. We started with a kind of desultory discussion of the election results during which I managed to read through my Ministry papers and prepare myself for the day. So I sat in the Executive and digested the views which Dame Evelyn had given me about the line I should take at the Cabinet meeting at 3.30 this afternoon.

I was able to get away at 11.15 for an important meeting with Jones and James MacColl* on the Span Company's proposal for a new model village in the green belt in Kent.[1] I had read in the papers in my red box about Kent County Council's refusal to permit this development. The company appealed against this refusal, and the Ministry had as usual appointed an Inspector. He had upheld the county council and now my officials recommended me to reverse this finding and permit the new model village to be built. This was the first major planning decision I had and I knew I had to think it over very carefully. The Span case was that one just had to have villages like this in the green belt to deal with the population explosion in London and prevent it spilling out further and creating even further urban sprawl. My instinct was to disagree with my officials, partly because it meant I was overriding the decision of the inspector and one shouldn't do this without substantial reason, and partly because it seemed to me that the amenity reasons for not allowing

* James MacColl was my Parliamentary Secretary, whom I had got by great good fortune. When I rang Harold Wilson that Monday morning about the future of the Ministry, he had offered me Jennie Lee. I had replied that she would be rather good for opening bazaars, and he then said, 'Who *do* you want?' Casting my mind about, I suddenly remembered this right-wing reactionary high churchman who really is an expert on housing and local government and I said 'MacColl', and by Monday evening I had got the man who would prove to be an absolutely first-rate number two on all my legislation.

[1] The village was Hartley. Later entries show how much trouble this case provoked in the Department.

the village in the green belt outweighed the case for exporting surplus population from London.

I also learned as a result of this excellent discussion that the trouble about planning permissions is that there is no clearly defined legal doctrine or principle; the Minister just has to decide for himself. So I left it that James MacColl should go and see the site of the village and I would make a final decision next week.

Then I went round to the Farmers' Club for lunch with Thomas Balogh and Peter Shore. I had hoped we could resume our old lunches of the kitchen Cabinet with Peter and Tommy and John Allen,[1] now in the Cabinet Office, and Tony Benn and George Wigg. But Harold got wind of this, said it was too large a gathering and too prominent, and had forbidden it. So Thomas and Peter and I met and it was a pretty good frost because with Peter still in Transport House there was no possibility of a frank talk. Tommy and I were hopelessly inhibited by Peter's unbriefedness. But one useful thing happened at this lunch. Tommy Balogh tipped me off without any doubt that George Brown was thinking of introducing licences for office building. This was invaluable since I was just due to hold my first official press conference. At two o'clock I went back to the Ministry to find about a hundred journalists waiting for myself and Mellish and MacColl. I had to handle them for thirty-five to forty minutes and as the conference went on I think I warmed up a bit. I was certainly pretty nervous at the beginning, despite the hours I had spent yesterday with Peter Brown, who was briefing me for the conference and warning me of all the things I could say wrong. Peter Brown is my senior Press Officer. He is a remarkable fellow; I am told he is the best public relations officer in Whitehall, and he certainly made his name by helping Macmillan launch his plan for 300,000 houses and bring it off.[2] However, his first job with me was to teach me how to deal with the conference and after it I felt very grateful to him. It wasn't a disaster and, thank heavens, I had Tommy Balogh's tip.

Of course, I was speaking against the background of the Government policy for the crisis, which had already been launched by George Brown and James Callaghan at a press conference on Monday morning and by Harold in his television appearance on Monday evening. I admit that their proposals for handling the crisis were pretty well the same as Maudling had been proposing under the previous Government and they struck me as extremely undynamic and dull. But Harold's performance on Monday night had been powerful, a lead for the nation, suggesting that we were prepared to be really tough: for instance, by tackling a scandal like Concorde or stopping the waste of building resources on office building. So at my conference I was careful to refer to

[1] Son of Sidney Scholefield Allen Q.C., the Labour M.P., John Allen had been an adviser to the Labour Party in Opposition and worked as a political adviser in the Cabinet Office October 1964–May 1965.
[2] See Harold Macmillan, *Tides of Fortune* (London: Macmillan, 1969), Chapter 13.

2

Harold's statement and to say that office building was an area where, despite my dislike of restrictionism, I might be seriously prepared to think of physical controls to deal with the scandal.

After I had finished the press conference I went straight on to the Cabinet meeting and while we were waiting outside I learned almost by chance that next Monday Home Affairs[1] will be discussing building licences for office building and that therefore this is a firm decision by George. I don't know how on earth a man who is not in the Cabinet can really get any idea of what is going on. I already hear from Tony Wedgwood Benn how utterly isolated he feels in his Ministry. It's only in my Cabinet Committees and even more in the informal meetings before and after the Cabinet that I am really able to keep in touch.

So I come to this afternoon's Cabinet meeting. What happened is really only intelligible in terms of the Cabinet Committee on the financial implications of the Queen's Speech which I went to yesterday. This was chaired by the Chancellor and he had with him all the Ministers concerned with expenditure. We had a frank discussion about old-age pensions, prescription charges, subsidies for mortgages, all the claims for money which had been in the manifesto and which might have been covered in the Queen's Speech. It was clear that whereas we all wanted a 12s. 6d. increase in the old-age pension and the abolition of prescription charges, the Chancellor would only go as far as 10s. and no abolition of prescription charges. At this Committee meeting I had made it clear as Minister of Housing and Local Government that I was not pressing at the moment for any concessions to mortgagors or to the ratepayer since it was important to get our priorities right. Indeed I argued we should make a virtue of necessity by saying that we should give everything at present to the old, the sick and the unemployed and ask everybody else to hold back.

Now we were in full Cabinet and the whole argument was rehearsed once again. This time it was started with a paper by James Callaghan insisting that 10s. was all he could afford and nothing else. After he had made his case Douglas Houghton made a speech saying why he wanted 12s. 6d. (Douglas Houghton as Chancellor of the Duchy of Lancaster was the representative in the Cabinet of two social service Ministers, Peggy Herbison, the Minister of Social Security, and Kenneth Robinson, the Minister of Health. Douglas was therefore an old-fashioned overlord, i.e. a Minister without departmental responsibility but responsible for two Ministries.*) Peggy Herbison and Kenneth Robinson were both present at this meeting though they were not members of Cabinet. Peggy Herbison supported Douglas on the 12s. 6d.

---

* As usual the arrangement worked very badly indeed.
[1] A Cabinet Committee. These committees are established on either an *ad hoc* or a permanent basis to consider the details of legislation and the intricacies of policy before the matter comes before the whole Cabinet. The Prime Minister appoints the members and chairman of each Committee, chairing some of the most important himself.

and then Kenneth Robinson gave the case for abolishing prescription charges. The Cabinet slowly warmed up and it was soon clear that the overwhelming majority took the view that a 10*s.* increase and nothing else was neither one thing nor the other. It would not be enough to dam the tide until national superannuation was introduced: there would have to be a second flat-rate concession at incredible expense. As for prescription charges, our package wouldn't impress anybody if we failed to abolish them right at the beginning. Those were the two main arguments employed. I was absolutely staggered at what happened because I am used to the idea that the Cabinet doesn't discuss a budget before the budget takes place. Yet here we were discussing budget secrets, considering what concessions should be made and to some extent discussing the taxes by which we should raise them, in full Cabinet — although Harold warned us about leaks which had occurred over the weekend. I thought he conducted this meeting in the most extraordinary way and shouldn't have allowed all this to happen. I should be amazed if some of it doesn't leak into the press and it might even leak out that only Frank Longford supported the Chancellor in the end — Harold Wilson, having waited, sided with the rest of us. Like us, no doubt, he remembered Hugh Gaitskell in 1951 and how he made the saving of the £11 million on teeth and spectacles a matter of principle when his calculations were actually £300 million out.[1]

All this occurred in full Cabinet with Harold Wilson chatting away, adding up the figures himself, and the Chancellor adding up the figures himself. It was staggering, as I said to Frank Longford who was sitting next to me; he also, with his experience of Cabinet, said he had never observed anything so extraordinary as this way of conducting business. By the end we had almost decided that this must be the policy even if it means raising enormous sums by further taxation in an autumn budget. And it was at this point that Harold brought in the idea that sacrifices must be imposed on private enterprise as well as on public enterprise and that one sacrifice would be the cutback in ostentatious office building in London. He turned to me and said this was something *I* was responsible for.

When I got back to the Ministry I warned them what was on and said I must have another paper on building controls. They weren't very pleased because they had briefed me firmly against them. I hadn't told the Dame that I had discussed this idea on the telephone with Harold Wilson on Sunday and suggested it as an example of the kind of tough measure that we should introduce quickly, or that I had gone on, on Monday, to discuss with Douglas Jay the practical methods of doing it. Nevertheless, by the time I got back to the Ministry on Wednesday the Dame's line had changed, the Whitehall grapevine had worked, she knew that building controls had to come in, and she said she would get me a paper ready for next morning.

[1] It was on this issue that **Aneurin Bevan** and Harold Wilson resigned from the front bench of the Labour Government.

Thursday, October 29th

Since the main item of Wednesday's Cabinet agenda, the Queen's Speech, had been squeezed out by the economic crisis we had to take it this morning at 11.30. We were pretty busy at the Ministry because we were discussing building controls; already by the time I got there the Dame had the paper showing the practicability of the method Douglas Jay had suggested to me on Monday and which she had told me was totally impractical. So then I went on to the Cabinet meeting on the Queen's Speech.

It was just like a meeting of the National Executive. There we were, twenty-three people, sitting down as a drafting committee, taking the Queen's Speech line by line. It was fantastic to see the Prime Minister sitting there, doing the drafting, and other people joining in. The meeting with its interminable amendments, redraftings and incompetence drooled on and on. I got so bored that I went in to talk to Marcia and Brenda in the little room behind, and waited there for Harold who was due to lunch with me at the House of Commons that afternoon. At 1.25 he came through rubbing his hands, saying what a splendid Queen's Speech we had got, and I was just thinking what an appalling performance the morning had been. Still, he felt he had got what he wanted and he was supremely confident. In came George Wigg, limping still from his broken ankle, but extremely happy. One of the things that has happened this week is the establishment of George Wigg and Tommy Balogh as figures in the No. 10 power structure. George is safely there as Paymaster-General, advising Harold on everything but particularly on security. Tommy is there as a civil servant, attached to the Cabinet Office but close to Harold. Close but not quite so safe as George Wigg. Both of them, particularly Tommy, along with Nicky Kaldor have received an enormous amount of publicity this week as Wilson's boffins. Indeed one of the big stories this week has been that Patrick Blackett[1] has joined Charles Snow[2] and Frank Cousins at the Ministry of Technology, that Alun Gwynne Jones, *The Times* defence correspondent,[3] and Tommy Balogh are our Prime Minister's intellectual advisers, and that Nicky Kaldor has become the taxation adviser to James Callaghan. All the cartoonists and columnists are having a fine time either laughing at us or comparing the Wilson regime with Kennedy's New Frontier.

Harold and I walked out with George Wigg to drive across to the House of Commons. There once again were crowds of people jostling and cheering. I remembered writing an article in the *Sunday Mirror* just before the election saying that one difference the election would make was that if we won politics would become interesting and lively again. Well, this has certainly happened.

---

[1] Professor Emeritus and Senior Research Fellow, Imperial College of Science and Technology since 1965, and part-time adviser to the Ministry.

[2] Extraordinary Fellow, University of Cambridge, and novelist. Parliamentary Secretary, Ministry of Technology 1964–6. He was made a life peer in 1964. See page 42.

[3] Since 1961. He became Minister of State at the Foreign Office in 1964, with special responsibility for disarmament, sitting in the Lords as Lord Chalfont (created 1964).

There are now crowds in Downing Street and queues outside the House of Commons. My letter bag is much heavier. There is a real sense of newness, an impression that the Government is doing something, that Harold Wilson is behaving well. And this has been particularly heightened by his brilliant success at handling the Rhodesian crisis. Here was an issue on which in Cabinet I advised far greater caution. But Harold told me at lunch that, thanks to the skilful drafting of Gerald Gardiner, our Lord Chancellor, he has been able to call Ian Smith's bluff and has made him try to run for cover and climb down. This I reckon is Harold's first big success.

When Harold asked me to lunch he said, 'We have to go over to the Commons,' and as he sat down in the corner of the Members' dining-room he said to me, 'The cook at Downing Street is ill so we can't manage it there.' I thought, 'My God, here is a Prime Minister who can't eat in his own house because his cook is ill.' But Harold was obviously pleased with everything. In the course of my report to him on what was going on in the Ministry he said, 'Well, you people must be desperately busy. I'm having an easier time now than for ages because I am no longer a one-man band. I've got my staff and advisers.' He also added that he was going to leave us all to run our Departments pretty freely. All he wanted was to know what was going on and he hoped that when he got Chequers going we would come down with our wives and spend the day with him and he would acquaint himself with all the details of the departments.* I said to him that it was a little too early for us to be able to say much about housing but I thought the press conference I had held the day before, to judge by the morning papers, had been a modest success.

We had only started lunch at 1.30 and we had to break off at 2.20 so that I could go to George Brown's meeting on licences for office building. This was an odd meeting because George Brown just started by saying, 'We have to do something sudden and dramatic. Is there any objection?' And he treated me as a colleague he wanted to carry with him on the point. As a matter of fact, a ban on office building in London could only release building workers for further house building, so it wasn't anything a Minister of Housing could possibly object to. I did mention, however, that there were grave dangers that we should enable some people to lose millions and some people to gain millions unjustly and unfairly. This was a point Dame Evelyn had made to me on the way in.

I didn't get away from this meeting until 2.55 and I then rushed round to a meeting of the Legislation Committee[1] which had been called to deal with my interim Rent Bill. This interim Bill was one of the ideas we thought up in the Ministry. We decided that while we were preparing the long Rent Bill and getting it through Parliament by next Easter we would need a short Bill to

---

* This idea never in my experience materialized.

[1] A Cabinet Committee which discussed the details and priorities of legislation.

provide security of tenure in the interval.[1] But my knowledge of geography failed me, and I found myself going to the wrong place so that I was ten minutes late for the meeting. The atmosphere was very frigid and I was ill prepared when I came to expound the nature of my one-clause Bill. I had an excellent brief from the Ministry but I wasn't very good and I had a rough time from Elwyn Jones, the Attorney-General, and the Lord Chancellor. I didn't answer their questions very adequately and I thought I might be in trouble later on.

However, with that meeting over I was able to relax and go back to the Ministry to talk things over with Dame Evelyn, and then I asked Charles Pannell and his Permanent Secretary to come across and discuss the building problems arising out of George Brown's proposal. Of course, top security was required since any breath of a leak in the press would enable people to start building offices and so make large sums of money. However, I did feel it necessary to tell Charles Pannell, though my officials warned me against it. Dame Evelyn insisted that she could talk to his officials and I needn't mention it to the Minister. I said this wouldn't do. The idea of officials talking together below the Ministers is something distasteful to me.

I was just able to clear everything up, then get to my car and drive down to Olympia to meet our farm manager, Dennis Pritchett, and spend two hours at the Dairy Show. This was a pleasant thing to do because we have decided at Prescote[2] to go pedigree and we wanted to confirm our judgment of the quality of our cattle. We did so. We felt the display at least of Friesians was pretty poor; our own herd was good enough; but what mainly interested us were the steers being grown for meat, where we saw some interesting experiments. After this I took him back to eat steak at the Carlton Towers.

Friday, October 30th
I decided to take the 4.10 to Banbury and spend a little time at home before going to Birmingham on Saturday. This meant I had a rushed time in the morning because Callaghan and I were to meet the building societies and ask them not to raise their interest rates.

This in itself is an interesting story. As Minister of Housing I am vitally concerned with the rate of interest, expecially the rate for future mortgagors. Since over half the houses built are now those for private sale to mortgagors the rate of interest largely determines the size of the building programme. I had heard some days previously that Callaghan was due to see the representatives of the Building Societies Federation, and my officials got him to ask me to come and see them as well. I had discussed all this with Harold at lunch the previous day and told him how horrified I was that Callaghan should consider talking to the building societies about concessions on profits

---

[1] The short Bill was called the Protection from Eviction Bill to distinguish it from the major Rent Bill, which dealt with rent controls.

[2] The Crossmans' farm, Prescote Manor, at Cropredy, near Banbury.

tax. 'We need to read the riot act,' I said, 'and tell them that if they dare to raise interest rates we will take Government action to stop them. This isn't the time for weakness.' Harold had agreed and I asked him to speak to Callaghan, and in the special briefing discussion this morning it became clear that he would be prepared to take his line from me.

We finally met the building societies at eleven o'clock. They had been warned by Dame Evelyn what was in store for them, but even so they were taken aback and a little baffled. I hope we were able to put it over to them. Certainly, I felt hopelessly amateur and I felt Callaghan was weak and ineffective. It was a curious sensation to feel that we were speaking for Her Majesty's Government and telling this vast organization not to raise its interest rates when it intended to do so. Of course they replied that if they didn't raise the interest rates and get the money in there would be fewer houses built and there might be a sudden upsurge of unemployment in the building industry. Nevertheless, we kept the instructions very strong.

This meeting with Callaghan and the building societies, following George Brown's meeting on office building, made me realize how we were evolving our Government policy. What we lacked was any comprehensive, thoroughly thought-out Government strategy. The policies are being thrown together – but still, that's better than nothing.

Saturday, October 31st
Birmingham was my first official visitation. Harry Watton, the Leader of the Labour Group, was in Dame Evelyn's office last week and came across to see me, and on the spur of the moment I said I'd like to go to Birmingham. He took it up and so there I was this morning driving in a Government car, being escorted by the police from the outskirts of the city, received by the Lord Mayor at the town hall. Lunch was a banquet for a hundred. I had accepted the invitation on the understanding that there would be no speeches, but it was quite clear from the speeches that the Lord Mayor and Harry Watton made – they each spoke for ten minutes – that I would also have to say something, and I think I made a fairly good spontaneous, yet carefully prepared, reply, beginning to develop the ideas of a Labour housing policy based on realities and not on emotion. In the morning the areas I visited had been curiously enough those which I last visited when I was Labour candidate in the 1937 by-election after the death of Austen Chamberlain. I was able to remark how one of the streets was in exactly the same state as I had seen it in 1937, which meant nearly thirty years worse. In the afternoon I was taken into the council chamber where some fifty officials and councillors put their case. I had a full note made and answered questions. I went straight on to a press conference where some dozen journalists talked to me for half an hour, then a tea-party and an informal talk with the Labour Group, and thence by *Birmingham Mail* car to Coventry for our victory celebrations at Coventry East.

For this little show we had asked some 150 members of the constituency Party to an informal evening. We held it in the council chamber. Anne and I provided the drink, and the Party provided the food. Anne drove over bringing Jennie and her husband Chris Hall. Winnie Lakin, my Party agent, arrived characteristically one hour late having done her insurance collection. Albert Rose, the Party secretary, was in fine form, having got himself re-elected against the opposition of the Walsgrave Ward; and after the formal show, which lasted from 7.45 to 10.00, a few of us went to the lovely room above the medieval gateway where Ron Morgan and his wife (Ron is a brilliant potter and craftsman) live and have their showrooms and we had the most amiable cup of tea before driving home to Prescote through the fog, where I found that another pillion rider had come down with my third red box.

I must add here that on getting home the night before I had found my keys were missing. What had happened was that in putting my papers together in the railway carriage when I got to Banbury I had locked one of my brief cases and the key had slipped out. I had to telephone George Moseley and the key ring was discovered by the railway police at Wolverhampton, much to the shock of Moseley, Ponsford and Peter Brown.

Sunday, November 1st

I was hoping for a fairly free day today but I found the whole morning pretty well engaged over problems of the Protection from Eviction Bill. The draft Bill was sent down here late last night and I was asked to confirm the paper, which the officials obviously thought was a mere formality. But when I looked at it I was worried about it, especially when I found that there was no kind of protection for tenants during the period between publication of the Bill and its being made law, which might be five or six weeks. I was anxious to find some way of making the Bill retrospective or at least effective on the day of publication. I rang up first of all the Under-Secretary at the Ministry, who said no lawyers were available on a Sunday, and I then tried to get the Attorney-General, Elwyn Jones, who was not available. And finally I rang Arnold Goodman. That resourceful man was once again full of ideas and by the end of the morning I had got a number of these clear in my head and I talked them over with the Ministry and at least had worked out a possible device for filling the gap. It was rather a thing, I suppose, for a new untried Minister to intervene at this late stage in the drafting of the Bill and clearly the Ministry didn't expect it. I dare say I shall find some difficulties tomorrow morning when I get back.

The First Secretary and the Chancellor continued to grapple with the trade figures and to lament the unhappy state of the pound. Early in the month the 'Paris Club' of central bankers agreed to make $400 million (£142 million) available immediately and the I.M.F. promised another $600 million (making £357 million in all). The autumn budget did little to reassure foreign observers.

Pensions were raised by 12s. 6d. a week for a single person and by 21s. for a married couple, and prescription charges were abolished. To cover the cost of these measures the national insurance contribution was raised, the tax on petrol was increased and the standard rate of income tax increased from the following spring. Income and profits taxes on companies were to be replaced by a capital gains tax and a corporation tax. The stock market sagged but at least the October trade figures, published in mid-November, were encouraging. Patrick Gordon Walker and Douglas Jay tried to reassure the EFTA countries that the surcharge was only temporary but European bankers and investors were uncertain and the pound continued to weaken.

In these circumstances, the Prime Minister felt justified in sanctioning the sale of sixteen Buccaneer aircraft to South Africa, a contract that was worth £20 million but contravened his declared policy of an embargo on arms sales to South Africa. This, as much as the matter of the postponement of the pension increases until after the winter, threatened to cause a squall in the Parliamentary Party.

Defence policy, too, was a problem for the Prime Minister. The new Labour Government had hoped to abandon the independent deterrent. Nor did they wish to join the Americans in a multilateral force (M.L.F.) which might include Germany among the nuclear powers. Harold Wilson was due to go to Washington for talks with Lyndon Baines Johnson, the newly elected American President, to discuss the Atlantic Alliance.

Monday, November 2nd

I've been learning some of the problems of ministerial responsibility. This started at the railway station where we were met by the station-master and all the other people were looking at us and saying, 'Why does the confounded fellow need a whole compartment to himself?' The explanation is absurd. The security people have laid it down that if we are to open our red boxes and read our documents in the train this can only be done in a reserved compartment; a reserved seat will not be sufficient. However, having made a big fuss about national security to George Wigg I have decided to be extremely careful in everything I do personally so I've had scramblers and big safes installed in London as well as here at Prescote and I have agreed to reserve a whole compartment despite the fury of the commuters.

It was a bit nerve-racking on Monday morning because there had been a thick fog and I wondered whether I would be late for my first Cabinet Committee. This was on economic development and I was able to see the relative performances of George Brown and James Callaghan, George in the chair as the First Secretary and Minister in charge of the D.E.A. and James Callaghan as Chancellor of the Exchequer. It was pretty clear from the first that George is the man of action. He decides, he does things, and James sits beside him sort of bleating amiably what he feels.

I had lunch with Vivian Bowden and Tam and his wife Kathleen. I had organized this lunch to try and help Vivian get his feet on the ground in the

2*

Department of Education and Science. He is an enterprising, talkative, brilliant, technological creature whom we brought into our councils as the result of his being mentioned to me by Tommy Balogh and coming to one of our Reform Club dinners.[1] At this dinner he happened to sit next to Harold Wilson, who was enraptured by him and immediately captured him as a possible member of the Government. When Patrick Blackett refused to go to the Lords[2] Vivian Bowden quite suddenly got the life peerage and the job as Minister of State at the D.E.S. The trouble is that there is a fairly close coterie there with Michael Stewart, Reg Prentice and Jim Boyden, all N.U.T. and trade-union types, while poor Vivian Bowden sits in his lonely office in Richmond Terrace completely out of touch. Here is a man who knows his way about the academic world and the U.G.C. and who finds himself absolutely powerless in the 'corridors of power', to quote from Charles Snow's new novel.[3]

At lunch I tried to persuade him to insist on seeing Michael Stewart alone for an hour each week to put up his projects to him, and I reminded him that he knew all our projects for higher education by heart and Michael Stewart didn't. But I had an uneasy feeling that somehow or other he will find it difficult to get on. That feeling was certainly strengthened in the evening when I went to a celebration party at the Blacketts'. There was a small group, Alun Gwynne Jones — previously an adviser to the Liberal Party and now, thanks to George Wigg, our new Minister of State at the Foreign Office dealing with disarmament; Patrick Blackett also, enormously happy now he has got the job he wanted in the Ministry of Technology; it became clear that poor Vivian was a fish out of water. I wonder how long he will last.

Maybe it's convenient here to add an observation on the new Minister of Technology, Frank Cousins. He is one of the great unknowns in the Cabinet. His appointment was a big shock, though I think it was absolutely first rate. He has considerable qualifications through his membership of D.S.I.R. and N.R.D.C. and also because we need a leading trade unionist in the Cabinet. He in fact refused to take Transport or Labour and only wanted Technology. What was a bit crazy was to put Charles Snow in as his Parliamentary Secretary. This again was the result of one of the Reform Club dinners at which Charles Snow took the chair and captivated Harold Wilson. Only I who had him here for a weekend at Prescote know that at fifty-nine he is not very effective in action and it's most unlikely that he will give Frank Cousins, who has no experience of the House of Commons and hasn't a seat there yet, the contacts at Westminster needed to make the Ministry a success, despite his novelistic talk.

[1] Meetings at which Crossman, as Shadow Minister, had entertained leading scientists and engineers to discuss Labour's future science policy.

[2] He relented in 1969 and became a life peer.

[3] This was the most recent of a series of novels describing different aspects of British society. *Corridors of Power* (London: Macmillan, 1964) purported to describe the intrigues and conventions of Whitehall.

Frank, who I see now at several Cabinet Committees (he usually sits beside me) is jolly good—sensible and not nearly as talkative as one might have expected. He took the chance to tell me that he wouldn't really have taken the job except on the assumption that I would be his Minister of Education and Science. Looking back, I wouldn't have allowed myself to be switched to Housing if I had known Frank would be Minister of Technology. I would have adored working with him and I think we could have made a go of it. Since Michael would have come into Housing knowing a lot about rent control and the law of town and country planning, he could have taken control much more quickly than I am doing and imposed his policies, too. My main difficulty in the Ministry is that I am taking time to find out what everything is about. I am beginning to discover for example that the name 'Ministry of Housing and Local Government' is an extraordinary misnomer. In fact the Ministry does no house-building at all. The people who build are either the local authorities or private-enterprise builders. Our Ministry is a Ministry for permissions, regulations, an administrative Ministry where the Minister should be someone passionately interested in the judicial activities of making decisions or giving planning permissions or the future of New Towns. It's a Ministry very remote from anything Harold suggested when he talked about organizing a housing drive. Of course, Ministers in the past have always talked about housing drives and pretended to carry them out. But what they have really done is to add up the figures and take credit for the creation of houses which are largely the responsibility on the one side of the Ministry of Public Building and Works, who deal with the housing industry, and on the other of the Chancellor of the Exchequer, who fixes the rate of interest which largely determines how many private-sector houses are built. One of the things I've largely had to decide is whether I should attempt (because I am not likely to be in the Ministry very long) to reorganize it as an effective production Ministry or whether I should just make the best of it as it is, and improve its public relations.

That brings me to the next thing I am beginning to discover about the life of the Minister. He is very largely concerned with public relations and with the fight inside Cabinet for his share of legislation and publicity. I can now see the job of a Minister from the civil servants' point of view. It is not merely to fight successfully at Cabinet, which I can do. It is not merely to get himself across in the House of Commons, which I am still not sure I can do. He is also required to sell himself to the public with announcements and pronouncements which, though they are not making any new policy, give a sense that he is doing something. And so I see around me in Cabinet all my colleagues struggling and pushing to get in and speak on the Queen's Speech, putting up papers in Cabinet Committees which really say nothing but which are intended to get the Minister on the map.

Strangely enough, whatever else may be said about my thrustingness and self-assertiveness, in these ways I am a very poor pusher. I am not a political shover. I have a positive phobia about appearing at public dinners and I am extremely unpopular in the Ministry for getting out of attending the County Councils Association's dinner on Wednesday, when the Queen will be present, on the ground that I have to have tea with her that afternoon and can't see her twice. In all these questions of public appearances I am pretty well a non-starter. Then I am also deeply inexperienced on the front bench and therefore reluctant to plunge in at the House. And as for making pronouncements, or getting things put on the agenda of Cabinet Committees in order to get on the map, I have a snobbish aversion from doing anything as phoney as that. I want to do what it's good to do; and for my Ministry now, frankly, the only thing I have got to do immediately is to deal with rent control.

What about the housing drive which Harold talks about? I have now reached the conclusion that 400,000 houses will probably be built in the next twelve months unless we have a financial crisis which prevents the building societies getting the money; or unless political decisions, like the one to control office building, create a crisis in the building industry; or, finally, unless the industry itself falls down on the job by not producing the bricks. Unless one of those three things happens—and I can't control any of them—the houses will get themselves built. Any decision I *now* take to make a new kind of plan which shifts the balance of housing between the public and the private sector beyond the next twelve months involves me in a very complicated calculation. I am pretty clear what the long-term plan should be. I am pretty clear that the decision means comprehensive urban renewal. We have to concentrate on six or seven places, Liverpool, Manchester, Birmingham, Glasgow, London, where the problem of housing is so bad that the local authorities simply can't grapple with the job. Ironically enough it is almost the same group of areas in which we need rent control. A Labour Minister should impose central leadership, large-scale state intervention, in these blighted areas of cities, the twilight areas, which were once genteelly respectable and are now rotting away, where Commonwealth citizens settle and where there are racial problems. Outside these great conurbations, the present housing laws, the present kind of development of new housing and the present scheme for improvement of old housing are all pretty well O.K. and should be allowed to run on unchanged.

But that's the kind of policy decision from which no serious effect could be seen in under eighteen months. And even to make a responsible speech about it one has got to get further in planning than I could have got in these first three weeks. So if we had had a day on housing in the Queen's Speech debate I would have found myself partly antedating my Second Reading speech on the anti-eviction Bill and partly just patching up, making vague statements about the future, and that is something I don't like to do. That's why I haven't pushed for a day on housing.

The other problem I have is that in addition to creating a new housing drive in these great conurbations and getting my two rent Bills through, I also have on my plate leasehold reform. I managed to see to it that the order of priority in the Queen's Speech should be rent control (that's my affair), Land Commission (that's Fred Willey's) and leasehold reform (that's back to me). Even so I am under ceaseless pressure from the Welsh group to bring on leasehold reform early. Of course, they couldn't care less that millions of people are affected by rent control, and that the Land Commission is absolutely vital for reducing the price of land, and that it is absolutely meaningless to do leasehold reform before the Land Commission is set up. The Welsh group brush all these considerations aside because they pledged themselves to leasehold reform years ago and it's got to be done quick to please their backers. Now, in fact, there is no way of bringing about leasehold reform and arranging for people to buy up their long leases which won't impose on the people who buy a far bigger cost than they will be willing to bear. We foresee in our Ministry that there will be keen resentment if we allow the cost to be related to the real market value of land, but equally if we try and fudge it in some way we shall find it very difficult to get the Bill through. So there is an overwhelming case for postponing leasehold reform to the second Session. I tried and tried and I pleaded with the Cabinet, but the pressure is too great and it's on me that they are pressing. I suppose I can say I have done something to prevent it being given an earlier priority than my Rent Bill; even so I'm not sure I have succeeded. It may well be that the Sunday papers will say Harold is planning a spring election and he will want to insert a quick leasehold Bill before the second major Rent Bill is introduced.

I should add here that my behaviour on Sunday over the anti-eviction Bill had caused Dame Evelyn absolute consternation. This evening she stayed behind to talk to me about other things, then said she had never been so insulted in her life and had very nearly resigned when she heard of my conduct. The very idea of consulting Arnold Goodman when she should have been consulted was intolerable. I said I was angry with her because I thought the Ministry had let me down very badly. The Bill was entirely unsatisfactory. Since I tried everybody round and there was no legal advice available I had to go outside and she would have to get used to the idea that I would always regard Arnold Goodman as an invaluable adviser and be bound to use him. She said nothing except that she would have to have a quiet talk with me about her future. I am not sure what her future will be.

Tuesday, November 3rd
Today I had my second appearance before the Legislation Committee on my anti-eviction Bill. I had quite a rush. The meeting was at 9.30 in the Ministerial conference room at the House of Commons and here I found round the table the usual battery of lawyers. I had taken precautions this time to wake up early at 6.30 and brief myself in the greatest detail. I must have done fairly well, because in reply the Lord Chancellor mentioned eight

points he wanted to have discussed, four of which had been dealt with satisfactorily in my speech. And we then went through it. There wasn't much time; in fact we only had twenty-five minutes' discussion of the Bill before Cabinet, which only lasted an hour because of the State Opening of Parliament at 11.30.

Cabinet was almost entirely devoted to the secret plan George Brown and I had worked out for stopping all office building in London. This was suddenly presented to Cabinet. George spoke. I gave details on the factual case for doing it, and despite the predictions in my Ministry that there would be tremendous opposition there was none at all. Nobody in a Labour Cabinet is going to object to an action which is extremely popular outside London and which will only ruin property speculators; actually, it probably won't even do that because a lot of them will make money out of the rising rents paid now for offices already in existence.* It all went with a bang, and we got it through comfortably. They all went off to the State Opening, and I went back to my Ministry to report, and then at 12.30 I went down to the D.E.A. to work out the details with George Brown of the actual text which we thought was due on Thursday afternoon.

From there I rushed off to lunch with Judith Hart at the Farmers' Club and then back to the debate on the Address. After Douglas-Home had made quite a nice little speech, Harold made his first speech as Prime Minister; it included the notorious attack on the Member for Smethwick,[1] whom he called a political leper, and set off a real House of Commons scene. I talked to him afterwards; it was undoubtedly a planned passage in the speech but it was intended to embarrass Sir Alec and to split him from Boyle[2] by showing the differences in the Tories' attitudes in Birmingham. Harold certainly didn't foresee that after the howling outburst caused by this remark the main content of his attack on the Tory Government was never listened to and didn't even get printed next day. It was an example of how one pays for the irrelevant minor episode which eclipses the main purpose of a speech.

Wednesday, November 4th

Yesterday evening George Wigg and I went on to the *Newsweek* party for the American election results in the Abraham Lincoln suite at the Savoy Hotel. The results were boring because we knew from the beginning there was

---

* The second of these speculations proved correct. In fact certain property-owners, including Mr Hyams, made vast sums out of the Labour Party's ban on new office building. I presume that I was able to make the guess because of my talks with him.

[1] Alderman Peter Griffiths had been elected Conservative M.P. for Smethwick in 1964, defeating Patrick Gordon Walker, with considerable support from constituents hostile to coloured immigration. He lost the seat in 1966.

[2] Edward Boyle, Conservative M.P. for Birmingham (Handsworth) from 1950 to 1970, was considered to have liberal views on such questions as immigration and education. He left the House of Commons to become Lord Boyle of Handsworth. He became Vice-Chancellor of Leeds University in 1970 and chairman of the Top Salaries Review Body in 1971.

a Johnson landslide,[1] but Arnold Goodman, George Wigg and I had to stay and breakfast at 3 a.m. before we could totter home and go to bed. A good object lesson, one shouldn't go out if one is a Labour Cabinet Minister—I felt pretty dreary this morning although I had been scrupulously careful in what I ate and drank.

Today we suddenly found George Brown was to speak this afternoon and not on Thursday, and everything had to be prepared for the great declaration on office building. We had another work-over of our brief in my Ministry because I was due to take a Lobby conference with George Brown afterwards. Then in the afternoon I went and sat beside him, the first time I had really taken my place on the front bench. At the Lobby conference afterwards George took the main brief and did very well. When he had finished I filled in with a number of details which I had collected very carefully. While I was doing this George said laughingly, 'Don't give away the whole of my Second Reading speech.' But I was sure I was right that the time to put out the justification is on the morning after you have made the announcement. In fact this was a terrific success. It gave a tremendous sense of the Hundred Days, to have the press giving this sensible account of what we had done and to have no criticism of it at all. I got no credit outside, though I may have got just a little inside the Cabinet.

In the evening I had dinner once again with Donnison. I am thinking of him more and more as the man I want to use full time.

Thursday, November 5th
Reading my papers early in the morning I suddenly realized that the White Paper which accompanied a Bill for the underground storage of gas would actually increase the alarm it was supposed to allay. I made this point at the Home Affairs Committee and as a result poor Fred Lee, the Minister in charge, had to withdraw the White Paper. Well, I won. But did I gain by it? On reflection I realize that all I've done is to make an enemy. Why should I sit there and do this? I realize now something about Cabinet Government: one should always be looking for friends and allies, not making enemies. That's why a Cabinet Minister is reluctant to weigh in on too many things. I daresay Aneurin Bevan used to and Manny Shinwell used to. Should I be the sort of Minister who weighs in on everything and doesn't calculate on friends and enemies? Or shall I be the careful kind of calculating man who puts up papers so as to get himself on the map, supporting or opposing not on the merits of the case but on the effect on his allies or his enemies? It seems to me clear that two-thirds of my colleagues here, as on the N.E.C., are going to act in the second way. I hope I shall act in the first fashion but with a great deal more caution and restraint than I would have done, say, five years ago.

[1] Lyndon Baines Johnson, who had become President after the assassination of John Kennedy in November 1963, was now elected to serve his first full term. The Democrats were given the largest poll ever recorded, 61 per cent of the votes cast, and the largest Democratic majority since 1936 was sent to Congress.

When I come to the end of this week I realize I've had some extremely depressing patches. I've very often felt completely isolated, felt that Harold has really ditched me by putting me into a job where I simply can't win. I've had difficulties with Dame Evelyn: she's a magnificent woman but she wants her Ministry run in her own way and there is a constant struggle between us. Every single person I want to bring in she opposes. This week my friend Hyams, the millionaire director of Wimpey whom Arnold Goodman suggested, came along to the Ministry. Unfortunately, the time I fixed with him was when I had to go and sit on the front bench by George Brown for the Building Control Bill.[1] I had to leave Hyams for twenty minutes to the tender mercies of Dame Evelyn plus Waddell and I gather they are wholly hostile to using him in any possible way. On the other hand I have I think made them realize that Arnold Goodman is the centre point of my outside advisory group on rent reform. But by and large it's been a difficult week, and I haven't done too well. I haven't even made sure of my two Bills, though I've made some advance there. I haven't made any impact on housing, I haven't got myself into the Queen's Speech on these six days, I haven't made my initial impact on the Commons. It's all still to come.

Saturday, November 7th

This is the most perfect autumn I can remember—on and on, lovely warm sunshine, mists in the early morning, the farm amazingly dry. This afternoon we and the children had our splendid Saturday walk. I've never seen a more beautiful crescent moon rising in the sunset behind the dairy. Coming to Prescote isn't running away from work but a way of doing it. I bring down all the stuff I have to reflect on, all the planning permissions, for example, because there is so little writing involved. And I shall look forward more and more to loading myself with boxes and coming down here as early as possible each weekend.

That is, of course, if we have more than a few months before the election or if *I* have more than a few months as Minister. I'm not at all sure yet whether I am a born Minister, not at all sure whether I shall come off in the House or even want to. In a curious way I'm not fully engaged in the work. Yes, I am engaged on rent controls already and maybe that is the one thing I've got to do in this Session, to put the Rent Bill on the statute book and make a job of that.

Monday, November 9th

After the morning's work in the office I went home to give lunch to Bob Mellish and Jim MacColl, my two Parliamentary Secretaries, with whom I have now arranged a weekly meeting at 1 p.m. to check things through and see how they are going. I've described Jim MacColl already, my prim, prissy,

---

[1] After a difficult Committee Stage, the Bill was dropped. It was re-introduced in the new 1966 Parliament, and eventually became law in August 1966.

high-church expert on local government. I think he is fairly happy with me though he dislikes being number two to Bob Mellish. Bob, breezy trade unionist, is a typical product of the London Labour movement, one of the men who were most anti-me when the trade unions took umbrage at my remarks in the *Daily Mirror*, made when we were in Opposition, that there were only four of them capable of being a useful member of a Labour Cabinet. Now he has got a job in my Ministry, and as long as I am successful and my success is something he depends on he is going to be loyal to me. Certainly he now goes round saying what a wonderful chap I am. He is doing a jolly good job himself in keeping contact with the London boroughs. I don't think I like him any more or any less than I did when he treated me as a dirty bastard. I think I really prefer MacColl, though I don't know whether I am getting any closer to him.

After these three weeks what do I know of other personalities in the Ministry? George Moseley is a grammar-school boy, grim, grey, retiring, diplomatic, able, skilful. At heart fairly nice and fairly loyal. I have a suspicion I may get on with him extremely well. At least I am going to like him more and I think it's possible that he may like working with me and learn something from me. I have a feeling that underneath he may be on our side politically and is anti-establishment. Very different from Brian Ponsford, an Oxford First in Greats, prim, priggish with immense moral courage in standing up to me. Along with him there are the two girls, Miss Green and Pamela something-or-other, who sit about in the Private Office doing, as far as I can see, pretty little. Finally I managed this week to say to George that I wanted Jennie Hall. To my great relief he thought it a first-rate idea. He wanted to put Jennie right in the Office to replace one of the girls and I was able to ring her up and tell her. I think Jennie and George will work well together; they are both similar types in certain ways and obviously like each other. But though I achieved that I did create a crisis by introducing Tam Dalyell to help to do my correspondence with Ponsford. I have been trying to explain to my Office that when people write to me personally I have to write back but I don't expect either to dictate the letters I sign or even to read them carefully. Once I have got staff who understand how I feel about these letters they must really write them for me. Now Ponsford says this is totally impossible and Tam Dalyell himself makes it very difficult. He is as awkward, stubborn and lovable as ever and I doubt if he will ever really succeed in writing the kind of letter I want any more than Ponsford will. But don't let me complain. Tam and Kathleen are lovely to have in the flat above me at Vincent Square; they look after me beautifully when Anne is away, make breakfast for me and have me up for a cup of tea at night. When Anne is up in London they leave us alone, so I get the best of both worlds.

Having diverged a bit about the Ministry personalities, let's get back to Monday. The *New Statesman* held one of its big parties in Stationers Hall in the evening. It was the first important party I've gone out to since becoming a

Minister. Harold was there, the whole Left establishment was there. And I found it quite pleasant to be one of the people courted and talked to with interest and respect while I held my glass of champagne in my hand. From there I went back to the House for dinner with Eddie Shackleton.[1] While we were sitting together Harold Wilson came in to dine with Frank Cousins. As I was going he called me over and said, 'Why on earth are you giving dinner to Shackleton?' I said, 'He was my old lodger,' and we went across and sat down with Harold and Frank for twenty-five minutes. It's the longest time I've been with Harold informally since we lunched together. He talked absolutely without a break, with enormous self-confidence. The main thing he said was, 'Well, now I can sit back and study strategy and leave you chaps to do the tactics and the detailed work in your Departments. My strategy is to put the Tories on the defensive and always give them awkward choices. Now, for instance, they have an awkward choice on the budget. They have an awkward choice voting for or against the pension increase. We have given them an awkward choice on office building and, Dick, you'll be giving them an awkward choice with your Bill for preventing evictions. Whatever we do we must keep the initiative and always give them awkward choices.' He was also full of the possibilities in foreign affairs. I only had half an ear for his long talk about the tremendous chance he now has to become the mediator in the deadlock in the Western alliance over nuclear weapons. The main impression I got was of enormous exuberance, self-confidence. He felt the Government had been established and we could continue like this for as long as we liked and then have the election at the moment of our own choosing.

After this we went in to vote on the steel resolution which had been moved that afternoon by Macleod and opposed by Fred Lee. Iain Macleod had made a very disappointing return to the Tory front bench because he had chosen to do a very technical, quiet, non-obvious speech. Fred Lee replied with what I thought was an utterly deplorable speech, but it went over fairly well. Certainly the contrast wasn't as bad as we expected. We achieved our first majority of seven.

Tuesday, November 10th
At 9.30 we had a crucial meeting, for me, of the Legislation Committee where the revised version of my anti-eviction Bill was being considered. Once again I had taken a great deal of trouble and sweat over it. I was delighted when the Bill got through with virtually no change. I went straight on to the Cabinet on the budget. This was extremely interesting. Callaghan read aloud the budget proposals,[2] which I felt straight away didn't make a budget at all. There was only one proposal in it, the tax on petrol, which was imposed

---

[1] Lord Shackleton (made a life peer in 1958) was Minister of Defence for the R.A.F. October 1964–January 1967. He was a former lodger at No. 9 Vincent Square.
[2] See pp. 40–41.

straight away. Everything else either had been already announced in the Government's first week or was a pre-announcement of something to come next April, i.e. new scales of social security benefits, the new capital gains tax, the new corporation tax and the increase in the standard rate of income tax. There we were. I said rather bluntly that I wondered if this budget was tough enough for the crisis; if we were going to have a budget at all shouldn't we ensure all the imposts, all the unpopularities were got into it, and I asked this particularly in view of Callaghan's remark that his budget was the very minimum we could afford to do. 'Why should we be doing the minimum?' I asked. We should be doing the maximum now. Harold replied that we must take care not to do a stop–go–stop budget and not to make the mistake of creating deflation. Production wasn't going forward very well; we had to raise production and we must be extremely careful not to depress the economy. He thought it just about right.

It may be so. But I must say, looking back from now I feel that my comment wasn't too bad. However, it wasn't confirmed when we got to the budget speech next day.

For the rest of the day I found myself virtually unemployed as far as the Ministry was concerned. There were quite literally no engagements for me. George Moseley said the only thing to do was to go off and sit in Parliament and listen to the debate on the Address. I had been increasingly uneasy about the absence of work and this was too much. I sat around in a fury and listened to a knock-about debate with Ted Heath and George Brown getting into a terrible tangle at the end, and I felt deeply depressed that evening.

Wednesday, November 11th
The first thing I did was to ring up Harold Wilson and explain to him that work was being kept from me and that I had had enough of the Dame. I then went and saw Dame Evelyn at 10.30 and told her this was an impossible situation. Straight away she said, 'I haven't seen anything of the real office work either. I have been entirely diverted from my real responsibilities by the great battle for the future of the Department,' to which I said, 'Well, that may be so. But I'm not sure we've done very well in fighting the battle during these last weeks. The main job was to get your Minister into his work and see that he was taking over responsibility. That you've failed to do. I insist on having regular staff meetings, regular decisions put up by you to me and I insist on having it done in the way I want it done.' She said she knew it was her fault and we must work out a system. And I found as one often does that I couldn't ask her for an explanation that day because she was so busily pleading guilty to all the crimes but also pleading extenuating circumstances. And I daresay the circumstances were extenuating, because it's true that the eruption of Wilson into Whitehall, the creation of the new Ministry, the uncertainties of the future of planning and land sales must all have been vastly disturbing to any mandarin, particularly to someone like Dame Evelyn who does really

care passionately about her subject. Whereas most of the Permanent Secretaries move from Ministry to Ministry and feel professional in them all, she stayed twelve years in Housing and she is a dominant character within this field. It's quite clear to me now that in the Ministry, especially in the planning section, there are many who feel her era of despotism should be brought to a close and would like to see her go. But I don't think they would want to see a person as ignorant and as out of touch with planning as I am get rid of her.

Lunch was a rather woebegone episode. I had been invited by Sydney Jacobson,[1] and I found myself in two private rooms with him, Hugh Cudlipp[2] and Harold Hutchinson.[3] We talked a little about old times and they pressed me very hard about the role I had played in the election. I told them the truth, that I played a very small part. But the main thing I felt was that three weeks had removed me utterly from them and the whole thing was a little forced.

After lunch I went across to the House as George Moseley had told me I must 'nod' for my first Bill. I got myself squeezed into the front bench just before the budget and then my name was read and I nodded. So I sat there and listened to Callaghan deliver his speech. It was an extremely good speech, extremely well delivered. Indeed, the speech was far better than the budget.* After this I rushed back to the Ministry to have another talk with Hyams. I like him. He is extremely innocent about government. And after some thinking it became clear that the best thing to do was to have him as an adviser, studying our methods and writing reports for me since it was impossible actually to introduce him into the organization. This is what I put to him and I hope it is satisfactory.

Then I had to rush out because I had agreed to take Anne to the Queen for a drink. Molly drove us along the Mall and we drew up outside the Palace. The equerries were there to receive us and take us into a magnificent room and serve us quite ordinary gin and tonics. In due course the Queen entered. We had some amiable conversation with Sir Edward Ford who, as a farmer in Northamptonshire, is our neighbour at Prescote,[4] and in turn each of us was taken up to talk to the Queen. There were some half-dozen Labour Cabinet Ministers, the Gunters, the Crossmans, the Greenwoods, the Cousinses, the Castles. In our ten minutes she talked, as I am told she always does, about her corgis. (Two fat corgis, roughly the same colour as the carpet, were lying at her feet.) She remarked how often people fell over the dogs. I asked what good they were and she said they were Welsh dogs used for rounding up cattle by biting their legs. So we talked about whether cattle

---

* Though I must say that the reaction of the press the next day to the actual budget was the same as mine had been in Cabinet.

[1] Editor of the *Sun* 1964–5, and Editorial Director of I.P.C. Newspapers since 1968.

[2] Deputy chairman of I.P.C. from 1964 until 1968, when he became chairman; and chairman of I.P.C. Newspapers since 1970. He retired from I.P.C. at the end of 1973.

[3] Political correspondent of the *Sun*.

[4] Secretary to the Pilgrim Trust and former Assistant Private Secretary to the Queen.

stepped on them and I said our Suki, a poodle, was much quicker than a corgi at evading the cows. Then the Queen got on to talking about cows and said how terribly pleased she was when she had entered for the Dairy Show for the first time and won the championship for Jersey cows. Then she talked about Charles at Gordonstoun and whether it was a good school, and remarked that Charles had taken his O-levels young for his age.

It was a fairly forced performance but I think Anne quite liked it; she looked stunning with a little black net over her hair and a little black dress with a magnificent jewel, but she felt she wasn't rightly dressed for the evening. Originally I had refused to go to the 65th anniversary dinner of the County Councils Association which was taking place at County Hall across the river. However, I had been pressured and bullied and finally agreed to go when I found that George Brown was also going but not in a tailcoat. I haven't got one and didn't want to hire one. Dame Evelyn, who had to go too, said she was going in a long dress and it would be impossible for Anne to go in a short dress; so after the party at the Palace I went home and changed and was taken across to the G.L.C. with Jim MacColl, both of us in dinner-jackets, and I left Anne at home. When we arrived I found Sophie Brown, George Brown's wife, in the same dress she had been wearing at the palace. Anne could perfectly well have gone and I believe she would have rather liked it.

It was really very useful to me since everybody was there who matters in the local government world; I was introduced to the chairman of the A.M.C., the chairman of the C.C.A., the head of the Local Government Boundary Commission and the head of the Parliamentary Boundary Commission. Most of the local authority town clerks were there too. Just the right assembly for me to meet and say how-do-you-do. The only nuisance was that the food was extremely difficult to get and I drank with very little food and felt terrible next morning.

Thursday, November 12th
Another Cabinet. This time devoted to whether we should increase the salaries of M.P.s and Ministers. It was a very interesting meeting. The Prime Minister wanted us to accept the Report of the Lawrence Committee[1] and give the Members of Parliament an increase backdated to the beginning of the Session. Secondly, he wanted to halve the increases proposed by the Lawrence Committee for Cabinet Ministers, taking nothing himself and having us voluntarily abstaining from taking any increase for the length of this Parliament. In this he was broadly supported by a very interesting group. Not unnaturally he had Barbara Castle and also the Minister of Labour, Ray Gunter. The Chancellor of the Exchequer was also, for obvious reasons, on

---

[1] *Cmnd. 2516.* This Committee had been established by Sir Alec Douglas-Home when he was Prime Minister with a general all-Party understanding that whichever Party was in government, the recommendations would be implemented. It proposed that M.P.s' salaries should be increased from £1,750 to £3,250 p.a.

his side as well as Michael Stewart, Arthur Bottomley, Frank Soskice and Frank Longford.

The opposition was started by George Brown. He said bluntly that he thought if M.P.s had pay increases Cabinet Ministers should have them too, and it was vital to have the Ministerial increases voted immediately because, after all, the Lawrence Committee had been set up to decide this issue and if we didn't accept their impartial recommendation we would never get the increases for Ministers at all. George Brown said he would accept a 50-percent reduction but on the other hand he thought the increase should be paid straight away, possibly on April 1st, at the same time as the old-age pensions, but that no effort should be made to persuade Ministers to make the moral gesture of abstaining from accepting an increase. He also pointed out that if some Cabinet Ministers did abstain, they would get less than other Ministers; and if other Ministers abstained they would get less than Parliamentary Secretaries. So the question was whether we should take or leave the whole recommendation for the salary structure. He was strongly supported by the Lord Chancellor, and then Frank Cousins weighed in with a speech about the rate for the job and an assurance that incomes policy would not be decided by the rate of Ministers' pay. I pointed out that if there were a Tory government the scale of salaries now recommended would not be attractive to them. It was fully adequate for us and I thought therefore that 50 per cent paid on April 1st was O.K. George Brown, Frank Cousins and I were then supported by Fred Lee, Tom Fraser, Willie Ross and Tony Greenwood. When it came to adding up the votes, to my great surprise Harold Wilson calculated that our side had distinctly more votes than his. We had defeated the Prime Minister.*

I was due to meet Harold Wilson after this fascinating Cabinet meeting but it had lasted a long time, until 1 p.m., because the discussion of Members' pay had been followed by a short, very important discussion of arms to South Africa. Harold reported verbally, and I am afraid I paid hardly any attention —except that I did notice with approval that some anxiety was being expressed lest by banning arms to South Africa we were cutting off a valuable part of our export trade which could help us on the home front.[1]

I was due to go to the theatre to see *The Boy Friend* in the evening but I found myself taking Dame Evelyn out to dinner at the Farmers' Club because she had invited herself in order to discuss the crisis between us. Directly we sat down she put the situation to me with her usual bluntness. 'Well,' she said, 'you are a lucky Minister. You've the choice either of keeping me or getting rid of me. Which do you want?' I knew this was a trap and I couldn't

---

* Within a few days it became very clear that we had completely misjudged one thing. Whereas we had assumed that nobody could deny the right of the M.P.s to a backdated pay award, there was in fact strong opposition to any increase for them and an unpleasant contrast made between our treatment of M.P.s and our treatment of old-age pensioners.

[1] See page 41.

possibly say 'Get rid of you', so I said, 'I want to have you working for *me* for a change,' and I again put it very bluntly that I wanted her to treat me as a chief of staff treats his general, to prepare things for *me,* and see that I really was taking charge of the Department. I also told her I thought she mishandled our relations in Whitehall by fighting too hard (this is something George Moseley himself said to me the other day), and I thought in some things I could do better than her since a word in Wilson's ear at the right time might be worth five of her stormy meetings with her fellow mandarins. The fact is that throughout these three weeks her personal battle for the future of her Department has antagonized most of the Civil Service and a number of my colleagues, particularly George Brown and Fred Willey. Even worse for me, it's made everybody say, 'There is Dame Evelyn running round, but what is her Minister doing?'

As dinner went on, I came to see that though I had convinced myself on Monday and Tuesday that I was going to insist on getting rid of her and though she had convinced herself she was ready to go if I wanted it, neither of us was actually likely to do it in this particular year of grace 1964 or in this particular week of November 1964. We weren't prepared to break, partly I think because we really do quite like each other and regard each other as exceptions to a dreary rule; we are two people who know their own value and know the other's value. And on my side there is another reason. Dame Evelyn stands high in Whitehall and if I were to throw her out and make an enemy of her, if it were on my initiative she were expelled, I know quite well (Harold warned me when I rang him up on Wednesday morning to say how impossible life had been) the whole of the Whitehall hierarchy would be against me. There would be Questions in Parliament and a hell of a row. So I came to the conclusion that what I needed was to get on with her as well as I could, and to use her as far as I possibly can. Then if she feels she can't fit in I will make it possible for her to go. By the end of the evening I was clear that we were working quite well together and she had given a good deal to meet my point of view and would try to give even more. In fact since last Tuesday she has already tried to work the way I want her to work.

Friday, November 13th

I was due to go down to Prescote for the annual shoot, but as I was going up to Liverpool on an official visit it really wasn't worth going home just for an hour. Thank God I didn't, because Friday was an absolute drencher. It poured all day at Prescote and also here in London and I had the full profits of virtue by going off to Liverpool on the 6 p.m. train after doing a useful day's work.

In the morning we had a meeting of the Home Affairs Committee at which the Lord Chancellor tried to get us to accept his Bill for establishing a Law Commission. I think this is a perfectly sensible idea and I welcome it. I had told the Lord Chancellor so, with the result that I found he was quoting me constantly in arguing the case for his Bill to the Committee. He is an extraordinarily inept politician. He had told somebody just before that he was quite certain he would have no difficulty in getting consent in half an hour. Actually at the end of an hour it was clear that his Bill would be totally rejected unless it was sent to a sub-committee and saved there. He had the Home Secretary,´ Frank Soskice, saying he wasn't going to have his criminal law mucked about by law commissioners and he also had Douglas Jay making the same kind of objection for the Board of Trade. These objections were partly the result of the bad drafting of the paper; but there was also a vague feeling that the law commissioners might be intended not merely to be a consultative advisory body but to have some kind of executive power. That the Departments wouldn't have and they had briefed their Ministers to say so. However, we saved the Lord Chancellor from himself by setting up the sub-committee and I found myself a member of it.

I rushed back to Vincent Square and gave Jennie the news that George Moseley had agreed that she should come into the Private Office as my secretary. Donnison came there to lunch so that I could hear more about rents and rent control. Then I went back to the office to tidy things up, see the Secretary again, see that everything was in order for the preparation of my big speech next Wednesday, when I move the Second Reading of the anti-eviction Bill. Then I was off by the 6 p.m. train to Liverpool for my visitation.

There had been a somewhat comic prelude to this Liverpool visit. I had been asked by the Labour Council to come and I had told them I would postpone my visit until Bessie Braddock[1] told me she wanted me there. When I got the double invitation I accepted, whereupon Bessie thought *she* had invited me and could run the visit. And Alderman Sefton, the leader of the Labour Group, thought he was running the visit, which he actually was. Three days had been spent in the most furious altercation: Bessie wanted me to be photographed for the press and on television seeing the scandals of Canning Street, a slum street in her constituency; Sefton wanted me at all costs not to give Bessie her regular publicity in Canning Street, since it is absurd that each Minister should be photographed in this particular street. Of course he was right. But on the other hand M.P.s, Bessie or any other M.P., have the right to ask a visiting Minister to go and see something in the constituency. So I had to try to make peace between them. When I arrived in Liverpool at ten o'clock on Friday evening I found the battle still in full swing. Bessie was on my doorstep threatening to cause a demonstration and block the street and stop the charabanc in which I and the councillors were going to make our visit. I had to think up a compromise which was that she should enter the bus when we entered her constituency and leave the bus when I left it on the other side. This satisfied her pride. She agreed and to my amazement Sefton also agreed.

---

[1] Much-loved M.P. for Liverpool Exchange from 1945 until her death in November 1970. She was also a member of Liverpool City Council 1930–61.

Sunday, November 15th
This diary seems to be going in regular weekly spasms. I have got to another Sunday, another exquisitely beautiful afternoon. This time I've got a gyppy stomach and I've let my two nephews Nicky and Tom walk out with Anne over the farm whilst I stay behind in the warmth of the house and dictate this diary. It's a little affliction I woke up with at the Adelphi Hotel in Liverpool yesterday.

On November 21st–22nd defence matters were discussed at Chequers. Mr Wilson proposed to replace the M.L.F. with an Atlantic nuclear force, which would include American Polaris submarines, British V-bombers, 'some kind of mixed-manned, jointly owned elements' and the British Polaris submarine that Labour was not going to scrap after all.

On December 6th the Prime Minister flew to Washington, with Patrick Gordon Walker, Denis Healey, the Secretary of the Cabinet, the Chief of Defence Staff and a party of senior officials from the F.O. and the Ministry of Defence. He discussed political and economic issues with the President, but their talk was largely of defence and foreign policy. The President and his advisers seemed to agree to the proposal for an A.N.F. The Prime Minister returned to London on December 11th, after two days of talks in Ottawa. But the A.N.F. issue was by no means settled. The Labour left wing had always condemned the independent deterrent and had been unhappy about German rearmament, and many back-benchers were also troubled by the Government's failure to condemn American policy in Vietnam. Some of the Cabinet now wondered how the Party would receive the new defence proposals. The row about the pension increase was already rumbling in the P.L.P.

The worsening economic situation was also discussed at the Chequers weekend at the end of November, and on Monday, November 23rd, bank rate went up from 5 to 7 per cent. But the pound continued to slide, and though devaluation was a forbidden subject in Cabinet the idea was certainly aired in public. The situation was saved, temporarily at least, when on November 25th the Bank of England arranged a $3,000 million credit with other central banks.

It seemed all the more important, therefore, that the Government should carry out its intention of scrapping the expensive Anglo-French project to build a supersonic aircraft, Concorde.

Monday, November 16th
I went up as usual by my morning train and found myself just in time for a meeting of the Economic Development Committee on Concorde. This was almost the first subject put to Cabinet at our first meeting; we were told that something dramatic must be done and Concorde should be scrapped because of the economic crisis. Since then, more cautious counsel has prevailed. It has been found impossible to scrap it without tearing up not merely a

commercial contract but a treaty, so possibly making ourselves liable to pay bigger compensation to the French than the cost of going ahead. It has also been found that the French are delighted to make it as difficult as possible for us and at this meeting Roy Jenkins (he is not in the Cabinet and at a grave disadvantage for that reason) put forward a paper on what should be done.

I think this was the first time that a really important issue had been put to a Cabinet Committee since we took office. What it means is that Harold Wilson has decided that if he can get an agreed solution in the Cabinet Committee he won't have to waste his time dealing with it in Cabinet. The paper of Roy's we were discussing offered us five alternatives ranging from cancelling completely to trying to interest the Americans in a tripartite project. It was soon obvious that our two main economic Ministers, the Chancellor and the First Secretary, were determined to cancel the contract at any price and to pooh-pooh the Attorney-General, Elwyn Jones, when he gravely warned them about the effects of treaty-breaking. On the other side it was clear that Douglas Jay, who as President of the Board of Trade had had a terrible time defending the 15 per cent surcharge against the infuriated members of EFTA, was appalled at the possibility of breaking another treaty. Here we had the two sides lined up, the brutal economizers on the one side and the more internationally minded people on the other, including the Foreign Secretary. Between them the rest of us were watching and carefully considering what should be done. I found myself rather on the side of Tony Crosland. Both of us thought George Brown was pretty free and easy about the cancellation of the contract and also unduly defeatist in writing off Concorde completely. On the other hand, he was strongly supported by Frank Cousins who said that by concentrating all our technological resources on to aircraft the contract was distorting the economy and everything would be gained technologically by getting rid of it altogether. Perhaps the most interesting feature of the meeting was Roy Jenkins's performance. He had quite strong support from Douglas Jay and one or two others, including Tony Crosland and myself, for a moderate view. If he had been prepared to propose that we should produce the two prototype aircraft, I think he could have got a firm commitment from the Committee. As it was, he went away with instructions to negotiate from an almost impossible position.

I had my weekly lunch with Bob Mellish and James MacColl at Vincent Square. Bob is settling down, getting a real housing drive going in London, going round the boroughs, assessing each one and making contact with them. He is also pretty shrewd at the important operation of keeping good relations with the Parliamentary Labour Party. Jim MacColl is a much more inhibited, retiring man; but I still feel he is far the best Parliamentary Secretary I could possibly have. He is concentrating on the planning work I delegated to him and I think he is enjoying life. We decided that on Wednesday, when we are to have the Second Reading of the anti-eviction Bill, Jim MacColl, who had been invited out to one of those endless dinners, should keep his engagement and Bob Mellish would wind up. So it was Bob and I who went to see the officials in the afternoon to be briefed on the Bill. I suggested to the officials that they should provide drafts of four passages in my speech for Wednesday while I would do the political introduction myself.

After this I went out to dinner with George Weidenfeld.[1] I had been invited to the Lord Mayor's dinner but since I haven't got a white tie and a tailcoat I had refused to go. And I must admit that this has been noticed already on the television by more than one commentator. However, I did have an extremely pleasant evening. Pam Berry was there and I sat next to Noel Annan's[2] wife, Gaby, and altogether it was the kind of party I enjoy. If I am going to relax that's the company I prefer to keep.

Tuesday, November 17th

I stayed at Vincent Square and Jennie came; together we prepared the first part of my speech. I had just about completed this when I went off to lunch and afterwards to the House of Commons where I had to be at 3.15, for Questions. Once again my Questions weren't reached.

Then I had to go to a meeting of the Legislation Committee on future legislation. This was quite illuminating. A vast concourse – some thirty people – had been gathered together, and some eighty to ninety Bills were listed in various classes of priority. I was staggered to see that whereas I had safely got top priority for the Rent Bill, the Land Commission had been pushed down to third priority and leasehold reform had been put second. I knew quite well that this was the result of the Welsh pressure group led by Jim Callaghan and Jim Griffiths operating on a weak Lord President of the Council. The meeting was a bit ludicrous: we were supposed to consider priorities but couldn't, since it was obvious that everyone there was deeply committed to his own particular measure whether it was a minor piece of legal reform or a little Bill to give independence to Gambia or a really major piece of our pro- gramme. If you go there briefed by your Ministry you can only say 'My Bill is equally important'. However, I was able to make a stink about the Land Commission being put down so low and strongly supported Fred Willey that it must be brought up higher. On this I got full support from Michael Stewart, my predecessor as Shadow Housing Minister, from the Secretary of State for Scotland, Willie Ross, and, rather surprisingly, from the Attorney-General. So it wasn't wasted time for me.

Then I went across to the office where I had asked George Moseley to have a shorthand-typist and Jennie available to get the speech done. We started

---

[1] Chairman of the publishing house of Weidenfeld & Nicolson, and noted for his literary and political parties.
[2] At this point Noel Annan was Provost of King's College, Cambridge. In 1965 he was created Lord Annan and in October 1966 became Provost of University College, London.

off at about 7.15 and we finished at about 1 a.m. while the discussion on immigration was still taking place on the Expiring Laws Continuance Bill.[1] It took a great deal longer than I thought to prepare the speech because all the passages drafted by the Department were totally useless with one minor exception. Though I had assumed, for example, that someone could write for me a clause-by-clause description of what was in the Bill, when the draft actually came up it was exactly like the memorandum from which it was drawn and I had to do the whole thing myself. I did it.

Wednesday, November 18th

When I got to the office at eleven o'clock the draft was ready and I knew that I had got a speech I could deliver. The process had been an object lesson. The fact is that a Minister who relies on a departmental brief is going to have a very dull exposition of his Bill.

However, even when my whole mind and emotions were geared to my debut at the dispatch box as a Cabinet Minister I had to concentrate on one of those dreary subjects which come up and harass a Minister. In this case it was the future of the children's service of the L.C.C. when the G.L.C. takes over.[2] One of the first things I did as Minister was to ask the Labour leaders of the L.C.C. to come over and tell me what they wanted. In this talk they said they were very anxious to get an amendment of the G.L.C. Act into the Queen's Speech. I explained to them that this kind of legislation was most unlikely to be included and we agreed that I should make a general statement of intention and then let them do the change when the educational provisions of the Act are reviewed after five years.[3] Some days later I found that they had been ferreting round with old friends like Frank Soskice, Michael Stewart and particularly the Lord Chancellor, an old member of the L.C.C., and the pressure was on me in Cabinet. Everyone began to feel that however short of time we were we ought to introduce a Bill to amend the G.L.C. Act and restore control to the boroughs of the children's service, which had been handed over by them to the top tier, i.e. the G.L.C. Well, my own Department dug their toes in; and though I was quite in favour of the idea, I didn't see why this should come first in my Ministry of Housing legislative programme because I wanted at least a dozen things a great deal more.

So a kind of deadlock arose and this morning a meeting had been called by the Home Secretary in the Lord President's room with only Ministers

---

[1] This renewed, each Session, legislation in force for one year only. Though unhappy with the Conservative 1961 Commonwealth Immigrants Act, the Government continued it as a holding measure.

[2] The reorganization of London government had been enacted in 1963, and the Greater London Council and the new London borough councils were to assume their new functions on April 1st, 1965.

[3] For an initial period the G.L.C. was to be responsible for education in the London area. The review could conceivably include child welfare services.

attending. Once again Alice Bacon, who is number two at the Home Office, reminded me of the pledges given by Michael Stewart and Arthur Skeffington to the Labour majority on the L.C.C. Once again I said I had nothing against giving the children's service back: it was simply a question of timing and priority. Once again I saw Frank Soskice squirming; whenever he asks for something to be done it is always because of his personal difficulties. We have to abolish capital punishment so that he won't have to execute a bank robber. We have to deal with immigration because his conscience is stretched by the Expiring Laws Continuance Act. Now we have to suit his friendship with Gerald Gardiner and the other old L.C.C. men by getting this Bill into our legislative programme. In defence I could only say that a new situation had developed now—a number of the Tory-controlled boroughs had made it clear that they would oppose the Bill since it was no longer a simple little Bill but controversial, and there simply wouldn't be time for it. I don't think I had persuaded anybody before I went back to the Ministry to find the civil servants had seen my draft speech and had found nothing wrong with it. I then worked away at finalizing it and went home to lunch with Anne and Jennie, who were going to come and listen to the debate.

My Second Reading went fairly satisfactorily. I planned a half-hour speech but as I was interrupted seven or eight times it ran to forty minutes, which was a bit too long. Nevertheless, it was about the right mixture: it ensured that the Bill was non-controversial and accepted by the Tories and yet gave our own back-benchers some feeling that the Minister was on their side. I don't think a single Cabinet Minister waited to listen to me. George Brown had been there at the end of Question Time and said, 'You can hardly expect me to wait for this, my dear brother,' and I said, 'Of course not.' In fact all my colleagues were too busy, though it would have been nice to have some support because I was extremely nervous. This was virtually a maiden front-bench speech. The fact is I've been almost totally absent from the House recently and have less front-bench experience than any other Cabinet Minister. That was why I was so nervous and why I had written out the speech in full, every word. I much prefer speaking ad lib and I always did on the back benches, but I think I shall have to do this in future on any complicated Bill because a written script does enable one to get everything in, which is certainly something one can't guarantee when one ad libs.

There was also the alarm that in dealing with a subject which I've only been looking at for a few weeks I might be caught out by the questions. So it was an enormous relief that I got through and Tam Dalyell after a round of the House said there was no doubt our side had thought it a good show, although they had taken this for granted. Most of the rest of the debate seemed to be maiden speeches and Bob Mellish wound up with a really rumbustious, knockabout speech that went down extremely well. Then I took Bob and his wife and Jim home for a drink at Vincent Square and we all felt the kind of enormous exhilaration one does feel when a first night is over.

Thursday, November 19th

The morning papers were satisfactory in a very modest way. Charles Snow had made his debut almost at the same moment as I had been speaking, with the result that I got virtually no publicity. That was quite a good thing. What was important from my point of view was that no journalist thought of describing my appearance as a first performance or reminding people of how little I had been in the House recently.

In Cabinet this morning the main subject was pensions. A few days after the budget debate it became clear that our own back-benchers were not at all pleased and would start insisting that the pension increase should not be postponed until April but paid out much earlier. Sydney Silverman,[1] for instance, and Ian Mikardo[2] could remember very well that this was the first subject on which there was successful rebellion under the Labour Government of 1945, and they hoped it would be the first subject under this Government too. Apparently at the first meeting of the new Parliamentary Party there had been an unfortunate fiasco because Douglas Houghton, who was the Cabinet Minister in charge of pensions, had been away and poor Peggy Herbison had been all alone there. She was attacked and chivvied and had gone away highly disconcerted. At Cabinet we decided quite rightly that if the pensions were put up earlier, the contributions must be raised earlier too. However the final decision would be deferred until our meeting on Tuesday next week.

We had our usual talk about parliamentary business and in the course of it I said I had some difficulties about the anti-eviction Bill, in particular the problem of the agricultural workers[3] where the Tories had made real difficulties. I said this clause wasn't essential to the emergency Bill and if necessary it could be dropped. Harold Wilson said rather sharply, 'That would give an impression of dithering,' a word he had borrowed from Lord Attlee. I replied that I was delighted to fight it out. I just wanted a Cabinet ruling that we should do so, because that might require an all-night sitting next Thursday when the Bill goes into Committee on the Floor of the House.

The last subject we dealt with was the legislative programme. Once again I was able to insist that whatever happened, the Land Commission must come on early and it seemed to me significant that Harold Wilson very carefully stated that it would be convenient to run the Steel Bill and the Rent Bill

---

[1] Left-wing M.P. for Nelson and Colne from 1935 until his death in 1968. In 1965 he succeeded in his ten-year battle for the abolition of capital punishment.

[2] Labour M.P. for Reading 1945–59, and Poplar since 1964. A notable extreme left-winger, and a member of the N.E.C. He became chairman of the Select Committee on the Nationalized Industries in 1966 (until 1970) and was chairman of the N.E.C. 1970–71.

[3] Farm workers living in tied cottages were particularly vulnerable to eviction. This issue had always been politically contentious, especially as the N.U.A.W. spokesman on Labour's N.E.C. came from East Anglia where agricultural labour was highly organized (in this region there was little alternative employment). Crossman inserted in the Protection from Eviction Bill a clause requiring a six-month delay before farmers could legally evict their tenants, during which the magistrates court would assess the balance of interests.

parallel, introducing them both at the end of January and keeping the Committee Stages simultaneous. Obviously he was thinking it would be a good idea that if we were defeated it would not be specifically and solely on steel but on rents as well. So he is still not excluding the possibility of a May election—a possibility that was strengthened this week by the results of the Gallup Poll, the first since the election. It gives Labour a lead of 11½ per cent compared to the 1½ per cent we had in the actual election.

In the afternoon I had the first of my staff meetings. Dame Evelyn and Waddell and Jones sat together with me. I discovered that there are regular meetings between Dame Evelyn and the Assistant Secretaries in charge of divisions, meetings which I shall obviously attend from time to time. I then put my first point, about the need for a progress-chaser who would deal not with the four-fifths of the work which comes up from the Department below but the one-fifth of the work—the policy decisions—which come down from the Minister to the Department. I said I wanted to bring somebody in from outside who would see that my ideas really got properly considered in the Department. No reaction. I was not surprised. But I did get an important agreement about planning decisions. At present those which come up to me for final decision are presented in an intolerable form. Just a mass of bumf in the file. I am now insisting that the papers should always have in front of them a two-page staff study, the shape of which I've borrowed very largely from the SHAEF soldiers.[1] So in future I shall be told at the beginning what the vital problem is and how the Department suggests it should be solved. And then at the back there should be all the documents for me to dig into.

Finally I asked how the Department was getting on with preparing the paper which will present the basic thinking and policy recommendations for the Rent Bill. I was told a draft was nearly ready but was quite unsuitable to send out to Goodman and the others to whom I wanted to show it. However, they would like me to see it and I was to take it away. I have now studied the draft and it seems to me very much the kind of thing we *can* send out to Goodman and the others, so long as we take the word 'Secret' off it! In the course of the meeting I did make it clear that, whatever happened, I was going to have all our policy ideas for the Rent Bill discussed by two separate outside groups, the first group to be the Labour lawyers headed by Ashley Bramall[2] and including Jim MacColl, and the second group headed by Arnold Goodman and including his friend Dennis Lloyd[3] and one or two other experts. I want to use both of them and bring them fully into my confidence. The Department hate it but I think they now see it's got to be done.

Indeed it seems to me that Dame Evelyn is gradually getting accustomed to my methods. Up till now she has held the traditional Civil Service view

[1] Crossman advised on psychological warfare at Eisenhower's H.Q. in Algiers in 1944.
[2] A barrister and former Labour M.P. for Bexley, 1946–50; now a member of the G.L.C. He became leader of the I.L.E.A. in 1970.
[3] Professor of Jurisprudence at University College London, and a member of the Law Reform Committee. He went to the Lords in 1965.

that a Minister mustn't complain if he doesn't know about a matter until it is ready for him to digest. My view is very different. I am not prepared to have things pre-cooked and to find that I am only a final court of appeal about matters which have virtually been decided before I've ever had access to them.

Friday, November 20th
I spent the whole day on departmental affairs, starting with a meeting of the Home Affairs Committee where I put forward a paper on leasehold reform. It outlines a way, suggested to me by one of the Welsh Whips, to pacify the Welsh lobby while not introducing the actual Bill. The pacification would come from a statement that leaseholders whose leases run out before the Bill's enactment would be able to receive all the advantages of the Bill. Characteristically enough, the moment I put forward the proposal the lawyers began to find all sorts of difficulties in the draft statement, but I finally got what I wanted – permission to call a meeting of the Welsh group to put this statement to them and to say that I was willing to make it if they felt that it didn't cause more perturbation than it allayed fears.

The other important meeting that Friday was a long-delayed meeting on local government, which the Dame has been very keen to hold. She had presented me with a long official paper which I had studied the night before. The more I looked at it the more I realized that this is one of my most important responsibilities. The problem is roughly this: for some eight years now the Local Government Boundary Commission (which was reconstituted after Aneurin Bevan tore it up) has been at work, going round the country making specific recommendations for revising local government boundaries, mostly those of boroughs and county boroughs, leaving the counties fairly well alone. Some of their most ambitious work has been done in the West Midlands conurbation and in Tyneside. They have also recommended the revision of the boundaries of Leicester city and of Nottingham city as well as my own city of Coventry. All these proposals are now coming up to me, because in the last period before the general election my predecessor, Keith Joseph, found an excuse for postponing any decisions.[1] So suddenly I have a whole series of extremely important decisions to make – in each case I have to decide whether to carry out the recommendation of the Commission or whether to modify it in any way. Dame Evelyn is naturally concerned to get me to make these decisions as soon as possible. On the other hand, I soon discovered that as a Labour politician these are for me not merely decisions about the boundaries of *local authorities* but decisions which will influence the boundaries of *constituencies*. The reason for that is simple: constituency boundaries are drawn broadly in conformity with the boundaries of county

---

[1] The Minister of Housing was responsible for adjudicating on the reports of the Local Government Boundary Commission. The directive to the Parliamentary Boundary Commission (the Home Secretary's responsibility) meant that local government constituency arrangements affected parliamentary constituencies.

boroughs; that is to say, the Parliamentary Commissioners try as far as possible to keep Coventry a unit divided up into two or three constituencies and to avoid having constituencies which are partly Coventry and partly Warwickshire. This fact means that every time, as Minister in charge of local government boundaries, I alter a county borough boundary I may affect the fate of the M.P. sitting for this borough.

Very soon after I became Minister I had been approached by Bert Bowden, Lord President of the Council, and told that if the reform of the boundaries of Leicester went through, at least two of the Labour seats would be in danger, including his own. I also discovered that in Coventry there were risks involved, but that I could by a minor amendment make practically sure that Coventry remains our way. So I find myself as Minister of Housing a powerful politician in my own right. Of course, it's a little improper to see these local government boundary changes in relation to parliamentary divisions and we must remember that the Parliamentary Boundary Commission responsible to the Home Secretary won't be reporting until five or six years' time, i.e. after the next election.[1] Nevertheless, my colleagues are bound to consider the impact of local government boundaries on their constituency boundaries; and I also have to consider what general attitude I should take to the Local Government Boundary Commission as well as how I shall handle these particular decisions. Frankly, the more I looked at what the Commission has been doing the more futile I found their work. I had a very challenging meeting with the local government section of the Ministry at which I said that I would like to see genuine local government reform on the agenda of the next Government with a big enough majority, and that we should now prepare for that as a real possibility.

It was this challenge that made the Dame produce the paper on the basis of which we were having the discussion this Friday. The paper was a skilful argument in favour of letting things go on as they are at present. It included a statement that the Boundary Commission was doing the best it could possibly do in tinkering along, working on the broad principle that where a city swells, the conurbation should extend its boundaries. I find this very unsatisfactory since it means accepting the war between the county councils and the county borough authorities as endemic in our national life, something I find one of the most stultifying things in our whole governmental system. So after our talk, I said we should look into this much more thoroughly and I wasn't going to make up my mind until I had had a chance of talking to members of the Local Government Boundary Commission and had heard again from the local government section of the Ministry what they would like to do if they had a Minister who wanted to undertake a major reform of local government.

I'm not sure whether the Dame doesn't crush all new ideas when she is at

[1] James Callaghan (by then Home Secretary) attempted to delay the implementation of the recommendations. This was to be a constitutional *cause célèbre* in 1970.

3

one of my meetings. She is so clear in her mind that she knows the answer to everything. She is so lapidary in her view that it's rather like turning a stone over and finding what animals are living underneath when I push her aside and try to get the junior members of the Ministry to talk freely. She hates it, they are scared of it, but unless they do talk I can't really discover what are the issues involved in any problem.

A good example of this came up this week with regard to Stevenage. Shirley Williams asked to see me urgently and said she wanted to give evidence at the public inquiry on Stevenage. This relates to a proposal to enlarge three of our New Towns, Basildon, Harlow and Stevenage, as part of the method of dealing with London overspill. The idea has been accepted without too much opposition by Basildon and Harlow. But Stevenage has reacted furiously against the proposal that their town should be doubled in size by the device of adding a kind of twin town on the far side of the motorway and the railway track. And of course Stevenage is right. What sane planner would place a motorway and a main railway plumb between two halves of a city? All my sympathies are with Stevenage, one of the few New Towns which really has achieved a genuine community civic sense. Now they are apparently going to be ordered by the Ministry to accept an enlargement which in their view will destroy their whole unity as a town. When I heard about this from Shirley I ordered a seminar, where Mr Beddoes and the Chief Architect put the case to me. I then tested it out by asking all the Ministry officials sitting there what they thought. James, our Chief Planner, said he was schizophrenic and two others were highly doubtful. Really the only supporter of Dame Evelyn was her ambitious Deputy, Mr Jones, and the Engineer. By the end I realized that the atmosphere was very sultry and that Dame Evelyn hated my technique of making her quite junior people speak up for themselves. I fancy she and I are going to have a major row about Stevenage. She sees the New Towns as the great creations of her Ministry and she loves them because they have been created autocratically from above. She is determined to keep that tradition, and although it is high time some of them were turned over wholly to their local authorities, Crawley and Hemel Hempstead for example, she is determined to keep the New Town Commissions almost permanently in being. In this she comes completely up against Labour Party policy, which expressly states that we should hand over to the urban district council as soon as they are ready to take over, and as soon as we've found a solution to the difficult problem of what happens to the assets.

Saturday, November 21st

I got back to Prescote on Friday night and worked through Saturday morning at my boxes, wading through the planning cases and seeing for myself what was wrong with the method of organizing planning decisions. Ever since I've been Minister I've noticed that each morning the papers carry news of a planning decision I have taken, usually stating that I've considered it sympathetically before turning it down. So there is a whole mass of stuff in the press about what the Minister has been doing and feeling where in fact the Minister hasn't been consulted at all. I therefore gave instructions that for one month all the press releases and all the actual letters to authorities written in my name on planning permissions and compulsory purchase orders should be sent to me. Reading them through, I am struck by two things. Firstly, there is nothing wrong with the press releases. They are sensible and well written. Secondly, there seems to me no rhyme or reason about the way the Minister's name is brought in by the various officials who write these instructions. Certainly, it's plain ridiculous that a decision which depends entirely on seeing whether a particular design for improving or enlarging a house looks well or badly in the middle of Suffolk should be said to be finally decided by me without me or any of my officials going near the spot. One of the obvious ways of ending this would be to say that no planning permission with a value of, say, under £100,000 should come up to me at all. Then we should have to set up some regional court of appeal to take the place of the Minister. I can see there is a problem here; but I do know that far too much comes up to the Ministry and there are delays of up to a year or eighteen months in the granting of permissions. Here is an area where I know that administrative action is really needed.

Sunday, November 22nd
On Saturday afternoon the family made a splendid expedition to the open-cast iron mine up north of us at Byfield, which may or may not be under my control. We dug fossils out of the newly exposed strata and had a wonderful afternoon. Today I was busy with Pritchett about tree-planting on the bends of the Cherwell between Upper Prescote and Prescote. We had Richard and Ann Hartree to lunch with their children, both families all together. Life here at Prescote gets lovelier the longer it goes on. Really, the more I am a Minister the better I feel physically, the more stimulated I feel. Work doesn't exhaust me at all. It feels far lighter in a way and it's far easier work than the arduous strains of writing for popular papers. Life personally for me is going magnificently. I'm not being a particularly successful Minister in the sense of throwing my weight about or getting known, but I think I am settling in to the Department. With so few weeks behind me it is almost incredible how quickly I have got into the Ministerial swing, become accustomed to the tempo and style of the work, with motor-cars and Cabinet Office and Private Office. It's a routine which moves so smoothly and envelops one so completely that it's difficult to remember I have ever done anything else. Of course, this doesn't mean that I'm not aware of how inexperienced I am in the politics of the Cabinet and the intrigues of Whitehall. There is an enormous lot to be learnt about running the Department and handling the House and putting one's case in Cabinet. But it still remains true that the routine has now got into my system. After twenty years of journalism I don't feel it strange that I

am not writing anything, or that I hardly read the newspapers apart from the subjects I am interested in, or that my work consists of office work, administration, decision-making, conferences. Indeed, in all of this I feel perfectly at home now and far less tired than I did in what you might call my free independent life as a working journalist.

What about the Cabinet? I notice there is some talk in the press about an inner Cabinet, no doubt partly occasioned by the Chequers weekend which is now taking place with all the Defence people to brief Harold for his visit to Washington. I don't think there is really any evidence of the existence of an inner Cabinet. What is clear is that Harold himself is taking a predominant interest in foreign affairs and defence and George Brown is becoming the Deputy Prime Minister, in charge of the home front. That suits me perfectly well. But there is a very delicate relationship between George Brown and myself because he, as head of the D.E.A., is interested in developing economic planning and I, as Minister of Housing, am in charge of physical planning. Almost inevitably there is a collision between my well-established job and George Brown's new ideas. I have been trying for a long time to persuade him that he and Willey and I should sit down together without officials for a couple of hours and ask where we are. I rather suspect that if I do, I shall find that on the whole subject of regional planning and regional organization he has left Bill Rodgers to do the job[1] and that he really knows very little about it. And that's typical of Cabinet, too. It's now a specialist Cabinet. We haven't any conflicts which have lined us up into Left and Right groups. We've had two tremendous arguments, one about pensions and the other about the budget, and we've had the disagreement about M.P.s' salaries. But in each of these cases there seemed to be a line-up of realists against gesture-makers, and in each case the P.M. failed to get his way. No, I can't now say that Harold is a presidential Prime Minister. On the contrary, he has done what he said he would do, genuinely delegated so that each Minister can run his own Ministry without running to him for assistance. As long as I carry on satisfactorily and don't cause trouble he will be satisfied with me. The difference for me of course is that I see him much less, even less than I did when he was leader of the Opposition. He is now very remote indeed. Even knowing Tommy Balogh and George Wigg really well doesn't help me much because I don't know what either of them is doing.

This evening Nicholas Davenport[2] and Olga have come over to see us from Hinton. He rang me up this morning to tell me he wasn't going to support Harold's Tory budget, and I said on the spur of the moment, 'Why not come over and see us,' and they turned up at six o'clock. And before I knew it we were in a furious argument. Nicholas's theme was a simple one. The City,

[1] M.P. for Stockton-on-Tees since 1962. Parliamentary Under-Secretary at the D.E.A. 1964–7 and at the F.O. 1967–8. He became Minister of State at the Board of Trade in 1969, and at the Treasury from 1969 to 1970. Since 1971 he has been chairman of the Trade and Industry Sub-Committee of the Expenditure Committee.

[2] Distinguished financial journalist, of left-wing inclination, writing for the *Spectator*.

he said, have lost confidence. After all, Callaghan threatens the City daily with the corporation tax and the capital gains tax, and the City feel they don't know what to fear; then they lose confidence. 'You are heading', said Nicholas, 'straight for devaluation.' And then something happened to me. For the first time since I became Minister I woke up out of my departmental seclusion and looked at the world round me and realized that in the Cabinet I had been as far removed from reality as Olga sitting painting a picture in Chelsea. I went up to town that evening by the nine o'clock train uneasy for the first time and wondering whether we had come unstuck. It was pretty clear from what Nicholas said that Callaghan's budget speech really had been a flop. Confidence had not been restored, at least not in the City; and with heavy selling and speculation in Zurich we were in the kind of classical financial crisis socialist governments must expect when they achieve power and find the till empty.

Monday, November 23rd
And, sure enough, when I got to my office I had a message that the Chancellor wanted to see me before the meeting of the Economic Development Committee. I went round to No. 11 and there was Callaghan, heavy and gloomy as ever. 'I am the Selwyn Lloyd', he said, 'of this Government.' He was obviously overawed by the situation and full of self-pity. There was to be an announcement of a 7 per cent bank rate at eleven o'clock, he said to me, and he wanted to warn me of it. He was in a terrible state and couldn't really tell me anything. We walked across to the Economic Committee where he gave the announcement again to the whole Committee before we got down to our ordinary business.

In the afternoon I sat on the front bench and heard Callaghan making the announcement to the Commons and emphasizing that he would try to mitigate the effect of the bank rate on housing and in particular on public-sector housing. What he meant by this God only knows. I thought it was quite unnecessary, and if he had asked me I would have told him not to say it. I gathered that Harold Wilson and George Brown had also been going round pacifying the comrades in the tea-room and trying to take the edge off the measures designed to soothe or at least to reassure the City and the Zurich bankers.

Tuesday, November 24th
Cabinet day. After a brief account by Callaghan of the reasons for the 7 per cent bank rate we had a long discussion about pensions, which revealed a great deal about what was wrong with our Cabinet. The previous week we had been under great pressure from the back-benchers, who wanted the pension increase backdated at least to Christmas. Last Thursday's Cabinet therefore decided to pay out £4 a head to everyone on national assistance, something I personally protested would do a great deal of damage since millions of pensioners aren't on national assistance and would keenly resent

getting nothing. Cabinet had instructed Peggy Herbison to work out a scheme of back-payment. I was very much against this, too, since I thought we had done quite enough for the pensioners. The whole mood of the Cabinet last Thursday had been one of readiness to surrender and appease the back-benchers, but now, between the two Cabinet meetings, we had been faced with a sudden economic crisis and we could hardly fail to realize the obvious fact that if we implemented our decision of the previous Thursday we might well have a 9 per cent bank rate or a devaluation.

So what was really striking was the difference between the mood of the two Cabinets. Peggy Herbison had worked out a backdating scheme as instructed but she got nothing but almost universal hostility. She was extremely angry at this and said she wouldn't explain it to the P.L.P. meeting this evening.

This was really the first Party meeting of the new Parliament under the new Labour Government. It was an alarming experience. It revealed once again the utter weakness of this Government. Really there are two weaknesses. The Government is very weak on foreign affairs—its three foreign representatives, Patrick Gordon Walker, Douglas Jay and Arthur Bottomley, are really all pretty hopeless. The second weakness—the one which concerns me chiefly—lies in the relation between the Cabinet and the Parliamentary Party, for which the Chief Whip, Ted Short, and the Lord President of the Council, Bert Bowden, are responsible. As far as I can see, these two men are really little disciplinarians with no idea of imaginative leadership and no real contact with the back-benchers, and as a result a great deal of ill will has crept in between the Cabinet and its supporters. We've been there five weeks. Yet not one of the Party groups has yet been re-established. I think I'm the only Minister who has got hold of his interested back-benchers and started them working. As a result of the frustration they feel a splendid lot of back-benchers are forming indignant pressure groups, grievance groups, and inevitably the pension issue has been the one taken up by John Mendelson,[1] Tom Driberg, Ian Mikardo, the people you would expect. They have gone round busily saying that in 1945 the pensioners were helped by a revolt of the rank and file against the Cabinet and this first rebellion could be repeated in the 1964 Government.

Well, it was a packed meeting and Douglas Houghton, in his usual rather pedestrian, pedantic way, gave an elaborate speech about Peggy's plan and what the difficulties were, and then he referred to the Cabinet decision and told the Party that despite the fact that the plan for backdating was technically possible the financial situation forbade it. After this questions were allowed for ten or twelve minutes and Douglas then made a lengthy reply. It was pretty obvious that the Party was out for major concessions, and that the danger outside, the danger of devaluation, wasn't real to that packed, smoky Party meeting. I was sitting on the platform, and as George Brown came in he said to me, 'The situation is desperate. It's the worst we've ever had.' Then

[1] M.P. for Penistone since 1959.

Jim Callaghan came in and sat down on the other side of me and he said the same thing, and I sat there realizing that we were absolutely on the edge of devaluation while the Party talked about getting more concessions for the old-age pensioners and upbraided the Government for its failure to do its duty by them.

It was a fantastic situation when one realized that the whole major crisis had been caused by the Government's attempt to do justice to the pensioners. The situation was grim. George Brown got up and did magnificently. He rallied the Party, he indicated the danger without actually describing it in so many words, and he pulled the back-benchers round and made them feel they had to accept the leadership of the Government and drop the idea of any further concessions to the pensioners.

After this meeting I took Anne in to dine alone with me in the Strangers' dining-room. When we had finished I looked into the other part of the room and found Harold and Tommy Balogh and I went to have a chat with them. This was really a fascinating occasion. I had hardly said a word to Harold before he gave us all brandies twice round. He seemed cool and collected and we discussed the situation we were in. Then the bell rang for the division and as we were walking along the corridor he said, 'You know, Dick, in any great campaign like the Peninsular War the commanding general has to know where to retreat to. He has to have his lines of Torres Vedras.'[1] 'Well,' I said, 'a number of people want devaluation now.' I had been talking to Thomas who, like Nicky Kaldor and Robert Neild, felt that devaluation was the only thing left and should be got over as quickly as possible. But Harold Wilson would have none of it. 'You're talking nonsense,' he said. 'Devaluation would sweep us away. We would have to go to the country defeated. We can't have it. No, I have my lines of Torres Vedras which I am retreating to, and I'm popping off now along the lobby to carry out the retreat.' And along the lobby he popped.

Wednesday, November 25th
I had been asked by George Brown to see him yesterday evening at 10, but I had Anne there and I didn't feel like going. I know now that during that period from 11 at night till 1.30 in the morning George and Harold, with the Governor of the Bank of England, worked out a magnificent appeal which rallied £3,000 million to our aid and really saved the Labour Government as well as saving the pound.[2]

I went to see George today at 9.20; at 9.35 he turned up, bleary-eyed. I thought at first this was because of drink, but no, he had of course been with Harold and the Governor the night before and he told me that he wasn't yet sure the trick had worked. Fred Willey came in and we got down to talking

[1] During the Peninsular War the Duke of Wellington foiled the French attack by secretly constructing enormous earthworks around one of the besieged cities. They were known as 'the lines of Torres Vedras'.
[2] For the Prime Minister's story of the 'desperate meeting with the Governor' see *Wilson*, pp. 35–8.

about planning. I explained what my Ministry wanted; I don't think George Brown had fully realized before that the creation of the Land Commission was a major factor in the whole planning operation for which he at the D.E.A. should be responsible.

From there George and I drove across to Smith Square to the N.E.C. meeting which we found three-quarters empty and absolutely flat, a long post-mortem on the election to which nobody was paying any attention. This is another of the dangerous weaknesses of our Party today. If we as a Cabinet have neglected our relationship with the Parliamentary Party we have equally neglected our relations with Transport House and the Party outside. Frankly, Transport House is dying on its feet because we are not facing up to the problem of giving it a job to do. What that meeting of the National Executive proved was that there really wasn't a function for the Party. Half the members who are Ministers weren't there, the trade unionists had their little chats and the whole situation was dead and, for that reason, dangerous.

Back to the Ministry for a big meeting with the local authorities about this year's General Grant. This is one of those tortuous administrative monstrosities which a Minister of Housing has to understand. The General Grant, as I've now learned, is the block contribution which central government pays to local authorities and it covers more than half their costs. This General Grant is fixed by Ministerial Order[1] every second year in December and it so happens that this December is the first of the two-year cycle. We as a Government have no time to change the General Grant fixed by the Tories and this year we are giving the local authorities a Grant £17 million less than they think they are entitled to. When the Ministry told me all this I accepted it and gave Callaghan an assurance that I wouldn't ask for any concessions on rates this year, although it was clear in our election programme that we are firmly committed to relieving the burden on the ratepayer during the course of this Parliament. The Order which I have to present to the House commits me not only for this year but for next year, not only for 1965–6 but for 1966–7, and for the second year, too, we are committed to cutting back the Grant and making the ratepayer pay even more. So under this two-year Order we are not only failing to carry out our promise but we are reversing the promise and shifting more of the burden on to the ratepayer and off the shoulders of the taxpayers. This was the situation I had to handle in the great formal meeting to which I was rushing, in the Ministry's huge conference room at the top of the stairs. I entered flanked by Michael Stewart from Education, Kenneth Robinson from Health and Alice Bacon from the Home Office, and found arrayed on one side of the huge long table some thirty gentlemen standing in silence as I entered. Quite a formidable gathering. However, I got without too much difficulty an agreement that the local authorities would

---

[1] Orders give authority to legislation delegated to Ministers. In some cases they must be approved by Parliament, but in others, unless there is a positive objection, they come into force automatically.

accept the cut of £17 million in the first year if in return I would make a really sincere effort to persuade Cabinet to allow them their full estimates in the second year and not to impose the £17 million cut again. This seemed to me a reasonable compromise and immediately after the meeting I gave instructions that a paper to this effect should be presented to Cabinet which we would try to have discussed on Tuesday.

When I had finished this rather arduous meeting with the local authorities I had to hold no less than three other meetings of that sort in the Ministry – and it was a day when I was still pretty anxious about the fate of the Government. However, these are the kind of meetings I can do fairly easily. And after dinner I had called a meeting of all the back-benchers who were interested in my little anti-eviction Bill. To my surprise the meeting lasted some three hours and during it I found I had a wealth of Labour lawyers there – Sam Silkin[1] (John Silkin's elder brother), Michael English of Nottingham,[2] Ivor Richard of Barons Court,[3] perhaps ten of them, with Harold Lever as well – all determined to move amendments to improve the Bill and all not quite realizing that with a majority of four the Government must demand of its own back-benchers that they support it and that they shouldn't provide encouragement to the Tories to move their amendments.

Later, I listened to the midnight news and heard that the £3,000 million loan had been granted and realized the devaluation crisis was over.

Thursday, November 26th
Cabinet was almost entirely devoted to defence, with Harold Wilson reporting on the great defence weekend at Chequers.[4] I soon realized that the Prime Minister was trying to get a mandate for proposing a British alternative to the American M.L.F. when he got to Washington. What interested me was the implication that we intended to retain nuclear weapons, not only the means of delivery but also the warheads, and that Harold Wilson and Denis Healey wouldn't regard this as incompatible with our election pledges because they would claim that our Government was consciously giving up the attempt to have an independent deterrent. Indeed, what they were keeping the weapons for was to try to persuade NATO that in return for our providing weapons as a contribution to the NATO nuclear deterrent we should be permitted to cut down the British Army of the Rhine. I must say I felt extremely dubious about whether our allies would take this proposal very seriously.

However, after the defence item there was another item which interested me, and that was of course the fate of the children's services in the London area.[5]

[1] Second son of Lord Silkin, and a Q.C. Labour M.P. for Camberwell since 1964, and an active member of the Council of Europe.
[2] The new M.P. for Nottingham West.
[3] The new M.P. for Barons Court. He later became Denis Healey's P.P.S.
[4] For the Prime Minister's account of the 'thorough' review, see *Wilson*, pp. 39–44.
[5] See p. 60.
3*

My God! The L.C.C. pressure group is a formidable thing in a Labour Cabinet. There they all were, Gerald Gardiner, our Lord Chancellor, once an L.C.C. member; Barbara Castle—her husband Ted on the G.L.C.; Michael Stewart, with his wife a member too; all there pressuring, levering, to try to help the G.L.C. to get its way against the Lord President and the Chief Whip and myself, who continued to say we quite liked the idea of an amending Act but we just haven't the time for it this Session because the Tories would oppose it. Well, we were pressured and pressured but at least we kept them at bay.

I then had to rush off to lunch with the building societies and found them very anxious about the rate of interest and wanting to hear from Callaghan. From there down to the House for the Committee Stage of the Protection from Eviction Bill. If I were honest I should have to admit that this was the first Committee Stage of a Bill that I had ever sat through in nineteen years of membership of the House of Commons, so I was pretty inexperienced. We were expecting an all-night sitting because there were some fifty amendments down, over half of them from our side. It was lucky I had had my three-hour discussion with the back-benchers on the night before, because if I hadn't they would really have blown their top on Thursday afternoon and kept things going all night. As it was, for the first three or four hours we had a whole series of minor debates on minor amendments in which our side took just as much time as the Tories. So at seven o'clock we had only reached Part V of Clause 1, and here we came to the controversial subject of agricultural workers; and we switched from the lawyers' paradise to a really big debate between the Tories and ourselves. Bert Hazell, the trade-union organizer,[1] speaking on our side, joined the Tories in denouncing me for dragging this issue of the tied cottage[2] into a Bill on rents. Now, as a matter of fact, it *had* got dragged into the Bill and I wouldn't have been sorry to see it removed; indeed, I don't understand how it got there—it certainly shouldn't have been in an emergency measure. However, I had thought very hard and I managed to concoct a pretty ingenious argument that the agricultural tied cottage had been in our election programme as well as the repeal of the Rent Act and I was therefore equally bound to protect both the agricultural worker and the tenant in this intervening period before the big Rent Bill became law. The whole Committee Stage lasted from about four o'clock in the afternoon till two thirty in the morning. In fact after the debate on the tied cottage the Tories got tired and it petered away. Heavens, we were an amazingly incompetent team on the front bench. I made the great mistake of telling the Attorney-General, Elwyn Jones, that we didn't need a lawyer and as a result time after time we were caught by Sir John Hobson,[3] who was leading for the

---

[1] The new M.P. for Norfolk North. A member of the National Union of Agricultural Workers, he soon became vice-chairman of the P.L.P. Agriculture Group.

[2] See p. 62.

[3] Conservative M.P. for Warwick and Leamington from 1957 until his death in 1967. He was Attorney-General 1962–4.

Tories as Shadow Attorney-General alongside John Boyd-Carpenter. I must make sure we have a lawyer there in future because we couldn't really expose ourselves like that again and get away with it. As for our Whips, they were also amateurs at the game. Still, we got the Bill through and at two thirty in the morning I tottered home and found myself feeling that we'd done the job and I had been blooded as a Minister in Parliament. I had made my Second Reading speech, I've got the Bill through Committee Stage and really I needn't worry about the Report Stage at all.

Friday, November 27th
I got to the Ministry fresh and hearty and spent the day on office meetings, staff meetings, progress meetings, dealing with the routine of the Private Office as well. They seem to have a better idea of what my policy is and I have got them to agree to an elaborate programme of informal consultations and discussions on the content of the Rent Bill. Monday, Wednesday and Thursday will be totally allocated to discussions in two groups, one headed by myself and Arnold Goodman, and the other headed by Jim MacColl and Donnison. These two groups will study one paper prepared by the Department. I am really pleased I have got this fixed.

I caught the train to Coventry on Friday evening where I had to make the first speech I had ever made in my life at a public dinner. I suppose I provided what was required. Then I motored home to find Anne lying upstairs in bed listening to the new B.B.C. programme which has now been put on instead of TW3, and finding how vacuous it was.[1]

Saturday, November 28th
At eight o'clock I had to be off to Leicester for one of my visitations, from nine fifteen in the morning till four o'clock in the afternoon. They have become quite a routine for me now and I had my long discussions on the usual subjects, multi-occupation, the new Government subsidies, land policy. The interesting thing at Leicester, I thought, was the admirable way they are trying to deal with the problem of the people who grow elderly on their huge housing estates and then under-occupy their three-room council houses. Here they are taking a certain number of the houses in each area and turning them into flats by the most ingenious method of putting one old person upstairs and one downstairs in each house. They were also putting the old people's bungalows next door to old people's homes so those in the bungalows could have meals if they wanted in the old people's homes. They all seemed to me humane and civilized schemes.

Monday, November 30th
The only thing I need really mention is the dinner held at Arnold Goodman's house for my Rent Bill study group. We got together there while Jim MacColl

[1] It did not last long, despite its title: 'Not so much a programme, more a way of life'.

was getting his group of Labour lawyers together, and after that meeting on Monday we all decided the thing to do was to pool our resources on Wednesday evening.

Tuesday, December 1st

I had a bleeding row in Cabinet Committee about the General Grant. This was of course the issue I was having with Callaghan, and a furious argument developed between myself and John Diamond. After that Callaghan weighed in with a great big speech about how we must hold down social services; but then at once Douglas Houghton and George Brown pointed out to him that the issue we were there to discuss was not the holding down of the social services but the balance between what the ratepayer and the taxpayer pay towards them. Harold Wilson—who was in the chair—finally said, 'I've never heard such a total disagreement of this kind. We really must get the facts right,' and so finally the issue was referred to a special sub-committee which I gather was called the Public Sector Development Committee. We were told it would meet on Friday, December 4th.

The other subject on Tuesday, which cropped up for the first time, was gypsies. I had a meeting between the Strood Rural District Council and the Kent County Council. I had invited them both to come and see me because they had got into an open war on how to handle the gypsies who plant themselves within the area of the Strood R.D.C. Listening to them, I discovered that the gypsy is now becoming a serious problem on a national scale owing to the unfortunate fact that a county like Kent which decides to be humane and prepare ten hard surfaces where gypsies can camp actually provides the honey which draws the gypsies from all over Britain. So Kent permits the bad counties like Essex to evict their gypsies and to add them to no less than thirty gypsy families waiting outside the camp now being prepared at Sevenoaks. It's obvious, therefore, that something will have to be done nationally if Kent is not either to attract all the gypsies in Britain or else to abandon its humane policy and become as reactionary as Essex.

Wednesday, December 2nd

I had asked the two Labour M.P.s concerned in this problem of the gypsies to come and see me. One of them is a very old adversary of mine, Mr Norman Dodds.[1] He is one of the most exhibitionist of our Labour M.P.s and he hates my guts. He has become a kind of hero of the gypsies, and he is also one of the hardest-working constituency members. He came along with his neighbour, Albert Murray,[2] a comic little untidy red-haired chap; the two of them really look rather like Laurel and Hardy because Dodds is enormous and

[1] A P.P.S. at the Commonwealth Relations Office. He entered Parliament in 1945 and sat for Erith and Crayford from 1955 until his death in August 1965.
[2] The new Cockney M.P. for Gravesend, which he represented until 1970. After 1965 he served as a P.P.S. and junior Minister in the Ministry of Defence, the Ministry of Technology and the Ministry of Transport.

stately and Murray is small and comic. Still, they stuck together very well. Norman Dodds was very hectoring at first while Murray was new and young and cautious. I think I gradually persuaded them to listen, and got them to understand that something could possibly best be done by me, through bringing the Home Counties in immediately. But I told them also that in the long run nothing much could be done except on a national plan, and that's what I would go for.

I went along to the House of Commons at twelve o'clock where a Party meeting had been summoned to hear Harold Wilson before he went to Washington. He spoke for thirty-five minutes and answered questions for twenty minutes, giving a picture of how we had advanced forward on the home front and how we had suffered a reverse in the rally we had been making. What he didn't admit was that we had been forced to choose between devaluation and deflation, that we had chosen the second and that we were in for a period of exactly the worst kind of 'stop' against which we had so passionately protested throughout the election. However, his speech and the answers to questions were extremely skilful and they were well received and he was given a wonderful farewell for his trip to Washington. When we had finished (I was the only Cabinet Minister there, by the way, which seemed to me a very bad thing) I listened to Emanuel Shinwell in the chair being urged to concede a regular weekly Party meeting, and treating this request in a completely insane way, which does no good for the relations between Parliament and the Cabinet. In Manny Shinwell we have a man of imagination, of enormous vigour, but somehow he has always impressed me as shiftless and unscrupulous. Certainly on Wednesday he convinced none of them—Peter Shore and David Ennals,[1] to take two examples—that we shouldn't have regular Party meetings every week. Indeed, there is everything to commend it. If we had a regular meeting every Wednesday people would know it and come along at the regular time. And contact between Government and the Party would be maintained. But Manny wouldn't allow it, for fear—as he put it—that the questions raised would be used for trouble-making. I regard this as one of the weakest aspects of our Government today and I predict it will prove disastrous.

Wednesday evening was the big evening for our rents policy meeting. I was pretty anxious when I went over to my room in the Ministry after dinner and found some fourteen people there. We were late as usual because we had had to do a division on the Finance Bill. I got them all round a table and we sat down to work, discussing the Rent Bill on the basis of the paper provided by Arnold Goodman and Dennis Lloyd as a result of our meeting on the previous Monday. It was a paper in which the idea of the fair rent was sketched out for the first time. It really was an astonishing meeting because we managed to

[1] M.P. for Dover 1964–70. He had been Secretary of the United Nations Association and between 1957 and 1964 was Overseas Secretary of the Labour Party. In 1964 he was P.P.S. at the Ministry of Overseas Development; he moved to the Ministry of Transport in 1966.

get something like agreement between these fourteen people, many of them lawyers, all of them knowing a great deal about the subject and with experience ranging from that of Arnold Goodman, a commercial lawyer in Fleet Street, on the one hand and his friend Professor Dennis Lloyd, a pure academic, on the other. Then we had, at the other end of the scale, young Labour lawyers, and one property speculator. And finally our own officials, Waddell and Rogerson, and we had Jim MacColl and Dame Evelyn and myself. We started at 8.15 and at 11.45 we sat back because our job had been done. Of course, it says a great deal for Arnold Goodman's powers of persuasion, but basically it was the idea of the fair rent that he had worked out which made it acceptable to this mixed gathering. I was also relieved to find that on other secondary issues, like the problem of service cottages, furnished lodgings and so on, we were very near the kind of detailed policy agreement that I desired.

I couldn't help feeling proud as I saw us there working together, our ideas men from outside the Ministry and the officials from inside, moulded into a team. And I must confess I couldn't help smugly reflecting on the contrast between what we were doing in the Ministry of Housing and the miserable performance going on at the Ministry of Land and Natural Resources. Only that morning I had read the draft paper which Fred Willey had produced with the help of his Permanent Secretary; to be frank, he had just given the officials the Labour Party's plan to work on, whereas we in the Ministry of Housing have really thought out policy from the bottom. In the case of rent control this was relatively easy because there were no ideas to which we were committed by the election manifesto. So I was able to produce a new creative debate between our outside advisers headed by Arnold and the Ministry officials, something that is much more difficult in the case of the Land Commission because of the finished document.

I've been thinking over this a great deal, wondering when the time would be ripe for me to propose to Wilson and Callaghan and Brown that, instead of trying to introduce the Land Commission ready-made in this Session, what we should do is to create something you can call a Land Commission but give it as its sole function at this stage the job of raising the tax on the betterment of land. We could argue that this was the first stage in our progress towards the establishment of a real Land Commission which would have a monopoly power to buy all building land. This would, of course, be something quite different. Introduced now, it could gum up the whole works and destroy our housing programme. But later on it could conceivably be the beginning of land nationalization and control of land prices. The trouble of course is that none of these long-term questions have been dealt with in Fred Willey's paper or really discussed at all. He is merely putting up the election manifesto proposal without discussing the basic idea.

I was thinking about all this as I went home after our meeting. I got into bed and got down to my box. For some reason I was lively and wakeful. I usually fall asleep and do the box at six next morning, but on this occasion I went right through my papers. I've had some trouble with my Office, who were inclined to pile every kind of junk loose in the boxes, and I have tried to insist that they should sort the papers out into 'urgent', 'less urgent', 'background' and so forth. Well, this they proceeded to do by having enormous cartons which overfilled the box. So I got them to stop doing that. They had then gone back to throwing the junk in and this evening at the bottom of the urgent letters I found a 'less urgent' paper, a sheet on which Brian Ponsford had written, 'You might like to see what will be said on your behalf by the architect at the Stevenage inquiry.' I glanced at it, very late at night by then, and saw to my astonishment that our Ministry architect was going to Stevenage next day to make the most powerful case for doubling the size of the town. I had already had a seminar on this and made it quite clear I was personally not in any sense committed to the Ministry proposal to double the size of Stevenage and was going to leave myself open to make up my mind after the inquiry. After I had made my position clear I had been asked by the Ministry whether I would cancel the inquiry. I had said, 'No, I don't mind holding it; it would be extremely useful because then we would be able to look at the whole case again and I could announce my decision independently at that point.' I remember the Dame said, 'But you know there will have to be a statement by the Chief Architect. We must just make sure it's neutral.' Remembering this conversation, I was absolutely infuriated by the discovery that this little document had been put in my less urgent papers as a mere formality and that the statement had already gone out and the Chief Architect was due to make it in the morning.

Thursday, December 3rd
So I came into the office this Thursday in a fury. I was being frustrated by the Department. I poured out my fury on poor George Moseley and I then insisted that there should be inserted at the top of the draft statement by the Chief Architect the words, 'The paper which follows shows the Ministry policy as it was before the change of Government. It is not to be understood to prejudice the present Minister's view on the matter.' George Moseley looked a bit shamefaced and said, 'But, Minister, you had better be careful because I am afraid it has gone out in your name already.' I realized that I had merely been shown a *fait accompli*. I sent for Jones and told him what I thought of him. He immediately said, 'There's only one thing – you can either cancel the inquiry though it's starting this morning or you can have the words you have drafted said at the inquiry.' I said I wouldn't cancel the inquiry, so it was decided that this astonishing statement should be made on my behalf as the opening words of the inquiry. And it was, though no newspaper noticed it.

I went to Cabinet at eleven o'clock. Nothing of interest there. Harold Wilson was just off to Washington; and we had some discussion about the

700th anniversary of the Parliament of Simon de Montfort. There was a general sense of finishing, winding up, with Harold going off. Again I had the uneasy feeling that we weren't grappling with central problems. To make Cabinet government work as against Prime Ministerial government, Cabinet should really discuss general policy. Whereas in our case all that happens is that twenty-three of us come, each with his particular pressures and problems, trying to get what we want. And we do avoid any collective discussion of general policy except perhaps on defence and foreign affairs. On the essentials of the home front there doesn't seem to be any general discussion at all — general issues just aren't raised. I have discussed this with Thomas Balogh before, and after Cabinet on Thursday I went along to his room in the Cabinet Office to talk it over. I think what has happened during this last ten days is that there has been a real row between the D.E.A., headed by George Brown, and the Treasury, headed by Callaghan. That would be tolerable if the D.E.A. and the Cabinet Secretariat was strong enough to insist that — once having taken it out of the Treasury hands — planning would *really* get done by the D.E.A. and presented via the Cabinet Secretariat to the Cabinet for consideration. That would mean, for instance, that as a Cabinet we would now be discussing the broad allocation of our resources in the new situation created by a 7 per cent bank rate and the period of deflation which is now setting in. It's no good Michael Stewart working up his expanded education estimates, me working up my housing estimates, Kenneth Robinson working up his health estimates, if we all know that in this deflationary period we'll have to hold back expenditure in the public sector and plan for the *cutting* of the social services, not their expansion. Now, so far there has been no suggestion by Harold or by James that we should actually cut social services. No wonder we are still faced with this complete lack of confidence in the pound abroad. We can't persuade the Zurich bankers that we are sound because we won't carry out the genuine old-fashioned deflation, and we are not prepared to carry out that deflation because we won't face a retreat on the social services front. I should add here that all this is something I can now say in private to myself, talk to Tommy about, write in my diary. It's also something I can read, for instance, in this week's *Economist* and hear from Nicholas Davenport. It isn't something which has as yet impacted on the Parliamentary Party or which we have ever discussed in Cabinet.

In the afternoon I was feeling pretty depressed and cursed it when I saw on my engagement list that I had to visit something called the Development Group. I found myself going to a new office block down by Dartmouth Street, the Fabians' old meeting place. I knew nothing about this but I found there Oliver Cox, the Deputy Chief Architect, with some twenty architects and six or seven sociologists, a brilliant group of young men and women actively at work developing two methods of system-building, 5M and 12M. One of these they are actually trying out now in Oldham where they are building the first 750 of these system-built houses, having just cleared an area.

I can't understand why it is that the Ministry have got this extremely good group working in its midst, but they gave me the most exhilarating time. I spent two or three hours getting to know their methods, seeing how they make their sociological studies and being told something of the technical side. In conversation I asked why it was only 750 houses they were building at Oldham; why not rebuild the whole thing? Wouldn't that help Laing, the builders? 'Of course it would,' said Oliver, 'and it would help Oldham too.' 'Well, why don't we do it?' 'It depends on the Minister.' And Whitfield-Lewis, the Chief Architect, smiled, and I said, 'Why shouldn't we? Why shouldn't we assume that instead of doing one little bit of the centre of Oldham we should use the whole 300 acres and have a real demonstration that our system-building can work and really does reduce costs? Let's see that one piece of central redevelopment is really finished by us.'

I drove back to the Ministry (it's only just round the corner) warmed and excited. I'm going to insist if I can that we should persuade Oldham to let us do the whole thing; there's no doubt that Laing would be delighted because they will be mass-producing for a longer continuous run, so that costs can be cut.

I got back just in time for my routine staff meeting with the Dame, Jones and Waddell. And I soon turned to the problems of Stevenage. I showed my anger and they all sat, very uncomfortable, and then the Dame said, 'I must take full responsibility,' and looked very sulky. That was that. Turning to our usual agenda we first went through the paper on the General Grant which was to be my brief for the crucial Cabinet Committee on Friday morning and then we turned to look at George Brown's policy paper on regional government. Now, in the division lobby I had been talking to George, who said, 'I'm having trouble with your Dame. She's organizing a cabal against me, all the Permanent Secretaries. You and I know we have to have a West Midlands and an East Midlands organization but she insists that there should be only one Midlands organization. Will you stand up to her?' 'Of course I will,' I said. 'It's absolutely insane to think the East Midlands would accept any organization whose headquarters were in Birmingham or that the West Midlands would accept any organization whose headquarters were in Leicester.' When we got to George's paper I repeated this story to the Dame. She said the staffing of two Midlands regional organizations would be out of the question and for half an hour we had a futile argument. This is very characteristic. Once again she was causing endless trouble by trying to change the regional reorganization which George had worked out in the D.E.A. I felt more and more angry and more and more inclined to hope she would clear out.

That evening Anne and I gave dinner in the House of Commons to Peter and Jean Lederer. Jean was one of the girls who shared digs with Anne when she lived in Queen's Gardens and she met this sensible, extremely anglicized Czech Jew and married him. Peter Lederer has now become one of the top men in Costain and we had a fascinating evening. I have known him partly because he is Jean's husband but rather more so because he built the jack-block building in Coventry, a fifteen- or sixteen-storey tower block built by a new technique of jacking each storey up after it has been erected. This was a first try-out for Britain and had cost Costain a lot of money because they couldn't get a continuous run by repeating it anywhere else, and I began to see the difficulties of system-building when you have hundreds of local authorities which all want to make each building just a little different and claim credit for it.

Friday, December 4th
By far the best day in my brief career as a Cabinet Minister. It started at the Home Affairs Committee at ten o'clock. That was over in five minutes and there we were in the Cabinet Office with half an hour to spare. I asked for a canteen and I was directed, but I lost my way and no one in the building seemed to know. At last I was taken to a drivers' canteen, an extremely nice place which was opened specially for us, and there Michael Stewart, Judith Hart and I had a cup of coffee together. It proved an invaluable interlude since I was able to brief them in full on my intentions in the big meeting on the General Grant. Judith was representing the Secretary of State for Scotland and Michael Stewart had naturally a great deal at stake since Education forms three-quarters of local authority expenditure, i.e. three-quarters of the General Grant goes on that. So, over our cup of coffee, we prepared our ground together and then we went to Room C where the special Public Sector Development sub-committee was meeting to discuss the General Grant.

Rather to my surprise I found there were twelve ministers there, including such diverse souls as Barbara Castle from Overseas Development, Fred Peart from Agriculture, Douglas Houghton, the co-ordinator of Social Services, Judith from Scotland, John Diamond, the Financial Secretary from the Treasury, Jim Callaghan of course, and the First Secretary, George Brown. The meeting started with George Brown saying to me, *sotto voce*, that he had been brought there to support Callaghan but felt very uncomfortable and anyway would have to leave in half an hour to meet the Indian Prime Minister. Then Callaghan started off with a long spiel which he read aloud from a Treasury brief on pale blue paper, describing the extreme gravity of the economic situation. He said he had come to remind us that the crisis was not over, that social services were increasing at the rate of 4 per cent annually when we hadn't anywhere near approached a 4 per cent productivity rate, and that sooner or later we would have to face reality – namely that there had to be a drastic cut in the overall figure for public expenditure. I then said his remarks had nothing to do with the issue of the General Grant which concerned only the balance between rates and taxes and not the gross amount of taxation. Then I said I wondered whether it wasn't for George Brown and his Ministry to work out the National Plan and include in it, I suppose, the plan of priorities for Government expenditure. To my surprise George Brown replied that this had not been decided between him and the Chancellor. So now after six weeks – is it? – of Labour Government they were still apparently waiting to exchange letters agreeing whose responsibility it was to plan the priorities of expenditure. However, that discussion having been got over, we then started on the General Grant and I was asked to put my case. I had been *very* carefully briefed and I knew the case pretty well. I put it as strongly as I could. In fact, I repeated very largely what the local authorities had said to me in our meeting the previous week. They had made a most powerful case in which they explained they weren't of course asking for a bigger grant in the second year (that would be illegal): they were only asking for an increase for a special reason, and the special reason was that whereas estimating for the first year could be extremely accurate there was a tendency in the second year for the cuts to be overdone – resulting in a divergence of something like 2 to 2·5 per cent, some £20 million, between what was estimated for the second year and what was spent. There was, therefore, always over-spending and they pleaded that the £20 million we cut out of the second year should be restored to them. I said that I wasn't asking for a single penny extra for the social services but merely that we should concede the £20 million in the second year *now* in order to prevent ourselves increasing the burden on the ratepayer as against the taxpayer.

I was answered by Diamond who said my picture was totally remote from the facts and that the Treasury couldn't even consider the possibility of conceding my demand. The General Grant, he said, must be recognized as the most effective way of holding down local government expenditure and that device would be undermined if we suddenly granted £20 million in the second year. This £20 million was a sheer inflationary concession which nobody could seriously consider. A pretty good row developed and I was fairly offensive. I pointed out that the real aim of the Treasury was not to defend the national income but to defend the taxpayer against the ratepayer and it really was very extraordinary to claim that taxes were somehow more sensitive and that rates could be increased without anybody worrying. I was supported by Fred Peart, Judith Hart and, finally and decisively, by Douglas Houghton. At this point Callaghan suddenly did the incredible. 'Well,' he said, 'that's it. You're all against me. Better face it. All right, but you won the battle not the campaign.' I was amazed. 'Does this mean that we won't go to Cabinet about this?' I asked. 'No,' said James Callaghan. 'It's unnecessary.' And that was the end.

John Diamond was flabbergasted. I was flabbergasted. I had never conceived the possibility that I should win an outright victory and I fully expected to find myself told by Harold Wilson at Cabinet, 'Well, Dick, you've made a very good case but frankly the situation is too grave to allow your demand.' Yet here suddenly the Chancellor had caved in, making nonsense, by the way, of all John Diamond, his subordinate, had said about the Treasury position.

What made him surrender? I think I know the answer. He may well have borne in mind that Harold Wilson would be away in Washington next Tuesday when the issue would be decided and George Brown, who would take his place, was already firmly on my side. Rather than be defeated at Cabinet he decided to throw in his hand at the P.S.D. sub-committee.

As a result, the affair will never be recorded in the Cabinet minutes. This is one of the odd things about our system. All that is recorded in Cabinet minutes is what actually is decided in the Cabinet. If a matter is referred to a Cabinet Committee and doesn't have to go back to Cabinet then the Cabinet minutes record nothing about the outcome of that particular discussion. You might think that nobody would know. On the contrary, everybody in Whitehall, where rumours go round, will hear of Callaghan's defeat.

I discussed the whole thing this evening with Tommy Balogh on the phone, and the more I reflect on it the more uneasy I become. Of course, I shouldn't have been allowed to win. In a sense I had a strong case, but if there had been a collective Cabinet policy I wouldn't have stood a chance. Yet because a Cabinet sub-committee was discussing only a departmental issue, a clash between two Ministers which had been brought to it, I felt no sense of responsibility for the general Cabinet policy and just pleaded my departmental case as well as I possibly could. In fact I was not the least concerned about the good of the country. I was solely concerned with looking after my Department. But isn't there an inner Cabinet to make sure that there is a Cabinet policy? No, I am afraid there isn't. There is no inner Cabinet, no coherent inner policy on home affairs and we are drifting along. That's really the lesson of this deplorable show.

Saturday, December 5th
My official visit to Dudley and Stourbridge. I decided to travel via Redditch, where a New Town is to be built, and then take a look at Wythall, an agricultural area near Birmingham which Birmingham Corporation is trying to acquire for land purposes. Unfortunately it was a day of drenching rain: Jimmy James, whom we picked up at Coventry, had a terrible time trying to show me anything, though we did get just a glimpse of lovely rolling country round Redditch. We should be able to make an immensely impressive town of 80,000 people here. Then we went up through the so-called green belt to see Wythall. What we often forget when we talk about the green belt is that large portions of it aren't green at all! As for the actual problem of Wythall right up against the boundaries of Birmingham, I soon came to the conclusion that if we did give way there we would let the whole conurbation break outwards and very soon Redditch New Town would be a suburb of Birmingham.

From there I went on to Dudley and Stourbridge, George Wigg's constituency. What an amazing contrast between those two boroughs! Earthy Black Country, Arnold Bennett atmosphere, councillors quarrelling, saying what they mean to each other, abusing me, cursing their officials, but all this with a splendid kind of Black Country heartiness and mixture of good humour and grittiness—that's Dudley. And then eight miles away, Stourbridge, with a real town clerk and a real rich businessman as the mayor, the whole atmosphere stiff, stuffy, stuck-up, because Stourbridge is outside the Black Country on the edge of Worcestershire, with a totally different genteel atmosphere.

This motor-car journey gave me my first chance of a real day's discussion with Jimmy, who is one of the most attractive of my civil servants, not a professional administrator but a planner deeply resenting the domination of the administrators in the Department. Talking to him I was able to try out all the ideas I've had about simplifying the system of planning, and also to suck in ideas from him. As a result of my talk with him, it's my impression that really we should have no aesthetic control in the Ministry but only functional control. I also think it ridiculous that, as he tells me, one-third of the planning permissions which come up to the Ministry are permissions to build or alter a single house. All those should be dealt with by an Inspector.*

Another problem I was able to discuss with him was one which has increasingly worried me, and that is how do I, as Minister, take my decisions? Let me clear my mind here. Technically, every single planning decision is taken personally by the Minister, although in fact in nine cases out of ten I don't really deal with them. But when one *is* important enough for me to deal with, how do I take the decision? There is no law here, no mass of legal precedents—decisions are taken basically in terms of common sense, personal judgment; and therefore it is really absolutely vital if I am taking a big decision on whether to allow building in the green belt that I should see the area for myself. I put all that to J. D. Jones, the Deputy, and said I should like to go and see the actual situation before I make up my mind. 'Oh, you can't possibly do that,' he said. 'The Minister must judge without going to see for himself.' 'But,' I said, 'that's judging without understanding. That means incompetent judgment.' And of course I was right. If I can't openly go anywhere to see what the actual situation is I can't have a basis on which to give a sane judgment. But the officials object that if I see one I shall have to see them all and they also have a legal argument that by seeing it for myself I might obtain new evidence which was not available to the Inspector and that would require another public inquiry. However, I refuse to be bulldozed on this. In fact, in the case of the Span Company's model village in Kent,[1] I sent Jim MacColl to see it for himself; and I have already begun regular quiet visits, like this one with Jimmy James, and by going quietly without any fuss my being there isn't noticed.

I should add that the Span decision at Hartley has caused consternation,

---

* These changes were recommended in a Bill which Anthony Greenwood produced after I was made Lord President of the Council.
[1] At Hartley. See p. 32.

and a tremendous row is building up. Indeed, I shall have to defend myself at the first meeting of the Labour Party housing group next week. In this particular case I am sure I'm right. James has enormously strengthened my view in this regard. He has made me see that one can't really preserve all these green belts intact; if one tries to, seepage occurs. The best thing to do is to allow planned incursions into them in certain concentrated developments, with model villages like the Span village or a New Town, and then to keep the rest truly green. Nevertheless, the row about Hartley is going to be awkward because it involves Irving,[1] who is our Deputy Chief Whip and the M.P. for the area, and Arthur Skeffington, one of our most influential members of the N.E.C. and a junior Minister: both live there and neither was consulted! I am pretty sure that Jim MacColl put his foot in it. After taking a look at it, he told me to accept the officials' advice, but didn't warn me of the political wrath to come. However, I'm not particularly afraid of it. Indeed I am positively looking forward to the confrontation in the Party.

Sunday, December 6th
Another lovely day. As the children have colds we decided to stay in, and had just settled down after lunch for a snooze when the doorbell rang and in came a man and a woman, and Anne said, 'Great Scott, here's a cousin of yours who rang up. I had forgotten he was coming.' So we walked round the farm and then at tea the man settled in and said he wanted to talk business because – and then he suddenly revealed it – 'I come from your Ministry.' I learned that he works in Great College Street where he is 'listing' historic buildings. Now, this is something I really hadn't heard of as being part of the work of the Ministry and it was a revelation that this division run by a cousin of mine existed. Then he explained to me at length that when a house has been listed two months' notice has to be given before the owner can do any alterations and he said, 'Yes, your house, Prescote, is a listed building.' Little did I know it.

What do I feel on reflection over this last week? First of all, my own Ministry. We don't argue too much and at last I think they are accepting leadership as far as I can give it. But I am having more and more difficulties in my Private Office. For example, this week I caught Brian Ponsford in an incident which nearly caused his downfall. I had a difficult task when I had to go to the R.I.B.A. and give the certificates and prizes for the best-designed houses of the year. It was a tricky speech to make and I had asked for a great deal of work to be done on the briefs. They weren't satisfactory and I had to knock them round at the last moment. I found myself ringing up Lord Esher (my old friend Lionel Brett who will be in the chair at the meeting)[2] and when I asked him about the speech he said, 'Oh, why not put in a paragraph

---

[1] Sydney Irving, M.P. for Dartford since 1955.
[2] Architect and planner of such major projects as Hatfield New Town, and since 1971 Rector of the Royal College of Art. He had succeeded to his father's viscountcy in 1963.

about the superiority of public-sector housing to private-sector housing, because you know, it is superior.' So I wrote in my notes 'Public superior to private housing. Why?'. When the final draft came I rushed back from lunch to have a look at it before going out and I found that this shorthand passage had been omitted. 'Ponsford,' I said, 'why has that been left out?' 'Because it's wrong, sir,' he said. 'It's wrong, Minister.' 'What do you mean, wrong?' I said. 'Even if you think it wrong you should do as you're told and prepare the notes for me as best you can in true Civil Service style. And you should say: Minister, I've done it for you but I warn you it's wrong. Why didn't you do that?' 'I didn't do it, Minister, because it's wrong. I couldn't do it.' At this moment I walked out of the room in fury and found the Deputy Chief Architect, Cox, and I brought him in and said, 'Tell me, as a matter of fact, is it absolutely lunatic to say that public-sector building is better than private?' 'Of course not,' he said. 'It *is* better and everybody knows it. Who has told you the opposite?'

So I had got Mr Ponsford in a corner. I told George Moseley about it and then I told the Dame about it and I rather expected them to agree that he ought to be moved out of my Private Office; but they are both extremely reluctant, they feel he is an able man, that his career and prestige would be wrecked if failure were admitted and he were moved. So we'll see how Brian Ponsford will do.

As for the work in the Ministry I am slowly getting down to formulating an attitude on planning. I've decided to give Birmingham a huge area of housing in their green belt at Water Orton,[1] and last week there came the announcement of my decision to create Hartley, the Span model village, in the green belt in Kent. I'm moving the same way on another big decision whether or not to give Sheffield a large amount of housing land in their green belt area. I'm making these three planning decisions quite deliberately because I've decided, if rigidly interpreted, a green belt can be the strangulation of a city. With so many people to house we can't put them all in New Towns thirty miles away on the other side of the green belt. We have to find places nearer the cities to house them in, even if this means that in some cases we shall trespass into the green belts or turn a green belt into four or five green fingers. I know this will cause me my first major row but I'm pleased about it. I've decided to do it and I think it's good ground on which to fight.

So much for the Ministry. As for the House of Commons, I've got the anti-eviction Bill through the Committee Stage. I've not done particularly well, but well enough. I've also had to deal during these first five weeks with the whole question of the Local Government Boundary Commission. I mentioned this subject since discussing this at length with the Dame some days ago, I've talked to my colleagues about it and I've got them to agree after a great deal of humming and hawing that I can't delay my decisions on the recommendations of the Commission any further and that I am bound to make and

[1] This was later called Chelmsley Wood.

announce these decisions in the near future. They are my personal decisions. Not even the Prime Minister can influence me in them. My colleagues know this and this gives me an odd detached power in dealing with them. After all I can make or mar George Brown at Belper, Bert Bowden in Leicester, Bill Wilson in Coventry,[1] Ted Short in Newcastle; each of them now knows that as Minister of Housing the decision I make may be life or death for them in terms of representation at Westminster.

What about the Cabinet? Well, the pound is still being nibbled away and I feel the Cabinet isn't very firm or very stable because the central leadership isn't there, the sense of priorities, the sense of grip that you need. Yes, we've got a remarkable man in Harold Wilson and a good man in George Brown, and both have already got some tremendous individual achievements to their credit. But what we still lack is that coherent, strong control which is real policy. Least of all do I feel that our legislative programme makes any sense whatsoever. I know now we shall be able to formulate a decent rent reform which will do us credit, but Fred Willey's Land Commission Bill is laughable. He hasn't done any basic thinking and if he puts the Bill forward in its present form and it becomes law it will get unstuck. As for Fred Lee's steel nationalization, that's got to be postponed until March because it has run into difficulties too. In these major reforms we are suffering from sheer lack of brains and imagination. And then of course there is the quite unsolved problem of handling the Parliamentary Party on the one side and Transport House and the Party in the country on the other.

Well, there is my diary for this week. I've settled in now pretty thoroughly as Departmental Minister; indeed I'm beginning to wonder whether I shouldn't become a Cabinet Minister, organizing some kind of movement in Cabinet to ensure that we do face up to our problems before they overpower us in a smash and sweep us away.

Monday, December 7th
An important meeting of the E.D.C. today, at which George Brown was putting forward his paper on regional organization. This was vital to me because it affects the relations between his new D.E.A. and my Ministry in the sphere of planning. I myself am very much in favour of George Brown as First Secretary getting this absolutely key economic responsibility and making a success of the D.E.A. because I am convinced we ought to downgrade the Treasury. And in the last week or two he has in fact downgraded the Chancellor. But as always happens in these cases someone has to pay a price, and part of the price for George's carving out this new empire is that he has become ambitious to take over *all* planning, not only economic planning but physical planning, both centrally and regionally. It was clear that Dame Evelyn was going to fight for her dear, beloved Ministry of Housing. I took

---

[1] M.P. for Coventry South since 1964, after unsuccessfully contesting Warwick and Leamington in 1951, 1955, 1957 and 1959.

rather a different view. I thought that so far from getting into a departmental battle between the D.E.A. and the Ministry of Housing I ought wherever possible to side with George and back his getting overall powers in the planning sphere. Now has come the next stage: George Brown is trying to establish regional government, and this is something on which the Ministry of Housing and Local Government really has to be consulted. I had begged him and prayed him not to make any grandiose announcement about regional government at all. But here he was with his twelve colleagues round the table, determined to get his way. I am afraid I had to behave in a pretty reactionary way, stand on my Ministerial powers and simply say, 'Look, whatever economic planning you may choose to do, First Secretary, you can't touch our power in the Ministry of Local Government to plan the land resources of this country.' The result was O.K. I was assured that I would have the last word on the Statement and be able to take out of it anything I didn't want.

In the afternoon came something really important, my first meeting with Sir Milner Holland, Professor Donnison, Mr Waddilove, Mr Pilcher and Mr Ruck, the members of the Milner Holland Committee. This committee had been established by my predecessor, Keith Joseph, at the time of the Rachman scandal.[1] Their terms of reference were to inquire into the conditions of landlords and tenants of private property in London and to report on the facts without recommendations. Sir Milner Holland turned out to be an extremely verbose and rather self-important lawyer who obviously couldn't write, but he dominated the committee and was delaying publication of the report by trying to write it himself. It also became clear to me that the report wasn't going to be published in time for our big Bill, i.e. in January or February. And that was very bad news. However, I was pleased to find that Milner Holland and his colleagues agree with us on two central principles – firstly, that in our new system of regulating rents there should be two tiers, conciliation followed by a tribunal; and secondly, that we must find a formula which was not related to gross rateable value. But on a third controversial point, whether we should include furnished accommodation in our Bill or not, Milner Holland came down wholly on the side of furnished dwellings being included, thus giving me a tremendous headache because the Ministry had hoped to have them excluded from the Bill.*

Then I asked him whether the tribunals should be legal tribunals or not and he said on no account should they be legal. Tenants wouldn't trust them.

---

* The exclusion of furnished dwellings from the Bill proved to be its fatal flaw and did untold damage. It was urged on me by the officials for purely administrative reasons. They said they couldn't get the Bill done in time. I should have been tough and insisted on including them on Milner Holland's perfectly correct advice. However, this was the recommendation of the Francis Committee in 1971, and the new Conservative Administration promised to implement it.

[1] Rachman had exploited the provisions of the 1957 Rent Act to flourish as a slum landlord in the area of Notting Hill and Paddington.

Here he was on my side against Dame Evelyn. 'No, they should be composed of ordinary people, surveyors and housewives, and one should do everything possible to keep them out of the legal set-up.[1] Indeed,' he said, 'they should be called rent assessment committees, not tribunals, to avoid a legal appearance.'

Just as I finished this meeting I found the Deputy, Waddell, hanging round and he said to me, 'Minister, will you just O.K. this paper for Cabinet?' He pushed into my hand a draft Cabinet paper on the Rent Bill. We had finished our main discussion of the policy issues in my grand late-night meeting last week with Arnold Goodman and all the outside advisers, but I had left the actual drafting of the agreed policies to Waddell and told him to take our minutes and Arnold's admirable paper and transform them into a single Cabinet paper. As I was standing in the doorway of my room I took one glance at Waddell's draft. Practically everything that we had achieved in the late-night meeting with Arnold had been removed from this paper, which was now a civil servants' document. It wasn't only written in Civil Service style; we had slipped back four-fifths of the way to the policy the Ministry wanted from what Goodman had recommended. Into the new draft had been written Dame Evelyn's ideas and Waddell's ideas but not Donnison's ideas or Goodman's ideas, or indeed my ideas.

I was furious. I went back into my room and went through it paragraph by paragraph with Waddell, realizing I was due for a dinner at 6.45 with the six big civil contractors who work on local authority housing. Dame Evelyn had staged this at the Oxford & Cambridge Club. Well, I couldn't help that. I had to stay and sit down with Waddell and massacre their paper. I really behaved like a savage editor. There was nothing for it. Once again they were deliberately and obstinately trying to get the departmental view adopted in spite of the clear directive from the Minister. It was the same kind of behaviour I had found over Stevenage.[2] Whenever one relaxes one's guard the Civil Service in one's Department quietly reasserts itself. And so the eternal process goes on. Just as the Cabinet Secretariat constantly transforms the actual proceedings of Cabinet into the form of the Cabinet minutes (i.e. it substitutes what we should have said if we had done as they wished for what we actually did say), so here in my Department the civil servants are always putting in what they think I should have said and not what I actually decided.

I finished well after eight and rushed out to the club where I found Dame Evelyn entertaining Maurice Laing, McAlpine and the others. We had a lively little dinner. If we are really going to get industrialized building going it will only be through the collaboration of these men. Donald Gibson, who was our old city architect at Coventry and is now the boss of the Ministry of Works, has been insisting that we ought to establish at least sixteen factories for the

---

[1] While Dame Evelyn felt that they should be legal bodies, she nevertheless shared the view that the tribunals should be composed of 'ordinary citizens' rather than the town-hall establishment.

[2] See p. 79.

basic parts of industrialized building, and here I found Laing and McAlpine saying the same thing. But the difficulty revealed itself when all of them at that dinner expressed doubts as to whether the Government would be prepared in a period of crisis and economic difficulty to sustain the industrialized building, and whether we were going to cut back the building programme.*

Tuesday, December 8th
We got the Report Stage and Third Reading of the anti-eviction Bill and sent it up to the Lords. The Tories had given us the assurance that if we delayed it for two days and took it on this Tuesday they would let it go through by eight o'clock, so getting it through by nine thirty wasn't too bad. This time we took the precaution of having the Attorney-General on the bench with us, which kept Sir John Hobson in his place. The only really important debate was an unexpected one, begun by the Tories, on furnished lodgings. The Tories from the seaside resorts came forward to say that under my Bill all the landladies would be ruined because the people who came in for winter lodgings wouldn't give way voluntarily so that summer people could come in at the higher prices. I was able to indicate that this was sheer nonsense.†　Moreover, I expect to find that this little Bill has been a successful operation with the public outside. Certainly it's popular with the Parliamentary Labour Party.

Wednesday, December 9th
I had a meeting at Transport House, a confidential discussion with Len Williams on the Local Government Boundary Commission. Len Williams confirmed that if I implemented the recommendations of the Commission, we were likely to lose Herbert Bowden's seat in Leicester, two seats in Nottingham, and Bill Wilson's seat in Coventry South. Lose them, of course, not in the next election but in the next but one election, after the Parliamentary Boundary Commission has revised the constituency boundaries.[1] I then went on to the R.I.B.A. where I was opening an exhibition of the work of our own Ministry R & D group, the group I visited last week when I got so excited about the Oldham scheme.

Back from there through the Christmas shopping scrum, to see the Local Government Boundary Commission itself. Fussy old gentlemen, full of themselves, somewhat disconcerted by meeting a Minister with strong ideas of his own where they have been used only to dealing with the Permanent Secretary. After lunch I had a talk with the official who is writing the two big planning decisions on Wythall and Chelmsley Wood. I told him what I wanted said and

* They were wise in their scepticism. The programme was cut back when the economic situation got difficult.

† In fact it was. I never had a single complaint about this, despite the confident predictions of several Conservative Members with seaside constituencies. This was my first reasonably effective parliamentary performance as a Cabinet Minister.

[1] See p. 64.

gave him pretty exact instructions how on the two decision letters should be written.

Next, a meeting with the National Association of Property Owners about the Rent Bill: a lot of charming men concerned to see that the fair rent clause would be fair to them. Then along to the Chancellor's room to discuss the building societies' rate of interest. Since the economic situation is still not very good and there is continued lack of confidence, there is, of course, pressure on the societies to raise the rate and the Chancellor had to plead even more strongly with them to hold back and to urge them at least to postpone the decision until after Christmas. It was obvious we were fighting against the tide.

After the building societies had left I sat with Callaghan and had a chat. I didn't feel that his heart was in his job. Indeed, I thought he was thoroughly unhappy and I tried to stiffen him and to discuss the kind of fighting, back-to-the-wall speeches we should make to the Party Conference at the end of the week. It's a good idea to cultivate Callaghan; I find he tells me a good deal.

After that, a whole series of departmental meetings, of which the most interesting was on my third big planning decision – the Sheffield proposal to build in their green belt. Dame Evelyn tried to shove me into a snap decision to violate the green belt round Sheffield as I have done in Kent, but by now I had reflected carefully and said, 'No, that's going too far.' I have decided to go there and see for myself.

Then I went to the House of Commons and gave Tommy Balogh and Peter Shore dinner – another unhappy occasion. Peter's uneasy and not too happy now he is a Member of the House; as for poor Thomas, he is in real trouble. He's now officially a member of the Cabinet Secretariat at £6,000 a year, a temporary civil servant. He has a beautiful office, which I visited the other day, and he is in fact Harold's private adviser. But, alas, he has decided to attack the whole Civil Service. He's already told Harold he ought to sack Helsby, the chief of the Civil Service, and he's also got himself up against George Wigg, who is Harold's other private adviser at No. 10. I found Tommy feeling isolated and miserable.

Tuesday, December 10th

The big thing for me this morning was the Ministerial Committee on the Rent Bill. I had persuaded Harold to let the Bill go not to the ordinary Home Affairs Committee but to a committee specially selected to see that we got it through. Among others, the committee consisted of the Lord President; Michael Stewart; the Secretary of State for Scotland, Willie Ross; the Attorney-General; the Attorney-General for Scotland; Douglas Houghton; and the Financial Secretary to the Treasury, Niall MacDermot.[1] Michael Stewart has of course strong views as an old L.C.C. man and Niall MacDermot is very opinionated and talks not as Financial Secretary but as an expert on

[1] M.P. for Derby North 1962–70. In 1967 he became a Minister of State at M.H.L.G.

rents. The meeting took two hours; it was really tough and I enjoyed it. It was the best Cabinet Committee meeting I've had because the opposition was formidable and expert. The Bill survived fairly well.

After that was over I had the two Parliamentary Secretaries to lunch. Then we all went over to the House to hear George Brown's Statement on 'regional economic planning'. In the course of yesterday and this morning I had been continually negotiating on the draft. It had come across to us with the word 'economic' added in in longhand before the word 'planning' as a concession to me, so that it read not just 'regional planning' but 'regional economic planning', ha, ha, ha! I also wrote into the Statement the explicit assurance that nothing in this scheme would affect the existing powers of the local authorities with regard to planning. It seemed to go down fairly well in the House, mainly because it will take some time for people to discover how inadequate and meaningless it has now been made.

Then I had my most ticklish meeting of the day, the first meeting of the housing and local government group of the Parliamentary Labour Party. Sixty or so people turned up. I made a carefully prepared statement on housing policy in general. However, I knew I was in for trouble with the Kent members about Hartley. It had been tremendously attacked in a good many of the papers; and the Rural District Council there is a Labour one, and many of the Labour M.P.s, particularly the Deputy Chief Whip, are enraged. I had just finished the easy part of the meeting when the division bell went. When we came back the Kent M.P.s started operating, particularly Sydney Irving and Norman Dodds, with a wild and whirlwind attack. Watching how the non-Kent Members were reacting, I began to realize what a sacred cow the green belt has become in progressive circles and how difficult it is for a Minister to deal with a special case like this in a large committee. I sat back patiently waiting for the storm to blow out and afterwards Bob Mellish loyally went round the London Members and told them to behave. I am glad to say that despite the row we didn't give way one inch.

Friday, December 11th
We started with a Cabinet at which Harold Wilson reported on his Washington visit. It doesn't show up much in my diary but in fact the week has been dominated by news of this first visit of the Prime Minister, the Foreign Secretary and the Defence Minister to Lyndon Johnson in Washington. They had flown back on Thursday and were coming to Cabinet to report to us in full. On this occasion I took notes at Cabinet and I am going to put down here my summary of his initial address. It will be interesting to compare what I recorded as having been said and what the Cabinet Secretariat said he said.[1]

He started by saying there were two conferences, one which took place and one which the British press reported. And he rebuked the *Sun* for sending

[1] For the Prime Minister's own account, see *Wilson*, pp. 46–51.

back fictitious reports, in particular for suggesting that he had already sold out on the issue of the M.L.F. He also said it was quite untrue that a pistol had been put to his head on Vietnam. The conference, he said, was more like an onion being peeled; the outer leaves came off and you gradually reached Europe at the centre. The most encouraging fact about the conference was America's emphasis on Britain's world-wide role; this line had been taken in particularly moving terms in a talk Denis Healey had had with McNamara on the plane to Omaha. McNamara had gone out of his way to emphasize the importance of Britain's role east of Suez. Harold went on to say that the whole conference moved away from any inward-looking worry about the alliance to positive discussions on peace-keeping and new disarmament proposals.

Then he turned to the economic problems. The Americans, he said, had shown much understanding of the point he himself had made about the danger of our over-commitment. President Lyndon Johnson had shown himself deeply concerned about our situation and virtually promised us all aid short of war. He also expressed an appreciation of the help which we had given him in the election and all that Harold Wilson's speeches had meant for him. (I found this extremely funny but I fear the humour was entirely unconscious.)

Harold said that he himself had made no request for a fresh loan, that he had discovered that the Americans were ready to help, that they were cutting their own defence costs and were therefore not unsympathetic to our doing the same. So Harold then turned to the problem of reducing costs by pooling. This he said was the most fruitful possibility, pooling weapons, pooling research and development; we must have a really constructive Anglo–American rationalization of defence budgeting. Broadly speaking, they led on air-frames, we led on air-engines, and that gave us a chance of useful co-operation.

Turning to Europe, he said the atmosphere was different from what he expected. The President feels as strongly as we do the danger of proliferation of nuclear weapons – and then Harold made a long reference to the problems of China and India, saying that the great watershed of proliferation would be if India were compelled to make a nuclear weapon under threat from China. The Indians, he said, could become a nuclear power in eighteen months once they had decided to do so. That is a very real danger.

Harold then turned to Vietnam and said that the President himself is deeply committed to Vietnam and asked him outright for a British military commitment. Harold had resisted, apart from offering the use of our jungle training team in Malaya and also our teams for anti-subversive activities. He didn't think the Americans really expected him to concede; they wanted not so much the presence of British soldiers as the presence of the British flag. He had persuaded the Americans not to embarrass our Foreign Secretary who, with the Russians, is co-chairman of the Geneva Conference. He ended up by referring to the importance of the communiqué and drawing attention to the last paragraph, emphasizing continuing discussion at all levels so that we, the British, are to be in on all the transatlantic conferences. 'They want us with them,' Harold said. 'They want our new constructive ideas after the epoch of sterility. We are now in a position to influence events more than ever before for the last ten years.'

That's the end of my note of his half-hour survey. When Gordon Walker had made some not very important points, Healey was given his turn. He talked at length about his five hours with McNamara on the way to Omaha during which they sorted out alternative weapon systems for the British to choose between. He said that McNamara was a man after his own heart and they were working together admirably. Then the subject was thrown open to discussion and Callaghan at once asked in his usual way, 'Well, where's the cut going to come in Defence?' Wilson replied that first of all there would be a cut in the weapons costs, thanks to our system for pooling R & D; and second, there would be a cut in overseas military commitments. Healey then remarked that hundreds of millions of pounds can be saved on weapons by pooling and added that there can be savings by co-operative work in the Indian Ocean and other spheres outside Europe. Callaghan then made a speech about the costs of our troops in Germany, which had jumped from £20 million to £65 million as the result of the disastrous agreement signed by the last Government in July 1963.

I then asked about our world-wide role: 'If the Americans like us to have a world-wide role what does this mean for us in terms of military commitments?' Healey replied that what they wanted us to do was not to maintain huge bases but to keep a foothold in Hong Kong, Malaya, the Persian Gulf, to enable us to do things for the alliance which they can't do. They think our forces are much more useful to the alliance outside Europe than in Germany.

Well, that's the end of my note on what happened in Cabinet. It's quite interesting to compare what Harold told us in confidence with what I could read next day in John Freeman's[1] account of the Washington conversations in the *New Statesman* or Henry Brandon's in the *Sunday Times*. Harold has told nothing to Cabinet which hasn't been told to the press.

I picked up Anne at Vincent Square and we drove to Victoria to catch the 4 p.m. train to Brighton for the Labour Party Conference.[2] We got down there in lovely weather but that was the last we saw of the sun. From then on the wind blew and for the next two days we were in a sea mist.

By 6 p.m. we were plunged into a terrible row with the union members of

---

[1] Labour M.P. for Watford, and a Bevanite, from 1945 to 1951, when he resigned his post at the Ministry of Supply on the rearmament issue. Like Crossman, he was a *New Statesman* journalist and in 1951 he became assistant editor, succeeding Kingsley Martin as editor in 1961. He served as High Commissioner in India 1965–8 and as Ambassador in Washington 1969–71. Since 1971 he has been chairman of London Weekend Television.

[2] Because of the general election the Labour Party's annual Conference had been postponed from October to December. It was held over a weekend, rather than the usual week.

the Executive as the result of Harry Nicholas retiring from the Treasurership. The details don't matter.* But this does show one how the old conflict of trade unions and intellectuals still carries on.

Saturday, December 12th

Filthy weather and a dreary morning in the conference hall. But I found myself seated on the platform between Barbara Castle and Jim Callaghan and as a result I was able to get quite a lot of information about what was going on in the Treasury and in Overseas Development. While the Young Socialists' discussion dragged on James was telling me of the seriousness of the economic situation. Poor James, he is off to Paris to try and get some more money and I think he told me (I heard this always against the noise of the speeches) that the reserves would only last ten days and if the wound can't be staunched by then, we shall be forced to have a devaluation and a general election straight away. All these were bits and pieces which came out during the session. Anne and I lunched with Sydney Jacobson, Pam Berry and Harold Hutchinson. I warned Harold Hutchinson how critical Wilson had been at Cabinet of the *Sun* and how angry he was. I came out of the lunch and Harold met me and said, 'So you've been dining in the enemy camp.' I thought he was laughing but he wasn't, which shows how passionately he objected to the criticisms of the press.

All this became more intelligible when I went down to the Conference and heard his speech that afternoon. There is no doubt it was a brilliant Conference performance. He had only had a day to prepare it since returning to London. He did extremely well. But it was a grievous disappointment to me because it *was* just a Conference performance, a lightweight affair with a great attack on the *Evening Standard*, quite unworthy of a Prime Minister. It didn't seem to me that he struck the right Prime Ministerial note and he certainly didn't steel our people for the difficulties ahead. As Minister of Housing I know quite well that I've got to explain the fact that the local authorities aren't going to get the money to build the houses. They will have to cut back their housing programme; and the building societies are going to charge 6¾ per cent and deter private building. The fact is, deflation is really starting. That's what I feel in my bones. But it hasn't been said and Harold Wilson blithely denies it. That's what I found unsatisfactory in his speech.

We had a gay dinner with the Llewelyn-Davieses. I took Pat Llewelyn-Davies into the Pavilion. We crept in through an unlocked side door and showed her round the state rooms.

Sunday, December 13th

I must say I expected a pretty miserable debate this morning but to my surprise it was a great success. I won't record it because from my point of view what really happened was that Callaghan went on talking to me during

¹ Anyway, they were fully reported in the papers next day.

the speeches about the terrible situation. When I wasn't listening to that, I was talking to Harold Collison, the General Secretary of the Agricultural and Allied Workers,[1] about a way of resolving the problem of the tied cottage. The only other thing I remember is watching Harold Wilson climbing up to the platform and standing like a little Napoleon while being photographed. In fact he talked to me for three or four minutes on the steps while we were photographed together. 'You got your £20 million off Callaghan,' he said. 'You are pleased about that, I suppose; a big victory for you. And your anti-eviction Bill is pretty popular, isn't it?' I said, 'Yes, that's true, but I'm in trouble about getting money from the building societies and I want you to make quite sure I can get some money for local-authority building apart from housing,' and he replied, 'Well, Tommy and Robert Neild said the budget wasn't deflationary enough but I told them that by April we shall need some reflationary expenditure. So it looks as though you will be able to have your public-sector housing financed after all, my dear Dick.'

What a contrast between the attitude of Harold Wilson during those four minutes on the steps and that of James Callaghan, his Chancellor! When I said something about Callaghan, he said, 'Yes, I'm having to hold his hand. His nerve isn't very good these days.'

The morning ended with a magnificent speech by George Brown in which he did all the things which Harold Wilson should have done. George Brown DID talk about the difficulties, he did warn people, harden them, and the Conference ended up in pretty good form.

After that Anne and I lunched with Liz and Peter Shore and the Croslands and Wedgwood Benns, and we all came back in the train together. Conference this year was more enjoyable than I had ever known it and really we all needed it. I think it made us realize how isolated we have become in our Ministries and how much we needed a sense of getting together, of good humour, of companionship which really we don't get in our Ministerial lives.

The fact is we are a fragmented Government. In the middle there are Harold Wilson and George Brown, each giving us a lead in his own way and often in his own direction. And around them are the rest of us, each on his own, not working as a team but working in towards either Harold or George Brown. Our relations with the Party in Parliament are already very bad and our relations with the Party in Transport House and outside are much worse. What we really need is somebody whole-time in the Cabinet – as a Tory Government always has – dealing with the Party, dealing with the presentation of Cabinet policy. One of the things I shall have to do, and Tam Dalyell is prodding me to do it, is to try to put over to Harold and George the need for integrating our Cabinet policy with Transport House policy and through Transport House getting it across to the Party outside and to the general public.

[1] He held this post from 1953 until 1969, when he became chairman of the Supplementary Benefits Commission. In 1964 he was made a life peer.

4

Looking back on this first stage of the Labour Government—from our election victory to our victory conference—I would say that on the whole the Government has established itself extremely well in terms of departmental efficiency. On the other hand, I'm not sure we have done very well in terms of our own socialist strategy or of our integrated leadership. I don't think Harold has really established himself as the leader we need. But he has certainly grown a great deal more Napoleonic. The trouble is one never sees him except when one needs to. He is therefore getting more and more apart from us all, relying more and more on his own ideas, and I think Tommy is probably right in saying that he is more and more in the hands of his civil servants. Indeed, I get the impression this Government isn't running itself in but just running along; maybe it's doing this for the reason Callaghan gave. Maybe until we know whether we are going to have a devaluation and election before the spring we shan't get very settled.

Difficult for me, therefore, to believe that the work I am doing in my Department has any very enduring value. I'm learning my job; I've got a certain amount of praise for the anti-eviction Bill; all that is useful. I don't feel I've sunk many roots, and I still feel a sense of unreality when I make my speeches in the House, when I answer my Questions, when I hold a press conference, when I sit on the platform at Brighton; I still feel I am taking part in a book I've written about the constitution and not actually playing a real part in real politics. And meanwhile I'm getting more and more separated from the children and from Anne. Ministerial life is totally absorbing. As one is cut off from one's home and at the same time cut off from one's colleagues one really is isolated, to an extent I had not thought possible.

How important it was for the Tories when they were in Government to relax for the weekend in those great country-house parties! How much we in the Labour Party miss the country houses which we don't have! How much Harold's personality accentuates the fragmentation to which we've been submitted by his refusal to have any cliques or coteries, his refusal to have a meal with one informally or an informal talk, his determination to have everything in terms of business.

As for my own career, I think I can say that so far the report is not too bad. I've established myself inside my own Ministry and in the House of Commons. I've kept Harold Wilson's confidence. I've made a bad start with planning permissions—I shan't say this to anybody, but the green belt decision in Hartley was a mistake. I was wrong to let Jim MacColl go down there and advise me on it; if I had gone myself I would have handled Hartley as I handled the Sheffield decision. Well, I've learnt my lesson.

Finally, as to my private life and my relations with Anne, I know she was extremely alarmed that my being a Minister would cut her off. At first I think she felt very strongly that it had and that I had become so 100 per cent a Minister that I was hardly a human being and hardly had any contact with her. But whereas this happened at the beginning, it's my impression that my sheer absorption into the job is wearing off. As a married couple we are absorbing the new activity into our joint private life. This weekend I am more convinced than ever that if I am going to be a success as a Minister it will largely depend on the way we are living together and the way we are loving each other. I am also pretty sure that my getting this astonishing fulfilment in this new life is not going to damage our relations, and may possibly deepen them.

I really didn't have any idea when I went into the Ministry whether I would like it, whether I would be a success. I knew pretty well what a Minister's job was; and now I find myself inside I haven't been surprised at what goes on in Whitehall. However, I am surprised at how well I fit into it and how naturally I have switched from a life mainly devoted to writing and criticism to a life wholly inside the Whitehall machine, where I am not a cog but an important part. I find all this perfectly natural, haven't a pang of regret for the writing I have completely given up. I had been writing for nineteen years as my main occupation and I thought I would miss it. But I don't. Indeed I find it very difficult to imagine going back into political criticism from the life of political action in which I am now engaged. This new kind of world in which I sit in conference, take the lead in committees, formulate policies, take decisions, requires that all the writing be done for me by other people. And though it is not done very well, surprisingly I don't find this exasperating, although I do try to persuade the civil servants to write better and I am afraid I am getting quite a name in the Department as a schoolmaster who gives tutorials in style.

There are also interesting physical changes. Before I became a Minister I used to worry, wake up early in the morning in a panic about whether I had done something wrong. Now that I have so many more things to worry about, so many big decisions to take, I find myself worrying much less. I have already made one decision which has made me in a major way unpopular, but it hasn't made me worry. Taking decisions seems something I can do easily and quickly once I have digested the essential information. I had always suspected when I was working in Eisenhower's headquarters that the job of a general was relatively easy. Well, I find the job of a Minister relatively easy. It suits my temperament. When I sit at my desk here at Prescote and pull out a mass of papers from the red box and see that I have to decide on the boundaries of Coventry or on where to let Birmingham have its new housing land, I find these decisions easy, pleasant, and I take them in a fairly light-hearted way.

When I went to *The Economist* to lunch last week I was asked what it felt like to be a Minister and I replied I hadn't realized how frustrated I was before I got office. I feel better, physically healthier, far less tired, on top of my form by day, even though I have very long days—I may sit in conference almost without a break from nine in the morning until six in the evening. But this doesn't tire me. It exhilarates me and I feel the better for it, whereas a morning at one's desk writing an article is nearly always exasperating and frustrating because one is always striving to improve it and one always knows it *could* be better than it is when one's finished it. In my life as a journalist I used to wake up after a night's sleep to find I had been pounding away at an article all night, writing, rewriting paragraphs in my sleep. I haven't so far found myself taking planning decisions in my sleep. Indeed I sleep all the more soundly for having had those decisions to take during the day, for having written 'O.K.' on that policy document, for having been a man of action in that sense of the word.

Is this a ridiculous, dangerous, unrealistic euphoria which I'm suffering under, am I really having an easy time because I've been put into an easy Ministry? Or is there something in the job which suits my temperament? When I ask myself these questions I naturally look at some of my colleagues and make comparisons. Now, there is George Brown. He is a man who thrives on responsibility; yet he is very different from me. He is a pure man of action, intensely unreflective, who bashes ahead. He is doing a wonderful job. He has come naturally to his new job as Deputy Prime Minister. He is happier, he drinks less and I daresay it's even true that what he drinks he now digests better. In fact he is a better man for the weight of responsibility on his shoulders. Just as Harold Wilson is obviously a better man and so is Tony Crosland and so is Roy Jenkins; one can see they are all obviously the better for it. The only person I see a lot of who doesn't seem to me to be really enjoying his job is poor Jim Callaghan.

Monday, December 14th
Callaghan was off to Paris today to try and persuade the European bankers to stand by us, after what had been a terrible week, and I'm afraid that anything he does personally will produce exactly the opposite effect. There is a man who simply isn't enthralled and stimulated and excited by the challenge of his office. He feels unhappy and insecure, and I sometimes suspect that he feels he has been hoicked up above his level and given a job which he has no taste for because he feels he can't get on top of it.

The most interesting thing which happened today was the meeting of the E.D.C. The last item on the agenda was the proposal to have a new Beeching Report on the railways.[1] I had better go back a little here. For a fortnight now I have been watching develop in the press a story about Dr Beeching's future when he retires from his position as head of British Railways. It's been fairly obvious that Harold Wilson has been talking to the journalists, since the Minister of Transport, Tom Fraser, wouldn't conceive of taking an initiative of this kind. So it was also pretty obvious that the item on the agenda was also backed by Harold. The actual detail was that Beeching was to resign on January 1st and from then until May 31st was to prepare a report on co-

[1] Dr Beeching was appointed chairman of the British Railways Board by the Conservative Government in 1963. His first report, published in 1964, recommended a drastic pruning of the railway network in the interests of economy. When he left the Board in 1965, Dr Beeching was made a life peer.

ordination of all transport, and was then to go back to I.C.I. Now, over the weekend I had had a word with Thomas Balogh about this. He also thought it a barmy idea. So I went to the E.D.C. determined to raise the issue. We had a very long agenda, with plans for boosting exports, introduced by Douglas Jay, and a good many other serious items. Nevertheless, I stayed on right until the end of the meeting and the moment this item came up Tony Crosland jumped in (and this in fact is significant because Crosland is George Brown's number two) and said that this was the most dangerous proposal he had yet seen made, dangerous to the whole image of the Government and dangerous to the future of transport. Thereupon Tom Fraser immediately intervened and said that he had done this with the full backing of the Prime Minister and the whole thing had reached a point where it was impossible to reverse the decision. So that was that.

At this point Frank Cousins and I both blew our tops. Frank Cousins talked about it in the kind of way an ordinary rank-and-file Labour person would; he said, 'Here's a man we have denounced up hill and down dale, a man who is a bureaucratic enemy of public transport. Why should we give him this job? Any idea Beeching proposed would be discredited among the trade unions by the very fact that he proposed it.'

The only people who really supported Beeching were Charles Pannell, our Minister of Works, and Fred Lee. So the voting was roughly 12 to 2 on the Committee. Callaghan was away, George Brown was in the chair and he said, 'Well, to avoid all further embarrassment I'll talk to the P.M. about it and tell him what's on, but I think it's too late to stop it.'

After the E.D.C. I had just time to get to Fred Willey's room for a meeting on the Land Commission. I found myself alone with Willey himself, Jack Diamond from the Treasury and Maurice Foley from the D.E.A. I explained the alternatives before us as I saw them. We could either have a big Bill creating a Land Commission with monopoly powers, or we could have a more modest measure in the first instance and create a Land Commission whose first job was to collect the tax on betterment and do some permissive buying of land. The second was a measure we could easily introduce, which would be popular and which we could carry through. The first seemed to me an immoderate policy which might gum up the works and destroy any chance of building the houses we require. As I expected, Maurice Foley from the D.E.A. backed Willey's demand for the big Bill whereas Jack Diamond from the Treasury was 150 per cent on my side. At the end of the discussion it was understood that Fred Willey was now to produce a second draft of his policy paper. It was obvious, however, that the line I took had infuriated Willey and that he would go straight to George Brown, who would be equally outraged by what he would regard as Dame Evelyn Sharp's opposition to the Labour Party's policy of the Land Commission. But I really had very little choice in the matter. One can talk gaily about backing Party policies but in this case the whole of my housing programme could be scuppered if we were to launch the wrong Land Commission measure. To take these enormous powers could prevent all sales of land in much the same way that the Silkin measure prevented them in 1946.[1]

However, I am not at all certain I shall win, because I am going to present to my colleagues the picture of someone going back on a very firm election commitment. The only thing on my side is that the Treasury will wholly support the cautious line, and I hope that more and more colleagues will get alarmed at the thought that what we are producing is administratively chaotic and impracticable.

Tuesday, December 15th

I was greatly tickled this morning to find in my red box that our Tuesday Cabinet meeting had had added to its agenda the issue of Beeching and transport. This was the first case where Harold had been committed in advance to a policy which was not popular with the rest of the Cabinet. I have known personally that he wanted a postponement in the increase of Ministerial salaries, and 10s. – not 12s. 6d. – for the old-age pensioners. But in both these cases he had remained cagily in the middle and had not committed himself until he could see which side was winning. However, here he was personally committed to backing the Minister of Transport and it was fascinating to see what happened.

Well, what happened was this: Harold Wilson straight away said that George Brown would report on the views expressed by his colleagues. George did so and then Harold chipped in before Tom Fraser and said he thought it important to have strong economic assessors and he mentioned the names of Teddy Jackson[2] and Christopher Foster,[3] given to him by Tommy Balogh. Secondly, he said it was unwise to commit ourselves to publication of the report and thirdly he recognized that the time proposed, five months, might be inadequate. These were all objections which had been made in the Committee. Harold had conceded them before the debate started in an effort to appease us. Then came the Cabinet reaction. Sitting round the table were twelve people, ten of whom had expressed themselves in strong language twenty-four hours before, condemning the whole proposal. How many of those twelve would now in Cabinet repeat their open opposition? The answer is that two – Frank Cousins and I – did so. Apart from us no one else was willing to stand up and fight the Prime Minister. Of course, one or two of them made a mild observation but that's not the test in Cabinet. The test is whether one is prepared to enter the contest with the P.M. or with the First Secretary, the two dominant forces in the Cabinet, and in order to do that one

[1] The provisions of the 1946 Town and Country Planning Act can be found in *Cmd. 6537*.

[2] Director of the Oxford University Institute of Economics and Statistics since 1959.

[3] Economist and Fellow of Jesus College, Oxford, and, since 1970, head of the Unit for Research in Urban Economics at L.S.E. After the 1966 general election he joined the Ministry of Transport as Director-General of Economic Planning.

hasn't just got to make a comment, one has to come back at them again and again and again, expressing dissent and getting one's way by will-power.

Now, this was the first Cabinet where we had had a row of this sort. Of course it was all terribly polite and 'Prime Minister this and Minister of Transport that and Minister of Housing this'. But it went on for three rounds with Frank Cousins and myself on the one side and the Prime Minister and Tom Fraser on the other. Tom Fraser made it exquisitely embarrassing to the Prime Minister by disowning all the concessions the Prime Minister had made and saying that he didn't want to have Beeching with a lot of experts hung round his neck and that he thought Beeching was really the only man who could do the job and that five months was ample time for him to do it in. Everything the Prime Minister had conceded in order to square us was taken back by Tom Fraser in his first-round speech. When it came to my turn I very carefully pointed this out and said that all the anxieties allayed by the Prime Minister had been reawakened by the Minister of Transport. Then Harold made another intervention to try and save Fraser, and Fraser behaved worse than ever, revealing himself as even more fervently and pathetically reliant on Beeching as the only person to do his job for him. Finally, when the Prime Minister obviously wanted to end the discussion, I pressed him further on the vital point. 'I'm sorry,' I said, 'but I want it absolutely clear that the assessors will have a genuinely independent position; and we are to have an explicit assurance that there will be no publication.' Somebody remarked, *sotto voce*, 'Well, the effect of that will be to keep Beeching out,' to which Frank Cousins snorted aloud, 'That would be a damned good thing.' In his summing up the Prime Minister did give an explicit assurance to Frank and me that all these things would be written into the minutes, and that was that.*

After Cabinet I went to see Burke Trend because I had something to put to him about the text of the Cabinet minutes of the previous Thursday. I had read them with special attention because I wanted to compare them with my own note of the meeting and I had been struck by the sentence in which Harold was stressing the importance of the British Government centring its attention on the prevention of nuclear proliferation. I noticed that in the minutes a second aim was added, 'the aim of satisfying the nuclear aspirations of the Federal German Government'. As soon as I saw this I was sure that Harold had never said it and that, if he had said it, he would have caused a stormy row with at least Tony Greenwood and Frank Cousins. In fact, the impression he had left was that he was determined to frustrate the nuclear aspirations of the Federal German Government. So I pointed this out to Burke Trend and I said, 'Harold can't have said this.' To which he replied, 'Ah, of course he never said it, we never do give verbatim what people say. We précis the sense and give the substance of what they say.' To which I

---

* This discussion leaked and the upshot was that Beeching was so insulted that he absolutely refused to accept the appointment.

replied, 'This is not the substance of what he said, and if it had been the substance he would have divided the Cabinet.' 'Well,' said Burke Trend, 'what would you like? Would you like me to have "deal with" instead of "satisfy"?' I replied that this indeed would change the whole tone of the passage and its meaning. 'I don't mind giving you "deal" instead of "satisfy",' said Burke airily and friendlily.

I should round this off perhaps by an incident which occurred next day when I ran into Burke and he asked me whether I was content with the minutes of the Cabinet dealing with the Beeching incident. I said I was, and he twinkled. What all this shows is the importance of being the kind of awkward Cabinet Minister who reads Cabinet minutes carefully. But it also shows that it's important not to raise the issue in Cabinet but to raise it verbally after Cabinet with the Secretary, so as not to embarrass him publicly, and then having done that to mention it to the Prime Minister.

Wednesday, December 16th

Today I met Vivian Bowden in the park and he walked me back from the Athenaeum. He told me how much better he was feeling, since he had just moved into Curzon Street and he was at last getting to feel at home in his job.[1] While he was dilating on how much happier he felt he added, 'And by the way I had better tell you, I've sacked my Permanent Secretary.' 'You've sacked your Permanent Secretary?' I said. 'But have you told Harold that you've done so, or Michael Stewart?' 'Oh, no,' he said, 'I just sacked him. Ought I to have told them? Well, anyhow, I've done it now and I hear that the intention is that when Dame Evelyn goes you should have my Permanent Secretary, Sir Bruce Fraser, in her place.' It was just after this conversation in the park that I heard from George Moseley that Harold wanted me to lunch next day and I assumed at once that he wanted to discuss Bruce Fraser. I took Bowden's remarks quite seriously because I now know about the grapevine in Whitehall, and I talked the whole thing over with the Dame. I asked her point blank when she wanted to go, and she said she would like to go in the summer. That would be long enough for her. I said, 'Fine, that gives me time to think.' And then I added, 'I have no doubt Harold Wilson wants me to take Bruce Fraser straight away in order to relieve him of embarrassment.' The Dame then said that she had heard the same thing; and when she had gone out I checked with George Moseley and he told me that everyone knew I was going to be asked by Harold Wilson to take Bruce Fraser instead of Dame Evelyn as my Permanent Secretary. Meeting Vivian in the park was quite a stroke of luck!

Thursday, December 17th

Lunch with Harold was quite eventful. Just as we were sitting down, Jim Callaghan came and sat beside Harold and said, 'Well, I'm afraid I must

[1] See p. 41.

mar your joy in your success in the defence debate yesterday by telling you that we have had the worst morning to date. We have lost £36 million this morning, my dear Harold.' And after that we got down to business. But before Harold would talk about Vivian Bowden he spent the first half of the lunch telling me about the speech he was going to make that evening in which he would annihilate Sir Alec Douglas-Home (as he duly did!) by demonstrating that the independent British deterrent was a complete myth.[1] At last we turned to the real subject and Harold said, 'Well, Dick, Vivian is the only misfit we have had in our Government, and as you and I are partly responsible I thought I would discuss it with you. Don't you think I could move him now to the Ministry of Technology and switch him with Charles Snow? After all, Snow would be ideally suited to Education and Bowden to Technology.' I reacted coolly to this idea, saying that if Bowden had been a failure in Education, he would probably be a failure in Technology as well. Moreover, I thought it would be very unfair on Frank Cousins to burden him with Vivian as his junior Minister, particularly in view of Frank's parliamentary inexperience. After discussing Vivian, Harold went on to say that there was a further complication in the Ministry of Education. Under the set-up created by Quintin Hogg in the previous Government there were two Permanent Secretaries in the Department of Education and Science, and Sir Bruce Fraser was the second one. Harold told me that this wasn't working and he wanted to move Bruce Fraser somewhere else. I then said that I had of course heard this on the grapevine, and indeed Vivian had told me that Bruce Fraser was to come to my Ministry as soon as Dame Evelyn had gone. I then told Harold that I had agreed with Dame Evelyn that she should go in the summer, since that would give me plenty of time to find a good successor. I didn't want one pushed on me, as Bruce Fraser would be if I took him straight away. I waited to see how Harold would react. He took it without any demur. But I was fairly sure that that wasn't the last I'd heard of the proposal.

Today was the day the Lords were discussing my anti-eviction Bill. There had been rumours that they would oppose it and send back amendments on furnished dwellings and on tied cottages. Actually they didn't dare to move a single amendment at Committee Stage and by four o'clock on Thursday it had became law. As a result, the programme I had arranged weeks ago to do in the B.B.C. *Gallery* programme became topical. I went round there imme- diately after the ten o'clock vote on defence, having just heard Harold's destruction of Douglas-Home. I got into my car and sped down with my bodyguard, Brian Ponsford, to Lime Grove where I was told I was going to be cross-examined by a representative of the property owners as well as by

[1] In the two-day debate, on December 16th and 17th, following the Prime Minister's visit to Washington, the Conservatives criticized the Government's proposals for an Atlantic nuclear force. On the first day, Harold Wilson answered the Opposition in an hour-long speech, defending the 'inter-dependent' deterrent. On the second day, the Prime Minister summed up the Government's case; his own account (*Wilson*, pp. 54–7) describes his 'towering attack'. The Opposition motion was defeated by 311 votes to 291.

4*

Audrey Harvey[1] representing the Left. Bob McKenzie[2] would be in the chair. As it turned out, so far from there being a cross-examination, Bob McKenzie handled the whole thing in a most courteous way. Audrey Harvey was allowed to make a couple of remarks and the property man was allowed to make three or four remarks, but apart from this the whole of the evening was devoted to enabling me to explain what the anti-eviction Bill was about, what the aim of the big Rent Bill would be and to discuss the housing situation. What I got was really a party political broadcast and I couldn't help remarking that Bob McKenzie treated me with the proper deference he accords to the reasonably successful Minister.

Friday, December 18th
I had been due to make one of my official visits—this time to Leeds—but this had to be cancelled because a Cabinet was suddenly put on with my rent policy on the agenda. It took place in the P.M.'s room in the House, which was terribly crowded; and it was the first time that one of our major reforms had been submitted to Cabinet. I was interested to see how Harold would treat me after I had stood up to him on Tuesday on the subject of Dr Beeching and also on the Thursday when he had offered me Sir Bruce instead of Dame Evelyn. Actually, he couldn't have been more helpful. He started by having a look at his own brief, obviously prepared for him by Burke Trend, and instead of allowing any general discussion of this paper he simply listed the items on which he thought a firm decision was required. Each of these ten items he read aloud and then asked me to say a sentence or two. (This was after I had given a clause by clause account of the Bill and how it worked.) One, two, three, four points were clipped through at top speed and anybody who wanted to criticize me, especially Michael Stewart on the subject of my substitution of the fair rent concept for gross rateable value as a basis for fixing rents, found themselves unable to do so without causing the kind of friction and resistance which Ministers are unwilling to cause in our good-humoured Labour Cabinet.

Today was one of those marvellous autumny days when the Horse Guards look at their best. I felt in tremendous form when my item was over and I sat back in my chair, looked out of the window and vaguely listened to the report which Denis Healey and Patrick Gordon Walker had brought back from Paris on the Western Alliance. Apparently although a fortnight ago we were regarded as the bad boys, deliberately out to delay the construction of the M.L.F., we were now heralded as the people who put forward constructive proposals and had become the blue-eyed boys of the Western Alliance. I had another reason for feeling cheerful—I was taking the children to the Bertram Mills circus in the afternoon. I had been personally invited to the

---

[1] Chairman of a voluntary body which advised London's homeless.

[2] Professor of Politics at L.S.E., author of such classical textbooks as *British Political Parties* (London: Heinemann, 1955). He had a reputation as a kindly but penetrating interviewer.

famous circus lunch but I had decided instead to get tickets for the whole family. I rushed to Vincent Square to have lunch with Anne and Jennie and the children, who had come up specially in the train. And then Molly arrived at two o'clock and we swept down to Olympia in the Ministry car. One of the few really nice perks a Minister gets is that black saloon car always at his disposal. In London, where parking is a nightmare, this is a tremendous thing. The children can sit in front with Molly and I can start pressing on the handle and make the glass screen move up and down. So the children like being in the Minister's car.

We had a fine time at the circus. We had to leave a little early and Molly then took us to Paddington. There, waiting with my red boxes by the reserved compartment, was Arthur, the doorman from the Ministry. And in the compartment was the fellow from the restaurant car, saying that a section would be reserved for the Minister and his family. And there we finally were, dining together in great state. We drove home from Banbury Station in fine fettle that night. It was a *splendid* outing and the extra splendour of the Minister's car and the Minister's reserved compartment made the children for the first time see the point of their father being a Minister.

Sunday, December 20th
I was pretty tired when we got home on Friday evening, and I really spent Saturday doing nothing until we had the Farm Dinner in the evening. That, too, was a pretty exhausting performance which started at 7.30 and finished after midnight. Today, Sunday, the Hodgkinsons—George and Carrie—came over from Coventry for lunch and it has been a lovely, lovely day, walking in the sunshine at Prescote.

One last reflection on the economic situation. This would have been a very good week for the Government, with George Brown's Incomes and Prices Statement[1] and our success on defence, if it hadn't been for the ghastly financial situation. Throughout the week it became clearer and clearer that confidence had not been restored, that the new $3,000 million loan was being rapidly eaten away, that the City of London and the bankers of Zurich just weren't prepared to give this Labour Government their confidence. However, I think it is fair to add that it may not be all their fault and that our efforts to appease them have been singularly unconvincing. The autumn budget which was designed to please in fact infuriated them. Then there came the second attempt, by outlining the taxes—the corporation tax and the capital gains tax.[2] The moment each detail was announced people wanted more, and we are really watching the Chancellor of the Exchequer giving his budget

---

[1] He had persuaded the C.B.I. and the T.U.C. to sign the Declaration of Intent on Productivity, Prices and Incomes, at a great conference at Lancaster House on December 16th.
[2] The Chancellor still gave no specific details of the eventual rates of these taxes but declared that Unit Trusts would not be hit unfairly and that building societies might even benefit. Some firms would be exempt.

away little by little and in no way gaining the confidence of those whose alarm he seeks to allay. Nevertheless, as I say, apart from the appalling financial crisis, this has been a splendid week. On Friday the Gallup Poll showed us still with a 10 per cent lead and indicated that if an election came along we should find ourselves with a greatly increased majority.

And that of course is Harold Wilson's secret weapon. I notice that the *Observer* is now talking of a snap election this spring, and I know from things that Harold has said to me – he said them again at lunch on Thursday – that a snap election is still very much in his mind. If it becomes clear that confidence cannot be restored and that devaluation threatens, he will go to the country before the devaluation, asking for a vote of confidence, and in so doing will put the Tories into a devastatingly weak position. There are two reasons why it will be weak. The first is because though they have decided to get rid of Douglas-Home, they haven't yet done so; and there's nothing weaker than a party which has decided that its present leader is a failure and is still considering who his successor should be. The second reason is because they have been very inept in Opposition. They have been licked on the independent deterrent and, even worse, they have given the impression of nagging on the financial situation. If the Opposition were to come out and say there is every reason for confidence in the pound, the crisis would be over, and this is what Harold Wilson has been insisting they should do. If they do, his position is strengthened. If they don't, he goes to the country on the grounds that they haven't done their duty. Both ways he has them in a vice. So this is his tactic: to keep the Opposition always with this unenviable choice between either supporting the Government, and thereby strengthening it, or seeming unpatriotic by opposing it.

I might just add for the record that after the special Cabinet on Friday when we discussed the Rent Bill I came back into the office to celebrate our victory with the Dame and George Moseley over a drink. Then I dictated a memo for her to issue to the Department, thanking all those who had helped me with the anti-eviction Bill and looking forward to collaboration on the bigger measure. But I was able to tell her something much more important – that at long last we are going to move forward on the housing front too. One of the things I was able to talk to Harold about over that lunch was the need to increase public-sector housing next year in order to make up for the gap caused by the fall-away in private building as the result of high interest rates. I'd talked this over with the Dame before lunch and cautiously suggested that we should make our target 135,000 houses – an increase of 20,000 over the figure for this year. Harold immediately upped me to 150,000 and of course I think this would be wise. So now over Christmas we are to work in the Ministry on the details of the short-term housing programme of 150,000, and are also to work out the circular to the local authorities asking them to put forward four-year programmes for upping the whole of their local-authority housing. It is a great thing to have a Prime Minister on your side.

1965

Sunday, January 3rd

I have had my first Christmas and New Year break as Minister. Rather to my surprise I found that the Ministry and I agreed that they didn't want to see me for the whole of the first week after Christmas. So I had a complete break until last Thursday when Jennie Hall came down for a light day's work. For the first time in a good many years I have been able to read without thinking of reviewing. I chose the huge life of Balfour by Kenneth Young, the editor of the *Yorkshire Post*,[1] and *Rupert Brooke* by Christopher Hassall,[2] which came out a few months ago and which Jennie gave me for Christmas. It's a pity that Kenneth Young's books, which are written at inordinate length and in great detail by a political journalist, should have no feeling for the real life of politics. The Rupert Brooke book, on the other hand, which had been fairly badly reviewed as far too verbose and detailed, I found an absolutely fascinating picture of the life of Cambridge in the last years before the 1914 war. I suppose I liked it partly because the kind of revolt against home which I had in the 1920s was comparable at least to what Brooke went through in the first decade of the century. And there was something else which young Oxford of the 1920s shared with young Cambridge of the 1910s: an extraordinary combination of heartlessness and youthful appreciation of beauty.

By the time Jennie arrived I was beginning to brood over the problems of the Ministry. But the week had been a wonderful relaxation. Over Christmas it was getting colder and by Boxing Day we had 25° of frost registered at Upper Prescote. We had one lovely walk with the children, testing the ice on the Broadimoor and then walking on it, and then crisply moving over the arctic snowfields as explorers, with Suki bounding on ahead because she adores the snow as much as we do. That night the weather suddenly changed. Next day was an incredible day of spring warmth and for the last three days we have had successively perfect cloudless days getting steadily rather colder. Today we woke up to a thick white hoar-frost.

We hadn't felt terribly Christmassy, though this year we did decide to break the church convention and I took Patrick and Virginia to chapel. We did it because the confounded vicar, year in, year out, has refused to provide a service on Christmas Day which the children could conceivably enjoy. So I decided that while paying our whack towards the church expenses, we would go to the little chapel and we really quite enjoyed the service, which lasted forty minutes and included hymns, a sermon and a Bible reading. On Boxing Day, as usual, we had a few people to drinks before lunch including Major Donner, our county councillor, who fell off his horse when he was in the Cavalry thirty years ago and ever since has been a sweet-tempered beekeeper. He has also managed to produce an exquisitely pretty and very nice daughter and a very talented boy—he at Eton and she at Wycombe

---

[1] *Arthur James Balfour* (London: Bell, 1963).
[2] London: Faber, 1964.

Abbey. They were both at our party along with the Hudsons, who live at the bridge across the canal — he being a Conservative and a great friend of Mr Pritchett, who also of course is a leading Conservative. It was pleasant and unassuming and unexciting and comforting and comfortable and homely. No doubt about it, here one acquires bourgeois values. Wherever I started off from in life, I am now a person who enjoys his creature comforts, his food, his drink, his fitted carpets, the sense of spaciousness on the farm, the sense of belonging to the village without any great obligation. These are the things I intensely and enormously enjoy. What a relaxation of tension there is for me in knowing that the moment anyone says that my life at the Ministry has got to end there is an alternative life ready.

The only worries we had during this recess were, curiously enough, about money. I had earned virtually nothing during August, September and October and I find that my Ministerial salary leaves me with far less than I earned before because of course I now have no expense account. As a Minister I am supposed to live in London so I don't get any living-away-from-home allowance. I have no meals paid for now. There is absolutely nothing on expenses for a Minister, and this means that even on a salary of £6,000 I shall be very hard up. Actually, we are going to have our salaries increased to £9,000 in April and then I reckon I shall get just about the same take-home pay as I had before as a working journalist and back-bench M.P.; this has meant that I have temporarily had to reduce my monthly allowance to Anne. But all this is possible because financially the farm is going from strength to strength. We have got a new accountant here in Banbury and we have decided to turn the farm into a limited liability company in order to make sure that we don't pay everything back to Her Majesty in tax.[1]

Perhaps I should add one thing to this picture of our life at Prescote — the children. Huge great bounding blonde monsters, they grow and they grow, and they become that wonderful blend of babyishness and child. In certain ways Patrick is now a very developed boy. Now he is a baby with his toys and then he is again a boy playing football or appreciating 'Kubla Khan', or reading to himself the intense complexities of Tolkein's Ring books.[2] But simultaneously he is getting me to read him the simplest babies' books as well. Virginia is jealous of Patrick and is having rather a rough time being kicked and knocked about a good deal, something she passes on to her poodle, Suki. But she is enormously appealing and, as Pam Berry says, she is the perfect Renoir child with that extraordinary colouring and bloom of the eyes. They are satisfying children and they are doing quite well at school. Miss Samuels came up to supper one night during the recess and we had a long chat about the school possibilities. It's just possible that the reorganiza-

---

[1] Actually, as a result of the changes in the treatment of private companies introduced in the Callaghan budget this step was disastrous and after a couple of years Prescote had to be turned back into a partnership.

[2] *The Fellowship of the Ring*, 3 vols. (London: Allen & Unwin, 1954–5).

tion of education in North Oxfordshire—taking place by the way under a very gifted man called Harry Judge, who is the headmaster of the grammar school[1]—will come in the nick of time. If it does Patrick may be able to leave his junior school at nine, and go on to a middle school from nine to thirteen before finally getting into the grammar school. This would certainly suit him very well because he will need a bigger kind of school when he is nine, with masters as well as mistresses.[2]

I have been thinking a lot about my first major upset, the Hartley affair. Of course, I have mentioned Hartley from time to time but since it is looming up bigger and bigger in my political life I'd like now to summarize what really happened in this case. It will be interesting to compare the picture I present of the Hartley case now with how I have spoken about it in previous weeks. It seemed to me, when I first began to look at the problem, that getting houses built must involve breaking into green belts and enabling cities that are being strangled by the green belt to get room to breathe. Of course, there can be some urban renewal in the centre of conurbations if one uses high-rise housing; but there will also have to be 'overspill' housing estates outside, which would make me unpopular. What I didn't realize at the time (though I was warned about it) was the strength of the army which could be mobilized in defence of any green belt. Up came the first case, whether or not I should reverse my own Inspector's decision against the Span village at Hartley. I was strongly advised by J. D. Jones to reverse it. Being new to the job, I asked Jim MacColl to go down in the Ministry car for me and survey the area. When he came back he said that I should realize that our colleague Arthur Skeffington lived there and had made speeches about it, and I should know that there would be a great row in the Party if I reversed the Inspector's decision. But he said that the area was very small and that on balance, with our new policy, he thought we should give Span the approval and take the punishment we should get. Mistake one was to send him down. Mistake two I see in retrospect was that I didn't look at all carefully at the decision letter which had been drafted for me. In my other two green belt cases, Chelmsley Wood and Stannington, near Sheffield, I took those letters in hand and rewrote every word of them and made both of them policy letters which clearly stated my wishes. But in the case of the Hartley letter I just took over and signed the very poor document presented to me by the Ministry. This stated at great length all the reasons why permission should not be granted and then added very baldly one or two reasons why it should. I just let that go out because I wasn't advised by the Ministry of the danger of doing so. At the time, I wasn't too alarmed when Alderman Reeves, the chairman of

[1] He became Principal of Banbury School in 1967 and a great friend of the Crossman family, a member of the Public Schools Commission in 1966–70 and of the James Committee of Enquiry into Teacher Training in 1970. He succeeded Alec Peterson as Director of the Department of Education at Oxford University in 1972.

[2] The reorganization which finally took place was rather different. There was no middle school but one large comprehensive to which the children went when they were eleven.

the R.D.C., called the decision the worst he had ever seen, though I did notice that one or two papers seemed a bit shocked by it. Soon it was obvious that the decision hadn't gone down very well, and it became even more obvious at that first meeting of the housing group where our Deputy Chief Whip, Sidney Irving, along with two other Kent M.P.s, Norman Dodds and Albert Murray, made a tremendous row, accusing me of surrendering to private enterprise in an area which is already overcrowded and where the commuters are packed in trains like sardines. 'Isn't it absolutely crazy?' they say. 'How could you have given your consent to this when you turned down local-authority building in that same area?' When I reflected on what I had done and on the row it had caused, I did realize that my handling of Hartley, as distinct from Birmingham and Sheffield where I was giving land for public-authority building, rendered me open to criticism, particularly since I had done it in defiance of my own Inspector.

However, I thought we had weathered the storm when there came a debate in the House of Lords on the initiative of Lord Molson, the chairman of the Town and Country Planning Association.[1] One of my first engagements as Minister was to be the guest of the T.C.P.A. at their annual dinner and there I found myself sitting next to Molson. Perhaps I had drunk too much, perhaps I was merely irritated by his stuffy manner, but I defended the Hartley decision very strongly to him over dinner. Three weeks later I got all this back a thousandfold when he launched the debate in the House of Lords and was supported by Lord Morrison and Lord Chorley from our side of the House. Altogether, it was an extremely damaging debate—it made Hartley a national and not merely a local parochial issue. Finally, just before Christmas, there was a vicious and brilliantly clever cartoon by Osbert Lancaster in the *Daily Express* headed 'Double Crossmanship', and also to my surprise I found a strongly worded leading article in the *Sun* inspired by Sydney Jacobson.

The new line of attack they all directed at me was to say that Span is a speculative group of builders who bought up the land at £70 an acre and would make vast profits. Though this sounds terrible, it is in fact an absurd charge, because what Span did was to buy the land at a low enough price to enable them to use only one-third of it for house building and to allocate two-thirds of it for public spaces, schools, hospitals, in order to create their model village. That's a perfectly adequate reply, but alas, as the Minister who is in charge in a judicial capacity, I haven't been able to reply.

What I *was* able to do was to have a special conference about my Chelmsley Wood decision just before Christmas. This time I took good care. I carefully briefed the Midland press; I got hold of Brian Redhead of the *Guardian* and gave lunch to the architectural correspondent of *The Times*, who is also editor of the *Architectural Review*, and as a result—with great luck—on the day of these attacks on me by Lancaster and Sydney Jacobson I actually had leading articles in the *Guardian* and *The Times* defending what I had done as a

[1] The debate was on December 21st.

short-term measure but warning that it would be untenable in the long term. I am also planning to publish my third big decision, on Stannington near Sheffield soon. It will be very difficult to attack me on this.

However, I am still highly vulnerable on Hartley; and over this recess I have been wondering whether instead of merely having a press conference about Sheffield I shouldn't have a press conference on the whole issue of the green belt, which would include Hartley as well as Stannington. I shall also have to work out methods of consultation far more effective than those I have had with the Kent County Council about Hartley. And I shall have to have firm agreements between Span on the one side and the L.C.C. and the R.D.C. on the other, in which Span offers to let each of them build a large number of houses to let inside their model village. I think if I do all that I may get through the Hartley affair without too much discredit.[1]

In the course of it I have learned something about the difference between my two Parliamentary Secretaries. Jim MacColl has shown himself a terrible coward. On the other hand Bob Mellish, that rough-neck from Bermondsey, has been loyal and I find him politically absolutely first-rate. Of course, he is an L.C.C. man who needs places for L.C.C. overspill and so has a strong London interest in supporting me on the Hartley decision against Kent County Council and the R.D.C. Nevertheless, he has done a lot more than that; he has gone round the Parliamentary Labour Party smoothing my way and defending my action.

Reflecting on the Ministry after ten days' absence, I find that distance doesn't increase my respect. No, the personnel is second-rate and unimpressive. They are extremely good at working the procedures of the Civil Service. What they lack is a constructive apprehension of the problems with which they deal and any kind of imagination. Also they are resistant in the extreme to the outside advice which I think it is my job to bring in. So the battle between me and the Ministry will go on as I try to get these admirable officials, conscientious and thorough people, somehow widened, and a little blood pumped into their veins by people from outside who know the realities which they handle in such an abstract and aloof way.

As a Minister of course I am still desperately remote. When she was here at Prescote, Jennie and I spent most of the day preparing a memorandum dealing with the problem of my correspondence, something which has been rumbling between myself and Brian Ponsford week after week. I must have told him four times at least that I wished, for even a trial period, to see all the letters on one day which are addressed to me personally. Each time he has answered 'But this is impossible', and still to this day most of the letters sent to me personally never reach me. They go straight into the Department and

[1] Crossman had hoped that instead of becoming a purely middle-class suburb in the green belt, Hartley would provide a mixture of private and public development. Alas, the scheme petered out because the local council refused to build houses there, and the model village is now a purely middle-class area known as Ash Green.

are 'processed' there without coming near the Minister. It is extremely difficult to get this changed. Indeed, the official attitude to a Minister is rather paradoxical in this respect. In really big decisions I have found up till now that the Ministry – having fought me resolutely – at a certain point sees that I am serious, accepts my view and sets about carrying it out. But on a little thing like changing the way my Private Office runs or getting my telephones put in the place I want, or reorganizing the packing of my red boxes, the civil servant is nearly always unbearably sticky, prickly and determined to keep to what he regards as the only possible procedure.

So much for the Ministry. Now what about the Cabinet and the Government's record? Looking back to October, I am impressed by our extraordinary innocence when we took over. We proceeded to do a number of things by almost instantaneous decision, all of which seem to me now to have been ill-judged, and of which Harold and George and Callaghan, the three men chiefly concerned, failed to foresee the consequences. For example, the 15 per cent surcharge, which is still causing us the most appalling trouble in Europe, was blatantly a flagrant violation of the EFTA treaty; and Douglas Jay at our first Cabinet warned us of all the trouble it would bring. Yet it was pushed through by George Brown and Harold Wilson. Then there was our innocence in insisting on the 12s. 6d. increase in the old-age pension and the abolition of prescription charges, despite the warnings of the Treasury. In both these cases, if I remember aright, Harold Wilson and James Callaghan were overruled. Cabinet wanted them and was allowed to carry out its wishes without anybody seriously warning us of what would happen. As I recall it, nobody expressed the fear that by carrying out these increases in pensions and announcing the tax increases which would pay for them we should unloose a crisis of confidence, provoke a 7 per cent bank rate and upset the foreign bankers. Harold Wilson was so experienced and shrewd and calculating throughout the election; yet when he actually entered No. 10 and tried to show himself a man of action and tried to vie with Kennedy's Hundred Days, he became unstuck on the very subject where he should have been expert – on economics.

But there is one case where he has had a stroke of luck. We came into office full of doubts about George Brown. Harold had said to me more than once before and more than once after the election that we would have to get rid of G.B. within six months. Actually, his leadership has been outstanding. He has created the new D.E.A. and got a number of excellent people into it; he has done a tremendous job on the prices and incomes policy in getting the employers and trade unions to sign the Declaration of Intent; and there is no doubt that as First Secretary and Deputy Prime Minister he is absolutely dominant over poor old James Callaghan who trails along as number three.

Of course, Harold himself has been good, above all in his handling of the Rhodesian crisis. He called Mr Smith's bluff brilliantly. I think he has also been extremely successful on his visit to Washington in convincing the

Americans that Britain is a loyal junior partner. By getting Lyndon Johnson firmly on his side he has convinced himself at least that we can get through without the devaluation of the pound because we are now built into the American system. But here again we have to pay a price for our success. There's no doubt about it that one of the things we really hoped for when we came to power was a substantial cut in defence expenditure. Yet as we have looked at each of our overseas commitments—at Hong Kong, at Malaya, at the Maldive Islands, the Persian Gulf and Aden—the Defence Ministers have been overwhelmed by the advice of their experts, who say 'Oh, Minister, you can't cut that.' As a result we are moving up to the period of the Defence Estimates without any serious cut being carried through by Denis Healey and his staff. Indeed, it now looks as though in 1964 Harold Wilson was responsible for an over-commitment in overseas expenditure almost as burdensome—if not more burdensome—than that to which Ernest Bevin[1] committed us in 1945, and for the same reason: because of our attachment to the Anglo–American special relationship and because of our belief that it is only through the existence of this relationship that we can survive outside Europe. And here is something we have to remember. While we have been establishing our Labour Government here, tremendous events have been taking place in Europe, including the final agreement on grain prices between Germany and France, which creates the foundation for the common agricultural policy. I think we are going to find that the European Community will now forge ahead and there will be no place for Britain in it. Our last chance of joining has gone unless some convulsion were to follow General de Gaulle's death.

So much for Harold Wilson's handling of foreign affairs. We have yet to see how good he is on the home front. So far he has shown a singular failing in dealing with general economic policy. Nor do I think he has been doing very well in the great upheavals in Whitehall. Though George Brown is a great success, the division of power between the Treasury and the D.E.A. is a development for which we are having to pay a heavy price in divided authority and dissension in central planning. I have some grave doubts about the new Ministry of Technology under Frank Cousins and Lord Snow. As for the new Ministry of Land and Natural Resources, carved out of my Ministry as a separate creation, it is purely unnecessary. There's no doubt that if the Land Commission had been handled by M.H.L.G. with Fred Willey as a Minister of State, we could have got a far better Bill prepared in time. Another equally idiotic creation is the Department for Wales, a completely artificial new office for Jim Griffiths and his two Parliamentary Secretaries, all the result of a silly election pledge. No! I don't think Harold Wilson has done too well in Whitehall. Certainly he has caused an enormous strain on the staff, which poor Dame Evelyn curses every day.

However, we are settling down now and I oughtn't to give the impression

[1] When he was Foreign Secretary in the post-war Labour Government.

that these weaknesses are clear to anybody outside. I don't think they are. On the contrary this Government seems to ordinary people to have a new look. We have just seen the Gallup Poll showing that we are far more popular than we were during the election and that Harold Wilson is in a position to force an election any time he likes against a Conservative Party ruined by internal competition over the succession to Douglas-Home. That's the other big fact that one has to take into account in weighing the strength of the Government – the break-up of the Tories in Opposition. They haven't held together and been stimulated by our tiny majority; they have fallen to quarrelling. The leader, Alec Douglas-Home, is an amiable, pleasant figure but totally ineffective as leader of the Opposition; and already there are ostentatious to-ings and fro-ings about who shall replace him and how it shall be done. In fact the Tories are behaving in Opposition with the same unimpressive disunity which we showed after 1951. It still seems to me absolutely on the cards that we shall have an early election which Harold Wilson will win comfortably. Alternatively, he may prefer to postpone it for two or three years, in which case he will be able to carry on while the Tories bicker and find tremendous difficulty in deciding on a policy.

What worries me, looking at things from inside, is whether we shall work out a satisfactory solution to a number of our central problems. First, shall we have a steel nationalization Bill which makes real sense? Second, shall we have a Land Commission Bill which makes any sense? And third (something I have hardly mentioned in this diary), shall we have an incomes guarantee that makes any sense? Indeed, it is clear once again that a socialist Opposition in this country comes into office with very half-baked plans. True, this time we have done far more work than the 1945 Government on social security, in particular on the incomes guarantee and on national superannuation. But already I hear it said that the incomes guarantee, which was Douglas Houghton's special contribution to our policy, is not nearly sufficiently worked out to be put into practice. I strongly suspect the same is true of steel nationalization and I know it to be true of leasehold reform and the Land Commission, where at first glance in Whitehall the Party policy was seen to be unworkable or futile.

With this lack of clearly worked-out policies, even more depends on Harold Wilson's leadership. He has been eleven days in the Scillies and he's back now, no doubt busily at work. It's a tremendous disadvantage that he has no social life. Every time one meets him, it's a formal interview and I refuse to ask for a lot of formal interviews because that gives the impression that I need his help. The only two people who really still see him privately are Thomas Balogh and George Wigg. The former has discredited himself by his attacks on the Civil Service; and as for the latter, I suspect George Wigg has become the Lindemann of this Government.[1] He really sees Harold four or

---

[1] Professor Lindemann, later Lord Cherwell, was Churchill's personal adviser and, to some degree, his confidant.

five times a day and is virtually living with him. Somebody said that he is Sancho Panza to Harold's Don Quixote, but I can't think of anyone less like Don Quixote than Harold Wilson or less like Sancho Panza than George Wigg. What is true is that these two really do stand together in the middle of this Government. There is no other coherent grouping in the Cabinet because the rest of us are in our own Ministries getting our Ministerial briefs, doing our own jobs, behaving as Ministers, not as politicians.

Will there be a crisis in February when we come to the Estimates? I think there will. Will there be another devaluation crisis? I think there might be. We shall have a pretty rough time between now and the budget, and I wouldn't be surprised if we have an early election. Equally I wouldn't be surprised if H.W. carries on for two years.

Monday, January 4th
I was aware as I travelled up by train that I would have to get in and see Harold Wilson about the Hartley affair as soon as possible in order to get his backing before somebody else got it. As a precaution I rang up George Wigg and after we had discussed his problems about aircraft and the decision on the new strategy East of Suez, I asked him about this. He said, 'Make no mistake about it, Dick, the Hartley decision has got you into a lot of trouble. There are many important people who are worried by it.' He made it pretty clear that Harold Wilson is also worried. Then I said, 'Shall I go and see him?' And he said, 'Of course you should go and get his backing. By the way, don't forget that if you have that as the first item on the agenda he will put as second item the person to replace your Permanent Secretary.' 'Oh,' I said, 'the question of Dame Evelyn?' 'Don't ask me any more,' he said. 'I just tell you the replacement of your Permanent Secretary is very much on his mind. You must put it second on your agenda.'

As I have said before in this diary the Whitehall grapevine is an extraordinary phenomenon. When I got into the office this morning I saw the Dame about a mass of business (my first day back after ten days of Christmas holiday). She told me at once that the Prime Minister had asked that Sir Laurence Helsby should see me about my agreement to take Bruce Fraser and kick her out. She said all this in perfect good temper. After all, she was past resignation age and on the point of going when the election took place. She is merely waiting in order to find a good replacement. She told me that Helsby would be coming to see me in a day or two. In return I told her I was going to discuss her future with the Prime Minister and insist that she should wait and only leave in the summer, giving me plenty of time to find a suitable replacement. Dame Evelyn said that I would find the Prime Minister a bit more pressing than that.

Next I saw Peter Brown, my press officer. He confirmed that the storm over Hartley had been steadily growing in intensity and had now turned into something like a national incident. But it's not only the amenity lobby which has been gravely upset. Now the popular press—the *News of the World* and the *Daily Express* for example—have begun to see this as a good issue for belabouring the Government. It was clear to Peter Brown as well as to me that we had to do something about it and do it quickly. So we decided to cancel Tuesday's press conference on the Sheffield decision and instead to hold a quite different kind of press conference next Thursday morning at which I will announce the Sheffield decision but as part of an expression of my whole attitude to the problems of the green belt. When I worked this idea out with Brown I told him I would check it with the Prime Minister. Meanwhile, Jennie rang up Marcia who replied that I should go round to No. 10 at three o'clock in the afternoon. So after I had taken Bob Mellish to lunch at the Farmers' Club in Whitehall Mansions, where I often hide out these days, I walked across to Downing Street. It was a good day to go since he was just back from the Scillies, there was no Cabinet, and no Cabinet Committees, and he had nothing to deal with until Indonesia at four o'clock.

So there I was at three o'clock, sitting beside him. When he receives you he is standing alone in the big Cabinet room. I started off on the green belt and asked him whether he was worried about it. 'No,' he said. 'I only thought this was a job which Fred Willey should have had, not you. I wanted him to get all the bother I knew there would be about green belt decisions. That's why I originally wanted to shift planning to him and leave you only with housing.'

This confirmed something that I have often noticed about Harold. He never really changes his mind. He is a Yorkshire terrier and having got his teeth into an idea he worries at it and never gives it up. Originally, he had been determined to split housing and planning and still that is his *idée fixe*. So I wasn't too surprised when he went on to say, 'Why don't you leave all that bother to friend Willey and concentrate on the real job of the housing drive?' I said rather briefly that it was Charlie Pannell's job as Minister of Works to deal with the bricks and mortar, and he said, 'Charlie Pannell's no good. I want you to take personal responsibility for the housing drive and I also want you to appoint a housing administrator, a real tough guy who will get it going.' Then I knew of course that he had been talking to Arnold Goodman about his pal Hyams. I must admit that the more I have reflected on Hyams the more dubious I have become whether this multi-millionaire property speculator could really serve a Labour Minister of Housing. However, I went back to the green belt problem and tried to expound it to him. He showed not the faintest interest. And I asked him again, 'Are you worried at all?' 'Not at all,' he said. 'I'm sure you're doing it perfectly all right.' And with those grey, cold eyes looking me full in the face I was aware what this meant. I had seen Harold already dropping Tom Fraser's idea of a Beeching inquiry as soon as it got really unpopular and I realize now that if I get myself into serious trouble about the green belt, the fact that Harold hasn't either criticized or opposed me won't prevent him from letting me meet my fate single-handed at a Cabinet meeting. So I did go on to press him and get his agreement that it would be wise for me to submit to the appropriate Cabinet Committee a paper about the future policy on housing and the green belt, and get Cabinet approval for it.

Then we turned to the problem of Dame Evelyn's successor and he indicated once again that he wanted Bruce Fraser to succeed her within a few weeks. 'We must find Dame Evelyn a good job,' he said, 'she's a fine woman.' 'Well,' I said, 'it's not as easy as that. I don't want to have some cast-off Permanent Secretary imposed on me with all Whitehall knowing what has happened. I'd rather keep her till the summer and give myself time to look at Bruce Fraser carefully, and also to take a look at Philip Allen, whom the Department would prefer. You know the Department rather resents first having a politician with no knowledge of housing like me being palmed off on them and then being given a Permanent Secretary like Sir Bruce Fraser.' 'Philip Allen?' said Harold. 'Yes, he's Helsby's number two, he's possible. Yes, I can see the chances of a shift round. All right, my dear Dick, you try and do that.' Harold then began to talk about the Opposition. How sorry he was for them and what terrible problems of leadership they had. Next he spelt out to me his proposal that we should run the steel nationalization Bill and my Rent Bill in double harness, providing a single guillotine motion for both of them and then sending them both upstairs. 'But surely we can't get away with that?' I asked. 'We can,' he said. 'With the Tories in their present state they won't dare to prevent either of those Bills being put on the Statute Book. And if we have two or three defeats in Committee we can put matters straight during the Report Stage.' I then put to him my concern about the Land Commission Bill, and told him that it seemed to me something of the most tremendous importance on which we were having really rather half-baked ideas thrown at us. I begged him, as I begged George Brown, to take the Land Commission seriously. 'Here,' I said, 'is a Bill which in the extreme form which Willey wants will force the House of Lords to repudiate it. In which case we might have an election on this issue.' At once he was interested and I could see him brooding over the possibilities of an election next autumn.

Finally, we talked a good deal about the electoral prospects of the Party, and he made it pretty clear that his election threat is nothing more than a secret weapon for disciplining our back-benchers. He isn't intending to have an election at all this spring and he told me that he saw the Tory division continuing happily and that his main anxieties were about the possibilities of unemployment and a difficult economic situation next autumn. This enabled me to put to him the idea that we could fill in the gap in private-enterprise building which will come with deflation by announcing our plans for local-authority building. In that case the local authorities would want financial assistance; could he help me in persuading the Chancellor to give us what we need through the Public Works Loans Board? He assured me that directly Callaghan was back he would give him his instructions.*

Wednesday, January 6th
Punctually at ten thirty Sir Laurence Helsby arrived to have the expected conversation with me. When I looked at him I suddenly realized I had been at Oxford with him where we had both done Greats. He's a curious character, amiable and apparently pleasant, but with veiled eyes. He came straight to the point. He wanted to announce Sir Bruce Fraser as my next Permanent Secretary, though he was prepared to let Dame Evelyn stay on for a few months of transition. I said I was interested in Sir Philip Allen. He told me that Allen was more suitable for the Home Office and Bruce Fraser for my Department—though he didn't say the latter very convincingly. We sparred a good deal and I finally said I was prepared to give dinner to both men and then to give Helsby my opinion. He said I must appreciate that a Permanent Secretary would last longer than a Minister and that therefore he was concerned to find one who not only got on with me but who was suitable for the Department. I said that if he was not concerned to appoint someone who got on with me, I had to be even more concerned than ever to get someone who suited me. We then had some talk about the Prime Minister's views on planning, where Helsby clearly sided with Dame Evelyn, and we also had a useful chat about the Land Commission, where I primed him about the alarm we felt. I found we had had quite a decent meeting together by the time he left at eleven.

Then I had to be off to the Cabinet Office for the Committee on the Land Commission. This time officials were present, and Fred Willey presented his second try at a major policy paper. I had been extremely well briefed by my Department and was able to make the required technical points. I went on to say how desperately alarmed I was to discover how vague we all were about the impact which this vast new instrument would have on the economy and in particular on the building programme. I suggested that before we went any further a paper should be prepared by either the Treasury or the D.E.A. on these repercussions.

I rushed off at one o'clock to a charming old house with an underground cellar in Queen Anne's Gate where I had a very gay lunch with the *Architects Journal* and the *Architectural Review*. They broached a bottle of champagne, a bottle of claret and a bottle of sherry. I only took a glass of claret as I was due to see the Dame at two thirty. I discussed Helsby with her and I think we both realized that it's extremely unlikely that either Philip Allen or Bruce Fraser will suit me, so she will stay with me until next summer, come what may.

* I was amused to discover when I opened my red boxes on the following Sunday morning a draft circular from the Treasury doing precisely what the Prime Minister suggested should be done.

I spent most of that afternoon preparing for my press conference on the green belt. I was just about to go off at five thirty and had cleared my desk altogether, when George Moseley came in and said we had had a missive from George Brown — an extraordinary, violent minute of the most staggering economic and political illiteracy attacking me for Hartley. There are many things wrong with my handling of Hartley but not the things George Brown charged me with. I realized a reply had to go off as soon as possible and sat down to draft one. When he saw it George Moseley said, 'That's too soft, Minister. I can tell you privately his own officials thought the First Secretary's attitude so silly that they refused to draft this minute for him. You can afford to send a tough one back.' Incited by George Moseley, I drafted an even tougher minute.* I got back to Vincent Square for dinner at eight o'clock. At ten o'clock, Oliver Cox, the Deputy Chief Architect of the Ministry, arrived to brief me about Oldham before he and I went up to Marylebone, where we found Peter Brown and George Moseley waiting and also Mr Hyams, who I had asked to join me for breakfast at Oldham next morning.

Thursday, January 7th
I duly sat down at 7.45 a.m. for breakfast, with Mr Hyams and the director of his property firm on the one side and Oliver Cox, George Moseley, Peter Brown and our regional organizer, Mr Hughes, on the other. It was amusing to discover that for three years Oliver Cox had been working on the central housing redevelopment of Oldham, getting the compulsory purchase orders through and making all the arrangements for the industrialized housing of the Ministry. All through these three years Mr Hyams has been clearing an area about four hundred yards away for the development of an enormous shopping centre. Before that breakfast neither man had met the other, although both of them were working for the Oldham Borough Council.

I then inspected Oldham in a thick fog for a couple of hours. The councillors are an attractive group but, oh dear, their borough engineer was dim to the *n*th degree and the general body of their officials drearily incompetent. Apart from the borough treasurer there was really no quality there at all, and I began to realize one of the problems of local government is the real, inherent weakness of administration. Even if you get a body of excellent, dedicated councillors what can they do? After the tour I sat down with the councillors for an hour and they told me that their financial situation was so grave that they would have to throw in their hands unless they got a firm

---

* These minutes from Minister to Minister are important in the formation of policy. They are personal and can be written in a fairly informal style. I receive, say, a minute from George Brown containing a bright idea. If it is simply and solely about my own Department, it comes to me alone; but if it refers to any other Department there is always a 'copy to' attached. The main thing, as I have discovered to my cost, is to remember that if you mention anybody he gets a copy of it. You may imagine you can send a strictly personal communication to a colleague in another Ministry, but in fact you can never be sure that your Private Office hasn't copied it to someone you mentioned undiplomatically.

promise of support. I don't think they were exaggerating! They just had cold feet.

From Oldham I drove across to Salford, bitterly hostile to Manchester in which it is encapsulated. I had an excellent lunch and then saw how they are trying to use the new law passed by Keith Joseph to compel landlords to improve their property.[1] It is far better to give thirty years' more life to some of this existing central property than to let it become a slum and then have to pull it all down. In Salford I found that for £200 they were making people happy. Since I don't like the idea of people having to live in huge blocks of high-rise housing, I found the Salford efforts extremely attractive. From there at about five o'clock we went on to Manchester where I was due to stay with the lord mayor. The town hall is a fantastic piece of romantic Victorian architecture – far more romantic than the House of Commons, which is in a kind of classical Gothic whereas the Manchester town hall is Radcliffe Gothic, spiral staircases and every other kind of extravagance. Right at the heart of this crazy building is a very comfortable Victorian suite of rooms where I was to spend the night as the guest of a charming lord mayor, Dr Chadwick, with whom I had last talked in 1947 at a Zionist demonstration. He is now a completely non-partisan local politician and his new young Jewish wife was there to entertain me. I had half an hour with them before I was taken round to the Queen's Hotel to a reception organized by our regional organizer, Reg Wallis, for some sixty or seventy local worthies to meet the Minister of Housing. I tried to give them a vivid inside picture of how we, a socialist Government, were trying to maintain the confidence of the international bankers while coolly carrying our social policies through. If one is going to keep any contact between government and the Party outside, this is the kind of inside view of politics a Minister should provide; but of course to do it is a risk.

I got back at nine o'clock to find the lord mayor had laid on a big dinner with the town clerk, Sir Philip Dingle, and four or five leading members of the council, which lasted till midnight. So if I look back to nine forty-five on Wednesday morning, when I started my first meeting in the Ministry, I realize that I had a fifteen-hour day, and that on Wednesday and Thursday I had worked pretty hard.

Friday, January 8th
A pleasant breakfast with the mayor. Manchester City is a bit blasé about Ministerial visits: it's had nine in the last seven or eight years. However, they briefed me very well in the town hall and then took me to the top of a sky-scraper to see the great area of slums they have cleared in the centre of the city. A few months ago I visited the new space cleared for the university campus. This slum clearance area is five times as large and adjacent to it.

[1] The 1963 Housing Act contained provisions for local authorities to enforce improvements to houses built before 1945.

It must be the largest hole ever created in a big city in the history of modern conurbations. I found myself impressed by the clearance but depressed by the standard of the houses with which they are filling it.

The main purpose of my visit, however, was not to see Manchester but to visit Risley, the site of the New Town selected by Keith Joseph. I had heard that Manchester detested the site and wanted another site at Lymm, in Cheshire.[1] When I saw Woolley, the President of the N.F.U., the other day,[2] he told me that Lymm was the apple of the N.F.U.'s eye and would be fought for tooth and nail. So now on a very lovely day after the awful fog at Oldham I was coasting out in a huge bus with the Manchester councillors to see Risley. We motored over the Ship Canal and found a ghastly flat area, partly cabbage-growing land like Middlesex, partly peat bog, full of duck shooting and 150 acres of devastated ordnance factory where naval bombs were made throughout the war, and which had been left to go to rack and ruin ever since. This was the site selected by the Ministry planners for the New Town, and I took one look at it and came to my conclusions! I got home at nine thirty that night with Anne meeting me at Birmingham to tell me about the marvellous excitement of Virginia seeing *Peter Pan* that afternoon.

Sunday, January 10th

A long, wild, stormy day with the river rising. This morning we got up nice and late – hearing the wind driving outside so feeling comfortable in bed. Then, everybody having done their little bit of work, I took the children and Suki to walk across the home pasture and give Suki her exercise chasing hares and plovers, up to Upper Prescote for my weekly Sunday visitation to Mr P., which takes place while the children play with the Pritchett children on the hay in the barn. Mr Pritchett and I came out and leaned on the gate looking at our cross-bred Hereford bullocks which are now being fattened indoors, comparing them with our pedigree Friesians, just bought to improve the herd. He discussed his anxieties, because we are deeply overdrawn, and then we waded right through the accounts.

After lunch Tommy Meffen, the old miner and Wyken councillor, brought Harold Green over from Coventry. Harold Green is the only farmer in my constituency and is now a member of the Milk Marketing Board; he has wanted for months to come over and see me. When they had cleared off we read the papers and had our tea. What a tremendous difference Prescote makes to me. I feel it all the more strongly now that we have had a week of family life in London. I went up last Sunday on the night train. The children followed next day with Anne by car and they spent the week doing the usual Science Museum visits. In the evenings we saw *Toad of Toad Hall*, which we found rather poor, and *Mary Poppins*, and on Friday Virginia

---

[1] Yet a third site, Chorley, had been suggested by George Brown. See pp. 138, 149.
[2] Harold Woolley was President of the N.F.U. 1960–6. In 1967 he was made a life peer.

was taken by her godmother to *Peter Pan*. Finally, on Saturday we all returned, and now we are deliciously at home at Prescote, glad to be back.

Monday, January 11th

I got off the train, not at Paddington but at Princes Risborough, to be met by Mr Ward of the Canadian High Commissioner's office and taken by car to Abbots Langley to see the Canadian timber houses there. The Canadians have at last recognized that the way to get more of their timber sold in Britain is to make us see that wooden houses built in modern techniques are just as safe in terms of fire damage as brick houses, infinitely warmer in terms of insulation and about the same price even with imported Canadian timber. However, on looking round them I found that these Canadian houses for the British market had been made to look as much like English council houses as possible, which destroys their whole colonial attraction. They had been boxed in, in fact, not in wood but in brick and roughcast. It's also wholly characteristic of what now goes on in the construction industry that the two best aspects of the North American house – the asbestos roofing and the piping of the water straight from the mains and not through a cistern in the roof – although they provide an enormous economy in building, are both forbidden here under our by-laws! I have been trying to have the by-law revision hurried up and I will talk again with Charlie Pannell at lunch tomorrow about it.

In the afternoon we had yet another meeting of the Committee on the Land Commission and plunged deeper and deeper into confusion. It became only too clear that even with the officials present practically nobody except the lawyers has a notion of what it is about. As a lawyer Fred Willey certainly understands it from a strictly legal point of view, and so does Niall MacDermot who represents the Treasury. I'm gradually beginning to twig a little tiny bit from a general, practical point of view, but for most of the colleagues around the table it's a subject completely beyond comprehension. We have got to decide how on earth to get it straight.

Tuesday, January 12th

This was a New Towns day for me. I had deputations to see me from the U.D.C. of Harlow New Town and then from Basildon U.D.C. The Harlow people couldn't have been nicer or more agreeable or more civilized. They had actually come to see me because they wanted to spend more on amenities than the New Town Corporation claimed it was entitled to spend, which was only £4 per head. I explained that this was only a rule of thumb which we had given the corporation, but I was disturbed by the curious distance which seems to exist in every New Town between the elected representatives on the local council and the members of the corporation appointed by our Ministry.

New Towns of course are Dame Evelyn's greatest creation. She is enormously proud of them and convinced that they wouldn't have been built without the completely autocratic constitution of the corporations, which we finance and whose members we appoint. The fact that they can get on with their job without consulting public opinion is the great thing in their favour, according to the Dame. Maybe this kind of autocracy was necessary in the first generation of New Towns. But it is also true that the Ministry, which is autocratic anyway and very remote, has displayed far too obvious a prejudice in favour of its privileged children and against the local authorities. This has made the U.D.C.s intensely jealous and difficult to handle; I am pretty sure changes will have to take place here as soon as the Dame disappears. And that feeling was confirmed in the afternoon by the Basildon U.D.C., whose delegation was headed by a tremendous old villain called Morgan—a real knockabout Labour demagogue who thundered and bellowed against the commission.

Wednesday, January 13th
The day for my official visit to Leeds, which I know by repute as a famous housing authority in the 1930s when Alderman Jenkinson was chairman of the housing committee. Now there is another dominant personality controlling Leeds housing, Councillor Karl Cohen, and I soon discovered that Leeds is as proud of its policy of improving the old central areas, wherever possible, as Manchester is proud of its policy of total clearance. I must say here I am wholly on the side of Leeds. It was really a pleasure to see how happy old people are when their old traditional slum houses are transformed by being given a bathroom and a skylight in the attic and proper dry roofing and modern kitchens.

In the evening I had to go and have a private discussion about local government boundaries with the Labour organizers in Yorkshire—one of those minor improprieties I allow myself in order to show my confidence in the Labour Party and win their confidence in me. After that I went to Karl Cohen's home. He lives with his sister Sylvia in a very comfortable house, and there we sat down for a talk with six members of the Labour Group, all taking our hair down together. One thing which seemed to me wrong was the group's decision that the chairmen of key committees can stay chairmen for a long time. Cohen has been chairman of housing for ten years and he runs it very much as his personal possession. If he's ever robbed of the chairmanship, he will feel that his personal property has been taken away. I am convinced that things would be far better for Leeds and far better for him if he had been moved on to the chairmanship of planning this year instead of continuing in housing. Nevertheless, as I left the city I had to realize that here, as in Sheffield, the Labour council is doing a physical transformation. What they need more than anything are architects of genius and they haven't got a single one.

There were two important by-elections in January. Patrick Gordon Walker, the Foreign Secretary, needed a seat, and a vacancy had been created at Leyton by giving Reginald Sorensen a peerage.[1] Frank Cousins, the Minister of Technology, still had no seat in Parliament and, equally reluctantly, Frank Bowles had gone to the Lords to make room at Nuneaton.[2] The Leyton result was a blow to Labour morale and, in the process, their majority in the Commons fell to three.

The aircraft industry continued to present problems. The future of the TSR2 was very doubtful, and the Aviation and Defence Ministers seemed to favour the American swing-wing TFX (renamed F-111). Employers from the British Aircraft Company protested to the Minister of Aviation, and 10,000 aircraft workers marched through London on January 14th. Richard Crossman was especially concerned because there were many aircraft workers in his Coventry constituency.

In his own Whitehall Department, the building societies were giving trouble. Some societies raised their mortgages early in the year and on January 15th the council of the Building Societies Federation raised its recommended rate for mortgages from 6 to 6½ per cent. This would affect new borrowers from February 1st, and 2·7 million existing ones from May 1st. The Chancellor scolded the chairman of the Association, but the societies replied that with a 7 per cent bank rate they could not otherwise find funds.

Thursday, January 14th

This was my big press conference day and I went into the Ministry at nine thirty for a last briefing before going on to Cabinet. Of course, I had spent a lot of time on my way up and down to Leeds in looking at the final draft of our press release and the background material that our people had been working out. Peter Brown is a first-rate press officer, probably the best in Whitehall. But on these subjects a Minister has to be very active in making sure that all the facts are precisely right and in working on the actual text of the press release. On the other hand, I leave entirely to Peter the job of organizing the conference and building up expectations.

From the Ministry I went on to Cabinet. It was our first meeting since the recess and I thought that at least the TSR2 would be on the agenda. Not at all. Cabinet dealt with two relatively minor issues. One of them was the problem of postal rates, which produced a clash between Tony Wedgwood Benn and Frank Cousins. Frank Cousins was back from his by-election campaign at Nuneaton where he is obviously being a first-rate candidate, unlike Gordon Walker at Leyton. He talked a great deal of nonsense on this occasion. Indeed, I feel he is rapidly developing a standing in Cabinet not unlike a cross between Nye Bevan and Manny Shinwell in the Attlee Cabinet. However, having said that I must add that we need people like Frank Cousins in

[1] M.P. for Leyton since 1929. He died in 1971.
[2] M.P. for Nuneaton since 1942. He died in 1970.

Cabinet, we need more of them. He is on the side of the angels. He is a very rare kind of man – one who still has a combination of real idealism and vitality and experience of practical power. We have to harness men like him and prevent them going the way of Nye and smashing things up. Well, on this occasion the clash went fairly well. Tony Benn was trying to persuade Cabinet that we ought to put up the cost of letter post from 3d. to 4d., and also increase the cost of parcels. Frank Cousins was against. Tony, with the help of Crosland, had wisely got George Brown on his side before the meeting started; but George, after all, is the man who wants to keep prices down, so Tony Benn can't have been surprised that his request that the announcement should be made on the 18th of this month was turned down. He was told that though the policy had been decided, the announcement had been indefinitely postponed!

The other issue we had at Cabinet was my recurrent problem of child care under London government.[1] On the instructions of the Cabinet, Frank Soskice had gone to the Greater London Council and the boroughs to ask whether they would like legislation dividing the responsibility between the G.L.C. and the boroughs. Ideally, this would be better than the complete transfer to the boroughs, but it just isn't practical to jam this into our legislative programme now. The case was really unanswerable, but poor old Frank Soskice's paper was terribly indecisive. True, it came down against legislation but it was so slanted that it was not difficult to draw the conclusion that legislation would still be possible. He talked about it rather feebly, and then Bert Bowden, the Lord President, boomed in and said it was absurd to go on trying to do this; it would block the Session – possibly for five days – and we ought to drop it altogether. At this point the L.C.C. pressure group joined in. The Chancellor, once a member of the L.C.C., Douglas Jay, whose wife is a prominent member, Michael Stewart, whose wife is also there, and Barbara Castle, whose husband sits on the G.L.C. – all of them weighed in and said we ought to do what is morally required of us. But on this occasion Harold Wilson as Prime Minister made up his mind and behaved perfectly correctly. He came down decisively on our side – not of course in principle but simply because of the parliamentary timetable.

Apart from agreeing to a proposal to set up a Royal Commission on the trade unions, these two items were the total Cabinet agenda in our first meeting since the recess. So once again all the major issues of politics and economics had been shelved or rather kept out of Cabinet. Right at the end the Prime Minister said he wanted to discuss Party tactics and the general election, though he added there wasn't time for a full discussion now. He let it out very carefully and calculatedly that he wanted a stop to all talk about an imminent election in the spring. On the other hand, we must soberly consider the pros and cons of an election either in the summer or in the autumn, although we should go on working on the assumption that we were

1 See p. 60.
5

carrying on for three years. He said it was most important that this point in our discussion shouldn't leak, because there had been some curious leaks on other issues which had caused a great deal of trouble, particularly on the proposal for a Beeching inquiry.

After Cabinet I went back to the Ministry and had lunch with Peter Brown and the rest of them; and then at two thirty I walked into our big conference room and found about 110 people there, gathered together for a long one-hour conference. I couldn't help remembering how only a few months ago I had presented the Labour Party's press release on teacher training to a conference at Transport House, and had in my innocence assumed that since they had been given the document in advance all I need do was to answer questions. As a result I got a thundering bad press. Well I wasn't quite so innocent that Thursday. I had been briefed right up to my neck by Peter Brown, who really knows how to teach Ministers their job. I didn't merely deliver a speech, I thundered it. As a result we got a goodish news story in every paper and five leading articles. I had also on the previous night given four interviews, two on television and two on radio, as well as appearing in the ten o'clock B.B.C. programme. Our achievement was to get the impression over that I wasn't just throwing away the green belt but developing a land acquisition policy essential for the housing drive, and I think I got Hartley put a bit more behind us by telling the conference that Span has now agreed to increase the number of houses allocated to the G.L.C. and the local R.D.C. from 10 to 20 per cent.

After the press conference I had my first interview with Miss Hope-Wallace. For thirty years she had worked in the National Assistance Board and ended up as the number two, an Under-Secretary. Now, quite suddenly, Dame Evelyn wants to make her the head of our New Towns division. After I had talked to her I didn't find the proposal any less astonishing. She is not only extremely intelligent but extremely cultured, and moves in artistic circles. But it's certainly a strange notion that we should bring her in and I am pretty sure that it's because she can't stand staying as Under-Secretary in the National Assistance Board and seeing a man promoted over her. I wouldn't dream of accepting Miss Hope-Wallace if it wasn't for the Dame. On this occasion I had special reasons why I had to oblige her. I learnt today that she is now prepared, even though it infuriates the Prime Minister, to stay on till the summer while I try and get Philip Allen as her successor instead of Bruce Fraser.

While the Dame and I were discussing this, she told me in passing that during the week George Brown had gone off to Austria and Sweden. There is a great crisis in his Department because he wants a new head of his Private Office, having sacked the present one on the ground that he is a Treasury man who isn't to be trusted. (I have some sympathy with him about this since I too find civil servants with a Treasury background unreliable.) The Dame told me that no less than five Assistant Secretaries were offered the job and all refused it on the ground that they wouldn't work for George Brown. So she was asked to submit a name and has already offered somebody out of Water. That would mean transferring George Moseley and then finding someone to take his place in my Private Office. All this is very unsettling just when I am getting used to the Ministry. One of the troubles about the Dame is that while she is extremely tough in negotiation she is extremely public school when she's asked by the Treasury or by Helsby to make a sacrifice in her departmental interests for the good of the nation or for the convenience of the Civil Service.

Friday, January 15th
Another meeting of our Cabinet Committee on the Rent Bill. This is now going pretty well routinely and we are getting through the Bill without any serious opposition. Gerald Gardiner came up to me on the way out to ask whether we shouldn't lunch together. He said he is getting more and more appalled by the way Cabinet business is done. Of course, the fact is that, though he is Lord Chancellor, he is a real political innocent, uncertain and unsure of himself and nearly as out of place in our world as Vivian Bowden. But he is so good and so noble and so much in Harold's good books that I will do what I possibly can to help him.

After lunching with Maurice Foley, who is George Brown's Parliamentary Secretary, and who I was anxious to get on my side about the Land Commission, I was involved in a series of office meetings of which the most important was on the National Building Agency. In describing my visit to Oldham in this diary I tried to indicate how important industrialized building is to us. Since I wrote that, the Prime Minister has committed us to industrialized building, and I see nothing to lose if we make the local authorities turn over to it since conventional architecture is so terrible it couldn't be worse. If we are going to do this, the agency through which we have to work is the National Building Agency. This afternoon we discussed how we should handle the N.B.A. and I was very tickled when I found that my idea of getting an outside expert to run the housing drive is now departmental policy. They are beginning to realize that they have got nobody in the Department to put in charge of a housing drive and they remember what Macmillan did when he got his 300,000 houses. I have got to have my man! They didn't like Mr Hyams so I suggested Peter Lederer, and now I am told by the Dame that he is regarded as one of the ablest young men in the whole construction industry.[1] We've agreed that I should suggest his being loaned to our Department for a year or two – to become the man responsible for pushing and shoving and getting industrialized building off the launching pad.

I caught the 5.45 Pullman to Bath where Anne and her aunt, May Cowper, met me and where we had a lovely dinner at the Hole in the Wall. It was a beautiful moonlight night with exquisite views of Bath. Ah, it is going to be nice weather tomorrow, I thought.

[1] See p. 81.

Saturday, January 16th

But today turned out to be full of driving rain and westerly gales. I was picked up at 9.30 by my official, Mr Pearce, and we spent three hours of the morning slogging round the city suburbs looking at the problems of the boundary in the rain. One of the things I had been thinking about in the last fortnight is how to get the Boundary Commission's directive reshaped and refurbished, not merely politically where all I have to do is prevent thirty or forty Labour seats going to the Tories, but also in terms of the efficiency of local government. Bath is a wonderful example because here the Commission has recommended bringing inside the boundaries of the borough two suburbs into which Bath people have overspilt. Going round these suburbs on Saturday – up the steep valleys and down again – I was appalled at the quality of the housing. In each case a very pretty and elegant piece of Bath runs along one side of the valley and lines of cheap, horrible houses along the other side. I can't conceive why Bath Council should want to take over such a liability area where the roads need to be redone, the houses are falling down and the services must be brought up to the standard of a county borough. Anyway, my feeling is that so far from backing one side against the other, I have got to find a *modus vivendi* between county and county borough. These feelings were entirely confirmed by our three-hour trudge in the rain. I am quite clear now that I can conscientiously reject most of the extension proposed by the Commission, and I shall do so expressly on the ground that where there is really powerful local feeling and a deep sense of continuity, county boroughs shouldn't be allowed to expand indefinitely into counties. I went back to lunch with May Cowper at Cavendish Crescent and then Anne and I drove home to Prescote in the driving rain and found our bouncing, booming children waiting for us. It was a delicious relaxation after quite a successful week.

Sunday, January 17th

This last week I have been outside the mainstream of politics. The papers were full of reports about the TSR2 and discussion of whether we are going to cancel it or not. Day after day I read this in my morning paper but as a member of the Cabinet I know *absolutely nothing* about it. Even on Thursday when we had Cabinet the issue wasn't discussed. I read in the papers that it is being discussed at Chequers this weekend, with George Wigg and his pals present and people like me completely excluded. So much for Cabinet responsibility. Actually, I am not against what is going on and I shan't complain; but it is true that when the issue comes up to Cabinet for final decision, those of us who were not departmentally concerned will be unable to form any opinion at all.

Tuesday, January 19th

We had our agenda for Cabinet at the weekend – comprehensive education.

Reading Michael Stewart's paper I saw straight away one fatal flaw. It was excellently written but the tough conclusion didn't follow from the sweetly reasonable argument, which laid down a generous definition of comprehensive education and included a refusal to legislate on direct grant schools. Yet, despite this mildness, the recommendation was that we should firmly commit ourselves to legislation making the comprehensive compulsory in the next Session. It seemed to me that this made no sense at all and I got down to work over the weekend and wrote out my views; and directly I got to London on Monday morning I rang up George Wigg and said to him, 'How can I get my views to Harold?' George said he would have a word with the P.M.; he rang through to me in the evening to say he had just seen Harold, who accepted my point of view. Could I let him have a paper straight away? I was just completing a very busy day in the office and said I couldn't manage to get it ready for an hour. However, I stopped work and rushed it off as fast as I could, but when this was done we found that George had left his office and there was nobody there. With George Moseley's assistance I decided to send the paper to Harold with a covering note which ran: 'Here is a note to George Wigg such as you asked for.'

This morning, Tuesday, I rang up George Wigg only two hours before the Cabinet and told him what I had done. He whistled and said, 'My God, I must get that out of the machine. Don't you realize, Dick, any piece of paper which you send to No. 10 addressed to the Prime Minister is got hold of by the Cabinet Secretariat and circulated to everyone concerned? So Michael Stewart will be bound to see what you have written.'

At the Cabinet Harold Wilson started by describing Michael Stewart's paper as the model of what a Cabinet paper should be – something he approved in every way. Then he added that he wondered about the end. Should we really commit ourselves to this legislative compulsion in the coming Session? This seemed to him possibly to be a mistake. He used almost the words I had written to him. If Michael Stewart had got a copy of the paper that morning, the fat would have been in the fire. When Harold Wilson finished Douglas Houghton came in on roughly the same lines, and it was clear that the only support Michael Stewart got was from the old schoolteachers like Fred Peart and Willie Ross. Even the other members of the Social Services Committee immediately withdrew when the Prime Minister made his point of view clear. Instead of trying to dragoon the schools into action by legislation, the Government would take the line that while we weren't afraid of legislation in the last resort, we didn't think it necessary now, since our plans for encouraging the local authorities to go comprehensive of their own free will were going so well.

Wednesday, January 20th

I went down to Nuneaton for the eve-of-poll meeting in Frank Cousins's by-election. Conditions were foul since there had been a heavy fall of snow the night before. I had intended to travel with Anne by the motorway (she had been up in London on Tuesday because the Donaldsons[1] had invited us to see a gorgeous performance of *Rigoletto* in the Royal Box at Covent Garden). With all that snow I decided to go down by train.

Of course, I had known for a fortnight while the by-election campaign was going on that there had been difficulties. It wasn't so easy to find two constituencies whose Members were even willing to consider going to the House of Lords in order to make room for Frank Cousins and Patrick Gordon Walker. Finally two old stalwarts, Sorensen of Leyton and Frank Bowles of Nuneaton, were put under tremendous pressure. Both of them are loyal Members and both are rather on the Left. Each in his own slightly sulky way finally agreed to go to the Lords and leave room for the two Cabinet Ministers. I assumed the majorities were so big that there was no conceivable chance of their not being elected, though there might be a small drop in the majority. As the election campaign developed the impression I got was that whereas things were going very well at Nuneaton, things were going very badly indeed at Leyton. Having taken the taint of Smethwick[2] with him into this gloomy North London suburb, of which a quarter of the population is old-age pensioners, Patrick Gordon Walker was doing a thoroughly dreary job of putting himself across.

Arriving at Nuneaton, I had a pleasant dinner with Frank Cousins and found him in an elated mood. He told me there had never been an election campaign where there had been such a tremendous response. I did just notice that the agents were not over-enthusiastic—they stayed quiet while Frank talked in this way, and so did Norman Pratt, the miners' agent. And when I got to the meeting I was extremely disconcerted to find that only about a hundred people were in the huge school hall and they were just Party stalwarts. I did my best, but it was an extremely flat meeting. I went back to London thinking, 'Well, it isn't very bright at Nuneaton but Frank seems to have done quite well.'

Thursday, January 21st

The debate in the House had been on education.[3] When I got there for the ten o'clock vote everybody told me what a tremendous success Michael Stewart had been. In the lobby Harold Wilson came up to me and said in a loud voice, 'You see what we can manage, my dear Dick, by a combined operation.' Of course, he was referring to the message I had got to him via George Wigg and he was enthusiastic about what he had done. He also

---

[1] Lord Donaldson of Kingsbridge was a director of the Royal Opera House.
[2] See p. 46.
[3] The Conservatives lost their censure motion by 279 votes to 306.

agreed that, though Michael Stewart had made a brilliant speech, he had failed to carry out the Cabinet decision; in fact he had talked in the most acid, Robespierre tone and revealed his determination to use legislation. Obviously, he had deeply annoyed the P.M. After I had gone through the lobby and talked to Harold I ran into Tam, who suggested that I should stay up and listen to the *Gallery* programme on B.B.C. television that night. I thought that marginally it would be worth it and so I undressed and then went into the sitting-room and there were the TV cameras at Nuneaton showing Frank Cousins looking somewhat grim. When the result was announced with a 6,000 slump in the Labour vote,[1] I realized something was pretty wrong and thought I had better stay up and see what had happened at Leyton.

It was one of those occasions when TV really does bring the viewer right into the event. I could see the Tory candidate not really believing his ears and watch Gordon Walker acting with melancholy dignity—and also revealing his deep inner defeatism.[2] It was an awful evening. I felt an epoch had ended—ironically enough this was the ninety-ninth day of Harold's famous Hundred Days. It was a shattering of our complacency and also a shattering of our Government's authority. I rang George Wigg and found he was still round at Downing Street. But, no, wiser not to try and talk to him.

Friday, January 22nd

So I waited till next morning and then spoke to Wigg on the phone. We agreed there were really probably three factors at work. First of all the resentment in the constituencies at having a Cabinet Minister foisted on them and a respected senior Member turned out. Secondly, we are as a Government in a very bad patch owing to the unpopularity of our mortgage programme, our attack on the aircraft industry and so on. And thirdly, the smear which Gordon Walker had carried with him from Smethwick probably accounted for the fact that the swing at Leyton was 8 per cent, whereas it was only 4·5 per cent at Nuneaton.

The main thing we agreed was the need for the Government to establish its authority, and I had to go to the Ministry to do my share. This wasn't so easy. Jennie Hall described to me how, sitting in the Private Office, she had seen the extraordinary supercilious detachment of the other officials. On the night before, I had had them in for a session on the organization of the Private Office and again insisted that I wanted to sign my own letters. Finally I had lost my temper and had said, 'You bloody well do what I tell you. Get out and do it.' That was what had happened on Thursday evening and there they were today looking at Jennie rather smugly and smirkily. The confidence that we could carry on despite our slender majority which had been building

[1] Frank Cousins held Nuneaton but the majority was reduced from 11,702 to 5,241.
[2] Gordon Walker was defending a majority of nearly 8,000 but the Conservatives won the seat by 205 votes. Wilson would have to find another Foreign Secretary.

up in the previous weeks was suddenly no longer there. Now they were hedging and feeling 'They'll be out soon.' I knew I must reassert my personal authority in the Department.

The trouble was that I had to spend the whole morning on a Party speech. While I talked to George Wigg I suddenly remembered that I was speaking in Coventry on Saturday evening and that I might be able to be useful there. George agreed I must get something drafted as rapidly as possible, so I scrapped my lunch and everything else, knocked off a press release and sent it round to Harold at 2.30 in the afternoon. This is not the kind of conduct which Ministry officials like, particularly since I had to scrap the business they had planned for me, but that couldn't be helped – I rushed over to the Commons and walked straight into Harold's room where he was standing with Marcia, Percy Clark and George Wigg. They had already prepared two drafts of speeches which were to be handed over to Ray Gunter and Tony Greenwood. I then produced mine. Harold glanced through it and told me to delete a passage in which I referred to racialism and Smethwick. Otherwise he seemed to like it. Then he said, 'Stay behind a moment. I want to talk to you.'

When Marcia and Percy had gone out he turned to me and said, 'Look, Dick, we have decided on Michael Stewart for Foreign Secretary and he has accepted. He and his wife are quite pleased.' He didn't ask my opinion. I said that I realized that he couldn't do what I would have liked and make Denis Healey Foreign Secretary and Roy Jenkins Minister of Defence.[1] 'No,' he said, 'I wouldn't trust Healey in the Foreign Office with all those professionals. And anyway we can't let him run away from the Defence job. It's something he has to wade through. No, we can't do that. That's why I chose Michael Stewart. You'll laugh, Dick, but when I talked to him he said he felt like crying at having to leave Education.' I looked at Harold and said, 'Well, I would actually have cried if I had lost M.H.L.G. owing to this shemozzle.'

He then said, 'Who shall we put at Education? We could of course take Reg Prentice . . . No, it's too big a job for the boy, though he made an excellent speech last night.' Then George Wigg said, 'What about Fred Willey?' looking at me. And I said, 'God, not on your life. That would be a nightmare – though from my own point of view I would be glad to get Fred out of Land and Natural Resources.' Then Harold said, 'What about Tony Greenwood?' And I said, 'Frankly, you know he's not up to it.' Then George came up with Anthony Crosland, and he said immediately, 'That's the right choice. If we can't have Roy Jenkins, let's have Crosland.[2] He's got a good brain, he's written well about education and he will be a positive addition to the Cabinet.' We all agreed that if George Brown would release Tony Crosland this would be the right solution. The Prime Minister didn't show

---

[1] Wilson gives his reasons in his own record. See *Wilson*, p. 66.
[2] Wilson had already offered the job to Roy Jenkins, who had turned it down.

much sign of any personal agony at Gordon Walker's plight. He obviously felt, as I did, that he really had been no good as Foreign Secretary and no great strength in the Government.

That forty minutes I spent with him, drinking a glass of brandy, was really like going back to old times. It was the first time since we took office that he and George Wigg and I, the old gang, had been on the job together. As I left Harold said to me, 'After such a long time it's been really exhilarating,' and I too felt exhilarated, keener, more excited than I had been for some weeks. Outside the door I found Sara Barker, the national agent, nearly crying because she had been down at Leyton the night before. For the right wing and the staff of Transport House this defeat had been the most ghastly blow, far worse than for Harold, George and me. I went back to the Ministry and found I could do no more than hand the draft speech over to be corrected and typed by Jennie because I had to rush to catch my train at Paddington.

It was very important to catch that train because Peter Lederer was waiting in the compartment for me. I was taking him down to spend the evening at Prescote. Having successfully stalled Mr Hyams, the Dame was prepared to accept Lederer now that I had redefined his job in a modest way and centred it on the need for industrialized housing. We had an excellent evening at Prescote. Peter seems to be gratified though I am afraid he won't accept the job. But he will be prepared to help me find the right person.

Sunday, January 24th
Yesterday, Saturday, I had to get to Coventry at 9.15 a.m. for my first official visit to the city. This went pretty well. Coventry were nice to me in an un-enthusiastic way and gave me a pleasant lunch. To be frank I think they would have entertained me more regally if I had been the Minister of Housing but not their local Member. They don't like their M.P.s hogging the limelight. At the lunch I made the big speech in which I gave an official Government reaction to the defeat at Leyton.

To my great embarrassment, later that afternoon I found that the *Coventry Evening Telegraph* had taken the odd relative clause out of my press release and made it their main lead by announcing that I was preparing legislation on mortgage payments. This might well be difficult since no Cabinet Minister is allowed to announce legislation in advance. I got hold of Peter Brown at the Ministry and instructed him to issue a correction. But I very much doubt whether he did so because I find today, Sunday, that most of the papers have given this announcement very great prominence.

However, that difficulty may be eased by the death of Winston which was declared this morning at eight o'clock. It has of course been macabre that his illness, which lasted for ten days, went on so long that the bulletins finally faded out because people got bored or sick or embarrassed by the whole affair. At Cabinet on Thursday the Prime Minister told us that this would be

5*

like the death of a monarch and that every Prime Minister in the Alliance would come and there would be important conversations for which we must all be ready and at their disposal. And he warned us that we would virtually have a week of respite from party politics for the funeral and the state mourning.[1] Well, the respite should make things easier for me in this mortgage affair. If we had had the debate on Wednesday I should have had some explaining to do.

Looking back on this week I have no doubt that this was the biggest crisis we have had and Harold Wilson came out of it as well as we could possibly hope. He was tough, he was exhilarated by the unexpected disaster and he handled it as thoroughly as anyone could.

Monday, January 25th
The main item I was concerned with at E.D.C. was the discussion of a joint paper put forward by George Brown's officials, my officials and Douglas Jay's officials on a proposed New Town in Lancashire.[2] George Brown supported the New Town and Douglas Jay fiercely opposed it on the ground that Lancashire is not a development area and therefore there shouldn't be any help of this kind given to it. Characteristically, George Brown bashed and smashed his way through and Douglas Jay bleated and was defeated. I saw once again that what matters in Cabinet government is personality. Whatever Douglas Jay says, this dry, bony Whitehall wonder, he turns people against any idea he represents.

In the afternoon Parliament met for tributes to Sir Winston. By then I felt we had already had enough tributes, but here they came, Wilson, Douglas-Home, Jo Grimond. I sat on the front bench squeezed between Barbara Castle and Tony Crosland and fell into a quiet slumber while the lugubrious process went on. In the evening I had dinner with Richard Llewelyn-Davies, and found Nicky Kaldor there. They spent most of the evening talking about a Lib–Lab pact, and I found the whole argument pretty futile. What mattered to me was that at eleven o'clock I was due to meet Fred Willey, who had asked to see me about the Land Commission Bill. At once he said to me straight out that he wanted my support for his paper. I replied, 'Let's agree to put a paper to Cabinet in which we indicate that there is a major political decision to be taken. They must decide whether they want the Land Commission with monopoly powers right now, or whether they are prepared to have a much more modest Bill at the beginning.' Willey found no difficulty in agreeing to this—at least so I thought—and I reported to Dame Evelyn that it was now all right for the officials of both Departments to draft the Cabinet paper presenting the issues to be decided.

---

[1] Parliament customarily adjourns for the day on the death of a former Prime Minister; but in this case the Prime Minister, Leader of the House and Chief Whip had decided to adjourn for the period until Churchill's funeral.
[2] See p. 149.

Tuesday, January 26th

At our first Cabinet since Leyton we were ostensibly discussing Winston's funeral arrangements; actually we were discussing the Leyton defeat. Harold made a very long and not very persuasive *plaidoyer*. I don't know quite what he was trying to achieve, but at least he did one thing that George Wigg and I had insisted on when he emphasized the need for contact with Transport House and communication with the Party in the country. I backed him up on both points and did it all the more confidently because my Saturday speech at Coventry had had a very big press, not only on Sunday but also on Monday, and was being treated as the dominant Government speech on the crisis. As I have mentioned in this diary, it had been headlined with firm promises to mortgagors and so I had expected fierce resentment in Cabinet. Not at all. Not one word was said—presumably because everybody was so frightened by Leyton.

The long, random discussion which followed was enlivened by a confrontation between Callaghan and Brown. Callaghan's line was that we must end illusions and tell the people honestly that expenditure was exceeding economic growth and that this couldn't go on. George Brown replied that too much probity would destroy us; if we took Callaghan's advice we should be ruined. We now had to make a short-term calculation and dispense with the assumption that we were going to stay in office for three or four years. The new situation was such that a couple of appendicitis operations could destroy us, or a single car accident. So our whole tactic had to change. We must now have nothing but short-term tactics and prepare an offensive designed to put the blame back on the Tories.

It had been a desultory, unsatisfactory and also somewhat defeatist Cabinet. I went up to Harold afterwards and found him for the first time really angry with me. 'Well,' he said, 'You're a fine one. First of all you do your best to destroy my new Ministry of Land and Natural Resources. Then you take even the control of water from Fred Willey. And now I gather you've destroyed his Land Commission Bill as well. I can't think what you're up to.'

I learned that after leaving my room on the previous evening Fred Willey had gone round to No. 10 to see Harold, ostensibly about the nationalization of water, where he was to deal with legislation, though my Ministry stayed in overall charge. In fact, he poured his heart out about how through the Dame I was bullying him and wrecking his Ministry and his only Bill. Harold demanded an explanation and an immediate meeting with the relevant Ministers.

Having listened to this, I went back to the Ministry somewhat shaken. It was the first time I had been given a really angry rebuke. What was I to do? Before I had even finished pondering the problem, I received a note from No. 10 in which Harold insisted that 100 per cent mortgages and immediate cuts in the cost of conveyancing were two positive proposals that he required straight away. I scrapped my appointments that afternoon and sat down to write a memo in reply. I told the Prime Minister that 100 per cent mortgages might act as an irritant rather than as a palliative when the rate of interest was 7 per cent. I thought our main job was to reassure borrowers that we were going to get the rate of interest down. As for conveyancing, I pointed out that that was a matter for the Lord Chancellor and not for me. The memo went off in the afternoon.

Wednesday, January 27th

A working lunch with my Parliamentary Secretaries today, and a whole string of routine jobs in the office. All the time I had at the back of my mind the knowledge that Harold Wilson was against me, that I was in hot water, that I had to get clear with him about this first difficulty. So I was glad to meet Tommy Balogh and his wife Penelope and be taken to *Camelot* at Drury Lane. Magnificent settings and a futile, stiff kind of Anglo-American music drama. But it took my mind off things and we had a delicious dinner at Rules.

Thursday, January 28th

This was my critical day with in the morning Cabinet—at which I had been told by Dame Evelyn that James Callaghan was to launch an attack on my housing programme—and in the evening the crucial meeting about the Land Commission. Just when Cabinet was starting I got a note from Harold Wilson congratulating me on agreeing to accept Bruce Fraser as Dame Evelyn's successor,* and concluding by saying that he was going to back my housing programme. So there it was. The row was over before it started, which was satisfactory for me! The evening meeting was also satisfactory. I found myself in the Cabinet room, Harold in the chair, with the Attorney-General (I had insisted on our lawyer being present) and Fred Willey. George Brown came in for a moment and walked out again. That left four of us to have the most vague informal discussion. After a couple of hours it was decided that Willey should draft a White Paper defining the policy he believed in for the Land Commission. O.K. by me!

Friday, January 29th

I lunched with Gerald Gardiner in his lodgings in the Victoria Tower. His wife Lesley seemed a trying woman—she was always stopping him from telling his favourite stories. However, one thing he did say was interesting. I asked him whether he liked all the protocol of the House of Lords and he said, 'I always wanted to be an actor so I really like dressing up a great deal.'

My last meeting of the day was with George Brown to discuss industrialized

---

* What I'd actually done was to put up to Helsby the proposal that if Fraser was to come to the Ministry of Housing he should spend the next six months working on local government finance at the Treasury while the Dame stayed on until the end of July; this was the condition on which I accepted Fraser. Harold was pleased with this.

building. It was the day on which all the foreign delegations were arriving for Churchill's funeral and he was so pissed that he straight away insulted Charlie Pannell. No doubt he was tired after a tremendously important meeting with the employers to discuss the incomes policy.

Saturday, January 30th
Winston's funeral. All through the week London had been working itself up for the great day. The lying-in-state in Westminster Hall had taken place on Wednesday, Thursday and Friday. I went on all three evenings, taking Molly and our doorman, Arthur, on one night, and Anne and Tommy Balogh the second night, and then on the third night Mr Large who cuts my hair. Each time one saw, even at one o'clock in the morning, the stream of people pouring down the steps of Westminster Hall towards the catafalque. Outside the column wound through the garden at Millbank, then stretched over Lambeth Bridge, right round the corner to St Thomas's Hospital. As one walked through the streets one felt the hush and one noticed the cars stopping suddenly and the people stepping out into the quietness and walking across to Westminster Hall. We as Members of Parliament could just step into the Hall through our side door.

I really hadn't wanted to go to the funeral. But it was obvious that I couldn't be known to have stayed away and I was a bit surprised, but also relieved, when Anne finally rang up and said she would like to go too and would come up on Friday. We spent the evening with Mark Childs, who for some years has been, I suppose, the number three American political columnist.[1] He had come over to cover the funeral. We discussed old times, particularly his visit during the Suez crisis when he had been, on request, first to see Anthony Eden, who told him nothing, and then to hear Harold Macmillan give him a hair-raising interview in which he was requested to send a personal message to the American Secretary of the Treasury begging him to go easy on the pound. He told us how next day, when he was seeing Anthony Eden, Macmillan had come into the room and said to him, 'Have you sent that telegram yet?' He then began to ask me about Gordon Walker, who had been built up by the American press as a strong, courageous man, almost a statesman. I am afraid that I said that he is really a pretty poor politician who got into Herbert Morrison's good books as a result of his attitude in the Oxford by-election at the time of Munich.[2] Having got into the Attlee Cabinet as a Morrison man and risen to be Commonwealth Secretary, he was a solid Gaitskellite until Hugh died; and then during the

[1] Marquis Childs' reputation had grown out of his work as a correspondent with the *St Louis Post Dispatch* from the late 1920s to the end of the war. Now living in Washington, he continued to write articles and books about politics and current affairs.
[2] In 1938 A. D. Lindsay stood against Quintin Hogg on an Independent anti-Chamberlain platform and Patrick Gordon Walker stood down as the Labour candidate. As an Oxford City councillor, Crossman played a large part in the campaign, and a large number of undergraduates, including Edward Heath at Balliol, worked for Lindsay.

contest for the leadership switched from George Brown to Harold Wilson at the critical moment.[1]

We had a pleasant evening dining at Overtons. Then Anne and I went back to bed, or rather to find Kathleen and Tam sitting quietly by our fire and we chatted before going to sleep to prepare for the great day.

On Saturday Molly called for us at 9 a.m. in the morning, because instructions were that we had to get past Aldwych by 9.40. We were through Trafalgar Square by 9.20 and then we joined the stream of establishment cars wending their way, down the Strand, down Fleet Street, to St Paul's. We got there about 9.55 and were decanted suddenly and unexpectedly. We crept past various kinds of guards and found ourselves with places right forward under the dome. Anne was sitting next to Ray Gunter, our Minister of Labour, and I next to Field-Marshal Harding, who I had last seen in Cyprus[2] when I was lunching with him, and his wife had turned to me and said, 'You're a very wicked man, Mr Crossman, last time you were here in Nicosia you were the cause of murder and destruction.' Harding is a little man who is always falling over his sword every time he gets down on his knees to pray. However, he relieved my boredom by conducting a conversation with me throughout the whole service in a fairly high-pitched, audible whisper. I had brought with me Conrad's *Youth* to fill in the intervals but I didn't read anything because the whole period before the service started was taken up by arrivals – the arrival of the lord mayor; the arrival of the procession of foreign ambassadors; then the foreign kings; they came at ten- or twenty-minute intervals and filled up the stage. Meanwhile there was also St Paul's to look at. Thanks to TV and the lighting, one could see the mosaics which one had never seen before and the whole decoration of the chancel. The mosaics were not very good but the general appearance under the lighting was magnificent. As for the service itself, it was fairly straightforward and very badly conducted by the Dean. My chief memory is of the pall-bearers, in particular poor Anthony Eden, literally ashen grey, looking as old as Clement Attlee. And then of the coffin being carried up the steps by those poor perspiring privates of the Guards, sweat streaming down their faces, each clutching the next in order to sustain the sheer weight. As they came past us they staggered and they weren't properly recovered when they had to bring the coffin down the steps again to put it on the gun carriage to be taken to Tower Bridge. My other chief memory was the superb way the trumpets sounded the Last Post and the Reveille. The trumpeters were right up in the Whispering Gallery, round the inside of the dome, and for the first time a trumpet had room to sound in a dimension, a hemisphere of its own. But, oh, what a faded, declining establishment surrounded me. Aged marshals, grey, dreary ladies, decadent Marlboroughs and Churchills. It was a dying congregation gathered there and I am afraid the Labour Cabinet didn't look

---

[1] In 1963.

[2] Where he was Governor and Commander-in-Chief between 1955 and November 1957.

too distinguished either. It felt like the end of an epoch, possibly even the end of a nation.

When it was all over and we got out and stood on the steps at the west end I feared the worst, and the worst came. The procession had of course been magnificently organized to the last split second so that the coffin arrived at the Tower of London, was got on to the boat and off the boat at Waterloo perfectly on time. But once the procession was over the Earl Marshal couldn't have cared less about those who had taken part. There we were, a couple of thousand people, waiting on the steps of St Paul's for cars which came one by one inconceivably slowly. We stood there for thirty minutes in a bitter wind and then Anne and I walked for five minutes to the underground at Blackfriars and I left her to go back to Vincent Square and on from there by car to the country, while I went to the Garrick for lunch with my publisher, Jamie Hamilton. The Ministry was shut so I slipped into a cinema after lunch and saw a slick, novelettish little Terence Rattigan show called *The Yellow Rolls Royce* which amused me a great deal. Then I walked home to do an hour and a half's reading and preparing papers before I went back to the House of Commons to the southern region of the Labour Party's annual dinner, which was being held in the Members' dining-room. I was only there because Harold Wilson had to look after the foreign guests at the funeral and gave instructions that I should take his place. I don't think he could have been conscious that the chairman would be Sydney Irving in whose constituency I had given Span permission to build the model village of Hartley!

Afterwards I walked home and found Tam and Kathleen sitting watching for the second time the film of Churchill's funeral. I could see the things I hadn't seen – the scene at the Tower and the boat on the river and the landing-stage. I must say it was impressive. There was a stature, an ashen magnificence about the whole thing which made me think of Tennyson's 'Passing of Arthur'. But chiefly I reflected on the mood of the regional dinner I had just been addressing. And I asked myself, are we going to be driven out of office? because if there were an election now there would be a landslide against us. I believe we shall get through this awkward period mainly because the Conservatives are still disunited and unable to strike. So if we keep our heads and do our job, there is no earthly reason why we shouldn't fight on into the summer, losing a lot of the local elections on the way I daresay, but still surviving. And once we get through to the summer and things pick up again we can settle down to go on for a year or two.

Sunday, January 31st

I came down to Prescote with Dame Evelyn because I wanted her to see the place. When we arrived at Banbury Station there were the children running to meet us on a perfectly lovely winter day, white clouds, pale-blue sky, and poplars looking as though the spring had given them that golden, red flush. I took her for a splendid walk to Upper Prescote to see the dairy herd there and the beef calves being fattened up. And then we walked back along the other side of the Cherwell. This evening we had the Hartrees to dinner to meet her and I think she now realizes I have an alternative life to fall back on.

Meanwhile, I have used the opportunity of her being here to discuss housing policy. This is something which has been formulated in the Ministry throughout the week and we are now safely committed to my ideas of differential interest rates. The Dame, of course, was keen on the policies of the Department and has her own plan for reorganizing the housing subsidies. At Prescote I think I managed to persuade her that we should try to fix the interest rates for housing across the board and have a subsidy which prevents the rate paid for building council houses rising above 4 per cent whatever happens. Then on top of this one could have special subsidies for high-rise building and so on. Each year (and this is my second main idea) I think we have to fix the total volume of houses we build by agreement between the Government, the industry, the building societies and the local authorities. I have a concept here of a house-building review rather like the annual farm-price review. Dame Evelyn sees a thousand administrative difficulties. She is a good civil servant but she knows I am set on this, and I think we shall work out something constructive and have it ready for Harold pretty soon.

Finally, a look back to a historic week. It has been dominated in terms of our Labour Party politics by the inquest on Leyton and Nuneaton, and, in terms of national politics, by Churchill's funeral. Judging by the mood inside the Government the Leyton by-election has punctured a myth, blown away an atmosphere of self-confidence defying reality which Harold created with his talk of the Hundred Days. This received its first bad knock with the economic crisis and the increase in bank rate to 7 per cent. But it survived and the Cabinet settled down into a mood which said 'We are doing a decent job here in Westminster', and neglected the effect we were having on public opinion outside. I think the defeat at Leyton shows that the Government has now lost one invaluable asset – the public belief that the Conservative Government was responsible for our present difficulties. During our first three months we had no machine for maintaining contact with the people outside, and we made no propaganda effort to keep up the political offensive which put the blame on the Conservative Government and the thirteen wasted years. And quite quietly during these three months the responsibility for the evils created by the thirteen years has been transferred to us. Now *we* are the people responsible for high prices, for the cut in pensions, for the failure to keep mortgage rates down.

The basic reason why this has happened is that there isn't a member of our Cabinet, as there was in the Macmillan Cabinet, responsible for relations with the Party. I have discussed this every day this week with George Wigg, who at long last has informally been given the job by Harold of trying to bridge the gap between No. 10 and Transport House. I have also discussed it a little with Wedgy Benn and with my own staff, and I am more and more convinced that this is really our major survival problem. Until we tackle it drastically this Government will be shaken, divided and increasingly disintegrated. I say disintegrate and I mean disintegrate, because morale, which had been so miraculously preserved before Leyton, has been shattered. Everybody in the Government is nervous. And, of course, the worst thing of all is the shock administered to the Party outside.

Dealing with this has been rendered no easier by the gigantic national celebration of Churchill's death, which was started by the decision of the House of Commons to go into purdah for a whole week and culminated on Saturday in a day of orgiastic self-condolence on the end of our imperial destiny – with Churchill as its symbol. All this hasn't helped the Government. What it has done is to give us a breathing-space and to that extent the five days have been useful. But tomorrow we shall start finding out what really has happened to us as the result of Leyton.

The three by-elections in February, at Altrincham and Sale, Salisbury and East Grinstead, were all in safe Conservative constituencies and the seats were held. Two weeks later Sir Alec reshuffled his Shadow Cabinet, moving Reginald Maudling from the Treasury to Foreign Affairs and promoting Edward Heath to take his place as Shadow Chancellor. Christopher Soames took on Defence and Peter Thorneycroft became Shadow Home Secretary. Later in the month, Sir Alec announced the new arrangements for electing future leaders of the Conservative Party, a system of three ballots of all Conservative M.P.s, supervised by the chairman of the 1922 Committee.

Meanwhile, the Labour front bench wrestled with the economy. The January trade figures that were published in February showed a deficit of £34 million and although the February figures showed an overall credit of £11 million, much of that proved to be a short-term statistical improvement largely accounted for by an American dock strike that had halved imports from the United States. On February 10th the I.M.F. extended their $3,000 million credit until the end of May, and on the following day George Brown published a White Paper setting out his proposals for a prices and incomes board to encourage voluntary efforts to stabilize wages and prices.

There was still no public announcement about the TSR2, but the cancellation of two other aircraft, the P-1154 and the HS-681, was an uncomfortable omen. The Prime Minister claimed that these two decisions would save £300 million over ten years, but in the censure debate on the issue the Government's majority fell to five.

Monday, February 1st
Straight from Prescote to the Cabinet which had been called on a Monday because it was necessary to get clearance for a provisional Statement on aircraft which Harold Wilson wanted to make in his reply to the censure debate tomorrow.

This was the first time Cabinet had discussed defence. I took virtually no part because it was clear that once again a postponement of a decision on the TSR2 was to be announced. I found the discussion as unilluminating as usual except in that James Callaghan revealed that he had already made up his mind firmly against the TSR2. It was also clear that the Prime Minister was against *him*.

I spent most of the day preparing for Question Time on Tuesday and the Statement on the future of the London children's service which will follow Harold Wilson's Questions and then also preparing for the Statement on the South-East which I shall make on Wednesday.

In the afternoon, however, I spent a couple of hours with our young architects and Oliver Cox being briefed on industrialized buildings and getting to know the two systems they are using, 5M and 12M. I had just got back to the Ministry and was tidying things up when B.G. came in.[1] He sat down and lectured me at length on being a good European. I found myself saying, 'Look, I'm not concerned with Europe now,' and I realized how departmentalized I have already become and how little the role I am playing in foreign affairs.

In the evening Anne and I had a really enjoyable outing—a Ministerial perk. We went to the Festival Hall for the concert celebrating the reopening, at which the Queen Mother was due to be present. I imagined lots of Ministers would be there. But I was the only one, along with Jennie Lee. We heard a splendid performance of Brahms' Piano Concerto No. 2. In the second half I had to sit next to the Queen Mother, who was large and cuddly and comfortable and easy. Afterwards Jennie, Anne and I went back to supper with Arnold Goodman—a really pleasant evening out.

Tuesday, February 2nd

This was the big day: a vote of censure on Harold Wilson preceded by Question Time, for which I was first on the list. Amazingly enough, the Dame was quite concerned about me. When we were sitting preparing for Questions over a working lunch in my room she seemed to feel distaste at the idea that I should have a rough time about the Labour Party's pledge to reduce interest rates for mortgagors. She is still living in the era of Keith Joseph—a fine, sensitive soul who didn't like rough questioning and needed her protection. I don't see any point in Question Time unless it is rough. On this occasion I felt pretty sure of myself and I managed by a carefully calculated, self-controlled riposte to knock out John Boyd-Carpenter. He was asking me an extremely impertinent question about the delicate subject of how much I consulted Fred Willey on planning decisions. The truth is that,

[1] David Ben Gurion, the Israeli statesman. Crossman had been a friend of Israel since 1946 when, as a member of Bevin's Anglo–American Palestine Commission, he advocated British support for the new Jewish state.

although the P.M. has often suggested I should be tactful and talk to Fred, I haven't done it on a single occasion. So I had to get out of answering that one and I think Hansard shows that I was not unskilful in so doing.

After I had announced our very unpopular decision that we weren't going to legislate on the London children's care service, the big censure debate started.[1] Douglas-Home's speech was really quite good, though he didn't deliver it very well and he was barracked a great deal. Harold's speech was hardly put together at all. It consisted really of two speeches, one provided by George Wigg and Roy Jenkins on the aircraft and the other provided by Tommy Balogh. Harold himself had added a rough knockabout defence of the Government's Hundred Days. It was a pretty tumultuous debate, but this kind of knockabout with the Opposition crashing and bashing does us more good than harm. I sat through it and studied it and after that I spent the evening in the Chamber, the smoking-room and the tea-room and found the Party wasn't in too bad a shape.

Wednesday, February 3rd
I spent the morning trying to win support for my new fair-rent formula.[2] There seemed to me two men I ought to get on to my side: Eric Fletcher, who is the Lord Chancellor's number two, and Niall MacDermot, Financial Secretary to the Treasury and, even more important, an able lawyer who really understands rents. I knew I had to persuade him, so I spent most of the morning doing this. At 3.30 there came my second major Statement of my career as Minister: this was about London overspill and the use of New Towns to deal with it. I announced the New Town at Bletchley.[3] And also another kind of New Town, which consists of doubling the population of a town by the device of setting up a New Town commission to work with the county borough authorities – we are to start with three famous boroughs, Northampton, Peterborough and Ipswich. I found our own people a little bit doubtful about this Statement and I had a number of constituency questions at the end, but, thanks to the work of Peter Brown, we had pre-released the news to the *Daily Express*, the *Guardian* and the *Evening Standard* and all this build-up helped the Statement and made sure that it went across pretty well. My colleagues in Cabinet were not too jealous, since on the whole a successful Minister of Housing does them good, even if he gets far more than his share of publicity – enough to be listed in the *Observer* as one of the four Ministers whose popularity is worth assessing (the other three are of course Harold Wilson, George Brown and Frank Cousins).

---

[1] The Government survived by 306 votes to 289.
[2] Local rent officers were to establish 'fair rents' based on a complicated assessment of such factors as the value, situation and condition of the property. Landlords and tenants would both have the right to appeal.
[3] Later named Milton Keynes.

Thursday, February 4th

That evening I had to go to a farewell dinner at the German Embassy given by the rather unpleasant Ambassador whom we once invited down for a night at Prescote. He was repaying that hospitality and he must have given me something fiendish to drink. Anyway, I woke up at three this morning with a splitting headache – a particularly horrible kind of hangover – from which I had only just recovered by midday, and as a result I was not very well prepared for a particularly heavy day's work. In my present job I find I am miraculously healthy as I just have work and nothing but work. I can't indulge in pleasure or entertainment without the possibility of dangerous consequences. I certainly have to be much more careful about what and how much I eat and drink in company. I am perfectly all right in private company with Tommy Balogh or with private friends like Noel Annan. It's the kind of formal dinner at an Embassy which does occasionally get me down.

Despite the hangover I managed to get through fairly well. It was a typical day of my life, starting at 9.30 at the office. I brief Nora Beloff of the *Observer*, who had asked for an interview, and talk to her until 10.30. After that just time to go over to the House to hear the P.M. address the Parliamentary Labour Party. Sit beside him to support him. After that rush back for a briefing on a meeting of my own Central Housing Advisory Committee, which is due on Friday. That done, to the Athenaeum to give Charles Pannell lunch in order to sort out a whole number of minor items including why the appointment of Peter Lederer was announced without consulting him in advance. At 2.45 receive the Executive Committee of the N.F.U. for forty-five minutes to try to find a new formula for tied cottages in the Rent Bill. After that, an hour's conference with the County Councils Association on relations with the Boundary Commission, and immediately after that a meeting with all the local authority associations in the big conference room in order to expound to them George Brown's prices and incomes policy. That is followed by a 45-minute briefing on the New Town near Manchester, on which a statement is due in about three weeks' time.

It wasn't surprising that after this, when Bob Mellish got me to see an excellent film of Harlow, I found my eyes tight closed at the end. Nevertheless, I woke up and helped him to give Bill Fiske[1] and Mrs Dennington, his housing chairman on the G.L.C., dinner before tottering back to Vincent Square. I was just going to bed when I remembered about the by-election and sat up with Tam to hear the result of Altrincham and Sale.[2] It was very much better than we expected and made us realize that Leyton was really an erratic response and one need not conclude that there has been a complete turn of public opinion against us.

---

[1] A member of the L.C.C. since 1945 and Leader of the G.L.C. 1964–7, when he was created Lord Fiske. From 1968 to 1971 he was chairman of the Decimal Currency Board.

[2] Following the translation of Frederick Erroll to the Lords. Anthony Barber held the seat for the Conservatives with a slightly reduced majority.

Friday, February 5th

The day started with a visit to Douglas Jay in his office in the new Board of Trade building at the corner of Great Peter Street and Victoria Street. He really has a magnificent view, and you can see the dome of St Paul's behind the tower of Big Ben. He wanted to see me alone about the Chorley site for a New Town, which George Brown has put up to E.D.C. as a joint proposal of the five Ministries concerned. Manchester has needed a New Town for years and the Ministry has found them a completely dud site at Risley which I visited a few weeks ago.[1] Fortunately, just after I had been there the geologists found there was a flaw and the area was full of potential subsidence. So there was Manchester with no site for any overspill except the ghastly place they themselves had found at Westhoughton. That's why I had decided to back George Brown, who had come to the conclusion that the right site was much further north in the Preston/Chorley area—he was backing the project because he wanted to see a new growth point in Lancashire. It was this idea of the growth point which had stimulated Douglas Jay's opposition. As I sat there in his room he said to me, 'It can't be a growth point because growth must only take place in the development areas; and we must not grant industrial development certificates in the Chorley area because that will take them away from the areas of unemployment.' Douglas Jay is obsessed with development areas because under the Attlee government he was one of the people responsible for initiating the whole policy, and he is the kind of man whose good ideas ossify into prejudice. I said in reply, 'Look, Douglas, if we don't ever allow growth areas to grow and if we divert all industry from them to the old development areas, we shall have a terrible situation where growth is penalized and failure is encouraged.'

So we went across to Cabinet and Chorley finally came up after a longish discussion on incomes policy. There was a good deal of bleating, but I got my way and was able to snaffle the Statement for myself in the process.

When I got back to the Ministry I found that George Wigg had rung up asking urgently that when I went to Stoke at the weekend I should do a hand-out on immigration. We have been having sittings of the Cabinet Committee on Immigration for week after week under Frank Soskice's chairmanship—poor Frank Soskice with his arthritis and his twisted shoulder and his amiability and his self-centredness. He is a disaster as Home Secretary and he has to deal with the hottest potato in politics—the problem of immigration. As the Committee has proceeded under his chairmanship he has been gradually dragged out of his purely liberalistic attitude to a recognition that we have to combine tight immigration controls, even if it means changing the law, with a constructive policy for integrating into the community the immigrants who are there already. This has been my line as a Midland M.P. and here I really do represent my constituents. Ever since the Smethwick election it has been quite clear that immigration can be the greatest potential

[1] See p. 125.

vote-loser for the Labour Party if we are seen to be permitting a flood of immigrants to come in and blight the central areas in all our cities. I told George I would certainly try and draft the speech for Stoke and I worked away at frantic speed during my lunch. I only just got it done and round to Frank Soskice, with a copy to Harold, before I went into the big Cabinet Committee on the Ministry of Technology, which was a pretty good waste of time but which I had to sit out before catching the Pullman for Coventry.

It was the night for my surgery and I found a long queue and sat there for two and a half hours, seeing finally a delegation of aircraft workers from Armstrong-Whitworth. They represented the 8,000 workers at the factory, which is now threatened with total closure by the announcement Harold Wilson made at the end of Tuesday's debate.

This was the first occasion on which I found a real conflict between my responsibilities as Minister and my responsibilities as a constituency M.P. I was interested to see how I could handle this split, all the more because ever since the first day of this Session Maurice Edelman has been taking the lead in organizing the aircraft workers and becoming the spokesman of the air-craft industry in protest against any kind of closure. He had quite a success when we all thought Concorde was due for cancellation, because he stood up for Concorde and, through his close contact with the French, made a great impression on the Coventry workers. And now once again, with the threat of the closure of Armstrong-Whitworth, he has been leading the workers' marches – 10,000 were in procession last week – and proclaiming his readiness to die with them on the barricades. Naturally enough, he has not done anything to help the other M.P. for Coventry – the Minister in whose constituency the A.W.W. factory is and who has so far been unable to open his mouth in public.

Well, they all filed into the big room at Coundon Road and I had a good rough meeting with them while six or seven journalists waited outside along with photographers in order to get a picture of the row. I thought the only thing to do was to talk pretty frankly and so I started, 'You understand that I am in favour of drastic defence cuts. It's impossible to buy British planes if they cost twice as much as American planes and if they are not ready at the right time. On the other hand, I will fight like a tiger to see that if any unem-ployment does take place, Coventry doesn't get more than its share.' I think – though I am not sure – that I managed to get through a very difficult meeting; though it is quite true that when A.W.W. closes down – as I think it will – I shall be in an impossible position. The truth is that one loses votes by being in the Cabinet because one has to keep one's trap shut. In the last general election the Conservative Cabinet Ministers by and large did worse than the back-benchers because the back-benchers were able to talk more freely and say the things their constituents wanted to hear. And though my own particular job should give me some popularity, it certainly prevents me from making the kind of hearty, calculated indiscretions which I had been able to indulge in as a back-bencher for twenty years.

After the meeting with the shop stewards I went round to George and Carrie Hodgkinson's house. I found a message waiting for me that Harold had decided that my speech, though good, should be postponed for a week, so all my effort had been wasted.

I got back to the Leofric at 10.45 and found the Silver Grill still open, so I had a bite and then went off to my bedroom where I sat and worked till 1.30 a.m.

Saturday, February 6th
An early start to Stoke with Molly in the official car. As I was driving through it I suddenly felt, 'Here is this huge, ghastly conurbation of five towns — what sense is there in talking about urban renewal here? Other towns have a shape, a centre, some place where renewal can start, perhaps a university. But if one spent billions on this ghastly collection of slag heaps, pools of water, old potteries, deserted coal mines, there would be nothing to show for the money.' There is nothing in Stoke except the worst of the industrial revolution and some of the nicest people in the world. Alas, there are no modern sophisticated industries. There is just a vast equalitarian working class living in cheap council houses and with very low wage-rates. I didn't see much of the town but I had a good discussion with half a dozen councillors in the lord mayor's parlour. When it was over I felt even more strongly that it was impossible to revive Britain without letting such places as Stoke-on-Trent decline. Indeed, I began to wonder whether it wasn't really better to let it be evacuated: renewal is an impossibility, or alternatively a fantastic waste of money.

In the afternoon I did a Labour Party regional conference in Hanley Town Hall, where I used to give my local government W.E.A. classes in 1936. There were some 250 delegates there and I tried to raise their morale with a fighting speech, telling them frankly of the difficulties of the Government, of the legacy we inherited from the Tories, explaining how we couldn't reveal the worst of that legacy for fear of destroying the value of the pound, and saying that the time had come now to fight back and to put the blame where it really belongs. I was amazed and relieved to find that morale, which I thought had been shattered, was still very solid indeed. These people were quietly and placidly discussing with me how to strengthen their support for their Labour Government, and none of them seemed unduly alarmed. The Young Socialists were bleating but there was no shriek from them, and even the old-age pensioners weren't shouting their complaints.

On the way back to Prescote I reflected on that splendid meeting. Of course, Stoke is particularly solid Labour. Nevertheless, if its morale is anything to go by (and it is confirmed to some extent by the results of this week's by-elections[1])

[1] On February 4th, at Altrincham (see p. 148); at East Grinstead, where Geoffrey Johnson-Smith kept for the Conservatives the seat left vacant by Mrs Emmet, now in the Lords; and at Salisbury, where Michael Heseltine retained the Conservative seat held by John Morrison, now Lord Margadale. In all three cases, the Conservative majority was slightly reduced.

we shall be able to carry on for as long as we require in order to get some achievements before we go to the country. Tommy Balogh and the economists seem to think that the pound is really fairly stable, though I must add that James Callaghan met me in the lobby last week and said that even a neutral budget would turn the bankers against us; what they are demanding is a savage budget. As if to confirm his words, on the very next day at the dinner Callaghan was attending for the Government, the Governor of the Bank of England made a speech saying that the only thing that mattered was the defence of the pound, and for that everything, including social services, must be sacrificed. I am pretty sure that in all he said he was reflecting not only the views of the City but the views of the Chancellor of the Exchequer.

The value of going out into the constituencies, as I did today, and talking to our people is that one tests grass-roots morale. Provided we can carry the Chancellor with us and provided Harold can get some strategy and coherence into our policy, there is no reason why we shouldn't get through this very bad patch and settle down to do a decent job. What we need now (and this was the lesson of this regional conference) is to use the Labour Party as our main instrument of communication with the rest of the electorate. That's now George Wigg's main job as the person who is doing the liaison between the Cabinet, Transport House and the constituencies, one of the most important jobs in the whole Government.

Monday, February 8th
The first Cabinet meeting of the week was quite unexpected. When I got to London in the morning I was told it was on at eleven, because a new factor had suddenly turned up in the defence problem. Outside the Cabinet door I met Roy Jenkins, the Minister of Aviation, who said to me, 'I'm afraid I'm not going to please you.' And he quickly informed me what I had half guessed—that Hawker Siddeley had suddenly, after three days' and three nights' unbroken work, come up with a new proposition—a proposal for a hybrid plane which did provide a real alternative to the American plane. I had heard about this Hawker Siddeley proposal when the delegation came to see me in Coventry last Friday evening. In Cabinet the discussion was started by Roy Jenkins, who described the firm's offer, saying that it was almost embarrassingly good and that Hawker Siddeley had now cut down its price, cut down the period of manufacture and put themselves really in a position comparable to that of the Americans. It was only because the delivery date was two years later than the Americans' that on balance he recommended rejection of the firm's offer. Roy was then supported by Denis Healey, who put the issue rather more crudely. He just said that if we wanted the American package we couldn't go back on it and start thinking about making one British plane which would upset the whole deal. It was obvious from the start that Harold Wilson, George Brown, Denis Healey and Jim Callaghan, whatever their disagreements, had made up their minds on the

American package and wanted to be authorized by the Cabinet to turn down this embarrassing Hawker Siddeley offer. There were only two people prepared to ask for it to be seriously considered – Frank Cousins and myself, who, of course, are two local M.P.s for Hawker Siddeley workers. Against us was ranged practically the whole Cabinet. I remember Barbara Castle made a very high-minded speech telling us that we must face the need to cut back the production of British planes. I couldn't help wondering what she would have said if the plane concerned was manufactured in her constituency and her biggest factory was due to be closed down and could have been saved if we had accepted this last-minute offer. Nevertheless, I didn't really fight hard because it was quite clear that all that was being asked for was formal Cabinet consent to a package which had been signed, sealed and delivered well before Christmas.

Thursday, February 11th
Today we had a second exciting Cabinet. I think it was the most dramatic meeting we have had and it revealed for the first time the way this Labour Cabinet splits on a really important socialist issue. The whole discussion centred on the proposals for expanding the housing programme. In these last weeks various Ministers – Kenneth Robinson, for instance, and Anthony Crosland at Education – have come forward pleading for small supplementary estimates. Each Minister has been told that he is only allowed the increased estimates allocated to his Department by the Tory White Paper last year. This means that over the next four years, if we keep the priorities unchanged, Transport would get an increase of 30 per cent, Education 30 per cent and Housing only 10 per cent. The reason is simple. In order to win votes in that last period before the election the Tories were prepared to announce a rapid expansion of higher education, a huge hospital-building programme, a huge road-building programme. The one social service they felt it was popular to cut back was public-sector housing – the construction of rented houses by local authorities, in contrast to the construction of owner-occupier houses by building society mortgagors. As a result of their policy, though council-house production was somewhat bigger than in the previous year, in 1964 it was still far less than it had been under Nye Bevan in 1949.

It was my contention that whereas the other Ministers could fairly be asked to be content with the amount of money in the Tory estimates, this was quite unreasonable in the case of housing where we were pledged to reverse the Tory policy and expand council-house building. I was therefore putting forward at this Cabinet a modest proposal. In 1964 the Tories had budgeted for 135,000 council-house approvals and the actual number of approvals was 144,000. I proposed to raise 144,000 to 156,000 – the figure Harold Wilson had privately suggested to me. I spoke extremely moderately. I was followed by Callaghan who in a long, violent harangue said that we were going to crack up and crash unless the increase in public expenditure could be halted. He could not permit any increase in the housing programme because he was facing a budget situation in which even a neutral budget would fail to win the confidence of the bankers. So we must all wait until July and then housing must be reviewed along with the other claimants. George Brown spoke next. He replied very well indeed, stressing, as I had also stressed, that the whole increase in the housing programme could be put through by expanding our industrialized building. This would not put a strain on our resources but simply employ unused capital resources in which millions had been invested, and production could now take place.

So it was a straight conflict between the Chancellor and the First Secretary and it was very clear indeed that, despite all the efforts to ensure that D.E.A. was the real planning Ministry, the Chancellor of the Exchequer in Britain today, with all the authority of the Treasury behind him, still holds the power. I suspect Jim Callaghan had done a great deal of quiet lobbying. On my side I had George Brown, the Lord Chancellor, Frank Cousins, Fred Peart, and Jim Griffiths, but very little other support. This was partly because the other Ministers were bound to support the Chancellor. Tony Crosland, for example, was obviously afraid that if housing got more money it would be taken from Education. Tom Fraser at Transport felt the same and so did the Minister of Power. All round the table this was the situation. Only Douglas Houghton was deliberately ambiguous, and Ted Short, the Chief Whip, was a little bit on my side because of the huge industrialized-building programme in the North-East. When I counted the votes I saw there was a heavy majority against me.

But then Harold started to speak, saying that he personally favoured increasing the council-housing programme to 150,000 straight away. So there! I had the Prime Minister, the Deputy Prime Minister and the Lord Chancellor on my side, and James Callaghan had most of the rest of the Cabinet on his. However, the Prime Minister can always decide how to count. He told Cabinet that he had added up the votes and found that there was a tie and then he made a powerful speech in favour of the housing programme. I waited in suspense. In this open conflict between Callaghan and Brown was he really siding with Brown against his own Chancellor? At first it looked as though he was, and then suddenly he switched and began to attack us all for not knowing our figures, and he demanded precise statistics about this and about that—figures we couldn't possibly give. Then he asked whether there shouldn't be licensing of private building, whether we shouldn't cut back office building and luxury houses still further in order to release the labour force and the materials necessary to sustain the council-house programme without inflation. Next he said that I must show how it was possible to get these 12,000 extra houses all built by industrialized methods and built in the right places. He ended by demanding two things. First, an inquiry into the control of private building, so as to cut back office building, and, second, proposals for the control of the production of industrialized houses to ensure that they would be produced and built in the development areas. This was a piece of brilliant stalling: next time it comes before Cabinet we shall get the increase I demanded.

Since I was going out to lunch, I ran back to the Ministry to try to get hold of the Dame. I knew we would have to have a meeting at once with Charlie Pannell in order to produce the two papers for the next Cabinet meeting. The Dame was engaged and so I said to George Moseley, 'In that case I will dictate to you a note of what happened in Cabinet and of the things which have to be done, so that directly I am back we can start the meeting at 3.30.' When I got back I found that the Ministry of Works people had already arrived and, to my horror, that a most vivid note describing what had happened in Cabinet, showing the split and recording the votes, had been circulated by George Moseley to Jim MacColl, to Bob Mellish, to four officials in the Department, and was lying before Charlie Pannell. This was all top secret Cabinet material—I really felt white to the gills and weak in the stomach, and I ordered all the copies to be burned. Afterwards I said to George, 'Heavens alive, you must know perfectly well that I wouldn't want all that top secret stuff circulated.' 'Oh,' he said, 'many Ministers previous to you have dictated things much more indiscreet than that and had them circulated.'

This Cabinet meeting was important for two reasons. Firstly, it showed the depth of the Brown/Callaghan split.* Secondly, it showed that the Prime Minister is siding with Brown, cautiously but decisively. Harold Wilson, I think, is aware that his Chancellor is open to precisely the pressures which a socialist Chancellor must resist. On the other hand, he must also be aware that George Brown is unable to gain the respect of the City of London and that his incomes policy is becoming more and more of a personal hard-sell, a virtuoso performance of exhibitionist politics which no one can take very seriously. By sheer personality, by drive, by imagination, George Brown has in an astonishing way managed to challenge the orthodoxy of the Right and I think Harold by and large supports him against Jim.

And a good thing too—because Callaghan is really representing the MacDonaldite attitude to the bankers in 1931. Like MacDonald he is open to moral blackmail by Lord Cromer[1] and the Bank of England, and so are most of my working-class colleagues. One could see at Cabinet how, whether they belong to the Right or to the Left of the Party, they can be terrorized, and how weak and pliable they are in the hands of the City and of the Bank of England when a crisis of this kind blows up and they feel they must put the country before their class. In this struggle I can see that Harold Wilson is having a very difficult time indeed.

* A split, by the way, which was reported in most of the main Sunday papers at the end of the week.
[1] The Governor of the Bank.

There is a lesson also to be drawn from that first and unexpected Cabinet meeting on Monday. Harold has devoted most of his time in the last three months to defence. Naturally, I trust George Wigg and I believe he has done a wonderful job. But this defence package which he has served up—the tremendous decision to buy American and cut back the British aircraft contribution, which he forced through or at least half forced through (everything still depends on whether the TSR2 is dropped or isn't dropped)—has put us temporarily completely in the power of the Americans. I am not so much alarmed about this politically. It is perfectly possible, even in Coventry, to win respect for this policy and even to get votes. But I am alarmed at the feeling that we have put ourselves in the hands of the American politicians—an uneasy feeling which I share with Frank Cousins. Nevertheless, I have to face that in all this Harold Wilson has played the leading role, and that Denis Healey and Roy Jenkins have really only acted as lieutenants. Harold has shown a solid determination to recreate the Anglo–American axis, the special relationship between Britain and America, very much along Bevinite lines. The more I think of this gamble the more I dislike it. We are cutting back the British aircraft industry in order to concentrate on maintaining our imperial position East of Suez. And we are doing that not because we need these bases ourselves but because the Americans can't defend the Far East on their own and need us there.

After we came to power in 1945 I attacked Bevin for not adopting a firm line towards the Americans;[1] and now Britain is not taking the mediating role in Vietnam which we always demanded in Opposition. Once again we are taking the subsidiary role, the pro-American line, and Michael Stewart as our new Foreign Secretary is following it very faithfully indeed. And in all this Harold is deeply, personally committed. His actions show that he didn't have any particular sense of being on the Left, or indeed any particular desire to act as mediator and to get an independent policy between the blocs. He just saw that one must either go into Europe or become a subsidiary of the Americans, and he chose the latter.

There's another comment I can make on looking at these two critical Cabinet meetings together. Despite all the talk just after the Leyton result, we have avoided considering the tactics of survival. For example, Fleet Street is now suggesting that steel nationalization may be postponed. I am pretty sure that no consideration has been given to this at all—and for a very simple reason. Harold Wilson is a curiously methodical, unimaginative, inflexible person. Once we have decided to put a measure in the Queen's Speech, Harold Wilson can't consider any possibility of postponement or delay. He's not implacable—that's too emotional a word—he is just a man of routine, carrying on with the agreed policy.

[1] In an amendment to the King's Speech in November 1946, and in the famous pamphlet *Keep Left*, April 1947, Crossman condemned the Government's excessive devotion to the Anglo–American 'special relationship'.

And that seems very strange because we know that Woodrow Wyatt is going to vote against the Steel Bill and that a couple of other people, including George Strauss[1] and Desmond Donnelly, will at least abstain; and we also know that the Liberals are all committed to vote against it. So, with a couple of appendicitis operations, we might find ourselves defeated on the Second Reading and suddenly forced to go to the country this spring, which would put us into very grave trouble indeed.[2] Yet despite all this we carry on in this routine, plodding way. Despite all the Fleet Street rumours, I believe that the Prime Minister still believes that we should run the Steel Bill and the Rent Bill in double harness and that the same motion should provide the guillotine for both Bills.

Friday, February 12th
Another example of Harold's plodding routine is his attitude to the Land Commission. As a result of the meeting which Harold called at No. 10,[3] Fred Willey did put forward a draft White Paper in which he stated the aims and the procedures of his Bill. It was an extremely polemical document in which he drew a contrast between a real Land Commission with real powers and a watered-down Land Commission with no powers, such as he said I proposed. I was very angry when I saw the draft yesterday, and I suddenly decided to write a document of my own for a change. I sat down at my desk and wrote a ferocious reply, pointing out that the only issues we disagreed on were tactical not political. I rang Tommy Balogh later to ask him whether he had seen the two papers yet. He seemed to be embarrassed and then said he thought the papers were not satisfactory—indeed, they were so bad that a proposed meeting of Ministers shouldn't take place. I said, 'Oh hell, you can't do that.' But today when I went into the office George Moseley said he had had a message from the Cabinet Secretariat—in view of the representations made by Dr Balogh to the Prime Minister, it had been decided that he should come and see me at once because he had said my paper was incompetent. This made me still angrier. I had an extremely busy day ahead of me. I had to cancel a lot of things in the afternoon and then sit there with Balogh and his number two, young Michael Stewart.[4] Thomas is a dear, brilliant man but he knows extremely little about land purchase and town and country planning, which really are very special subjects, and his adjutant Michael Stewart didn't know much more. I had no difficulty in bashing them and I am afraid I accused Thomas of personal disloyalty in writing a minute to Harold denouncing the paper as incompetent. It was disloyal, I said, because

---

[1] M.P. for Lambeth since 1929, a Minister in the 1929–31 Governments, and Minister of Supply 1947–51. He had been chairman of his father's steel company.
[2] After the Leyton defeat, Labour had a majority of three.
[3] See p. 140.
[4] A Treasury economist until he became an (unsuccessful) Labour candidate in 1964 and 1966. He worked with Thomas Balogh in the Cabinet Office 1964–7, and in 1969 because Reader in Political Economy at University College, London.

this kind of thing gets round Whitehall and it had forced me to hit back.

In the evening we had the meeting. It went on for an hour and a half; and on the major issue Fred Willey prevailed, since the Committee saw that he couldn't go back now on the election manifesto. Indeed, as the meeting went on it became clearer and clearer how important the manifesto is to our Cabinet—everybody feels that because the Land Commission was in the manifesto and because it promised to reduce land prices and enable local authorities to get their land cheaper, we must have a Land Commission whatever happens. Of course, there is the difficulty that the Land Commission, as envisaged in the Goodman memorandum, is a sheer nonsense, a non-starter, because it is impossible to create a monopoly purchaser as was planned in the memo. And directly one gives up the monopoly purchaser and introduces betterment tax to deal with a two-tier price system all the advantages of the Land Commission disappear. The truth is that even with the powers Willey wants, the Land Commission will increase prices, not reduce them, and hinder our housing policy, not help it.

I fancy this dawned on some of my colleagues as the argument raged on. More and more people began to see that this confounded Land Commission was an albatross hanging round our necks. We ought to cast it off but we couldn't do so. Under Harold we were carrying on. At the end of the meeting Gerald Gardiner came up to me and said, 'Is it really impossible for a Labour Government ever to drop an idea because it is found to be impractical?' It's a valid point. If the Land Commission were not in the manifesto and we didn't have to legislate, we could simply improve the present planning Acts by the addition of new compulsory-purchase powers for local authorities which would achieve far more than the Land Commission can in lowering prices and assisting urban redevelopment. All this is true, and yet I have no doubt that after this meeting Harold will side with Fred Willey and say, 'We can't go back on it now.' Indeed, I suspect he is perfectly prepared to fight the next election on a repetition of our last Land Commission pledge and to push through Parliament a Bill which repeats all the mistakes that have now been demonstrably proved to be part of this confounded plan.

Sunday, February 14th
I spent yesterday in Cumbernauld New Town, which is the creation of Hugh Wilson, the architect we've chosen to reorganize the architectural side of our Department and build up our work on urban renewal. Cumbernauld is built on the top of a long, high, bleak ridge. It's a very grey Scottish town, which has settled into the ridge with an enormous lot of roads and a fascinating variety of modern houses. Up-and-down houses, vertical houses, horizontal houses, and everything, including the churches, fitting into the style, everything done in a tremendously austere, exhilarating, uncomfortable style. I thought Atticus this morning in the *Sunday Times* was extremely apposite when he pointed out that this was the kind of thing which Dame Evelyn and

I are excited about, in contrast to the cosy garden suburb atmosphere of Stevenage or Harlow or Basildon. In the evening I addressed a big rally for Tam, with 500 elderly ladies and gentlemen crowded into a hall and my speech spatchcocked in between songs and dances. Looking down from the platform on this audience, I realized it was exactly the audience I addressed in Coventry when I first went there as candidate in 1936. But under the pressure of affluence Coventry Labour has changed whereas Scottish Labour remains much the same as thirty years ago – this is one of the reasons why it is so much more reliable and easier to manage than Labour Parties in the South. Sophistication has undermined the solidarity and the simplicity of Midland Labour Parties, whereas in Scotland one can make the old traditional speeches and the audiences are content to sing the old traditional songs which Coventry would laugh out of court.

I got back from Scotland to Prescote to find Anne and Patrick both in bed with flu. A pity, since it's a lovely day with the sunshine and the moonshine and the river just dribbling along at the bottom of its banks because of the remarkable dryness of the winter. We haven't had nearly enough rain but still Prescote Manor Farm is doing fine. Physically, a day at Prescote makes me feel wonderful and yet there is this sense of economic crisis which hangs round me there as well. A sense of dissatisfaction. Everybody tearing his hair, doctors, farmers, all complaining, a sense of disturbance. It makes me have an uneasy feeling. For a long time I felt that being in Government wasn't real, or that I was in an unreal Government. Now I find the Government real, but appreciate that it isn't getting a grip, that we haven't grappled with our problems – and I can't help feeling that Frank Cousins may well be right when he said to me the other day, 'My dear Dick, I don't think this Government is going to last long, frankly, do you?'

Wednesday, February 17th
A visit to Stevenage. On the way we took a look at Welwyn which, with Letchworth, was the first of our garden suburbs, built at the same time as Hampstead Garden Suburb. And then Welwyn was enlarged into a New Town in 1947 and 1948, and became part of the first generation of olde-worlde red-brick New Towns. I find it charming and I am sure it is a delightful place to live in. The Dame, of course, is contemptuous. She loves Cumbernauld. I also like Cumbernauld as architecture, but I see that the vast majority of British people would probably prefer to live in Welwyn with its red bricks and its North Oxford lilac.

The contrast with Stevenage is astonishing. Stevenage is modern, full of glass and chromium. In the centre, a shopping precinct about as good or about as bad as that at Coventry, about as undistinguished in its architecture and as excellent in its planning. However, as we motored away from the centre on a lovely, cold, sunshiny February day and saw the neighbourhood units and the terracing of the housing I felt no doubt that the modern style of house-building in our New Towns is something original and creative. Then we went across the industrial area to the proposed new area on the other side of the motorway and the railway, and I saw what was wrong. The fact is, you *can't* double the size of Stevenage. What you could do is to put another New Town on the other side of the railway tracks, with another shopping centre of its own. Then we crossed the Chilterns, driving about eight or nine miles through lovely remote country like my old Town End at Radnage,[1] until we got to Luton where I wanted to look at the aerodrome because we were having a dispute about planning permissions. An astonishing phenomenon! The aerodrome, jammed right up against Luton on the one side and the Vauxhall works on the other, is an outrage, and it is even more outrageous that one should propose to expand it. But shall I be able to use my authority as Minister to stop the extension of the runway? That's what we weren't sure about. It was a splendid, enjoyable morning.

In the afternoon I went across to the House of Commons for a secret meeting with the Labour members of the A.M.C., the Association of Municipal Corporations. I found myself meeting some fifty to sixty people who were tremendously keen on seeing their Minister. This was a Transport House idea which certainly worked. It was all the more important because the Labour local authorities are having an extremely rough time under our Government. They are bearing the brunt of the higher interest rates and having a difficult time even with their staff. We need their loyalty.

In the evening I had to sit on the front bench for a debate on the Northampton Boundary Regulations. It's a long story but quite amusing. Of course, I am responsible for issuing the decision on the boundary extensions and I have taken the greatest care to see that politically they were acceptable to the Labour group on the town council and to the Labour Member, Reggie Paget. So I was surprised to be rung up by Paget, who asserted in a fury that we had approved a Conservative plan for making a built-in Conservative majority on the Council. Alas, he was right. The Inspector had reported in favour of the Conservative plan for ward reorganization on the ground that it had no political implications, and Frank Soskice had accepted it without question. Then under pressure from Reggie Paget, he changed his mind and appointed another public inquiry. Of course there was trouble and the Tories were trying to exploit it in this debate.[2] Hobson, the Shadow Attorney-General, made a very clever speech and I soon saw that his aim was to suggest that there lurked behind Soskice that sinister political boss, the Minister of Housing. I was the man they were really hoping to get at. They couldn't because I quite literally had nothing to do with it. Soskice had a rough time; but he will get away with it because everybody will say 'He's an honest man. *

---

* The leading article in *The Times* the next day showed that if I had been Minister in charge I would have been for the high jump.
[1] Where Crossman and his second wife, Zita, had a cottage.
[2] A vote of censure on the Home Secretary followed on February 25th. See p. 170.

Thursday, February 18th

Another confused Cabinet meeting, this time on the draft Statement James Callaghan put forward, in which he hoped to explain away the enormous increase in this year's Estimates. The Cabinet meeting took place against a background of news stories in all the papers about the great contest between the Chancellor and the First Secretary on the character of this year's Budget. I must say I have been wondering what is the duty of a Cabinet Minister who doesn't belong to the inner circle and yet must see and hear the sort of stories I had been reading in the papers this week. Should one insist on discussing those stories in Cabinet? Should one put them down on the agenda? The thought came into my mind very strongly when I read Lord Cromer's astonishing speech on Tuesday. Indeed, I was so outraged by it that for the first time in my Ministerial life I wrote a minute to the Prime Minister asking him what steps would be taken to shut up this one-man May Committee.[1] I sent this minute off, after talking to George Wigg and Tommy Balogh so as to make sure it impacted on No. 10. And sure enough on three occasions when we were walking through the division lobby the Prime Minister came up to me and said, 'I've got your minute, and I am dealing with Lord Cromer in my weekend speech.' And on Wednesday I found that there was a longish passage by David Wood in the centre of *The Times* describing how senior Cabinet Ministers were protesting about Lord Cromer and using the actual substance of my minute, which had been obviously shown to him in an off-the-record briefing.

This is typical of Harold's handling of politics. He still thinks he can settle problems just by talking to the press. As for the press reports of the Brown/Callaghan struggle, I suspect they are chiefly supplied by George, who now seems to be relapsing into his old habits. There's no one more talented in the whole Cabinet or nicer or more loyal or more basically constructive. Frank Cousins and I feel ourselves on his side. But he is schizophrenic, and once again the wear and tear is showing in him after the first four months. Leaks and drink will in the end get him down; and we shouldn't reckon on our First Secretary being there overlong unless he mends his ways. Whether Callaghan has talked to the press I rather doubt. He has become a very staid, prim, Bank of England type, almost a parody of the Labour man taken over by his officials – by the Treasury officials in this case. I should say that most of the pro-Callaghan stories are leaked through the Treasury Press Office.

Well, that's the background to today's Cabinet discussion. The Statement was drafted in such a way as to make clear that its main aim was to curb public-sector expenditure. It showed that despite all our efforts the Estimates had gone up by 6 per cent, which of course was substantially less than the 9 per cent the Tories had planned. It also included a firm commitment to

---

[1] In 1931 the National Government set up the May Committee to propose cuts in public expenditure. The storm that followed its recommendations, which included a reduction in unemployment benefit, led to MacDonald's resignation.

permit an increase of only 23 per cent in public expenditure during the next four years, an annual average increase of 4 per cent. This was written into the Statement as a Cabinet objective.

Frank Cousins started the opposition by expressing his dislike of the Statement in rather vague terms. I pointed out that if the Chancellor specified a maximum rate of development for the public sector without displaying an equally iron determination to control the expansion of the private sector, we should have an economy in which wildly extravagant and unnecessary growth of the private sector went unrestrained and in which, whenever we were in trouble, we only cut back the public sector. In fact, we should be making the same disastrous mistake the Tories have been making for the last ten years. Then Tony Crosland said that we shouldn't commit ourselves to a maximum rate of expenditure in the public sector, and the real criticism started. Round the Cabinet table it went and the Statement was torn to pieces paragraph by paragraph. Even Tom Fraser said it was unfortunate that the principles enshrined by our predecessors in the Tory Estimates were those we socialists were maintaining in office. The truth is that Callaghan just took over the Treasury policy of the Tory Estimates and is trying to hold expenditure down within this Conservative framework. He had fought a stalling battle the previous week on my public-housing programme. I counter-attacked this Thursday, slashing his Statement to smithereens, so that finally he got up sulkily and said, 'Well, since every paragraph has been found fault with, I hardly think it's worth having a Statement.' However, he apparently got down to work later on. When I went to see George Brown about industrialized building he told me that none of the officials were being consulted about the redraft—Callaghan was doing it himself. George went on to tell me that the figures for the Budget had now been agreed. 'God forbid that you should tell me what the figures are, George,' I said before he could pour them all out, but I did get the impression that the crisis between him and Callaghan had been resolved, and this is just possible.

In the afternoon I went into the House to hear Frank Cousins making his maiden speech.[1] I found he was showing, much more than Ernie Bevin ever showed, a sense of the House—a kind of conversationalism and a natural modesty. He seemed to me to be doing extremely well.

Back in the Department I had a difficult meeting with the Dame. She brought eight officials to try to persuade me to accept a last-minute amendment to the Rent Bill. The Bill, of course, restores security of tenure. The suggested clause says that tenants could still be evicted if a private developer needed the land for redevelopment—even if he was unable to provide alternative accommodation. I had told her long before that this was quite impossible but she insisted on arguing it out, all because of her great friend the builder Norman Wates, who I know has been putting up to her the idea that private development will be scotched by our Rent Bill. Of course, it's

[1] On the Second Reading of the Development of Inventions Bill.

perfectly true that the private developer may find it impossible to develop a valuable piece of land because a couple of old people are awkward and use their powers under our Bill. But if we are to make this change, it can only be in a Bill dealing comprehensively with redevelopment; and this is what I told her. She said curtly, 'Well, we didn't expect you to change, but we thought it worth a try.' So I said, 'All right, now you've tried that on me, I'll try my favourite idea on you. Let's deal with caravans.' This is something I have long wanted to get into the Rent Bill: the 100,000 people who live in caravans can be evicted by their landlord because they are not strictly tenants, but that is a problem that our Bill ought to deal with. Of course, I was right; but she was as sticky about the caravanners as I was sticky about redevelopment and the whole atmosphere of the meeting turned sterile, and she went away sulky and angry as a result.

Friday, February 19th
I was very pleased to find that the London evening papers today were carrying banner headlines to my 'Open Letter to Londoners' and giving the full text. In it I told people exactly what they should do if they were threatened with eviction or had a friend in that position. This is a new idea I was trying out not only in London but in Manchester, Birmingham, Liverpool and Glasgow. There had been not unjustified complaints that we hadn't had nearly enough publicity for the Prevention from Eviction Act. Peter Brown originally proposed that we should spend £10,000 on an advertising campaign. I said that an open letter would be printed without our having to waste money on the advertising space.*

I spent the whole day in my office. The Cabinet paper on housing was finally agreed between the D.E.A., the Ministry of Works and ourselves. I also completely recast my Statement on Chorley New Town, which had to be agreed with the D.E.A., the Board of Trade, Scotland, Wales and the Ministry of Works. I also slogged away at my own special problem – how to implement the pledge we made to help borrowers. I saw the first draft of the paper and sent it to a brains trust which includes Donald MacDougall at the D.E.A., Neild at the Treasury and Tommy Balogh. I hope the technique will succeed again. Finally, I approved my local government boundary Order for Bath and Bristol, the first really controversial decision I have taken.[1]

I managed to catch the 5.10 train home where I found the family recovering from the flu which put Patrick and Anne into bed last Sunday. I was now the one who was voiceless; I found myself hardly able to speak a word by the

* Sure enough, this was a tremendous success and at our Coventry dinner the next evening Bob Chamberlain, the regional organizer, said that at his Birmingham Regional Rally the day before this letter had been the talk of the rally and was said to be the best thing the Labour Government had done. Of course, the lesson is that I should take far more trouble about the publicity in the Department.
[1] Crossman appears to have forgotten about Hartley. See p. 32.

time I got back to Prescote, although I had to face the Coventry East constituency annual dinner on Saturday evening.

Sunday, February 21st
Frank Cousins and Nancy, his wife, duly arrived, and although the dinner itself was a bit frigid and formal the turn-out was wonderful and they all seemed very pleased to have two leading Cabinet Ministers there. We both made speeches. George Wigg will have been pleased that Crossman and Cousins were stiffening people for the tough time ahead and telling the aircraft workers to be sensible. Of course, they have become, as I feared they would, a major problem for me in Coventry East.[1] There is now no doubt that the transport plane Armstrong-Whitworth are making will be cancelled and the factory at Baginton closed completely as soon as possible. On Saturday night both Frank and I talked very straight on the problems of defence. We said we had always stood for cuts in defence and that we had to carry these cuts through. We knew that Coventry would accept this provided we looked after redundancy properly.

I have had quite a lot of talk with Frank. He and his wife are enormously nice people. We have agreed to have dinner tonight with Michael Foot and Barbara Castle — a little left-wing confab, the first we have ever had. We both think the time has now come to form something like a left-wing alliance, because there is no doubt that James Callaghan lobbies a great deal to achieve his aims and we shall have to do the same. This weekend I have no less than four red boxes to work through; one of them contains the redraft of the Statement the Chancellor is due to make. It still includes the most dangerously firm commitment to cut back the speed of development in the public sector. True, it has had written into it a section about the control of the private sector but the phrases used are very inconsistent. On this I really rather agree with the Accountant-General in my Ministry, Crocker. He is an able Tory and he is right when he says 'Qui s'excuse s'accuse' and tells me that the whole Statement in its latest form will neither impress the bankers nor impress the home front. I am looking forward with keen anticipation to what happens in Cabinet tomorrow. I shall be in a weak situation with George Brown and Douglas Jay away at the EFTA meeting[2] and with the Prime Minister saying that they had agreed the draft before they left the country. However, I shall have a go.

Monday, February 22nd
There I was yesterday, actually believing that the dinner with Michael Foot and Barbara Castle might produce a left-wing conspiracy in the Cabinet.

---

[1] It had become clear that all three aircraft (HS-681; P-1154; TSR2) would be cancelled. The leaders of the aircraft industry had already discussed their problems with the P.M. at Chequers on January 15th.
[2] A crisis meeting in Geneva.

Heavens alive! When Frank and I got there last night at six o'clock we began an excellent talk with Michael, but as soon as Barbara came life was impossible. She's a good sort and I am fond of her. She really does have certain left-wing views and she has done a fine job in her Ministry, bringing in a whole number of solid socialists (including Chris Hall, Jennie's husband, who now, thank heavens, has been got off the staff of the *Sun* and has become one of Barbara's press officers at the Ministry). All that she has done jolly well. But heavens alive! she has become difficult in the process. She spent that evening lecturing us on our responsibilities. Before the evening was out it was perfectly clear that there was no question of a left-wing alliance between us.

I was so sick and disappointed by her attitude that I went home early and rang up George Wigg and poured out my heart to him. I told him I found life unbearable and the situation in the Cabinet hopeless. There I was, a senior departmental Minister, with great decisions being taken over my head. What was the good of my trying to do anything about them? George berated me as he always does and told me to pull myself together. Then he asked me what in particular I was beefing about. I said, 'Well, for example, the first thing we have tomorrow morning is a Cabinet meeting to discuss the Chancellor's Statement. I have seen the revision and it is almost as bad as the first draft. My stuff has been spatchcocked in, but the central weakness is still there—the theory that one should cut the public sector and leave the private sector untouched.' George's reply was to ask why the hell I didn't redraft it myself. I said that was impossible and then I suddenly thought, well, why shouldn't I? This morning I rushed into the office and did a redraft of the vital passage, got six copies made and went round with them just in time for Cabinet at 10.30. As I was going in through the door the Private Secretary, Mitchell, took me aside and said that the P.M. would like me to have lunch with him in the Members' dining-room. I knew at once that George Wigg had told Harold of my bleating and that Harold had thought, 'Well, if Dick feels out of it I will invite him to lunch to give him the feeling that he is in.'

Cabinet went pretty well. It started with an item about the surcharge that we had imposed as one of our first actions on imported goods, which has caused the most appalling trouble with the EFTA countries.[1] Cabinet was now being asked for formal approval to a 5-per-cent reduction in the surcharge at the very moment George Brown and Douglas Jay were announcing it at the EFTA conference! The only exciting part of this item was the lecture the Prime Minister gave us on the leaks which have been coming out of Cabinet recently, one of which anticipated the announcement on the surcharge. I chose my moment and went in to bat. I said I was heartily sick of leaks and I wanted to know how it was that the battle between Callaghan and Brown had been reported round by round in the papers. The reply I got from

[1] The 15 per cent surcharge announced in the Statement on October 26th, 1964, was reduced to 10 per cent on April 27th, 1965, and finally abolished on November 30th, 1966.

the P.M. was that there wasn't a word of truth in the story. So far, nothing had been discussed by Ministers. The officials were still at work and he could say quite sincerely, with the support of the Chancellor, that the whole thing was the invention of the journalists.

Then Harold Wilson raised the issue of Anthony Howard. He has just been appointed by the *Sunday Times* to be the first Whitehall correspondent in history, looking into the secrets of the Civil Service rather than leaking the secrets of the politicians. His first article had been an analysis of the relationship between the D.E.A. and the Treasury.[1] The P.M. said this was outrageous and he was going to accept the challenge of the *Sunday Times*. In order to kill Tony Howard's new job he forbade any of us to speak to him.

Then we turned to the Chancellor's Statement. Pretty soon I waded in and threw one copy of my amendments to the Chancellor, whom I had already seen before the meeting, and another to the P.M. While I was talking the P.M. had my draft duplicated and gave each member of the Cabinet a copy. To my amazement it formed the basis of the amended version.

I went back to the office to tell my people what had happened and then walked over to the House for lunch with Harold. I found him walking up and down the corridor outside the Members' dining-room. He started off on leaks and said that they had probably come from George Brown and that in his view the First Secretary had lapsed right back to his old ways, and that quite likely we would have a leak and a Budget inquiry and the end of George Brown. He spoke about this with extraordinary frankness, and he also referred to Douglas Jay's misbehaviour in leaking the story of the surcharge. Then he turned to my affairs and repeated to me a remark that he had made in Cabinet about the need to stop demolition of houses. He asked me to check very carefully whether a house could be demolished without planning authorization. I knew vaguely that whereas you have to have planning permission to put up a building, you don't have to have it in order to pull one down unless it is a listed building. Harold made a tremendous point of this demolition problem and said that if we were going to obtain the increased housing allocation, we must stop the demolishing of habitable houses and the building of luxury houses. He then turned to legislation and I told him we were on time with the Rent Bill but it might well be that we should find the Tories refusing to vote against us on the Second Reading. Immediately he said, 'Draft a White Paper which forces them to vote against you by describing the iniquities of the Tory Rent Act and the need to repeal it.' That's typical of Harold's tactical ingenuity; and I am immediately taking it up in the Ministry. He also told me that the Steel Bill wouldn't be ready and that I should have to run my Bill separately. Finally, we discussed the general situation and he gave me the very clear impression that he doesn't want to go to the country now and that we must win time—possibly until May of next

[1] He wrote one more piece, on the Ministry of Technology and the Ministry of Aviation, before abandoning the attempt.

year. I got a tremendous impression (he was talking very intimately) that he was treating Frank Cousins and me very much as his allies in the line he was taking.

Straight after lunch I went across to Caxton House and had two hours with my urban planning group, the people who are doing the research into urban renewal and comprehensive development. I listened to them and then pushed them very hard on the idea of producing a pamphlet of instructions to local authorities on how they should handle private developers. I am keen on this because of something Lord Thomson of the *Sunday Times* told me at lunch last week. He said that the seamiest thing in British life today is the money being made through planning permissions and by private developers buying up and selling land. This is something which we in the Ministry must cope with.

After that I went home and we had the Wedgwood Benns to supper. Tony and I compared notes while Carol and Anne compared notes. Tony was as frustrated as ever in the Post Office, and he finds the difficulties in that Department even greater than those I confront in mine. He told me what he thought should be done about the B.B.C. He feels the licence can't be increased from £4 to £6 at the moment without upsetting people. Instead, we ought to try to raise the money by giving the B.B.C. the right to raise some of its revenue by advertising on television.[1] He is also anxious that the B.B.C. should run radio with advertising as a main source of income. I had to tell him frankly that I thought these ideas would be unacceptable to Cabinet, who had simple views about the B.B.C. as a public service radio and wouldn't see his proposals as progressive. And I didn't see our colleagues wanting to introduce legislation to ban Radio Caroline—the pirate radio station— unless and until the B.B.C. produces as good pop music itself.[2] It was a pretty good evening—I knew Wedgy Benn was enjoying it because he is one of the few politicians who likes taking punishment.

Tuesday, February 23rd

In the morning I was mainly concerned with the situation in Smethwick. Some time ago the Smethwick Council announced that it wanted to buy houses in Marshall Street in order to stop the street being blighted by coloured immigrants taking over the houses one by one. I received a delegation from the council, accompanied by their new M.P., Peter Griffiths, and gave them a lecture. I thought I had made some impression upon them. However, in yesterday's papers I learned that they had now decided to buy

---

[1] The B.B.C. had a large deficit, unlike the Independent Television service, which was financed by advertising.

[2] In March 1964 this pirate station began transmitting pop music and advertisements from a ship anchored outside territorial waters off the Essex coast. The Postmaster-General was dissuaded from intervening, and the station proved so popular that by the summer a second Caroline was anchored off the Isle of Man; and the Egg Marketing Board bought air-time.

the houses and would ask me for loan sanction. It seemed to me essential that we should turn down the loan sanction, but that we should let it be seen to be part of a positive policy; so I sent a memo to the Prime Minister to this effect.

While I was getting this memorandum into its final shape, I had my new Private Secretary with me. I'd only just got used to George Moseley, who has now been transferred, and Ponsford when this one was wished on me by the Dame. What I really would have liked was to keep George and get rid of Ponsford, a gifted but difficult, complex young man. Indeed, I had asked the Dame to have him moved and was horrified to find that she had sent for him and told him I found him unbearable. He had come back to me and pleaded for his life and ever since then he has been my faithful swain. Now, having had the new man for a week, I know I would have been content to keep Moseley and Ponsford unchanged.

In the afternoon we had another meeting of the Cabinet Committee on the Land Commission and made a little progress. Indeed, we got far enough to let the officials formulate a paper for the Cabinet this week. Some of my colleagues are beginning to realize that, whatever its merits, the Land Commission isn't going to be effective for the first three or four years after the Act has been passed. Indeed, if only we didn't have to legislate for the Land Commission, I could have had a new planning Bill which would have enabled us to stop the racketeering in land prices far more effectively than the Land Commission could possibly do — at least in the short run.

Back in the Ministry I had called a meeting on rating. I had noticed in the papers this morning that the Allen Committee, set up by my predecessor, was publishing its report on Thursday in which the incidence and impact on households of the rates were analysed for the first time. This gave me an idea for a big speech on Friday night. Why shouldn't I make an attack on the rating system, and get across to the ratepayer that rates at their present level are a legacy we have inherited from the Tories and that we can't be blamed for them? So I set to work to try and get the facts together and made up my mind that I would make the speech at Huyton — I had suggested to Harold over lunch that I should join him at the Annual Civic Dinner of the Huyton Labour Party, and it seemed an ideal place to make the speech. Of course, I found as I always do in the Department that if I want a speech with strong political content the officials refuse to help. Crocker, the Accountant-General, is an extremely able, alert man and he quickly submitted a draft with absolutely none of the information I had instructed him to give. Not one of the points raised in my written directive was answered.

Wednesday, February 24th

A battle royal with the Department. I started with a quiet talk to James Margach of the *Sunday Times* about my rating speech. Then I got Crocker in and battled away to try to get out of him the facts that would enable me to show the wickedness of the Tory legacy of rating. He held his ground, I held mine. It's the kind of row which I don't resent a bit. I now know that there isn't anybody in the Department who will help me on this kind of issue without forcing me to go through this difficult and rather rude process. I had to say to Crocker, 'Look, I know what your politics are, and I know you disagree with me, I don't want to waste time arguing with you. I want you simply to tell me whether the facts in my draft are right, not whether the opinions are right.' By this treatment I managed to extract from him, as from others, the teeth I need for fighting the enemy. So that's how I spent the day till lunchtime. And then it was time for me to go down to the Commons to make my Statement on the New Town in Lancashire.[1]

Thursday, February 25th
This was the day of the big Cabinet meeting on my public-housing programme. Harold and I agreed later that it was far the most important and far the best Cabinet of this Labour Government. At long last we did take decisions; and for the first time Harold Wilson came out as a leader – a man who wasn't just content to sit back in the chair and see what happened but was prepared to make sure that things happened the way he wanted.

The meeting had been preceded by a lot of jockeying. My officials and Charlie Pannell's had got together to produce a joint paper on how we could get all the extra 12,000 houses built in development areas by using industrialized building methods. Meanwhile, Pannell himself had got another paper done on physical controls – an insane paper, by the way, simply proving that they were totally impossible; and my Department had done a brief, cautious note on financial controls, saying they were possible but very difficult and if they were introduced it must be in conjunction with differential interest rates, on which I would produce a paper in a few weeks. At Cabinet there wasn't a very good turn-out. Gerald Gardiner and Arthur Bottomley were away in Rhodesia. Fred Peart wasn't there. Barbara Castle wasn't there. Only two-thirds of Cabinet were present when I started the debate. I had been very carefully briefed by the Department and I realized that the main point I must make was that we were now building fewer council houses than were constructed under the last Labour Government. Whereas the private sector had increased output considerably, the public sector had sagged back, despite the desperate need of cheap houses to rent.

So we were talking about a vital social service – the only social service the Tories had ruthlessly cut back. I was asking for a small increase in 1965 to enable the local authorities to make this the first year of their four-year plan. If we denied them any increase this year, I pointed out, we should lose a whole year of house production. I was also able to say that there would be no increased cost to the Chancellor in the budget, and that all the new houses

---

[1] The Statement explained that geological subsidence made it impossible to develop a large part of the Risley area. Chorley would therefore be the site for the New Town, and the supporters of Risley would be placated with a development project.
6*

would be put up by industrialized system-building which wouldn't put an undue strain on the construction industry. I was briefly supported by Charlie Pannell. Then the Chancellor made exactly the same speech as before. He disregarded my whole case and said we must have a general review in July and that we couldn't afford to let any Ministry increase its estimates before that review. If the Minister of Housing had his way, how would the Chancellor manage to deal with all the other claims that would be put forward?

I was nervous that Harold would let the debate go on, but at this point he jumped right in and laid down his own line. He said that it was quite impossible for a Labour Government to let public housing continue to run at a lower level than that in 1950. We simply had to jack it up even if it meant cutting back luxury building and using physical controls. And suddenly he said that he had found the solution to the problem in Clause 8 of Charlie Pannell's paper. Poor Charlie did not know whether he was standing on his head or his heels. He wriggled, because he is a passionate opponent of physical controls and here was his paper being taken by the Prime Minister as the text on which to preach a sermon to the effect that by imposing physical controls on the private sector we could permit ourselves a moderate increase of production in the public sector. Harold's speech completely cut away the ground under the opposition. Nobody spoke against us. The First Secretary helped us along, and within an hour the issue had been settled. Afterwards Harold said to me, 'Well, aren't you pleased? That's the best meeting we've had. I enjoyed it.' There was no doubt I had enjoyed it. My whole attitude to life which had been so dejected on the Sunday was improved.

In the afternoon I had to sit on the front bench beside Frank Soskice while he was censured for his conduct with regard to the 'warding' of the County Borough of Northampton. Frank, being a man of exquisite liberal conscience, had havered and hovered. In my view, once you have accepted a report you can't go back on it. If I had been him, I would have said to Reg Paget 'Sorry I made that balls-up, old boy. But that's it. I can't do anything about it now, because if I went back on it I would put myself in an intolerable position.' Peter Thorneycroft[1] made a lengthy, formidable attack. When he rose to reply, Soskice said quite simply that no political pressure had been used on him and that he conscientiously felt there was time for a second inquiry. This is something I couldn't possibly have done but—because he is dearly loved as well as good and honest—he got away with it.[2] He was followed by Michael Foot, to whom I had told the story on Sunday night at dinner. He now got up and said that what was wrong with the debate was that the vote of censure was moved against the wrong Minister. It was as though St George had chased the virgin maiden tied to the stake instead of chasing

---

[1] A Conservative M.P. since 1938, since 1945 for Monmouth. A former Chancellor of the Exchequer (1957–8), Minister of Aviation (1960–2) and Minister of Defence (1962–4), he became a life peer in 1967.

[2] As Crossman had predicted on February 17th Soskice survived, by 299 votes to 291.

the dragon. One can't conceive, said Michael, of our Home Secretary behaving like a Tammany boss. But the Minister of Housing—now he's a very different kettle of fish. There was enormous laughter at this—in which I joined. The whole House thought it funny because it was true. Of course, Frank Soskice is completely ineffective. If I had been found out doing that kind of thing I would have been forced to resign—and that's that. Something to reflect on.

After the debate I had dinner at University College London with Richard Llewelyn-Davies, who wanted me to meet Margaret Mead;[1] and then I got my things together, got into my sleeper and was off to Preston for two days. This Lancashire official visit had become beautifully timely as a result of the announcement in the House on the North Lancashire town which I had made on Wednesday. That is the kind of good public relations for which Peter Brown is so often responsible.

Friday, February 26th
I arrived in Preston to find all the Lancashire people delighted with the news about the New Town, and I spent the morning in a bus with them, taking a look at that dreary Lancashire plain, quite nice country but appallingly built over and its villages totally undistinguished. I found I had designated the New Town in an area with at one end a really ghastly town called Chorley and at the other end a slightly less ghastly expanded village called Leyland, home of the big Government tank factory, where Leyland now make buses. I came back in time for a long, arduous press conference, a long, filmed television interview and a very long lunch with the Lancashire County Council. After lunch we plunged into complex boundary problems which we discussed in private. When I came out, there were the evening newspapers with BOMBER CROSSMAN WITH HIS BOMBSHELL ANNOUNCEMENT right across the front page. An hour or two later there was an eight-minute television interview, at the same time as the Prime Minister was given a couple of minutes for his ceremony of receiving a degree at Liverpool University. Once again good old Peter Brown had scored. After that I was rushed down to Harold's constituency dinner at Huyton.

I must explain that he used to have the Ormskirk constituency, which is mainly agricultural, with Huyton at the southern end of it, a Liverpool overspill area which just gave him a small majority. Then the overspill was extended and Kirkby was added to Huyton so that Harold's constituency changed from a marginal seat into a 20,000 majority, with a 60-per-cent Catholic vote and, I think, some of the roughest and most criminal Liverpool elements. It was at this dinner that I had decided to deliver my big onslaught on Tory rating. When the car drew up at Huyton, I said to Peter Brown's number two, who was still with me, that I would be obliged if he would hand

---

[1] Professor of Anthropology at Columbia University. Her best-known book is perhaps *Coming of Age in Samoa* (London: Jonathan Cape, 1929).

over copies of the press release to the journalists who were waiting for it. To my amazement he said he couldn't possibly do this since I was making a political speech and it was a Transport House press release. This of course was a continuation of the row I had had in the Ministry with Crocker! Civil servants won't touch anything they think political.

I had been a bit surprised when Harold said I ought to wear a dinner-jacket but, by jove, when I got into the primary-school hall where the dinner was being held I found I was jostling shoulders with the Catholic Archbishop of Liverpool, the Anglican Bishop, who sat next to me, some twenty-five mayors and their wives, clerks of the county, all bigwigs with chains of office clattering round them and all in dinner-jackets. It was a tremendous Arnold Bennett occasion and a great evening. Harold couldn't have been more pally with me, talking to me right across the chairman of the U.D.C. and his wife, both aged over sixty-five and fairly deaf and infirm. Heavens, the dinner went on for ages, and the speeches, including my long speech, went on until 11.15. Then afterwards he said he would drive me back in his car to the Adelphi Hotel in Liverpool.

Before we got back there, however, there was a curious interlude. We had been asked for a quick farewell drink in the council rooms. I said, 'For God's sake, Harold, let's get back to the Adelphi.' But Harold won't ever refuse anything; so we were whirled off in his car to the council rooms to find ourselves outside with no key, far in advance of the rest of the guests and their crowd of cars. Finally, we were got into the building and found upstairs a lot of empty glasses and no bottle-opener. A quarter of an hour later one councillor turned up and twenty-five minutes later a bottle-opener was found. Finally five minutes after they had given Harold a drink, I persuaded him it was time to leave. During this long process the room had gradually filled with members of the Huyton Urban District Council and their wives, some twelve or fourteen people. Nobody noticed the peremptory way the P.M. had been handled—indeed these Lancashire people were obviously determined to show that they were on a level with their M.P. It was an interesting example of a Northern egalitarianism and bloody-mindedness which I found almost intolerable but which Harold took very quietly with his usual iron self-control. Finally, we got to the Adelphi where we had quite a gossip. He was flatteringly indiscreet and gave me the feeling of how important I was to him, and how close a personal friend, and he left me going to my suite in the Adelphi basking in the warmth of his favour while he and Mary caught the sleeper to Chequers, where he was due to spend all Saturday discussing the budget.

Saturday, February 27th

I spent this morning at Skelmersdale New Town, just outside Liverpool. In most New Towns the relations between the U.D.C. and the corporation are appalling. Here from the start the corporation has made tremendous efforts.

I was very impressed and greatly looking forward to seeing the first new houses they had built since I knew Hugh Wilson, our architect at the Ministry, had done them.[1] Alas, they seemed ghastly to me, like back ends of factories, and they didn't recommend themselves any more when the architect said, 'I tried to get the strength and the sheer character of Lancashire.' However, the area of the New Town is lovely and it has got a real chance. We went up to the top of a hill from where we had a magnificent view right over to Ormskirk and Wigan and Liverpool, and the other way to the moors. Lovely in dappled sunshine.

Lunch afterwards with the corporation; and kindly enough they sent me down the M6 in the chairman's Daimler and I managed to get home by 5.30 and have a romp with the children before they went to bed. Thomas turned up at Prescote about ten o'clock that night, straight from Chequers. He was full of Harold's brilliant success in reversing Callaghan's views and persuading him to accept the public-housing programme.

Another problem was especially worrying in Midlands constituencies, of which Richard Crossman's was one. Immigration from the West Indies, India and Pakistan had increased considerably, despite the existing controls of the 1961 Commonwealth Immigration Act (renewed by Labour in November 1964). Quite apart from the 'racialist' resentment shown by some native residents towards the immigrants, the numbers also exacerbated the difficulties that central and local authorities already found in supplying schools, housing and hospitals at a time of economic squeeze. On March 9th, Maurice Foley, Under-Secretary of the D.E.A., had been given responsibility for co-ordinating official action to improve the situation of the immigrant communities. And in late March the Prime Minister had announced the appointment of Lord Mountbatten to head a mission to Commonwealth countries to re-examine the present immigration arrangements. Back-benchers from both sides of the House, led by Norman St John-Stevas and Roy Hattersley, argued against the restrictionist policies for which both front benches reluctantly saw the need. To some extent the liberals were successful and in April the Home Secretary, Sir Frank Soskice, introduced a Race Relations Bill, making discrimination a criminal offence. But there was strong opposition from the Conservatives and at the end of May, these provisions were replaced by a system of conciliatory boards to deal with complaints. Meanwhile, the Government were beginning to feel that at some point they must, unwillingly, impose further controls on entry from the Commonwealth.

Monday, March 1st
I started reading the Milner Holland Report at Prescote on Sunday.[2] At our

---

[1] And architect of Cumbernauld, which Crossman regarded as more of a success.

[2] On housing in Greater London. It showed that 190,000 London households were in urgent need of rehousing, and an additional 61,000 single persons lacked proper accommodation.

first meeting I hadn't thought very highly of Milner Holland. On the other hand I had fallen in love with Donnison, who I felt might be the Titmuss of Housing, and I quite liked the other members of the committee. It was therefore an enormous surprise and relief to discover that the report itself is extremely good. And already by today I knew that I could look forward to the publication of something which would bluff the Tories and force them to vote against the Second Reading of my Bill. When I got to the Ministry, full of nothing but Milner Holland, I found them quite pleased but also a bit annoyed. I suspect they are not used to a Minister who reads faster than they do, although it is something that they really quite want. I had just time to talk to Peter Brown and tell him how carefully the Press Office must work out the campaign before rushing off to the Cabinet Immigration Committee, chaired now by Bert Bowden, which for weeks and weeks has been mulling over the immigration issue.

It's the problem of Smethwick which has made me more deeply engaged than ever with this. After the deputation from Smethwick came to see me last week I had dashed off a minute to Harold saying we should link the refusal of loan sanction with our own positive policy. Well, today I got a definite snub, and I think it was deserved. Maurice Foley, who sat next to me at the Cabinet Immigration Committee, rebuked me and said of course we shouldn't link our policy to anything so negative as Smethwick. The moment he said it I knew I was wrong. I don't in any way resent its being said. Indeed, it seemed to me perfectly sensible when I heard later that Maurice is to be the chairman of a new committee in order to get a new policy for immigration worked out.

In the afternoon I had a long briefing meeting in the Ministry in preparation for the crucial Cabinet on the Land Commission. There was a long Cabinet paper prepared not by one of the Ministries but by the Lord President and the Cabinet Office, a completely objective study of Fred Willey's proposals and those of our Department. After the meeting the Secretary came in to see me and said, 'Oh my dear Minister, don't let's bother to fight this Land Commission any more. There are more important things in life.' I must say I agreed with her.

Tuesday, March 2nd
But when we came to Cabinet this wasn't so easy. Bowden made a long, perfectly fair statement of the problem. Then Fred Willey explained his position in his usual precise yet vague way. Then I had to defend my position. I started by saying that I didn't pretend to understand the Land Commission fully but I suspected nobody else round the table did and that was half the trouble. We were trying to introduce a very rough-and-ready social instrument into the extraordinary delicate operation of land purchase and I was nervous whether this wouldn't be a spanner in the works. On this occasion Harold Wilson was wholly against me. Having heard both of us, he said we

ought to take 'the more courageous' solution. The moment he said 'more courageous' I knew he was backing Fred. But, to my surprise, it was clear as the meeting went on that I had some supporters. First of all Denis Healey came in – this was almost his first intervention in home affairs – and formulated extremely accurately what he believed me to have been saying. Then Douglas Houghton said he had been embarrassed to hear me disown the position he was so anxious to support. But James Callaghan and the whole Treasury were on my side, and it became clear that more and more people were gradually coming to realize that this was a question not of showing courage or lacking courage but of whether we should commit ourselves to something practical which we could actually put into effect or whether we should go on making a lot of vague and dangerous noises.

It's still anybody's guess who won that Cabinet. On three of the issues things seem to have come my way, and I was aware that the Prime Minister was reluctantly forced into admitting that I had been talking good sense on a subject on which he has always been both vague and extremist. On this whole question of land and planning Harold Wilson is really a complete innocent. And this is all the worse because as an economist, a statistician and an ex-civil servant he tends to think he can understand anything. This segment of life is perhaps the only part of the administrative process of which he is totally ignorant and for which he has no feeling at all. I can say this because four months ago I was just as ignorant as he is. The fact is that on the executive we always left this area to people like Arthur Skeffington and Fred Willey to deal with, and they have made Harold believe I was in the pocket of the Dame and battling for reaction against their honest-to-God socialism.[1] Indeed, this picture of the battle has got into the press and there have been a series of not very important but annoying leaks about how I have been trying remorselessly to water down Fred Willey's Bill.

After Cabinet, talking to the Dame, I mentioned that I found my new Private Secretary extremely unattractive and I didn't want her to take it for granted I was going to keep him. She was very upset. 'He's perfectly all right,' she said. 'You mustn't be so difficult. You do treat our people so badly.' I replied, 'Sorry, Secretary, but it's my Private Office not yours, and I have got to be sure that my Private Secretary is somebody who I feel is on my side. I must warn you that I will keep Moseley if this one is unsatisfactory.' I now know I was too obliging in promising that I wouldn't oppose George Moseley's move, and I am finding it difficult not to renege on that promise despite the trouble it will cause the Department.

Wednesday, March 3rd
First of all I had to deal with the local government boundaries of Plymouth. I have been thinking and thinking of how I can best adjudicate to avoid bringing Conservative suburbs into Labour cities like Leicester and Nottingham

[1] Harold Wilson's suspicions still lingered in 1971. See *Wilson*, p. 9.

and so undermining safe Labour parliamentary seats in four or five years' time. One reason I spent so much trouble on Bath was that here I had a Conservative county borough and a Conservative county at loggerheads. In Bath I decided to leave the two semi-suburbs outside the borough, and that was fine. But when on Sunday night I began to study the Plymouth recommendation – to bring the two Conservative overspill suburbs into Plymouth – for the life of me I couldn't find a case for keeping them out. However, to make sure, I saw the two Plymouth M.P.s, both Tories – Joan Vickers, the formidable woman who knocked Michael Foot out of Devonport,[1] and a little lame man called Ian Fraser.[2] I met them in the lobby on Monday night and Joan Vickers at once said, 'Oh, don't give those socialists on the city council anything. They don't deserve an extension.' Fraser was more careful, and I wasn't surprised when today he asked for a private interview and said that as a responsible Plymouth M.P. he couldn't deny the right of the city council to those two suburbs. After all, he said, the population of Plymouth is falling and the city inside the boundary is being eroded as the people move across the frontier into the county suburbs: he felt that Plympton and Plymstock should become part of Plymouth. The next person I talked to was Len Williams at Transport House. He made contact with our regional organizer in the South-West and came up quickly with the firm opinion that, from a parliamentary point of view, the addition of these two Conservative suburbs to Plymouth might well lose us the seat, so he wants them kept out. This really makes it easier for me to see the problem on its merits. And on local government merits it's clear that Plymouth needs this rateable value whereas Bath didn't really need the Easton suburbs.

I gave lunch to Bullock, the old Professor of Naval History for whom I used to lecture at Greenwich for years. He wanted to talk to me about the preservation not of a single 'listed' house but of a group of buildings on Blackheath. Curiously enough, when I went over to Caxton House last week I met yet another research group called the Townscape Group. They were working on a new policy document which suggested that preservation of ancient buildings should be concerned not merely with individual listed buildings but also with groups or streets or small areas of old towns. There may be four listed houses, for example, and scattered among them one or two not particularly valuable houses whose demolition would destroy the aesthetic value of the group.

I spent some time trying to persuade Dame Evelyn and J. D. Jones that this idea is of great importance and that we should legislate on it.

But alongside this question of preserving ancient buildings from demolition has now cropped up the more topical and politically important question of the demolition of modern houses, which Harold Wilson raised with me at lunch last week. Before twenty-four hours were passed his Secretary had

---

[1] Dame Joan Vickers had won the seat for the Conservatives in 1955.
[2] M.P. for the Sutton division 1959–66.

1 Richard Crossman outside No. 10 on his appointment as Minister of Housing and Local Government on October 18th, 1964.

2 Leaving No. 10 with Barbara Castle (Minister of Overseas Development), October 18th, 1964.

3   The official Cabinet photograph, 1964.
Left to right (standing): Fred Lee, Frank Cousins, Douglas Houghton, Anthony Crosland, Douglas Jay, Barbara Castle, Anthony Greenwood, The Earl of Longford, Richard Crossman, Ray Gunter, Frederick Peart, Thomas Fraser, and Sir Burke Trend.

Left to right (seated): William Ross, Sir Frank Soskice, Michael Stewart, The Lord Gardiner, George Brown, Harold Wilson, Herbert Bowden, James Callaghan, Dennis Healey, Arthur Bottomley, and James Griffiths.

4 With George Brown and Harold Wilson, talking to Her Majesty the Queen at the 75th Royal Anniversary reception of the County Councils Association in November 1964. Michael Stewart is in the background.

written to my Secretary recording what was said at lunch and insisting on a quick answer. So this afternoon I found myself at my big table with Dame Evelyn and the full retinue of officials. This is the sort of occasion when the Dame is at her worst. She was furious with me for having so much as discussed the matter with the Prime Minister without previously mentioning it to her. She was furious with him for intervening. She was convinced that the whole thing was a mare's nest, and she hadn't much difficulty in showing that there was no reason to believe that of the twelve to fourteen thousand houses demolished by private developers last year the vast majority of them had been demolished for perfectly good reasons – because of road building, for example. I replied that Harold had raised a rather more subtle point. He had asked me to explain why we should in general waste our resources pulling down a block of flats or a house with thirty years' more life and replacing it with a slap-up modern building. She pushed this aside impatiently, whereupon I said, 'Anyway, local authorities are far worse than private developers. They will often destroy buildings and leave a huge open space for years afterwards because they have planned things so badly.' 'You're attacking my local authorities again,' she said. 'There's nothing in what you say.' I then had to insist that anyway we would have to reply to the Prime Minister.*

Today was one of my 'difficult' days in the Ministry, and the next subject I was difficult about was gravel pits. The officials wanted me to give consent to new pits near Egham in Surrey. I noticed that the Inspector's proposal had been to create an artificial lagoon once the gravel had been extracted. The Department wanted me to overrule him and say that the hole should be filled in over a period of twenty years. So I summoned all the officials and said I was worried by the obvious fact that there were huge areas round London which had been devastated by gravel pits. Why shouldn't we take seriously a proposal for turning one into an amenity. Whenever I put forward an idea of this sort the Department's hackles rise. The senior official present solemnly attacked me on the strange ground that the man concerned with the Egham case had died only yesterday and I shouldn't have raised this just after his death. However, I persisted. I wanted to know what plan we had as a Department for creating a blue belt around London in addition to the green belt. I am pretty sure that an enormous lot could be done if we were to put to the gravel merchants the idea that planning permission would be given only on condition that they would pay the cost of turning those ugly holes into real boating, water-skiing or fishing amenities.[1]

I had been invited along with the Prime Minister to be a guest of honour at the farewell annual dinner of the L.C.C. Labour group, which is now being disbanded and replaced by a G.L.C. group. I have an immense admiration

---

* By the end of the week a reply still hadn't been sent.
[1] As Secretary of State for the Environment, Peter Walker was able to announce this very policy in August 1972.

for the Morrison tradition of local government.[1] I saw something of it when
I was dealing with education as Shadow Minister last year. I have seen a lot
more dealing with housing and homelessness this year. Nevertheless, what an
inhuman show the London Labour Party is! The food at this dinner was
horrible, the atmosphere chilly, nobody seemed really grateful and the
speeches of Harold Wilson and Ike Hayward[2] were devoid of humanity.
There was a huge reception afterwards at which I was of course bombarded
with abuse for my decision about Hartley, and I just ran off home, sick at
heart, grey and tired and put myself to sleep reading Milner Holland. I have
now read the report twice through, starting each day about five o'clock in the
morning, going on until breakfast at eight o'clock. It's a most absorbing
document and on the second occasion I found it better reading then ever.

*The Labour Left were growing increasingly angry about Vietnam where they
alleged America was waging a colonial war. Since early February the United
States had been bombing North Vietnam and on March 4th over fifty Labour
M.P.s called on Mr Wilson to declare unequivocally that Britain could not
support United States policy. This was politically difficult for the Prime Minister,
who had emphasized good relations with Washington as a cornerstone of his
foreign policy and who realized how dependent Britain was on United States
support for sterling. He resisted his back-benchers, but in Cabinet Mrs Castle
continued to assail him.*

*The Government were also having trouble with the general practitioners, who
refused to accept the recommendation of a review body of a pay award of
£5½ million rather than the £18 million for which they had asked. On February
17th the B.M.A. asked 23,000 G.P.s to resign from the Health Service on
April 1st, but the Prime Minister stood firm at £5½ million and a promise of
negotiations for a new contract. Squabbles between the B.M.A. and the Ministry
of Health were to persist until June.*

*Farmers, also, were dissatisfied with the terms of the annual price review,
published on March 17th. They claimed that the increase of £10½ million in
price guarantees did not go far to meet an increase of £29 million in production
costs. Fred Peart, the Minister of Agriculture, would not concede more than
the original small rise in producer prices for milk and in the guaranteed price
for fat cattle, sugar beet and potatoes. As Richard Crossman confessed, this
particular policy suited his own personal farming interests very well.*

*There were two by-elections in March, both in Conservative-held consti-
tuencies: at Saffron Walden and at Roxburgh, Selkirk and Peebles.*

Thursday, March 4th
The second Cabinet meeting this week. There seemed to be nothing on the

---

[1] Herbert Morrison had profoundly influenced the development of London government
as an L.C.C. member from 1922 to 1945 and its leader from 1934 to 1940.
[2] Sir Isaac Hayward, leader of the L.C.C., 1947–65.

agenda until George Wigg rang me up and told me that what was at stake was the future of the army museum due to be built in the back of the garden at the Chelsea Royal Hospital. He'd heard that it was to be dropped because the Treasury didn't like it and the First Secretary didn't like it. True enough, it was the first item on the agenda and Harold Wilson had already been got at by George. As for me, I found amongst my Cabinet papers in the red box a single sheet of brief with a note at the bottom from my Department: 'The Treasury passed this on to you and would be grateful if you would use it in debate.' It was in fact an exact description of the Treasury proposal to have the museum outside London and sell the land and ground rent for thirty-four luxury flats.

Many Cabinet members were incredulous when I asserted this but I pegged away and managed to get clear what the First Secretary and the Chancellor really wanted: the alternative to the army museum, which was thirty-four luxury flats. The most interesting feature of this Cabinet was Harold's behaviour. He showed himself once again curiously solicitous to see that we came to a full Cabinet decision. You could see him ticking off the names, counting up the heads on each side and finally coming down himself just, but only just, on our side.

While I was thinking about the army museum at Chelsea, Barbara Castle was once again raising the problem of Vietnam and its repercussions. The subject has been discussed pretty often, but nearly always I have had my mind on something else and have taken no part in the discussion. Indeed, I think I can say that I haven't spoken on foreign affairs since I became a Minister, and I am now beginning to wonder whether one should insulate one's mind as completely as this. Vietnam might become an issue as awkward as the Korean war was for the Attlee government and even more divisive. Certainly there is a growing suspicion in the P.L.P. that we ought to be playing a much more active mediating role, along with the Russians, instead of siding so closely with the Americans. Of course, the Cabinet has the enthusiastic support of the Opposition. But this week we've got open rebellion on the back benches: some forty-five left-wingers are putting their names to a motion insisting on a far more decisive effort to stop the war in Vietnam.[1]

I had lunch with my two Parliamentary Secretaries and discussed how we were going to handle the Milner Holland Report and the Second Reading of our Bill. On all this my new Private Secretary has been quite competent, coming as he does from the Cabinet Office.[2] On his suggestion, I sent an urgent note to the Prime Minister asking that Milner Holland should hold his own press conference next Thursday and that a week later we should debate his report and then have our Second Reading debate ten days after that.

---

[1] The Chief Whip was even more anxious than Crossman about the back-bench rebellion and its effect on the Government's precarious majority of three.
[2] And therefore knowing the Whitehall ropes for securing Parliamentary time.

That gives us two bites at this cherry. Of course this has meant all this week a great deal of negotiation. I had to go and see Frank Longford, our leader in the Lords, who, in the course of talking about the Bill, congratulated me on always getting my way in Cabinet and said he had been particularly impressed by my handling of the problem of the Land Commission. I replied, 'I didn't get my way there.' 'Oh yes, I've never heard anybody in Cabinet before claiming, as you did, that you knew nothing about it, that's a brilliant technique.' I must say I had never thought of it as a technique, but Frank is, whatever else he is, an old hand at Cabinet techniques.

In the evening I was due at the dinner of the Institution of Municipal Engineers. This was the first official dinner to which I had very reluctantly agreed to go. I have turned down all the rest, including the lord mayor's banquet at the Guildhall, and given them to my Parliamentary Secretaries, both of whom like dining out. So back I went to Vincent Square to change. It was filthy weather and when I had taken all my clothes off I found that my dinner-jacket had been taken by Mrs Meek (our housekeeper) to the cleaners. So there I was with no clothes and no dinner-jacket. I was due at 8 p.m. and it was already 7.40. I had to get back into my old dark suit, and I went off miserably equipped to find the dinner was taking place in a very smart new hotel with some 400 guests all in full evening-dress and decorations, the men of course in tails. What made it even more embarrassing was that the dinner was served very slowly. It was 9.20 when I looked at my watch, stopped talking to the chairman, and discovered that we'd only got to the end of the turkey course and I had a three-line whip which required me to leave at latest by 9.35 in order to vote on defence.[1] They had to stop the dinner half-way through and the chairman made a little speech and I made a nice little reply. It was just all right but it was one of the most uncomfortable evenings I have had. The only relief I got was when Molly said to me on the way back, 'Well I suppose you're a politician because you can master that kind of a difficulty.'

The defence debate itself was a strange affair. The Tories have finally given up pretending that there is such a thing as an independent British deterrent and we've finally given up pretending that we are going to get rid of British nuclear weapons. Which surrender is the more awkward? Certainly ours. Our back-benchers are deeply disturbed.

Friday, March 5th
A trying day in the Department. In the afternoon I had my weekly meeting with the Secretary, Jones and Waddell. First of all I raised the issue of the Ordnance Survey, run, I've just discovered, by the Department. There has been an appalling delay in revising the One-Inch map owing to totally inadequate staff. But I got nowhere. Then I asked again about the survey of

[1] At the end of the two-day debate approving the 1965 Defence Estimates. The vote was 299 to 293.

the gypsy problem. I got nowhere. Finally, I raised the problem of listed building and group buildings. I realized that in each of these cases the irritation of the office is due to the mere idea of any intervention by the Minister. They think this is the kind of area which Ministers should leave to them.

We were just breaking up when I had a sudden call from the National Union of Agricultural Workers—they had to see me that afternoon. At three o'clock young Dennis Hodson, the secretary of the Union, came in without my old friend Collison, who is his chairman. The trouble, of course, is the tied cottage and the long-standing Party pledge never to throw a man out of a tied cottage unless the local authority can provide him with a house. This was impossible to implement because if farmers knew that anybody they evict would automatically get a council house, they would evict all the more readily. Now Collison understands why I had to implement the spirit of the Party policy but couldn't implement the letter of the resolution.[1] I was furious, therefore, when Mr Hodson came to tell me that the Agricultural Workers Union were not prepared to consider my reasonable compromise and had reverted to their irreconcilable original position. I sat down to it and argued it out, and about every ten minutes Mr Hodson said to me, 'You're wasting your time, Minister.' And I said, 'No I'm not.' Finally, I told him that if the Union are serious about this I simply shall not include the topic in the big Bill at all. He replied that in that case I will be hounded and harried in every rural constituency for failing to keep the Party pledge.

This really did rile me and when I got to Paddington for the 5.10 train I was still hot under the collar in a way I haven't been since I became Minister. This is the first thing which has really upset me in the way that I was constantly being upset when I was a back-bencher and a journalist before. It made me realize how much I enjoy my job, when I reflected that this is the first occasion I have felt 'How awful my Ministry is, how awful my Private Office is. The job's not worth it and oh! curse the Agricultural Workers Union for finally spoiling a terrible day.'

Saturday, March 6th
I woke up to find there had been heavy snow during the night and there were big drifts round Prescote, ice on the canal and brilliant sunshine. Anne motored me over to Coventry to a meeting of the shop stewards to discuss the closure of the Baginton works owing to the cancellation of the HS-681 transport plane. I had been expecting the Armstrong-Whitworth works to close down ever since 1946. It has tottered along mainly on sub-contractual work and the fact of its closure surprised no one in Coventry. Nevertheless, it has been a devastating blow. But there was a bright side. It was clear that all the young people had got jobs elsewhere already. The people who clung on and were now threatened with redundancy were those with ten or fifteen years' service, people fifty years old or more. The meeting was officially a

[1] See p. 62, n. 3.

meeting of the shop stewards, but actually it was virtually confined to people from Baginton and the room at the A.W. hall was only half full with about two hundred present. I started with a matter-of-fact speech, defending what we had done as right and inevitable; I left it to Bill Wilson to handle the redundancy problem. Then Maurice Edelman made an inflammatory half-hour attack on the Government, charging me and Frank Cousins with every kind of crime, including a sell-out to the Americans. His speech was followed by hostile questioning for about forty minutes. At the end I managed to get them round a bit by expressing my surprise that only four months after we had won our election victory Maurice should claim that Frank Cousins and I were prepared to sell out Coventry to the Americans and ruin the aircraft industry. I think I gained something by having attended the meeting at all, and I drove back home fairly contented. In the afternoon we took the children for a marvellous walk in the snow-drifts.

Sunday, March 7th

I had a fairly free day except that I had to spend two hours listening to the Redditch Labour Party telling me what a bloody awful New Town the Ministry had wished upon them. I find that the problem of the New Towns is the most time-consuming of all I face in the Department. One of the troubles is the personnel of the corporations after thirteen years of Tory selection. There are certain standard types. There is nearly always a colonial governor. There is nearly always a woman from the W.V.S. and a surveyor with strong Tory sympathies. On the other hand, you have in the urban district councils an ingrained opposition, quite often run by Labour groups who detest the snobbishness and up-staginess of the corporations' attitude, which by the way has been strongly backed by the Dame and whole Ministry. In the case of Redditch the problem is particularly acute because the town itself has some 30,000 or 40,000 inhabitants—for the most part people who have escaped from Birmingham, only ten miles away—who don't want Birmingham slum dwellers dumped on them as overspill. I spent two hours pleading and arguing with these indignant Labour Party members. I secretly sympathize with them a great deal and I am beginning to realize that one of the jobs I must do is to find a way of discovering sufficient talent for me to make some really good appointments to the corporations.

Sunday, March 21st*

There have been two episodes in my own semi-private life as Minister which are worth mentioning. The first was the publication of my book *Planning for Freedom*[1] which took place quietly on Thursday, March 11th. I had assumed

---

* I let the rest of March slip by without recording anything on my tape. At the beginning of April I looked at a list of my main engagements and at the Cabinet minutes and described the most significant events, to bring the diary up to date.

[1] Collected essays written between 1938 and 1964 (London: Hamish Hamilton, 1965).

that the book would be extensively noticed. Actually, it has been a quite pleasant, harmless flop. Things started off with a jolly well-written review in the *New Statesman* by David Marquand, which was hostile but recognized the book's importance. The only other serious review was in *The Times Literary Supplement*. The full-page anonymous reviewer is obviously Michael Oakeshott,[1] who was so upset by my anonymous review of his book in the *T.L.S.* Apart from the *New Statesman* and the *T.L.S.* nobody has taken the book seriously. It has been glanced at and pushed on one side. It may well be true, as both the *T.L.S.* and the *New Statesman* suggest, that by collecting in one volume my more theoretical essays I have exposed the fact that I am not a serious thinker but a political journalist who takes himself a bit too seriously. Also reviewers may be reluctant to look at a politician in two ways simultaneously—as a writer and as a Minister. Frankly, the feeling is that Ministers should be Ministers and writers should be writers, and Ministers shouldn't write books until they have retired.

Do I mind the flop? In this respect I am a split personality. If I had been offered the chance I would have thrown away practical politics and concentrated on writing. Equally, if Attlee had given me a job fifteen or twenty years ago I'd have been a whole-time professional politician. But then after the fall of the Attlee Government I'd have had twelve years sitting on the Opposition front bench instead of enjoying myself as an active political journalist and back-bencher in the way I have actually done. So I have a lot to be thankful for. Maybe I have got this job a few years too late. But I am at the top of my powers and I think I now have enough experience and maturity to avoid some of the clangers which I'd have made if I'd been promoted earlier in my career. Anyway, I couldn't care less about the fate of the book.

The other personal experience I have to record is the trouble I have had in my Private Office, which culminated in my getting rid of my new Private Secretary and getting in his place, thank God, John Delafons. The more I think about it the greater the loss of George Moseley, that owl-eyed, dark, quizzical character who had been Private Secretary to my two Tory predecessors and who was thoroughly tired and wanted to get home occasionally to dinner. The moment the Dame replaced him I was as isolated in my Private Office as I had been on my first day in the Ministry.

In relaxing the strain on a Minister and enabling him to do his work, the Private Secretary can do an enormous lot of good or no good at all. George Moseley had been invaluable because he knew everybody in the Department and because he would comment intelligently on everything I wrote and tell me if he thought I was going wrong. So he gave me a sense of assurance that I wouldn't ever go very far wrong. And at times he could also be candid and critical of my behaviour. Now all this suddenly disappeared and all I had was an elegant young man who came wafting into my room and stood about the

[1] Professor of Political Science at L.S.E.

place and never did a damn thing. I suspect his lordly manner, as often happens with civil servants, actually concealed uncertainty and insecurity. But that didn't help me. After a fortnight I went to the Dame and said, 'He just won't do.'

Within a week a young man was hauled out of the Planning Department and delivered to me. Actually, I had spotted him for the first time during a seminar on the West Midlands Review. He has been the Secretary to the Planning Advisory Group (P.A.G.), which is a stunningly able and successful group of town clerks, treasurers and planners who have been working in the last year with the Ministry's planning officials on a drastic revision of all planning procedure. He is tall, almost as owlish as George, but more vital, keen and alert. Within a week he has wholly transformed the Private Office. I brought him down to Prescote yesterday on my way back from an official visit to the Black Country. He clicked with Patrick and Virginia; and he told me that he had never had such a week in his life as his first week running the Private Office. I now know I am all right. I have somebody who can talk to me, somebody I can talk to completely freely, somebody enormously ambitious who also thinks it exciting to work with me, and above all somebody who knows his way about the Department and is prepared to be loyal to me in his relations with other civil servants.

Having read Hassall's *Rupert Brooke* over Christmas I decided to read his life of Sir Edward Marsh, who was not only Brooke's patron, but was also a kind of professional Private Secretary.[1] He started as P.S. in the Colonial Office and thereby became Churchill's Private Secretary; later he became Jimmy Thomas's Private Secretary. So you can get from his life a picture of what a Private Secretary was before 1945. Certainly in the days before World War I it was a kind of social job. Marsh's main responsibility was to travel with Churchill on the Admiralty yacht, the *Enchantress*, and to go to the grouse moors with him in the summer. In those days he really was a *Private* Secretary to the Minister. It was a time when the Minister could be absent from his office for weeks and weeks on end. Indeed, one of the things Marsh always did was to attend all the by-elections at which Churchill was making a speech and be with him throughout all the general elections and write drafts of his speeches. And that went on right through his period with Jimmy Thomas, after World War I.

The functions of the Private Secretary have changed a good deal since then! The idea that I should ask Delafons to draft a speech for a by-election, or to take any part in a general election, is utterly fantastic today. The modern Civil Service is extremely rigid in its determination not to permit party politics to get mixed with departmental politics. Of course they will help me to a great extent in my parliamentary life or in answering questions. But they would absolutely refuse to have anything to do with a by-election, and indeed

[1] Christopher Hassall, *Edward Marsh, A Biography* (London: Longman, 1959). Marsh had been the author's patron too.

they refuse to help with any speech they regard as political. The second big difference is that the Private Office is a far larger place now than it was before the war. John Delafons is in charge of quite a large slice of the Department, and under him are the other two Private Offices, those of Jim MacColl and Bob Mellish. Then across the corridor he has the whole parliamentary section and another section dealing with correspondence. I suppose there are some twenty-five people in that office all working for the Minister and his two parliamentary lieutenants. The young man who heads the Private Office has to be able to run all this. As a result he jumps ahead of all his contemporaries, earning another £250 a year even if he remains a Principal; and he is marked for promotion.

One of Delafons' main jobs is to organize my relationships with the Dame, J. D. Jones and Waddell. I am now pretty clear that Waddell is a conventional administrator and that J. D. Jones is an extremely talented, adroit Whitehall schemer with whom a Minister must deal very carefully indeed.

As for the Dame, the more I see of her the more remarkable I find her. She is as resourceful as ever, and her skill and speed of drafting and her power to take an idea of mine and think it through and write it out impresses me more the more I see of her. I still have very great difficulties with her when it comes to bringing ideas and people in from outside. I thought I had overcome her opposition by the success of Arnold Goodman and David Donnison in dealing with Clause 22 of the Rent Bill.[1] But no. There is still tremendous resistance, as I found only this week when I suggested that in working out the jobs of the new rent officers and rent assessment committees I should make use of our usual outsiders. I got a very frosty response from the Dame, although she knows she will have to agree in the end. That problem is accentuated in my mind by my gradual acceptance of the extreme second-rateness of most of the people working for me in the Department. I had a little party in the office when we had finished drafting the Rent Bill to celebrate the Second Reading. There turned up, of course, from the Lord Chancellor's office, the parliamentary draftsman, the famous Mr Rowe. But I discovered that although we had thirty lawyers in the Department only one was allocated to the Rent Bill. The rest of my advisers are administrators who know nothing about the law. No wonder we make mistakes, no wonder we are inadequate. But it is the basic conviction of the Civil Service that Assistant Secretaries and Principals are capable of dealing with any problem, including the preparation of a Rent Bill, even though they have no legal training. I realize now that one of the main reasons why the planning side of the Department is so much stronger than the housing side is that the professionals – the architects and the planners – are at least on equal terms with the administrators. James, Chief Planner, and Oliver Cox, Deputy Chief Architect, are both absolutely first rate; and every time I meet their young men I get more

---

[1] Clause 22 set out the principle of 'fair rent', which was to be established by local assessment committees.

impressed and excited. But on the housing side of the Department there literally isn't anybody who knows anything about building a house. That's why I have had to bring Peter Lederer in as my progress-chaser on system building. That's why I am getting more and more aware of the danger of relying entirely on the Department's advice on anything to do with the world outside Whitehall.

During this last month my whole life as a politician has been dominated by two things: the launching of the Milner Holland Report and the preparations for the Second Reading debate on my own Rent Bill. I think I can take some personal credit for what happened. Directly I became Minister I made contact with Milner Holland and got to know the individual members of his Committee, particularly David Donnison and Pilcher.[1] I also took their advice at length, not only about the Bill in general but about the fair-rent clause in particular, and as a result I was able to persuade them to change their publication plans. Instead of waiting till the summer to publish their report, they agreed to get it out as a matter of urgency *before my Bill*, even though this meant printing each chapter as it was finished. Everybody now realizes the Milner Holland Report and the Crossman Bill are parts of a single operation. The Report was published on March 11th, and my next task was to launch it in the House of Commons.

Monday, March 22nd

Apart from two days' electioneering in Saffron Walden and on the Scottish border[2] I spent a whole week almost entirely in preparations for the debate on the Report. But when the weekend came I still hadn't got a speech ready. I had hoped that most of it could have been prepared in the Department, but again they were quite unable to do so. It rained practically throughout the whole weekend so I worked all Saturday evening and for twelve hours on Sunday and produced a complete written speech in time for the debate today.

Poor Anne was due to be in the Commons for the debate but at the last moment she had to stay at home because Patrick and Virginia both went down with a mild virus. So she missed hearing what turned out to be the first effective political oration I have made as Minister. I had thought over my tactics very carefully indeed and I decided to launch an all-out attack on the Tory record and put the whole blame on them for the rent crisis we inherited. For weeks now, George Wigg and I have been discussing our failure to pin the responsibility on the Tories for the troubles we are coping with.

---

[1] See p. 89.
[2] The Saffron Walden by-election followed the resignation of R. A. Butler and his elevation to the Lords and the Mastership of Trinity College, Cambridge. There was a by-election in Roxburgh after the death of the sitting Conservative Member, Commander Donaldson. At the poll on March 23rd Peter Kirk held Saffron Walden for the Tories; David Steel, a Liberal, snatched the Scottish seat from the Conservatives with a majority of 4,607 votes.

Here is a case where we really could do so, and so the speech was a ruthless party political attack on the Conservatives, with my own side roaring enthusiastically behind me. Probably in the long run it was marred by a remark I made about my natural prejudice against landlords. I had put it into the text at the last moment so as to make sure I would carry my own back-benchers with me.

Tuesday, March 23rd
My speech in Monday's debate had a mixed reaction from the press. The *Daily Telegraph* described the speech as the most merciless parliamentary performance. On the other hand, my demagoguery lost me the support of *The Times*, for example, which not unreasonably regarded it as vulgar. However, I had no time to worry because today was the day for my second big Lobby conference within a week—this time explaining in detail the Rent Bill, which I had timed very nicely to come out just a week after the Milner Holland Report.

The Lobby conference took place at four o'clock. I had been asked by Harold Wilson to hold it then because he wanted one as well and Douglas-Home was also having one that day. So I had my forty-five minutes with the Lobby explaining the Bill and the White Paper. I had taken tremendous trouble with the White Paper, writing most of the first half of it myself, and the Dame and I had really slaved away to make the exposition of the Bill in the second half both intelligible and highly political.

Wednesday, March 24th
I completed the double presentation this morning at the Parliamentary Party meeting, when fifty or sixty people turned up to hear me particularly on Clause 22. I've made it clear in this diary that the fair-rent clause and the machinery of rent officers and rent assessment committees was almost entirely the invention of Pilcher and Arnold Goodman and his friend Dennis Lloyd. At first sight it does seem an extraordinary thing that we have done. What we have said is that we would not try to define a fair rent by any normal method and we wouldn't relate it either to a fair return on the landlord's money or a standard rent or anything else. Instead, we would simply say that if either the landlord or the tenant requests it, a fair rent must be fixed— with the one proviso that in fixing it the rent officer must eliminate scarcity value. Otherwise we have left it up to him to do the job, with the option of an appeal to the rent assessment committees if his solution is found to be unsatisfactory by either party. What Arnold Goodman has in fact said to me is, don't try to invent a formula. Get the right people and let them do the job by setting a series of precedents in their early decisions. It was obvious from this morning's discussion that this fair-rent idea was regarded as highly dubious and I shall have a very rough time in Committee, fighting for it against my own back-benchers.

Friday, March 26th

At Cabinet yesterday morning we discussed the awkward problem of Airey Neave's[1] Private Members' Bill, which provides redress for all those people who were excluded for a variety of reasons from receiving a contributory old-age pension. This Bill, which was due to be moved today, would put our marginal back-benchers in great difficulties because many of them felt they couldn't vote against it. Now it so happened that the Consolidated Fund Third Reading was taking place on Thursday night and normally it carries on until five or six in the morning.[2] George Wigg had the bright idea that we should deliberately carry the debate on until eleven on Friday morning and so knock the whole of Friday's Private Members' business out and dish Airey Neave.[3] I thought this was a pleasant idea. As six of the subjects put down for debate belonged to my own Ministry and poor James MacColl would have to sit through the night dealing with all of them, I said that after going to a formal dinner we were having at the Dorchester for the Israeli Prime Minister I would clock in in evening dress at, say, ten thirty in order to see how things were going.

When I did clock in only one subject—Oxford rating—had been taken and the second of our Ministry's debates, which was on planning and listed buildings, had started. I sat there listening for three hours and then I gave an impromptu seventy-minute reply to the debate before going home to bed preparatory to catching the train to the North next day. After that, the debate went on and on and on. Friday's papers were dominated by this parliamentary outrage. We had succeeded in that we had talked out the Airey Neave Bill. What had gone wrong was that our leadership in the House of Commons had failed us. I was the only Minister who took part in the operation, although Callaghan turned up for two or three minutes. But the Leader of the House and the Chief Whip, who had both been at our Dorchester dinner, just went home to bed and turned up at eight o'clock or nine o'clock next morning, leaving the back-benchers to fight on throughout the night. This morning there was only George Wigg to reply for our side. George had enjoyed organizing the whole show, but you don't put up your secret conspirator to speak from the front bench. So we got a bad press for what was a perfectly legitimate manœuvre.

Tuesday, March 30th

At ten o'clock we had a short meeting, called by the Prime Minister, to

---

[1] Conservative M.P. for Abingdon since 1953. Member of the Select Committee on Science and Technology since 1967, and its chairman since 1970.

[2] The Consolidated Fund is the Exchequer's account, kept at the Bank of England, into which all revenue is paid. The Commons' vote on supply is purely formal, and on the occasions when the Bill is debated, normally three times each Session, Private Members can by convention discuss their chosen subjects with the Minister responsible. The order is determined by ballot.

[3] For George Wigg's account of how he thwarted 'Tory capacity to sustain their humbug', see *Wigg*, pp. 319–20.

review electoral boundaries before Cabinet at ten thirty. The only people present were the Attorney-General, the Leader of the House, the Home Secretary and myself. Harold was obviously concerned to make quite sure that I was doing my job as a politician on the local boundary decisions, that no adjustment was politically disadvantageous to us. He was equally concerned to make sure that the Home Secretary was doing his job with regard to the warding of the reorganized boroughs. But poor Frank Soskice suffers desperately from arthritis and he's ageing. As soon as he had slipped out the Prime Minister raised his hands to me in horror.

Today we had the long-delayed discussion on foreign policy which Barbara Castle has been asking for. Cabinet meetings have not been very important for me since I got my way about the housing programme and obtained the Prime Minister's backing. I must say I felt that this one was the sheerest waste of time. Long papers had been prepared for us on Vietnam, on the Middle East and on Europe. My only conclusion was that a Cabinet consisting of busy departmental Ministers can't make much impact on how foreign policy is conducted. Proceedings stopped punctually at eleven forty-five to enable us to go to Westminster Abbey for a memorial service to Herbert Morrison.[1]

In the afternoon I had a very interesting job. At the previous week's Cabinet we had approved the incomes policy. Now I had the job of presenting this policy to the local authorities, who are the employers responsible to me. George Brown had wanted me to use all my influence to persuade the local authorities to refuse the dustmen and the lower-paid workers an extra 2d. an hour on the ground that they had signed a three-year contract and couldn't break it before the end of the three years. This was intolerable: the cost of living has gone up and they are the lowest-paid workers in the country. When I received this request I first talked to Bob Mellish and then said to the Dame, 'I'm not going to agree to this.' I wrote a very hot letter to the First Secretary, saying that I couldn't conscientiously put pressure on the local authorities on this issue. And I didn't. After the meeting I found myself being congratulated although my letter to George Brown had been strictly private. Nothing is private in Whitehall! Everybody on the local authorities knew that I had stood up for the lower-paid workers and respected me for it.

Wednesday, March 31st
Today was notable in my life mainly for the appalling experience I had of receiving Manchester Corporation's deputation to protest against my behaviour in the matter of Westhoughton.[2] We had encouraged the

---

[1] He had died on March 6th.
[2] In February 1965 the Minister had confirmed, with substantial modifications, Manchester's compulsory purchase order for land at Westhoughton. When Manchester found themselves unable to accept this, the Minister offered to contribute to the cost of employing consultants to produce a master plan that all the authorities concerned could accept. Differences of opinion between Manchester and Westhoughton were so fundamental

corporation to go in for this not very satisfactory solution of where to put some of their overspill. But now we have just announced my decision to exclude nearly a third of the 1,000 acres they wanted from the compulsory purchase order. Manchester felt that we had wrecked the scheme and I realized that we had laid ourselves open to being massacred by Sir Philip Dingle, the formidable Manchester town clerk.

The meeting was a ghastly experience and after it I summoned the Dame and J.D. and said there musn't be another meeting with a delegation for which I was so badly briefed and in which I felt myself so absolutely out-witted and outgunned. J.D. looked very miserable and the Dame very sour, and I decided to see the Manchester people again and patch things up in the absence of both of them.

However, after this ghastly meeting I did have a rather pleasanter occasion. Many weeks before I had been asked to wind up the staff's series of discussion meetings. I had assumed that I would be talking to a discussion group and didn't do very much preparation. I found myself, however, in Caxton Hall at one o'clock with 600 ticket-holders there, and lots queueing outside as well. I described to them how the staff looked to a Minister. They were like fish swimming about in a goldfish bowl and I was the cat looking in from outside. Then I put up to them a number of awkward ideas. I ended by suggesting that in terms of structure they were a self-perpetuating hierarchy. When it came to question time I knew that my provocation had been a success.

Thursday, April 1st
I went to see Tommy Balogh this morning in the London Clinic. A fortnight before we had been together one evening and he told me he had had a twinge of heart trouble. However, the following day I was lunching with Pam Berry and there he was cheerfully telling me that the doctor had given him a clean bill of health. Then I rang up on Saturday to hear from his wife, Pen, that he had had a ghastly attack of angina pectoris and had been shipped off to the Clinic. However, I found him in marvellous form having been visited by Harold — despite the fact that he was paying £60 a week.

This was the day of our first major Cabinet crisis. It had been brewing for a long time. We had already had the cancellation of the HS-681 and the closing down of the Armstrong-Whitworth factory in my constituency. Obviously that meant we should have to cancel the TSR2 as well. So I was not surprised when Cabinet were suddenly summoned to approve the cancellation. The discussion showed there had been a certain divergence amongst those concerned. James Callaghan, as Chancellor of the Exchequer, wanted to cancel the plane altogether for purely financial reasons. Ranged against him

---

that no acceptable scheme could be devised, and in October 1966 the Minister reluctantly withdrew his support for any Manchester town development scheme in the Westhoughton area.

were (a) Denis Healey, who wanted to cancel the TSR2 and to substitute the American F-111-A, which would mean a certain saving of money but an enormous increase of outlay in dollars; and (b) Roy Jenkins, who wanted to cancel the TSR2 and replace it with a British plane—which was roughly George Brown's view as well; and (c) George Wigg, who held the view that we might have to cancel both but we mustn't make any decision until we had finished the strategic reappraisal which would show what kind of plane was required. George had briefed/convinced me (among others) that our main object must be to avoid committing ourselves to the American plane; and this could best be done by postponing the TSR2 decision until we could decide whether we needed any plane of this kind. Long before midday it was clear we weren't going to get very far that morning. We had a long speech from Denis Healey; and a rambling speech from Harold Wilson in which he seemed to be against Healey, but it wasn't clear what he was for. Healey talked a lot about the wonderful option he had got for the F-111-A. As the morning went on it was more and more clear that he has become a McNamara boy and that the Chiefs of Staff hate the TSR2 and are determined to get the F-111-A as a replacement. With Callaghan saying he wanted no new plane at all and George Brown saying he didn't feel sure either plane was essential, things got very confused and the meeting had to be broken off because of the funeral of the Princess Royal.

It was continued after the foreign affairs debate on Vietnam at ten o'clock that night in a meeting which lasted two and a half hours. In the end, after another confusing discussion, Harold Wilson summed up: there were three possibilities.[1] Possibility 1 was to cancel TSR2 without taking up the American option. Possibility 2 was to cancel while taking up the option. And possibility 3 was to keep TSR2 for the time being and make our final decision after we had finished the strategic reappraisal. About ten of us, including Fred Peart, Willie Ross and myself, supported possibility 3. We were defeated because a strange alliance had been set up between the morning and the evening meeting. The basis for the alliance was an assurance by Denis Healey that in taking out the option for the F-111-A we need not assume any obligations or commitments of any kind. Was this assurance true or not? I don't know. I doubt whether it was. But it was sufficient to enable Roy Jenkins, George Brown and James Callaghan, each for his own reasons, to support cancellation now that it left us free of any American commitment. I happened to know from George Wigg that Harold was for postponement, but he didn't put his view very clearly and allowed us to be defeated. He took very great trouble on this occasion to ensure that each member of the Cabinet committed himself. Round the table he went, totting up the score in the most amusing, cynical, detached way and forcing everyone to declare himself personally and precisely on the three possibilities. Why did he behave in this

[1] And, according to the Prime Minister, 'a clear majority was for cancelling TSR2'; *Wilson*, p. 90.

way? Did he align himself with Denis Healey because after this particular decision the idea of our ever taking up the option is out of the question? I just don't know.

Sunday, April 4th

What has happened inside the Department during March? Well, I think I have managed to get the section dealing with 'listing' of buildings reorganized. At least, I have doubled the clerical staff and so reduced the time in which the list can be prepared from ten to three years. On the Ordnance Survey side I have got no change, and I now propose to hand over the whole of this work either to Fred Willey at Land and Natural Resources or to Fred Peart at Agriculture. And then, as I have mentioned, there is the work of P.A.G., the Planning Advisory Group. At the end of last week I first of all addressed the Town Planning Institute and gave what was really an inaugural lecture about the relation of politics and planning. And then I gave a dinner for the members of P.A.G. and told them that I would accept their report on planning procedure once certain inadequacies had been made good, and that we would turn it into legislation. This is easier for me to do now because I have been able to put Richard Llewelyn-Davies in charge of the research work, so now I have R.A.G., the Research Advisory Group, and P.A.G., the Planning Advisory Group, working hand in hand.

What about the impression we are making on the outside world? I think everyone now thinks the Ministry of Housing is one of the dynamic Departments. We have issued our first directive to the local authorities about their housing plans, and we have made a whole series of pledges about the work we are going to do. I've promised to reform local government finance. I've promised to introduce a scheme for differential rates for borrowers, I've promised to reorganize the housing subsidies. That's a lot of hostages to fortune! But at least we have begun to start showing that we can keep our promises: we have got the big Rent Bill through its Second Reading and now we are starting on the Committee Stage.

As for the electorate, it is clear that housing counts for more than any other single issue. Harold Wilson often says 'We can win or lose the next election on housing.' And that's why he likes to have me there as Minister of Housing, outside the inner Cabinet where things like defence and the budget and the TSR2 are discussed. There is a question in my mind now as to whether, in addition to doing my present departmental job, I shouldn't try to force my way rather nearer to the centre of things. At present I don't think I shall because I am doing quite enough already.

I spent most of the past week preparing for the Second Reading debate which is due to take place this Monday, April 5th, the day before James Callaghan's budget. This time I can't make a political oration, I have to make a speech which was accurate and precise and really based on the advice of my civil servants. Rogerson and Waddell spent four hours on Wednesday and

four hours on Thursday night struggling with the drafts. But I wasn't really
satisfied, and I got Jennie to come down to Prescote on Saturday afternoon.
We worked through Sunday and got the Second Reading speech pretty well
finished.

Monday, April 5th
The budget Cabinet was a pretty formal proceeding. In fact, it turned out to
be a pretty good budget without any of the rows and alarms the press had
taught us to expect as a result of the deadlock between George Brown and
James Callaghan.

Though I wasn't paying much attention, I did realize that all the tax side
had been done by Nicky Kaldor, and that Tommy Balogh's great success
was in the decision to limit foreign investment and reimpose investment
controls.[1] Of course the decisive role had been played by Harold Wilson.
He'd had two long meetings at Chequers and this budget was his real achievement[2]—yet it was also an immense personal success for the Chancellor.
Callaghan is a man with great popular appeal. He is so good on television
and he is quite competent in the House; and of course he has become the
darling of the Treasury. George Brown, on the other hand, has become
rather dissolute lately, not his usual self. Also he is no good at running a
planning Ministry. So in the battle between the Treasury and the D.E.A., the
Treasury is coming out on top in terms of prestige and status. Harold, I
suppose, has been content to watch this going on while he makes sure the
budget is according to his wishes. After the budget meeting I moved the
Second Reading of the Rent Bill.

I had been pretty anxious over the weekend because there was a rumour
that a Statement on the Government's decision about the TSR2 would be
made today at 3.30. I got hold of George Wigg on Sunday and he got hold
of Harold (just back from a successful weekend with General de Gaulle in
Paris).[3] At once the Prime Minister said 'No, the Rent Bill must be given
Monday afternoon. However awkward it may be, the Statement on TSR2
must be made in the course of the budget speech.' So I got my way and I gave
a completely unemotional exposition of the Bill centring on the controversial
Clause 22.[4] It certainly flummoxed poor John Boyd-Carpenter and reduced
Quintin Hogg in his winding-up speech to sounding entirely in favour of it.

---

[1] Wilson veils the Hungarians with a reference only to the Treasury, the revenue departments and the three Treasury Ministers. *Wilson*, p. 89.
[2] 'My advice was limited to a few thoughts on the economic aspects—especially on
overseas financing—and on what we might hope to get through in an unusually long Finance
Bill, with a majority of three.' *Wilson*, p. 89.
[3] Harold Wilson had spent a long weekend with the French President and his Ministers
discussing the economic situation, especially French gold holdings, and foreign affairs. The
Prime Minister warned the French that the British Government was about to announce
arrangements to purchase weapons from the U.S.A. See *Wilson*, pp. 89–93.
[4] The Second Reading was carried by 306 votes to 286.

7

The budget was introduced on April 6th; and in the same speech the Chancellor announced the dropping of the TSR2. There was still little foreign confidence in sterling although export figures were looking up. It was a deflationary budget, and, as well as the 6d. increase in income tax that had been published in the autumn, there were increased taxes on beer, spirits, tobacco and motor-car licence duties. Foreign exchange regulations also hit private foreign travel and private investment abroad. The City was aggrieved by the Chancellor's strictures on business entertaining, which would no longer be an expense allowable for tax relief, and criticized as doctrinaire Mr Callaghan's capital gains tax, which was set, in 1965–6, at 30 per cent for individuals and 55½ per cent for companies. After 1965–6, companies would pay a consolidated corporation tax at a rate as yet undivulged but not exceeding 40 per cent. This would hit distributed profits and, immediately, would devalue the existing investment allowances to industry. Overseas investment was also discouraged. This was criticized as a shortsighted way of cutting off profitable and useful income from foreign dividends, and as discouraging overseas investors from reciprocal investment in this country.

Tuesday, April 6th
I had an easy morning and then I lunched with Lord Holford[1] and James MacColl in order to have more discussion about listed buildings. After that a haircut while Jim Callaghan made his speech – I looked in about 5.30 to see how he was doing. Then back to the Ministry to meet Peter Lederer and on to a party. A pleasant, ordinary kind of day I had while the budget was thundering out in the country.

Wednesday, April 7th
I had to make two important speeches: the first in the morning at the Housing Centre, on housing associations, which was followed by a formal lunch, and the second at six o'clock to the Town Planning Institute. Both went fairly well; the town planning speech was a kind of inaugural address followed by an official dinner.

Friday, April 9th
On Thursday there was an interesting first item in Cabinet. We had all received a paper on the issue of whether we should re-arm the Indians and in particular on whether we should supply them with submarines. For the first time I led the general discussion. I said I couldn't see any point in giving the Indians a submarine if you had to give the Pakistanis a submarine as well, though I didn't mind selling them thirty Hunters on the cheap. Anyway should we really be committing ourselves to an East of Suez policy before the

[1] Architect and town planning consultant. Professor of Town Planning at University College, London, 1948–70. He had been a member of the Historic Buildings Council for England since 1953.

strategic reappraisal had taken place? I was supported by a number of others and we managed to postpone the decision on the submarine in Harold's absence (he's away with flu).

In the afternoon I had a delegation from the women of Marshall Street in Smethwick. This has been a problem for me for some time.[1] The council wants loan sanction for buying up houses in Marshall Street in order to keep the coloured people out. We are introducing a Race Relations Bill with special clauses against discriminatory covenants.[2] So it is obviously impossible to permit loan sanction. Nevertheless, young Peter Griffiths, the fellow who defeated Gordon Walker, asked me in a letter whether I would go and see the five complaining ladies of Marshall Street for myself. The last thing I wanted was to agree and I thought it clever instead to tell him to bring them to see me at the Ministry. On Thursday afternoon at 4.30 he brought them in. They were hysterical and shouted at me a good deal. While I was seeing them I thought I heard a lot of *sotto voce* muttering by Bob Mellish, who was sitting beside me; but I didn't think much of it until I got into the train the next morning to go to the Black Country with my new Private Secretary, John Delafons. Every paper had front-page headlines saying that Bob Mellish had insulted the women of Smethwick. By the time I had got to Halesowen, where I was making an official visit, everybody was on my tracks for an interview. I had to stick up for Bob at a long press conference and give a long interview on the telly before motoring on to Ditchley Park[3] for a great housing conference.

Tuesday, April 13th

I had the first meeting of the Standing Committee on my Rent Bill this morning from 11.30 till 1.00. I tried to arrange with the Whips, on George Wigg's advice, to have a big Committee with fifty members in order to give opportunities to our back-benchers, and I got Tam to do all the work of collecting the twenty-six Labour volunteers. We were amazed to discover on Monday when I got back from a day in Coventry launching an improvement grant campaign, that the Committee was only going to total thirty-five. And I was even more amazed when I learned that without a word to me the Lord President and the Chief Whip, acting on the advice of Freddie Warren,[4] had proposed twenty-five on the Committee—the number had only been increased to thirty-five by the demand of the Opposition.

[1] See p. 167.
[2] It received its Second Reading on May 2nd, 1965, and was given the Royal Assent on November 8th, 1965. Its provisions were insufficient, and supplementary measures to deal with discrimination in housing and employment were set out in a further Act in 1968.
[3] A large and beautiful house outside Oxford used for conferences and international seminars.
[4] Private Secretary to the Chief Whip. The position's permanence provides shrewd and intimate knowledge of the 'usual channels' through which parliamentary business is arranged.

All this is indicative of what's wrong with our parliamentary leadership. Bowden and Short are run by Freddie Warren just as William Whiteley[1] was run by his predecessor, Charles Harris.[2] They were simply told by Warren that the right number of members for this Committee would be twenty-five and they didn't stop to calculate, as George Wigg and I did, that by having fifty members we would have embarrassed the Tories, who would have found it difficult to man a Committee of fifty, and we would probably have got a better majority than we will with a smaller one. As for the first meeting of the Committee, it was routine Second Reading stuff and it was clear that the Tories were not in an oppositional mood.

Wednesday, April 14th

I had a meeting today with Boyd-Carpenter to discuss the future of the Standing Committee, and suggested to him three meetings a week up to Whitsuntide in order to get the Bill finished. His counter-proposal was two meetings a week, which he said would be convenient to him because he is the chairman of the Public Accounts Committee and if we met on Tuesday it would have to be in the afternoon. I made it clear that I thought we ought to start with three; but I have to admit that after the first meeting I couldn't really complain about any filibustering. Finally Boyd-Carpenter virtually promised to let me have the appallingly complicated Clause 1 of the Bill as well as the first Schedule by the end of the first week after the recess. If he delivers we could hardly move faster by introducing a guillotine. However, I am expecting that when it comes to the point we *shall* have to guillotine the Bill, and indeed the Finance Bill and every other Bill, as soon as we get back from the Easter recess.

In the afternoon I went along the passage with Dame Evelyn Sharp to the Chancellor's room in order to have a discussion on home loans with officials present. We had produced a paper and he had produced a paper and straight away he said he was quite willing to take our paper first and consider our proposals for fulfilling the election pledge as cheaply as possible. But he added that he also wanted to see a paper from us on the total volume of the housing problem. We said we had no objection to doing this — and I observed that he was speaking with a new authority as a result of his budget success. He was virtually saying to me 'Before you discuss this in the E.D.C. under George Brown's chairmanship you must come to a private understanding with me about the total amount of public expenditure you'll be pre-empting for housing in the next four years.' Having given him his point, we came back to our own paper and had a fairly reasonable first talk.

[1] M.P. for Durham 1922–31 and 1935–56, and a Labour Chief Whip between 1942 and 1951.
[2] Sir Charles Harris was Private Secretary to successive Chief Whips from 1919 to 1961.

Saturday, April 17th

We took the family up to London at the beginning of the week, and Patrick and Virginia had Monday, Tuesday and Wednesday in town and then motored down with me on Thursday afternoon for a fairly restful Easter weekend of mixed, blowy, brilliant, shiny, thunderstormy weather. The London holiday was the usual mixture. They did the zoo and the museums, and I took them on Thursday morning to the Natural History Museum where we looked at fossils and prehistoric monsters before having a splendid birthday lunch for Anne in the House of Commons. As Thursday was the day of the Easter adjournment there was virtually nobody there; and the only people in the restaurant were those, like ourselves, with children. It was fun and we ordered ourselves a great *bombe surprise*. From there we drove straight up to Hampstead to see Tommy Balogh, who is now recovering well, and thence came straight to Prescote, getting here with extraordinarily little trouble and no traffic, starting from Hampstead at four and reaching home at six o'clock. Good Friday we spent pretty quietly. Today we went over to my eldest sister, Bridget Bardsley, at Odell near Bedford, where there was a real family gathering. Bridget had her two children, Sue and Nicholas, and Mary, my other sister, and Charles Woodhouse had their Anne and we had our two, who were the youngest there. It was a pleasant lunch. Charles Woodhouse, who teaches at the Dragon School in Oxford, was very anxious to know whether Patrick would go there next spring. I was unable to say.

After an exciting climb up the church tower we drove back through an enormous thunderstorm to give dinner to the chairman of my constituency Party and his wife – Mr and Mrs David Young, who are both schoolteachers. He is now not only the chairman of my Party but also a potential parliamentary candidate.[1] From them we learned that we are in the middle of a tremendous scandal in Coventry because my election agent, Winnie Lakin, has been expelled from the Party on the allegation that she fiddled the votes in some election at the regional party conference a fortnight ago.[2] Actually, this is all part of a struggle between the borough Party, run by Roy Hughes, and our Coventry East constituency. So Coventry is in a pretty unhealthy state a few weeks before the municipal elections. Fortunately that isn't true of the country as a whole. Indeed, I should say now that in this Easter recess we have wound up in a much stronger position than we have ever had except perhaps during the first fortnight of this Government. Harold Wilson has made a tremendous success of his sixty-hour trip to New York and Washington[3] – just as he made a tremendous success of his visit to General de Gaulle three weeks ago. James Callaghan's budget has obviously gone over

---

[1] See p. 279.

[2] The allegation was later proved to be false.

[3] On April 14th Harold Wilson flew to New York and Washington for talks with Mr Fowler, the new Secretary of the Treasury, and for discussions with President Johnson on the situation in Vietnam. He also saw Willy Brandt, at that time Mayor of Berlin, who was also in the U.S.A. See *Wilson*, pp. 94–5.

and put him right on top of the world. And so has George Brown's incomes policy (he has now got Aubrey Jones[1] and Hilary Marquand[2] in charge of the Prices and Incomes Board).

Sunday, April 18th

David Butler[3] came over to see me today. This was one of his routine visitations. I suspect he has a diary which says 'See Crossman every four months'. As usual he put his questions to me and put down his answers in his little book. However, his visit did remind me that it was about time that I reflected on these first six months of Labour Government.

Broadly speaking, the analysis I made in the Introduction to Bagehot is being confirmed. Certainly it is true that the Cabinet is now part of the 'dignified' element in the constitution, in the sense that the real decisions are rarely taken there, unless the Prime Minister deliberately chooses to give the appearance of letting Cabinet decide a matter. I was also right to recognize the importance of Cabinet Committees. I am a permanent member of two, the Home Affairs Committee and the Economic Development Committee. In addition, I attend the Immigration Committee and the Broadcasting Committee as well as the Legislation Committee. But I am not a member of the Social Services Committee.* Nor, of course, am I a member of the two really important Committees, on Defence and Foreign Affairs. From these I am totally excluded. So I am very much a home-front Cabinet Minister.

The really big thing I completely failed to notice when I wrote that Introduction was that, in addition to the Cabinet Committees which only Ministers normally attend, there is a full network of official committees; and the work of the Ministers is therefore strictly and completely paralleled at the official level. This means that very often the whole job is pre-cooked in the official committee to a point from which it is extremely difficult to reach any other conclusion than that already determined by the officials in advance; and if agreement is reached at the lower level of a Cabinet Committee, only formal approval is needed from the full Cabinet. This is the way in which Whitehall ensures that the Cabinet system is relatively harmless.

Another big surprise was the discovery that Cabinet minutes are a travesty, or to be more accurate, do not pretend to be an account of what actually takes place in the Cabinet. The same applies to the minutes of Cabinet Committees. Normally, what they record is not what was actually said but a

---

* I was made a member shortly afterwards.

[1] Conservative M.P. for Birmingham (Hall Green) 1950–65. He was Minister of Fuel and Power 1955–7, and of Supply 1957–9, and was the chairman of the National Board for Prices and Incomes from 1965 until 1970.

[2] Labour M.P. for East Cardiff 1945–50, and for Middlesbrough 1950–61. His wartime service as an adviser in the Ministries of Labour and Production and his work as the director of the International Institute for Labour Studies in Geneva (1961–5) made him an ideal choice for deputy chairman. He died in 1972.

[3] Fellow of Nuffield College, Oxford. Psephologist, and author of *Political Change in Britain* (London: Macmillan, 1969) and studies of successive British general elections.

summary of the official brief which the Minister brought with him, the official papers on the original policy, and the official conclusions. The minutes never describe the real struggle which took place. That struggle is only abstracted in the form of 'in the course of discussion the following points were made ... '. And in this summary the name of the Minister who made the point is rarely mentioned.

The combination of this kind of Cabinet minute (which provides the main directive for Whitehall) and official committees enormously strengthens the Civil Service against the politicians. Here are three examples of this system working.

1. We have been busy for some time in my Ministry trying to work out the best method, either fiscal or physical, of controlling the total volume of housing, including private-enterprise housing. All this work has been done following discussions at E.D.C. and in Cabinet, and the responsibility has been taken over by the official committee. In fact, this started when Harold Wilson, in Cabinet, backed my increased housing programme but only won his point by saying that we must look at physical controls in order to manage the total. The moment he said this the whole of Whitehall alerted itself, and an official committee began to work on a paper dealing with physical controls. This paper was then presented to the E.D.C. as an 'official' paper. It was a very odd paper, because though it theoretically came down in favour of physical controls the case was never made out; and Charlie Pannell was able to blow it sky-high with the simple observation that we can't anyway have physical controls for eighteen months because they require legislation. So the whole idea of relying on physical controls before the election was a pipe dream. The lesson of this story is, first, that whatever a Prime Minister says goes in Whitehall, in the sense that if he proclaims himself in favour of something, Whitehall will do its best to make sense of the proposition; and second, that whatever we say as Ministers, or even as Prime Minister, the actual work will be done by the officials.

2. This example relates to local government finance. I think I have recorded already that, much to my regret, I am having Sir Bruce Fraser to replace Dame Evelyn in the autumn, and as a method of appeasing me I was told that he would spend the intervening months in the Treasury doing the initial spade-work on the reform of local taxation, i.e. rates. I had him to dinner along with MacColl the other day, and we had quite a pleasant evening during which he told me his view, which turned out to be wholly negative. He saw no chance of any additional local taxes and he ruled out any prospect of a local income tax as well. 'I'll be putting up a paper,' he said, and I replied, 'Well, for heaven's sake, show it to me first.' But I soon discovered that the paper had been prepared in the Treasury weeks ago and had been seen by the Chancellor and I think by the Prime Minister, but not by me, the Minister most vitally concerned. So the official paper is now in circulation in Whitehall, and unless I am extremely strong-minded it will have pre-judged the whole issue of

local government finance to a point where I shall find it impossible to resist.

3. Another very obvious example of how official committees work has been in something I have been watching over the past two months: the development of the Land Commission Bill. Of course, this is an appallingly difficult measure on which poor Fred Willey has been spending nearly all his time. Whenever we have had a disagreement in the Cabinet Committee, the matter has been referred to the official committee. In due course they produce a solution in a six- or seven-page paper which we Ministers then discuss. Naturally, a solution hammered out by the officials is extremely difficult to overturn.

One surprising effect of these official committees is that still greater influence is given to the Treasury. Why? Because the kind of official who sits on these committees is either the Permanent Secretary himself or the Assistant Secretary in charge. When they all get together, though they dispute with each other, they try as far as possible to even out their disputes and then to produce a coherent Whitehall view. And a coherent Whitehall view is nearly always a view dominated by Treasury thinking.

So what this comes to is that there are two ways in which officialdom impresses its views on Ministers. The first pressure comes from inside the Department where the officials try to make one see things in a departmental way. Ministers tend to have *only* a departmental briefing. The second pressure is inter-departmental, coming when the official committee brings its inter-departmental cohesive view to bear on the Ministers in a single official policy paper. I have yet to see a Minister prevail against an inter-departmental official paper without the backing of the Prime Minister, the First Secretary or the Chancellor. And this is where one's relationships with the P.M. are so all-important. If one doesn't have his backing, or at least the Chancellor's or First Secretary's, the chance of winning against the official view is absolutely nil.

But though Cabinet Ministers have this enormous limitation on their power of decision-taking, still their standing is infinitely superior compared with that of the non-Cabinet Minister. The unfortunate Tony Wedgwood Benn as Postmaster-General, Kenneth Robinson as Minister of Health and Peggy Herbison as Minister of Pensions have a far more difficult time than we do. And I am sure they find it much more difficult to impose their views on their civil servants. Because though the discussions of the Cabinet Committees and Cabinet very often don't have much reality and are simply rehearsing departmental points of view, nevertheless we Cabinet Ministers do have status within Whitehall, in Parliament and in the nation at large. A Cabinet Minister counts for something and a leading Cabinet Minister can certainly get his way far more easily than a non-Cabinet Minister, both in his own Department and of course in the Cabinet.[1]

[1] Crossman discussed these ideas in his Godkin lectures, given at Harvard University in 1970. They are published as *Inside View* (London: Cape, 1972).

Having looked at the constraints on Cabinet's power, I want to try and reflect upon its function. Of course, it isn't a coherent, effective, policy-making body: it's a collection of departmental Ministers who are in practice divided into groups, and with all of whom Harold Wilson maintains bilateral relations. Most important of all, there is the defence and foreign policy group, from which I and over half the Cabinet are totally excluded. Secondly, there is the economic planning group, which consists of the Prime Minister, Brown and Callaghan and whoever they like to call in – pretty often Douglas Jay, occasionally me, occasionally Frank Cousins. Then there are certain segments of home policy, such as the housing segment which I run as overlord with two Ministers under me, Charlie Pannell at the Ministry of Works and Willey at the Ministry of Land and Natural Resources. Quite separate from us is Douglas Houghton's social security segment and of course, equally separate and quite in a corner, agriculture under Fred Peart. All these segments are given a very free hand provided they run smoothly. For example the P.M. has only called one Cabinet Committee meeting in No. 10 to look at housing since he became P.M.

As for the Cabinet agenda, Harold Wilson is keeping to the rule that we should only discuss things in Cabinet which we can't resolve in a Cabinet Committee or which the Prime Minister thinks so important that we must make our individual decisions upon them. In fact, there is nothing decided at Cabinet unless the P.M. specifically wants to have it discussed there.[1]

It looks to me as though this P.M. very much likes fixing things up privately with Ministers by bilateral discussions if he possibly can. On the other hand, he is extremely conventional in his desire to make the Cabinet system work in the traditional way. He is equally conventional with regard to legislation. We prepare our Bills in our Departments; then if they are major Bills we submit them to special committees of Ministers with parallel special committees of officials; and then there comes out a White Paper which is discussed line by line by the Cabinet. After that, the Bill is got ready and presented to Legislation Committee, presided over by the Lord President or the Lord Chancellor, and Legislation Committee is supposed to go through the Bill in detail before it goes to the House.

I give that description because my Rent Bill has gone through this process and I have been able to see how effective it is. If the Prime Minister is on your side, you can get your Bill right through with the minimum of bother from your colleagues. No serious effort was made to change my Bill in any important particular at any stage. The same was true of the Steel Bill. We did have a couple of discussions at Cabinet but not of the contents of the Bill; and when the White Paper came up to Cabinet I was one of the few who made suggestions. But they were entirely about the presentation of the Paper, and no policy issue was raised by anyone at all. As far as I can remember there are

---

[1] Harold Wilson sets out in his book his principles for the preparation and expedition of Cabinet business; *Wilson*, pp. 18–19.

only two Bills which have been substantially changed in Cabinet—the Land Commission Bill and the ombudsman Bill.[1] In the former case the issue had to come to Cabinet because there was a disagreement between Fred Willey, who is in charge of the Bill, and me, his overlord. As for the ombudsman, this we did discuss at great length only last week in Cabinet. There were two reasons for this. In the first place, Harold Wilson was in bed with flu; and in the second place, the Lord Chancellor, who is sponsoring the Bill, is very weak. He had had great difficulty with his Law Commission Bill, though it was an excellent proposal. Now he is having difficulty with his ombudsman Bill, not because Cabinet didn't like it but because he is so ineffective.

Has the Cabinet changed during these first six months? On the economic crisis Cabinet didn't do anything in the so-called Hundred Days except rubber-stamp. The only decisions we were allowed were on prescription charges, pensions and M.P.s' salaries. And the decision in which I was involved, with George Brown, to stop all office building in London, was largely arranged after a telephone conversation between Harold and myself at breakfast-time.[2] But even since the Hundred Days, Cabinet hasn't really become a collective decision-taking body—we have been mainly dealing with secondary disagreements which have to be resolved. We were promised a discussion of general economic policy before the budget, but that discussion never took place. Instead, we had endless leaks in the press about disagreements between Callaghan and Brown which were apparently being fought out partly at Chequers and partly in the special economic group Harold Wilson had established. All I knew of this was what I learned from Tommy Balogh and from the press. Cabinet only heard about the budget on the day before it was presented to Parliament. So we were completely excluded from the general economic planning.

This was equally true with regard to defence policy. I admit that before he went to Washington the Prime Minister did give us an account of his view of the independent nuclear deterrent. But there was no paper and he spoke his piece very rapidly in Cabinet and got it agreed to. After that, two defence issues were brought to Cabinet: the future of the HS-681—brought to Cabinet too late to reverse—and the future of the TSR2. On the TSR2 I have described how each of us was made to make up his mind on three alternatives formulated by the P.M.[3]

The other big issue brought up to Cabinet was my housing programme. The reason it came to Cabinet was of course because there was a disagreement between the Chancellor and myself. I got the policy through as a result of the firm support of the P.M. and an alliance with George Brown. But even so we had some difficulty, because all the other departmental Ministers

---

[1] The measure establishing a Parliamentary Commissioner to examine complaints of maladministration by the Civil Service.
[2] George Brown, Harold Wilson and Crossman all played a part in this.
[3] See p. 190.

resented seeing Housing get more money at the cost of their own budgets. That is why Barbara Castle is against me, for instance.

I think I have listed the main decisions which were the result of genuine collective Cabinet action. Harold Wilson, at the centre of things, has certainly allowed some of us a great deal of Ministerial freedom in forging our own departmental policies. Nevertheless, I would say that he has completely dominated foreign affairs and defence, as well as all the main economic decisions. Here the Cabinet has been excluded and the P.M. has played the formative role by arbitrating the struggle between George Brown and Callaghan.

However, even in the areas in which he runs his Prime Ministerial government a few formal occasions have been interspersed on which he has chosen to have a demonstration of Cabinet government in action. On these occasions he hasn't 'taken the voices'. He has added up the opinions and listed them on a piece of paper. Indeed, I have seen him take pleasure in getting a tie and then forcing us to resolve a closely fought-out decision by a personal vote from each of us.

Let me try to rate the Cabinet Ministers in terms of the power we wield. Well, there's the Prime Minister: not *primus inter pares* – not at all. He is Prime Ministerial in his supreme authority. Below him there is a contest between Jim Callaghan and George Brown. Of course George has emerged as complete king in incomes policy and he has run it on his own, brilliantly successfully. But although he counts for a lot, I should say that in the White-hall struggle the views of Jim Callaghan have prevailed and the views of George Brown have not. The planning of economic policy, which was supposed to be Brown's essential contribution, has hardly started in the D.E.A. – what planning there is is still basically done in the Treasury. It is the economists and officials there who have had all the influence, not those who were taken out of the Treasury and put on Brown's staff at the D.E.A. So we have the P.M. and the Chancellor counting a great deal.

Who else counts? I suppose the Minister of Defence could count. But it is my impression that at present the only man who has come out on the defence side with a will and a mind of his own is Roy Jenkins at Aviation. I have said that non-Cabinet Ministers don't matter, and certainly they don't elsewhere. But Roy Jenkins is an example of a non-Cabinet Minister who has steadily raised his status. Roy refused the offer of the job of Secretary of State for Education and let Tony Crosland have it – at least he says so. Certainly, he has made his mark at Aviation; so that if George Brown falls he might quite likely become head of the D.E.A. But he has been able to play this role because Denis Healey has not been dominant in Defence but has let it be run for him by the P.M. and George Wigg.

As for foreign affairs, I suspect that under Michael Stewart, even more than under Patrick Gordon Walker, the Prime Minister has been the prevailing, dominant personality.

What about the social services, where Douglas Houghton is the overlord in the Cabinet, with Peggy Herbison and Kenneth Robinson working underneath him as non-Cabinet Ministers? Well, Douglas is certainly respected in Cabinet. He is an eminent trade unionist and an important man and he has been put in charge of the agricultural price review, with Fred Peart below him. So he is a top-ranking Minister in that sense. I don't find him very impressive, and certainly he is a dreadful chairman. Nevertheless, he's made clear to the rest of the Cabinet that he is very much in charge of Peggy and Kenneth, and we have let him implement our social security policy in a way which seems to me to have destroyed the whole of our strategy. But if I were to say so in Cabinet I should come into direct conflict with a personality strong in his own right. Indeed, I suppose in Cabinet he and I are about level in power.

Who else really matters? On the Commonwealth side there are three Ministers, Barbara Castle, Arthur Bottomley and Tony Greenwood; and the last two are mere henchmen of the P.M. Barbara talks a great deal in Cabinet about other things than her own small Department. She doesn't yet cut any ice, but she will. I have talked already about the ineffectiveness of poor Frank Soskice at the Home Office. At Education Tony Crosland is now much more confident than he seemed likely to be a few weeks ago, and is emerging in Cabinet as a man with something important to contribute on the economic side.

Of course, one must not forget the people who have no power, for example Fred Lee and Tom Fraser, the Minister of Transport. Fraser's pretty disastrous. He is the only Minister I have actually seen reversed in a Cabinet Committee. A few weeks ago, on his Department's advice, he came forward at a Committee meeting and said he didn't want the railway workshops given the right to compete for orders outside. Here was a gratuitous violation of a socialist pledge which the Committee couldn't stomach. So the E.D.C. ordered the Minister to change his mind, and change it he did.

I have left Frank Cousins to the last because he's a real mystery man still. He sounds like a terrible old blatherer, talking on every subject and usually saying the obvious thing. But he does say it in a working-class way and that's important, because nobody else talks in that way in this Cabinet and we ought to be reminded of what sensible people think in the Labour movement. This he reflects very faithfully, and he also displays every now and then the kind of expertise which the General Secretary of the T.G.W.U. should show on a subject such as the docks. What kind of a new Ministry he is building in Vickers House on the Embankment I have no idea. All I know is that he is occupying more and more floors and getting tremendous backing from Harold Wilson, who believes passionately that his new Ministry of Technology has got to succeed if he is going to keep his promise to modernize British industry. And of course there is one other thing to say about Frank: he is the only trade-union leader introduced by Harold Wilson into his Cabinet. As such he exerts at minimum a very powerful veto.

The Government staggered on with its small majority, increased to four while Aubrey Jones's seat at Hall Green, Birmingham, was vacant. A major parliamentary test came at the beginning of May in the debate on the White Paper on the renationalization of the steel industry. The Labour left wing had been appeased by proposals to nationalize the fourteen biggest companies, which altogether produced over 90 per cent of the country's iron and steel and employed 70 per cent of the industry's work-force. Shareholders were to be generously compensated with £650 million of Government stock. However, opposition was not confined to Conservatives and Liberals, for some Labour right-wingers, notably Woodrow Wyatt and Desmond Donnelly, threatened to abstain and even to vote against the three-line whip. Conciliatory words from the First Secretary only precipitated objections from the left, notably from Ian Mikardo, Michael Foot and Tom Driberg, against any interference with nationalization doctrine.

Nor were things smooth outside Parliament. In May South Wales coal pits shut down over a trivial swearing incident. There were sporadic strikes and walk-outs in Midlands engineering industries—the Royal Commission on the Trade Unions, led by Lord Donovan, was not expected to report until 1968 or so. Meanwhile, some highly paid car workers objected to George Brown's policy of voluntary incomes restraint.

Such troubles were all made manifest early in May, when Labour suffered stunning losses in the municipal elections, with many boroughs showing a swing to the Conservatives of as much as 7 per cent.

Sunday, April 25th

Anne and I have had a lovely week of sunny, cold days in Mullion. While we were there my mind was mainly on the coastline, and we spent all our time walking the coast and seeing the appalling excrescences of Mullion Cove and the Lizard caravan sites. Preservation has been fairly successful up till now, but it's bursting at the seams. Surely there must be something really big we could do.

Some months ago I was asked as Minister to attend a lunch with Prince Philip to launch Operation Neptune, the publicity stunt by which the National Trust is trying to buy up the remaining 900 miles of unspoilt coastline. I turned the invitation down almost automatically because the whole project seemed to me misguided. If the National Trust advertises that it's in the market, all it will do is to put up the price of coastal land which is virtually valueless unless there is planning permission. When I talked to Anne about this one night she said, 'Why don't you freeze the coastline as you froze office-building in London?' I replied rather abruptly that that was a silly idea which would require further legislation. But Anne's remark has given me an idea and I have been brooding over it and trying to think of a way of striking for the coastline this summer as dramatic a blow as we struck for office building in London last autumn.

The red boxes started arriving at the hotel to the predictable excitement of the proprietor. But I didn't find myself worrying about them until news began to come that the building societies' deposits were drying up because investors were transferring their money to more profitable areas of investment, such as the new 9 per cent local government loan. As a result the builders, who rely on the mortgage money when building the new houses, and also the house-owner who is selling his house on an old mortgage, were both suddenly short of funds. By the end of this week I knew what trouble I was in for. The Tories thought they had got me. They put down two successive votes of censure, one on home loans, for April 29th, and the other on rates, for May 5th (carefully timed to coincide with the municipal elections).

Monday, April 26th
I didn't come back by sleeper from Cornwall because it costs too much (I was on holiday so there was no free pass) and it would waste time. Instead, Anne drove me back through a day of driving rain all the way to Prescote. First to see the children, and then after a brief few hours I set out for London. My first appointment was a talk with the Prime Minister about our policy in the home loans debate. I found him, as he always is, very anxious to discuss the general political situation. I finally got round to airing my ideas on dif-ferential interest rates – my main ministerial preoccupation at present. I have got to work out a way of implementing the Party manifesto which promised to give reduced interest rates to the owner-occupier and to the local authority which builds houses. I explained the outline of my idea to the P.M. – a 4 per cent interest rate for house building right across the board, valid for the owner-occupier, valid for the local authority as well. Then he turned to discuss the first censure debate and said that he thought James Callaghan ought to wind up. I said that would be a jolly good idea if Mr Callaghan was really prepared to do it.

Tuesday, April 27th
I should have gone to the Rent Bill Committee, but Jim MacColl is perfectly all right and so I was able to go to Cabinet instead. There the Prime Minister started by saying that he thought I should open the censure debate on home loans for the Government and Callaghan should wind up. Callaghan, as I expected, neatly opted out. He thought he should leave it to me as a pure local government subject. I had to accept that. With an effort I got some kind of authority for telling the House that we would have to have a national plan for integrating housing in the private sector and the public sector. The Cabinet obviously realized that I was in for a bad day on Thursday and when one of us is in for a bad day he doesn't get much sympathy. I was certainly aware that Callaghan was opting out of speaking because at present his image is jolly good, as a result of his budget success, and he doesn't want it tarnished by coming to my help. But it is only a half-day's debate and it has

been agreed that Jack Diamond should give what kind of reply is necessary at the end.

Meanwhile, in the Ministry I was receiving the most alarming reports about home loans. First of all Bill Fiske and his colleagues on the G.L.C. reported to me that no less than half their capital investment this year is going into home loans, most of it on 100 per cent mortgages on old houses. They just borrow the money from the Treasury and pass it on. I can understand why the Chancellor can't take that: it's an anomaly that should not have been permitted. Dame Evelyn wanted me to accept the Treasury policy and rebuke Fiske for his misbehaviour! I realized that with a vote of censure ahead of me I couldn't possibly have it known that I was trying to dry up the supply of money for local authority mortgages at a time when the building societies were drying themselves up. I also received a deputation from the National Federation of Building Trades Employers, headed by Kirby Laing, the chairman of the Laing group of companies. They produced an equally sensational picture, of building societies cutting down their funds altogether, and they actually told me that 50,000 starts were being stopped. I must say that when I cross-examined them carefully it was clear that their only knowledge of these stops came from the newspapers—the panic in fact is partly self-induced. Nevertheless, it provides the atmosphere in which the debate will take place this week.

Wednesday, April 28th
Yet another deputation about the home loans situation. This time it was the building societies. I discovered from them that what is happening varies greatly between the various societies: the Halifax is cutting back very little, and it is the Abbey National, a society which largely finances new housing in the south of England, which is the main cause of the alarm. This delegation told me that the Abbey National, bearing in mind that they have got a Labour Government to deal with, had simply rung up their clients and said, 'No more money.'

All that day I struggled with the drafting of my speech. As the debate got nearer I became more and more concerned about the line I was being pressured to adopt. I wanted to take a tough anti-Tory line, attacking the Opposition for their lack of patriotism and their refusal to defend the pound. As I had no reply about the home loans, surely attack was the best defence. But Harold Wilson and Jim Callaghan tried to dissuade me and by 10.30 p.m. I still had no speech.

Thursday, April 29th
I woke up at six in the morning with an idea for the end of the speech. Why not broach the notion of a national building plan? This is an idea I have aired with the builders and with the building societies and I have had some degree of positive response. I decided to use it for the peroration. All that morning

I worked away, knowing that I was due to appear on *Gallery* immediately after the debate that evening and then to catch the 9.10 to Stafford for a full Friday's work at Newcastle-under-Lyme.

I did just manage to finish the speech and went down to the debate knowing I was going to have my first real taste of punishment.[1] Ted Heath made an extremely powerful oration, accusing us of welching on our pledges and deceiving the public. What was I to reply? What he said was quite true. I had been rather puffed up after lunch because when Peter Brown read the draft he said it was an outstanding declaration of policy which would hit the headlines everywhere. I was quite certain it wouldn't! But his comment encouraged me. Yet when I had made my speech I realized I hadn't pulled it off, mainly because I had failed to attack hard enough. I had made a reasoned, sensible explanation of the situation, followed by a cautious suggestion as to how one might tackle the problem. As a reply to a ferocious vote of censure I am afraid it sounded flat—decent, laborious, but a gimmick thought up at the last moment to get me out of the difficulty. What's more important—in the long run—I had chosen the wrong atmosphere in which to launch my new idea. I hope I haven't kiboshed it altogether.

It doesn't take long in the Commons to realize that a speech hasn't been a success. Today none of my colleagues were there to sit by me and sustain me. When I sat down it was clear enough that I had flopped. Our own people had felt embarrassed and unhappy, precisely because they thought highly of me and were expecting a hard-hitting, confident attack on the Tories. What they got was a diffident, unsure speech, not at all what the situation demanded.

However, I hadn't time for reflections since I had to rush off to Lime Grove for the television show. On the way I had a talk to Tony Shrimsley, the political correspondent of the *Sunday Mirror*. In the car I gave him all the details of my big long-term solution for the home loans problem. Then within minutes I was in a *Gallery* discussion with Ted Heath. I was tired by this time—I had worked since six o'clock that morning. However, I think I seemed to the viewers quiet and collected and Heath was relatively quiet too, so we had a decent discussion. But I am afraid the general impression on the following day was that my *Gallery* appearance had been like my speech, a bit cowed. I don't think I have ruined my personal position but it has been a set-back. My friends have felt sorry and said, 'Dick's up against it.' As for my colleagues in Cabinet, their sympathy has been tinged with the malicious thought, 'Well, there's that confident bugger and he has not done all that well.'

Friday, April 30th
The usual official visit, this time to Newcastle-under-Lyme where I laid the foundation stone of the new council buildings. The mayor was an extraordinary character, straight out of Arnold Bennett, with a grey topper, a

[1] The Government survived by 296 votes to 284.

soiled white shirt and a waltzy manner—a racy, left-wing radical with whom I had a tremendous time. After the official opening we went down to Trentham Gardens, once the Duchess of Sutherland's palace and now a bingo palace on weekdays with grand entertainment suites for use at the weekend. There we stood drinking for an hour before a great meal was served in a highland banqueting hall surrounded by portraits of the Sutherlands and served by Stoke girls in kilts. After a brief official visit to Leek—Harold Davies's constituency[1]—I caught a train to Birmingham where I was due to speak in the Hall Green by-election.[2] I made what may well be the best speech of my whole life—lively and completely confident—but, alas, it was to some fifty or sixty people in an empty hall with no press present. I was motored back to Prescote by a rich Jew with a Rolls Royce, a candidate in the Birmingham municipal elections. I arrived there at 11.30 to find that the Hartrees had brought Anne back already from a film in Banbury and we had a pleasant end to the evening.

Sunday, May 2nd

I had to go back to Birmingham in order to make the main speech at the May Day demonstration at the town hall—about eight hundred people in the audience, not a bad number, but the mood was terribly piano. Again, I had the impression there that the atmosphere is wrong and I suspect it is just as bad in Coventry. Albert Rose rang me up only a few days ago, desperately anxious for a leaflet with my photograph to encourage the candidates, who have been devastated in Coventry East by Winnie Lakin's expulsion from the Party.[3] I did what I could but it's not a good sign and I am expecting bad results.

Wednesday, May 5th

This was my big day—the vote of censure on rating. A good deal of preparatory work had been done in the Ministry, providing briefs for Bob and myself. But I had decided that in my own personal interest I would let Bob start the debate, a full day's debate, unlike the previous one. I would then end up with a party political speech, and since I wouldn't be tied by a script I could hit harder and be more like my natural self. On Monday and Tuesday it had become clearer and clearer to me that, despite Tam's complacent judgment, I really needed to restore my reputation with my own back-benchers and get on top of the Tories, who hoped to capitalize on their success of the previous Wednesday and pull me down if they could. They wanted a kill in the chase for the Minister of Housing. So a lot depended on my success.

[1] Davies held the seat from 1945 until 1970, when he was created Lord Davies of Leek. See p. 269.
[2] Caused by the appointment of the sitting Conservative Member, Aubrey Jones, as Chairman of the Prices and Incomes Board. In the by-election on May 6th Reginald Eyre held the seat for the Conservatives with a 3 per cent swing from Labour.
[3] See p. 197.

However, today was a pretty full day because in addition to the debate at
3.30 I had to take a big conference on the planning proposals for Piccadilly
in the morning. For some weeks we have been working in the Ministry on the
presentation to the press of an expert report which suggests that the new
Piccadilly Circus should be built on stilts. I took a great deal of trouble about
this press release and the briefing for the press conference, mainly because I
was hopeful that the proper publicity for it in Thursday's papers would push
the Commons debate out of the headlines. Well, I had a jolly good press
conference.* I had seen all the weekly highbrow press on Tuesday, and today
I held the big press conference at eleven o'clock and then did television and
radio interviews until nearly one o'clock. It was a good thing I didn't have to
prepare a full-scale opening speech for the afternoon.

After I had finished the Piccadilly press conference I went across to the
House of Commons to hear the end of the P.L.P. meeting on steel, held as a
run-up for tomorrow's debate. I got there in time to hear Desmond Donnelly
making a very careful, cagey speech before Harold Wilson wound up. His
speech was a combination of (a) a piece about steel, (b) a piece about the
second Hundred Days, and (c) a peroration in which he emphasized to the
Party the danger of being dictated to by minorities, and said that rather than
let that happen, whether it was a steel minority, or a pacifist minority or any
other minority, he would tell them to go to blazes. Though I found the rest
of the speech, particularly on foreign policy, fairly nauseating—especially
the assertion that Britain holds the initiative all over the world—I was relieved
to listen to the assurance in the last passage that, whatever happened, the
steel minorities, such as Desmond Donnelly and Woodrow Wyatt, would be
kept in their place.[1]

Now for my rating debate. I was glad that I had given the opening to Bob
Mellish: he made a very characteristic speech, good knock-about stuff,
although he had received the same brief as I had. Bob has become a stalwart
lieutenant. He is a very rough diamond, a working-class chap from
Bermondsey, a T.G.W.U. organizer at one time, an officer in a transport unit
during the war, and a real professional politician today. He's a bit crude, a
bit slippery, a bit vulgar-minded and very much the supporter of whoever is
his boss at the moment. Let me say, however, that, despite hating me before,
he has become extremely loyal; and that afternoon he did as well as he
possibly could. As for my own winding-up speech at the end, if I won the
debate it was because I had to fight for my life, and by means of a conscious
rhetorically- and demagogically-forced row with the Opposition I won back
both their respect and my popularity among my own Party.[2]

* And actually succeeded in my objective.
[1] According to Wilson, George Brown had 'sweated blood with Donnelly', and he
himself had found Wyatt extremely persuasive; see *Wilson*, pp. 100–101. Woodrow Wyatt
gives a rather different account of his role in the affair in *Turn Again Westminster* (London:
Deutsch, 1973), pp. 156–7.
[2] The Government survived with a narrow majority — 279 votes to 275.

These two censure debates have made me realize that for the first time I really have been up against it, struggling for my political existence. And I recognize for the first time that if the pack gets me down and undermines my self-confidence it could be very difficult to regain that confidence and restore my position.

Thursday, May 6th
Convinced by Harold's speech to the Party that there wasn't going to be a big Cabinet crisis I allowed myself all day for departmental worries. I spent the whole of the afternoon, when I could have been listening to the steel debate, sitting with Dame Evelyn, John Delafons and the rest of them, trying to work out a way of putting the Party manifesto into practice by assuring low interest rates both to local authorities and to private-house purchasers. Here I must add a word about John Delafons. He is proving a magnificent Private Secretary, devoted, enthusiastic and, though he doesn't know an awful lot about housing, enormously helpful. Before the meeting started he warned me that the Dame had been tearing her hair out all that morning about my ideas. I told him to tell her and the rest of them beforehand that I would lay down the law – that this was Party policy and we would have to carry it out – and that is just what I did, reading aloud, as though it was the sacred Bible, the passage of the manifesto on housing finance, and saying that it was our job to try to carry this out competently. Looking round the room rather severely I added, 'I would like to hear what objections there would be in strict terms of feasibility to 4 per cent interest rates across the board.' That made it fairly simple and I soon got agreement that the Department should provide a paper for me for submission this week to the Chancellor, with a copy to the Prime Minister at the same time.

In the evening I gave dinner to Richard Llewelyn-Davies in order to discuss R.A.G. After dinner we went in to the House for the end of the steel debate. There wasn't all that much of a crowd in the Chamber. He went up to the gallery to watch and I went down below and was sitting there quietly listening to George Brown's wind-up. I was not apprehensive, having heard Harold Wilson's categoric assurance to the Party meeting. True, I remembered that he had said to me in private conversation that, yes, he had had three or four talks with Woodrow on his idea that a 51 per cent shareholding was a sufficient degree of Government control to exert over the steel industry. But I hadn't taken this too seriously.[1] So when I heard George Brown at the end of his proper speech give himself an extra five minutes in order to address a special message to Woodrow Wyatt and Desmond Donnelly, I was flabbergasted.[2]

[1] Nor, it seems had Wilson.
[2] At the very end of the debate Wyatt asked the First Secretary, ' "if the industry will come forward, [is he] prepared to listen?" ' George Brown replied, ' "Listen" is the word. Listen, certainly." ' The Government survived narrowly with 310 votes to 306. The Prime Minister's view of this was that '[George] appeared to incline more to their views than anyone expected.' See *Wilson*, p. 101.

Friday, May 7th

At breakfast I rang up George Wigg as I very often do and asked him what the hell was going on. 'Look, George,' I said, 'the P.M. had better know that he and the First Secretary can't get away with this kind of behaviour. It undermines the whole basis of unity in Cabinet.' George Wigg bit my head off. 'Don't be so silly,' he said. 'Harold was consulted by George Brown just afterwards and I have talked to him since. He thinks that good can come out of what happened.' That was characteristic George Wigg. Whenever you take your own line he tries to swamp you.

I had to break our talk in order to go to the office before catching the train to Cambridge, where I was due to make an official visit with J. D. Jones and John Delafons. In the train I talked to J.D. about Anne's suggestion of a complete freeze on all coastline planning permission. As usual his first reaction to the idea was pretty negative. But Anne was right. So far from a total freeze being impossible, it is well within my legal powers to 'call in' in future every planning permission which affects the coastline. Naturally, J.D. explained, I wouldn't be able to do this unless I had the administrative capacity to deal with all these planning permissions. Then we checked over the whole Cambridge planning problem and he warned me about the inner ring-road controversy. He is brilliant at briefing his Minister and I felt pretty sure of myself before I stepped into the mayor's car and went off to open a block of old people's flats. But throughout my day of visits and discussions with the Cambridge Council I was brooding on the steel debate and feeling more and more upset. I had a feeling that in the last fortnight it wasn't only Dick Crossman who was in personal trouble at Housing. Public opinion was getting impatient with the whole Labour Government and now with this steel affair thrown in we were bound to face serious trouble outside as well as in Cabinet. I couldn't see how Harold and George could get out of it. They had made these concessions to Woodrow Wyatt and Desmond Donnelly, a back-bench minority, within hours of absolutely and completely denying that any such concessions were on the map. My impression was not removed when after the day's work I went to stay with Nicky Kaldor and his wife, Clarissa. When I got there Nicky was away in London talking to James Callaghan. But Clarissa, who is a Cambridge councillor, had a long talk to me about the local situation – the difficulty of getting canvassers out and how the whole élan had gone out of the city Party. There was no lift, no sense of participation in the affairs of the Labour Government, she said, because the Government wasn't communicating with the local Parties. Later in the evening Nicky arrived, and Victor Rothschild came in to dinner.[1] Not having devalued, said Nicky, we mustn't have any illusions. We shall have to go through a long period of savage deflation and mass unemployment in order

---

[1] Lord Rothschild was a distinguished zoologist at Cambridge and, until 1970, the chairman of Shell Research. He then became the director-general of the Central Policy Review Staff established in the Cabinet Office by the new Conservative Administration.

to purge ourselves. I argued against this pessimism, furiously and probably rudely, but I knew I couldn't really answer the case which Nicky put.

I drove back to Prescote on Saturday in time to receive Tommy Balogh, who had been convalescing at Gavin Faringdon's place in Berkshire for ten days.[1] Checking over with him I found he shared Kaldor's view. He agreed that, having failed to float the pound, we should have to deflate on a major scale and for that reason my chances of getting Cabinet to adopt low interest rates for housing were nil. In fact, we wouldn't gain anything by letting this Labour Government linger on. The sensible thing was to have an election as soon as possible.

Well, that may be true. I have thought for some time that an election in May or June would probably be the best thing for us. But we won't have one, if only because of the municipal elections next Thursday when we are liable to lose 300 or 400 seats throughout the country. A Tory victory of these dimensions wouldn't be a good prelude to an election campaign.

Monday, May 10th
We set out for the station nine minutes before the train was due and had a terrible rush on an exquisite early summer morning through the back lanes to get there on time. Once safely on the train, I looked at my engagement list and found that by good fortune I had an interview with the Prime Minister at 10.30, half an hour after the train got into Paddington, at which we were due to discuss parliamentary boundaries. Instead of letting him quiz me on boundaries, I had to tell him that at all costs we must have a Cabinet meeting on the steel crisis before the Party meeting on Wednesday. Directly I got to my office I saw Delafons and said, 'Well I shall be seeing the Prime Minister in half an hour.' And he replied, 'It's been cancelled already.' When I heard this I didn't quite know what to do so I sat down at my desk and finally took the phone and rang Frank Cousins. He sits almost opposite me at the Cabinet table and though I don't see much of him I feel we have a good deal of natural sympathy. When he heard I would like to see him, he was obviously glad. So I said I would come round straight away. Then I rang George Wigg and left a message at his office that my meeting with the Prime Minister had been cancelled and I wanted it restored.

I found Frank Cousins full of himself. He told me that he had been thinking of resigning for some time owing to his dissatisfaction with his job. He also revealed that he had spent Sunday evening with Mikardo and a number of other left-wing socialists and that his view, like theirs, was that the whole issue must be settled at the Party meeting. I said I thought this was a great mistake: it was a matter for Cabinet decision and we two ought to requisition a Cabinet on Tuesday morning. Would he support me in that? He said he would. That was about all I could do before George Wigg came through on the phone and began a long explanation to Frank Cousins, assuring him how

[1] Lord Faringdon's house at Buscot Park, Faringdon.

everything was in order. When Frank told him I was sitting there beside him, George said he had arranged that I should see the Prime Minister after all at 11. So back I sped to Downing Street pretty pleased that my cancelled meeting had been put back on the agenda so quickly.

I found Harold sitting in the Cabinet room. He at once said he had to be careful that officially he was only seeing me about housing; he also explained why he couldn't keep his appointment with me at 10.30 — it would have been thought that he was discussing George Brown with me. I said we could certainly discuss housing and I began to talk a little about the Department's new interest-rate policy, but Harold soon switched to George and the steel crisis. I said straight away that the essential thing was to call a Cabinet on Tuesday and then to get the backing of the Party meeting on Wednesday morning. He replied that he intended to hold a Lobby conference that day in which he would explain how George Brown had done it all entirely on his own and how he himself had had nothing to do with it. I said this couldn't be more unfortunate for his own image. The press was already implying that he was backing out of his responsibilities, and an off-the-record conference of this sort might give them an excuse for saying that the Prime Minister was leaving the First Secretary in the lurch. At one point he asked me, 'Do you think I should be left alone to bear the brunt of this?' 'No,' I said, 'I think it is our job in Cabinet to back you up. The moment you bring us together tomorrow, Cabinet will realize that it can't jettison George. We must agree to support what he said and allow him to waste his time listening to the steel magnates. Having given him public support, however, we can trounce him in private about his unfortunate performance.'

We discussed this round and round for some time until a message was brought in that Callaghan and others were waiting to see Harold. At once I went out and mentioned to Callaghan in passing that I had been having a discussion about housing (sure enough in the morning papers next day there was a statement, released presumably from Downing Street, that the Prime Minister had spent a long time discussing the urgent problems of housing loans). I went straight up to George Wigg's room and told him what had happened. George Wigg blew up. 'Who are you to say there is anything wrong with the George Brown line?' he shouted at me. I said it was outrageous that George Brown should take this line with Donnelly and Wyatt just after the Prime Minister had assured us in the Parliamentary Party meeting that he would send all minorities to blazes. 'That's your view, is it?' said Wigg suddenly. 'Well in that case we are fighting each other and that's the end of it.' I began to realize that in this episode George and I were giving opposite advice. Wigg's advice was that George Brown had done nothing very much wrong and that the thing to do was to brazen it out throughout the week and not to have a Cabinet meeting. I was saying that it was essential to have a Cabinet on Tuesday. During the day I was interested to wait and see which of us would win. In the afternoon Barbara Castle came to me about a planning

permission for development in central Blackburn. I told her about my talk
with Frank Cousins and asked her whether she would support me in
requisitioning a Tuesday Cabinet meeting. She said she would. A little later
John Delafons came in to tell me that a Cabinet meeting had been called for
Tuesday morning at 11.

Tuesday, May 11th
The Cabinet meeting meant that I was only able to look in at the Committee
Stage of my Rent Bill; I have been neglecting it a good deal. Harold started
with a longish, rambling account, and was followed by a very attractive
apologia from George Brown which included the frank admission that he
should have informed the Minister, Fred Lee, before he made his Statement.
At this, Harold signalled to me and I weighed in, making a full statement with
three points. I said first that what we had to decide was whether to jettison
George Brown or whether to support him. There couldn't be any half
measures. We must either unreservedly accept that we were bound by his
offer to listen to the steel magnates or throw him overboard. I personally had
no doubt that we must accept what he said as said on our behalf. My second
point was that, although I held this view, I also thought that he had done
something very unwise because it was in complete contradiction to the Prime
Minister's assurances to the Parliamentary Party. It was this, I emphasized,
which had undermined the morale of the Party. Finally, I concluded that it
seemed to me essential that, when Cabinet had decided its line, the Prime
Minister should go to the Party meeting on Wednesday morning and make a
statement, but—and here I corrected Harold Wilson—he shouldn't just make
a statement; he should subject himself to questioning, because the Party must
feel that they have the right to be consulted.
    I was pleased when Thomas Balogh rang me up in the evening to con-
gratulate me on a speech which Harold Wilson had described to him in a most
enthusiastic way. Apparently he felt the Cabinet meeting had been a success,
and I felt so too.
    I had a long and hectic afternoon in the Ministry. Then I had to rush off to
London University to debate a motion on racial discrimination with Iain
Macleod. It is always a bit of a risk speaking off one's subject when one is a
Minister, and I had tried to prepare this speech adequately in the intervals of
a long series of meetings. I had asked Iain Macleod to pick me up at the
Ministry so that I could take him up to Gower Street in the ministerial car
because I didn't want to go and dine with the young men at five thirty. So at
six o'clock he came in while I was changing into my dinner-jacket. I gave him
a drink and I took up my speech notes from the desk. It was only when I was
sitting in my place at the debate that I noticed that by mistake I had picked
up not only the speech notes and Hansard but some sheets of Cabinet background papers on race relations. The debate itself, a motion of no confidence

on the Labour Party's policy on racialism, went pretty well and I managed to win by two to one. Then I took Iain Macleod back to his flat in St James's Street. I had been interested to meet him for the first time since we had come to power, and I told him how much I enjoyed being a Minister. 'Of course you do,' he said. 'Being a Minister is the only thing worth doing in the whole world.' I said I wouldn't go so far as that but it was enjoyable. 'Of course,' said Iain again, 'you and I are politicians. A Minister's life is the only thing in the world worth having.' I realized that he meant it.

I was going to ask Molly to drive me home when I realized I was hungry – I hadn't eaten since lunch-time. Since it was now eleven o'clock and I was in St James's Street, I went to Prunier, where Anne and I always celebrate her birthday. There I found myself sitting next to four people who I thought to be hunting people – silly, stuck-up, well-dressed and slightly bibulous. I felt uneasy sitting beside them and I put my little sheaf of Cabinet papers below my feet and pretended to read my Hansard while I ate my supper slightly sanctimoniously. Then I went out and walked home across the park.

Wednesday, May 12th
This was the morning of the Party meeting, and I went across at eleven to hear Harold Wilson make his speech. He was given his success on a plate by William Warbey,[1] who with a single question turned the ire of the whole Party against *himself* and took the heat off Harold. By the end of the meeting I knew that the tactics I had advised had worked to perfection. The steel crisis was over.

In the afternoon we had the first afternoon session of the Rent Bill Committee. Despite a great deal of Tory fuss I had in the previous week carried the motion extending the number of sessions of the Committee from two to three, the third to be fitted in on Wednesdays at four o'clock. As I sat through this first meeting I was puzzled by a series of messages that I must talk urgently to my Private Secretary. I was in the middle of addressing the Committee on one of the amendments when another message came through that Cabinet papers were missing. Slowly it dawned on me that I had left at Prunier the sheets I had snatched up to take with me to the debate with Iain Macleod.

At six forty-five, when I moved the adjournment of the Committee and went out into the corridor, I was told that I had to go back to my office and wait for an urgent appointment with the Prime Minister, who was then broadcasting a party political – a last-minute appeal before Thursday's municipal elections. However, I said I didn't see why I couldn't go home and see my dear Anne while I was waiting for him. This was the evening when we

---

[1] M.P. for Broxtowe (Nottinghamshire) 1953–5 and Ashfield (Nottinghamshire) from 1955 until his resignation in 1966. He took an extreme left-wing line on Vietnam and in 1965 published *Vietnam, the Truth* (London: Merlin Press, 1966).

had decided to accept an invitation to see an American play at the World Theatre season at the Aldwych. We don't often go out to the theatre but on this occasion we had been invited by the American Ambassador to a party at the Embassy in order to meet the cast. When I got home I told Anne about the extraordinary *contretemps* and what I now realized had happened at Prunier. It wasn't long before a message came from George Wigg that I must go and see him immediately. When I arrived, he was all seriousness. He explained to me that nothing could be more inconvenient for the Prime Minister and him than that I should be guilty of a lapse of security. On the previous Monday the Prime Minister had, in order to get a diversion from the steel crisis, announced new security regulations for which George Wigg would be the chief co-ordinator. I then told George exactly what had happened. He looked very grave and said I must wait and see the Prime Minister.

In due course he went down, and I sat on alone in his room. After twenty minutes Derek Mitchell, the Prime Minister's Private Secretary, came and said, 'Come and see him. I don't think it's very serious.' As he went into No. 10 through the back door from George's office I saw the P.M. disappear into the lift. The lift was halted and I just caught it. He laughed when he saw me, saying he had heard from George Wigg what had happened and he would be delighted to answer any questions the Tories liked to put. 'I am in a great state of euphoria,' he said to me. 'I have just given the finest party political broadcast in history. I have really trounced the Tories. As for you, well, thank heavens you weren't dining with Christine Keeler. There's nothing in it, my dear boy, you can go away happy.' So I went to the theatre and on from there to the American Embassy, where there was a vast crowd queueing for food. Anne and I went home to have some there. We had scarcely got to Vincent Square, at about twelve o'clock, when the telephone began to ring. By then the first editions had come out: and Chapman Pincher had a story in the *Express* that had impacted on the rest of Fleet Street. Each of them wanted to write a story of their own for their second editions.

I said nothing to any of them except the man from *The Times*. To him I revealed the key fact that I had been debating with Iain Macleod and that the papers referred to race and had nothing secret in them.

Thursday, May 13th
I woke up this morning to find that Chapman Pincher had written a piece about how someone had informed against me. Apparently this fellow had spotted the papers under my chair, and had taken them home, kept them until twelve o'clock next day and then handed them over to the police. But before doing so he had shown them to the *Daily Express*, Nothing more unpleasant could have happened.

Apart from my own personal Prunier crisis, I had a busy day finalizing my home loans policy for circulation to Cabinet and getting on with my coastline policy. I also had my Rent Bill Committee. Frankly, I hardly had time to register the fact that it was polling day in the municipal elections before I went off to Lime Grove for a debate with Eric Lubbock and Enoch Powell on the rates. In this broadcast I had decided to really push my policy on local taxation. I was still furious that in the censure debate on home loans I had got the rough end of the stick because James Callaghan had refused to speak and left me to carry the can. I wanted to send him a message that I didn't want any more nonsense but a genuine reform of local finance, and to do it in the only way I knew how—by saying it publicly. In fact, I really had a mouthful to spill and perhaps this is why I did so much better that week on *Gallery* than I had done a week before, battling against Ted Heath. Anne told me at the end that it was one of the best things she had heard me do, and certainly I knew that I had been quiet and competent and effective, and that Lubbock and Powell had been very pleasant to me before I got into my car to go along with Peter Brown to King's Cross to catch the night train for Newcastle. On the way to the station I went to Vincent Square to pack and just had time to switch on the television and see the second edition of the *Gallery* programme, which was dealing with the municipal elections. Right at the beginning it was quite clear that Labour was in for a hell of a hiding.

Saturday, May 15th
I wasn't too surprised when I got into my bath on Friday morning to read that we had lost between three hundred and four hundred seats, and that the results in the North-East were something of a disaster.[1] These times are difficult for a Minister. I had a press conference arranged for eleven that morning and the last thing I wanted to talk about was the municipal election results. Mistakenly, I did find myself talking about them, and, even more mistakenly, I decided to tell people what had really happened at Prunier earlier in the week. I don't know why I did this. Anyway, this morning that story was vying with the municipal election disaster in filling the news columns.

This was another official visit which I enjoyed intensely. I spent Friday morning with the Newcastle housing people and did a tour of the city to see something of their problems. The afternoon was scheduled for a visit to the Durham County Council in their magnificent palace of a building just outside Durham. The men in charge were willowy Englishmen from down south, ruling over a great civic establishment and greatly enjoying the hunting and fishing and shooting which seemed to be part of their job. I sped back from Durham to see one of the most difficult planning problems of Newcastle, Eldon Square—a beautiful Georgian square which they are going to destroy for a new shopping centre. I am passionately opposed to this and I blew up

---

[1] The Conservatives gained 552 seats; Labour lost 374 and the Liberals lost 174. In the Scottish borough elections on May 4th Labour had lost 4 seats and the Scottish Nationalists had gained 4.

our regional staff in Newcastle and told them they were vandals for giving my consent. But I knew that it was already a *fait accompli*, and when I get back I shall be forced to draft the directive letter saying they should have permission.*

That evening the Lord Mayor of Newcastle gave a dinner at which we were able to discuss the coastline and local government boundaries. He is a Labour mayor, and later in the evening the devastating shock of the elections was also a subject of conversation. I tottered to bed at eleven o'clock knowing I had to be up at eight thirty.

Today, Saturday, a cold, thundery, darkish morning. I was taken out by Alderman Sir Nicholas Garrow, chairman of the Northumberland County Council, and his planning officer. Like the Durham officials, they were terribly anxious to impress their personalities, corporate and individual, on me, in order to dissuade me from creating a Greater Newcastle which would have to be carved out of the richest rateable area in the two counties. I found the Northumberland 'New Towning' efforts pathetic, but I did my best for them, opening their new factories and visiting their bogus New Town. Then I was speeding off to Sunderland where I found in addition to a shipyard, a lovely sea-front, an excellent lunch and a splendid afternoon with a council which has the best house-building record in England and is really warm-heartedly Labour. We toured the countryside in a bus and saw where they are going to build a satellite town. Then I motored forty miles to Darlington to catch the train, arriving at Birmingham at nine o'clock where a car was waiting to get me back to Prescote at ten forty-five. It had been quite a week and I wanted a day of relaxation.

Sunday, May 16th
I have had time to reflect and recover from the shock of the municipal elections. Although I anticipated the total of the losses, somehow when some of the losses happen to you it feels much worse. Birmingham, twelve seats lost; Coventry, four seats lost—this is tremendously serious. This evening I have had Albert Rose and Winnie Lakin over to discuss the problems of Coventry, because three of the four defeats were in Coventry East and two at least were largely due to the scandalous decision to expel Winnie from the Party during the election campaign.[1] But whatever the local Coventry difficulties, it seemed to all of us quite clear that one can't expect the electorate to vote Labour after nearly eight months of Labour Government when, despite sowing a lot of seed, we have reaped nothing. Of the package we promised the elector—including low interest rates and reduced rents—nothing so far has been delivered, even by my anti-eviction Bill. So naturally enough we had a mass of abstentions and a vicious swing to the Tories. No doubt, as

---

* It is a major scandal that the development never materialized. The destruction of Eldon Square was a tragedy.
[1] See p. 197.

seen by the outside world, the effect of municipals will be to knock out a summer election. But that's a fallacy since a summer election was out long before this catastrophe: Harold Wilson clearly prefers spring. No! what this municipal defeat did was to emphasize the precarious situation of the Government. If two of our people die, that could destroy our majority. In the last division we had poor Hayman, the M.P. for Falmouth, ill,[1] and Leslie Spriggs lying in an oxygen tent in an ambulance in Speaker's Yard.[2] We are terribly near the edge of the abyss and it is my impression that if things are at all favourable we shall seize an opportunity in October, having ended the Session in July.

But we shall still have to get the Steel Bill, the Land Commission Bill and my rating legislation ready. As a result of the row I had with the Dame, my officials have now got down to the job. With very little help from me the Dame has turned out a clear-cut, hard-hitting Cabinet paper in which she has had the sense to put the four-year housing plan at the top and merely ask for authority to go ahead on the new system of 4 per cent interest subsidies for local authorities and a 4 per cent slice for the houseowner as a means to this end. Fortunately, in the first twelve months it doesn't cost very much and that's what interests the Chancellor. Moreover I am in a strong bargaining position with him because I must start negotiating with the building societies and the local authorities at once if I am to get the policy ready for the summer recess.

As they had promised, the Government cut the import surcharge to 10 per cent at the end of April, but simultaneously the Bank of England had to call for special deposits. On May 5th Lord Cromer, the Governor of the Bank, had asked the clearing banks to restrict all bank advances, save to exporters, to only 5 per cent until March 1966. But the clearing banks made no promises to prune their lending.

The April trade figures, published on May 13th, showed a further rise in imports and the trade gap continued to widen, as imports rose to £501 million and as exports fell to £392 million during May. This was coupled with unhappiness in the City at the Chancellor's corporation and capital gains taxes and disbelief in the First Secretary's hopeful prices and incomes policy. Voluntary restraint had been undermined by a wage award to the postmen in mid-April and it was now threatened by claims from the miners, railwaymen and London busmen. Not surprisingly, the pound continued to drop on the exchanges although the Prime Minister still refused to breathe the word devaluation.

He also remained adamantly opposed to any demand for a general election. Labour Members were driven through the lobbies and both sides endured all-night sittings on the details of the Finance Bill, which was to take until the end of

---

[1] Frank Hayman, Gaitskell's former P.P.S., had been M.P. for Falmouth since 1950, and was now aged seventy-one. He died in February 1966.
[2] M.P. for St Helens since 1958. He survived the experience.

*July to pass, with some 440 amendments from the Government alone. But
divisions were a close business for the Government, with its precarious majority.
Richard Crossman's Rent Bill presented the same problems of time-tabling and
manning the benches. The Minister of Housing also found that his efforts to
build more houses were being frustrated. Mortgage rates were by now at 7 per
cent and the Chancellor was unable to give the Minister the financial support
he required.*

Monday, May 17th

The meeting with the Chancellor didn't really add up to very much. I had
given him my paper in advance, and with Willie Ross's help I presented it
briefly. In reply, the Chancellor started by saying that if we got what we
asked for there wouldn't be room for an increase in any other social service
and that's a position he couldn't possibly consider. Then he proceeded to ask
a few desultory questions about why we needed more housing and whether
we couldn't solve the situation by taking over old houses and putting young
people into them. I suppose they are the questions which Conservative
Chancellors always ask of their Ministers of Housing. It was a little depressing
that James made no effort to judge our plan from the point of view of Government strategy as a whole, but saw it in strict Treasury terms. It was also depressing that he was inclined to tell us all our plans were pie in the sky in
view of the crisis. Oh dear! I do understand why George Brown detests him
and why Harold feels embarrassed by his behaviour. I can also understand
why Nicky Kaldor, Tommy Balogh and Robert Neild – who were in his room
when we were talking – are all unrepentantly saying that we should have
devalued last October and that the deflation which we are now beginning
must go inexorably on.

In the evening I had a meeting with the Labour members of the Standing
Committee on the Rent Bill. They had asked to see me about Clause 15, which
deals with the machinery for transferring controlled houses into the
regulated sector. What this Bill does is to freeze all controlled rents so as to
give people complete security, unless the tenancy changes. But once the
tenancy changes under this Bill, the houses automatically become regulated
and not controlled. On the other hand, this is all designed as a first stage;
and I said in the Second Reading that there will come a second stage. When
we have finished dealing with the houses out of control and have got the
rent system in order, we intend to transfer whole sections of controlled
houses to regulation, and Clause 15 deals with this. Of course, there are a
number of my back-benchers who really hate my whole Bill because what they
would have liked was a return to rents fixed in relation to rateable value. They
hate the whole idea of a moveable fair rent, which can be put up as well as
down by the rent officer. And so four of my Committee, Frank Allaun,[1]

---

[1] Labour M.P. for East Salford since 1955. P.P.S. to the Secretary of State for the
Colonies 1964–5.

Eric Heffer,[1] Lena Jeger[2] and Julius Silverman,[3] have been waiting for the moment when they could test the Minister. It came on Monday evening. They told me they would have to dig their toes in and prevent this Clause going through because it was a tacit admission that once I had dealt with the uncontrolled houses, controlled rents would have to go up. I told them this was quite true and added that it was obvious that many controlled rents today, particularly in Scotland, are fantastically low. I had a two-hour struggle and I thought at the end that I had got them round. Anyway, I had to rush off to dinner with the Dame, who was in splendid form. She entertained me at her home in Kensington; the other guests were Jimmy James, our Chief Planner from the Ministry, and a man I had wanted to meet for a long time, Dan Smith, the Labour boss of Newcastle who is a great personal friend of the Dame.[4] I felt that she was really beginning to enjoy me as Minister and I am certainly enjoying her enormously as Permanent Secretary.

Tuesday, May 18th

When we began to deal with Clause 15 in the Rent Bill Committee today it was, alas, our people who dug their toes in; we spent the whole morning quarrelling, with the Tories looking on in pleasure. This could turn out a disaster. If our people delay me on Clause 15, I can't reasonably blame the Tories if they also start filibustering, which they are not doing at present. They sat there delighted while Frank Allaun, Julius Silverman and Lena Jeger all made long speeches saying they would vote *against* the Clause – not merely abstain – if I dared to put it to the vote. As the morning wore on, I was faced with my first parliamentary crisis. There was I in complete charge of the Bill and having to take a decision on tactics. Dick Mabon, the Scot,[5] who is one of my two junior Ministers in charge, moved along the bench and whispered, 'I'd make the concession to them: let the Clause be talked out now so that you can meet them this evening and make the concession they need.'

I was just wondering whether to take Mabon's advice when the Tories very stupidly declared their intention of voting against the Clause on their own. I saw my chance and decided to force a division. Obviously it was better to be defeated by my back-benchers on a division, in which case I could report the

---

[1] A Liverpool councillor 1960–66 and Labour M.P. for the Walton Division of Liverpool since 1964.

[2] Labour M.P. for Holborn and St Pancras South 1953–9 and since 1964.

[3] A barrister. Labour M.P. for Birmingham 1945–55, and for Aston, Birmingham, since 1955. No relation to Sydney Silverman.

[4] A county councillor in Newcastle upon Tyne 1950–66, he was chairman of the Northern Economic Planning Council 1965–70 and of the Peterlee and Aycliffe Development Corporation 1968–70, and a member of the Royal Commission on Local Government 1966–9. Under his energetic direction much of Newcastle and the surrounding country was redeveloped and resourcefully exploited. In October 1973 he was arrested on a charge of conspiracy to corrupt.

[5] Joint Parliamentary Under-Secretary of State for Scotland 1964–7, and M.P. for Greenock since December 1955.

whole matter to the Prime Minister, rather than cave in privately behind the scenes. Alternatively, the division might call their bluff. I didn't think there was much chance of this happening but it was worth a try.

At about 12.45 the division took place and, though the three of them had sworn they would vote against the Clause, they voted for it when it was put, and I had a majority of two. I had called *their* bluff and got over my first crisis. However, I did meet them again that evening to discuss the much more critical Clause 22, the famous fair-rent clause, which we might possibly reach next week. I spent two and a half hours with them and I thought I had convinced them that I might be right about the fair rent. At least I had made them realize that they had a fairly strong Minister in charge and they had also got an idea of the basic thinking which had inspired Clause 22.

In the afternoon Harold Wilson insisted on taking Questions about my affair at Prunier even though it involved his making a special Statement at the end of Question Time. He really lambasted the Tories and pointed out that an 'officer and a gentleman' really wasn't behaving in a very officerly or gentlemanly way in handing secret papers over to the *Daily Express*. None of the front-bench Tories took any part in the affair. Indeed, some of them were extremely embarrassed and came up to me afterwards to say that this was a case where a personal incident which could have been disastrous was being transformed by Tory mismanagement to their disadvantage. As we walked out of the Chamber Harold said to me, 'Well, I had the pleasure of rehabilitating you and George Wigg simultaneously.' Indeed, George has been in bad odour recently with the press and also with the Parliamentary Party. The Prime Minister had replied by contrasting his treatment of security with that of the 'officer and gentleman' in question.

Thursday, May 20th
I was only able to look in on Cabinet this week because I was busy with the Bill. There is certainly a feeling among more and more Ministers that our whole tactics have been very odd. In this particular year it seems crazy to have a Finance Bill two hundred pages long[1] creating every kind of difficulty in the City at the very time when we want to regain the confidence of the capitalist world. Also, coupling the Finance Bill with steel nationalization does seem an odd way of keeping going a radical government with a majority of three. Of course, the situation is made far worse by the complete ineffectiveness of our Party propaganda and the total lack of co-ordination between Transport House and the Cabinet. I was able to make this point in Cabinet before rushing back to my Bill. It may all get better now that George Wigg has been made unofficial liaison officer between Transport House and the Cabinet. But I am doubtful about it. What we need is what the Tories have always had—a Cabinet Minister responsible for relations with the Party. The Chancellor of the Duchy of Lancaster, for example, instead of having

---

[1] It had ninety clauses and twenty-one schedules.

social security as his job, should be charged with responsibility for the liaison with the Party and the press without which any government, but above all a Labour government, lives in a state of permanent embarrassment.

My conversation with the back-benchers on Tuesday didn't have any immediate effect. Three hours on Wednesday afternoon and three hours on Thursday were largely consumed by their speeches and as a result we made virtually no progress last week. I shall have to stage my first all-night sitting on Wednesday of next week if we are going to keep to the time-table we have planned. However, I am meeting the back-benchers again next Monday and I hope to get them on my side; their morale has certainly been improved this week. How much has this back-bench bloody-mindedness to do with the disastrous results of the municipal elections? Directly, not much. But there is no doubt that the defeat unsettled everybody, unsettled even the Department. I felt the difference in their attitude to me throughout this week.

Friday, May 21st
Well, we have just had our first all-night sitting and pretty uncomfortable it was in my room with Tam lying on the floor in a splendid sleeping-bag and me on the couch without even a pillow. If we are going to have these all-nighters once or twice a week for the next few weeks I shall have to make myself a great deal more comfortable than I was last night. We got back to Vincent Square at five o'clock in the morning and had two hours' sleep. Then I got up and prepared to go to Oxford to open a supermarket in Cowley. This turned out to be a very enjoyable occasion. Oxford City Council has had the courage to create a new shopping centre and it is a successful affair, done not by private developers but by the city itself. Moreover, I was being treated as an old boy coming back to his old council.[1] This was really a delightful day and it ended perfectly by my looking in on the Woodhouses and then driving on to Prescote for the weekend.

Sunday, May 23rd
Alas, the last part of the week has been absolutely ruined by a second confounded incident, which will be far more embarrassing than my losing my Cabinet papers at Prunier. It concerns a cottage, or rather half a cottage, in Creampot Lane, which runs down to the canal on our side of Cropredy. For thirty-five years now we have had a family, the Spencers—a man and his mother—living in one half of the cottage, unmodernized, while we have modernized the other half for one of our farm-workers. We have been unable to get rid of the two Spencers because when Anne's father bought the pair of cottages they were sitting tenants and he wasn't permitted to move them. Since Mr Pritchett's been here we've twice offered the man to have his half modernized and the roof mended and a bathroom put in, in return for the normal increase of rent; and he has replied that he would rather go on living

[1] Crossman was leader of the Labour Group 1934-40.

in the dilapidated cottage with a rent of five shillings a year. When I was in
Oxford on Friday I learnt that one of the *Oxford Mail* journalists had been
out in the village talking to the people in the cottage and had got hold of a
story which he proposed to publish. I tried to remedy things with the *Oxford
Mail* but when I found out the journalist's name and made him ring me up
he was cagey, and I knew I could do nothing. So that was that. We came
back yesterday, Saturday, from a beautiful day we had spent with my cousin
Michael Howard, who lives at Lambourne, to find a car with three or four
journalists, including the *Express* and the *Telegraph*, waiting for me by the
corner of the garden wall. I knew the worst. By the time they saw me they had
got their stories and no doubt we shall read them on the front pages of the
papers tomorrow morning—stories which will say how the Minister of
Housing is permitting a villager to live in a slum cottage while he improves the
other half for one of his tenants. It will be interesting to see what the press
makes of it. But I can't help feeling raw because, since we have owned the
farm, we have built four first-rate modern houses in the village for our men
and at the bridge we have knocked three old cottages into two in order to
provide bathrooms. All our men therefore have modern houses free of rent;
and as for the dilapidated dwelling, it has been like that for thirty-five years
because of the sitting tenant who was in possession when the house was
bought.

I must add one other depressing incident. All this week I have been worried
about the future of Winnie Lakin, my agent at Coventry East. Last Monday
Mr Moon, the *Coventry Evening Telegraph* Westminster correspondent,
came to see me and told me that the Organization Sub-Committee at Transport House would be deciding her case on Tuesday afternoon.[1] I got hold of
Sara Barker and told her the facts as I knew them and she assured me they
were practically certain to reinstate her. On Wednesday morning I heard that
Transport House had reinstated her. But then the *Coventry Evening Telegraph*
announced on the same day that the expulsion had been confirmed by the
Coventry borough. This means endless trouble. We have got her back into the
Party, but a battle royal will now start which won't do us any good in
Coventry.

Monday, May 24th

Anne is very shaken by the press we are having about our cottage in Creampot
Lane. She dislikes it all the more because she feels we have been remiss and
thereby made ourselves guilty. I must say the Sunday paper stories were pretty
horrible, a nauseating one in the *News of the World* and a fairly outrageous
one in the *Sunday Express*. But then our farm manager, Mr Pritchett, got to
work and certainly Monday's papers were far better. The *Daily Telegraph*,
though it had a horrible contrasting pair of photographs (the Georgian mansion on the one side and the slum cottage on the other), ran a story which

[1]See p. 197.

was not too bad. The *Sun*, the *Daily Mail* and *The Times* never mentioned it at all, nor did the *Coventry Evening Telegraph*. So it really meant that the story was only covered in the *Express* and the *Telegraph*.

As soon as I got to London I tried to find out what people thought. The first discovery I made in my own Ministry was that neither the Dame, nor Jones nor Waddell had even seen it. When I got to the House of Commons my colleagues merely took it as another of those poisonous, lying attacks, and George Brown said to me as we sat on the steps of the Speaker's chair waiting for a division, 'Well, Dick, you are taking some of the load of bombardment off me for a change.' On our side of the House no one seemed to think for a moment that the story might be true and in that sense no damage was done. In the rough-house of politics today it doesn't really do much harm and is forgotten in forty-eight hours.* Indeed, it wouldn't have had any significance at all if it hadn't followed so quickly on my affair at Prunier. That, by the way, seems to have done me much more good than harm. It has been the kind of joke the public enjoy and ironically enough it actually made me for the first time seem a human being with human weaknesses and not an acidulated adding-machine.

We started to make our preparations for another all-night sitting on the Rent Bill because after a really bad week's progress the only way to get ahead was to force the issue. After spending Monday making our plans and squaring our back-benchers we proposed to start a session at four o'clock on Wednesday afternoon and carry it right through without a break to one o'clock on Thursday afternoon. As for the progress we required, it was agreed that we would tell the Tories that we were determined to get the whole of Part III through by Thursday lunch-time, leaving only Part IV, the Schedules and the new Clauses to be dealt with the week after next. We got all our officials lined up in the office and made them see how fast we could go. They had a lot of ground to make up because at the beginning of the week we hadn't got near the famous Clause 22—the main hurdle we must get over before we settle down to our all-night session.

One interruption I had today was from a deputation from the builders headed by Kirby Laing. Their complaint was the desperate shortage of mortgage funds. Just before the meeting I'd been handed the latest figures of starts, that is until April of this year. It showed that in those four months building starts were 4 per cent higher this year than in 1964, by far the highest in the history of building in this country. I said, 'Let's start with the facts. Here they are.' And when I had read those figures aloud I said, 'Now are those figures agreed?' Of course they had to agree. So I said, 'Well, on the basis of those figures the building society threats about a mortgage shortage last March had no effect on starts.' To which Kirby Laing replied, 'But the little

---

* This proved true only in our own village, where the facts were easy to establish. Elsewhere the smear was permanent and the story was vaguely remembered for years—with embarrassment by friends, with pleasure by enemies.

builders are slow off the mark in seeing what future they are in for.' It was clear that, whereas the big contractors have begun to cut their programmes back, the small builders who build the majority of houses for sale haven't yet felt the hot air coming down their necks.

However, it is obvious that, with the building society funds available for advances nearly £300 million down this year compared to last, the shut-down will soon come if something urgent isn't done about it. After the meeting Charlie Pannell was urging me to publish the true figures. 'Not on your life,' I said. 'I'm not going to rush into print saying what liars the builders are. I prefer to let them accuse me of being incompetent and inefficient now because they may be right and we may get into great difficulties at the end of this year. But if they are wrong then it is better to let them make fools of themselves.'*

My other interruption was from a meeting of the Cabinet Committee on Broadcasting. Tony Wedgwood Benn put up an elaborate paper in which he proposed to get a firm commitment that the B.B.C. should finance its expanding programme partly by advertising, while on the other hand we should introduce legislation to ban Radio Caroline, the pirate pop-radio station.[1] I was decisively against him on Radio Caroline because I didn't see any point in losing the votes of young people before the B.B.C. had any real alternative to it. As for B.B.C. advertising, I am for it in principle but I am not at all convinced that it is a wise thing to propose just now. If we tried to persuade the Party to commit itself in advance on this issue, we should split it wide open. What we ought to do is have a severe investigation of the B.B.C. without commitment on Government policy.

I like Tony Benn a great deal and I had every hope of him when Harold appointed him Postmaster-General. It's a queer thing but I am not very happy about him now I see him at work. To begin with, on every single occasion when he is about to bring a plan to Cabinet a leak occurs giving the full details in advance. In the second place, there is an odd hardness about him which makes him sometimes unattractive as a colleague. He has certainly got himself detested by the Tories—though that's nothing against him—but even among us in Cabinet he doesn't inspire conviction, partly because, although I doubt whether he is a believer, he has at times a kind of mechanical Nonconformist self-righteousness about him which seems to come out even more strongly in office. I was terribly keen at first that he should be Minister of Transport, but I am not so sure that he will get his promotion when we move into the next stage of this Government. He may have to wait and to learn.

I left the Ministry at 4.30 and went across to the House for a meeting at 5 with my Rent Bill back-benchers. They seemed extremely keen and willing;

---

* I was following one of the rules I learnt during the war as a psychological warrior. After Charlie Pannell had put this to me the Prime Minister also pressed it on me, and I had to write a special minute saying why I was cagey about doing it.
[1] Benn had been mulling this over for months. See p. 167.

and the very people who have been making life impossible for me only a week before were now eager to smash the Tories with the all-night session.

After the meeting I stayed at the House for dinner and then went home about midnight, leaving the Finance Bill still being debated on the Floor of the House. It's anybody's guess what benefits, if any, we shall draw from this complex, controversial measure. But the more I reflect on it the more puzzled I am that, with a majority of three and so many enormously important things to do, Harold Wilson and the inner group who decide things should have risked everything on the most complicated fiscal reform for thirty years, a reform from which in the case of corporation tax we shall see no benefit at all until the year after next. Perhaps the fact that James Callaghan was an Inland Revenue officer and Nicky Kaldor, his chief economic adviser, is a tax expert — a job at which Harold Wilson fancies himself too — is why they got themselves committed in the autumn budget speech to a capital gains tax and a corporation tax in their spring budget. I suspect the pledge was made in order to placate the unions and so make them more likely to collaborate in George Brown's voluntary incomes policy.

Tuesday, May 25th

I had to be back at my Rent Bill Committee at 10.30 a.m. I'd had quite a fuss with Tam Dalyell and John Delafons because I found they had paired me, assuming I would be away at the Cabinet Committee on the Social Science Research Council. But I felt I couldn't be away from the Rent Bill on such a critical morning, particularly since I ought to wind up the debate on the rent officers and personally tell Boyd-Carpenter about our plans. I managed to do all that during the morning session before going to the Albert Hall where I was due to address seven thousand people from the Women's Institutes at their annual conference. I drove there with Anne and we wondered together what the feeling of all these women would be since many of them would have read by then the terrible, disgusting story about me as a slum landlord. It was an incredible sound when we entered the hall, those seven thousand women tittering and susurrating together. I came on, following the recitation by Cecil Day Lewis[1] of a noble poem written for the occasion. After my speech to my amazement they asked me the right kind of questions and I found myself answering them quite naturally.

Back to the Ministry to see an American called Gordon who is Shepherd Stone's number two for Europe in the Ford Foundation. He is the man we have to persuade if we are to have any hope of getting financial assistance from Ford for launching our British Centre for Environmental Studies.[2] I arranged to give Gordon dinner on Thursday evening with Richard Llewelyn-Davies.

[1] He became Poet Laureate in 1968, and died in 1972.
[2] The Minister and R.A.G., led by Richard Llewelyn-Davies, hoped to secure matching grants from the Government and the Ford Foundation for such an organization.

Wednesday, May 26th

This was quite a day. I started at 10 a.m. in the N.E.C. round at Transport House. We were soon in the middle of one of those good, old-fashioned N.E.C. rows. Mikardo started an attack on the sub-committee headed by Bessie Braddock (the 'Org. Sub.'), which controls the list of recommended candidates, on the ground that a left-winger from the T.G.W.U. who had been a parliamentary candidate at Wembley had been deliberately removed from the list. I finally had to slip out at the end of an hour, having voted with the Left in the traditional way, and so I wasn't there when the Executive formally endorsed the 'Org. Sub.'s' acquittal of Winnie Lakin. I had to be back in the Ministry by 11.30 to see Sir Sydney Littlewood, a distinguished solicitor, and the ex-head of the Law Society, who is proposed very enthusiastically by the Dame as the President of the London rent assessment committee.[1] I found Sir Sydney very stolid and extremely reactionary, but a pretty good character and probably the kind of person I want. I should be happier if I could get David Donnison teamed up with him as the other key personality on this vital committee.

But my main preoccupation that morning was in preparing the big speech I had to give at 2.20 to the County Councils Association. This is one of the three or four really big annual set occasions for a Minister of Housing and Local Government. For days the Department had been busy sending me briefs. Finally I told them I would do a big piece of my own on preservation of the coastline, and rely for the rest on improvisation. But I didn't get much time that morning, partly because I had to go across to the House twice to vote on the capital punishment Bill Committee Stage which was going on at the time.[2] I had left lunch-time free for final preparation but was suddenly told the Prime Minister wanted me to lunch with him in No. 10. I found him sitting in the room down below. We had a glass of sherry with Marcia and then he took me upstairs in the lift to the flat above the official reception-rooms on the first floor. There I found in a little sitting-room a couple of dirty plates with bread and butter on them and a glass half full of milk. Obviously Mary Wilson had had her lunch before rushing out. We had another glass of sherry there before moving into a little dining-room where an Irish maid slammed down in front of me a plate with a piece of steak, two veg and a bit of cold salad. On the table were two tins of Skol beer, which I don't like. Harold saw this and while he took water gave me a glass of claret. After lunch we went along to his little sitting-room and there he offered me a

---

[1] The decisions of the London committee were to be particularly important in setting precedents for the working of the Act. Undoubtedly many hitherto 'controlled' rents would be increased.

[2] In December 1964 Sydney Silverman introduced his Murder (Abolition of the Death Penalty) Bill as a Private Members' Bill. The Cabinet resolved to provide time for the Bill to be debated every Wednesday morning, and it was passed in July 1965. The Lords then carried a Conservative amendment that the measure lapse automatically after an experimental period of five years unless both Houses passed motions for permanent abolition. Such motions were carried in December 1969.

glass of brandy which he likes very much. I refused the brandy and accepted a second glass of claret.

Nothing could be more deeply *petit bourgeois* than the way he lives in those crowded little servants' quarters up there. But the fact that he doesn't, unlike Sir Alec Douglas-Home, use the state rooms for sitting in after dinner is only a proof that he is not corrupted by his new station in life. No. 10 doesn't change him, he changes it so that its rooms look exactly like the rooms in his Hampstead house. Harold's strength is that he has no kind of inferiority complex but lives his own real, natural life. He doesn't respect the upper classes for having superior cultural tastes which he would like to share. I didn't ask him what he thought about the horrid story of Prescote Manor and the slum cottage. But he talked to me about it as a typical Tory lie. He won't hold it against me that I live in a lovely manor house in the country and he doesn't.

He had got me there to tell me his plans about housing. He has decided that all other social services must be cut back in order to have a magnificent housing drive and bring the annual production of houses up to 500,000 by 1970. 'This is it,' he said. 'We'll make housing the most popular single thing this Government does. We won't build another single mile of road if a cut-back is necessary in order to get that half-million houses a year. That's what I believe in,' he said. 'I have already had the Chancellor here and written him a paper and talked about it. He knows perfectly well now that this is what we have got to persuade Cabinet to accept.' When he had finished I found myself complaining to him about the irrelevance of the Finance Bill. 'Oh no,' he said, 'the Finance Bill is very useful. It fills in time. We have got five weeks ahead of us to deal with the Committee Stage of the Finance Bill and we shall hold out successfully. That's the point. To fill in time and to win.' It struck me as an odd description of the Bill which has been causing alarm and despondency in the City, but of course there is always something in the tactical arguments Harold Wilson puts up. If the Government can survive these five weeks despite a majority of three, and complete the Committee Stage on the Floor of the House, it will be a crushing defeat for the Opposition and a strengthening of our authority.

At the last moment I mentioned that Bob Mellish thoroughly deserves to be Minister of State. 'I mean to go further than that,' he said. 'Bob should become Minister of Works when old Charlie Pannell moves out. He's getting on in years and he isn't too strong.' So there is something in the rumours of a reshuffle this summer!

I found him throughout this meal extremely friendly and forthcoming. So, venturing very greatly, I finally said, 'Well, if housing is going to be all that important I really can't accept Bruce Fraser as a replacement for the Dame.' I summoned up the courage to tell him this because the more I look at the Department, the more I realize, and so does the Dame, that the arrival of Bruce Fraser is going to be a crushing blow—particularly since neither of the Deputies can stand up to a powerful figure. I said all this to Harold and then added, 'If you want the Department really to work you can't give us a Treasury man instead of the Dame. I want the Dame for another year.' This was an idea which came into my head quite suddenly when Charlie Pannell suggested I might have a great farewell dinner for her at Lancaster House and I found she hated the idea. So I had been preparing a little dinner for her with her ex-Ministers and now, thank heavens, there was a chance of her carrying on if only the P.M. would agree.

By now it was 2.20 and I had to rush downstairs, get into the car and be whirled across the river to County Hall where within thirty seconds of my entering the great council chamber with them all standing up to receive me, Lord Heathcoat Amory had sat them down and introduced me. I've never started off so stone cold on a major address. I talked to them for forty minutes and, thank God, I had got some of it written out. It may make quite a good speech in print. At any rate it was better than anything I had been given in J. D. Jones's brief.

I had to be back in the House by four o'clock for the beginning of our big all-night session on the Rent Bill. I was going through the division lobby downstairs when I ran into the Chief Whip, who said he had just had a message from the Tory Chief Whip saying they were willing to give us our Bill by the Thursday after the Whitsun recess – give it to us signed, sealed and delivered – on the condition we didn't try any late-night sittings. He told me all this as we went through the division lobby during the Finance Bill Committee Stage, which was as usual going on. (We do this day and night now, and at least it means that you bump into people like the Chief Whip.) So one threat on Tuesday morning of an all-night sitting has been sufficient to bring the Tories to heel. But on that Wednesday afternoon John Boyd-Carpenter hadn't had time, poor man, to adjust to these new instructions from his Chief Whip or to tell his own people what had happened. So they went on filibustering when we started the consideration of Clause 22, the fair-rent clause. This went on for three and a half hours and then I took Anne to dinner in the Strangers' dining-room. Afterwards she motored back to the country and I stayed till five o'clock in the morning at another all-night sitting on the Rent Bill, which I found very trying indeed. I had had quite a day, with a major speech to deliver at County Hall and then a major speech in the Committee and then sitting in for hour after hour.

Thursday, May 27th
I was pretty tired when I got back to the Ministry after three hours' sleep. Cabinet, thank God, had been cancelled,[1] but I knew that Clause 22 was still going on in the Committee upstairs. However, I had to go to the Ministry to

---

[1] Cabinet was postponed until Friday morning. The Prime Minister had spent the night of Wednesday, May 26th, discussing the lowering of bank rate with James Callaghan and George Brown. See *Wilson*, p. 107.

prepare for the great confrontation with Callaghan about my housing policy which was due to take place in the Prime Minister's room in the Commons at 5 p.m. My paper had been circulated, his paper had been circulated, Willie Ross's paper had been circulated, and in addition there had of course been briefs and counter-briefs. It was one of those big occasions when the Ministers are put into the ring like boxing champions after weeks of training for the big fight. Directly I heard that it had reached 'that Clause 22 should stand part' I went across to the Committee and we had a two-hour debate at the end of which I made my big summing-up, which was reckoned a fairly powerful speech. Then the division came and we carried this absolutely key clause by only a single vote. We couldn't get a bigger majority because we only have a majority of one in the Committee.

Directly the division was over I drove along Victoria Street to the sky-scraper on the right where the Westminster City Council have their new offices. I was shown a magnificent view from the top of the rain-clouds clearing into sunshine (the weather had now changed). The Mayor of Westminster and a few friends were entertaining me at a very pleasant, informal lunch. I then had to go back to the Ministry for a characteristic interview with a deputation from the Crawley New Town U.D.C. I spend a great deal of time listening to U.D.C. delegations complaining about the New Town corporations or listening to the chairmen of the New Town corporations complaining about the impossible conduct of U.D.C.s.

When I had got rid of the delegation I went across once again to the Commons to attend the crucial meeting in the Prime Minister's room. It was soon clear that, despite the expectation of the civil servants, there wouldn't even be a shadow-boxing match since the Chancellor had surrendered before the discussion began. I decided not to make another speech and very soon it was basically agreed that the scheme my civil servants had worked out should be presented to Cabinet roughly as it stood in our policy paper, both with regard to mortgages and with regard to local-authority loans. Well, if that's so, that's that. In fact very little was done. We just chatted round the subject and I didn't really have to fight.

So I was able to leave pretty soon and go back to the Ministry and report to the Dame who was waiting to hear the result of the contest. She told me that my lunch with the Prime Minister had worked like magic. Helsby had sent for her and told her what the Prime Minister had said I wanted and asked her whether she would stay on and, as he put it, 'share the Ministry with Sir Bruce Fraser'. The Dame told me there had been a great deal of talk in the Treasury along the lines of 'Wait till we get Bruce Fraser into the Ministry of Housing, then we'll bring them to heel'. The Treasury hates the feeling that I have got the backing of the P.M. for this enormous housing programme. Now it looks as though the Dame will stay on and we shall be able to postpone Bruce Fraser for a year. And after all, a lot can happen during the course of a twelve-month postponement.

By then it was time to clean myself up and go out to a very important dinner-party at the house of Richard Llewelyn-Davies. The plan was that we should talk to this fellow Gordon from the Ford Foundation and make sure that he would back our idea. What Richard and I were planning was an institute which would do the kind of long-term thinking, planning and research for physical planning that the research councils are doing for the natural sciences and that the new Social Science Research Council is due to do for the social services. We knew that it all depended on getting Foundation money since the Treasury wouldn't move a foot unless we could go to them and say we'd got the main amount from a private source.

I was appalled to find that Victor Rothschild and his wife Tessa were also there. This didn't create an easy situation because Gordon is a cagey little man, like all the professional American foundation men who go round deciding whether to give you money. They have the greatest pleasure in keeping you on tenterhooks and you have to guess how they react. The job of hooking him wasn't made easier by the presence of Victor, who is one of the most brilliant (and sometimes malicious) conversationalists in the world but who didn't exactly stimulate Gordon to come out of his shell. By the end of the evening I felt our chances were growing remote.

I had sent my car away and agreed that Richard should drive me down from Hampstead. On the way we had an experience which left a nasty taste in my mouth. We were driving through Regent's Park at about eleven o'clock when suddenly a car cut in front of us and three youths got out and came towards our car shouting at Richard in broad Irish accents and ordering him to get out on the ground that he had endangered their lives by his bad driving. Had he been alone I have no doubt these hooligans would have dragged him out in that dark avenue of the park, broken him up and left him lying on the side of the road. As it was, they insisted on taking him to a police station whereupon I said, 'Drive on.' So we tried to escape and they chased us for a mile down towards Baker Street tube station and then cut in once again in front of us. We sat in the car and shut up the windows. They shouted at us through the windows and Richard got out; I thought he was going to be assaulted so I slipped out on the other side of the car, strolled across the road to a garage and rang up the police. But I found it very difficult to explain what was the accident or the incident they should come to and it took quite a time to persuade them to come at all. When I got back and said the police were coming the youths went off and Richard brought me home.

How placid our life is in this country and how completely the sense of the danger of violence has been removed from our minds! To Richard and me it was an appalling shock that these three young men could have been ready to beat us up though, of course, they were restrained by fear of the law. We were both still very shaken when we reached Vincent Square.

Friday, May 28th

I had to catch an 8 a.m. train from Paddington in order to be on time for my official visit to Swindon. I had decided to go there and see the contrast between a town which has undertaken its own expansion and a New Town created under one of our magnificent, dignified New Town corporations. Of course, I had been told by my Ministry that Swindon was a terrible place: though the people were charming and keen, everything they had done was inferior to what was done in a New Town. I soon discovered that their housing is shabby and their planning is not first-rate; nevertheless, as I toured the town I felt that they had done a tremendous job. The population of Swindon has increased by 30,000 or 40,000 and they had in fact created a New Town without spending a penny of Treasury money and without creating the expensive paraphernalia of a New Town corporation and the friction which exists everywhere between the New Town corporation and the local U.D.C. Moreover, the councillors are not so stuck up as the New Town appointees. In fact they are nice, unassuming Labour people, a lot of them railwaymen, and personally devoted to me because I used to lecture regularly in Swindon in the 1930s when the Swindon W.E.A. was at its height, under that great old man, Reuben George.[1]

From Swindon I drove off a bit late to Newbury. We've already appointed Richard Llewelyn-Davies's firm of architects as the consultants to produce a report for us on the possibility of a New Town in the area of Newbury and Swindon. From everything I saw I am sure we don't need a New Town and it would be wildly extravagant to try to build one. All we need do is let the old towns expand themselves and frankly I don't see why Swindon shouldn't go ahead. When I got to Newbury I found that they were extremely reluctant to expand to the extent the Ministry wanted. Their idea is to go up from 20,000 to, say, 40,000. The last thing they want is to become a town of 80,000, and I must say that having gone round their pleasant place with them I tended to agree.

Sunday, May 30th

This Government is in rough water. It is doing extremely well in the House of Commons, but outside it is rapidly losing momentum. Indeed, all that sustains us is the reluctance of the country to go back to the inadequacies of Alec Douglas-Home and the incompetence of his Government. But, my God, the situation is against us. The pound has not been stabilized, despite the deflation we are carrying through. Economic confidence is not being restored and the Finance Bill is doing nothing to help us in this particular regard. So it is difficult to see our way. We are just struggling; and I shouldn't be in the least surprised if we have an October election, because we are running on too fine a margin to risk anything else.

[1] Crossman lectured for the W.E.A. from 1938 to 1940.

I had thought that one guest we had this weekend would help me to relax from politics. But it didn't turn out that way. The guest was Celia Strachey, the widow of John Strachey who died so suddenly and completely unnecessarily a couple of years ago because he chose to have a minor operation to relieve the pain in his leg although he had had a coronary thrombosis before.[1] A clot appeared and that left Celia a political widow in a really desperate sense. She had been devoted to John all her life and she was pretty nearly betrothed to him when he was captured by an American millionairess. Celia fought back and rescued him from the millionairess and after she had married him she defended him against a good many other female affections with which he was afflicted in the course of his married life. She has been a wonderful wife in the sense that Dora Gaitskell and Jill Foot are wonderful wives. All of them are possessive women who fight for their husbands like tigers, and all of them, unlike Anne, are politicians themselves and not merely interested in politics. Fortunately, in the latter part of John's life Celia also became a very keen artist. They were here at Prescote once when he was speaking for me and she loved the look of the place and said she would like to come and paint it; so I asked her to come whenever she felt fit enough after John's death. And this was her weekend. She was a tremendous success with the children and had painting sessions with them, sitting on the window-sill looking out across the Cherwell. But what she really wanted was a political gossip, something she doesn't get in her remote part of Essex, and this made it a very painful and exhausting weekend for me. It made me realize what a difference it is for Anne that we have two young children, seven and five this year, and whatever happens to me there will be plenty of love in her life for the next ten years; also, unlike the Stracheys, we have this place.

By the way, I must write now about what we have been doing to the house. A month or two ago we found that the nails were rusting in the roof and we had to remove all the slates and put new nails in. While the scaffolding was up we gave instructions that eight five-foot Victorian chimney-pots should be heaved down. They made the house look, I always said, like a sheep, upturned and clawing into the air. To our delight we found that little pots some six inches high provide an equally good draught; so now half a dozen of the five-footers are standing on the terrace looking like Corinthian pillars and acting as stands for flower-pots. Another went off to my stepdaughter, Venice Barry, for her home at Stokenchurch. We have also taken the opportunity while the scaffolding is up to paint a false window on the east side of the house where the old four-foot outer wall made a real window impossible, as well as painting in false tops to the windows on the south side, which removes the blind look the house had. It is more settled into the landscape rather than

---

[1] Labour M.P. for Aston Birmingham 1929–31, and for Dundee from 1945 until his death in 1963. He was Minister of Food 1946–50 and Secretary of State for War 1950–51 in the post-war Labour Government. He wrote several important books on the theory of socialism.

clawing up at the sky as it used to be. I was able to write a letter this weekend to Clough Williams-Ellis[1] thanking him for suggesting the chimney-pots should come off when he was staying here years ago.

Monday, May 31st
In the afternoon I went into the Prime Minister's room punctually at four o'clock for a meeting with Callaghan. The summons had come by telephone on Saturday and at the same time I was asked to cancel an article on housing which I have given to the *Sunday Citizen*. Suddenly Harold had had cold feet about whether we could announce my mortgage scheme without undermining the pound. So there I sat with the P.M. and the Chancellor while the Finance Bill divisions clanged around us. They first asked me about my time-table. I explained that I must immediately send out a confidential circular to all the borough treasurers calling them to a meeting to discuss the new form the housing subsidy would take. Harold immediately said that in these talks I couldn't make any reference to my proposal to limit the percentage they paid to 4 per cent. I must also be careful to have no meetings with the building societies about mortgages. It was obvious that something had happened to shake his confidence because only a few days before he had been talking as though, now the I.M.F. loan was already safely in our pockets, we could go ahead with our own plans and launch the housing campaign. Now, although the I.M.F. loan had been delivered, it looked as though the pound had become very dicky and the Prime Minister and his Chancellor were preparing for another bout of emergency measures. As I sat with them I became more and more aware how utterly remote I am from the inner group who plan the economic policy. They discussed any number of things in my presence which I couldn't understand because I hadn't been briefed. Finally it was agreed (1) that I should make all my preparations inside the Ministry, and (2) that I should make no announcement to the local authorities until June 10th, the Thursday after Whitsuntide. Harold and Jim seemed to reckon this would just give them nice time for the announcement they intended to make. I presumed they planned to reduce bank rate on the Tuesday or Wednesday after Whitsun, when the present crisis would be over.

For me this was an unsatisfactory and disturbing talk. Harold was still determined to go ahead with the new housing policy; but instead of Harold dragging the Chancellor along, James was now dragging him back. It was only too clear that the Treasury regarded the whole housing policy as an act of financial sin, and were using this opportunity to have one more effort at sabotaging it.

I had to go on to the Cabinet Committee on the Land Commission. We hadn't had a meeting for some weeks — in fact not since Cabinet agreed the policy. A White Paper has now been prepared which I don't much like but

[1] A celebrated, idiosyncratic architect and town-planner, owner and designer of the village of Portmeirion in North Wales. He was knighted in 1972.

which I am not going to challenge.[1] We spent a whole morning upon it and nobody really quite understood except Willey and Niall MacDermot, who represents the Treasury and who is both an extremely able lawyer and a socialist as well.

That evening I gave dinner to Gordon, the fellow from the Ford Foundation. He was off next morning to America and needed the extra zip which a meal with a Minister gives. With the help of Tam Dalyell I ordered the best dinner the House of Commons could provide and hope he felt the Minister had treated him properly. While we were eating I went right through the proposals with him and got it quite clear that the Ford Foundation is prepared to help finance a Centre for Environmental Studies, established in Britain on the same lines as the National Institute in Tokyo and in some European capitals. From Ford's point of view the most important thing is to build up a network of these Institutes and for a British institute to be in line with all the others. On our side we have to make sure that it is useful to us.

Richard Llewelyn-Davies wants it attached to London University, where he is now a Professor. J. D. Jones rather suspects that Richard is looking after his own interests and prefers the institute run by someone under Ministry control. It was obvious to me that neither of these projects would satisfy Gordon. He wanted a genuinely independent centre which would not be attached to one university, and which would be heavily financed by the Government and yet completely independent of it. I finally agreed that we would try to set up a seminar early in August at which some twenty people would work out the details with him and the other Ford Foundation people.

On Monday night the House sat late again, ploughing through the Finance Bill. I sat in my room doing my boxes and moving out to vote time after time in endless divisions on obscure clauses which no one understands. However, I was paired that night and got home just after eleven. Tam only got home at six on Tuesday.

To create an impression of confidence, among foreign bankers as much as at home, bank rate was lowered to 6 per cent on June 3rd. But, simultaneously, stricter controls on hire purchase were announced. Sterling still gave cause for concern and, though the figures were not published until July 2nd, in June some £24 million of gold reserves drained away. On June 29th the Chancellor flew to Washington for talks with the American Secretary of the Treasury on dollar reinforcement for the pound. Cuts in departmental expenditure seemed inevitable, and the Public Expenditure Survey Committee, the 'five wise men', prepared to review Ministers' plans and programmes.

The Commonwealth Conference in London in June provided less distraction than the Prime Minister hoped. His master-card was to propose a peace initiative in Vietnam. The conduct of the war now horrified not only the Labour Left but the informed public as well. An Oxford Union 'teach-in' on June 17th, at which

[1] See p. 157.

*the Foreign Secretary, Michael Stewart, defended the Government's attitude,
became headline news. Mr Wilson's plan was for a peace mission to Vietnam,
composed of the heads of Government of Britain, Nigeria, Trinidad and Tobago,
Ghana and Ceylon. With the single exception of the President of Tanzania, the
Commonwealth Prime Ministers assented in surprise. The venture seemed about
to collapse when some delegates complained of the tactics used to secure their
approval and when the Chinese seemed reluctant to admit the visitors. But the
idea was kept up throughout the month.*

Tuesday, June 1st
I had to be up early to meet George Brown at 9.45 in the D.E.A. I found him
remarkably spruce although he hadn't gone to bed till 6.30 and had been
woken again at 8.30. The official purpose of our meeting was to discuss what
to do with the North-West and the Midlands Planning Reviews, both of which
had been submitted in draft to his Department and also, of course, to mine.
This is the area where we overlap. The West Midlands Review, conducted by
my Mr Pugh, was a far better document than the North-West Review, conducted by his Mr Mackintosh and rushed out to satisfy George's demand for
action. Neither of them is particularly profound. Indeed, they are horrifyingly
superficial—merely a collection of the facts available to central government
with one or two rush-job social surveys and some very hasty conclusions. One
only begins to realize in what a primitive phase planning is when one knows
as I do exactly how many people have been engaged on this work, what
quality of work it is, and what a vacuum there was before these reports were
done. I said little of this to George and merely advised him not to overplay
their importance; they should be circulated in the first place without being
put into print.

After this, as happens with George, we talked about the economic situation
and the development in the regions. I reflected on the extraordinary change
since last November, when the D.E.A. started off with such a bang as the
Department which would really do the economic planning while the Treasury
was relegated to finance. George, however, has concentrated on his incomes
policy and left the serious economic planning to tick over in his Ministry while
the Treasury did the job. He told me there was a meeting at Chequers last
weekend with the Prime Minister, himself and Callaghan, but I very much
doubt whether the D.E.A. will ever recover a dominant position. Perhaps it
never could have achieved it under the kind of leadership George Brown
gave—gifted, brilliant, ebullient, gay, erratic—not the kind of leadership
necessary to face the Treasury on equal terms. Indeed, in certain ways my
Department is a greater obstacle to the Treasury and stands more formidably
in its path than the D.E.A.

I went straight across from there to the Rent Bill Committee which had
reached the clauses on harassment. Because there are so many legal problems
about this idea we had the Attorney-General present and ploughed ahead all

the morning. The problem of harassment had become acute when I restored protection to the tenant in the Protection from Eviction Act. Some landlords took to the simple device of throwing the tenants out but not legally evicting them. So I told the Ministry that at all costs this must be made good in the new Bill. When it was published I was assured the new clauses did the job and I was furious when it was suggested, first on the B.B.C. and then in *The Economist*, that they weren't any good. Now when it came to the discussion in Committee it was awkward to find the Attorney-General admitting there were all sorts of holes and things wrong with these clauses which I had strenuously defended against attack. Once again one is struck by the curious patchiness in Civil Service efficiency. Whereas the parliamentary draftsman who has worked on my Bill is superb, in the Ministry I feel we could have got a far stronger team together if we hadn't relied so entirely on the administrative class.

In the afternoon we went on with the discussion of the Land Commission White Paper at the Cabinet Committee. I feel profoundly depressed at the thought that such great things are expected of this measure. It seems to me more likely that when it is put on the statute-book it will be very unpopular as well as ridiculed for its obscurity and for the insignificant contribution it will make to the solution of any of our problems. It is obvious now that the only thing the Bill will really do is establish a tax on betterment, which by the way could have been far better managed by the Inland Revenue. If the Bill had been the responsibility of my Ministry I would have made the radical decision to tell people candidly that we have cut back on our original big proposal and gone in for a moderate, practical, short-term Bill, while concentrating on giving the local authorities much greater powers of compulsory purchase of land. But this is not Fred Willey's way, and this Bill is a standing example of a measure which has enormous pretensions but which, at least for the first seven or eight years of its operation, will have an insignificant effect.

When I got back to the Ministry I found that J. D. Jones and Jimmy James had got to work on the Ford project. They had already hired Churchill College for four days in August and begun to send out the invitations. The Civil Service can act quickly when it sees something to its own advantage.

Since the House of Commons was still reeling after its all-night session, today was virtually a day off at Westminster and I was able to take Anne to the theatre where we saw a dramatized version of a novel by Ivy Compton-Burnett.[1] The dramatization was really a complete flop. But I had a very pleasant evening with Helga Greene,[2] her son Graham[3] and his wife Judy, the daughter of Patrick Gordon Walker. Afterwards we went to Prunier for dinner and the young people talked to me entirely about education—the only part of the Labour Government's programme they were really interested in.

[1] *A Heritage and its History* (London: Gollancz, 1969).
[2] Crossman's literary agent.
[3] A director of Jonathan Cape Ltd.

I was surprised to hear that Graham and Judy had been doing a lot of canvassing in Chelsea for the municipals. They are keen Labour people and greatly distressed by the present state of the Government.

Wednesday, June 2nd

I spent the whole morning preparing for the three big decisions I am announcing at noon on Thursday on the boundaries of Leicester, Torbay and Plymouth. First I received the Midlands press in order to explain my decision at Leicester. Then I had the Devonshire press for Torbay and Plymouth. And I also had special interviews with the *Guardian*, *The Times* and the *Financial Times* so as to make sure that in commenting on my decisions they would understand the general philosophy behind them.[1]

I have already described in this diary how I reached my decision about Plymouth,[2] and applied the same principles in Torbay. Leicester was my first case in which the party political issue was central. I read the Commission's report very carefully and found that the Leicester county had conceded at one point that Leicester city should have its overspill housing estates, which are at present inside the county. A new boundary based on this principle would at least be clear and unambiguous. In fact, the Commission's recommendation was a difficult compromise, neither one thing nor the other, which wouldn't satisfy the city and would infuriate the county.[3] I began asking myself whether there wasn't a good sound philosophical and practical justification for giving the city its own housing estates and leaving the rest to the county, saying to the county council, 'Now we have given you all this, get down to planning a sensible co-operation between yourselves and the borough.' Of course I realized that this solution would put the maximum number of Labour votes inside the borough and the maximum number of Tory votes outside in the county, and so save the Labour seats in the next parliamentary redistribution. This is the line I forced on the Department. It has been an anxious job because I have to be sure that no one can accuse me of gerrymandering the boundary for Party purposes. To this end I must make sure I do not infuriate Leicester City Council and find them denouncing the arrangements I propose. But mainly I have to be certain that this will create a genuine basis for ending the cold war between the county and the county borough.

In the weeks of consultation I haven't bothered to conceal the political factor from my officials but I was careful not to mention it on Wednesday morning in my press briefing.

In the afternoon at the Rent Bill Committee we completed the clause on harassment and began to consider service tenancy. One of the good features

---

[1] There was also the implicit fact that the Minister's decisions might jeopardize as many as thirty seats of his Labour colleagues in Parliament.

[2] See p. 175.

[3] Leicester was complicated because the city, Labour-controlled, still retained its grammar schools while the Conservative-led Leicester county practised a famous and popular experiment in comprehensive education.

of the Bill is that the security which we restore to all tenants of unfurnished
property is also accorded for the first time to so-called licensees, i.e. people
who live in tied houses, caretakers and agricultural labourers. I wanted the
agricultural workers, who demand the complete abolition of the tied cottage,
at least to obtain their full security. But the Tories were moving an amendment
which would introduce a time limit of twelve months into the clause.[1] Jim
MacColl, Davey, our Ministry lawyer, and the parliamentary draftsman,
were all deeply anxious about this amendment because they thought the
Tories had a very powerful case. I got away with it surprisingly easily, perhaps
because I am reckoned to be a farmer and can talk with some practical
experience of the problem. After that we settled down to another all-night
sitting on the Finance Bill.

Thursday, June 3rd
Helsby was due to see me this morning about the future of my Permanent
Secretary. He came at 10, having seen the Dame and Bruce Fraser. I had had
one long last talk with the Dame on Wednesday. She had urged me to tell
Helsby that Bruce Fraser was the wrong man for the Ministry of Housing
and that she was staying on to enable me to get someone better, if not Philip
Allen from the Home Office, then Dunnett from Labour. I had sense enough
to turn her down. I knew that my line should be that I had nothing against
Bruce Fraser personally but that since Housing was the absolutely key
Department in the Government's strategy this autumn and winter, we needed
to keep morale high and it was therefore the wrong time to change the leadership. That was the reason I wanted the Dame to carry on until the spring
and that was the argument I used to Helsby, who then said, 'Well, there's only
one other Department for him – the Ministry of Land and Natural Resources.'
He then asked me whether I knew that Bishop, the Permanent Secretary
there, was wanting to leave the Service. Out of this emerged a wonderful new
idea – that Bruce Fraser should go to Land and Natural Resources this
autumn and that while he was running that little Ministry he should take on
the Leasehold Enfranchisement Bill, which I don't in the least want to do.
Then when the Land Commission has been established and leaseholds
enfranchised Bruce Fraser should come into Housing bringing Land and
Natural Resources with him, as the Permanent Secretary of the new fused
Ministry.

'Can we get the Prime Minister to accept this?' asked Helsby. 'Don't for
heaven's sake talk about it to him yet,' I replied. 'Oh, we can't deceive him,'
he said. 'If we are sending Bruce Fraser to Land and Natural Resources with
the idea of his coming back to Housing, that has got to be sold to the Prime
Minister.' I persuaded him that we needn't go as far as that in explaining our
intentions. So Helsby and Bruce Fraser and the Dame and I are now all in a

[1] After which a farmer could legally evict a tenant even if there was no alternative
accommodation.

conspiracy to find the best way and the best time to persuade the Prime Minister to wind up his new Department as soon as possible. It certainly provides an ideal solution for me because it keeps the Dame in charge during this critical winter. As for the future, when Land and Natural Resources comes back to Housing I shan't have to worry about it. It's most unlikely I shall be Minister of Housing at that particular date.

After talking to Helsby I went to Cabinet – the last before the Whit recess. Directly we sat down Harold Wilson said he had urgent business which had to be finished before 11.30. He then explained that there was a chance now of a package deal under which the bank rate would be lowered from 7 to 6 per cent in exchange for new restrictions on hire purchase. He told us that this was probably the last chance before the autumn to bring the bank rate down. It was vital to do it but the Governor of the Bank would only agree if the reduction was combined with new hire-purchase restrictions sufficiently sharp to impress the Gnomes of Zurich. It soon came out that George Brown was strongly opposed to this policy on the ground that it would start the unemployment he feared. He was supported to some extent by Tony Crosland, who told us he was against the terms of the package because they weren't credible and he didn't think it was wise to link bank rate with restriction on consumer demand. Then the Chancellor spoke. He was very frank. He said the Treasury was firmly against the policy but he himself was unenthusiastically for it.

Then came the turn of the rest of us. It soon became clear that the majority were for the Harold Wilson line, despite the opposition of the First Secretary, the Chancellor of the Exchequer and Tony Crosland. I was with the majority. An important feature of this discussion was that in the course of it Harold had to make a number of admissions – something he doesn't easily do. What was unpleasant, he remarked, was that this time there was a great deal of truth in what the press were saying. We *are* being more and more boxed in and our room for manœuvre *has* been mercilessly restricted. Somehow we have to break out, and this decision to gamble on the effect of reducing bank rate suddenly at a time when the pound is wonky is a desperate attempt to do so at the last possible moment. All this he admitted and the fact that he did so made me realize that the Government is really up against it.

After this we had a dreary discussion on computers which lasted for an hour and a half. I have been away from Cabinet more than once during the last weeks owing to my Standing Committee on the Rent Bill, and I have missed two meetings on this subject, in which the argument goes on and on between Frank Cousins and the rest of the Cabinet. Harold backs Frank because he has committed himself to the scientific revolution. But it is obvious that one of the difficulties in the way is the marked inferiority of British computers to American. If we are going to force Whitehall to buy British, we are going to subsidize inefficiency in a way which may be difficult to defend.

I stayed on throughout the Cabinet because I saw that the last item was future Government business. Sure enough at 12.25, when this computer debate dragged itself to its end, Harold said he wanted to give us a little pep talk. We were all tired, he said, and needed a good week's holiday; and he referred to the rumours in the press that Ministers had been coming to him begging for an October election. Though this wasn't true, he didn't deny that one or two members of the Cabinet had been expressing rather desperate views about the future of the Government. There was no reason for despera-tion, he said. Once we got into the summer recess and could have two months ahead with no Parliament we should be able to recover. He was working on the assumption that we would carry on at least until next year because by then we would have good things to put into our shop window—the Land Com-mission, for example, and the incomes guarantee. We would also have a positive programme of reform worked out in detail, which would improve our relations with the public. So we weren't to go away depressed. I then repeated my complaints about the relations between Cabinet and the Party, and pointed out that it was useless to ask somebody to do this job *sub rosa*, alluding of course to George Wigg. What we needed, I claimed, was someone of full Cabinet rank sitting there with us but also in constant contact with the Party. Harold quickly said that he was doing a great deal to remedy this. He couldn't make an announcement now, but there would be a new man talking to the Lobby. I asked who it was and he said it wouldn't be fair to give a name. I said it wasn't good enough just to have another official in the Lobby; what we needed was someone in Cabinet. Harold was resistant and I knew why. In many of his speeches he had gibed at the Tories for spending Government money on a Minister solely devoted to party politics. Once he has committed himself to something publicly there is no one more obstinate than Harold in refusing to go back on it, however necessary it may be to do so.

Friday, June 4th
Yesterday I announced my three local government decisions, and my first job today was to see how the national press had treated them. I found per-fectly decent pieces in *The Times* and in the *Guardian*. Certainly, they saw nothing sensational in my decisions and they don't make any charges of gerrymandering. This is a case where the less said the better.

There's been an appalling anti-climax after yesterday's Cabinet. The appointment which Harold claims will close the gap between the Cabinet and the Party is the return of John Harris to the Lobby.[1] That confirms my view that he has not grown up since he went to Downing Street. Far from adapting himself to his new position he is adapting his new position to himself (No. 10, as I saw the other day, is the spitting image of his little house in

---

[1] Former research officer for the Labour Party and secretary to Hugh Gaitskell. He was the Party's press officer 1962–4; and after Labour's election victory he became an official adviser to Patrick Gordon Walker, Michael Stewart and Roy Jenkins.

Hampstead), and that is why he is not developing into a strong Prime Minister. He lets Jim Callaghan be a Chancellor under Treasury dictation and George Brown go a-whoring after his incomes policy while failing to produce the National Plan which is the real purpose of the D.E.A. Further, although he sees a number of senior Ministers pretty continuously he lacks both an inner Cabinet and a real strategy.

When I look back on him as leader of the Opposition I find I was making exactly the same criticisms then. I remember how I said to myself, Why can't he have the courage to form an inner group, why can't he have a consistent policy worked out by that inner group? The reason he always gave for not doing these things was that he was going to reorganize the Shadow Cabinet, but actually he never did. He just let each member go on within the conventional sphere of his own Shadow office.

Whit Monday, June 7th
A lovely day. The B.B.C. prophesy rain in the next few hours but the B.B.C. has been unsuccessfully prophesying rain on each day of this Whit holiday. I am just beginning to feel that sense of relaxation one gets when the bags and the boxes no longer appear. There have been none this weekend. Actually, the holiday started on Friday morning when I discovered that the office was not going to open because it was a holiday for all civil servants. So I was able to put Tam into my car and send him off to Kings Cross and I myself walked across the park to have a haircut. I caught the 11.10, looked out of the window at a June countryside richer and greener than I have ever known it, and got here in time for an early lunch with the children, who were rushing back for the last session of school before the Whit holiday.

Anne is still very distressed by the newspaper stories a fortnight ago about the Spencers' cottage. I seemed to have forgotten them altogether until I got home. They impacted on me at the time, but so much has happened since. Here at home the impact was much greater and is still continuing. Partly because of the scandal we have offered the Marriotts, who are living in the flat at the top of our house, the other half of the Spencer cottage. This is because we have now discovered the cause of Spencer's grievance, and why he talked to the press. He didn't complain so long as Joe, our cowman, was living next door. But then we built the new houses in the village and naturally offered the best of them to Joe. That left Creampot Lane vacant and I did something I had always wanted to do, which was to offer it to Tony Lynes who is one of the Titmuss young men and who has always wanted a cottage in the country.[1] Pritchett, who is canny on these things, was greatly against my doing so and kept on arguing that we would have to retain the right to throw him out if ever we wanted an agricultural labourer there. But Tony was all agreement and so he got it and soon settled down and began to have his

[1] A research worker in the social services. Later he was to spend time at D.H.S.S. as an adviser to Peggy Herbison.

friends for the weekends. He is a great left-winger and idealist and one of his friends was a Pakistani lady with a small baby. Tony used to wheel the pram while she walked beside him through the village and the village began to talk. As for Mr Spencer in the ruined part of Creampot Lane, he couldn't contain himself—hence the outbreak. Though it seems a bit weak I can't blame Mr Pritchett and Anne for doing what they did. The Marriotts, who have been working as housekeepers here, have been wanting to move into a house of their own. Indeed, the best way to hold him as our gardener is to give him the Creampot Lane house. So Tony is going and Marriott is moving in. And that should appease the Spencers for the time necessary to find them a council house.

Sunday, June 13th
I have had my Whit week holiday and feel entirely relaxed. I say a week's holiday but when I add it up I have had Monday, Tuesday, Thursday—three days—as Jennie came down on Wednesday and Friday and we did some work here. Nevertheless, we have been together as a family more than for a very long time, because my Easter holiday was spent away at the Lizard with Anne.

The weather was fairly difficult for the hay crop and Amos Meadow has only just been cut at last. It's still wet and we have had relatively little sunshine. But it's a great relaxation to be here, discussing the farm problems with Pritchett. One thing this week's holiday has done is to strengthen that sense of detachment which has never entirely left me since I became a Cabinet Minister. There is no doubt that getting the job when I was already fifty-seven and having very young children, as well as Prescote, and having written about Cabinet government for so long, all this together gave me at first a sense of being an inside observer, not a participator. Then there came a period when the Government was getting momentum and I became entirely absorbed in my own work. I lost my sense of detachment and that's why this diary became more spasmodic. But now it has come back, and I find myself saying to myself, and even sometimes to other people, 'Well, you know I have had my eight or nine months as Minister. Almost long enough for my purposes.' When I say that, there is quite a large slice of affectation in the remark, and there is also a little bit of insurance since I always like to make sure that whatever happens I shall enjoy it. But there is also an element of deeper truth. I don't expect to be a Minister for very long. I may be shoved round a bit but hardly promoted because I have reached the top and I am having my chance—and part of that chance consists of being an outside observer on the inside.

Now let me fill in the political events of this holiday week. First of all Thomas Balogh, Pen and Tessa turned up here on their way back from Pen's house at Loweswater where they had been spending two or three days. They arrived at 8.30 last Sunday and we had a talk that evening and another during the whole of the next morning before they drove off to Chequers. I feel a little jealous of Thomas that he gets asked to Chequers and I don't. Of course, I don't really want to go and I'm sure I would be bitchy if I were asked. I certainly wouldn't enjoy staying there and nor would Anne. Nevertheless, there is that feeling that one is left out of the inner group.

Thomas told me that he has had to abandon all his great hopes of building up a presidential system, so that the Prime Minister would have a real staff at No. 10 enabling him to control the activities of his Ministers and to develop a central strategy. I have always thought him over-optimistic on this point and remember telling him a story I got from Hugh Carleton Greene.[1] When Harold was leader of the Opposition he asked Normanbrook, then chairman of the Governors of the B.B.C.,[2] to come to lunch and told him about his ideas for expanding the Prime Minister's staff. Back at the B.B.C. that afternoon Normanbrook ran into Carleton Greene and recited to him vividly how he had persuaded Harold that it would be a great mistake to conceive of a presidential staff since this would create suspicions in the Civil Service. And in fact Harold has been deeply conventional in his acceptance of the Civil Service hierarchy, and is willing to leave all the key people in their key positions—Helsby as head of the Civil Service, for example, and Otto Clarke and Denis Rickett[3] as the two key men in the Treasury. Tommy believes that it is now too late for Harold to break out of this situation. There is nothing for it but to go on with things roughly as they are at present in Whitehall, where there has been a tremendous reassertion of Civil Service confidence and initiative, including a determination to prevent any more new ideas being launched. What chance we had at the beginning of the Government to introduce basic changes has now been removed by our first losing the initiative and then grinding to a halt. Unfortunately, instead of changing the key personnel, Harold chose at the start to busy himself creating unnecessary new Ministries. When I look round Whitehall and see the enormous shifts forced upon it by Harold's decisions, I realize what sisyphean labours he undertook or made others undertake to very little purpose. He could have achieved far more by changes in individual personnel.

It's also very difficult to defend these new, chopped-up Ministries in terms of their functional merits.[4] What is the value of a separate Ministry of Land and Natural Resources? We will have to get rid of it quite soon. What is achieved by creating Barbara's little Ministry of Overseas Development? Certainly it doesn't do any harm, but it remains true that in these overseas areas we have three Cabinet Ministers, Barbara Castle, Tony Greenwood and

[1] Crossman's wartime colleague. He had been Director-General of the B.B.C. since 1960. He became a Governor in 1969, and resigned in 1971.

[2] Norman Brook (created Lord Normanbrook in 1963) had been chairman of the Governors of the B.B.C. since 1964. As Secretary of the Cabinet between 1947 and 1962 and Head of the Home Civil Service from 1956 to 1962, he was the epitome of a Whitehall mandarin.

[3] Second Secretary at the Treasury, 1960–68. He became Vice-President of the International Bank for Reconstruction and Development in 1968.

[4] But see *Wilson*, pp. 7–11.

Arthur Bottomley, with three Ministries which could be rolled into one under one Minister perfectly comfortably. And that would leave room for a senior Minister of Pensions inside the Cabinet who really could have made a profound difference to the whole future of the Party by getting on with our reform of social security.

But of course the two most important new Ministries are Technology and the D.E.A. It looks as though Technology is pretty badly organized; and it was given a very poor start by the personnel selected as Ministers. As for the D.E.A., the choice of George Brown as the first Minister in charge made its failure certain. He completely failed to give priority to the economic plan under which the Labour Government should proceed – he preferred incomes policy.

One other subject which I discussed with Thomas because I knew he was going to Chequers was my own housing programme. I found that he entirely agreed with Harold on the risks of a Statement at the end of July about a new form of housing subsidy. I could of course start negotiating with the building societies and the local authorities about the housing plan, but finance should not be discussed. Just after Thomas left, I found in the first red box that came down from London a note from Harold Wilson to which was attached a copy of a minute he had sent to George Brown on this subject. In it he asked George to accept the idea of a national housing drive and then suggested that it should be taken out of the economic plan and given not merely priority in importance but priority in time over all other social services. This would mean that, although the National Plan as a whole might not be ready until the autumn, the national housing plan could precede it in July.

I am doubtful whether it is practical politics to expect Cabinet to give housing priority over all other social services. Callaghan has said more than once that the amount of housing I am demanding in the next four years would eat up practically all the resources allocated for expansion. Whatever Harold may say, I can't see Cabinet swallowing that.

So when Jennie came down to Prescote on Friday I polished up a polite reply to the P.M., welcoming the idea of a national housing plan but asking him whether it could be launched before September unless other Ministers accepted its urgency. Just when I had finished drafting my minute I found that my copy of George Brown's reply had already arrived, in which he stated that there could be no question of a national housing plan coming before September and raised the difficulty of getting other Ministers to accept the degree of priority required.*

Another subject dealt with during this recess was rating. On Wednesday Jennie brought down the Department's draft paper, which I am due to submit at the meeting the Prime Minister is calling next Tuesday. I am not in the least

---

* I was now beginning to appreciate the full importance of these personal minutes from Minister to Minister to Cabinet proceedings, and to the formation of Cabinet policy.

convinced, despite what my officials tell me, that a local income tax is impossible. But I am convinced that with these five months wasted we now have no time to get the foundation work done for a major rating reform Bill in the next Session. All I am left with is a small interim Bill in this Session. The aim of this Bill is quite simply to keep rates down next spring, because it is vital that there shouldn't be rate increases just before the municipal elections or, even worse, before the general election if it takes place. After that a long-term measure can be introduced later in the Session.

On the Friday of my holiday, June 4th, I went to Coventry to do interviews. Some thirty to thirty-five people had turned up from as far afield as Nuneaton and Rugby. They were there to see not the Member of Parliament for Coventry East but the Minister of Housing. Fortunately, I was able to deal with a good many of the problems quickly: they had come to ask about planning appeals and I had to say that I wasn't able to discuss an appeal while it was *sub judice* – as I was the *judex*. After those interviews I took Albert Rose and David Young and his wife out to dinner, with Anne, to talk about the situation in Coventry. The treatment of Winnie Lakin is appalling. The borough executive has merely taken note of the N.E.C.'s report acquitting her, and the G.M.C. of the borough merely took note of the executive's recommendation to take note! So poor Winnie received no apology and no decision and they haven't even written to inform her of the N.E.C. decision. Alas, there is not much more we can do. I told Albert I agreed with Bill Wilson that Winnie would be entitled to take a libel action against the *Coventry Evening Telegraph* – more particularly since the Party was unwilling to reinstate her in a clean and honourable way.

Apart from the Lakin scandal, the situation in Coventry is deeply depressing. I heard that evening that not a single meeting has been held in any of the three constituencies – not even in the marginal Coventry South – since the election. There was practically no canvassing before the municipals, despite the activity of the Tories. For the first time for many years – perhaps for the first time in history – the Tories won the majority of votes in the municipal elections in Coventry East. We have had a 16 per cent Conservative swing against us in Upper Stoke and we have lost Lower Stoke unnecessarily. What were we to do? We decided to have an autumn campaign and that I would do one meeting in each of the wards to launch the campaign.

Finally they asked me the question for which they had all been waiting: what was the future of the Government? What they wanted to hear was that everything was O.K. but they wouldn't have believed it if I had said so. I explained to them the danger we now faced of deflation and even of unemployment; and I disclosed that I wasn't enthusiastic, to put it mildly, about Harold Wilson's support for an East of Suez policy and for American policy in Vietnam. I went on to discuss relations between the Government and the Party, and told them that I had spent that day preparing a memorandum urging that the Paymaster-General should be made a co-ordinator with full

Cabinet membership. I must say that Albert Rose didn't seem passionately resentful about the relationship between the Government and the rank and file. Yet I am still convinced that this memorandum I am sending Harold is the most important thing I have done so far as this week's work is concerned. I have got to get over Harold's inhibitions and make him see the need for a co-ordinator of this kind. Only this morning the *Daily Telegraph* Gallup Poll reported a Tory lead of 4½ per cent, due not to a reduction in Labour support but to a switch by Liberals to the Tory Party. Much the most sinister thing about the poll however was the revelation that an overwhelming majority now expect a Tory victory. Expectation of victory has always been a far more reliable guide in the Gallup Polls than voting intentions.

There is one thing more which I want to put down. I am now wondering whether I haven't really got to try and use the Cabinet in a way I haven't used it before. Oughtn't I to make one real effort to get some sanity and central strategy into our conduct of affairs? Here we are, drifting along, with our momentum halted and the Civil Service taking over more every day. Policy is now formulated in the various Departments and merely co-ordinated by Harold at the last moment. There is no inner Cabinet with a coherent policy for this Government; and yet that is what we need more than anything else if we are going to regain the initiative this summer. We must have a clear-cut purpose.

This is one of Harold's weaknesses. He sees his job, not as launching a strategy, but as carrying out the manifesto. He is always getting George Wigg and Tommy Balogh to try and convince him that of the seventy-three promises in the manifesto, fifty-two are already being carried out. Yet from the point of view of the electorate this technical promise-keeping is quite unimportant. I have just been reading the draft White Paper on the Land Commission and if anyone thinks we are going to win votes by that document, they can think again. What we have failed to put over is that we have a purpose and a drive which will get the country on its feet. George Brown's incomes policy, in its present voluntary form, is over-boosted and has obviously come unstuck. The nationalization of iron and steel seems irrelevant, and so does our Finance Bill. Yet we must have a relevant policy which can be seen to be helping to deal with ordinary people's needs. That means incomes guarantee, housing policies and above all a strategy which links all this together in a central, coherent drive. I know all this. In a sense every member of Cabinet knows all this. Yet is it being done? And if it isn't being done, how can I persuade Harold that we need something more?

When I ask that question, I know the answer. If I do try to intervene along these lines, I have to face two things. On the one hand, I shall be accused of splitting the Cabinet and my action will be taken as anti-Wilson. The only way you can avoid being anti-Wilson is by going to him privately and letting him either take your advice or reject it. If I took an open initiative of this kind in open Cabinet, it would mean that I was apparently challenging his leadership. That is the eternal problem of the Labour Party – the problem of Labour leadership. One can't put any views strongly without being accused of factional strife. And that of course is accentuated by the danger that if I staged my initiative in Cabinet our private discussions would be leaked to the press. On the other hand, if I go through this June and July without any effort at all, can I think of myself as a responsible member of this Cabinet? Would I ever be able to forgive myself for my failure? That is a rhetorical question because really and truly I have no strong feeling of guilt and failure, and I don't regard this kind of initiative as my job. Harold hasn't put me in the Cabinet for that purpose. He is perfectly content with me if I do a good departmental job; and he has very carefully excluded me from central consultation and from his Chequers talks. So I can say to myself rather sulkily, why on earth should I make myself unpopular? But I have said that too often in the past. It is about time I made one real effort in Cabinet.

Tuesday, June 15th
Cabinet – and a characteristic one. I went there before going to my Rent Bill Committee despite the fact that there was nothing on the agenda which I cared about. Nevertheless, I was so worried by the Vietnam situation that I thought I had to raise it. It has been getting worse and worse with the Americans becoming more and more deeply committed; and I found myself yesterday looking back to a lunch party at Pam Berry's some weeks ago when Joe Alsop was the main guest.[1] I remember him sitting beside me and solemnly explaining to the assembled company that he was a happy man for the first time in years because in his view the President was now irrevocably and firmly committed to fighting the Vietnam war to the finish. At the time I was impressed and I believed Joe 75 per cent. Now, alas, I believe him 100 per cent and things look bleaker and bleaker. It is having its effect inside the Parliamentary Party, where the situation is growing very tense and not only left-wingers are beginning to organize letters and stage protests in their constituencies. So the squeeze on Harold is getting tighter. Michael Stewart being 100 per cent Anglo–American in a highly prim and proper way, feels no difficulties. With all this going on, I thought Vietnam must be raised in Cabinet. But it fell flat. This was mainly because, with the Commonwealth Conference just starting, Harold was able to say that a big initiative was now on the way – and he didn't want to say anything more about it for obvious reasons. That seemed to satisfy Cabinet, and I was content since George Wigg has been tipping me off about this initiative each morning on the phone and telling me the enormous success it is going to be.

At 5.30 we had a long-awaited Prime Minister's meeting on local government and finance. Harold had said he would lay this special meeting on for me because the Treasury was obviously muscling in on my province of local

---

[1] The American syndicated columnist who had been writing about political and foreign affairs since the 1930s. His views on Vietnam tended to be right-wing.

government finance. I was to submit our departmental paper and the Chancellor was to submit the Treasury paper. When I got to Harold's room in the House of Commons I found a crowd outside – some thirteen or fourteen people, including Treasury officials, Ministry of Housing officials, Scottish officials, Welsh officials and quite a bevy of Ministers. We stood there for about half an hour – an unusual delay in Whitehall life – while Harold talked to the Indian Prime Minister. It gave me a chance to chat with Bruce Fraser, and we didn't take long to agree that our aim must be to bring the Ministry of Land and Natural Resources back into the Ministry of Housing with him in charge. Having got his verbal agreement I was, by the way, very careful to back him up strongly whenever I could in the meeting itself. The proceedings were a bit rough. As soon as we had been ushered in and sat down, James Callaghan said that he didn't see the point of holding this meeting. Why, he asked, should the Minister of Housing and Local Government lay down the law about what he wants? This issue must go back into the normal channels and be dealt with by a committee of officials on the one level and by the Cabinet Committee at the higher level. Harold let him shout and sulk and then he slowly got the discussion going and I gradually got my case across. We must have the short Bill immediately to relieve the ratepayer next March and then next Session a longer-term reform to deal with rating. The discussion was very desultory because though the Prime Minister was genuinely trying to push things along he clearly didn't know where he wanted them to go. Indeed, I began to feel some sympathy for Callaghan's asking why matters should be conducted in this peculiar way. However, after the meeting I took the officials upstairs to my room in order to get the minute written right and to ensure it included the conclusions we wanted. What we finally decided was that Bruce Fraser should immediately write a long Cabinet policy paper analysing the issues which needed decision. All the officials agreed that this must come up next week to the Cabinet Committee. Next week? The sooner the better; after all, I had been asking for action on local finance and now it was being taken.

Wednesday, June 16th
In the morning I had a whole series of meetings at the Ministry. We began, for instance, to discuss the administration of rent control, the size of the areas for the rent assessment committees and how the personnel should be recruited. After that I had a big conference about the introduction of system-building, which resulted in a battle between Peter Lederer and our Chief Architect. Finally, just before lunch, came a little light relief – a protest delegation from the Council for the Protection of Rural England. The members of it were exactly the kind of people a novelist would put into a chapter caricaturing a protest committee. They were led by a bustling little business-man and a great smooth lawyer, and they placed before me a very offensive memorandum about how badly I had behaved in granting compulsory

purchases in the green belt. After they had gone out J. D. Jones said to me, 'You didn't realize but that chairman is a consultant who is constantly advising developers on how to get permissions granted for building in the green belt.'

All that afternoon I struggled with the Rent Bill and made very slow progress. When I had had four hours of that, I hurried along the Committee Floor to Room 14 where I found a packed meeting of the London Labour Party; I gave them an exposition of how the Bill will work and then answered questions. I have no doubt they were enormously impressed and pleased because, after all, in the realm of social service this is the first solid achievement of the Wilson Government. When they had gone, I went downstairs for a quiet supper and began to prepare for yet another Finance Bill all-night sitting. Thank heavens I was told I could go home at eleven because I was needed for the Rent Bill next morning.

Thursday, June 17th
I woke up early and began to worry whether we might fail to have a quorum when the Rent Bill Committee resumed at ten in the morning. I needn't have worried. Though most of my Members had been in the House all night I found them all sitting in their places at half a minute past ten thirty when I arrived. That's pretty good morale. There is no doubt that the hours we spend on the dreary corporation tax clauses of this Finance Bill are made tolerable by the fact that with a majority of three we are defeating the Opposition challenge night after night and winning the battle of the vote.

I had asked Peggy Herbison to lunch because I wanted to see how her plans for a minimum incomes guarantee would fit with my proposed rate rebates. She had nothing to tell me about that, but she poured out her heart to me on the subject of Douglas Houghton. I had imagined that what she resented was the fact of his being an overlord set on top of her. Her real objection was very different—that he didn't run things at all and did nothing except lift her ideas and take the credit for them. After she had gone George Wigg came across the Members' dining-room and sat with me to urge me once again not to push the Prime Minister too much at this stage. He also told me that the great Statement was due to be made at seven that evening and that I must be there without fail. I told him I was going to Nottingham on an official visit. Then Harold joined us and I told him about the turn-out of my Members in the Rent Bill Committee and he was enormously pleased. But he didn't stay long because he had to take George Wigg off to discuss this important event of which I knew nothing. I guessed by now that it must be a Vietnam peace initiative designed to calm the left-wing of the Party.

In the afternoon I began my negotiations with the building societies about the national housing plan. Representing the Treasury was Jack Diamond, who had written a very cynical paper about the whole idea. He came to the meeting after twenty-two hours on the front bench, so tired that he could scarcely move. Perhaps this was just as well since it enabled the meeting to go very smoothly. The building societies were not merely courteous; they were almost enthusiastic about the plan.

When they left I drove to St Pancras to catch the train to Nottingham. Directly I got there I was asked upstairs in the hotel for a drink by the city architect, who wondered whether I would like to see the television. So I went into another room and was just settling down to Michael Stewart's teach-in on Vietnam at Oxford when it was interrupted for a news bulletin. There was the Prime Minister announcing the Commonwealth mission to Vietnam and Bob Menzies[1] clapping him on the back and saying, 'I give this trip to you, old boy. Really it was your idea.' The political matiness and gimmickry of the proceedings were in startling contrast with Stewart's performance which preceded and followed it (he was a brilliant television success and put the American case more competently than any American has ever put it). I went to bed not very impressed and thinking, 'Poor old Harold. George Wigg has committed him to yet another of his stunts.'[2]

Friday, June 18th
When I looked at the papers this morning it was clear that my suspicions were justified – this was a last-minute dish, cooked up by George and Harold to get the Prime Minister out of his 'little local difficulties'. I find the whole affair immensely unattractive but I also know that I am being unfair to Harold in having this feeling. After all, he is the kind of man who takes these opportunities; and why, if Harold Macmillan can take them and win applause,[3] should Harold Wilson be despised or criticized for doing so? What really worries me is that the chances of success are so very slim and don't really justify the role he has allotted himself. I gather that it is assumed he will be a month on the job – and it will be the critical month when Cabinet has to take all the decisions about the future of the economy and the priorities between the various Departments. It is on the home front that Harold should be showing his leadership and displaying his courage; but he is going away on a Vietnam stunt.[4]

[1] Sir Robert Menzies was Prime Minister of Australia 1939–41 and from 1949 until 1966. He had also been Minister of External Affairs 1960–61. He himself had led such a mission as Wilson's – to Colonel Nasser at the time of the 1956 Suez crisis. In 1965 he was made Lord Warden of the Cinque Ports.
[2] According to Wilson the idea came to him when 'pacing the terrace at Chequers'. *Wilson*, p. 108.
[3] June and July 1963 were a time when disastrous by-elections and security scandals shook the Conservative Government. But the Prime Minister, Harold Macmillan, was able to offer the electorate distraction and hope when, on July 25th, representatives of the United States, Britain and the U.S.S.R. initialled a treaty banning atmospheric and underwater nuclear tests. Sir Alec Douglas-Home was dispatched to Moscow for the formal ceremony of signature on August 5th. Parliament was nearing the end of its term at that time, though no date had been announced for a general election.
[4] The mission was to visit Moscow, Washington and Peking as well as Hanoi and Saigon.

I spent the morning opening a swimming-bath at Beeston—which is virtually a suburb of Nottingham—and the afternoon at Derby. Beeston is not only the home of boilers but of British roses; and the council gave me thirty-six rose trees—a good deal preferable to the ghastly pottery which one usually gets at an opening. Their U.D.C. is middle-aged but vigorous and go-ahead. At Derby, of the six councillors selected to receive me when I got there after lunch, two were over eighty and all were over sixty-two. Oh dear, defunct Derby—that soulless industrial Victorian town with its pathetically ingrained Labour administration terrified of any change. It had been announced today that British Railways was going to give 800 scientists jobs there. I asked our Labour Mayor about it and he said, 'We shan't give them council houses. It's not our job to house them.' From there back to Prescote in a Ministry of Works car.

Sunday, June 20th
Early in the morning I rang up George Wigg because I was still worrying about the Vietnam stunt. So I said to him, 'We must now consider what to do if Wilson is out of action for a month.' He obviously saw the point and replied, 'Don't worry about it now. Let's face it when it comes.' This didn't make me feel any more enthusiastic. Certainly, in the short run it will relieve tension among our back-benchers. But there will be trouble in Cabinet. We were asked our opinion on bank rate before the decision was finally taken; so it really was ridiculous that last Tuesday we were not consulted before the news of the stunt was released. Characteristically, of course, when I read the *Observer* today I found in Nora Beloff's article a round by round description of Harold Wilson's secret preparations for the great coup and a statement that he had to keep it secret because he couldn't trust his Cabinet colleagues not to leak.

Sunday, June 27th
All last week the Commonwealth Conference was going on and also the reactions to Harold's peace initiative. This certainly reverberated through Whitehall and Westminster but it is now virtually over and the mission is dead.[1]

To be fair to Harold, it had the desired effect in the Parliamentary Party. I was lunching with my Parliamentary Secretaries, as I do each week, when Harold came in and asked me to walk down the corridor with him. I was feeling very critical of him for this political stunt. As we walked together Manny Shinwell came up and praised him in the most exaggerated way; when Manny turned off into the tea-room, I said to the Prime Minister, 'I really was anxious, Harold, that if this stunt had come off you might have been away

[1] Hanoi, Moscow and Peking rejected the proposed visit. However, the Prime Minister soon produced another initiative. See p. 269.

for a whole month.' 'Oh, I don't think it would have been a month,' he replied. 'At the most it would have been a fortnight.' And he added these significant words: 'Anyway, I think we have got most of the value we can out of it already.' This makes me wonder whether the factor which really persuaded him to take George Wigg's advice was the prospect of the Commonwealth Conference breaking up on the first day as a result of the furious row over Rhodesia. Black Africa is now virtually at war with Rhodesia whereas the white Commonwealth is still trying to keep the peace. In order to postpone that row and create a better atmosphere, Harold needed a personal initiative on the first day and in this sense I have no doubt the stunt was brilliantly successful. He got through the Conference without having to give anything away and he achieved what was a great feat of diplomacy in the circumstances — an agreed communiqué. He requested our permission in Cabinet on Thursday (the only important thing that happened there) to say in the communiqué that Britain would in due course consider the possibility of summoning 'a constitutional conference' on white Rhodesia. I doubt whether such a minor concession to the African viewpoint would have won him that agreed communiqué without the Vietnam initiative on the first day.

In domestic politics he has also gained quite a lot. The tension on the Left of the Labour Party has been eased and the Tories thrown on the defensive. Of course Douglas-Home knows that it was a political stunt, but so was Harold Macmillan's Moscow enterprise. Our Harold has pulled off a diplomatic coup which was popular with public opinion, eased the situation in his own Party and prevented a potential breakdown of the Commonwealth Conference. One can't be surprised if he is rather pleased with himself.

The initiative also made its impact on my personal plans, since in Whitehall everything is held up. The memorandum I submitted through George Wigg still hasn't been read; Helsby still hasn't had time to tell the P.M. about the idea we agreed of sending Bruce Fraser to the Ministry of Land and Natural Resources and keeping the Dame on till next spring. Even the very important meeting we were due to hold this week on the Land Commission had to be postponed because the Prime Minister was busy drafting the Commonwealth communiqué.

For those of us not concerned with that Conference, the week has been dominated once again by the Finance Bill — we have nearly finished the Committee Stage on the Floor of the House. The fact that a Government with a precarious majority got this inordinately complex Bill through Committee without a single defeat is a tremendous triumph. Harold was able to announce yesterday in Glasgow that the Government has no intention of going to the country this year since it has proved that the most contentious legislation can be got through the Commons and that, therefore, we can effectively rule the country. The man who should get the credit for all this in the Whips' Office is not Ted Short, who is efficient but uninspired. It is John Silkin, the youngest of the three sons of Lewis Silkin, the originator of the

1947 Town and Country Planning Act.[1] Another son, Sam Silkin, is a very
able lawyer and a solid chap, who has been working with me on leasehold
enfranchisement. John, his much younger brother, is a newcomer to the
House and a very new Whip. But he has shown such brains, charm and
diplomacy that he has been given the job of organizing the whole pairing
system during this critical period. Incidentally, he has been a very good friend
to me because I have only had once to stay through the night. Mostly he has
let me off at midnight or two in the morning. And although that is tiring
enough it makes a very great difference.

Harold's preoccupations have given me time to reflect and to prepare for
the battle ahead. From what I have learnt during the week I have no doubt
whatsoever that the period from now to the end of July will be an absolutely
critical time in the life of the Government. George Brown has told me in
private conversation what the plan is. First, there will be no Statement on
housing before the recess – that's definite. Second, we shall recess as
punctually as possible at the end of July. Third, the Government will use the
recess to finalize George's National Plan, in which there will be separate
chapters on housing and the social services. In preparation for this, a strange
new committee has been established consisting of five senior Ministers without
departmental problems, who are to make a searching examination of expenditure in the public sector;[2] so much for George Brown's National Plan. But
Thomas Balogh tells me that although he used to be my stalwart ally against
Callaghan, and supported an expanded housing programme, George Brown
now sides with Callaghan in thinking that, if there have to be cuts in the social
services, housing should take them and I, the Minister of Housing, should
take the consequences. Tommy sees this as a conspiracy, but there are really
quite sensible reasons why the First Secretary should change his mind about
giving housing top priority and decide now to avoid cuts in the social services
by letting the axe fall mainly on me. The political advantage of this procedure
would be that there would be fewer toes trodden on. All the other social
service Ministers inherited programmes of expansion to which the Tories
had committed themselves. Public-sector housing alone was held back by our
predecessors. The simplest way, therefore, of avoiding an unpleasant Cabinet
row would be to leave public-sector housing in a depressed condition, let the
crisis in the private sector of housing develop, and then – after we have got
through our deflation – to revive the housing programme and let it go ahead.
At least, that's the kind of way in which I believe George Brown has justified
himself in reversing his position. So over the week I have been thinking

---

[1] Sir Lewis Silkin, created Lord Silkin in 1950. A solicitor, he had been Labour M.P.
for Peckham since 1936. From 1945 to 1950 he was Minister of Town and Country Planning.
He died in 1972; and his eldest son, Arthur, a civil servant, disclaimed the peerage for life.
[2] The Public Expenditure Survey Committee, known as PESC. The first comprehensive
survey of the long-term expenditure plans and forecasts of growth had been made in 1961.
But 1965, as a result of the PESC deliberations, was the first year in which a Cabinet
decision on resources and priorities was made.

out how to defend myself against a combined attack by Jim and George. At least I know I have one ally. I talked to Frank Cousins, who feels more and more frustrated because he knows he was far more powerful as General Secretary of the T.G.W.U. than he is as Minister of Technology in a Department which is really not doing very much. He talks a great deal to Harold; and he made it clear to me that he is going to stand solid against the attempt to cut back housing which he thinks will be made by the new committee of five – of which, by the way, he is a member – and that is about all the support I have got, except of course the Prime Minister himself. When the crunch comes it will be interesting to see how strongly Harold will fight for the housing crusade as the central feature of the National Plan.

I must add one footnote. On Thursday after Cabinet I was drafted to attend a meeting of the Privy Council. This was the first time I had been compelled to go to Buckingham Palace. My job was to shake the hands of the three new Privy Councillors being introduced, and then to listen to the Lord President reading aloud to the poor little Queen a list of Orders in Council which have been passed. It is the most idiotic flummery and I must admit that I feel morally superior to my colleagues in despising it. I've carried this kind of self-conscious contempt a long way, and now they don't bother to send me invitations. Anne and I are completely out. We didn't even go to the Lancaster House party for Magna Carta or the proceedings in the Great Hall at Westminster.[1] I know my attitude is partly a piece of conscious arrogance – I want to prove to myself that I don't like these things, although I sometimes find myself mildly enjoying them and I even slightly resent myself for refusing ever to attend them. Nevertheless, this Privy Council made me realize how good it is to have a wife who genuinely doesn't want me to accept any of these official invitations and so lets me save myself a great deal of the time and energy which other Ministers waste upon them. This week for instance I have had quite a lot of time off as the result of refusing to attend any of the Commonwealth jamborees.

Monday, June 28th
I had to go up by the Sunday-night train since the E.D.C. meeting started at 9.45. My mind wasn't very much on the agenda since I was overwhelmingly concerned with preparations for the Report Stage of the Rent Bill. There are 8 or 9 new clauses and some 100 amendments down, most of the important ones being new Government clauses and Government amendments. Unfortunately I am also first in Questions on Tuesday and we have a censure debate on our failure to meet house-building targets on Thursday, so I am going to have three successive days sitting on the front bench, followed on

---

[1] The 750th anniversary of Magna Carta was marked with a service at St Paul's on June 10th. On June 22nd the Queen received an Address in Westminster Hall to celebrate the 700th anniversary of the first English Parliament, summoned in 1265 by Simon de Montfort.

9

Friday by a full day of official visitations and a surgery in Coventry, and on
Saturday the great country fair which is being organized in Cropredy for the
village hall fund.

I was pretty anxious and tense this morning about what would happen. So
I didn't play a great role in the big item on the E.D.C. agenda – the treatment
of the declining coal industry. We were confronted with a very characteristic
recommendation from Fred Lee, our trade-union Minister of Power. His
main concern seemed to be that we should on no account give any kind of
tapering subsidies to help declining coalfields such as those in Scotland and
South Wales. It's extraordinary how a Department can get a Minister down.
It would have been difficult to conceive nine months ago that Mr Lee would
have been opposed to any help for the coalminers and blind to the fact that
tapering subsidies are politically essential.

I had to leave before the debate was over for an important meeting at the
Ministry about accommodation for Commonwealth immigrants. There had
been an extraordinary incident last week when Maurice Foley, chairman of
the special sub-committee, had put forward to the Cabinet Immigration Committee (in my absence) a proposal for a twelve-month moratorium on all
entries, including wives, children and dependants. This would have been
perfectly insane since it would simply have increased the chaos by creating a
dam which would have been swept away twelve months later. I had discussed
with Bob Mellish an idea which had been put up to us that we should limit
the arrival of dependants to immigrants who could prove that they were
going to adequate accommodation. We liked it at first, but came to the conclusion that in practical terms it would produce the most extraordinary
difficulties for the local authorities. They would be very unwilling to take on
the job of vetting and, above all, of adjudicating whether the immigrant's
accommodation was sufficiently good to permit the arrival of his children.
At the meeting we opposed this as well as the moratorium.

I got a little time to take a look at the Questions I was due to answer next
day when the Department was first on the Order Paper, and then I was off to a
curious lunch with the Lord Chancellor. This is light relief, but it reveals his
strange character. I found the other guests were Ray Gunter, the Minister of
Labour, and Charlie Pannell, the Minister of Works. Why were we gathered
together? There was no great issue of policy he wanted to discuss. He and his
wife were just worried about the window-cleaners who deal with the windows
in the huge Victoria Tower where they live. Apparently they just put a long
board out of the window, weigh down the trestles inside, and then walk out
along it and where necessary put up a ladder at the end of the board and climb
up that. He complained that the firms who do this have already had deaths
and injuries and that there is no insurance for the men and no trade-union
protection. He thought this should be stopped, and showed us a New York
law which made regulations of a kind which don't exist in this country for
window-cleaning on high buildings. I dare say Gerald Gardiner's anxieties

were justified but they were received very negatively. Mr Gunter showed a great reluctance to deal with it departmentally and Mr Pannell merely gave the assurance that the Ministry of Works would 'process the problem in the normal way'. As for me, I had a perfect departmental alibi. It occurred to none of us that Gerald might really have exposed a social evil which a Labour government should deal with.

After that I got back to the Ministry and down to the task of going through all the amendments and new clauses of the Rent Bill, planning the time-table of the debate and dividing up front-bench responsibility. This I did with Jim MacColl, who has been absolutely invaluable on the Bill. We decided that we must get to the end of Part II on Tuesday night, however late we ran, if we were to have the Report Stage concluded by seven o'clock on Wednesday afternoon. A mere day and a half was a crazy time-allocation if only because the eight new clauses and fifty amendments the Government had put down — more than half the total — would take all the time available, leaving nothing for the Opposition. In any case, it was obvious that we should have to have something like an all-night sitting on Tuesday if we were to get through the job. At five o'clock I went across to the House to discuss our plans with a meeting of back-benchers interested in the Bill.

Unfortunately, the team which had been working with me throughout the Committee Stage had been wound up. I now had to meet any old back-bencher interested in rent. I found some thirty people there, of whom ten hadn't worked with us at all on the Committee. This made it difficult because I had had a good discussion with the team a few days ago about the two issues which I knew divided us. They had strongly objected to two clauses. One of them gave the Minister power to wind up the new rent-regulation machinery in any part of the country, or indeed throughout the whole of England and Wales. It seemed to them absurd that a Minister should be able to end an Act by an Order in Council, and I agreed that we must remove this from the Bill. The other clause on which I made a major concession was on the crucial subject of the second stage of the Act, when the controlled tenants are brought into the new system of rent regulation and their rents — at present frozen under control — are then revised by the rent officers and the rent assessment committees. It may well be that in this second stage rents will have to be doubled or more than doubled because the gap will be so wide. To deal with this humanely, the first draft of the Bill had given the Minister power to introduce progressive scales under which rents could be gradually increased. My back-benchers thought this was not nearly strong enough and I had promised at the Report Stage a brand new clause saying that the increase in any one year cannot be more than 15 per cent. They had asked for a 10 per cent maximum, Jim MacColl had suggested 25 per cent and I had settled for 15 per cent. Now I found that two members of my old team, Julius Silverman and Frank Allaun, had put down an amendment to my new clause saying there should be only one increase and after that nothing more. That, of course, would have been a completely wrecking amendment. I had to listen once again to long speeches from Eric Heffer and Frank Allaun, repeating that the whole idea of the fair-rent clause should never have been allowed since it was a betrayal of Party policy. After they had finished their harangues, I said, 'Look, you can't do this to me. Last week some of you proposed a 10 per cent maximum. I can understand your putting down a new amendment to substitute 10 per cent for 15 per cent. What I can't understand is this wrecking amendment which Julius Silverman has put on the Order Paper.'

There was a fairly rough atmosphere but I got through the evening pretty well and my impression was that they wouldn't resist too much on the Floor of the House. I then went back to Vincent Square and took Anne out to see a new John Osborne play at Wyndhams, *Inadmissible Evidence*—talk, talk, talk on the telephone by a no-good clerk. Technically a great performance, but curiously unmemorable. We had a quiet dinner at the Ivy and got home in good time because I knew I had to wake up early next morning to prepare my speeches on the new clauses.

Wednesday, June 30th
So there I was sitting up in bed at six o'clock on Tuesday morning finishing off the normal administrative work in the red box and then getting down to the three key speeches I would have to make this week.

I had to get into the office shortly after nine because there was a mass of routine work. We were preparing for the further negotiations with the building societies about the national housing plan; and of course we had to think ahead to the vote of censure on Thursday. Also we had to resolve endless difficulties about leasehold reform and the Land Commission. At eleven thirty the Prime Minister had his big meeting at No. 10 on this. I had been horrified by the draft White Paper which Fred Willey had produced because it seemed to me to threaten the use of the big stick when we secretly knew that there wouldn't be a big stick for seven or eight years at least. I had been briefed by the Department to support the Chancellor, who wanted to rely mainly on his new capital gains tax and to keep the betterment levy down. However, Harold was in his best fixing form. He straight away conceded to Fred Willey—in the absence of the Chancellor, who was away in New York—that the betterment levy must be levied on all betterment and there should be no capital gains at all. Then he satisfied me by agreeing that we should start with a low betterment levy and gradually work up. So we all went away satisfied.

I was due at the end of this meeting to stay behind and see the Prime Minister about the future of my Department, and I hoped to sell him the proposals I had worked out with Dame Evelyn and Helsby. However, he at once began to ask me about the housing figures, which were much better than we expected—a record number of completions in the first five months. I tried to warn him against making too much of these figures, and I reminded

him we were facing a tremendous crisis in the private sector owing to the
shortage of building-society funds. Having got this across, I then said, 'Is
Helsby coming in order to discuss the future of my Department?' And he
replied, 'Oh, I told Helsby not to come. I didn't think we would have time to
deal with it.' Then he went on, 'But I gather you want to talk about the
ultimate future of the Ministry of Land and Natural Resources.' 'Oh no,' I
said, 'I don't want to talk about that. I want to talk about the future of Dame
Evelyn and the proposition we put up to you that since the Permanent
Secretary at Land and Natural Resources wants to join big business he should
be sent off as soon as possible. Let's get rid of him this summer and put Bruce
Fraser in there to take us through the Land Commission Bill, which he will
do very well. Meanwhile, Dame Evelyn is prepared to stay until next March.'
'Well,' he said, 'are you prepared to leave it open?' 'Yes,' I said. 'I don't want
to discuss the ultimate future of Land and Natural Resources but I want to
warn you that we have all got together, Helsby, Bruce Fraser, the Dame and
myself, and we think that when the Land Commission Bill is through the
House and possibly leasehold enfranchisement too, you ought to wind that
Ministry up or else give it a great deal more power. But we don't think you
should have to decide that now. All you need to do now is to put Bruce Fraser
there and then if you do hand back Land and Natural Resources to us in
Housing I could take him too.'

To my amazement he said he agreed; and when I ran into him in the
division lobby that same evening he told me that he had fixed it all with
Helsby. 'It's all done,' he said, very pleased with himself. And I found it was
true.

All this had taken me well into lunch-time but I wasn't too dissatisfied when
I got back to the Ministry and sat down to prepare our Questions with my
Parliamentary Secretaries over a cold lunch. One is only first for Questions
once every seven or eight weeks, so in a sense it is equivalent to making a
major speech. We divided the Questions up among the three of us and I had
about half and they had the other half. Inevitably, I was as boring as I had
been on the previous occasion because all I can do is stand up and say, 'I have
nothing to say on mortgages yet,' 'I have nothing to say on local government
finance yet.' In fact, there is nothing I can make a Statement about and the
Tories are so unenterprising that they don't ask me about the difficult, controversial issues with which I am always dealing, such as planning permissions
and compulsory purchase orders. They leave out all that side of my work
because all they now care about is mortgage rates. So it wasn't very difficult;
and afterwards I sat by while Harold Wilson did his quarter-of-an-hour of
Prime Minister's Questions. Then there was a longish Statement on the
Commonwealth Conference and another Statement on medical research. And
after that I was up on the first of my new clauses in the Report Stage of the
Rent Bill.

This session, as expected, ran from 3.30 on Tuesday afternoon until 5.50

this morning. The group of clauses which enable owner-occupiers to get back into their houses when they have let them temporarily were expected to take three hours, owing to Tory objections. They did. Then came the famous clause on the transition from control to regulation which I had been discussing with my back-benchers on Monday evening. I knew that would take another three hours. And it did. I wound it up in what I thought was a brisk and amusing speech, which went down pretty well though I was aware that I had been rather sharp and arrogant in the rebukes I had delivered to the left-wingers for what I called their conservatism. However, it seemed to have all been taken in good heart. I took the precaution of going downstairs afterwards to have supper with Stan Orme[1] and Norman Buchan,[2] two prominent left-wingers. The resistance to this clause was one of the few rebellions on a home issue under this Government. But the speeches by Julius Silverman, Frank Allaun and the rest of them were a bit flat. It was obvious from the start that they weren't actually going to move their own amendment and that when the time came they would have to vote with me against the Tory amendment. This they duly did shortly after 10.

At about midnight we were getting near the end of the new clauses when John Boyd-Carpenter got up to move progress. I replied, 'No, no. We are getting on quite well.' And we ploughed our way through to the end of the new clauses at about 2 a.m. and then we started on the amendments. I was feeling perfectly well and I would have liked to carry through to the next afternoon and cancel the next day's business in order to finish the Bill. But here something rather interesting happened. As long as the Tories were keeping enough of their back-benchers in the House to be able to call a division and muster a respectable total in the division lobby there was no kind of filibustering. But at last they let their people go home and kept only a small party there simply to prolong business. From this moment we made virtually no progress; indeed, I think we only got through three amendments in three hours.

By 5 a.m. it was clear that we were getting nowhere and I talked it over with John Silkin. He is not Chief Whip or Deputy Chief Whip but it seems to me he is the man who really now manages our business. He strongly advised me to let him negotiate the best agreement he could with Boyd-Carpenter. I concurred — whereupon he soon came back to tell me that the Tory Whips had agreed to give us the Bill holus-bolus by 11.30 on Wednesday evening if we would let them go home at the end of that clause. John Silkin had extracted an extraordinarily generous concession.

I got to bed just before 6 a.m. and, thank God, I fell asleep. I had to wake up at 8 to get to the office fairly soon to deal with a mountain of work. I also had to hold a big press conference at 11 to announce my decision on the

---

[1] M.P. for Salford West since 1964, and an A.E.U. member.
[2] M.P. for Renfrewshire West since 1964, and a former member of the Communist Party and C.N.D.

West Midlands conurbation.[1] I found the press conference and the television interviews heavy going and I was told I looked a wreck. Nevertheless, I got through it all and then sat down in my room to prepare for the afternoon session which was due to start at 3.30. After that I strolled across to the House and there I made a great mistake. Tommy Balogh had come into my room to talk to me about the Sunday meeting I was to have with PESC. I gave him a glass of sherry and I had a glass of gin. Then I went down to the Members' dining-room and took a carafe of white wine with my lunch. Soon after lunch I was horrified to find that a splitting headache was coming on, as though I had drunk far too much and was starting the worst kind of hangover. And in fact until 7 p.m. that headache hung over me. I began to realize what it is that goes wrong with George Brown. I was so physically and nervously exhausted and so strung up that a couple of glasses of wine, which would have had no effect upon me if I had downed them at a dinner-party, had put me in a hell of a way. I found this all the more trying because from 3.30 till about nine I had to be on the front bench virtually the whole time, since this part of the Bill dealt with issues where the Minister had to reply. For instance, I had to deal with all the questions about rateable value and with the fair-rent clause. So I sat there feeling like death but apparently making a series of speeches which were perfectly adequate. I could only have done this because I really had the stuff off by heart.

Having agreed to give us the Bill by 11.30 p.m., the Conservatives organized the session most efficiently, dropping a great many of their own key amendments. They were pushing the Bill on all the time and so was the Chair; and yet we were dragging behind the time-table because there was genuinely so much to discuss. It was obvious to me that the time allotted should have been doubled if there was to be any real analysis of the new material. So there had been a pretty serious miscalculation by Bert Bowden (who will be in trouble again when we face the Report Stage of the Finance Bill unless he provides time for a decent discussion). I was in bed before midnight knowing that next day I had a full day's work in the morning followed by the big censure debate in the afternoon.

Thursday, July 1st
I could only look in at Cabinet and hear part of the discussion of Fred Lee's policy for the coalmines. Thank heavens Cabinet has seen the necessity for sensible tapering subsidies—it enabled him to make a perfectly satisfactory Statement in the House before my censure debate. It was Cabinet in fact that saved Fred from his Department.

Back in my Ministry I had an appointment with Helsby. He confirmed that

[1] The Local Government Boundary Commission had recommended in its 1960 report the creation of five new county boroughs. Some local authorities threatened with extinction had appealed against the change, but Crossman's decision was that the original recommendations should be carried out with all possible speed.

the whole arrangement had been firmly agreed with the P.M. Not only that, but the ultimate future of the Ministry of Land and Natural Resources had been conceded to us on the one condition, characteristic of Harold Wilson, that Fred Willey should not be informed. I found this very difficult to swallow; but it had nothing to do with me. Indeed, it was probably my biggest success as Minister so far. I've got what I wanted. I've got Dame Evelyn to stay on until next spring. I've got Bruce Fraser pushed into the Ministry of Land and Natural Resources. I've got the decision to wind that little Ministry up. And last of all I've got the arrangement that, before it is wound up, that appalling political embarrassment, leasehold enfranchisement, can be handed over to it.

The censure debate in the afternoon went fairly well. Fortunately for me the Tories had overreached themselves in having three days running on housing. In fact the House was empty and the atmosphere was totally different from the last censure debate only a few weeks ago. This was not because the situation had changed but because the back-benchers are exhausted and won't attend when they haven't got to tramp through the lobbies. Today they knew there was to be a vote at ten and most of them got there at ten. The censure motion was moved in an extremely dull speech by Page of Crosby, who had been number two to John Boyd-Carpenter throughout the Committee Stage of the Rent Bill.[1] And then Charlie Pannell got up to reply. I couldn't hear much of him because I had to go out to the Cabinet Immigration Committee in order to defeat the proposal to include housing in the Statement on immigration.

I got back to the front bench at about six o'clock and listened to the rest of the debate. I had been provided with a fairly good brief by the Ministry and, fortunately, that morning I had seen a new Tory pamphlet on housing produced by Corfield[2] and Geoffrey Rippon, which was ridiculous because it had nothing positive to say. John Boyd-Carpenter wound up with his usual competent efficiency. My reply was knockabout. I made one mistake which was to sit down and let Corfield get in and so stop me from making my peroration. Otherwise I got away with it.[3] George Brown came up and congratulated me on being loyal to the Treasury and not saying anything improper about housing finance. I had been careful to keep my trap shut because of the crucial meeting with the five wise men next Sunday.

I got into bed just before midnight and rang up Anne.

---

[1] Graham Page, M.P. for Crosby since 1953. He became Minister of Local Government and Development in the Department of the Environment in 1970.

[2] Sir Frederick Corfield, M.P. for Gloucestershire South since 1955. A former Joint Parliamentary Secretary in the Ministry of Housing and Local Government (1962–4), he became a Minister of State at the Board of Trade in 1970, moved to be Minister of Aviation Supply later that year, and was Minister for Aerospace at the Department of Trade and Industry 1971–2.

[3] The Government had a majority of 286 votes to 279.

Friday, July 2nd

There is nothing like a feeling of successful achievement to enable one to stand getting up at eight on a Friday morning to motor right down the M1 for an official visit to Meriden. I had treated this little rural district pretty harshly by sanctioning Birmingham's building of its new satellite town at Chelmsley Wood. I had also lopped off a piece on the other side and given it to Coventry. So I promised to come and see them and discuss green belt problems. I had quite a good morning with the council followed by a press conference, and then went on to Coventry to open what must be one of the most modern sewage works. I spent the whole afternoon walking round the plant, leaning about methods of sewage disposal. After that I had a surgery for two hours and finally Albert Rose delivered me to Prescote where I had supper and suddenly felt so tired that I could scarcely get upstairs to bed.

Sunday, July 4th

Yesterday we had our village fête. The show Cropredy put on was really tremendous. The village had built a seventeenth-century village street on the cricket field and organized a slap-up country fair to pay for a new village hall. Thousands of people turned up and I had persuaded John Betjeman[1] to come over from Berkshire to open it. He arrived for lunch and was absolutely charming with the children. While we were eating we told him that the only poem we could recite as a family was 'The Congo' by Vachel Lindsay. But we didn't have it in print. Whereupon John recited the whole poem by heart and reminded us of a few lines we had never heard and promised to send us a copy of his anthology containing it. In the afternoon, after he had opened the fete, I took him for a tour of Northampton villages and churches and then I trotted down to see the Coventry children dancing, which they did very sweetly. And then down came the rain, and Patrick and I ran home soaked to the skin. But we got both the crowd *and* the insurance money towards the village hall! This morning I am going up to see Mr Pritchett for a farm walk and then I shall be off on the 2.27 from Leamington for my meeting with the five wise men.

The Chancellor's success in arranging dollar support for the pound at the end of June only fostered rumours of devaluation. The publication of figures showing the drain of gold that had continued throughout June – some £24 million – put further pressure on sterling. Mr Callaghan's fears were made plain when he told the Commons, on July 15th, that he was resisting the temptation to rush into measures to restrain the economy still further. But since the beginning of the month Ministers had been scrutinizing their departmental estimates to see where cuts could be made with least damage.

The outcome was a Statement on July 29th announcing savings of some £350

[1] Who was to become Poet Laureate in 1972.

9*

million in public investment over the next year: £100 million was lopped from the 1966 defence programme. Local authorities were told to cut their building programmes and local-authority house mortgages were to be held at £130 million a year, compared with the £180 million Crossman had secured for 1964–5. Non-industrial capital projects, especially roads, were to be delayed for six months; there was to be no increase in housing, hospital or school building. Licences were to be introduced for new private-investment projects of £100,000 or more; hire-purchase repayment periods were cut. Exchange controls and import regulations became even more strict.

Devaluation was again avoided, though the price seemed to be a movement towards a complete economic recession. In Cabinet, Ministers were angry and frustrated at the cuts in their programmes and the Chancellor was accused of appeasing foreign bankers and the Federal Reserve authorities in New York by sacrificing essential socialist measures.

Monday, July 5th
The Sunday meeting in the Cabinet Office was a very strange performance. I was due to arrive at four thirty but my train was ten minutes early at Paddington and I was whirled along the Mall on a beautiful, fine Sunday afternoon so that I had to wait for some thirty-five minutes outside the door of the famous main Cabinet committee room. At last I saw Barbara Castle go away looking rather sad and depressed and then Ray Gunter and George Brown came out to spend a penny. It was my turn. I went in, dropped my papers on the table and sat down on the empty side. This is the committee room where the bust of the Duke of Wellington by Nollekens smiles down on you and you sit round an enormous, heavy, square table. The chairman, who in this case was James Callaghan, was facing the bust. On his left was George Brown. I sat round the corner, facing the Treasury officials on the other side. Beyond me was Frank Cousins, looking rather uncomfortable, and beyond him, facing across to the Chancellor, Douglas Houghton. On his right sat Ray Gunter and John Diamond. They were the five wise men.

To judge from what was said later, I must have given the impression of haughtiness and anger; but the real trouble was that I hadn't very clearly made up my mind what to say. My difficulties arose partly from the unpopularity of the Ministry of Housing and partly from the way the Treasury were presenting their case. The Cabinet had agreed that public expenditure must only go up by $4\frac{1}{2}$ per cent a year to keep it roughly in line with the $4\frac{1}{2}$ per cent increase in national income on which we were planning. To achieve this parallel we had to cut down public expenditure from roughly $6\frac{1}{2}$ per cent to $4\frac{1}{2}$ per cent. So the five wise men have had four-year plans submitted to them by Education, Health, Overseas Development, etc., and in presenting his four-year plan each Minister has tried to state the reasons in favour of his going beyond the basic programme allocated to him. Now this basic programme hasn't been planned by the Labour Government; it is simply the amount which the Conservatives had planned to spend on the various social services in the next four years. In our White Paper last October our basic allocation to each Ministry was the Tory allocation. By tradition the Tories believe in owner-occupation and prefer private- to public-sector housing. So they had planned for a considerable expansion in all the public services with one exception—council housing, which they had deliberately kept depressed until the year immediately before the election. All this meant that when the four-year expenditure programmes were compared, my basic line for public-sector housing was far behind the base line of any other social service department. This is the case I argued in two Cabinet meetings when I tried to persuade my colleagues to give me a 20,000 increase in housing starts this year. The five wise men agreed that this figure should be kept steady for some years ahead. They might possibly allow the total housing programme to move forward to 500,000 a year by 1969–70, as Harold and I have proposed. But during the period when money is tight (which may well last till 1966–7) public-sector housing cannot go beyond the figure I had already been given.

So the case was put by the five wise men—the Treasury case. My first argument against it, on which I had been carefully briefed by Thomas Balogh and with which Harold Wilson has a great deal of sympathy, was that the Treasury method of calculating the burden of housing is quite ridiculous. In a normal sense, there aren't any estimates for housing as there are for education or for health because the amount of money I draw from the Treasury is quite negligible. It is needed for subsidies and planning and such things. The real cost of housing is the capital expenditure of the local authorities on the one side and the capital expenditure of the builders and mortgagees on the other. Yet the Treasury separate council housing from private-sector housing, and reckon the council housing as public expenditure comparable with health and education while they don't reckon in the private sector at all. This is an unreal way of considering the matter for two reasons. First, even in the narrow terms of strict Government subsidy it is now admitted that each house built for sale receives more in tax concessions from the Government than the council house receives in subsidies. In fact, it costs the Chancellor more in current expenditure to have a house built for owner-occupation than to have a house built for renting to a council tenant. Second, in terms of the national resources expended it is obvious that private house-building uses up exactly the same amount as public house-building.

When I had put this case we argued for some time; but it soon became quite clear that the five wise men were entirely concerned about a book-keeping transaction. All they had to do was to see that the Cabinet expenditure—by which they meant expenditure defined in the Treasury style—was brought down to an increase of 4½ per cent a year. And that was to be done by the normal method of cutting back the expenditure of each Department. The fact that I started from a base far below all my colleagues simply didn't interest them. After a time I tried another tack. I can understand, I said, that you are afraid that the public sector will suddenly forge ahead next year under my housing drive. But it's also true that the private sector, which is going into a tail-spin at the moment, may be crumpling up next year. And if we are going to have some deflation, you may need public-sector housing to keep the economy going. So I have no objection, I went on, to agreeing that I should have nothing beyond my extra 20,000 next year, provided it is written into the National Plan that we are going to move up first to 400,000 houses a year and then to 500,000 by 1970–71. Provided that half-million is roughly divided into quarter-million private-enterprise and quarter-million council houses I am quite content to give way on the increase I had been planning for next year.

I hoped that this would sound quite reasonable; but it didn't placate my colleagues. Towards the end, when we had been sitting arguing for nearly an hour, Douglas Houghton said, 'I must say I don't like this at all. The others all came in here fearing their programmes will be cut. This fellow saunters into the room giving the impression that we dare not cut him for political reasons.' Of course, what Houghton said was the precise truth. I know I have the Prime Minister behind me. I also know that my housing programme is at the mercy not of any cuts they may wish to make but of economic forces which are threatening and pressuring and bullying this poor Government. The crisis has been hanging over it all this past week.

Tuesday, July 6th

I was having a meeting with the Dame and J. D. Jones when I was told that Waddell had been called away to the Treasury. Just as we were breaking up he came rushing back into the room with a quite extraordinary story. He said that when he got there a fellow called Petch[1] had announced to all those present that the Prime Minister wished to have worked out for him a plan for a complete three-month moratorium on all new contracts. Quite literally, for three months no one should, on behalf of any Ministry, sign a new contract. Petch had indicated that the occasion for this extraordinary idea was the fear that this month's balance-of-trade figures might again be very bad and set off another run on the pound by the Gnomes of Zurich: the Prime Minister wanted to do something which would impress them with our determination to curb incipient inflation. I cross-examined Waddell very thoroughly. There was no doubt about it. It was a serious proposal to be submitted to a meeting of Ministers called on Friday to consider various plans for dealing with the economic crisis. Waddell said that the Ministry of Works had blown its top; and he had blown his top about the housing programme – and it was not quite clear by the end of the meeting whether housing would or would not be included in the moratorium. Talk about 'stop–go'! This was the most violent,

[1] Sir Louis Petch was a distinguished civil servant who had entered the Service in 1937; he was at this time Third Secretary of the Treasury and the Treasury Officer of Accounts. In 1966 he became Second Secretary of the Treasury, and in 1968 Second Permanent Secretary at the Civil Service Department. Since 1969 he has been chairman of the Board of Customs and Excise.

primitive, stupid form of 'stop–go' ever thought of. I at once rang up Thomas Balogh, who came round to talk to me. He knew a little about the project but not much. He was sure that it had been falsely interpreted and that a vague idea of Harold's had been taken far too literally by the Treasury.

At lunch-time I went over to the House and once again found George Wigg lunching with Harold Wilson. We had a pleasant chat and naturally I didn't mention this project to Harold. Indeed, I waited until he had gone and then I checked with George and at once went back to the Ministry and drafted a vigorous minute to the P.M. I next alerted Charlie Pannell, who was actually lunching with me that day, and the whole machine began to get into motion. The moment my minute was sent across to the Prime Minister with a copy to Charlie Pannell it was distributed in the D.E.A. and the other Ministries and George Brown was soon asking for a copy of the original. Before the afternoon was out I got verbal confirmation from him that there had never been any thought in any circumstances of cutting the housing programme. Nevertheless, when I met the Prime Minister and the First Secretary in the lobby in one of our endless Finance Bill divisions that evening, George Brown remarked, 'There *was* one point, Harold, when we did think of cancelling all contracts.' And I suspect this indeed had really happened.

The Third Reading of the Rent Bill took place yesterday between 3.30 and 7.00. This was a quiet little occasion. Jim MacColl moved and I wound up. It was all very formal and almost pleasant.

After 7.00 when everybody's suspicions were lulled we reverted to the Finance Bill and then suddenly at about 1.30 a.m. fell into the trap the Tories had laid for us. It was an exact imitation of the trap George Wigg organized years ago, when we had all our people brought round secretly to Vincent Square and then rushed them back again into the House when the Government thought they had gone home.[1] Such tricks don't do real harm to a government. But this one of course will mean that we will have to have an extra two days on the Finance Bill: Monday next week for the end of the Report Stage and Thursday for the Third Reading.

Thursday, July 8th
Cabinet, with the main item immigration. But before we came to that the Prime Minister mentioned the Harold Davies mission to Hanoi which had been revealed in the morning papers.[2] Once again a peace initiative had been taken without consulting Cabinet. I didn't blame him too heavily for this, but again I am pretty sure this mission is only a gimmick. The Tories have reacted

---

[1] As part of George Wigg's guerilla war on the Tories in November 1953; the Government was defeated by four votes (on a resolution dealing with glass imports). This time the departing Conservatives lurked in near-by rooms and houses until the division bells rang. The Government was defeated by 180 votes to 167. See *Wigg*, pp. 165–7; *Wilson*, pp. 120–21.

[2] Harold Davies apparently knew Ho Chi Minh and seemed likely to get a visa to visit North Vietnam. According to the Prime Minister the visit was sabotaged by a disastrous leak in London. See *Wilson*, pp. 122–3.

very stupidly by attacking it, and Alec Douglas-Home is urging the necessity for secret diplomacy in a way which will upset public opinion. So Harold will once more gain by the gimmick. Nevertheless, it is very un-serious; he is just moving from emergency to emergency, picking up bright ideas as he goes along. It doesn't please me at all

For the immigration discussion we had two papers. Bert Bowden's draft conclusions, which had been prepared in the Cabinet Office, and poor Frank Soskice's lengthy departmental paper. The latter was pushed aside straight away and only dragged in when someone wanted to argue a point. The whole discussion took place on the ten concrete proposals put forward by Bowden. I have been regularly attending the Committee where these policies were being worked out under his chairmanship and in the (not very effective) presence of the Minister in charge – the Home Secretary. Even while we were sitting immigration gradually grew into a major political issue, and it now dominates politics in the West Midlands and in the West Riding as well as in London and the Home Counties. I have watched Bowden during the last four months becoming more and more inclined towards a switch to a much stronger policy. Like Bert, George Wigg and I are Midland M.P.s, and because we see the effect in our constituencies we all realize that we have got to control the rate of immigration into this country – we can't digest the number who are now arriving in the West Midlands. We didn't oppose the Mountbatten mission when Harold sent it out to find out what the Dominions were prepared to do at home about controlling immigration. It was a skilful move politically because we could switch our policy once we had demonstrated that it was no good relying on the Indian and Pakistani Governments. So, after months of discussion, the Bowden proposals, which include cutting down the vouchers and stiffening up control of dependants, were put forward.[1]

It was a rambling, strange discussion in which the only resistance to the Bowden line came from the three Ministers departmentally responsible for the Commonwealth and the Colonies: Barbara Castle, Tony Greenwood and Arthur Bottomley. But I noticed that even these three didn't adopt the 100 per cent pro-immigration line and arguments with which Hugh Gaitskell and George Brown opposed the Tory immigration Act lock, stock and barrel only three years ago. The atmosphere has changed since then! Perhaps Elwyn Jones, our Attorney-General, would have stood by the Gaitskellite line, but nobody did at Cabinet on Thursday. Tony Crosland, as Minister of Education, favoured tightening up controls. So did Maurice Foley, the young Under-Secretary who has been put in charge of the sub-committee dealing with the methods of integrating the immigrants into the community. So did Douglas Houghton. The only people who vaguely protested were George

[1] In November 1964, when the Commonwealth Immigrants Act was renewed, the Home Secretary had reported that each month 1,600 to 2,000 entry vouchers were being granted to heads of families.

Brown and the Lord Chancellor. But both of them were feeble because they couldn't really challenge the concrete Bowden proposals.

Indeed, the only dangerous point in the discussion was when the Prime Minister, prompted I suspect by George Wigg, suggested that a passage should be included in the White Paper requiring immigrants in future to provide evidence that they had adequate accommodation before their dependants received permission to enter the country. As I have noted, this is quite a nice idea in theory but it is administratively impossible to ask the local authorities to do it. In Cabinet I managed to fend it off and to obtain instead for the local authorities something they very much want – legislation which will make the registration of multi-occupied dwellings compulsory.

It was a desultory, unhappy meeting. Broadly, I am sure we have accepted the right policy. But it has been accepted far too slowly, with the Tories taking the lead all the time, and a lot will depend on how firmly it is put across.

In the afternoon my Rent Bill got its Second Reading in the Lords. To my astonishment it was warmly approved – indeed it was accepted by the official Opposition as a courageous measure, better than they could have expected from a Labour Government. If this had happened before I got it through the Commons I would have been in real difficulty with my own back-benchers, who have always suspected that this is really a landlords' Bill. However, that doesn't alter my view that it is in fact a courageous and a good Bill which in the long run will give us a lot of popularity because it will be fair to both sides. Meanwhile, I am glad to hear that we shan't have the Lords' amendments to the Bill back in the Commons until next October. So I shall have an extra two months during the recess in which to work up the administration, select the rent assessment committees, get the rent officers chosen and prepare the advertising and propaganda.

Tonight was supposed to be the final all-night sitting on the Finance Bill. But actually each evening this week we have got home earlier and earlier and today were were off at eleven o'clock and the Committee Stage was over.

Friday, July 9th
This week I have managed to get two days out of town, visiting Harlow New Town and Basingstoke town development in order to compare the two methods. I find I infinitely prefer the atmosphere of town development – in this case carried out by the Hampshire County Council, the G.L.C. and Basingstoke Borough; they are rapidly expanding a little town of 20,000 and bringing it up to 80,000 inhabitants. What I noticed at Basingstoke, compared with Harlow, was the lack of snobbery and autocracy and stratospheric good living which certainly exists inside the New Town corporations. The appointees who run those corporations are self-important people who do what they damn-well like and don't listen to the local people or feel any respect for the urban district authority. In Basingstoke, on the other hand, the G.L.C. and county council experts are much more subject to popular

criticism, and there is a much better relationship between the town planners and the elected councillors.

I heard a great deal of apparently well-founded complaint that town development isn't given the same favourable financial terms as a New Town. In the present crisis, for example, the interest rate which a New Town corporation has to pay for its money has been assiduously protected by the Department, whereas I discovered at Basingstoke that their interest rates have not been protected at all. This is something I will have to look into very carefully. If I do, there will be a great deal of resistance within my Department.

Saturday, July 17th
I have decided not to go into day-by-day detail about the past week because I find it boring to do it too many weeks on end. So this time I shall deal mainly with the big Cabinet meeting on Thursday, which was of absolutely major importance, and apart from this only give one or two impressions.

One expedition I made was to yet another New Town, Bracknell. About £22 million of capital has been put into this village and it has turned into a charming little garden suburb. I greatly enjoyed meeting the corporation, though I went on a very bad day because I had just given approval to their town redevelopment scheme which involves their destroying the whole of the centre of the old Bracknell and putting a modern supermarket in its place, though ten years ago the traders had been solidly assured that nothing of this sort would occur. Discussing Bracknell's problems with an amiable but ineffective chairman, I became more and more aware of the extreme dubiety of the view that the New Town system really eases the pressure on waiting lists for houses. I discovered that only 41 per cent of the people in Bracknell come from the London housing list; and after all, the purpose of the New Towns is to get people out of the cities and across the green belts. So we shall obviously have to consider how to improve our methods of doing this. But what are my chances of influencing the Department? I am having a great struggle to insert myself into the very powerful group, dominated by Dame Evelyn, which controls New Town policy. She regards New Towns as very much her personal creation and she controls policy very closely, along with J. D. Jones who is really her personal appointee; and now she has added to him Miss Hope-Wallace from the National Assistance Board who I discover comes very much from her intellectual coterie.* These three don't in the least want the Minister intervening and upsetting their settled procedures.

This is also true of the Ministry's relations with local government. Here, after all, the Dame has been the dominant character for many years and she has achieved a remarkable relationship with the local authorities. True, in the particular sphere of the Local Government Boundary Commission's work I have been able to insert myself effectively; but in most of my relations with

* See, for an excellent picture of this, Francis Meynell, *My Lives* (London: Bodley Head, 1971).

the local authorities I find it difficult to get my way. An interesting example
was the scandal about Bognor Regis. The town clerk accused the council
members of corruption. Then, when he was forced to resign, he started up a
society for cleansing local government. For many weeks I have wanted to have
an inquiry into the situation at Bognor Regis but the Dame was adamant.
It took me a fortnight to get a letter written to the Attorney-General asking
whether we could use the Tribunal and Inquiries Act of 1921. It took the
Attorney-General three weeks to reply that he thought this would be using
a hammer to crush a nut. Instead, he suggested that we should ask a distinguished Q.C. to hold an inquiry on the lines of the Denning Inquiry after
the Profumo affair. I had the letter drafted to the Bognor Regis authorities
and then the Dame said, 'I have been having a talk to them. We ought to
offer them half the cost,' When I said I was reluctant to do so it was clear she
had done it already and that she had also selected the Q.C. for the job.[1] She
was in fact in charge of the whole operation and I was not. I always have to
be careful not to lose my temper on these occasions. It's no good thinking
that a Minister who is only going to be there for two or three years can run
a whole mass of departmental policy in detail himself.

Broadly speaking, the civil servants will run the Ministry the way they
want; and if I am determined to have something changed it will take me a
long time. Months ago, for example, I wanted to give councillors the same
rights, privileges and responsibilities as M.P.s and let them speak their minds
freely when their interest is concerned, provided they declare it. At present
they have to get leave from me before they do so. The Dame wanted me to
give the permission only to council-house tenants, to allow them to speak
about council-house rents. I said if we were going to change things we should
extend it to the whole area of councillors' private interests; and though I got
the circular drafted and redrafted it still has not gone out and I am pretty
sure that this is the Dame's work. She had it sent to the local authority
organizations knowing that the A.M.C. would have strong objections.

The same is true of another circular in which Bob Mellish and I are keenly
interested. We want to tell local authorities that all the inhibitions imposed
by the Tory Government on direct building (that is, building done by councils
using their own labour force) have been abolished. At last the circular has
gone out to the local authorities for discussion and will no doubt come back

---

[1] Between 1964 and 1967 a Mr Campion, a ratepayer in Bognor Regis, bombarded local
councillors, council officials, the Director of Public Prosecutions, the press and others with
complaints that Bognor Regis U.D.C. was inefficient and undemocratic. Various actions
for defamation were brought by the council and its employees; and at one stage a newly
appointed town clerk resigned after he had objected to the council's handling of the matter.
At the council's request and at public expense the Ministry of Housing set up an inquiry
and the Hon. Mr Justice Ramsay Willis (as he then was) produced a report acquitting the
council and hoping that these domestic disputes would cease. Mr Campion persisted,
however, and in 1972 the council brought a private suit in defamation. Bognor Regis
U.D.C. were awarded £2,000 damages and £34,445·24p costs, exclusive of witnesses'
expenses. *Bognor Regis Urban District Council* v. *Campion* [1972] 2Q.B.169.

to us in due course. We have to fight very hard to get a change of this kind because every possible difficulty is discovered; and though each is duly surmounted it all takes time if the Department doesn't like the direction in which we are moving. But if I want something which the Department does want, I often find the tempo over-accelerated by the determination of someone to jump forward and win approval.

However, the main issue this week has been the public expenditure cuts and the housing programme. The result of the Sunday confrontations on July 4th was a Cabinet paper which only got to the Departments last Tuesday, July 13th. On the back of the paper was summarized the evidence each of us had given and, at the front, the recommendations PESC was presenting to Cabinet. In summary the Committee recommended that we could afford some £200 million of expenditure over and above the basic programmes we inherited from the Tory Party. Of this £200 million, £100 million should go to housing in the form of the 20,000 starts for which I had already obtained Cabinet consent. But the housing subsidy proposals I had put forward were halved. I have got sufficient to enable me to give the public sector the subsidies I really need, i.e. the guaranteed 4 per cent increase on new council-house building. But I can only do this if I leave nothing at all for subsidizing mortgages and so make certain that concessions to the private sector are postponed at least until 1968. Actually, this is no bad thing. If I want to curb the expansion of the private sector in order to increase the size of the public sector, it would be absolutely insane at the moment to stimulate owner-occupation by financial concessions to the mortgagors. So I can stand the cut of 50 per cent in my money allocation. On actual house production, the Committee recommend that it should be kept at the same level next year as this year but after that they give me the advance I want, namely half a million houses by 1969–70.

It's clear from the remarks of my colleagues that they think I have got the lion's share. Poor Barbara Castle, for example, came to see me almost in tears. She had just been dining at Buckingham Palace with the President of Peru, and she came in to plead with me to help her with her White Paper. Her trouble was that in the course of Tuesday's Cabinet, when we polished off the routine business, a decision had been taken to postpone the publication of all White Papers until September. There were obvious advantages in this for me since I wasn't ready to launch my White Paper now. But poor Barbara explained to me that her little Department had been sweating their guts out and working every Saturday on a great new White Paper on Overseas Development. 'The increase I wanted between now and 1970 has been cut back to virtually nothing,' she said. 'If I can't even have a White Paper, how can I justify building up the Department? What about Dudley Seers[1] and

---

[1] Director-general of the Economic Planning Staff at the Ministry of Overseas Development. In 1967 he became director of the Institute of Development Studies at the University of Sussex.

Marris[1] and the rest of the economists I have brought in? How can I face them? Andrew Cohen is on the edge of suicide. Dick, I plead with you. You have everything. You get all the money, you have all the big legislation, you are a rich, successful Minister. Do give something to poor little Barbara.' The emotions she expressed are shared to a greater or lesser extent by Kenneth Robinson at the Ministry of Health and Peggy Herbison at Social Security. Peggy is even more bitterly affronted than Barbara because she feels that Douglas Houghton, her overlord, is denying her the place and the importance which she deserves. At least in this respect Barbara is lucky.

Now for Thursday's big Cabinet meeting. In preparation, I had a long talk with the Department and decided that the best thing to do was, before Cabinet got to discussing individual estimates, to start the meeting by challenging the whole basis of the work of the committee of five. I got Thomas Balogh to warn Harold Wilson that I was going to do this. Harold started off with a little introduction on the limits of the work of the committee and then let me make my statement. I attacked the whole philosophy of the cuts and then gave my own departmental example. Once again I exposed the absurdity of treating public-sector housing quite separately from private-sector housing and then went on to argue that housing had been put into the wrong category. It had been wrongly put in with the social services, whereas it should be transferred, say, to the category which includes agriculture or the nationalized industries and looked at in that perspective.

When I said this, there was some protest from James Callaghan but not as much as you might expect because I have been working hard behind the scenes and so has Harold. Then George Brown intervened. He said that at first he thought my point was very much exaggerated; now he saw there was more to it. However, in his view the conclusions of the Cabinet paper didn't exclude what I wanted. I intervened and was able to prove that, although I seemed to have got my own way the paper in fact showed that my policy would be frustrated, and I insisted that I couldn't be content with a total figure of half a million houses a year. But if I had to, what was important was that the half-million must be divided, 50/50, between the private and the public sectors. At this point I waited because I really thought I had helped Kenneth Robinson and Barbara and the other spending Ministers a good deal by giving this example and pointing out the case for having the whole thing reconsidered. Not a peep came out of any of them. When I asked Kenneth Robinson afterwards why this was, he replied, 'I wasn't briefed on this.' That was rather illuminating. We come briefed by our Departments to fight for departmental budgets, not as Cabinet Ministers with a Cabinet view. Even Tony Crosland—I suppose because his education estimates were at stake—displayed a completely defeatist departmentalism.

[1] Robin Marris, Fellow of King's College, Cambridge. He became Reader in Economics in 1972.

At this point what happened was that, into the silence, Harold Wilson chipped in. 'There is something in what the Minister says. But surely if we are going to have half a million houses, a quarter of a million council houses and a quarter for owner-occupation, there clearly have got to be building controls.' And back we were in the old argument, because the Prime Minister had been slapped down on building controls by the E.D.C. when he urged the need for them a couple of months ago. On that occasion we had agreed that, while we might require building controls, the Minister of Works should go ahead and try to get a voluntary agreement. The Prime Minister now reminded us we must be prepared to institute controls if necessary.

This point having been laid down, we proceeded to a separate discussion of each estimate. I was a bit shocked by Tony Crosland. He pointed out that the cuts required of him would mean that the improvement of the primary schools which had been started under the Tories must be slowed down; he would have to do this because he accepted the view that he couldn't cut back expenditure on university education (as I would have done) and give priority to the schools. I would have liked to hear him protesting much more vigorously. He merely said that if that is the Cabinet decision, well, that's that but it will be very awkward and very unpopular. Next came Kenneth Robinson, who virtually said he was content with what he had got for Health. Frank Soskice was content with what he had got for the Home Office and the police. And then we came to Pensions. Now Pensions, of course, is in exactly the same position as Housing, with a public sector (national insurance) and a private sector, which includes all the private superannuation schemes. The contributions you make to your private pension do not count as taxation but your contributions to national insurance do. In the same way, the tax concessions which the Treasury makes to private superannuation schemes are not treated as a subsidy and so part of state expenditure, whereas the Exchequer contribution to national insurance is so treated. Did Peggy Herbison have the sense to chime in with me on this, or Douglas Houghton? Not at all. Instead, under cross-examination they got into a horrible mess and confirmed my fear that the whole strategy of our pensioneering, worked out for years before the election, had been jettisoned almost without noticing it by the Minister under the *diktat* of Douglas Houghton. The basic idea had been that we should switch as early as possible from flat-rate to earnings-related contributions and in this way pile up enormous sums in the pension fund which we could use to dynamize the existing flat-rate pension. That was cardinal. However Douglas and Peggy had turned things upside down, by first of all conceding an enormously increased flat-rate benefit financed by increased flat-rate contributions. The net result is the worst of all worlds as we can't raise the flat-rate contributions any higher without imposing an intolerable burden on the lower-paid worker. Even worse, the income guarantee which we had pledged ourselves to introduce would now be at an absurdly low level as the result of the money we had wasted on the huge initial increase of the flat-rate pension. After the Cabinet discussion I became quite sure that it was far too late to go back to the original strategy. The least damaging thing we could do was probably to abandon the income guarantee because the pittance we could offer would make a mockery of the whole concept.

By this time it was twelve o'clock and the Prime Minister had to go to the funeral of Adlai Stevenson,[1] who had come over to London, fallen down in the street and died rather dramatically on Wednesday. So we halted the discussion and will continue it next Thursday.

Meanwhile, a tremendous lot will have to go on behind the scenes. After this Cabinet discussion I feel even more strongly that, in the present climate of public opinion and the present state of the economy, an announcement of major concessions to mortgagors would be economic insanity as well as making nonsense of my own national housing plan. Because of the election pledges we gave about interest rates for owner-occupiers, the Cabinet is scared of public opinion. I want to persuade them to be courageous and to postpone fulfilment of the pledge until 1968, so that I can concentrate the subsidies on public-sector building. Somehow I have *got* to get them to decide not to pay the money out to the mortgagors and to make a virtue of what is really a sheer economic necessity. But can I risk doing something which my colleagues regard as so desperately unpopular? I shall have to do so; and, having decided that, I must consider tactics. I shall have to see George Brown first and foremost because I don't want to find myself up against him—and he's the man who is more deeply committed on mortgage interest rates than any other member of the Cabinet. Then I shall have to go to Callaghan and find out what I can get out of the Treasury. What will the Chancellor offer to the building societies in return for their acceptance of voluntary rationing of private-sector starts? None of these things has been decided although it is getting desperately late. The Dame tells me that by this time our predecessor's plans for the legislative programme for the next Session would have been virtually finished. We haven't even started getting policy clear, let alone the legislation. Indeed, the Cabinet discussion demonstrated our limitations. This is the first occasion on which we have discussed the National Plan. And it is clear that so far no effort has been made to do more than a kind of book-keeping job of accountancy; that has been the substitute this year for adequate economic planning. For this I suppose we must blame two things. The first is that George Brown at the D.E.A. just isn't a planner by nature. And the second is that James Callaghan has been far too busy on the Finance Bill to give any serious attention to economic planning. As for the Prime Minister, he is economically trained, God knows, but he is incapable of imposing a strategy. During this meeting on Thursday he just sat there letting the discussion go on and then, at the last moment, doing a fix. He has not insisted on

---

[1] The American lawyer and diplomat, Democratic Presidential candidate in 1952 and 1956. He had become the U.S. Ambassador to the United Nations in 1961.

a steady, controlled, concerted central purpose which could dynamize the whole machinery of Whitehall.

I must add in fairness, however, that within his limits he continues to be a very resourceful Prime Minister. I saw him at his best one afternoon this week when we received a delegation of Welsh M.P.s who wanted to discuss the problem of leasehold enfranchisement. How skilful he was in defending me against them and not committing me to anything. After that we had a word or two about my own housing programme. He is ready to help me, as always, but he now expects me to get my own way. So I must do a good deal of knockabout political warfare in Whitehall and fend for myself without calling on him for aid, as far as I possibly can.

Sunday, July 18th
The first fortnight of July has been one of the coldest and wettest I ever remember. St Swithun's day[1] came with relatively little rain, but the weather since then hasn't greatly improved. We had a fairly decent half-day yesterday and it's dry and cloudy today. But the farm looks greener and greener and the wheat grows heavier and heavier and the chance of a difficult harvest grows likelier and likelier. Meanwhile those children of mine seem to grow with the corn and the farm and the animals, bigger and more boisterous and tougher and healthier – in a way more difficult to manage, too. Last night we had the Hartrees in for dinner with the Judges, the headmaster of Banbury Grammar School and his wife Mary, and of course the conversation was about education, as it always is. One can now see that there will be reasonably good education on the Banbury campus where Harry Judge is now getting his tripartite system knitted into a new comprehensive school. On the other hand, we have paid Patrick's fees for his four years at the Dragon School, his place is already reserved, and Charles and Mary Woodhouse are enormously looking forward to having him there. With our connections with the Dragon and Winchester, our family tradition would be his natural way. Yet it seems totally unnatural when he is here at home and his mother wants him here and they are having a wonderful time. Of course there will be problems if he stays at home: the Oxfordshire County Council have a really excellent system of primary education, but there are no men teachers in prospect for Patrick until he is eleven; moreover, our primary schools work on an extremely advanced liberal theory which requires that no child ever be strained, that no effort be made to teach the children intensively. My two children require a school which demands something of them in order to get the best out of them. I feel this rather strongly and if we can't find them a satisfactory primary school in Banbury they may well have to go to boarding-school in the end. However, it is no good worrying about it. But we do worry and brood, especially when the Hartrees and the Judges are at dinner.

Curiously, the topic came up in Cabinet last week when Tony Crosland

1 July 15th.

presented a small paper asking authority to make a statement about the establishment of a public schools commission.[1] I wasn't very happy about it because I don't see much point in setting up a commission or trying to improve the link between the public schools and the state system. Nevertheless, I don't want to get into a fight with Tony; and he got his authorization quite easily. He is to make a brief Statement which commits us not to any particular version of a public schools commission but simply to having one within the next twelve months. I very much doubt whether this will make the faintest difference to Patrick's or Virginia's education.

I must record one other event of the weekend and that was the selection of a new Labour candidate for Banbury, which took the whole of a fine Saturday afternoon. I don't think I have ever been to a selection conference before. We were told that if we didn't get there in time for the first candidate's speech we wouldn't be allowed to vote, so we got there exactly at 3 p.m. There were some thirty-seven people, including Anne and myself as delegates for Cropredy. On the platform was the brand new secretary of the Party and the chairman, young Martin Ennals, as well as the assistant regional organizer, representing the N.E.C. Five candidates had been short-listed and two of them failed to turn up. That left us three, each of whom would be given fifteen minutes to make a speech and then ten minutes of questioning. Immediately this was completed there would be a motion that a vote should be taken. If we weren't satisfied, we could annul the motion and ask for another selection conference. If we were satisfied, we should then proceed straight away to a secret ballot. Throughout the selection there must not be, we were told, any discussion between the delegates; otherwise those with a stronger personality would have an unfair advantage.

Assuming that it would be very boring I had taken along with me the report of my Inspector on the Christ Church Meadow road.[2] But I wasn't bored. The young local man who is this year's chairman of the Banbury Labour Party was very nice, and he wouldn't have been a disastrous candidate. Then we had a young barrister from London, the kind of left-wing internationalist who always turns up. He was followed by a businessman from Bromsgrove who did himself in by saying that he travelled abroad often; he was clearly too busy to give us much time. Then the chairman of my own constituency Party, David Young. He told me afterwards that he had only learnt at lunchtime that the conference was happening and had to jump into his car immediately, totally unprepared. However, he was obviously far the most effective candidate.

After the speeches came the questions, neither very pressing nor very

---

[1] It was eventually established in 1968 under the chairmanship of Professor Donnison.

[2] Successive Ministers had grappled with the opposing views of the Oxford City Council and the University over the proposal to drive an inner relief road through Christ Church Meadow. On the evidence of the Inspector's report, Crossman ruled that further studies should be made; and as a result of the consultants' recommendation, the proposal for an inner relief road was abandoned.

embarrassing. Sometimes a candidate was asked how he would handle the constituency, sometimes how he would arouse enthusiasm. We weren't allowed to see the wives or even to know much about them. Indeed, we didn't know anything about the candidates except for the formal life history which they provided themselves, usually a long list of offices held in the local Labour Party. The aim of the conference seemed to be to ensure that the candidates were judged not on personal knowledge of them as individuals or as politicians but simply and solely on the impact their speeches and answers to questions made—not to get the best candidate but to ensure the strictest equality of treatment. A queer way of doing political business, but on this occasion we chose the right man. Anne and I were able to congratulate David sincerely. Certainly, if we had been away our absence would have been a disaster in Coventry East!

Monday, July 19th
I came up to London last night by the last train because I had to face a Monday morning of solid Cabinet Committees. As I sat there, first at the E.D.C. and then at Home Affairs, I reflected on the way that Cabinet Committees as well as the Cabinet itself are becoming part of the dignified element of the English constitution.[1] This is very largely because under this Government, maybe under all governments, Ministers are more and more departmentally conditioned before they come to these meetings. The E.D.C. under George Brown, with James Callaghan sitting beside him, is supposed to be the basic home economic committee, dealing with economic planning. Yet in fact it only deals with matters which a Minister wants to bring before his colleagues. On Monday, for example, the main item was Fred Peart's marketing scheme and, apart from myself, nobody had any basis on which to comment unless he had been given a departmental brief. And no Department will prepare a brief for its Minister on anything outside the departmental purview.

Tommy Balogh always says that in this lies the case for a Minister bringing an outside staff with him to work in his Private Office. And I think there is a strong case for doing so. If I started again I would like to have, as well as those I have already brought in, (1) a ghost writer, not for my speeches but for my letters and my Statements: he would be the kind of person who could take the Ministry's policy and translate it into the kind of words I would use; (2) perhaps an economist; and (3) a general investigator whose job it would be to brief me so that I could participate intelligently at Cabinet Committees and in Cabinet on subjects outside my own Department. All these men would not only write; they would also have to read, because the Minister is not able to read all the Cabinet agenda before he gets there, or even all the agenda of the Cabinet Committees; and if he does read the papers he reads them with an eye which often fails to understand and to spot the relevant. My successful

[1] See Crossman's Introduction to Bagehot, *The English Constitution*, pp. 20–22.

interventions in Cabinet Committees and at Cabinet are largely occasioned by a talk beforehand with a few people who have access to all the Cabinet papers—Nicky Kaldor, Tommy Balogh, George Wigg—and who want to have a certain view put forward. Because most Ministers aren't briefed in this way our discussions are lifeless; and the Whitehall view prevails even more than it did six months ago.[1]

Tuesday, July 20th
Our second Cabinet on public expenditure. There were only two programmes left to consider, Overseas Development and Housing. Harold Wilson started by saying, 'Now let's turn to Housing.' I wasn't prepared and replied, 'It isn't my turn yet. It's Barbara Castle first.' And so it was. It had been clear at the previous meeting that both Harold and the Foreign Secretary felt the cut in overseas aid was greater than we could defend as a Party or as a country. Something had to be restored to Barbara. On the other hand, the system under which PESC had been working guaranteed that if one Minister were to get more money another would get that amount less. There was no play here, just a fantastically rigid adherence to basic programmes we had inherited from the Tory Government. Tory priorities were prevailing over our own socialist loyalties, and all that we could hope to do was to continue a basically Tory spending programme with minor adjustments.

I'd said all this at the beginning of last Thursday's meeting and it had had its effect. Nevertheless, this Cabinet was in a mood to finish the job off and had no inclination to give anything away to Barbara. Their attitude was strengthened when she spoke for thirty-five minutes. The sensible thing would have been to speak for five minutes and then to ask Michael Stewart, Arthur Bottomley and Anthony Greenwood to plead her case for her. When she had finished Callaghan simply said, 'I'm sorry about this but I can't believe there is any special case here, and anyway, if there is, what other Ministry is to be cut back?'

At this point Harold Wilson intervened. 'We mustn't be absolutely rigid about these programmes,' he said. 'After all, they are not our own—we only inherited them. I suggest we set up a working party to see whether we can't give Barbara at least some increase in areas where the dollar spending is not too severe.' At this point Cabinet suddenly moved into a major row. Callaghan refused to serve on a working party of this kind. 'All these points have been argued out,' he said, 'and at the end of July it is far too late to go back on the basic programmes which we've assumed for the last eight months. You can't challenge them now.' On this he was strongly supported by George Brown, who reminded us that he had to have the final figures by the end of the week for inclusion in his National Plan. After this there came an altercation

[1] The Central Policy Review Staff was established by the Heath Administration in 1971 to provide Cabinet Ministers, it was said, with overall briefings on policy.

which took nearly an hour and a half and which most of us sat through looking pretty embarrassed. The First Secretary and the Chancellor, clearly in some sense working together, leapt on Harold like wolfhounds in at the kill.[1] That sounds a bit exalted for Harold, but that's what it was. They tore him from both sides. They insulted him, tried to pull him down in the most violent way, obviously both feeling that Harold was evading his responsibilities as Prime Minister and trying to do an unseemly fix. And of course that is what he was doing. He was trying to help Barbara without openly saying so and planning to get her allocated another £20 million or so and then later to save the money by cutting the road programme of Tom Fraser, who was sitting just beside me. When he was defeated he tried to pretend he hadn't made the proposal and had the whole story removed from Cabinet minutes—historic proof that those minutes never tell you a damn thing of what goes on in Cabinet unless the P.M. and Cabinet Secretariat want to publish it.

After this we turned to Housing and, unlike Barbara, I spoke very briefly. I said that the thing I cared about was getting a firm commitment to a rate of building in 1969–70 of half a million houses a year. Once I got that I would be content to forego any further commitment to increase the public-sector programme in 1966–7 when things were tight. But I added that I wanted the Cabinet to realize how dramatically private-sector housing was sagging (I read aloud the figures for June which showed a decrease for the third month running). Would Cabinet agree that if private-sector housing continued to slump, the deficiency in the grand total could be made up next year by public housing? I then turned to the decision to halve my money for subsidies and said I would accept it provided Cabinet agreed that there should be no question of honouring the mortgage pledge for two years. After this the meeting broke up. It was the worst Cabinet we have had, and the worst for Harold Wilson.

In the afternoon I heard rumours that the plan for a complete moratorium on new contracts was being revived in another form. Waddell came back from yet another meeting with the Treasury with the new version. This time he assured me that housing and schools were not affected. However, I immediately dictated a confidential minute to the Prime Minister urging him to make a virtue of necessity and, instead of letting his economies leak bit by bit, to make a big announcement at the end of September saying he was cutting everything back and demanding blood and sweat. This minute was sent off to him straight away.

Fortunately for Labour, but perhaps not fortuitously, the announcement of the Chancellor's July measures coincided with the Conservatives' ballot for a new

---

[1] There were newspaper rumours that the Chancellor was plotting to overthrow the leadership, and this had come to a head on July 16th while the Prime Minister was in Moscow at the British Trade Fair.

Party leader. For a month or more there had been rumours of Sir Alec's impending resignation and by July 22nd this was common knowledge. It was a sensible time for him to retire, well before the Party Conference in October and at a moment when the Party had been drawn together during the proceedings on the Finance Bill. Iain Macleod announced that he would not stand and the three candidates that emerged were Edward Heath, Reginald Maudling and Enoch Powell.

Mr Powell, the skilful protagonist of private enterprise, received fifteen votes; Mr Maudling, with 133 votes to Mr Heath's 150, stood down, so no second ballot was needed. Heath's victory was something of a surprise, for his background was not that of the 'traditional Tory' and his sturdy championship of the 1964 Retail Price Maintenance Act had not endeared him to the right wing of the Party. But he had been an efficient Chief Whip and had worked doggedly and untiringly in the Brussels negotiations in 1962. More to the point, he was closer in age (he was forty-nine) to Mr Wilson than Sir Alec had been, and he showed much of the same diligence as the Prime Minister. Maudling was made Deputy Leader, Macleod became Shadow Chancellor and Powell was given Defence. Sir Alec took general responsibility for external affairs.

Wednesday, July 21st
Another meeting of the Cabinet Social Services Committee. On this occasion we were presented with two alternative methods of achieving the cut which PESC demanded. Everyone round that table, with the exception of Douglas Houghton, realized that there was only one practical course of action – to postpone the incomes guarantee while introducing the graded benefits for sickness and unemployment and giving what flat-rate increases were necessary. Both Crosland and I, however, pleaded for a drastic change of strategy designed to introduce earnings-related National Insurance contributions as soon as possible. At this point Douglas Houghton burst out that he wasn't going to consent: instead he would file a minority report. And that's just what he did. If Frank Soskice is ineffective and ailing, Douglas Houghton is explosive, erratic and extremely self-centred – the worst possible kind of overlord for Peggy Herbison.

Later in the day I got from Waddell the latest details about the revised public expenditure plan, which confirmed that there were to be no cuts on the roads, housing and schools programmes. I found the plan more mad and gimmicky than ever and decided to send Harold a second minute. In it I urged him to put all the emphasis on three things: the postponement of the incomes guarantee, the postponement of our pledges to mortgage-holders and the cuts in overseas development aid. These are cuts, I said, that would really impress the foreign bankers if we want to save the pound. Having sent the minute across, I went to see Marcia and said, 'I simply must see the old man.' In a minute or two she had fixed a meeting for 5.30 on Thursday afternoon in his room at the Commons.

Thursday, July 22nd

Our second Cabinet of the week – one of those routine Cabinets which consist of a hotch-potch of contested items from Cabinet Committees brought up for final arbitration. Characteristically, we spent an hour and a half on the future of the family service. This is an interesting story. Frank Longford had been chairman of a Party study group on juvenile delinquency while we were in Opposition, in which the notion of a family service had been evolved: a special service to look after the problems of the child in the home and to keep the child out of the juvenile courts and give him a new kind of discipline. As soon as we took office Frank began insisting to the Social Services Committee that a family service Bill should be introduced at once and he threatened to resign if this was unduly delayed. The moment the idea was looked at departmentally it was clear that we couldn't introduce a family service without careful consultation with the local authorities. The first time I heard it mentioned was when I got a personal letter signed by Titmuss and practically every other social scientist that I respect, urging me to insist on a really independent inquiry into the local authority services to sort out how responsibility should be divided. Along with Kenneth Robinson and Anthony Crosland I found myself as Minister of Housing expressing grave doubts whether we could commit ourselves to a family service in a White Paper. At the very least, the local authorities would have to be consulted first; and probably there ought to be an independent inquiry. This package had been forced on Douglas Houghton, as chairman of the Committee, very much against his will. That is why the issue had been raised again in Cabinet. With three departmental Ministers lined up against them, Houghton and Longford really had no chance. There is nothing easier than to stop something in a British Cabinet. But of course in the background to that discussion was the thought, which everybody had, that the real row was being postponed till the following Tuesday.

I discovered in the afternoon that Marcia had allocated me half of Tommy Balogh's time with the P.M. I got to Harold's room at 5.50 and by then I think he had read both my minutes, as well as a similar minute which Crosland in Cabinet that morning had agreed to send. At first he seemed curiously complacent and unaffected. He is indeed an unaffectable man, partly because he is so unimaginative. I felt I had to stir him up and we began to walk about the room while I kept on saying, 'Don't have another gimmick. Isn't the best thing to do now to make a virtue of necessity? Since you have to postpone them all anyway, why not announce as a matter of policy the postponement of the incomes guarantee, of help to mortgagors and of overseas development money.' And quite suddenly he spotted the point. He got up from his chair and started walking round the table. We walked round two or three times, he in front, me pursuing him and trying to put ideas into the back of his head. I don't think very much more happened except that I complained to him about having all these cuts discussed behind my back by my own officials in consultation with the Treasury. 'Well anyway,' he replied, 'we shall be discussing all this on Monday at the meeting of Ministers.' That was the first I had heard of it and I said, 'Am I invited as one of the Ministers?' 'Yes,' said Harold. 'Your name is on the list.'

Of course, the main reason why our talk was so empty was because Harold had been thinking throughout about the resignation of Alec Douglas-Home. When I entered the room he told me that he was on the edge of resignation and we must have spent over half our time discussing something which had really taken his mind off the central issue. When I left his room I found that the resignation had taken the House of Commons by surprise and was the only topic of conversation.

It had one rather advantageous by-product. Tonight had been chosen for the great rebellion of the left wing of the Party on judges' salaries. The row started on Wednesday of last week when a Bill was introduced to increase the salaries by 25 per cent. This is a Bill on which the Lord Chancellor has always insisted; and I had always been told that there had been a package deal by which the Tories had agreed to an increase in Members' pay provided there was an increase in judges' salaries too. Suddenly last week the Tory front bench denied the package deal and said that they were not committed to it, and our back-benchers staged a violent revolt on the instigation of Reggie Paget, Michael Foot and John Mendelson. They kept it going until three o'clock in the morning and put down a series of wrecking amendments. They had committed themselves to another all-night sitting today, and I stayed until one in the morning to hear it start. It was pretty mild, largely because it had been overtaken by Home's sudden decision to resign.

Pam Berry rang me yesterday and told me that in her view Harold Wilson had played the most notable part in forcing the resignation because he had gone round saying that Alec Douglas-Home was his greatest asset. One of the people he had told it to was Adlai Stevenson a short while before his death, and Adlai had retailed it to every Conservative he met, including Douglas-Home. There may be truth in what Pam said. Home is a funny man. Perhaps he really *was* doubtful as to whether to hold on for another six months and the determining factor was the story that Adlai was going round London saying this.

Saturday, July 24th
On Thursday night I heard that George Brown had suddenly decided to call a meeting of the relevant Cabinet Ministers to discuss the PESC cuts. As the meeting was at 11.45 on Friday morning and I was due to go to Wolverhampton, I asked Bob Mellish to go. When I told George in the lobby on Thursday that I was sorry I couldn't come and that I was sending Bob, he said, 'It's no good sending Bob, he's worthless. If you don't bother to come to my meeting, it's up to you. I thought you really cared about things.' And he walked off. Oh dear!

I set out by the 8.20 train for Wolverhampton yesterday morning, where I was to open the ten-thousandth council house built since the war. The weather has been getting worse and worse this week and Friday opened with torrential rain. As the train rolled through the Midlands we saw the crops being ruined everywhere. We spent the morning viewing the housing estates in the rain. Wolverhampton is a characteristic Labour town. It has only had two short spells of non-Labour rule since the war; there is very little open space and all of it has been used for council building. Not brilliant architecture but decently done and constantly improving, and inspired by a real socialist sense of municipal enterprise. But, oh dear! The chairman of the Housing Committee who received me has been thirty-eight years on the council and eighteen years in charge of housing. The mayor, who is also chairman of the Planning Committee, is in his seventies. The whole atmosphere of the council is one of socialist decrepitude. They lost their majority last year and they are relying now on the aldermen's vote. They all feel on the down-grade. This is a bad sort of West Midlands politics.

When I had finished this official visit I had agreed with the regional organizer to do an evening Labour Party meeting for him. I was mildly surprised to hear that it wasn't a public meeting but that I was to go to a private reception for some two hundred members of the Party in the area. I hadn't a notion before I arrived of the one thing that was bound to happen. Everybody came that evening in a cold fury about my decision to order the complete reorganization of local government in the West Midlands, which I had announced a few weeks ago. It means that the whole of the Black Country, which at present is divided into sixteen local authorities, will be reorganized into five large county boroughs.[1] This kind of reorganization naturally upsets scores of existing councillors who, in the Black Country, are 100 per cent Labour. Indeed, an attempt to implement the decision was held up because three of the authorities had taken proceedings in the High Court against Keith Joseph and these are still being heard in the Court of Appeal—we shall have a judgment next Thursday. But despite the protests of the Labour councillors I had, after taking George Wigg's advice, decided that the politics of the Black Country are so utterly deplorable that whatever happens I would implement the recommendations lock, stock and barrel, from April 1st, 1966. Of course the reaction of many of these smaller authorities—Wednesbury, Sedgley, etc.—was furious. When I got to the reception, which took place at a big pub called The Hen and Chickens, I found a huge dance-hall and round the hall a series of round tables with eight or ten people at each sitting silently drinking. As I was introduced I began to realize that 90 per cent of that room was filled with councillors, with their wives and families, of the sixteen local U.D.C.s and boroughs I had decided to abolish. They had come determined to do me down. But I noticed something else. Each table had a separate community round it—one for

[1] See p. 263.

Sedgley, one for Wednesbury, one for Tettenhall, one for Darlaston, one for Rowley Regis, one for Oldbury. The separatism of the Black Country was revealed by those tables. And I saw the need for a shake-up: I have never met a more conservative collection of politicians than that gathering of Black Country socialists. Neither have I ever felt such a sullen, pugnacious atmosphere.

However, as often happens in Labour gatherings, it turned out a tremendous success just because they let off steam and attacked me and said I had stabbed them in the back and betrayed the Labour Party. In return I made it clear that the reorganization would take place next April whether they liked it nor not. They had to get down to making the best of it. After the first hour I got them to consider not its merits but its timing. Did they want it postponed in order to get time to reorganize? They said they couldn't possibly organize elections in January or February. I said I would like to have all that in writing since this was an administrative problem we could consider.

Walter Burley, who had been the agent here in Banbury and is now the assistant organizer in Birmingham, motored me back to Prescote afterwards and we talked all the way. I felt it had been an exhilarating meeting but it was also true that I had got up at seven in the morning and I didn't get home until midnight. When I had had my supper I got to bed and fell into the soundest sleep under the sun – or was it the moon?

Sunday, July 25th
This morning a dispatch-rider drove up to the house carrying a packet of top-secret papers. I have taken a look at them. It is quite clear that the Cabinet paper is a miserable document, a mere adjuration to cut back public spending. The moratorium is ruled out and all we get is appeals to the nationalized industries and the local authorities to try to stop spending except on housing and schools. So much for the great contingency plan about which I have been hearing so much from Waddell. I can't complain, as some other Ministers can, of not being cut in on the secret official consultations. Nevertheless, the secrecy does seem ridiculous in view of what happened on Saturday afternoon, when Harold blurted out an advance version of what he was going to put to his Ministers on Monday.[1] He revealed his determination to hold back public expenditure even if it meant abandoning certain projects, and apparently he made a special reference to cuts in the road programme. His ruling by press conference is becoming a positive menace. There is hardly a damn thing we are due to do of which he fails to give advance notice in the press. The Harold Davies visit to Hanoi, for example, was leaked by Harold Wilson talking out of turn. Now there is a leak about improving relations with Russia. As for Harold's Saturday speech I can't see any advantage in it and it is going to cause terrible trouble in Cabinet.

[1] Wilson writes, 'I foreshadowed [the measures] in a speech at a Party rally at Newtown, Montgomeryshire, on 24 July.' *Wilson*, p. 126.

I have little doubt that when his draft Statement is submitted to us tomorrow at Cabinet it will be as I want. But as a precaution I have decided to go up to London today, have dinner with Dame Evelyn and drive on to Tommy Balogh to brief myself as well as possible. In all this, George Wigg is very much on the anti-devaluation side. Indeed, I rather suspect that the emergency ideas cooked up by George Brown and presented at his meeting on Friday morning are really a counter-plan supported by the George Wigg side of the kitchen cabinet as contrasted with the Balogh/Marcia side.[1] That is just a guess, of course, but certainly Wigg has known much more about the contingency planning than Tommy Balogh, who was only cut in on the import/export aspects.

When I got to the Dame's house she at once told me that Bob Mellish had also been briefed. 'What brief?' I asked. And she said, 'The same papers as you got.' It took me some time to realize that the unconvincing Cabinet paper I had read was the product of the Ministers' meeting George Brown held on Friday morning after I had left for Wolverhampton. Bob had gone to the meeting and found everybody ferociously opposed to any form of building licensing as well as to any form of moratorium—which one of them described as literally putting a spanner in the works as the best method of overcoming an economic crisis. The Dame told me that, starting from last Sunday, officials have been desperately working on a new emergency plan because it is now feared that without even more drastic cuts we shall face devaluation. To some extent this was confirmed by Tommy Balogh when I motored on to his house in Hampstead. Thomas has always been friendly and intimate but that night there was a curious hitch in our relationship. We clearly weren't in the same team. This is one of the real difficulties of modern Cabinet government. I had been briefed with one lot of secrets dealing with public expenditure; he had been briefed on the international crisis. Neither of us was informed about each other's sector and neither was sure how much the other knew. This meant that our conversation was inhibited. I talked to him quite freely about the absurdity of the moratorium but I knew that he was terrified of talking back. Partly, I suspect, because I see George Wigg a great deal and they have come to hate each other in this particular crisis. George Wigg, whom I rang later on, was equally unwilling to tell me much, equally unsure of himself, and right to the end I couldn't make out whether he had been briefed about the whole home side.

Monday, July 26th
When I got to No. 10 this morning I found a great assembly of Ministers outside the door; all the spending Ministers—Health, Housing, Transport,

---

[1] George Wigg suggests that George Brown 'would have preferred to take the high line of devaluation' but that his attitude was 'one of complete loyalty to the Government', while 'Mrs Castle and Crossman ... were sound'. See *Wigg*, pp. 335–6.

Aviation, Overseas Development—were there. We soon discovered that Harold had set his eye on building licensing. After forbidding cuts in the housing programme he was determined to take the over-heating out of the construction industry and push the builders and building-material people away from the construction of inessential shops and garages and central supermarkets into housing, schools and hospitals.

In a crisis of this kind what a difference the personality of the Minister makes. I had often heard Nye say this about the Attlee Government but I had been a bit sceptical. It was literally true today. There is no doubt in my mind that if we had had a strong Minister of Transport he would have saved many of his essential roads. But it didn't happen. I had fought hard and saved my housing. Kenneth Robinson had fought hard and saved his hospitals. Tony Crosland had fought moderately hard and saved his schools at the cost of postponing his university and further-education building programme. And Barbara Castle had fought and fought and fought and got herself pretty soundly defeated up till now. Cabinet was desultory and disappointing, chiefly because Harold still felt unable to put us fully in the picture. We were discussing a Statement with no idea of how it would be timed. Indeed, I was assuming that it would go to Cabinet on Tuesday and then there would be negotiations before it was finally made on Thursday. But this actually wasn't the idea. Another cause of our unhappiness was the feeling of deep uncertainty we all had as to whether there was already a kind of cahoots between Callaghan and Brown against the P.M., which would produce a repetition of that terrible row in the last Cabinet.[1]

At 6 p.m. the Dame and I met Charlie and his officials in his room in order to discuss building controls. It was a rather pathetic meeting. The Dame was able to tell me that the Whitehall grapevine had it that the Statement would be made, whatever happened, on Tuesday afternoon because the Prime Minister, Callaghan and Brown were agreed on forcing it through. As we talked we began to see the redrafts of the Statement, which was being distributed in bits to Departments affected by it. Building licensing, for example, was to be far more drastic than the Ministry of Works had imagined, since the Prime Minister was insisting that contracts over £100,000, rather than over £250,000, would be licensed. As we sat there we heard that the Treasury had brushed aside all Charles Pannell's protests. It was clear that the careful PESC review of public expenditure had gone by the board. Now a Statement was being prepared as a real panic measure to stop a run on the pound which had started the previous weekend. This made nonsense of Callaghan's assurance a fortnight before that no further measures were contemplated. Yes! it was as short-term as that. And it became clear to me that this would be positively the last Statement before we went off the pound. The next Statement would announce that the pound was devalued, or floating.

It was also clear that devaluation was something Harold Wilson could

[1] See p. 281.

10

contemplate as little as George Brown and Callaghan. They were now united. The division was between, on the one side, these three plus their political advisers, such as George Wigg, and, on the other, the economic advisers. All the economists were urging that the pound should float, while the three politicians, strongly backed by George Wigg, were fighting for the pound on the ground that no Labour government could survive devaluation in 1965 after the devaluations of 1931 and 1949.

Tuesday, July 27th

Sure enough, when I got to my office at nine thirty I found a new draft of the Statement which had only been agreed by the Prime Minister, Brown and Callaghan at one o'clock in the morning. What happened then was as near to central dictatorship as one is likely to get in a British Cabinet. At Cabinet we were not given the time either to discuss the underlying strategy or even to consider the document as a whole. We were told to 'take it or leave it as it stands'. The Chancellor revealed that there had been a run on sterling in the previous week and that a huge part of our reserves, including the £200 million we had got from Germany as a result of our negotiations in Bonn, had disappeared. Unless a Statement was made that afternoon devaluation would be upon us. As well as the Chancellor, Harold and George Brown both spoke quite briefly. Each of them repeated that this was a package deal which they had worked out among themselves. I, of course, knew that Callaghan wanted a lot more, including the regulator[1] and a complete moratorium on all building contracts—and that these had been excluded by the efforts of Brown and Wilson. I also knew that building licensing was something which neither Callaghan nor Brown wanted, but on which Harold Wilson was insisting.

So there were rifts between the three of them. Callaghan, in particular, made it clear that if he'd had his way he would have done a lot more but that this had been prevented by the other two. As usual Harold allowed a lengthy Second Reading type of discussion. Frank Cousins was the only person who took up an extreme oppositional position. I said I was doubtful if the package was tough enough. It seemed to me that it would have maximum home disadvantages and would fail to impress the bankers abroad, and I didn't see why the Chancellor hadn't used the regulator. But my main feeling that morning was relief that my main suggestions had been accepted. The central part of the Statement included the announcement that we were abandoning the incomes guarantee for the lower paid, postponing cheap mortgages and cutting back local-authority mortgages. Of course, this would shock our own people to the teeth but it could also have the desired effect on the bankers abroad. Moreover, we would not really be giving up anything but merely

[1] The Chancellor of the Exchequer was able to increase or decrease certain taxes by up to 10 per cent at short notice, in order to 'regulate' the economy. An increase of 10 per cent would, for example, be anti-inflationary, in theory at least.

making a virtue of necessity. Most of the Cabinet did not agree. They objected with varying degrees of strength to the whole package; and there was a long and rather desperate argument about the relative importance of sticking to the incomes guarantee as compared to earnings-related short-term benefits. Anthony Crosland, however, was another who, like me, doubted whether the package would be particularly effective, and Roy Jenkins was also unenthusiastic about it for the same reason. The discussion drifted on till nearly twelve thirty, when it became obvious that we wouldn't have time to go through the draft in great detail. It would have to be bull-dozed through. And that's what happened.

By one o'clock something like agreement on the actual text was reached and then came the question of who should make the Statement. Suddenly Harold said that he didn't think he was the right person to make a Statement which included the abandonment of so many promises and pledges. He couldn't possibly do this. I guessed what he was thinking. By this time we knew that the Statement would be made in the House today, when the new Tory leader was to be elected. Moreover, we were having no less than three votes of censure, two during this week and one on the following Monday.[1] It therefore seemed obvious that the Chancellor should make what was basically a Treasury Statement and that Harold should reply to the big vote of censure on Thursday, when the new Tory leader would have been elected. But for some twenty minutes Callaghan wriggled. I at least was quite deter-mined to nail him to our cross—after all he had been mainly responsible for constructing it. Finally, Harold Wilson, who quite obviously wanted him to do the job, took a vote and called our names. There was a two to one majority for making Callaghan do it. And he did it, and the interviews on the wireless and on the telly, extremely well. In fact he got away with murder—very largely because the whole of the Tory Party was entirely distracted from the crisis by its own leadership crisis. I suspect that this was one of the main factors in Harold's mind when he insisted on having the Statement on Tuesday afternoon. If so, the calculation certainly worked.

In the afternoon I had an important meeting with the local authority treasurers to discuss local government finance. It was just getting under way when I suddenly got a message that I had to go across to hear the Callaghan Statement. As soon as it was clear that there was no risk of a division I went back to my meeting and took with me a copy of Callaghan's speech. This had a remarkable effect on the treasurers. By going through it with them, I was able to reduce the shock of the announcement of the cuts in local-authority building, apart from schools, hospitals and houses, and of the heavy cut-back in local-authority mortgages to private house-buyers. They were able to react to all this in my presence in a friendly way; and I think they knew that during

---

[1] The first two were on the cost of living and on the Government's failure to fulfil its election pledges. The third was a general censure motion on the day before the adjournment and it was the occasion of Heath's first speech as Conservative leader.

the discussions leading up to the announcement they had had a friend at court. Finally, by going back to see them I had saved them returning to London for another meeting.

Soon after that I had to go back to Harold's room for a further meeting at which we finished Cabinet business before seven thirty. Most of the time was spent on the draft immigration White Paper, on which I have consistently presented a West Midlands point of view, insisting that we must have really effective control and trying to choose a middle path between the liberal sloppiness of Frank Soskice and the extreme anti-Commonwealth immigrant feeling of Herbert Bowden. The meeting was bad-tempered because both Barbara Castle and the Attorney-General, Elwyn Jones, detest the philosophy behind the Statement. But it turned out well and a Statement will be made in the House tomorrow.[1] I feel it will do the job politically. In order to ease the situation with Barbara I helped to make sure that her White Paper appears at the same time. It was obviously sensible to publish them together as a defensive operation in order to prevent the Tories from winning too many votes on the race issue.

After that I drove home to Vincent Square where we were giving a dinner (Anne was up in London) for the Llewelyn-Davieses and Jimmy James to discuss the P.A.G. report, and also the work of R.A.G. I pulled this second committee together under Richard's chairmanship last January because I thought it was urgent to get a ten-year research programme for the Ministry. Getting a report from them was my first idea before I got interested in the housing programme and I am jolly glad I laid the foundations for it. Unfortunately, however, when it came the report of R.A.G. was an amiable, rather futile document which didn't list precise projects as I wanted. I was pretty angry with it. However, Richard is very quick off the mark when things have gone wrong. Straight away at dinner he said that he was perfectly willing, along with his colleagues, to make the suggestions specific and detailed as soon as possible. Then we turned to discussing the P.A.G. report, for which a press conference is timed for tomorrow.

Wednesday, July 28th
The news of the economic crisis was nicely balanced by the news that Heath had defeated Maudling in the leadership contest. Naturally, I wanted the good man to lose. I knew that Douglas-Home's departure was a real disaster for us (he was *our* asset) and I wanted Maudling instead of Heath because Heath would be the more formidable leader. However, I wasn't unduly surprised when the announcement came that Heath had got a majority on the first ballot, that Powell had come out very badly and that Maudling had at once conceded defeat. As a result we have curiously similar leaders in the Tory and the Labour Parties. Two wholly political politicians, much more tactically than strategically minded. Maudling would have been a far better,

[1] It was actually made on August 2nd.

wiser political leader. All the disadvantages of Harold Wilson seem to me to be incorporated in Heath—and most of the advantages as well—his drive, energy, skill in debate, his dedication to politics. These are all considerable assets; and I dare say it is quite good for the country, in a period when great, high policies are unlikely to be attainable, to have two tactical politicians of this kind in charge. Certainly, it means the electoral battle will be keen and there will be no question of a national government if we are driven into devaluation. Our parliamentary democracy will continue to run along the strictest Party lines.

The Tories were enormously confident. They felt strengthened, and that they had really got us on the run. I asked Tam how things were going and he admitted to me that Tuesday's Statement had been a terrible blow to our back-benchers. I should add that the actual Statement was of course designed for the bankers, emphasizing the negative side and sounding far worse than it actually was. I hadn't correctly estimated the shock to people like Tam of the abandonment of the incomes guarantee and the postponement of the mortgage scheme. That shock was far less for me because I knew that the incomes guarantee had already been abandoned by Douglas Houghton, and I had seen the papers and seen that what they *were* proposing was a disaster which they wouldn't actually dare to put forward. I also knew that the postponement of the private mortgages wasn't an abandonment but was for the time being essential to the expansion of the public-sector housing programme. But these are things known only to very few people in Whitehall. To many of our people it really was the limit. They were feeling, 'We're on the skids, slithering into devaluation. When we come back from the recess we shall find the pound devalued.'

Meanwhile, I was having a day of departmental worries—no, jobs, not worries. The press conference on the P.A.G. report was easy but the departmental committee on the Christ Church Meadow road was not. I had had time by now to study the Inspector's report—which really put us back fourteen years. At first I assumed that I could reject it and let the unfortunate city council get on with building the Meadow Road. But then I heard that Hugh Wilson, the leading architect who had been brought into the Ministry, shares the Inspector's view; and so we had to have a special conference on Wednesday with the Ministry of Transport represented by both Tom Fraser and Stephen Swingler.[1] They made it clear that their Ministry was completely opposed to my view. With my own officials at best divided, I was licked and I knew it.

But most of the day was spent much more cheerfully at the renewed

---

[1] Labour M.P. for Stafford 1945–50, and for Newcastle-under-Lyme from 1951. He was Joint Parliamentary Secretary at the Ministry of Transport 1964–7 and Minister of Transport 1967–8. He was to become one of Crossman's Ministers of State at the Department of Health and Social Security in 1968, where he stayed until his death in February 1969. He and Crossman were old friends: they had both been at New College, Oxford, and had both lectured for the W.E.A. in the late 1930s.

negotiations with the building societies. I didn't realize how happy they would be until I met them. First of all, they had been saved by the skin of their teeth from having building licensing applied to private-enterprise building and to housing. Secondly, we had clamped down on local-authority mortgage loans, something the societies have been asking me to do for months. So I found them eating out of my hand and very pleased to tell their council on August 12th that they favour my national housing plan and want to work out details with us. However, they were careful to give me two warnings. First, the plan mustn't be put forward in a political framework or made part of any party polemic. Second, I must appreciate how unpopular in their circle it would be to keep the private sector constant while I upped the size of the public sector. With these two provisos they gave me what I wanted. And I felt that afternoon that I had fulfilled what the Treasury, as well as the Tories in the Commons, had told me was a futile and inane ambition. Of course, it is very largely luck, due to the situation created by the crisis, that has made it possible for me to achieve it. But it wasn't *all* due to the crisis: a fortnight ago the Dame told me that in her private talks with the building societies they had said they were willing to come along. Now I have got to complete the talks over the summer and then approach the insurance companies and the building industry, which won't be quite so amiable.

In the evening I dined with Nicky Kaldor and he was able to fill me in on what he knew of events of the past week. He told me that last Friday he, Tommy and Robert Neild had made a joint *démarche* to Harold, urging him not to go in for repressive measures but to accept the floating pound. They had been turned down and on this occasion George Wigg's advice had been preferred.

Thursday, July 29th

I was due to see the P.M. at 9.30 to discuss the national housing plan and local government finance. However, I got a desperate message that I wasn't to go because he was still preparing his big speech for the censure debate. I realized that the speech must be his only concern during the morning. True, it was only Anthony Barber moving the vote of censure, but nevertheless everything depended on how Harold replied.

He didn't have much time, however, because Cabinet met to resume discussion on public expenditure, in particular to deal with the two un-resolved subjects — social security and overseas aid. This time Callaghan was on the side of Barbara — which shows how pertinacious Harold can be when he wants. To George Brown's amazement he had brought the Chancellor over and persuaded him to come out with a 'compromise', under which, as far as I could make out, Barbara would get about £10 million more. Callaghan said this was essential because we couldn't renege on firm Government commitments. This produced the expected explosion. Many Ministers pointed out that there were other just as firm Government commit-ments on the home side which had been abandoned in the Statement. Harold fought for Barbara; Barbara talked and talked – weakened her case – and then there came a farcical moment when John Diamond for the Treasury suddenly said, 'But I believe we have got all the calculations wrong. We have been calculating not on 1964 prices but on current prices.' So the issue was postponed again, and we turned to social security.

Douglas Houghton had put in a long memorandum protesting against the abandonment of the incomes guarantee. Having made his fuss he gave way sulkily. It didn't take long. So we came finally to housing. I said I agreed to forgo the increased figures for 1966–7, but only if I could have one clear ruling from Cabinet. Suppose by any chance that the private-enterprise starts should go on sagging, I must be able to fill the vacuum with increased housing in the public sector. Callaghan was, of course, vehemently opposed. I then had a row with him for three or four minutes, won, and got it minuted; so this critical point is Cabinet policy. What really clinched it for me was that the Prime Minister carefully asked me about the national housing plan and the state of play with the building societies. He said this, of course, because I had told him about my success on Wednesday in the renewed negotiations. I was able to give Cabinet a really optimistic picture.

When the others left the room I stayed behind and said to Harold, 'If you say a word about this housing plan in your speech this afternoon you'll kill it stone dead.' He looked very disappointed. Could he not mention the target of half a million? This appalled me. I had heard rumours that he wanted to do it and I said to him, 'For God's sake, don't.' When I got back to the Ministry I found the draft passage in his speech for that afternoon in his own long-hand with the corrections he had made and had photographed and sent over. (John Delafons has got it as a memorial of that morning.) He must have been rewriting right up to delivery that afternoon at 3.30 because I noticed that he delivered it from pencil notes.

I had another meeting with the local authorities that afternoon – this time about my draft circular on the ethics of councillors.[1] I was back in the Commons just in time to hear the end of Anthony Barber's speech – obviously not very effective. Then came Harold and he kept his word. On housing he took just the line I wanted and there was no mention of the half-a-million. So I have still got the announcement reserved for October – which is of crucial importance to me and the Ministry. I sat on to listen to the rest of the speech. He looked very confident leaning against the box, but from where I sat I could see that he was so tired he could scarcely stand up, and he was muttering and reading the speech fast and not doing it very well. Yet it was an astonishing performance because of his wit and agility, and also because he hit the level of the House exactly. 'I wasn't too serious,' he said to me as he sat down. 'I'll leave that for Monday. Let's make fools of them today.' And that, of course, is exactly what he did.[2]

[1] See p. 273.
[2] See *Wilson*, p. 127, for the Prime Minister's own account.

But he did something more. He also remoralized his own Party—gave them back their faith. This is an example of how one speech can really transform a situation. I have seldom seen it happen to the extent it happened today. But then I have seldom had a period in my political life when the Party's morale had reached such a low ebb. By the time he sat down they were all cheering and laughing behind him, and the Tories were totally discomfited. It was a tremendous show.

I had been due to see the Chancellor about local government finance at 5.30. But he and I sat on during the debate to hear Harold finish and to join in the applause before we slipped out to meet our officials. That meeting lasted an hour; and once again I bullied and battered James about the need for a short-term rates policy which would include rate rebates paid for by him. Dame Evelyn and Crocker helped me with the battering. When I went out of the meeting I ran into Harold Wilson. I said what a marvellous speech he had made; but perhaps I didn't congratulate him quite enough because he was indeed overwhelmed by his own success. He asked me straight away whether I still wanted to see him that evening in view of his failure to see me in the morning. I told him, 'There is nothing I need to say—you have transformed the situation. Now I must carry on as well as I can.' 'Yes,' he said. 'I think I did my job. I got the temperature down. I got it just right and now we are through the worst.'

I had made arrangements to motor to Salisbury after the division at 10,[1] because I wanted to have plenty of time to visit the rural district council throughout Friday and if I took the morning train I wouldn't have seen all I wanted. So at 10.30 I set off, with Molly at the wheel and John Delafons beside me. I looked in on the Longford party in Chelsea, taking John with me, and there I found a lot of the Cabinet, including Michael Stewart, as well as Paul Johnson from the *Statesman*; and the atmosphere was fairly good. Then off we went into the night and by 1.45 I was safe in a comfortable bed in a beautiful old hostel in the centre of Salisbury.

Friday, July 30th
I woke up at 6.30 to torrential rain. This has been an awful week for the farmers. We have still got plenty of time to avert a catastrophe with the crops if we can get a fortnight of dry weather now; but the wireless gives us little prospect of that. I had my breakfast in bed and had the morning papers brought up to me. It was clear that Harold has scored a most sensational triumph. Even the Tory press had to describe how he had detonated the Opposition, restored our morale and transformed the situation. And of course he had changed the value of the pound sterling too.

The weather improved and I had a delightful day on my first visit to a rural district council (I had let it be known that I would like to visit one or two).

---

[1] The vote was 306 to 285 in favour of the Government.

This one covers an enormous area, some 178 square miles all round Salisbury
—five beautiful forked river valleys stretching out from the town. They
wanted to show me some of the 1,000 houses they had built and the 900 houses
they've improved. After lunch, when I had opened some old people's homes,
I went to the council chambers for an hour's private talks with the councillors
and officials. I have a feeling that as Minister for Local Government this is a
job which is really worth doing. After I had finished with the R.D.C. I went
to look at some of the classic problems which the Salisbury preservationists
wanted to show me. Then Molly motored me back home to Prescote where
I arrived at 8.30.

Saturday, July 31st
We went over to see John Betjeman at his house in Wantage today because
I wanted to discuss the reorganization of the section of the Ministry which
deals with the preservation and listing of houses. I'd started on this last week
in a long talk with Lord Holford, in which I had told him how I wanted to
broaden the scope of his committee and try to make it less pedantic and more
concerned with real policy planning. Holford is a tired man and bit of a spent
force and he obviously wanted me to kick him out of the chair. I was clever
enough to keep him as chairman while I put the changes through. I discussed
the reorganization with John Betjeman, who is now quite a friend of mine,
and saw for the first time his strange wife, Penelope, who showed her ponies
and horses to an intoxicated Virginia and to a Patrick a good deal less than
intoxicated. Patrick, of course, found John Betjeman his best friend and I
think they both enjoyed each other's company.

Sunday, August 1st
Off to London today with the children to have four days' holiday there. On
the way we lunched with Pam Berry at Oving and she gave us all a bathe in
her swimming-bath. In fact we are having a few small family pleasures to
soften the arduousness of political crises. Inevitably, Anne has felt a little left
out recently; but I think we can ease off now August has come and with the
House rising on Thursday. I will get time to tidy up my housing White Paper
and prepare for the launching of the national housing plan in my speech at
the Party Conference. I can see my way ahead now without too much stress
and strain. Yes, this particular crisis is behind us. I suppose, objectively, there
is no reason why there shouldn't be another crisis in September or October—
with devaluation this time. Nevertheless, after Harold's Thursday speech I
personally feel more hopeful, really quite elated. Partly this is because I
estimate that the package we have put out is considerably better balanced
than anything Cabinet did before. For the first time we got priorities really
written into a Statement of policy and a distinction between essential and
inessential spending. On reflection, I don't think now that either of the
Callaghan budgets were as good! So we are learning a bit.

Official figures published on August 3rd showed that the reserves had fallen by £91 million in July. Since October some £1,000 million had been taken out of London. However, exports had risen by £44 million and although imports continued to rise (by £12 million in July) the gap was now reduced to £50 million. But during August the reserves lost, officially, another £140 million and the trade figures fell away. The Federal Reserve Bank swap agreement was by now exhausted and the Chancellor, on a visit to Washington, negotiated another $50 million. He also managed to persuade the building societies to keep their lending rates at 6¾ per cent.

The Chancellor appeared to be more successful than his colleague and rival at the D.E.A. George Brown was still working on the preparation of his National Plan, but meanwhile wages continued to rise. By August, weekly wage rates had risen by 4½ per cent in twelve months. But in negotiations with the unions, at least the Minister of Labour, Ray Gunter, had one success. Lord Devlin's report on the docks appeared in the first week of August and both the employers and the T.G.W.U. generally approved its recommendations. It advised the decasualization of employment, cuts in the number of employers, a new wages structure and improved methods of working. It was the 'wreckers', unofficial groups whose leader in London was Jack Dash (a Communist), who objected and continued to demand the nationalization of the ports.

Though wage claims ran high, prices held fairly steady, helped by the first reports of the Prices and Incomes Board. Road haulage rates were kept down and price rises in the printing industry were refused. In September, a rise in the price of bread was approved but a further rise deferred. However, the Government (and the public) were aware that prices had been only temporarily held down while earnings had risen steeply, and that a burst of price increases was inevitable.

Monday, August 2nd

I went back to Westminster confident that Harold Wilson's speech had really helped the pound. Well, it hadn't! The fact is that the whole package was not terribly effective. Today the pound is still dithering, Callaghan is still suicidal and Wilson is looking a bit harassed. We all, in both Whitehall and Westminster, have the uneasy feeling that this year's third budget still hasn't had the required effect. As for the Party in the House, it has the rather desperate feeling, underneath the end-of-term atmosphere, that something disastrous could happen while Parliament is in recess. On the other hand, the Tories seem completely confident that Parliament is going to be recalled. I don't think they expect or even want to come to power this October; but they feel the Government is being driven to the wall, battered by its failure to achieve confidence and by having to make concession after concession to reality. One looks back to Harold's immense triumph last Thursday only as an event in the past—yet another desperate remedy already being overtaken and overwhelmed by the events which followed.

This afternoon we had the Statement on immigration and the publication of the White Paper.[1] This has been one of the most difficult and unpleasant jobs the Government has had to do. We have become illiberal and lowered the quotas at a time when we have an acute shortage of labour. No wonder all the weekend liberal papers have been bitterly attacking us. Nevertheless, I am convinced that if we hadn't done all this we would have been faced with certain electoral defeat in the West Midlands and the South-East. Politically, fear of immigration is the most powerful undertow today. Moreover, we had already abandoned the Gaitskell position when we renewed the Immigration Act, and any attempt now to resist demands for reduced quotas would have been fatal. We felt we had to out-trump the Tories by doing what they would have done and so transforming their policy into a bipartisan policy. I fear we were right; and partly I think so because I am an old-fashioned Zionist who believes that anti-Semitism and racialism are endemic, that one has to deal with them by controlling immigration when it gets beyond a certain level. On the other hand, I can't overestimate the shock to the Party. This will confirm the feeling that ours is not a socialist Government, that it is surrendering to pressure, that it is not in control of its own destiny. If only we had had a Home Secretary who could have done this as a matter of principle and done it strongly and early! But it has been squeezed out of us, just as our economic concessions to reality have been squeezed out of us. I think it will be very difficult to deal with the thoroughly deplorable image we have created when Conference meets. When you add immigration to Vietnam you realize why the rank and file feel that we have abandoned our pledges and are retreating from socialism. The White Paper will probably have a deeper undermining effect on the moral strength of Harold Wilson's leadership than any other thing that we have done.

After the Statement on immigration came the great censure debate in which Ted Heath was to make his debut as leader of the Tory Party. Like so many debuts, this was a pretty good flop. Heath turned out to be a second-class orator, making his own second-class, highly competent speech in his own way. He was neither a tremendous attacking force nor a statesman, and there can't have been many Tories who didn't whisper under their breath, 'My God, I see the point of Maudling now.' Moreover, the contrast between Heath and Callaghan, who was replying to him, was very interesting. Callaghan did well. He has a good personality at the dispatch box: he looks the statesman and he has a calm authority.

Being Thursday, there was the usual Party meeting at six o'clock, but on this occasion we had been told that it was a farewell by the leader before the recess. I found Manny Shinwell's stage management a bit odious. Harold made a real end-of-term speech congratulating the Party on its marvellous work, talking about our confidence in the prospects ahead and committing

---

[1] Entry vouchers were reduced from 208,000 per annum to 8,500.

himself to fighting on until 1967. There were carefully arranged interventions by Walter Monslow[1] and Bernard Taylor,[2] two old-time left-wingers, giving fealty to their leader.

In the evening I had to accompany the Dame to a dinner with the Hampshire County Council. The point was to persuade me of the validity of their proposal that Hampshire should be considered as an all-purpose authority and include the two county boroughs of Portsmouth and Southampton.

I was tempted to allow this, but the dinner finally convinced me it would be unwise. In certain ways Hampshire is one of the best counties I have visited – particularly in its town development. Nevertheless, they are a tight little oligarchy, not the kind of unit I want to see as a paradigm of local administration. Over the past ten months I have been saying regularly that there is no question of our reorganizing local government; but the more I go round the country the more I realize how difficult it is to carry out my policy of ending the cold war and getting a genuine collaboration of county and county borough. However, I realized that even if I succeed in making a series of wise decisions on local boundaries they aren't really going to resolve this problem. If I really care about planning, I must find some legislative way of making regional planning effective while this Government survives.

I rushed back from the dinner to hear the last minutes of Harold Wilson's speech – what *The Times* described as a knockout blow to Heath slightly below the belt. And that was the effective end of this session of Parliament.[3] Now there is nothing left but bits and pieces before we recess on Thursday.

Tuesday, August 3rd
Cabinet. And the main item was George Brown's National Plan. We had four key chapters in front of us, including the summary at the beginning, and the question was whether, in view of the deflation Callaghan launched in his Statement last week, we should still publish the Plan next September as we had intended. Tony Crosland had this in mind when he asked how we could talk about a plan based on a 4-per-cent average increase of production each year when we now knew perfectly well that for the next eighteen months at least production wasn't going to rise by anything like that – in fact when the Government was actually cutting back production by its deflationary measures. Crosland is the only member of the Cabinet who comes right out with these honest-to-God economic judgments. He then went on, 'We are launched on deflation and I know I shall have to rewrite the whole of my

[1] The Organization Secretary of ASLEF, and Labour M.P. for Barrow-in-Furness from 1945 to 1966, when he became a life peer. He had been a Parliamentary Secretary at the Ministry of Aviation and at the Ministry of Food in the post-war Labour Government. He died in October 1966.

[2] A coal-miner, and Labour M.P. for Mansfield from 1941 to 1966, when he became a life peer. He had held junior office at the Ministries of Aircraft Production and of National Insurance in the wartime Coalition and the post-war Labour Governments.

[3] The Government had a majority of thirteen.

chapter in George Brown's National Plan. It makes no sense any more.' Frank Cousins, who followed, was as usual quite ineffective.*

The others sat round with their departmental briefs, and since there was no brief on the central topic nobody spoke until Callaghan said, 'All you've got is a postponement for six months and I can't see why any competent Minister can't plan a postponement if he has got his Department under control.' At this I remarked, 'As a matter of fact, for the last five days my officials have been discussing with your officials, my dear James, the text of a circular in which the Treasury has been insisting that this isn't only a postponement for six months but may well last longer. If you will assure me that it really stops after six months I will go out and tell my officials.' James said, 'You'll do no such thing. I am not going to be talked to in that way.' And that was that.

After this we moved on to another boring discussion of Frank Cousins's computers. I sat through it for an hour and then walked out before the big item on coal prices – a proposal by the Ministry of Fuel and Power to announce a huge increase in prices on September 1st. But I was away by then because I was determined to get back to the office and then take the children to the Crystal Palace. Our mission was especially to see the models of the prehistoric monsters on the island – the ones put there by the Prince Consort when the Crystal Palace was moved from Hyde Park in 1854. The children liked it all a great deal; and Patrick was enormously aware of being the son of a Minister, though I am not sure it is good for him. The other day when the family had a breakdown on the M1 he said to his mother, 'Will this be in the newspapers too?' I don't think it really does him any harm and he certainly isn't embarrassed by having a father whose name is always in the papers and who rides about in a ministerial car. In the evening we all went out to see the new Beatles film, *Help*. I thought it was going to be awful but it turned out the best thing I have seen since the Marx Brothers. I adored it.

Wednesday, August 4th
I had two crucial Cabinet Committees. In the morning Home Affairs was due to discuss my big paper on housing finance. And in the afternoon a special committee was going to sit under James Callaghan's chairmanship to discuss my paper on local government finance. It was vital to get authority to go ahead on these two Bills before we broke up for the recess.

The morning meeting of Home Affairs turned out to be a mere formality. Once the Treasury had given its consent to my plan to enable local authorities to borrow money for new housing at 4 per cent and receive the difference

---

* I liked Cousins personally and, in working with him at an interdepartmental level, realized how hampered the Minister of Technology was by having as his Minister of State Charles Snow (an effective scientist but no politician). However, I began to feel that Cousins was being exceptionally favoured by the Prime Minister in discussions on computer policy; and I regretted, while I respected, his intransigent stand against a firm prices and incomes policy. This perhaps explains my inconsistent attitude towards him.

between that and the prevailing rate of interest from the Exchequer, there was no further discussion.

The meeting in the afternoon on local government was much trickier because here I had deliberately forced the issue of rating reform by speaking and writing publicly about it—and this had upset my colleagues. However, the E.D.C. meeting that preceded it turned out to be far more important. I hadn't meant to go, but I got a message from George Brown that he badly wanted me to help him against Callaghan. So I turned up in the large ministerial conference room in the House of Commons where I found the usual gathering of the clans, with George in the chair and Callaghan beside him. After I had left Cabinet yesterday morning there had been a deadlock on coal prices, so the problem had been pushed back to E.D.C. this afternoon. Callaghan had all the arguments and the logic on his side. They were re-hearsed by Fred Lee, the Minister of Power, who reminded us that last March he had asked for the necessary increase and it had been postponed because of the municipal elections. He had asked for it again in June and on that occasion it had been postponed because of the incomes policy. 'Every postponement,' he said, 'costs us several million pounds a week. For God's sake give us the increase quickly and in the right places. Put coal prices up in the unremunerative areas—Wales and Scotland and Lancashire—while keeping them steady where the coal actually makes a profit, in the East Midlands and the West Riding.' George Brown's reply was that at the present juncture an increase would be tantamount to political suicide. He reminded us that coal prices had not been increased for four years under the Tories. How could we risk the T.U.C. blowing up in our faces at their Congress in September? Callaghan turned round and said, 'Some time we have to face reality. That time has come now. We ought to put the prices up and keep the wages steady.' George Brown replied, 'That will be the end of the incomes policy.' Callaghan: 'There comes a point when you have to do it.' Brown: 'You've no right to talk like that to me here.' I felt in my bones that George was right. For the second time Callaghan was demonstrating that he has become the Minister for Deflation, the kind of deflation Ramsay MacDonald tried to carry out in 1931.

So there was a terrible row between the two of them and then George Brown, from the chair, went round the table asking for opinions. The Minister of Labour was on his side, of course, because he is on the side of the T.U.C. So was the Secretary of State for Scotland, Willie Ross. On the other hand, Callaghan got the votes of Tom Fraser, ex-Minister of Power, and Fred Lee. Then it came to my turn. It was clear that what I said could tip the balance and I decided merely to ask a question. 'Is it true, as George Brown said,' I asked, 'that we could make this year's £50 million deficit at the Coal Board part of the general write-off? Can we do that? I can't make up my mind until I know the answer.' Callaghan, forced to reply, said, 'Well, of course it is technically possible.' So I then remarked, 'Well, in that case, I am on George Brown's side.' When he'd finished the count, George Brown said he had a majority on his side. Callaghan: 'I reckon I've got one more than you.' George: 'You're trying to take the chair as well.' Then he read out his list of names and he put in Fred Peart—who wasn't there. Callaghan: 'What about Fred Peart?' George: 'Oh, I've got a note in my pocket ... ' (I knew he had because Fred had written to me, too). Fred's was the extra vote which gave us the seven to five majority for economic madness but for political sanity.

All this had pushed off my special committee on local government finance for forty minutes. It turned out to be another farcical meeting. The main issue was whether I should be allowed a special short Bill introducing rate rebates *before* the long-term reform of rating. The Chancellor, who was in the chair, began by saying, 'We've just given away £30 million in coal subsidies this year. Now the Minister of Housing wants another £40 million for rate rebates.' I replied, 'I don't want a penny of extra taxation this or any other year. I merely want a transfer from one form of taxation to another. I want to lighten the burden on the ratepayer at the cost of the taxpayer.' I held him to this point and I got my way. The committee knew perfectly well that rate rebates were something we had to give the electors if we wanted to survive the municipal elections. But they weren't prepared to humiliate the Chancellor by giving me this formally. What I got was an agreement that I should be allowed to prepare the short Bill and let the Cabinet sanction it in October in time for the Queen's Speech.

I went home to have a little supper with Anne at 10.30, leaving the House as usual preparing for an all-night session. Tam Dalyell was there, suffering from a terrible stye in his eye caused by general end-of-term exhaustion. As one of the youngest people in the House Tam has been heroic. He has done every all-night sitting all through the night—all eleven of them—and meanwhile in the daytime he has got me my pairs and been the most devoted, kind, good P.P.S., as well as a very nice lodger who cooks my breakfast when Anne isn't here. Though I laugh at him sometimes, I am undyingly grateful to him for all he has done during these last eight months and if I had any appreciation of loyalty and friendship I would really tell him so oftener.

Thursday, August 5th
Our last Cabinet before the recess took place while the Commons was going through its last stages and winding up its recess adjournment debate. The whole place is completely conked out. But we still had to hold the Cabinet in the Prime Minister's private room because there were Questions at eleven o'clock and he and Tony Crosland and others had to go off to the front bench to answer them. Since both the First Secretary and the Chancellor had to be away at the beginning Harold had put in as a filler a paper proposing to reduce the ban on the publication of state documents from a fifty- to a thirty-year rule. This was a very modest reform, long overdue. Yet only Tony

Crosland and I were prepared to support the P.M. and Gerald Gardiner against the civil servants. We had read aloud to us, first by Michael Stewart and then by James Callaghan, the departmental briefs provided for them by their officials. Here was a Labour Foreign Secretary objecting that a reduction of the ban on publications to a thirty-year rule might damage the reputations of civil servants active during the Munich period while they were still alive. I pointed out that the present ban, quite apart from all its other drawbacks, was rendered intolerable by the permission which a Cabinet Minister, particularly a Prime Minister, can obtain to use official documents denied to academic and objective historians for writing his memoirs. If we are going to go on exercising the right to turn out memoirs which are often nothing but personal *plaidoyers*, there is a powerful case for letting the historians get at the documents as soon as possible. This formed the main discussion but I wasn't surprised to find that not a word of my argument was retained in the Cabinet minutes.

At last we turned to the main item on the agenda, the postponed discussion on the public expenditure cuts in overseas aid. Cabinet was presented with the final result of a lot of haggling behind the scenes. Barbara was to get £10 million extra in the really difficult year, 1966–7. Provided she didn't make another 25-minute speech to us, we were all prepared to accept it. But I did ask rather maliciously where the £10 million was coming from and whose estimates would be cut back. Harold explained that they weren't coming from anywhere. So the proposal went through.

Then we turned once again to coal prices. George Brown had written a report on the Committee that had taken place on the previous afternoon. It was a difficult item because of the absence of George, who stayed at Neddy[1] throughout the whole morning and left Harold Wilson to look after his side of the case. James Callaghan and Fred Lee repeated their speeches at length and asked whether we were prepared to simply subsidize the coal industry. Before anybody else could speak Tony Crosland intervened. 'I've got to go away to answer a Question,' he said. 'But before I go I want to say that Callaghan, of course, is absolutely right. If we are going to have a policy of deflation—which I don't agree with but which we have accepted—then we ought to have these price increases now. But,' and here he paused, 'we ought to have seen them as a part of last week's package. As it is, we have got to accept them in addition to the package.' Harold Wilson was obviously nonplussed and said he thought Tony had muddied the waters; it was unfair to suggest that coal prices had anything to do with the package. I then barged in and said, 'But let's look at the realities. How can you make this announcement before the T.U.C. meets next September? If you do you will destroy the incomes policy.' In fact, I put the case which had persuaded the majority to vote with George in the Committee. None of George's other supporters on the Committee said a word. Ray Gunter stayed silent. Willie Ross stayed

[1] N.E.D.C.

silent. They all stood back from the Cabinet battle. So I was left alone to speak for the Committee, strongly supported by Fred Peart, Barbara Castle and the Chief Whip. Harold Wilson then said it was quite wrong to consider coal prices as part of the package, and I said I wasn't prepared to accept this until we had had the economic strategy meeting which the Prime Minister had promised Barbara Castle. As a compromise, the Prime Minister then suggested that the decision should be taken now but that the prices should only be increased in December. After that he had to leave the room, and the chair was taken by Bert Bowden while the debate roamed on and on. It was soon clear that the majority in the Cabinet was behind George Brown, and Callaghan got sorer and sorer sitting there and seeing how little support he had. Even Michael Stewart came our way. As for the P.M.'s compromise, it was obviously impracticable since a decision would leak long before December. However, when Harold came back Bert Bowden said, 'I think there is a majority in favour of your proposal, Prime Minister, for a decision now to increase the prices in December.' This caused another row at the end of which the P.M. gave in. A special Cabinet is now fixed for September 9th (curse it, in the middle of my holiday) and on that day the decision on coal prices will be taken.

It was a trying Cabinet and one that revealed once again the underlying stresses and divisions. In the last resort, when the Prime Minister and Callaghan really act together, they may still just be able to carry a majority with them. On the other hand, there has now grown up a strong centre group in the Cabinet who refuse to be forced into deflation.

I talked to Tony Crosland afterwards and we agreed that the vital thing is to make Cabinet take the risk of deserting the pound for the sake of the social services. But that is a very difficult thing to do because both James Callaghan and Harold Wilson are personally committed to the defence of the pound to a quite extraordinary degree.

Looking back over this fortnight and putting together the bits and pieces, I now realize that the underlying issue has always been the fight for the pound. I heard about it for the first time at that dinner with Nicky Kaldor when he told me how he and Tommy and Robert Neild had written to the Prime Minister begging that the pound should float. When I reported the conversation to George Wigg he blew up and said I had been talking to Hungarian traitors. George has been one of the men most strongly advising Harold to stand by the pound and dismissing anybody with a different view as a dangerous Hungarian or a tool of the Hungarians. Talking to George Wigg has made me realize that if you commit yourself to the view that de-valuation is the end of everything and then fail to defend the pound, then it really is the end and you go down in catastrophe. I agree with the Hungarians. Failing to defend the pound would not mean the end of everything; we have already paid far too high a price in the effort to bolster it up. Indeed, letting the pound float and accepting straight away the measures we should have to take after a devaluation makes sense. Defending the pound by frantic cuts and then in the end finding one has to devalue makes no sense at all.

Tony Crosland is passionate about this, and I agreed that I would write a letter to Harold trying to use my influence with him on the side of letting the pound float when the next pressure comes. Of course, this would mean that Callaghan's personal reputation would be irreparably damaged and that is why he is so desperately concerned. What none of us know is what it would mean for Harold Wilson's personal reputation. I shall have to write to him and tell him that he is the only person flexible enough and strong enough to float the pound and survive. Nevertheless, Harold Wilson and George Wigg will see devaluation as a defeat far more than I do. Indeed, at this Cabinet meeting I was leading those who were saying no more abandonment of socialist policies in order to save the pound. I expect Harold Wilson will reply to me that Tony Crosland's interpretation of the last package is unfair and that it is not really a deflation. But the next package will be; and therefore what happens during this recess is all-important.

Of course, it is possible that the exchange rate will steady up after the House has gone into recess. If you have a tiny majority the instability it presents to the outsider is a bad factor. So when Parliament disappears for the recess and the instability is not demonstrated day by day at Westminster, the pound will stand a much better chance. Already I begin to feel it now, with everybody getting out and away. We have taken a terrible beating; and our own people are disheartened and the press is utterly vicious. Terrible times. We can still pick up but I am pretty sure we wouldn't be able to pick up after the next package Callaghan wants to put through in defence of sterling.

Saturday, August 7th
Harold Macmillan once said to me, 'When you have got a really good speech deliver it time after time until all of it gets printed.' So I have had a press release done, and approved by the Dame, repeating a speech I made last weekend on local authority housing and Peter Brown made sure the press, the radio and television were all present at Dawley New Town on Friday morning.

Getting all this done after Cabinet on Thursday has been a terrible rush. I just caught the 7.10 at Paddington and had a very pleasant dinner with the Dame, during which we went over a whole number of difficult decision cases — the planning permission for the Woburn Sands brickworks in particular.[1]

We were met at Shrewsbury by the deputy town clerk and taken straight to the Judge's Lodgings where we were spending the night. After fourteen years, the Dame knows how to work these things — no hotels for us. In each of the county towns there are Judge's Lodgings, paid for by the local authorities, where the judges stay in great creature-comfort on their twice-yearly circuits. The Shrewsbury one is a magnificent house, magnificently appointed with a magnificent steward, and we were looked after very well.

[1] See p. 310.

On Friday morning we drove out of Shrewsbury in exquisite weather, with the Wrekin on the one side, Church Stretton on the other and the Welsh hills far behind. It was a country recovering from the battering of rain and wind. Dawley corporation is in a characteristic phase of New Towning. There are more than a hundred staff in a large country house, each with his own car, and not a single house built or even in prospect. It was my job to put over a complete change of plan, the result of the publication of the West Midlands Review last week and the recommendation that Oakengates and Wellington, the old iron-ore area adjacent to Dawley, should also be developed for Birmingham overspill. I had to persuade the corporation to accept the idea that the area designated to them was the wrong one and that we should have a completely new New Town area, including Oakengates and Wellington, and probably a new name. At midday we reached the little town of Dawley where the press was gathered and I did my piece. Then we had lunch with all the local authority people concerned, councillors from Wellington, councillors from Oakengates, councillors from the Shropshire County Council. It was a buffet lunch and I was very skilfully steered round to talk to each section separately.

During the afternoon I began to realize how mad the old concept of Dawley New Town had been. I first visited the ravine of the Severn, spanned by the famous Iron Bridge – the first iron bridge in the country; it was at Ironbridge that Coalport china used to be made and the Darbys made their original discovery, how to smelt iron using coal. It is a curious bit of country, neither agricultural nor urban, but the area of perhaps the oldest industrial revolution in the whole country. People of this part have been miners and small smelters for more than two hundred years and it seemed to me crazy that the Ministry should have selected it as the site for the New Town, if only because the uneven surface is riddled with mining subsidence. And it is even odder now to add to it Wellington and Oakengates where some forty thousand people live, most of them in extremely dilapidated surroundings. I suppose the aim of the Dame was to choose an area which wasn't agricultural. Money could have been no object in her mind since it will cost a fortune to turn this into a modern urban area. As we went round I churned over in my mind once more the relative merits of the New Town technique developed by the Dame and the town development technique as exemplified by the G.L.C. working in collaboration with Hampshire and Basingstoke. The New Town is far the more ambitious concept but it is autocratic and can be completely dominated by the Ministry of Housing. But town development is essentially a local government affair, and I like it better because it is responsible to elected bodies. I am sure that at the back of the Dame's mind is the idea that unless the Ministry runs and controls the new building the local authorities will fall down on their job; and so she sets up these expensive New Town corporations. She is certainly worshipped in them wherever she goes.

I spent forty minutes at Oakengates with the local Labour Party, who enjoyed having the Minister to tea, and then drove back to the Judge's Lodgings at Shrewsbury for dinner with selected members of Shropshire County Council to discuss both the changed plan for the New Town and the West Midlands Review. The result of the evening was that the county representatives virtually accepted the Dame's New Town concept, even though I warned them that making a really big New Town of 200,000 people would mean very wide incursions into agricultural land. Of course we paid the price for their consent. When we came to consider their proposals for 'redistricting' Shropshire I quickly gave in and let them have what they wanted.

Then I got myself motored back to Banbury late at night. Looking at the morning papers today I realize that at my press conference I had at last got my point across. The speech was a lead story in *The Times* and the *Telegraph*. And I had for once been quite helpful to the Chancellor because I had emphasized the severity of the squeeze on local government projects for new town halls and swimming-baths, and argued that cutting back their luxury building would have a good effect on housing. This is jolly good socialism and it is also good sense; and it helps Mr Callaghan.

Sunday, August 8th
Walking round the farm I realized that in the last three or four days our weather had picked up. When I left here last Monday the farm was water-logged and the hay was rotting all around us. Now, with the better weather, we have got wonderfully green grass and wheatfields, battered and stormed on last week, but really beginning to ripen. I shouldn't think there has been a year when more hay has been lost by the farmers around us. We have got some good silage but not much hay and our men have just had to fill in time hedging and ditching. Poor Pritchett is very depressed but these last four days his morale has been picking up.

Meanwhile I can look forward to the first week of the recess when I get down to work in the Department. First the Rent Bill: having got it through the Commons I tended to put it aside. Nevertheless, it is by far the most important thing I have done and it was interesting last week to see its passage through the Lords. I think I have recorded how on the Second Reading I was praised for my courage by their Lordships in a highly embarrassing way. Then came the Committee State during which the Government had three defeats that will have to be dealt with when the Lords amendments come back to us at the end of the recess. Of course, we could have got it through the Lords and also dealt with the amendments in the Commons before we broke up for the summer. I considered the possibility but turned it down because I wanted an extra two months to plan the implementation of Part II of the Bill, the part that sets up the rent officers and the rent committees. One of the things I was able to do last week, by the way, was to announce the four key members of the London rent assessment committee, who, if our plan works out, will be setting the precedents in their decisions for all the other rent assessment committees in the country. Littlewood, the chairman, is now backed by two members of the Milner Holland Committee, Pilcher and Donnison, as well as by Edwards, who was the Deputy Valuer for the Government. Together they form a pyramid of respectability.

During August I must get down to the job of collecting names of suitable people to man the committees in the provinces. One thing I have discovered about government is how difficult it is either to find time for this oneself or to get one's colleagues to help one. Take Liverpool for instance. I have asked and asked, but I have only got one name out of Bessie Braddock and no suggestions out of Arthur Irvine.[1] I shall go to the Prime Minister and no doubt he will give me something. Nearer home, I am getting Butterworth, the Vice-Chancellor of Warwick University, over to lunch today and I am sure he will give me a few names for the Birmingham area. As for Coventry I have at least got the right rent officer, Dodson, who used to be the head of the local housing department. But when one sees how patronage is organized in other countries it is amazing how unorganized it is here. And as a result the Dame is getting her way on these selections. If I haven't got ideas, she always has names to put in and of course the people she suggests are extremely establishment-minded.

In the Ministry this August I hope to get ahead with preparing the legislation for the autumn Session: my Bill on housing finance and my two Bills on local government finance, plus the White Paper on housing which will provide the basis for my speech at the Labour Party Conference. When I said I wanted to stay throughout August the Dame complained; but she is valiant, she *is* staying on with me. We are terribly short-staffed; indeed, last week when I talked about preparations for the White Paper they very nearly struck—until I said I would do it myself, which grappled them down to support me.

Sunday, August 22nd

On Tuesday we are due to start our holiday in Polzeath where we have borrowed Wilfred Cave's cottage.[2] Since I last wrote in this diary I have been tidying up after the Callaghan squeeze Statement and trying to prepare legislation for the autumn. Tidying up after the squeeze meant issuing a directive to the local authorities on how to reduce public expenditure. That was done by the Department. As for preparing for the autumn, frankly it hasn't been possible. So many officials have been away and the Dame has been so tired that I have achieved very little by staying in London. On the other hand, it has been interesting to see how the office runs in a routine period and so to understand its working rather better.

[1] Labour M.P. for Edge Hill, Liverpool, since 1947. He was Solicitor-General 1967–70.
[2] One of the biggest and most successful farmers in the south-west, and an enthusiastic supporter of land nationalization. An ardent socialist, he failed to get into Parliament as candidate for Devizes, but continued to work on Labour's policy committees.

I have, however, been able to get through a number of difficult decisions. For example, I have quashed on appeal a surcharge on eight Oxfordshire councillors made by the district auditor. But perhaps the most difficult case was a proposal to build a huge brick kiln with an enormous chimney at Aspley Guise and Woburn Sands, which I knew so well during the war. By some extraordinarily ironical luck an Alkali Inspector, who was also acting as technical assessor, sent in an outrageous report of the inquiry where the decision was given in favour of the firm. Directly I read it through I knew I would cancel the inquiry, make the Ministry bear the bill, and set up a new inquiry with an independent technical assessor. I had tremendous resistance from the Dame and the Department, but it happened. Ideally, I would like to have refused planning permission altogether but I am afraid there would have been an appalling bill for compensation if I had overridden the Inspector's report.

With the Department running so quietly I have been able to stay a good deal at home and do a series of pleasant official visits. I had an excellent day last week with the children at Corby, studying open-cast iron-ore mining. Of course, we have a little open-cast iron-ore mining here in Oxfordshire where the churches are golden brown. Up in Corby the villages are white like the Cotswolds because the iron-ore is a layer under a tier of white limestone. My main interest was to see the way they make the land good and rehabilitate it after it has been scooped out in those enormous trenches, 100 to 140 feet deep, by diggers and winders which are reckoned to be the largest in the whole world. The children loved seeing them and actually sitting in them as they padded along like prehistoric monsters.

Over lunch I was reminded of how it was that these admirable arrangements for rehabilitating the countryside came about. It all arose from Hugh Dalton's visit in 1950 when for a short time he was Minister of Town and Country Planning.[1] He happened to visit Corby, and returned to London saying that it looked as frightful as the Mountains of the Moon and something had to be done about it. Out of this the Department evolved the Act of 1951. Under this Act a special fund was established into which Stewarts and Lloyds, the steelmakers, have to pay three-farthings for each ton they mine. The Treasury puts in its three-farthings and thereby the fund is built up for restoring the land at a cost of something like £300 an acre. As a result of this unique arrangement, there is the happiest relationship between the producers, the county council, who previously had the whole responsibility for dealing with the derelict land, our own Inspectorate of Mines and, last but not least, the farmers of the area, who get paid for the use of their land and have it fully restored.

[1] Economist and barrister, Labour M.P. for Peckham from 1924 to 1960, when he became a life peer. He died in 1962. He held several Cabinet posts, and was most notably the Minister for Economic Warfare 1940–42, President of the Board of Trade 1942–5, and Chancellor of the Exchequer 1945–7.

What baffles me is our failure to get similar arrangements for other forms of open-cast mining, especially for gravel pits. The problem of restoring the wreckage caused by gravel removal covers huge areas of the country, especially in the Thames Valley, and in fact some 200 million tons of gravel are extracted every year. Of course in the case of iron-ore, where the seam which you remove is only 4 feet deep and the trench you cut 140 feet deep, most of what you take out can be put back and the problem of restoration is that much easier. In the case of gravel, far more is taken away and the hole you leave is therefore far bigger. That's why I have been thinking for ages about my blue-belt idea. When I asked at the Ministry they told me, as I expected, that this problem has been referred to an official committee.

From Corby we drove on next day across Northampton, Rutland and Nottingham into the Peak District, where we stayed the night at Matlock. The weather had improved and we had a lovely day for seeing something both of the scenery and of the problems of the National Park. Appalling damage has been done to it by limestone quarrying, mainly for cement manufacture or for I.C.I. Something is now being done to prevent the worst effects on the landscape by placing the quarrying chimneys carefully. Nevertheless, this is the only industry in the area and it is allowed to do enormous damage without any serious attempt at restoration. Indeed, touring with the officials I found their main complaint a little surprising. They told me that their trouble is that the Peak district lies within fifty miles of over half the population – the people who live in Lancashire, Yorkshire, Derbyshire and the Black Country. So they get masses of pot-holers. But what they would really like, in order to keep the National Park looking nice, is the high-class guest, and of course the high-class guest won't stay there until there are high-class hotels. And the high-class hotels won't come there until there are high-class guests. *That* is their unsolved dilemma!

The other big event of the month was the conference at Churchill College, Cambridge, where we laid the foundations for our Centre for Environmental Studies.[1] It lasted for four days and we had a pretty distinguished company – as architects, Hugh Wilson and Robert Matthew from Edinburgh;[2] as town planner, Bor from Liverpool;[3] as economists, Teddy Jackson and David Worswick.[4] The Ministry was represented by Richard Llewelyn-Davies, who brought with him Professor Peter Self. Ford had sent a Japanese, a Dutchman and a very high level American professor. I found Churchill College itself absolutely unbearable to live in. It has obviously been designed at great expense by architects who hated college life or else knew nothing about it. It was rather ironical to discuss architecture and the planning of the environment

[1] See p. 237.
[2] Professor of Architecture 1953–68, President of the International Union of Architects 1961–5.
[3] Liverpool city architect 1962–6, and a member of P.A.G. 1964–5. He became a partner in Llewelyn-Davies Weeks in 1969.
[4] Director of the National Institute of Economic and Social Research since 1965.

in such a ghastly place and to sleep in a room where I had to get into the cupboard while undressing in order not to be seen by people in the court outside and where everything had been sacrificed to gimmickiness and a rather teutonic ingenuity.

The conference went pretty smoothly and I chaired it for most of the time. In the middle I went up to London, but came back to chair the concluding session. What made it worth while was that although everybody, being experts, came there with fairly set ideas, the conference really made us think. There were the people who wanted a research council on the pattern of the Medical Research Council; then there were those who insisted on an institute like the N.I.E.S.R.; and third, and not least, we had the Ford people, who simply wanted another organization like those they had already established in France and Japan. The Ministry sided with the Ford Foundation representatives. We urged we should press for an institution which was not attached to a university and which didn't do its own research. Its function would be to channel money to those doing research in the universities without arousing their suspicion and also to provide a forum for confrontation and libraries and information. If we get the £750,000 Ford grant which we are aiming for, I think I shall be able to claim that as Minister I had a great deal to do with the establishment of this institute.

After the conference I went up to London to give Margaret Green her party. She is the civil servant whose work has exclusively been arranging my appointments and she is now getting married to a fourth-year student and is therefore leaving my Private Office. I told her she could invite fifty people to a party in my room and I made it pretty slap-up. The Dame was rather taken aback and didn't come, but J. D. Jones and Waddell both put in an appearance and added tone.

Under John Delafons the Private Office is now running with extraordinary efficiency. He started wildly enthusiastic for me. He is not quite so wildly enthusiastic now but he has developed into a really outstanding Private Secretary. I have succeeded in making one change by insisting on signing more answers to the vast correspondence sent to the Minister or even to me personally, which is usually secreted from my eyes. But I have still failed to find someone who can write a personal reply from me in my own style, and that limits the number I can sign. I have managed to devolve London housing entirely on Bob Mellish and planning appeals almost entirely on Jim MacColl (only a very few important ones come up to me). I have kept entirely for myself the decisions on the recommendations of the Local Government Boundary Commission and that means taking it out of the Dame's hands.

The other change I made was that I introduced an outsider, Peter Lederer, who is still travelling around the country discovering the real building situation. He has already proved himself extremely discreet inside the Ministry and is now trying to improve our relations with the N.B.A., which is supposedly responsible to no one. Harold Macmillan found that he had to

have outside advice on building and so he brought in Percy Mills.[1] I believe
that Lederer in his own way can be just as good. I shall see a lot more of him
after the holidays when he has settled in. Indeed, I shall insist on having him
in at least once a fortnight to prime me with his news, although this will
cause cordial dislike among the civil servants.

Before Margaret's party I had received one surprising and very bad piece
of news, namely that the Council of the Building Societies Federation had
considered my national housing plan and had unreservedly turned it down.
This was the worst blow I had received since becoming Minister. The last
meeting I had with them just before Parliament broke up was first-rate and
indeed I felt confident that everyone present would go back and recommend
the Council to accept the plan in principle and help me to work out its
detail.[2] Here, however, was the letter telling me of their point-blank refusal.
The letter made it clear that it was a contested decision but also that it was
reached on political motives. Of course, I had always assumed that the
builders, whom I saw again last week, would be obstructive. But the building
societies had really been helpful and now they have gone the same way.

On reflection, however, I think I may be able to draw some advantage from
this disaster. I have probably been too innocent in the whole affair, believing
that I personally could pull it off, although the Treasury never believed it
would be possible and never wanted it, most of my colleagues didn't want it
either and the Ministry officials were sceptical. I now have the solid advantage
that I have genuinely tried to persuade the builders and the building societies
to work with me in a national housing plan. Having been turned down, I am
absolutely free to think out my own methods of fulfilling our pledge to build
half a million houses without worrying too much about working through the
building societies.

I have therefore written them a tactful letter expressing my sorrow and
regret and telling them that, whereas they can always come back to me, I
must now go ahead and work out my plan independently. I can afford to do
this with some equanimity because the chance of the private sector building
more than we allocated to them is now extremely remote. During the next
eighteen months we are likely to have a sag in private starts; and this gives me
time to build up the public sector and work out my plans. I talked all this
over with George Wigg; and before I go on holiday I shall send a note to the
Prime Minister, who is back from the Scillies next week, so that when I come
back on September 9th I shall have something concrete to discuss with him.

One other little tasty item before I forget. I have just been to lunch with

[1] Macmillan, as Minister of Housing, had appointed Percy Mills honorary adviser to his
Ministry in 1951, a position he held for a year. He had served in the Ministry of Production
during the war; and between 1950 and 1955 he was chairman of the National Research and
Development Corporation. In 1957 he was made a viscount, and was brought into
government as Minister of Power (1957–9), Paymaster-General (1959–61) and as Minister
without Portfolio (1961–2).
[2] See pp. 293–4.

Hugh Massingham[1] at the Savoy. He assured me over the phone that he didn't want to talk about politics and as soon as we sat down he said, 'I want to make you a cash offer for the use of your diary in the *Sunday Telegraph* as soon as the Labour Government collapses.' I found, by the way, that he has also made a cash offer to George Wigg for his reminiscences. I tried to explain to him that I wasn't writing for sale in that way and I probably wouldn't want to write the kind of article he would pay me a lot of money for. My diary was the basis for a serious book on the inside view of politics and was not designed as a sensational effort to cash in on topicality. I don't think be believed a word of it and his attitude only confirms my impression that Fleet Street, as well as Whitehall, has now got a settled conviction that this Labour Government isn't going to last very long.

This conviction that we have cooked our goose and that the Conservatives are coming back is being strengthened by the first effects of the Callaghan squeeze. For example, we are faced with short-time in the motor industry, and there is actually a slight rise in unemployment in the West Midlands. When Cabinet comes back for its discussion on September 9th the position of anti-deflationists like Crosland will be greatly strengthened. The Cabinet will have to face the view of people like Hugh Massingham and realize that if we really go in for a slow retardation of British industry and allow unemployment to rise to 700,000 we shall be committing political suicide.

On the other hand the immediate danger of devaluation seems to have faded away. Perhaps that has been the effect on the outside world of the Callaghan squeeze. But I suspect it is more the result of the disappearance of the M.P.s from Westminster, the disappearance of the P.M. to the Scillies and the disappearance of the public arguments between George Brown and James Callaghan. The absence of party politics has really eased the situation and certainly eased the immediate pressure on the pound. But no one can say that we are in anything but a parlous plight.

The recess was interrupted at the beginning of September when Cabinet Ministers were called to London to hear the First Secretary outline his plans for legislation to establish a compulsory early-warning system for price increases and wage claims. The voluntary policy had failed. Some Ministers thought the proposal would have small chance of success when George Brown put it to the T.U.C. General Council in Conference at Brighton on September 2nd, but after twelve hours of argument the union leaders accepted the policy by 21 votes to 6.

On the following day, however, the General Secretary of the T.U.C. General Council, George Woodcock,[2] suggested that the T.U.C. should run its own voluntary early-warning system. After much bargaining, the union leaders agreed to put a compromise plan incorporating both George Brown's and

---

[1] The novelist. He was formerly on the *Observer*.
[2] General Secretary of the T.U.C. 1960–69. He was a member of N.E.D.C. 1962–9, and chairman of the Commission on Industrial Relations 1969–71.

*George Woodcock's schemes before their members. On September 8th, the
T.U.C. voted to accept the General Council's report, by 5,251,000 to 3,312,000
votes; but the dissidents announced that they would simply ignore the voluntary
system. Moreover, the First Secretary now had to secure the approval of the
Labour Party.*

Wednesday, September 1st
We had planned our Polzeath holiday on the assumption that I should have
to go back on September 8th for the special Cabinet meeting I had demanded.
Actually I had to go on the 31st by the night train for a meeting of the
Cabinet on the 1st. This had been put forward a week mainly because it was
suddenly felt that we needed a new turn in the prices and incomes policy
before the T.U.C. General Council met. I at once asked to see Harold
Wilson before the meeting in order to discuss my troubles with the building
societies, and I got on to Jennie who in turn got on to Marcia and it was
arranged that I should have breakfast with him at 8.40 on the Wednesday
after getting into Paddington on the night train.

I dutifully clocked in and found him alone, with Mary still in the Scilly
Isles. We were rather at cross-purposes. I wanted to talk to him about housing
and he wanted to say that he wished the old firm – Benn, Wigg, Crossman and
Wilson – to get together again, and that he had decided that I should take
charge of Party propaganda policy in the liaison committee. I had known for
ages that our propaganda co-ordination was hopeless and had been insisting
that he should appoint a Minister in the Cabinet to deal with it. So I wasn't
surprised when he said, 'Of course, if it was a Minister, it would be you.
However, I don't want to have one now, though I think you have really
finished your job in Housing.' This disconcerted me because I had just begun
to settle down in the Ministry and thought that in the second year I could do
a really good job. He also made it clear that he wanted to transfer control of
immigration to my Ministry. This wouldn't suit me – or the Ministry – at all.
I said that frankly it wasn't right; the Home Secretary should be in charge of
immigration. And added that I didn't like being given the job because we
had got an incompetent Home Secretary; he ought to change the Home
Secretary. We left it there. He went on to outline to me the legislation
required for the new shift in incomes policy. Then we went downstairs at
9.30. Cabinet started at 10.30 so I just had time to go across to the office and
see what was on there.

Cabinet began with a longish, rather incoherent, review of the situation by
the Prime Minister. He said that the economic situation had greatly improved
during August and then launched into a very guarded account of the next
phase in the strengthening of sterling, which seemed to include a fresh bout of
assistance. I noticed that he told Cabinet a great deal less than he had told me
over breakfast. Then he called on Callaghan and Brown to reinforce his
account of the economic situation and explain the change in incomes policy.

Before they got going on this I intervened to say that I wanted to continue the general discussion of the economic situation. Certainly things were better now but what would happen if there was another threat to the pound? Would there be another package of deflation? When Callaghan said he didn't think this was necessary, I pointed out that though *he* didn't think it necessary there were important people outside that room who did think so. Would we be forced to do it? He said this was very insulting. But everybody in the Cabinet knew what I meant – that this new turn in incomes policy was linked with Callaghan's August visit to Washington and his talks with Fowler, the Secretary to the Treasury. It seems that Callaghan must have given Fowler assurances that in return for more dollars there would be an attempt to control wage increases.[1] But nobody else asked a question so we passed on to incomes policy.

It soon became clear that once again there had been a conflict between George Brown and Callaghan, with Callaghan fighting for his wage freeze and George Brown resisting on behalf of the unions. We gathered that they had reached a compromise: there should be statutory power not to regulate wages but only to provide early warning and delay. Here too, as usual with this Cabinet of ours, there was no real opposition. The proposals just went through and as a result the idea of increasing coal prices now, over which we had split at the previous Cabinet meeting, was simply pushed to one side as something inconceivable before the T.U.C. met and the prices and incomes policy was announced. Poor Fred Lee was left speechless, with the vast Coal Board losses piling up.

After Cabinet I had lunch with George Wigg in order to talk to him about the new job of which Harold had spoken. He at once said, 'We ought to share the chairmanship,' and I realized he felt bitterly the fact that I was to take his place. Harold had said to me that, loyal as he was to his friends, he felt George was a bit overwrought and needed a good holiday; anyway he wasn't good on propaganda policy. So he had obviously decided to remove George from this absolutely key position as the only link between the Cabinet and Transport House. Not wanting a quarrel, I agreed with George's proposal for a joint chairmanship and said I would write a minute to Harold about it. But rather characteristically George rushed round to Harold immediately I left him and I found myself summoned to No. 10 at 7 p.m., when the Prime Minister made it clear that it would be impossible to have the chairmanship shared. He wanted me to have a fortnight's holiday and then come back ready to take up new responsibilities as well as a much more intimate relationship with him.

With this at the back of my mind I went out to dinner with Thomas Balogh. I found he had seen Harold after I left and was full of this new job of mine. He also confirmed my impression that in Washington Callaghan had made a

---

[1] Wilson concedes that it was in the light of discussions with Fowler that 'we began to think in terms of statutory powers'. *Wilson*, pp. 131–2.

series of firm commitments to Fowler in return for strong American backing. It was largely in order to honour these commitments that Cabinet had been brought forward a week, so that G.B. could get authority for the new prices and incomes policy before presenting it the very next day to the General Council of the T.U.C. just before their annual Conference.

After dinner I caught the night train back to Cornwall for the rest of my holiday.

Sunday, September 12th
We had rather better weather in Cornwall than at Prescote where poor Mr Pritchett had rain every day except two. We bathed every day in bitter cold and I coined the phrase 'No man hath greater love than to bathe with his children.'

I was able to see a good deal of the chairman of the Cornwall County Council, Kim Foster, and on my last day went there for a meeting with him and a number of key officials to discuss my plan for preserving the coastline. I got the county's agreement to my ideas.

The rain was so bad that we motored home on Friday. I spent Saturday morning plodding over the farm, looking at the wheat, sodden and unripened and already widely laid in the damp fields. Today I had to be at Chequers by 9.45 for an all-day Cabinet. No one knows how to find Chequers. Thomas Balogh gave me exact details of how I could get in by the back entrance behind Great Kimble Church. When we got to Great Kimble we found two churches and finally got to the front entrance at 9.58. There must be hundreds of great country houses nicer than this. It is heavily restored and stuffy in atmosphere. After a day there one appreciates why everybody says they detest Chequers.

Before the meeting I just had time for a word with Callaghan. He had made his great statement on the Friday and obviously scored a tremendous success in beating the speculators off the pound.[1] But he had also announced that he had seen the building societies on the previous day and persuaded them not to increase their interest rates. This he had apparently done without consulting my Ministry. I asked him why, and he said, 'For political reasons. I just think the rates must not go up.' I take a very different view. If we want houses built, the building societies must get the cash in, even if the interest rates are rather high.

Today's meeting was due to Barbara's pressure for a whole day's discussion of economic policy. The Cabinet Secretariat was only present for a very short time. So I thought it worth while to make notes and record them this evening.

The first speaker was Callaghan, who of course started with his sensational success of Friday. He explained that when Fowler was in London he had

[1] On September 10th Callaghan had announced that he had secured a further $1,000 million international short-term loan.

listened to a wonderful presentation of our case by George Brown. This had so impressed him that he was ready to provide us with special financial backing. Callaghan also explained the stringent measures he was going to take to catch the speculators. He reckoned that 30 per cent of our losses were the result of speculative betting against the pound. He also said that Heath was not committed against deflation, so that we shouldn't assume that if a Conservative Government came to power it would not deflate. Altogether it was a competent report.

Harold Wilson then made a long speech. His first theme was that he thought that the right thing now was to settle down for another Queen's Speech and another Session; and to have one more year during which we should reach phase two, when we should move from defence of the pound into carrying out our positive policies. He said that no poll had been published for five weeks, a sign that things were going our way. Moreover, he himself was having excellent public meetings and so was George Brown. He was convinced in due course we would reap the benefit for our blood, tears and sweat. Churchill wasn't liked for his policy but he was respected for it. He then turned to his second theme—the parliamentary situation after the death of the Speaker.[1] Here again he thought we were coming into easier waters, since there was no prospect of another Bill as tough as the Finance Bill. 'Let's notice in passing,' he said, 'that we carried out a fiscal revolution in that Finance Bill—something we couldn't ever repeat with such a small majority.' Indeed, he seemed to hope for a dull Session in which the Tories would be embarrassed because they would have to commit themselves on a series of difficult issues. They would be having a two-day debate, for example, on the National Plan—should they oppose it? Or how should they react to the Land Commission? To our house-building policy? To rate rebates? These were all subjects which would be favourable to us this Session. Then he turned to the position of the Liberals and gave the assurance that he had had no talks with them about a pact.[2] He *had* seen Grimond on quite a different subject and then Grimond had observed that there could be no question of a Lib–Lab pact. 'Anyway,' Wilson added, 'if I had wanted one I couldn't have persuaded the Party to deliver.' He was convinced that the Liberals understood the need to postpone the election since they would be destroyed if it came early.

He then turned to the Speakership. 'We shouldn't start discussing it this

[1] Sir Harry Hylton-Foster, Conservative M.P. for the Cities of London and Westminster since 1959, had collapsed and died on September 2nd. Labour's majority would be unimpaired if they could secure not only the election as Speaker of Dr Horace King, Labour M.P. for Southampton since 1950, but also the election as deputy Speaker of Roderic Bowen, Liberal M.P. for the County of Cardigan since 1945. The Conservatives threatened to oppose Bowen's candidacy so that the Government would be obliged to lose the deputy Speakership to another of their back-benchers.

[2] The Government's dependence on the ten Liberal M.P.s to provide a deputy Speaker, which would maintain their tiny majority, had nourished speculation about a Lib-Lab pact.

morning,' he said. 'I am not going to meet Heath or Grimond about it. It is a House of Commons matter. If the Tories want to do some political manœuvring, let them discredit themselves. The Labour Party should leave it to negotiations between the Whips and we should keep our hands clear.'

He ended up with a warning about reflation. 'In our last Cabinet,' he said, 'when we were discussing incomes policy I myself talked of the possibility of reflation if deflation went too far. But we must be careful not to go too fast in this direction. Certainly we should concentrate on growth factors such as housing, and certainly we must turn the easier months which are coming to our advantage. Is this euphoric?' he concluded. 'No, I don't think so.'

George Brown said we were exaggerating the 'browned-offness' of the electorate. 'At my meetings I don't find any signs of it.' Then he turned to the new situation and repeated Harold Wilson's warning: we must be careful not to give the impression of switching suddenly from deflation to reflation. He then went on to the question Wilson had raised of going on for another year. 'Of course we should,' he said, 'but how should we handle the Parliamentary Party during that period? That's a difficult question. Why not a Beaver Hall[1] meeting before we get back to that dreadful place. Yes, I think it is a dreadful place, the House of Commons. Demoralizing, discrediting. I am not so optimistic about the parliamentary situation as Harold Wilson. I don't believe that the Tories are going to let us get our Bills through as easily as that. We mustn't underestimate the Opposition.' Next came Anthony Greenwood, who hardly ever speaks in Cabinet. Like Barbara Castle a little later, he made delicate left-wing hints about apathy in the Party and our failure to get our policy across, and he warned us of Conference difficulties.

At this point Wilson interjected very quickly that if there were faults in public relations—and there certainly were—the first way to deal with them was to see that our Ministers no longer made purely departmental pronouncements but became more political and made more political speeches every weekend. All of us, he said, had been far too Department-conscious. We must turn back into politicians.

Barbara took the Greenwood line. First of all there must be no abdication of socialist principle. If we are going to be thrown out we must be kicked out. Our real trouble is that we do things at the expense of our principles, and she illustrated this with three examples: the squeeze, immigration and Vietnam. She finally warned us of the danger of putting forward the incomes policy as something we had to do to appease the bankers. This was said in reply to something George Brown said in an August meeting. He had remarked that trade-union leaders were unwilling to accept the incomes policy on its merits and had actually asked him to present it as a necessary condition for satisfying the bankers. It would be disastrous, Barbara said, if it were put to the public in this way. Our incomes policy must be presented as a policy looking

---

[1] A large hall in the City of London where, in 1945, at the first meeting of the Parliamentary Labour Party, the new Labour M.P.s met Attlee and adopted him as leader.

forward to the new phase, not back to the old crisis. Then she asked what we could do to demonstrate our adherence to socialist principles. She quoted, once more, three examples: (1) If steel nationalization must be postponed, we should start buying equities in those industries which we aided. (2) We should impose sanctions against South Africa. (3) We should channel more of our aid through the U.N. (I found these a pretty feeble collection of left-wing demands.) She concluded by remarking that the Government is at the mercy of any one of our conscience-stricken cranks – Jeremy Bray or Reginald Paget.[1]

Callaghan spoke next and made one of the best contributions I have heard from him. He said Barbara was right to point out our dilemma – the conflict between what is popular with our Party workers and what is popular with the electorate. But the most important thing of all is that we must believe our policy ourselves. For instance, the immigration policy, which Barbara had attacked so fiercely, must be sold to the electorate as something the Labour Government really believes in. Our theme at the next general election must be our uncompleted mission. And he added that in his view we had kept our middle-class vote and our losses had all been among the working classes. Finally he said he would like to suggest the five themes we should concentrate on in all our speeches: (1) the National Plan; (2) paying our way; (3) modernization; (4) price stabilization; (5) industrial self-discipline.

This concluded the general political discussion. Brown was then asked to make his report on the economic situation. He made five points. (1) On present policies we could only expect a 1 per cent increase in production in the next twelve months. That was why we must plan reflation. (2) We must look forward to a modest increase in unemployment. It might reach 450,000 which would be 50,000 extra and not too bad. (3) Though he could observe no down-turn in investment, there was unfortunately no evidence on modernization and there was some down-turn in orders. (4) Import controls. After a very careful study of the case for import controls and the case for a surcharge, he and his colleagues had on balance come down in favour of continuing the surcharge. (5) The press had entirely misinterpreted what had happened at the T.U.C. Conference about prices and incomes. He had put the policy to the General Council on its merits, but most of those there had been unwilling to sell it to their membership on merits and had insisted that he should talk about a crisis and an emergency which they could then use as an excuse for conceding policies they were not prepared to accept and defend on their merits. However, they all understood perfectly well that the Government would legislate irrespective of what they thought. Finally, he referred to the National Plan, which he was due to announce on Thursday, and said that

---

[1] During the recess, Paget had been threatening to resign. Jeremy Bray, M.P. for Middlesbrough since 1962, and chairman of the Labour Party Committee on Science and Technology, had left his position as George Brown's P.P.S. in order to be free to make a series of speeches attacking the Government.

it was a national not a Party plan and we wanted to destroy the Tories by keeping it strictly national.

Then came the President of the Board of Trade. Douglas Jay made one point which blew the gaff about Callaghan's dealings in the U.S.A. He pointed out to George Brown that we can't reflate this autumn without breaking the pledges which James Callaghan made to Fowler in Washington. I wasn't surprised when Callaghan solemnly intervened and said there was some misunderstanding since he had made no pledges at all to Fowler; there could be no question of this. If a denial ever completely confirmed a statement it was Callaghan's on that occasion.

Crosland replied that reflation should take the form of quietly relaxing the cuts. This stimulated Harold Wilson into one of his optimistic wriggles. 'Yes,' he said to Callaghan, 'we must move craftily. If we find things getting a little slack we must take up the slack by providing more schools and hospitals without any drums or trumpets. We mustn't have a panic reflation any more than a panic deflation.' This started a discussion of priorities – schools versus housing. Callaghan rather sensibly said we couldn't go back to where we were before the cuts. There was a lot of surplus liquid to be squeezed out of the economy. I supported him on this because I realized that to achieve a house-building rate of half a million you have got to have a pretty tight ban on the building of offices and shops.

At this point Cousins broke in with outraged indignation. 'How hypocritical can we get! The trade unions really hate your incomes policy. I myself disagree with it so utterly that I can no longer make a political speech: I can only speak on technological problems. Why can't we swing our policy away from incomes control towards productivity, following the lead which Harold Wilson gave us at Bristol last Saturday?[1] Every time I am asked what I am doing here in the Cabinet, I keep on saying to myself that I should do more good outside getting production going in the unions than sitting here. I think it's time I resigned.' This was the first time he had openly talked in Cabinet of resignation. Harold Wilson didn't brush him off: he smoothed him off. And then Ray Gunter launched into a huge attack on the hypocrisy of those who talk about productivity and do nothing to end restrictive practices. This worked Cousins up into another outburst. 'The unions won't take cuts in manpower,' he said, 'unless the employers are prepared to pay for it by putting up wages. If manpower is cut by 30 per cent, wages must go up by 30 per cent.' Jim Griffiths then began to speak, but by this time Callaghan, Wilson and Brown had all gone off to appointments and the discussion petered out.

Over lunch I talked to Barbara Castle (as fierce as ever about immigration) as well as to Bowden. Harold, alas, is still determined that I should take over immigration policy from the Home Office and he now wants me to make the

[1] On September 4th Wilson had made a speech calling for specific productivity measures, including the establishment of factory production committees.

II

speech at the annual Conference as well. Somehow I have got to get out of both.

After lunch we started with a formal report to Cabinet on foreign policy. First we were warned that U.D.I. was due at any moment in Rhodesia. We are making all preparations for it, including the possibility of sanctions. But we must face it that if we were to cut off access to the copper mines we might have a large number of unemployed in this country. The second subject on the agenda was Kashmir and the war between India and Pakistan.[1] No discussion took place on either.

So we turned back to our politics, un-minuted. First, we had a report from the Chief Whip, who said that in order to survive at all with our illness record we had to get proxy voting permitted for the sick. Second, we had to deal with the awkward people in the Party. Of these awkward people he reckoned that right-wingers such as Paget and Bray were not really a danger. Nor were the so-called 'new purists' such as Reg Freeson,[2] concerned with immigration, or men like Arthur Lewis[3] who just go berserk occasionally. The only really dangerous, erratic man who might lose us our majority was Bill Warbey. However, the Chief Whip said that given loyalty and a bit of luck we had some chance of getting through, though he didn't feel nearly as optimistic as Wilson. Wilson then turned the debate to the quite different issue of morning sittings. 'If the Tories are bloody-minded,' he said, 'and won't give us proxy voting for the sick, should we not retaliate by having Question Time at eleven o'clock in the morning and starting business of the day immediately after it, running through to the early evening, say to six or seven?' Morning sittings had been ruled out under previous Governments on the ground that Ministers simply couldn't combine them with their work. This produced half an hour of ministerial expressions of opinion. On the whole the feeling was that if we want to modernize anything, the modernization of Parliament is an excellent thing to start with; and we should now begin to decide to work through the day and stop before dinner every night. Sensing the mood of Cabinet, Harold Wilson adroitly shifted his ground. He stopped arguing that we should introduce morning sittings as a retaliation against the Tories and began to recognize that this was something that could be introduced on its own merits.

The next subject he chose to raise was steel. On this, the Chief Whip and the Lord President told us roundly that it is now impossible to get a Bill through Parliament with our small majority. Cousins then said that anyway the nationalization of the docks was far more relevant to the crisis than steel nationalization, which could be postponed. Then came a long discussion on the reasons we should give for its postponement. Should we say quite frankly

[1] Despite the negotiations of Arthur Bottomley at the C.R.O. and Harold Wilson's personal intervention, India had invaded the disputed border territory on September 6th.
[2] M.P. for Willesden since 1964.
[3] M.P. for West Ham North since 1950.

that we just couldn't get it through this Parliament or should we make a virtue of necessity and say we had come to the conclusion that dock nationalization must be given top priority and steel postponed? Fred Lee, as Minister of Power, said you couldn't just postpone a steel Bill since there had to be a policy for steel in the interim. At this point Wilson talked a great deal about the steel-masters' row with the Tory Party, and began to show only too clearly that he had been discussing with Woodrow Wyatt and other people the various possible deals that could be made with the steel-masters. There was a dangerous moment here. However, it was left that we should have a new Cabinet Committee to study docks and steel. There was no Cabinet decision for postponement, but equally there was no doubt that the Bill will be postponed and that there is no opposition in Cabinet to this happening.

It was quite an interesting day. I felt what a humdrum Cabinet we are – a gang of competent politicians. Once again Harold Wilson showed himself without a trace of vision – no Kennedy touch, not even the dynamic of Lyndon Johnson. But if the Cabinet lacks spark and originality, that doesn't prove it's a bad Cabinet, it doesn't even prove it won't win an election.

I got home at the end of a cloudy afternoon to see our two combines out on the Wardington Land on the other side of the Cherwell trying to deal with the dank, sodden corn, mostly laid.

On September 16th the Government published George Brown's National Plan, which was designed to reinvigorate the economy and stimulate the electorate's faith in Labour's economic policy. It set a target of 25 per cent increase in national output, requiring an annual average growth of 3·8 per cent over six years. This demanded an annual rise of 3·4 per cent in productivity, even when underemployment in the North and West and any overall rise in total employment were taken into account. The Plan looked for a rise in exports of 5·2 per cent a year and a reduction in the visible trade deficit to £225 million by 1970.

But industrialists' expectations now differed from those of the First Secretary, the more so in the wake of James Callaghan's restrictionist measures of July. The Plan also lacked positive incentives and seemed to rely largely on consultation between little Neddies for each industry, the National Export Council and the regional economic planning boards.

Some Ministers were pleased. Defence spending was to be limited by 1970 to £2,000 million at 1964 prices. The housing programme was to rise to half a million houses a year by 1970. There was to be 40 per cent more invested in the road programme, and education spending was to rise by a third. In the light of the Chancellor's strictures, however, this all seemed very optimistic.

Cabinet had other preoccupations in the remaining weeks of the recess. The Indo-Pakistan war was a major problem. Fighting had broken out on August 5th and by September 6th the Indians had invaded Pakistani territory. Kashmir had been an intractable problem for many years and a settlement between President Ayub Khan of Pakistan and Mr Shastri of India seemed impossible. Both were pressed by nationalist groups at home. The British Government supported the U.N. Security Council's call for a return to the ceasefire line, but risked losing the confidence of both sides in its failure to intervene on behalf of either. The situation became even more worrying when the Chinese Government threatened India on September 17th. However, on September 20th, both Pakistan and India sulkily agreed to a ceasefire.

Monday, September 13th

Back to the Ministry after my holidays. The Dame is away on holiday for a whole month and it will be very pleasant running myself in. Though I shall miss her dynamism and drive in Whitehall, I shall find it much easier to work direct to Waddell and Jones. I got down straight away to checking on all the multifarious things I have undertaken—historic buildings for example, and the Meadow road at Oxford, and the Packington estate at Islington (where we are in a hell of a mess because we have objected on architectural grounds to a building which is to be built by an architect of our own choice).[1] Then there are the latest of my local boundary decisions—at Gloucester where I may lose Jack Diamond's seat if I don't get it right, at Teesside, where I am creating a huge new county borough, and at Tyneside where I am planning to move towards a Greater Newcastle in October. I am also checking on the trouble about the Alkali Inspector at the Woburn Sands inquiry.

Considering the instability of the political situation, the Department works for me dutifully. We spent some time preparing for the meeting with the building societies which is due tomorrow. This has been called at the request of Donald Gould, this year's chairman of their council, to reconsider their total repudiation of my plan at their August meeting. While I have been on holiday tremendous efforts have been made by the building societies and inside the Department to get this decision reversed, and at least to get the ten big building societies, who do 80 per cent of the business, lined up in principle behind the scheme.

In the evening I strolled round to the Athenaeum in order to discuss propaganda policy with Wedgwood Benn before going to Tommy Balogh's home to continue to talk on the same subject. I intended this as a quiet beginning to my new life as chairman of the liaison committee. One side of the work is liaison with Transport House on current political issues. On the other is the production of the outline election manifesto, and that is what I was discussing with Benn and Balogh. But it is the last thing we can admit we are discussing because if we do, Len Williams at Transport House will say that we are trespassing on the Party privilege. Each time the manifesto is written its first draft has to be done secretly. Last time it was written by Peter Shore and myself, and then the draft was formally presented to the Executive as though it were entirely the work of the Transport House staff.

[1] A public inquiry had been called by the Minister in February 1965 on the proposed redevelopment of this part of Islington.

I found that Balogh and Benn had each produced a good paper on the themes we need. I agreed that, having considered them together, we should now wait until after the decisive event—George Brown's launching of his National Plan on Thursday of this week. How the Plan went over would, I thought, be decisive for our future line. If it was a success with the press and welcomed by our Conference as well, that would fix the central theme for our current propaganda as well as for the election manifesto.

Thursday, September 14th
The conference with the building societies was held in our big conference-room at the top of the stairs on the first floor. The routine is that when they are all in attendance, sitting round the huge table, the little door from my room is unlocked. The Minister walks through and they all stand up and wait until he has taken his place at the centre of the table. I am getting used to this little bit of pomp which Ministers of Housing have to put up with. I had decided to conduct the whole proceedings myself and after sitting down, with Bob Mellish on my right, at once made a very carefully prepared speech—a real speech—presenting to them the whole idea of George Brown's National Plan and showing them the role they could play in the section devoted to housing. I indicated the dangers they faced by not coming in and the inference that the insurance companies and the local authorities, who had already agreed to participate, would draw if they were self-excluded. It was laid out as objectively as possible but with due emphasis on two things: (1) my plan is a plan for expansion in house production and is primarily concerned to increase the production of owner-occupied houses; (2) we only build council houses where it is clear they are needed, and we are prepared to assess that need objectively. My aim was to make owner-occupation a possibility for a whole group of average and below-average workers at present excluded because they can't afford the current mortgage rates. The meeting was very formalized. Two or three questions followed my speech—rather obviously prepared and over-rehearsed. Then Donald Gould read aloud a resolution they had passed that morning, when the big ten had met and decided in principle to accept my plan. That was for me something of an anti-climax. So all my efforts had been wasted: they had already made their decision before they had heard my speech. Cohen of the Alliance and Potter of the Halifax had been the chief supporters of the chairman, Donald Gould, in working for the reversal.

However, the speech wasn't really wasted. Afterwards, Newton of the Leek & Westbourne said to me, 'This is the first time a Minister has ever called the building societies in to consult about a major issue of housing policy.' I think that's fair. From the very start I have personally had to sell my ideas of the national housing plan to people who didn't believe in it, first and foremost my own Department (apart from Peter Brown) and then to the Treasury, the building societies and, most difficult of all, the builders.

In the evening I worked on until 7.30, tidying up in my office, and then went home by the 8 p.m. train to be ready to go to Warwick University early on tomorrow morning.

Wednesday, September 15th
Anne and I motored over to Warwick University, which is in a very pleasant Coventry suburb. Astounding progress has been made there in twelve months. They are using very modern techniques of industrialized building and the new sections are being run up incredibly quickly. I found it difficult talking to Jack Butterworth, who is a very old friend, because I knew too much about the relations between Warwick University and the city authorities. When I was Shadow Science Minister I became more and more convinced that one of the biggest jobs for the next Labour Secretary of State for Education was to break down the rigid division between higher education and further education and institute a unitary approach as against the existing binary approach. At that time I saw this extremely clearly in Coventry itself. It seemed obvious that one should try and integrate the Lanchester College of Technology, the new university and the first-rate teacher training college which for years has been on the site adjacent to the university campus. Indeed, one of the last things I did before the election was to ask Harold Wilson to come down and make a speech at the Lanchester *against* the binary policy, although I knew that officials in the Ministry were firmly committed to it. Alas! in 1964 when Michael Stewart took over, he quietly accepted the departmental line because there was nothing in the Party policy about committing us to repeal it. When Michael went and Tony replaced him I felt it was unfair to intervene, since I remembered how much I resented any intervention by Michael Stewart in my rents problem (he had been Shadow Minister of Housing). But I was disappointed to hear that he had decided to maintain the binary system, and I was greatly disconcerted when I learnt later on that he was by no means convinced in his own mind that it was right. I have always wondered since then whether he mightn't have changed his mind if I had really gone in to bat when he first took over.

Still, those are all speculations which one shouldn't waste time on. I had an excellent time with Butterworth, and informal talks with a number of his staff. I safely caught the 3.20 train and was up in time for my first meeting of the liaison committee at 6 in George Wigg's room.

Taking over as chairman was tricky because Transport House was deeply suspicious of me and George himself is a most erratic, difficult, crabby man. I went away after an hour and a half feeling fairly depressed, saying to myself, 'Well, I have either asserted my authority or I have got myself into an unholy row.' I was sure I had got Marcia Williams's support but I wasn't sure of much else.

I found it difficult to keep my attention fully on the meeting because of something which had happened just before I went across to Palace Yard.

Into my office came copies of the *Evening Standard* and the *Evening News*, each containing the announcement that the London boroughs had jointly decided on a common policy of requiring a five-year residence qualification for anybody to get a council house in Greater London. This shocked me. And not only that: I had spent a great deal of time working out a speech I was due to deliver on Thursday morning to the annual meeting of the Institute of Housing Managers in Brighton, which contained a slashing attack on the reactionary attitude many housing authorities display to immigrants and the point that cities laying down a five- or six-year residence qualification were objectively committing racial discrimination. Peter Brown and Bob Mellish were in a state of great excitement about the speech. All I knew was that the press release I had prepared would not do as it would be regarded by everyone as a direct reaction by the Minister to the announcement from the boroughs.

I had to leave the liaison committee meeting in order to go across to No. 10 for a cocktail party Harold was giving to the industrial correspondents. I stayed about ten minutes, long enough for Geoffrey Goodman[1] to tell me that he thought the reaction to George Brown's National Plan would be lousy. The press had had the plan that day and had been working on it in preparation for Thursday morning.

From Downing Street I went on to Crosland's house where I had a most amiable evening with him and his wife Susan—so delightful that I talked politics far too freely and felt a delicious, racy, scandalized joy in doing so.

Thursday, September 16th
I stayed awake most of last night for fear I would miss getting up early enough to catch the 8.24 to Brighton. As a result I was ready at 8.05, waiting outside the door with my papers, eager to start writing my speech in the train. At 8.20 Molly hadn't turned up and I realized that she had been very late the night before and must have overslept. So I had to get another car, missed the train and was late for the meeting. It didn't matter too much because the president was making a few remarks when I arrived, but I had to speak cold and from notes which didn't make the impact my hard-hitting press release would have had.

In the afternoon came my key Cabinet meeting on local government finance. I'd wanted to introduce a major reform of rating, and at first thought it would be possible to find new forms of local taxation—a local income tax, for example, or a share of the motor tax. When it was clear that I wasn't going to get my way here against the Chancellor, Bruce Fraser came up with an ingenious formula for relating the increase of rates to the increase of the national product and so enabling the Exchequer to take more of the cost. I had to accept this, and all I could do in Cabinet was to insist that in addition I should get rate rebates and a special short Bill in which to introduce them. Whereas the long Bill in the next Session would be uncontroversial and

[1] Industrial correspondent of the *Daily Mirror*.

dominated by Treasury thinking, at least the short Bill would be mine.[1] This policy was approved in principle. The big paper was a Bruce Fraser paper moved by Callaghan, and I must admit that I had virtually had no impact on it. Whitehall has got the rating reform it wanted, partly of course because it coincides with our Party policy to shift the burden of rates from the local taxpayer to the centre, and partly because there hasn't been enough time for creative political thinking to force a change.

Callaghan was eager to get some kudos for himself and he introduced our joint paper without any reference to me. Fortunately, he showed that he didn't understand it perfectly, and I was able to correct him and then go on to say that I had committed myself to rate rebates in my negotiations with the city treasurers and couldn't now hold back. So I did manage to get my own small Bill out of him. I also got an informal agreement that rate rebates would be financed 75 per cent by the Treasury.

After we had finished with rating we turned back to Kashmir, where the situation had grown extremely serious now that China has come in on the side of Pakistan and sent India an ultimatum. Listening to this debate I began to wonder whether we weren't behaving like the Liberal Government in 1914 before Sarajevo. In 1914 Sarajevo was as far away from London as Nepal is today. If the Chinese actually go to war with the Indians, the Americans will come to the help of India and the war with China might then be extended to Vietnam; Britain might be committed as well and a world war might be in the offing. But there is nothing we can do about it, we are too weak. However, the main feeling of Cabinet was an enormous sense of relief that we had got over our Chequers meeting on Sunday with only one leak—in the *Financial Times*. Moreover, it was obvious that the pound was now bounding ahead despite the extremely bad trade figures published last week. We all felt that we had turned the corner. It was also clear that Conservative ebullience was beginning to wear off. That morning we had read in the newspapers that the N.O.P. poll showed Labour in the lead and I gather that the Gallup poll tomorrow will show the parties dead even.

What we need now to complete our satisfaction is the successful launching of George Brown's National Plan this evening, and that is what we are all waiting for. Since I have only just been made chairman of the liaison committee it was far too late for me to take over from George Wigg, who has done a tremendous job in making sure that the First Secretary appears on the greatest possible number of TV and radio programmes as well as making a Ministerial broadcast. Earlier on, Transport House had decided that he must go on *This Week*[2] because the B.B.C. had turned down a Ministerial broadcast as unsuitable.[3] Thank heavens, George Wigg got this decision reversed.

[1] To distinguish between these two Bills, the short Bill is called the Rating Bill and the long Bill, the Local Government Bill.

[2] The Thames TV current affairs programme.

[3] The B.B.C. were anxious to pare down the number of Ministerial broadcasts as they required replies and comment from the other Parties and so disrupted television schedules.

As a result he had caused maximum irritation in the B.B.C. but he has got George a jolly good showing on all the media.

It so happened that James Callaghan had, to my great surprise, invited me to a buffet supper. It was the first occasion on which I had been invited to an evening party at No. 11 — or for that matter at No. 10. I was curious to know what it would be like. It started with us sitting round rather gingerly in that large, comfortable drawing-room decorated by Mrs Maudling when she was the Chancellor's wife. There we sat, eating royal venison and drinking a very sweet white wine. The Chancellor certainly has a far nicer house to live in than the Prime Minister, for the simple reason that Harold's state rooms are too large to be used and his penthouse is a miserable string of servants' bedrooms. Callaghan has only one state room but has a much larger number of rooms in his house for domestic purposes. Sitting there, I felt I couldn't stick living in furnished rooms with somebody else's paintings in them and everything borrowed. As for the company, we were a typical Labour Party gathering, which gave us a pre-taste of the Blackpool hotels when Conference starts in a few days' time. We discussed each other's children, but conversation was a bit difficult and it was a great relief when we were able to crowd round and watch George Brown on TV. I must say that when Cabinet discussed the National Plan I was inclined to swallow Geoffrey Goodman's verdict that it would be a flop. However, as I watched George on the TV it was clear that he was doing well and putting Ted in a fix. For even before he had time to read the Plan, Heath had let it be announced that he regarded it as a political gimmick. He had also made another mistake by putting Iain Macleod on to reply to George Brown with a purely vindictive party speech, whereas someone like Maudling would have dealt with the Plan on its merits. So it seemed to me that we were getting off on the right foot. We were behaving as a truly national party putting a National Plan forward, while the Tories were spluttering in party-minded opposition. That was all to the good.

When Harold Collison and I were saying goodbye, Callaghan turned to me and said, 'I am glad you were able to come, Dick, because I decided to have a party today for all the members of the National Executive we haven't yet entertained.' So that was why I was there!

Friday, September 17th
The morning press confirmed that George had done a first-rate job in launching the Plan. Now I had to put the housing section of that Plan across. It had suddenly occurred to me on Wednesday that with the National Plan released we should need on Saturday a statement on housing, however brief. Peter Brown worked away at it on Thursday, and today I held a press conference and put out the statement in which we explained how we were actually going to achieve our half-million target.

In the evening I was due in Coventry for a G.M.C. meeting with council members present. I knew the Coventry Labour Party was longing to grill their Minister so I went down with a copy of the Plan and my housing hand-out and found some forty-five people gathered in the council chamber after tea. I concentrated on the National Plan and the target of half a million houses. Though most of them had come determined to maul me and to get their Member down, by the end of the meeting they were, as often happens in Coventry, half-willingly raped by me into thinking 'Well, dammit, Dick did make a pretty good case and we couldn't really answer it.' Then at last I could go home.

Sunday, September 19th
This is an absolutely perfect autumn day after another disastrous harvesting week. Pritchett still has to do a bit of a field across the river as well as the Long Meadow and the big bank of oats before he completes the worst harvest in Prescote history. I wouldn't be surprised if we were a couple of thousand pounds down on our corn; and I now suspect we have made a mistake in turning ourselves into a limited liability company as we shan't be able to consolidate my income with these losses and ease income tax.

Yesterday was a brilliant, wonderful afternoon with huge storm clouds coming over, which made it even more beautiful. For the first time this year the children could be out in the cornfields, riding on the combine or riding on the sledge behind the bailer, or climbing up into the tanker and bathing in the corn as it was tipped out of the combine, or even going into the big barn and playing by the big drier. Privileged children who are allowed to play in a modern industrialized harvest do have a lovely time.

However, I had a very difficult morning at the village school. Months ago I had insisted on a school managers' meeting this September 18th because I had been appalled to discover that all last year no meetings had been called because the vicar was too lazy. As a result, the money for our school extension was not included in last year's estimates. I suggested the vicar should tell Oxford that owing to all these delays we insisted on having an architect at our managers' meeting in September, and that he should warn the architect that the Minister of Housing would be there. I know it was unfair but it had the desired effect. A very nice Mr Smith turned up with plans for two new class-rooms, lavatories, a better staff-room and a new garage, and we spent the morning discussing them with him. Now I think there is really some chance of getting the playground done next April and the extension finished by next September.

Monday, September 20th
My first job when I got back to the office was to deal with the press leak about my new position as chairman of the liaison committee. The story had been started by Walter Terry in the *Daily Mail*; but all the other papers had picked it up from the first edition, getting more information as they went along. So the damage had been done. I pointed out straight away to George and

Harold that I had taken the job on the condition that it was confidential and I couldn't possibly do it now. I further pointed out that the National Executive would be furious; and it was agreed that I would not be able to take the chair on Wednesday. The more I look at it the more relieved I am. It would have been a difficult job and it is a good thing I am out of it.

Tuesday, September 21st
The day of my speech to the A.M.C. annual conference at Torquay. I had to prepare the speech yesterday and go down last night because I was speaking first thing in the morning. I had previously agreed with the Department that I would speak on two topics: local government press relations; and the ethics of the councillor. However, yesterday I suddenly decided that I would add a third topic, the reform of local government; and I would announce that the situation was now getting unworkable and I was thinking of winding up the Local Government Boundary Commission. What should the next step after that be? I called in J. D. Jones, who was very good indeed, and with his advice I came to the conclusion that I should propose a committee of inquiry with very great authority and with terms of reference that instructed it to lay down the principles of local government reform. I rang up Harold to tip him off that I was going to do this and he liked the idea. There was a great rush to finish before I caught the train with John Delafons. We were met at the station at eleven o'clock by Francis Hill, the secretary of the A.M.C., and taken back to the hotel for a drink. In the early morning I prepared the final draft fitting the new section in with the old sections, and I delivered it at eleven, answering questions for a full hour afterwards and getting something like a standing ovation. I was quite sure that I had done well.

Wednesday, September 22nd
A glance at the newspapers this morning proved that I had done well. The White Paper on the Land Commission was released yesterday and I had knocked it off the centre page of *The Times*.[1] Once again I was forcing the pace and had made a definite advance in Government policy without consulting my Cabinet colleagues. This will make it possible to include the reform of local government in our next Party manifesto, which could be quite important to us in the electoral campaign.

The fiasco about the liaison committee has certainly brought me closer to Harold Wilson. I am sure now that he wants to have the old firm working together. But he is still showing as much nervousness in asserting his authority as he did when he was leader of the Opposition. He certainly hasn't changed for the worse in his personal relations—he is still as unassuming, as straightforward, as sensitive and also as tough as he ever was. But neither has he

---

[1] The White Paper proposed that the maximum levy on the development value of land disposed of for building should be 40 per cent. But the Minister intended this to rise to 45 per cent and, eventually, to 50 per cent.

grown into his job in the sense of increasing his dimensions of statesmanship or at least of losing his reluctance to have a scene or sack anybody. He should have had a scene years ago with Helsby at the Treasury, with Len Williams at Transport House, and he should have sacked Frank Soskice from the Home Office. He should have done a hundred awkward things which need doing, but he prefers to fix if he possibly can.

Today after a talk to Wedgy Benn, Tommy Balogh and Peter Shore, I was deputed to put to him the case for an early election and see how he took it. When I started he replied, 'Don't put it on paper. Why not travel up to Conference with me by sleeper and we will talk on the way?' So I have to prepare myself very carefully for that. We all feel that objectively the right time for an election would be this autumn, with the trade and gold figures good, and with the Opposition ill prepared. We are unlikely to get a better moment during the limited period when we are free to choose. Nevertheless, it is clear that Harold doesn't even envisage this. His image of himself is as a gritty, practical Yorkshireman, a fighter, the Britisher who doesn't give in, who doesn't switch, who hangs on. This is the Harold Wilson he believes in and we shan't deflect him because he is confident he can do it this way. So if we miss a golden opportunity this October it is because of the character of Harold Wilson.

At the Ministry my main job so far this week has been to clear up the mess about housing allocations.[1] I was horrified to discover that allocations at Dover (David Ennal's marginal seat) had been axed by my officials without any of us politicians at the Ministry knowing. When I looked into it I found the situation far worse than that. All over the South-East my officials had been axing allocations to local authorities.[2] Sure enough, I got a stinker of a minute from No. 10 enclosing a bitter letter from David Ennals.

So I summoned a big meeting, with all the officials present, and said to them quite simply that the situation was intolerable and that in future all allocations would have to be submitted to Bob Mellish. The official response was predictable — it would be impossible for him to cope with fifteen hundred allocations. To this I replied that he needn't see them where there was no change. But where there was a change Mellish should have the first sight and then they should come to me. The officials were very mulish, so I said to them, 'Look, the plain fact is that for me to achieve an annual figure of ten thousand below the hundred and fifty thousand I am allowed would be a disaster for which I would get the sack. To achieve the thousand above would make me extremely popular.' Waddell then said that this would upset relations with his Treasury opposite number because we would have been exceeding our estimates without an authorization from the Treasury. I replied that the

[1] Local authorities must have the Ministry's loan sanction authorizing their expenditure on housing. The housing allocation determines the size of the Ministry's promise of money.
[2] As a result of the Chancellor's statement restricting expenditure, the housing programme was restricted mainly to development areas, conurbations and the London area.

Prime Minister had made it clear that we might well have to have a creeping reflation next spring, based very largely on housing. We must have our approvals and housing starts so arranged that if it were necessary we could rapidly increase the number at very short notice. If things came to the worst and we over-allocated, we should have to cut back in the second half of the year in the less essential towns. All this had to be worked out in detail; but the main thing was for the officials to realize that in future the politicians would be in charge of all allocations.

Peter Lederer was there, as was Peter Brown. As I went out of the room after a very rough meeting Peter Brown said to me, 'The last time I had that kind of a meeting was ten years ago when Harold Macmillan did exactly the same thing with the officials. And had exactly the same scene.' Peter Lederer had a rather different reaction. 'You treated the civil servants appallingly. You dressed them down and didn't give them a chance to speak. I wouldn't like to have been treated in that way.' Then he added, 'But I must admit that the civil servants didn't complain. They seemed to think it perfectly normal.' I am convinced that unless a Labour Minister – indeed, any Minister – sometimes takes that line with his civil servants, he has no chance of prevailing against the all-pervasive Treasury influence in every spending department.

The Labour Left were spoiling for a fight and the Party Conference at Blackpool promised to be the battlefield. Mr Wilson seemed as ebullient as usual, and dismissed Liberal taunts that he could not contain his left wing and would be driven to a Lib–Lab pact in the next Session. And with the help of the chairman, Ray Gunter, he did indeed crush the three revolts that broke out. On September 29th, the Government's support for the United States in Vietnam was upheld and, in the afternoon, the Left lost again on immigration. And on September 30th George Brown and James Callaghan successfully appealed for support for the early-warning system for wage claims, although the outcome of the vote was ominously narrow – 3,635,000 votes to 2,540,000. Prices and incomes legislation was obviously going to bring further trouble.

Thursday, September 23rd
The Blackpool Conference for me really started when I said goodbye to Peter Lederer at Vincent Square and then with Tommy and his wife went round to No. 10 and up to Harold's room. There were Marcia and Mary (just off to break a champagne bottle on an atomic submarine at Barrow) and we had a really cosy family evening. Most of the things we had discussed behind Harold's back got discussed openly with him that evening. Was he too kind to civil servants? Thomas said he was. Shouldn't he have more outside advisers? Thomas said he should. To which Harold replied that he couldn't afford to have more than one Thomas since he wouldn't be able to read the stuff. No! he is not going to be a president and he is not going to have a presidential staff, and neither is he going to have any fundamental change in

the Civil Service. All these things are remote from his mind. As for party politics, he has the greatest contempt for Heath, greater than he has for Alec Douglas-Home. He was also, I remember, very critical of Anthony Greenwood for trying to get a decision to revoke constitutional government in Aden postponed until after the N.E.C. elections were announced next Tuesday.[1] But apart from that he was his friendly, cosy self with us all, and we sat round drinking brandy until we moved up to Euston and got on to the sleeper.

Friday, September 24th
We were due to be driven to Blackpool after the Prime Minister had been received by the Mayor of Preston on the platform. There he was on the platform at 7.30 punct., shaved, clean, sparkling and saying to me, 'Directly we get to Blackpool, come up to my room and have breakfast.' Unlike Harold I hadn't had either a shave or a wash and I said to Marcia, 'For God's sake give me forty minutes when we get there,' to which Harold said, 'But I always feel so much better after a night train.' Marcia whispered to me, 'He is always like that after a night journey. I can't sleep a wink.' So Harold and George and Sophie and the mayor all poured into one car and behind them Marcia and I travelled alone.

After a quick bath I went down to breakfast with him and soon it was time for the routine N.E.C. meeting which always takes place on the Friday before Conference. As usual we spent endless time discussing resolutions which would obviously never be reached. On the subject of Executive speakers I was greatly relieved that the suggestion for my taking Alice Bacon's place in answering the debate on immigration was never even put. What Len Williams and Harold Wilson had privately agreed was accepted unchanged. The only other news we had was that in addition to the expected emergency resolution on immigration we had another and possibly more difficult one on George Brown's new early-warning system.

Saturday, September 25th
I spent the morning reading the first draft of Harold's Conference speech, which is to be delivered on Tuesday. I found a passage at the end in which he was talking about introducing the new Britain and actually said 'Here we have stepped forward and done it.' I said to Harold, 'But we haven't done it. That's the trouble. And people know we haven't. We haven't even got across the image of a new era. Don't pretend. Let's say instead that we have only built up to the skirting, and ask people to give us a chance to build the whole house.' He said, 'That's a fine idea.' And I replied, 'You know, any idea of our

---

[1] The Speaker of the Aden Legislative Council had been shot by terrorists on September 1st. Meetings had been held at No. 10 to prepare for a military takeover and suspension of the constitution. A State of Emergency was declared on September 25th, two days before the Conference opened.

being a Kennedy regime is absurd.' He looked at me and he said, 'I suppose you're right, Dick. You can't really sell a Yorkshire terrier as a borzoi hound.' Fortunately, I was able to reply, 'In Britain we prefer a terrier to a borzoi as our leader. It's a clear electoral asset.' I went upstairs and worked away with Jennie (who travelled up with us on the train) to prepare him a draft.*

Freddie Ward from the Department – one of my more enterprising civil servants – had come up to help me. While I worked for Harold I set him to prepare two press releases for my own speech for Monday, on my agreement with the building societies and on housing finance.

The weather wasn't too bad and I had a magnificent walk in the evening along the beach to clear my mind after a day working on Harold's speech – and not on my own.

Sunday, September 26th

In the morning I got to work at last on my own speech with Freddie Ward, who went off at lunch-time. By then we had finished the press releases, but I still hadn't got the text of a speech.

In the afternoon we had the regular N.E.C. meeting to consider for the first time the composites[1] which had been worked out in discussions on Saturday afternoon.

I found the Executive still discussing the draft of the foreign policy statement to be presented to Conference. This had started as a miserable thing; but it had been worked on by Walter Padley[2] and Tom Driberg throughout Sunday morning and it had certainly improved a great deal. When that had been accepted we began to work through the resolutions and the composites and there was very little real disagreement until right at the end. Then came the emergency resolution protesting against George's prices and incomes policy and at once there was a flaming row, with Jack Jones[3] and Danny McGarvey[4] on the one side and George Brown on the other. Naturally enough, the row was fully reported next morning in the press.

Meanwhile, the Imperial Hotel had been filling up in the usual way with the usual guests. I am pretty used to Conference now, and being hardened I just opt out of the evening entertainments and the endless trade-union dinners.

---

* Of which as far as I can see he used nothing. Indeed, the only thing I managed to do was to knock out a passage on steel which seemed to me evasive and disingenuous.

[1] Motions amalgamating similar resolutions proposed by various trade unions or constituency Labour Parties.

[2] President of USDAW 1948–64, and Labour M.P. for the Ogmore Division of Glamorgan since 1950. Minister of State for Foreign Affairs 1964–70.

[3] After fighting in the Spanish Civil War, Jack Jones became a Liverpool city councillor in 1936. He left Liverpool in 1939 for Coventry, where he became the District Secretary of the T.G.W.U. He held this post until 1955, when he became the Midlands Regional Secretary. In 1960 he became the General Secretary of the T.G.W.U. He and Crossman had known each other for some twenty-five years.

[4] President of the Amalgamated Society of Boilermakers, Shipwrights, Blacksmiths and Structural Workers and a member of the T.U.C. General Council since 1965.

In the evening I ran into Uwe Kitzinger, a strange young man who is a Fellow of Nuffield College and whose speciality is social democracy.[1] He is also a tremendous European. I took him for a five-mile walk along the sands, which soaked his shoes, and briefed him about life in England while he briefed me on life in the inter-racial, lethargic sunshine of Jamaica where he has been for the last nine months. It was a very enjoyable couple of hours.

As a Labour Minister at a full-scale Party Conference, one certainly has a very different status from the other members of the N.E.C. Red boxes arrive from London regularly and are brought up to one's hotel room where one struggles to get through them. A Minister has to do all his work in his hotel room and that makes things difficult. I got through by having a little table stuck in the bathroom where Jennie could type, while Freddie Ward worked on the bed. Jennie is here for the whole Conference. I had Freddie Ward all Saturday and John Delafons coming at the end of the week. In fact, I insisted on keeping a nucleus of my Private Office functioning up here.

I told all this to Harold on Friday because I knew that he wasn't allowed to bring civil servants to a Party Conference, which meant of course that he had given way to Helsby's pressure again. I told him this was absolute nonsense. If I was to keep control of my Ministry I had to have the civil servants I needed here in Blackpool. Harold was quite impressed when he learned what the Minister of Housing was getting away with and allowed Tommy Balogh to come up on Saturday night.

Tuesday, Saturday 28th

My big moment at Conference was Monday afternoon. Once the housing debate was over I had no more Conference work to do. The awful thing was that at ten o'clock on Sunday night when Uwe Kitzinger left I still had no speech prepared, apart from Freddie Ward's press releases. So I woke up very early on Monday and worked hard and then I decided not to go to Conference that morning but to work with Jennie, and actually try to write out the speech and work in the press releases. At eleven o'clock on Monday morning an urgent telephone message came from the Conference asking me to rush down because my own subject had started. I knew this must be wrong and went on working. Ten minutes later came an even more urgent message. No taxis outside the hotel. I ran to the Winter Garden. Of course it was a false alarm. The debate that had started was the one on local government which Arthur Skeffington was answering for the Executive. Though I am the Minister of Local Government as well as of Housing, I wasn't making a speech in that debate. The explanation was dear old Bob Mellish. He was so anxious because I wasn't there when I was being attacked from the

[1] Uwe Kitzinger had been one of the earliest supporters of Britain's entry into the Common Market, and had worked in Strasbourg with the Council of Europe from 1951 to 1958. In 1973 he became the adviser to Sir Christopher Soames at the Commission of the E.E.C.

5   At his desk at the Ministry of Housing and Local Government.

6 and 7   On a tour of the Birmingham slums in November 1964.

8 and 9   Inspecting local authority housing at Romsey in July 1966.

10 With Barbara Castle (Minister of Transport) looking at the Oxford
Road Development Plan, January 1966.

floor that he had sent the message to me. This wasted an hour of my time and meant that by one o'clock my speech consisted only of a series of bitty notes. Jennie and I were very nearly in tears. However, I got something together by two thirty and went down to the Conference hall. Fortunately the debate on local government was still dragging on. Then Skeffington had to make his reply, and then there were fifty minutes of speeches from the floor before I made the reply to the housing debate. That gave me time enough to organize my thoughts.

Looking back on that speech I don't think it was very well delivered, and I know it could have been far better if I had had more time and done more work on it. Nevertheless, it really hit the headlines in the morning papers today and the TV headlines too. On Monday evening I did four TV interviews and one radio interview as well as a full-scale Lobby conference. In fact I was busy on these interviews from the moment I left the Conference Hall at five until eleven thirty at night. As a result of this work today's press at least gave the impression that Labour is determined to be building half a million houses a year by 1969.

Today was the day of Harold's big speech and we went down to the Conference Hall at nine thirty to hear it. But first came the results of the elections to the N.E.C. Throughout the weekend Barbara Castle was continually saying, 'Oh dear, Dick, what shall we do? I believe we are going to be knocked off the Executive this time. It's the young ones who are going to win.' I told her that the young ones wouldn't do anything this year; the Ministers would get all the votes. True enough. We did. Barbara of course was at the top of the poll, with Tony Greenwood close behind. I was down one place and James Callaghan was up one place. I was quite content with this. I am unlike Barbara in this respect: the elections for the National Executive don't dominate my life; in her case it is a chronic disease.

Next came Harold's speech, an immensely impressive performance. I knew most of it and was horrified to find that into a speech already far too long had been spatchcocked an enormous new section describing the Conservative Party as the party which sides with management against the workers in a new class war. When Thomas Balogh had finally been allowed to come to Blackpool he had gone straight up to Harold's room and spent a lot of time on the speech. Before he went back to London he had said to me, rubbing his hands, 'My God, this is a masterly speech which Helsby won't approve of. We've really put some teeth into it.' Nevertheless, the Balogh insertion sounded synthetic and made the speech an extra ten minutes too long. That evening Hugh Cudlipp told me that he was asked his opinion and said to Harold, 'Well, most people say that your speech was too long.' And Harold had replied, 'How many people?' Hugh: 'Ten people I have spoken to.' Harold: 'Well, now you've spoken to eleven. I think it was too long, too.'

Directly Harold's speech was over I motored over to Preston in order to try to mend some fences that had been laid low by my decision to abandon the New Town at Risley which my predecessor had planned. We were moving towards the idea that there should be a Greater Warrington, roughly on the lines of our schemes for doubling Ipswich, Northampton and Peterborough.[1] Doubling of this kind may work in the Midlands and in the South but it causes a hell of a mess in Lancashire. I found gathered in Preston county hall representatives of the county, of the Warrington R.D.C., of the Warrington Borough Council, all in passionate ructions with each other. Fortunately, McColl, the county clerk, had come across to Blackpool to pick me up. He briefed me on the way about the personalities in the town as well as explaining how the Lancashire County Council works. They have an agreement there whereby whichever side wins the election is guaranteed against defeat for the next four years, and the chairmanships for that period are divided up between the two main parties. No press is present at any of the main committees and the council meets in public five times a year. It must be one of the tightest corporations in the world.

My job was to convince everyone present that they weren't being tricked and that nothing would be decided until after the fullest possible consultation. In fact, as I later realized, there was going to be far too much consultation. Then we had lunch and I spent the afternoon seeing the coastline. It was a drenching afternoon. We went up to Morecambe and then down the coast from there, and I realized that there are 180 miles of unspoilt Lancashire coast, mostly estuaries and mudflats of considerably beauty. I am sure my idea of a really bold policy for preserving the coastline is a winner.

I got back to Blackpool in time for a really splendid *Daily Mirror* party. Afterwards a few of us sat down to dinner together – Hugh Cudlipp and his new wife, Sydney Jacobson and Alma and Ellis Birk[2] – and we had a really gay, old-fashioned *Daily Mirror* time together which I enormously enjoyed. After dinner I strolled into the hotel foyer. The talk was now about the immigration debate, and all the corridors were humming about the great sell-out of socialist principle in the White Paper and what M.P.s were doing about it, and how the T.G.W.U. were going to side with the anti-Government people. There was Vicky,[3] looking white with anger, sitting with Michael Foot. All the Left were up in arms against the betrayal the next morning.

Wednesday, September 29th
Before the immigration debate we had to debate foreign policy, so Conference listened to Michael Stewart for fifty minutes – that clear, precise, boring voice, competent and, oh dear, so lucid that you could see only too

[1] See p. 147.
[2] Alma Birk was leader of Finchley Borough Council 1950–53, and an unsuccessful Labour candidate at successive elections. A journalist, she was associate editor of *Nova* 1965–9. She became a life peer in 1967, and served as chairman of the Health Education Council 1969–72. Ellis Birk, her husband, is legal adviser to I.P.C.
[3] Victor Weisz, the *Evening Standard* and *New Statesman* cartoonist, himself an immigrant. He died in February 1966.

clearly how little he had to say. Nevertheless, in debating terms he made a powerful case. Then came the Left attack. John Mendelson led it. He centred on Vietnam and the Government's failure to get through to real American public opinion. Once again I realized that in the Labour Party the real division is between practical policy and emotional protest. Very rarely have we discussed alternative policies or even alternative attitudes. The Left don't say they have a different policy from support for the Americans in Vietnam. The Left say, 'That is the official line and we object to it.' This was very much what was happening this morning.

In the afternoon I got down to my red boxes and then went down to hear the immigration debate which started late at four o'clock. It was an interesting scene. I had noticed already that Ray Gunter was a dramatic, self-dramatizing kind of chairman. He had deliberately refused a card vote where he should obviously have given it, not because he didn't know the correct procedure but because he was trying to show himself able to impose his will. On immigration, too, he did a job I didn't like very much. He had obviously been tricky with some of the delegates, and he was bashing and banging away and cut short the debate after only twenty-five minutes. True, it was an emergency debate spatchcocked into the full time-table, but he behaved, I thought, in an abominable way and as a result the whole Conference was completely out of control.

The most awkward moment came when Bob Mellish got up and made a rip-roaring speech which might have been tolerable from a Bermondsey docker but was really impossible for a Parliamentary Secretary of Housing and Local Government. Altogether it was a pretty unpleasant debate, until it was saved by Alice Bacon, who did magnificently. The row in the Conference Hall stimulated her. In that grating voice, she gave her clear, schoolmistressy, common-sense view of the White Paper, demonstrating what was in it to people who hadn't bothered to read it. It really was quite impressive. When the final vote was taken the majority for the platform was overwhelming and it was clear that, despite the talk of betrayal, the majority of the constituency Parties accepted the White Paper policy.

In the evening I dined with Pam Berry, Hugh and Pauline Massingham, George Wigg and Manny Shinwell, and then we went down to the B.B.C. studios to see how things were going there. We watched Michael Stewart and then Alice Bacon.

Thursday, September 30th
There had been a good deal of talk about a platform defeat on the emergency resolution on George Brown's early-warning system. This was certain to be opposed by the T.G.W.U. and we didn't know how the A.E.U. would split this time. George Brown started and did a magnificent job. After a very fine debate, James Callaghan came in, weary from a flight back from America and carrying the weight of the Chancellor's responsibility. He gained another very

formidable triumph and the danger of defeat was averted. In the evening I went down to the B.B.C. studios to watch George Brown being interviewed. The room was nearly full when the P.M. came in. George Brown was doing extremely well. He had had a long and tiring day but this didn't upset him until, right at the end, Robin Day[1] popped a question about his attitude to immigration which he clearly hadn't expected. However, he recovered and responded well. I noticed that Harold took this very badly and told John Grist[2] before us all that it was an outrage to try and to trap a Minister in that kind of way. He added ominously, 'We shall be watching throughout the Tory Conference to see if you treat them the same way as you treated us.'*

Saturday, October 2nd
I left Blackpool at eight o'clock on Friday morning and spent the next two days at Rochdale and Wigan inspecting housing in appalling Lancashire weather—sheets of rain, driving wind—which made those pretty depressing towns look even worse. I went to Rochdale because there is an area in the centre of the city called Deeplish where we had been doing a special socio-logical study. This is a part of the town which is now going downhill, but the quality of its housing is good enough to prevent it being certified as a slum. It is therefore being classified as an improvement area and our survey was designed to find out how people actually live, how they work and what they want done to their homes in an area of this kind. I spent the morning holding a seminar with the people engaged on the study and the local officials, and despite what they told me I was shocked and surprised when I actually walked round Deeplish. This is a so-called improvement area and its houses have been given thirty more years of life; yet they are little dwellings, each with a tiny courtyard behind, the tin bath hanging on the wall of the court-yard and two steps across it the toilet in a shed. Upstairs in the houses there was a fairly stenchy smell, beds unmade in each house I visited and blankets with no sheets. It's a primitive, dismal life in Deeplish; and high above are the five great tower blocks which Wimpey have clamped down in the middle of the town.

In the evening I went over to Manchester to see some of the Labour people concerned in the Westhoughton dispute. This was my second visit about this unhappy development and I had with me Jim MacColl, who is part of this world of Lancashire politics. The Department was right to refuse sanction to the compulsory purchase order which would have given Manchester most of the centre of Westhoughton for redevelopment. Jim

---

* By the end of Conference week it was public property that a major row had blown up between the Prime Minister and the B.B.C. about their handling of Conference proceedings. A great pity.
[1] A former journalist who had gone into television in 1959 and acquired a reputation for provocative and determined interviewing particularly in the field of current affairs.
[2] Then Head of B.B.C. Current Affairs.

says they were asking for too much, far more than they needed, and I was bound to axe great chunks out of the order.

Since that appallingly embarrassing scene when I received the delegation from Manchester[1] nothing really has happened month after month. I have had placatory meetings, trying to persuade the Manchester people, and indeed I thought I had persuaded them, to agree to the appointment of a consultant who would advise us objectively about the feasibility of their proposals. But I now learn they have not agreed the consultant's terms of reference. Well, that night we had a stormy meeting, with all the Labour people shouting at each other. Westhoughton Labour versus Manchester Labour and both versus county council Labour. I only had to sit and listen to their row in order to make them understand my difficulty.

Then I rushed off to Manchester University where I found a big hall full of students and we had a fairly sober meeting on housing. I then got one of them to drive me to Wigan where I was to stay the night. Waiting for me this morning were the usual gang of officials ready to start on the tour of the town. Wigan is enormously overcrowded and since it is determined to be better than its jokes, the council has undertaken an enormous building programme; and, as a result, thousands of council houses have been built. Unfortunately, they haven't got a city architect or a town planner. The houses are of an appalling dimness and dullness, and I am afraid they have built a Wigan that in 2000 will look just as bad as the old 1880 Wigan looks in the eyes of the 1960s. For lunch the council took me to a large house they have bought, with its park, outside the town. But they don't know what to do with it. Then I went out to open the new housing block and down came the rain. It was an enormous cube of flats of very poor quality. After that, back to the council chamber where I addressed the councillors and received as a gift from the council something which for once was really nice and useful – a pewter jug and a set of pewter mugs. I repeated again my theme of the need for reform of local government. Then I motored to Crewe to catch the train back to Banbury and found Prescote soaked after an awful fortnight of rain.

Monday, October 4th
This Monday was very like the beginning of a school term. Our Party Conference was over and here I was, back in the routine, preparing for the new Session ahead. The chief jobs on hand were: (1) preparing the White Paper on the housing programme; (2) getting ahead with my two local government finance Bills, a short-term Bill (on rate rebates), and a long-term Bill (concerned with the reform of rating); and (3) completing the preparations for bringing the Rent Act into operation at the beginning of December. Yes, it was very much getting down to work again.

The Dame was back from a good holiday, but I found her very disturbed.

[1] See p. 189.

She had been appalled by my A.M.C. speech.[1] Not only did she find the content disastrous, because she was convinced it would destroy her dear Boundary Commission and all its works, she also felt that I must have deliberately waited until she was on holiday and done it when her back was turned. Of course, this second point was perfectly true, but I didn't feel shaken because on reflection I thought I had pulled off the coup. And that day my position was to some extent confirmed in her eyes when we had a meeting with the County Councils Association. They had come to see me about my speech, and they didn't react quite as she predicted. I was careful to tell them that I expected them to welcome the long-term decision for a Royal Commission, but in the short term I couldn't possibly make it an excuse for lethargy. I was going ahead with my boundary decisions and they would find a number of them very advantageous to themselves. I hoped I could rely on their support in getting the regulations drafted and all the statutory work done. They listened, they were pleasant and on the whole they were more agreeable than she expected.

Tuesday, October 5th
I spent the morning preparing for an important press conference on Thursday, at which I shall announce the creation of the Borough of Greater Teesside, the biggest borough outside London to be created since the war. But before I got down to this I had a characteristically difficult talk with Callaghan. He had asked to see me directly I got back from the recess; and when I went along the passage he hummed and hawed and I wondered what he was up to. Quite wrongly I had assumed he wanted to talk to me about staff, since the Prime Minister had told me recently how sick James was of Kaldor and how much Kaldor would like to transfer to the Ministry of Housing. I had liked the idea at first sight and broached it to the Dame but without much success. However, he chatted and chatted and finally said he gathered that I wanted ten thousand extra houses this year. Was that true? I was completely bewildered and frankly told him so, but added that it certainly wasn't true that I had asked for ten thousand more houses. 'I think you are going to do so,' he said rather grimly. And I said, 'Well, that only shows that your Treasury is at its usual practice of spying.' I would go back to the Department immediately and discover the facts.

Back I went and, sure enough, in the afternoon, when I had my meeting on housing allocations, Bob Mellish said that we needed an extra ten thousand approvals if we weren't going to have a first-rate political crisis. This is a very good example of the Whitehall grapevine. Bob had been having strictly private consultations in my Ministry before coming to me with a proposition; and yet the Chancellor of the Exchequer knew about it before I did. I had it out with the Dame. I said to her how deeply I resented people in my Department leaking in this way — because that's what it is — to the Treasury. Of

[1] See p. 331.

course, I see that the Department can't in fact approve extra houses without the Treasury discovering what we are up to and that our officials are honour-bound to tell the Treasury of any firm commitments we enter into. But I keenly resent the behaviour of officials who obviously feel that their first obligation is to the Treasury and their second to their own Minister.

I can talk in this way to the Dame but I am not thereby going to alter the structure of Whitehall. All my key officials, the two Deputies for example, know that promotion comes to them not from the Minister—he has virtually nothing to do with it—but from the standing which they have in the eyes of the Treasury and of the head of the Civil Service, Helsby. It is this relationship which makes so many higher civil servants willing to spy for the Treasury and to align themselves with the Treasury view even against their own Minister.

All the Dame could do was to listen to my outburst before we got down to business and decided to write the very letter that the Chancellor knew he was going to get. Actually, I toned it down a bit and said we couldn't possibly get on without seven thousand extra approvals. Before I knew what, the fact of this change from ten to seven thousand was circulating round Whitehall.

Wednesday, October 6th

I had one important thing to do—address the Council of the Building Societies Federation. What had seemed the previous week to be a formality had now become a major speech because of the disastrous reaction of the building societies and the builders to my Conference speech.[1] Waddell had warned me on the Saturday after the speech that the building societies felt deeply insulted, and even my friends were in great dismay at the arrogance I had been said to reveal on TV. Oh dear, how dangerous it is to be humorous. I had remarked that they had suspected me at first but had gradually found out what a simple man I was. It was this that was regarded as double-dyed duplicity and villainous arrogance. The explanation for the outburst was, I think, a bit more complex. Anyway, their hostile reaction, however synthetic, meant we were pretty well back at square one; and instead of making a pleasant, informal, after-dinner speech I had to redefine my attitude to owner-occupation once again and try to woo the building societies and the builders back into my confidence.

Speech-making is still one of the things I find most difficult to do as a Minister. I can do it as a back-bencher, I can do it as an academic, but ministerial speech-making is not my natural style; and I still resent having to prepare press releases. On this occasion the release wasn't ready until a few minutes before I had to deliver the speech at 2.30 to the somnolent members

---

[1] In which the Minister had announced the new option-mortgage scheme, providing subsidies on mortgages whatever the ruling interest rate if mortgagors would forgo tax relief at the standard rate. Local councils were promised new financial aid to protect them against high interest rates and to encourage council-house building.

of some twenty-six building societies. They couldn't have been less interested but they provided me with an occasion for enunciating a philosophy in favour of owner-occupation. Donald Gould, the chairman of the Council of the Building Societies Federation, ordered four hundred copies of the speech for circulation and it may really ease relations before we resume negotiations.

Friday, October 8th

Yesterday was the first Cabinet since our return from Blackpool. We started with a little epilogue on coal prices. In August and September we had a Cabinet crisis arising out of the proposal to announce an increase of prices.[1] The crisis was averted by postponement. Now George Brown was asking that after Christmas, when the announcement will be made, the issue should be referred to the Prices and Incomes Board. It was obviously a lesser evil to let the Board make the final decision and we gave George the support he wanted.

Then the Prime Minister turned to Rhodesia and made a statement describing how, if U.D.I. is announced, the Rhodesian government will be treated as traitors and the Queen will take over the government. This was the first occasion on which I was a bit of a bastard and did the kind of Socratic cross-examination which people expect of me. 'That doesn't mean very much,' I said, 'because what we want to know is whether the Queen will act through the Governor-General or the British Prime Minister?' The more I pressed the question the clearer it was that quite elaborate contingency plans for action existed but nobody wanted to reveal what they were. However, I managed to extract from Harold Wilson the admission that he was still determined not to send in troops even as part of a United Nations force. When I said I could accept the first but not the second I got some support from Denis Healey. But I didn't press it because I had achieved my object of demonstrating that Harold Wilson's policy is designed not to unseat Smith but to carry the Tories with him.

That evening I travelled up to Darlington, where I stayed the night, in order to open the Balderhead Dam – the largest earth-dam in Great Britain – this morning. I got to the hotel in time to switch on the TV in my room and see myself interviewed on Teesside. How localized interests are in this country! Though it was hardly mentioned in London, the story that the Minister of Housing had created a great new borough in Teesside dominated the press of the whole area – not only the morning papers but TV and radio as well. Today at the Balderhead Dam it was also the sole subject of talk – they obviously assumed I had timed the statement to coincide with the opening. Accompanied by the usual aldermen, and in a big Rolls Royce, I had driven up into the hills on a cold, bleak day – a little sunshine but mostly cloud – through that serenely beautiful Northumbrian landscape. After the

[1] See p. 302.

opening ceremony, some 130 of the elite of the world of water drove to Scotch Corner and sat down to lunch to celebrate the opening. I found myself being accosted not only by the councillors who wanted to come into Teesside, like those from Middlesbrough and Redcar, but also by those who didn't, like the Billingham councillors. From there I sped to Northallerton where I was due to see the North Riding Council about their coastline—a lovely stretch from Teesside right down to Flamborough Head. They had done an excellent job of preservation and fully support my idea of preserving the whole coast, not by National Trust purchase, but by effective planning control.

I motored to York and thence by train to Cambridge to stay with Nicky Kaldor and discuss his future. He gave me a tutorial on devaluation and deflation, after explaining that he would like to stay at Inland Revenue if he possibly could.

Sunday, October 10th

I had gone to Cambridge to address a regional Labour Party demonstration in the Guildhall. A thousand people turned up. There was tremendous enthusiasm and a standing ovation—for the first time in my life I heard people singing 'For He's a Jolly Good Fellow' after my speech. But what they were fêting was not the Minister of Housing but the Labour Party. In the last three weeks the lift in morale has been tremendous. We are not a good Party in adversity but we are an ecstatic Party when adversity seems to be behind us. I had a splendid time; and then Anne brought me home for a quiet weekend to slave away at my own housing White Paper.

This has proved to be quite a problem. I am clear what kind of White Paper I want—a clear statement of what has to be done in order to achieve an annual output of half a million houses, more like a military staff study than a Civil Service paper. These in fact were the instructions I gave. The result was a voluminous mass of officialese. In desperation I made an exact synopsis today—paragraph by paragraph—parallel with their first draft, showing how they should reorganize it. That was as near as I could get to forcing them to do the right thing.

Monday, October 11th

Molly and John Delafons met me and the boxes at Paddington. We sorted them out and I gave orders on how my synopsis of the White Paper was to be dealt with. Then I went into the Home Affairs Committee. It was concerned only with one item, the Countryside Bill.[1] This is Fred Willey's third Bill as

---

[1] The Countryside Commission would extend the functions of the earlier body established under the National Parks and Access to the Countryside Act of 1949, and would confer powers on local authorities for the protection and benefit of the countryside and its users. The Bill had to wait until November 1967 for its First Reading, and as the Ministry of Land and Natural Resources had been disbanded, the new Minister of Housing and Local Government, Anthony Greenwood, introduced the measure.

Minister of Land and Natural Resources; he has already got the Land Commission, and I have arranged that he should have leasehold enfranchisement. Now he wants this Countryside Bill as well. It establishes a commission, financing its operation with a 50 per cent grant. As all Fred's officials were drafted from my Ministry I was well briefed to reply that this was futile because the counties which most needed the work of the commission wouldn't be able to afford the other 50 per cent. We had been arguing about this for some time when Bert Bowden in the chair remarked, 'You two needn't worry about this Bill, there won't be room for it in this session anyway.'

I had a working lunch for all the people concerned with Party propaganda. When the transfer of the liaison committee chairmanship to me was leaked after the first meeting I had made a terrible row and told Harold I would have nothing to do with it unless he fixed it with the chairman and the secretary of the Party in Transport House. Well, he hasn't fixed it with them but I have been persuaded to do the job. So there I was, chairing the meeting in my room. All the Transport House people were present, as well as the P.L.P. officials from the House of Commons, Frank Barlow and Harry Mitchell.[1] I managed to persuade them that our job was not to advertise the activities of the Conservative Party Conference or the policy statement Heath had produced by speeches against them but to concentrate on our own National Plan. This was a change for most of them since George Wigg's idea of propaganda was verbal fisticuffs.

In the evening I had a meeting with Sir Sydney Littlewood and his three vice-presidents, and was more impressed with him than before. He is a superbly solid man, and is determined to create a London rent assessment committee which is a genuine tribunal full of *gravitas* and *Würde* which can set precedents for the whole of the country. I went through my ideas of the fair rent with him and felt relieved at the end. Later in the evening I took the train for two days in the North, one in Newcastle to discuss Tyneside reorganization and the second visiting the Northumbrian coastline.

The Conservative Conference opened on October 12th and Edward Heath presented delegates with a pamphlet of firm and thoughtful policies, including the promised trade-union reform, changes in tax structure and entry into the E.E.C. But the Conference was troubled by the growing crisis in Rhodesia. Not only did Lord Salisbury himself appear in Brighton to appeal to Conservatives not to desert their Rhodesian kith and kin but the limelight was stolen from Mr Heath on the first full day of the Conference by Mr Wilson's dramatic flight to Balmoral.

The Prime Minister's journey was not, after all, to discuss a dissolution and general election. It apparently concerned the Rhodesian crisis, for by now Mr Smith and his Rhodesian Front had won an overwhelming electoral victory and

[1] Deputy Secretary of the P.L.P. and Secretary of the P.L.P. respectively.

stubbornly insisted on the country's claim to independence before the African majority had voting rights.

Talks between Mr Smith and Mr Wilson in Downing Street on October 4th brought no agreement. Mr Wilson would not give way on the five principles which would guarantee an improvement in the circumstances of the African people, with unimpeded progress to majority rule, on terms that would satisfy both black and white members of the Rhodesian population. Mr Smith refused to accept the principles and, back in Rhodesia, sent on October 20th a somewhat obscure message offering Britain various alternative undertakings. The Rhodesian issue, therefore, took up much of Cabinet's attention.

Wednesday, October 13th

Yesterday's Newcastle session was quite a successful experiment. Tyneside has sixteen local authorities and my Local Government Boundary Commission had come up with a proposal for a two-tier county solution—the sixteen authorities to be grouped together into four boroughs with a county organization on top. This had not only infuriated everybody in Tyneside but also raised opposition in the two counties of Northumberland and Durham. After advice from the Dame I decided to do something unprecedented by staging a conference in which I as Minister would take the chair. I think it is the first time that a Minister has had a conference of this kind before making up his mind what to do. So up to Newcastle with me came all the officials of the local government division. On the way up I spent about three hours delving in the endless official reports and picked up enough to convince the people who attended the conference that I had read the half-million words. When I got there I discovered that the membership consisted of two or three representatives of the sixteen local authorities, plus observers from the two counties. The fact that they were only observers had infuriated the counties, and I at once decided to bring them fully in and ask them to start the discussion in order to avoid giving them a permanent sense of grievance.

The discussion went on from ten till twelve thirty and from two till four and took the form of my quizzing everybody there. I soon found that they assumed I was there to sell a particular solution, the creation of a one-tier Greater Newcastle. Actually I had gone to listen. The only thing I was sure of was that I couldn't accept the four boroughs which the Commission had proposed unless the centralized planning services at the top were far stronger than those of a county—unless in fact sewage, planning, police and fire services were all centralized.

At lunchtime I said, 'Will you appoint a committee to represent you when we receive the press?' They said they were confident the Minister could handle the press alone, so I did—as well as doing a long filmed interview with the B.B.C. and I.T.V. Once again the activities of the Minister of Housing had knocked out of the headlines on Tyneside both the Rhodesian crisis and the Tory Party Conference. It is this which enables him to be a comparatively influential member of any Cabinet—he is constantly in the public eye, not nationally but in the regions.

That evening I had a delightful dinner at Newcastle University as the guest of Charles Bosanquet,[1] with a select and lively collection of dons, all of whom seemed to be convinced that if I put forward the Greater Newcastle solution I can swing the whole area. Maybe, but it is also true that with the quality of officials available the Greater Newcastle solution might be a ghastly administrative mess.

I spent today visiting the Northumbrian coastline with the chairman and the clerk of the County Council, and the chairman of the Planning Committee. Magnificent beaches, sand-dunes, low cliffs and three famous castles; the first in the village of Walkworth; the second at Dunstanburgh, where you walk a mile and a quarter along the low green cliff to a terrific castle standing on a headland with the dunes dropping sheer behind it; and the third at Bamburgh, which looks terrific from outside but which has been so restored that it is utterly unbearable. On the whole the county council preserve their coastline very well indeed, and they were really enthusiastic about my idea. Here is an example of a Minister's plan being developed by very extensive consultations. I had started with the idea of calling in all the planning permissions and imposing control centrally. J. D. Jones rightly warned me against this. Now I am doing the thing voluntarily, going round from county to county and together with the local people seeing what development is needed—where the caravans could be concentrated, where the new chalet villages could be placed. We need to construct a policy of limited development in areas already blighted and a complete ban on all development along the unspoilt coastline. It is only by a balance of this sort, as I have learnt from J. D. Jones and from talking to the counties, that the programme makes sense.

This afternoon the Tory Conference began and Harold Wilson carefully took all the headlines by flying to Balmoral to talk to the Queen. Everybody immediately jumped to the conclusion that he was asking for a dissolution because this week's Gallup Poll and N.O.P. show Labour eleven points ahead of the Tories. Certainly, the circumstances are perfect: after weeks of awful rain we have had ten days of clear, beautiful, cloudless summer weather —a slight mist in the mornings and warm sunshine afterwards. The gold reserves are good and the Gallup Poll is good and I, of course, have been pressing him to have the election now. But in sober truth he had no reason to go to Balmoral except to bitch Heath's opening speech—a typical Harold trick.

Thursday, October 14th
The trouble about being away for two days from London is that your mind gets off politics. I went to Cabinet this morning at 10.30 for my rate-rebate

[1] Vice-Chancellor of the University of Newcastle-upon-Tyne since August 1965.

item much too free-and-easy in my mind. Indeed, I only started making notes on what I was to say while Harold was filling us in about the Rhodesian crisis. This was the first occasion on which I definitely misjudged Cabinet and did very badly. I mistakenly started by bluntly saying that politically we had lost five hundred seats in the municipal elections last March and that we should lose another five hundred if we didn't give some relief to the ratepayer and fulfil our election pledge to shift the balance of the burden from rates on to taxation. To do that on a large scale we shall first have to carry out our major reorganization of the system of central grants to local authorities. For that we need my big rating reform Bill which is due to be introduced in February but which can only be operative from the spring of 1967. It was therefore essential to have an interim rate rebate Bill—like my interim Protection from Eviction Act—to give some immediate assistance now. That was my case.

The moment I finished, James Callaghan weighed in. He said he didn't agree with my political argument; there were no votes to be got out of rate rebates since the people who got the rebates wouldn't be grateful to us.

I was taken aback because he had told me last week that he thought my rate rebates could come this year. Now he had gone back on this assurance, although he knew that it would be a personal defeat for me because I had been going round the country speaking in favour of a short Bill. More important, it would be a defeat for the whole policy of controlled reflation and another victory for the deflationists in the Treasury.

When Callaghan had finished, the Lord Chancellor said that the proposal was unjust, unhappy, unpopular. I realized that by talking about the elections I had upset a number of my colleagues. The Prime Minister came in quickly to put me right. He said that if it was a question merely of votes next March in the municipal elections he wouldn't consider the proposal at all; but what mattered was its social justice. So I then switched quickly into reverse and used the arguments one needs to win the support of Douglas Houghton and Willie Ross. Then Barbara waded in and said, 'Aren't we supposed to be in favour of helping the poor and the weak? Isn't it time we did something solid for them? The rates went up last year by 10 per cent and they will be up another 10 per cent this year. How can we leave the old-age pensioner in a high-rated house to suffer in this way?' Then things began to swing my way. James Callaghan was supported by the Lord Chancellor, by Arthur Bottomley, and by virtually nobody else. Finally, George Brown said, 'Well, if we are all declaring ourselves, I must admit that I came to this meeting thinking the proposal was too complicated and not worth doing. But I fancy I have now been convinced of its social justice.'

This experience was an eye-opener for me. I learnt that you must never go into a Cabinet meeting without carefully preparing your tactics. You must never take for granted that the battle is won merely because the Prime Minister is on your side and the Chancellor has hinted to you—but not sworn to you—that he will support you in the fray. However, after an hour it was through: Cabinet is committed firmly to rate rebates which will start operating next March. I thought it rather significant that the Prime Minister, in his summing-up, pointed out (although he had rebuked me for mentioning politics) that if we were going to have a general election before the municipal elections it might be a good thing to have the rate rebates in operation. It was the first time he had indicated the first week of May as being the time for the election. In my view it is the only date before October next year. We can't help losing the municipal elections but we can win the general election if it takes place first.

After Cabinet I saw Callaghan for a moment and he told me he was replying to my letter about housing allocations but he felt it essential to have a proper objective assessment of the state of the building industry. I at once agreed that the extra allocations should only be granted if it can be shown that this will really fill a gap.

Friday, October 15th

My official visit to the town of Banbury. I had agreed to do this months before, knowing that in the council the position is awkward because there is an equal balance between the Parties and the Labour mayor has the casting vote.

The great issue at Banbury is how much the town should be expanded and in which direction. The humorous fact is that the Minister of Housing lives five miles from the centre—and the town council's plan takes in Little Bourton, which is only one and a half miles from Prescote Manor on the other side of the Cherwell Valley. The council in fact wants its expansion to go north whereas every farmer in our area, including the owner of Prescote, wants it to go east into Northamptonshire and south down the river. When I mentioned it to the Dame she said that she had never had such an awkward situation with a Minister. We agreed that I had better state publicly that on this issue of Banbury's development I would leave it entirely to my officials when decisions have to be taken on the direction in which the expansion should take place. By making this announcement straight away I took the council's breath away and won the Tories over. I then went on to say that the Ministry reckons as an interim calculation that Banbury will increase from its present 20,000 not to 80,000 by 1981 as the town clerk wanted, but to 56,000, which seems quite enough. I also pointed out that the central redevelopment of the town will probably be planned on the assumption of an ultimate size of 70–80,000. This seemed to satisfy them.

Afterwards, I found myself lunching in a tiny room with the mayor, the chairman of the housing committee, the chairman of the waterworks committee, one trade-union official and the town clerk. What on earth had happened? I discovered that the Labour Party had decided not to stage a big civic occasion for me but to have a private lunch at which I should meet only the Labour members. This annoyed everyone else, all the more because at 2.30 I was due to open the new reservoir with all the county officials and county councillors present. Denying them lunch and telling them to arrive at the waterworks at 2.30 hadn't put them in the best of spirits! But it was a lovely day and we got through the thing quite successfully. At 3.30 I was able to drive back home to see the children for a couple of hours and then go off to Coventry, where the students at the Lanchester College had organized another discussion.

Sunday, October 17th
Charles and Mary Woodhouse came over for lunch and a walk in exquisite sunshine across the fields. We discussed Patrick's future. For the last twelve months to and fro in our minds has been tossed the question, shall he go to the Dragon School, where there is a place reserved and the fees are already paid and where he will be with his aunt and uncle, or shall he stay at school here? More and more Anne wants him to stay here. If she was in any way inclined to let him go to the Dragon I am afraid I would weaken. But since she is determined to have him here that's fine by me. The only difficulty is that though he is already eight he can hardly write, and I don't want him to fall far behind and fail the 11-plus. This personal family problem is a perfect illustration of the national problem of state versus private education. There is no doubt that if Patrick goes to the Dragon he will within a matter of months be learning Latin and Greek and forging ahead intellectually – but he will also be leaving home. If he stays in the state system – in the village school and then in Banbury – he will develop at a far slower rate and his whole social life will be entirely different. There couldn't be two more different paths for a boy to take. I feel as a socialist I must be prepared to stake enough on my principles to let him go through the state system today. Ten years ago maybe the state system wasn't good enough. Now there is no intrinsic reason why he shouldn't stay on in it.

Despite Harold's flight to Balmoral,[1] Ted's Conference speech was apparently a fairly satisfactory means of launching him as the Party leader. The next day he survived his first crisis, over Rhodesia, when he was bailed out by Douglas-Home. Lord Salisbury denounced the Labour Government for attacking our white brothers and an open split was only averted by Douglas-Home pleading with the Conference to disregard Lord Salisbury. I am pretty sure he couldn't have done this unless he felt there was a deep understanding with the Prime Minister that under no circumstances should we send troops to Rhodesia. But the general impression from the Conference is that Heath has not proved as immediately successful as we feared he might. He is dry, and too cold, and the policy he is putting across seems to me to be attractive only to young and thrusting businessmen. Certainly for the whole of what you might call the traditional, hierarchical, deferential Right, Maudling would have been far more attractive. One can't feel deferential to

---

[1] See *Wilson*, p. 151, for his remarks on its unsettling effects on the Conservative Party Conference at Brighton.

Heath; one is aware of him as a professional politician – cold, tough, efficient. In the public eye he is much colder than Harold Wilson, who has something rather warm and cosy about him compared to this calculating, driving politician. So though I am sure he is going to win tremendous enthusiasm among the business community and his own Party workers, I am more doubtful whether he will be able to pull out of their mood of abstention a number of Tory voters whose support he desperately needs and who are still out of sympathy with the kind of policy for which he stands. It is now clear that he has taken the very big decision to drop the socialistic attitude which crept into Tory policy in the last two years of Macmillan's regime. Heath is going to fight much more for free enterprise; his theme will be Into Europe where British free enterprise can survive, and we shall have to reply, We must have socialist planning in order to live outside Europe.

Looking at the situation after the two Party Conferences I am convinced that our situation has improved enormously. As a result of having won the battle of the pound, as a result of Harold Wilson's leadership on Rhodesia, as a result of the general feeling that this Government is settling down and is going to deliver the goods, we have staged an astonishing come-back. Of course this situation might change very rapidly and be undermined in a few days by the edgy narkiness of political life once Parliament resumes. The Government has had its summer recess – a delicious time for any Government. Now we have got to settle down to the dreary, nagging strain of Parliament.

Monday, October 18th

The reserved compartment which I have to occupy in lonely state each Monday morning is becoming quite a social problem. Often the train is full and I don't dare to keep everyone out. But that means that I can't read my papers (because of the rule that our red boxes can't be opened in a railway carriage if anybody else is there). So I am faced with an awkward choice. Should I offend people and seem self-important and hog the carriage? Or should I deny myself the chance to read my Cabinet papers before I reach Paddington? This Monday I had to rush through the minutes of the E.D.C. where the major item was Fred Lee's proposal for cutting back coal production.

This whole business of pit closures, far more drastic than those proposed by the Tories, is one of the most embarrassing duties our Government has assumed. And with some interest I watch Fred Lee trying to grapple with it. Certainly he is handling the miners far more savagely than I would ever dare to do. Is it because he is working class or is it because he is in the hands of the officials? I just don't know.

Back in the Ministry I was due to meet the clerk of the Oxfordshire County Council and the chairman of planning, Alderman Wise, and deal with that splendid subject, the toilets in Bladon village. As a result of

Churchill being buried in the graveyard, Bladon has become a place of pilgrimage; and some months ago I had to deal with the protesters who challenged the planning permission on the ground that the toilets and the car-park were in the wrong place. I suspected the protest was correct and spent a hot summer afternoon with the two who came to see me today pacing the distance from the car-park to the grave. We found it was thirteen hundred yards each way with four private car-parks in between. I also found that some sixteen hundred yards from the church on the other side there was quite a good place for a car-park. I told the Alderman that I wasn't prepared to give consent until he had reconsidered the matter. Well, here they were back on my doorstep, insisting on their proposal. Of course, as Minister I am the final judge in these matters and I have the power to order the council to revoke the planning permission. But the trouble is that if I trampled on them in this way they would claim that compensation would have to be paid. So I didn't take very long in giving way to the extent of a three-year planning permission.

I spent the rest of the day frantically trying to prepare a speech for the Town Planning Association's annual conference, due to take place tomorrow. I had told the officials exactly what I wanted, and on Sunday I got a fairly full text from them. When I read it I realized I couldn't deliver it without making myself a laughing-stock. Even more irritating, I discovered that at the same conference Hugh Wilson, who is our leading architect, was going to make a really interesting speech covering exactly the ground I was supposed to cover. I set to work on Sunday to prepare some ideas and when I came in today I cleared the afternoon and cancelled a broadcast I was due to do about Reinhold Niebuhr,[1] much to the irritation of the Religious Department of the B.B.C. Then at midday I set down to work. By midnight I had managed to compose a speech which seemed tolerably interesting.

Tuesday, October 19th
I worked on the speech until 11.45, when I had to attend the first Cabinet Committee on Fred Willey's Leasehold Enfranchisement Bill. I was delighted to find he had put up a powerful paper which really proposes something new and radical. In principle, it states that a house which a tenant has leased for more than twenty-one years shall be taken to belong to him and not to the ground landlord. I agree entirely that unless one accepts this principle the Bill isn't worth having. But having announced the principle, will Fred Willey be able to stick to it against the objections of his legal colleagues? If he succeeds we shall have an extremely useful addition to our electoral armoury.

In the afternoon I found a packed meeting at Church House, and delivered

---

[1] The eminent theologian and Professor of Ethics at the Union Theological Seminary, New York, since 1928. Crossman had been influenced by his early writings and had come to know him well.

my speech on town planning and answered questions for some forty minutes. I don't expect much press coverage but I have found with these long, careful speeches that if you get them printed in the specialist papers they do, in the end, make a difference.

From there straight back to No. 10 where the first meeting of the new liaison committee was taking place in the Housekeeper's Room. Apparently (I didn't know this before the meeting) my position as chairman has been regularized by the officers of the Party, so I found myself officially in the chair. All the Transport House people were there, as well as parliamentary officials like Harry Mitchell and Frank Barlow and of course Marcia and George Wigg. In this first meeting my aim was to give the Transport House people the feeling that their new chairman would really keep them in contact with Government strategy and provide the low-down on what was going on in Whitehall. When the meeting broke up Marcia asked me to go upstairs to see Harold. He was in his cosiest form. We sat and had a glass of sherry and discussed the manœuvres of Mr Heath on Rhodesia. We also discussed Powell's speech at the Tory Conference, in which as the new Shadow Defence Minister he proposed withdrawal from East of Suez. Harold and I agreed that pressure from our left wing and from Powell on the Right would have value since it would leave him free either to withdraw from East of Suez or to extract a higher price from the Americans for standing staunchly by them.

From there I moved one floor higher in No. 10 to Tommy Balogh's room where the strategy group was meeting to discuss the draft manifesto — Tony Wedgwood Benn, Peter Shore, Tommy, Marcia and I. We began to list the points at which the manifesto will have to go beyond the existing Ministerial and departmental policies. But soon we lapsed into discussing whether Harold has missed his chance by failing to have a snap election this autumn. I think all of us felt he had. On the other hand, we were pleased at Heath's failure to match up to him and that Harold had come through the Conference and the Rhodesian crisis with such conspicuous aplomb that he is now in a stronger position than ever. Like all close friends in politics, we were critical of him. But we were also basking in his strength and success.

Wednesday, October 20th
A terrible, long day which started with my catching the train at 8.15 from Euston and ended with Molly motoring me down the motorway from Coventry to arrive back in London just before midnight. My main job was an official visit to Corby New Town where there has been tremendous competition between the corporation and a very excitable U.D.C. This was a very big day in the life of the U.D.C. because I was opening a civic centre which cost nearly £1 million, and included not only the offices of the U.D.C. but a vast assembly hall, a brand-new theatre and a swimming-bath. The U.D.C. was showing that it really counts for something in Corby. I cut back the official tour and civic lunch in order to have time for informal talks, first

with the U.D.C. and then with the corporation. The councillors are nearly all Scots brought down by Stewarts and Lloyds to the steelworks. I sat with them for an hour in their extraordinary new council-chamber, created by an Italian architect as a kind of dramatic expression of a steel town, black and white and towering, and our voices all lost in the roof. Then I was hauled away by the corporation and went round the town to see *their* housing and to be shown how much better it was than the U.D.C. housing. Corby makes it pretty clear what psychological and political problems are created by planking a development corporation next door to a disgruntled, competitive U.D.C. I tried to make the corporation see it was *their* duty to make the running in friendly co-operation.

From Corby I had to speed off to Coventry, where I had promised to inspect in daylight a corporation caravan-site about which there have been complaints. In British law caravans are curious betwixt-and-between objects and the people who live in them aren't tenants and therefore can't be covered by the Rent Act. On the other hand, although the caravan is not a house most of the people in them are compelled to buy them on mortgage; and the moment they start their repayments, with a life of only ten years before the depreciation runs out, they are so deeply tied that they can't get away. Altogether it is a pathetic problem; and from what I saw I concluded that Coventry Council was quite right to say that you really shouldn't have caravans at all in a city this size.

Next, to the Chase Hostel[1] where I had promised to address a ward meeting. Two hundred personal invitations had been sent out and some ten or fifteen people turned up—not one of the young people came. But we chatted about Vietnam, housing policy and rents, in a pleasant atmosphere over coffee and sandwiches. Molly drove me back to London in well under two hours so as to be in time for Cabinet next morning.

On October 25th, the Prime Minister took another of his initiatives, a dramatic flight to Rhodesia. He returned the following weekend and reported to the House of Commons on Monday, November 1st. The visit produced a proposal for a Royal Commission under Rhodesia's Chief Justice, Sir Hugh Beadle, with one British and one Rhodesian member. They were to devise some acceptable form of independence. Mr Wilson insisted that the Report should be unanimous; Mr Smith disagreed.

Thursday, October 21st

I had expected Cabinet to deal entirely with the legislative programme. But I was rung up in bed by George Wigg and then Tommy Balogh, who both warned me that the big event would be Rhodesia. A glance at the morning papers showed why. The *Daily Express* had the full story on the front page:

---

[1] One of the hostels established after the Blitz for the workers rebuilding Coventry. During elections these hostels became centres of political activity.

Harold Wilson had decided to fly to Rhodesia to try to stop the disaster of U.D.I.

Sure enough, as soon as we started Harold made a longish statement as to why he had to go. He just couldn't let U.D.I. happen without one more effort to stop it. On Tuesday, when I was alone with him, he had told me how enormously aware he was of the internal, domestic problems involved in U.D.I. – particularly the danger of our getting into a state of war with the British white settlers, which would be ruthlessly exploited by Heath. That was one of his preoccupations. Another was the economic fear that if Rhodesia cut off the Kariba Dam we might have our copper supply cut off and all our economic plans brought to frustration. And the third was the sheer risk of world war. If the Russians were to take over the U.N. police force, they might end by trying to march into Rhodesia. Harold repeated to Cabinet all these fears, giving them as the reasons why he felt he ought to go. The discussion lasted some forty minutes. I started it by saying to vague murmurs of approval that I was doubtful. (After all I had talked to Tommy and to George, both of whom were very doubtful indeed.) Why should we allow the P.M. to risk not only his life but also his reputation? Instead, a delegation should be sent out which might well consist of Arthur Bottomley and Alec Douglas-Home, representing the Opposition, plus one other.

Harold resisted this very strongly and it soon became clear that he wasn't discussing the idea with Cabinet before making up his mind – he had not only made up his mind but committed himself. It was also clear that he had nobbled the Lord Chancellor and Frank Cousins, who both saw this as a dramatic piece of statesmanship. The rest of us were uneasy but not really willing to put up much resistance because we felt it was a *fait accompli*.

But the discussion was quite useful because it revealed that he wasn't doing what I at first thought he might be doing – he wasn't assuming U.D.I. must happen and so taking precautions to strengthen his position in dealing with it after the event. No, he was so appalled by U.D.I. that he was going all out to stop it.[1] And this is important because it makes it more like Munich. Just as Neville Chamberlain was horrified at the prospect of war and went out to Munich to try to stop it, so Harold is going out to Salisbury feeling that he must stop U.D.I. He talked about how he would see all the people he wanted out there and create conditions in which Smith would be driven off U.D.I. and back into negotiation. But has he any real chance of doing this? I doubt it. The moment he goes out there he puts himself on an equality with Smith and makes it seem as though he is being allowed to come to Salisbury, where Smith is king and lord.

What makes him go? He certainly didn't take George Wigg's advice or even tell George Brown before he made up his mind. So I am pretty sure Tommy is right when he says that Burke Trend was the decisive influence – more so than any of his political friends.

[1] The Prime Minister describes his attitude in *Wilson*, pp. 152ff.

The second item on the agenda was a forty-minute discussion on roadside drink tests for drivers.[1] We reached the conclusion that these clauses of the Transport Bill should be put to free vote. At this point I thought we were going to turn to the legislative programme, but Harold said, 'Before we come to that there is one thing we must clear out of the way—steel.' Then to everybody's amazement he argued that new factors had intervened and that we must reconsider our position because we mustn't look as though we were surrendering to Desmond Donnelly and Woodrow Wyatt. I don't think he really said any more than this in his quarter-hour speech. He was immediately supported by Frank Cousins and Barbara Castle. Both said that in their view honour and loyalty to principle required us to write nationalization of steel into the Queen's Speech. I weighed in and said I was amazed this should be raised now since we had had a whole day at Chequers when we had come to a firm agreement that there were a number of measures which were more urgent than this. What had happened since to alter this agreement? To change our minds now would be seen not as a decision to stand up to Wyatt and Donnelly but as a switch occasioned by pressures from a different section of the Party.

After this Fred Lee made one of his bumbling, confused speeches, arguing that the terms of compensation would be affected by another year's delay and that once the steel-masters knew the industry wasn't going to be nationalized they would start changing its structure and this would mean that we would need a Hybrid Bill.[2]

By this time it was nearly one o'clock and it was clear that we couldn't finish the discussion, so we decided to resume it at five o'clock in the afternoon. The moment we broke off I drove round to Cowley Street and had a pleasant lunch with Pam Berry, Maurice Edelman and the editor of the New York Times. It was a real relaxation from serious things.

Harold started our resumed meeting by telling us that he had already received Smith's ambiguous reply. Then we turned back to steel. It was an extraordinary evening because as the debate went on it became clear that apart from Barbara Castle and Frank Cousins (and, departmentally, Fred Lee) the Prime Minister hadn't a single supporter. For once George Brown and Jim Callaghan were united—against him. Even the Lord Chancellor and Tony Greenwood, who are sometimes radical on these things, said we ought to keep to the Chequers agreement. Then what on earth has made the P.M. suddenly switch? Denis Healey blurted out what was in all our minds. 'After all,' he said, 'we talk about surrendering to two people, Donnelly and Wyatt, but I think there are two different people who we might be accused of surrendering to,' and of course he meant Cousins and Castle. Actually, I

[1] This was the issue of whether tests should be made selectively or taken on a random basis.
[2] A Hybrid Bill is one affecting specific private or local interests. It must follow a special procedure, which allows for representations by those affected.

don't think Barbara had anything to do with it. So the only source the switch could have come from is Cousins.

I'd rather expected that after Conference Harold would take the opportunity of getting rid of him; but instead he tried to buy him in with a bigger job. I know now from Tommy Balogh that Cousins and Jenkins were both offered jobs, Jenkins the Home Office and Cousins an expanded Ministry of Technology, including Aviation. The plan broke down because it was announced in the press before it was firm and Harold refused to be dictated to in this way. Now apparently it is on again, presumably because he feels he can't afford the split which Cousins's going might cause. And so, to keep Cousins sweet, he said to him, 'I will try out your idea about steel in Cabinet, but I warn you what might well happen.' There is no doubt about it that this performance lowered his standing. A few days before he had been at the height of success after a wonderful broadcast on Rhodesia which made many Tories say they would vote with us. Now, suddenly, inside Cabinet he revealed a failure of leadership which took my breath away.

At last we got to the legislative programme, and Bert Bowden told us he had managed to produce a programme which would take eighty-two days on the Floor, although last year we had a maximum of fifty-six. So twenty-six days have to be cut out; would Cabinet please do it? Now one thing a Cabinet can't do is to sit round and cut a legislative programme back by 25 per cent. However, we started ploughing through the list and we soon got to immigration. Tom Fraser, who sits beside me, is usually inarticulate; but right at the beginning he had said, 'I am in favour of dropping steel, but I would drop immigration as well in order to give a balance.' I now took up his theme and pointed out that every single argument for postponing steel applied equally to immigration. Of course the Lord President and the Home Secretary were much against it but everybody else realized that this was common sense—if we were going to maintain the unity of the Party and get the Left to accept the postponement of steel, why not compensate them by postponing immigration as well? So this is what was finally arranged.

Harold had played no part whatsoever; but after we had dealt with immigration, he remarked that we need not cut the programme back since even if the Bills got no further, a number of Second Readings would be useful in the election manifesto. And before we knew what was happening we were discussing the legislative programme in terms not of a job to be done but of election propaganda. I couldn't help remembering how in the first Session we decided to sit down grimly and do a serious job. Now at the beginning of this second Session we have given up planning to do a job this year and are merely preparing for an election. Surely in that case it would have been infinitely better to have had the election this autumn? However, my immediate concern was to see to it that I got my own essential Bills put right at the beginning of the Session. I must get my rate rebates, building licensing and housing subsidies on to the Statute Book. And that doesn't leave much time if we are going to have the election before the municipals, i.e. at the very latest in the first fortnight of May 1966.

By now it was long after seven, when I was due to catch the train to Crewe, so I started back to the office, tidied up and went by the 9.10. When I got into bed I began to read the enormous briefs which the Department had prepared for my visits next day to Winsford U.D.C. and Cheshire County Council.

Friday, October 22nd
That brief was not only enormous, it was also boring. Nevertheless, Winsford, though a ghastly little spot, turned out to be an amusing as well as an interesting place. Originally it was a string of houses for the salt-workers at the mines north of Nantwich. But because the salt dried up as an industry only a hundred workers are now needed, and this little place decided to save itself: the enterprising town clerk launched an industrial estate rather like ours outside Banbury, and he soon began to do town development for Manchester without much help from the county. Winsford has already built a thousand houses and my job that morning was to open the thousandth. I soon realized my presence was due to over-ambition on the part of the U.D.C. and incompetence in my own Ministry. This thousandth house was falling down, partly because the contractor did not know his job and partly because the function of the clerk of works had been let out by the U.D.C. to a private company. This put me in a rather delicate position as I had been brought there to be photographed congratulating the authority on its success. However, life was made easier for me by the housewives of this new estate. They were so indignant about the new houses that they had put their dustbins all across the road to bar my progress and get me to have a good talk about the scandal. This I did and when I got back to the local government office I told the assembled councillors and their town clerk that they really must work with the county and not go so fast that they were tripping over their own feet.

From there to Chester, where a great lunch was to be given by the county council with all the town development people present. I was able to make clear that New Town corporations are terribly cumbrous things and that I liked seeing counties getting on with the job through town development. I then caught the train back to London. Anne had come up from Prescote to prepare a splendid dinner for Mike Bessie, my American publisher, and his wife Connie. He told me my book *Planning for Freedom* is due out in November. I couldn't care less.

Saturday, October 23rd
Another day of official visits, this time north of London, to Letchworth Garden Suburb and Stevenage. The wonderful autumn weather had degenerated, as it always does in the Chilterns, into an early morning fog. I was a very tired man by now and I was glad to get away with Anne at four

o'clock and to struggle on to the motorway still in that thick fog. Then suddenly, just as we moved into Buckinghamshire, we found ourselves in brilliant sunshine and we got home in time to have tea with the children and a splendid play before they went to bed. Pritchett has been away for a week's holiday and he filled me in before I gave my neighbour Tom Loveday, of Williamscot, a drink. It had probably been the most exhausting week of my ministerial life. What wears me out is the combination of early rising, official visitations and the grind of actually running the Ministry. In addition there is the anxiety about the new White Paper on housing which is always at the back of my mind.

Monday, October 25th
I worked most of Sunday on the draft White Paper and completed the whole of the first ten pages. Directly I got to London I delivered them to Jennie and went off to the E.D.C. When I came back later in the morning Peter Brown was waiting for me. He said he was deeply disturbed after reading the draft. He felt that the White Paper was unpublishable with the section on the national housing plan as it stands at present. All the plan is is an expression of good intentions, not a concrete policy. This is something I had been getting uneasier about all last week. So when Peter Brown chimed in with the same argument I was furious and really rude to him because I knew he was right! I can't make it sound satisfactory unless I get something out of the talks with the building societies and the builders, which are due to be resumed on Wednesday afternoon.

The chances aren't too good. Indeed, after lunching with the two Parliamentary Secretaries at the Farmers' Club, I decided the situation was so dangerous that I must get the officials together that afternoon. When they were gathered, I made them reassert their belief in our aims — which I am not at all sure that they feel. I also, I think, made them promise they would do everything before Wednesday's meeting to win the builders over. Of course, I know very well that some of them would be delighted to have this White Paper flop just at the moment when the Minister is so personally successful.

With this worry at the back of my mind, I had to speak at the by-election which resulted from the death of the gypsy's ally, Norman Dodds.[1] I went down to Erith and Crayford fully briefed on the local issues — town-centre development and housing. We were driven through the fog to the usual kind of school hall, and found the usual kind of crowd, seventy or eighty people, sitting disconsolately about. Then just before we started the hall suddenly filled. A lot of people filed in and it was whispered to me that they had come to protest about the county council's hostel at West Malling in Kent. I didn't think much about it during the speech of the candidate, Mr Wellbeloved, an extremely complacent man who has been on the council four years, exudes self-confidence and told me that everything was sure to be O.K. But my speech

[1] It was held on Thursday, November 11th.

was soon interspersed with a stream of ribald comments. The chairman wasn't used to disorderly meetings and there were only four stewards in the hall; but I managed to plough through my set piece and sit down for questions. After ten minutes the police had to be called in. But they stood about at the back of the hall doing absolutely nothing because they had been instructed (as I heard afterwards) not to intervene unless the chairman specifically asked them to remove certain persons from the meeting. Instead they tried to shepherd *me* out! I tried desperately to avoid being photographed surrounded by a police escort; but I went back to my train feeling pretty flat and realizing how little it takes to turn a Minister's appearance into a flop.

Tuesday, October 26th
Cabinet, with George Brown in the chair since Harold is still away in Rhodesia. It started with George reporting that things in Salisbury were extremely bleak and Harold on the edge of leaving with nothing achieved. However, there was one more card in his hand which he would play before he left. I am afraid I took all this rather for granted and thought it supported those of us who had been against his going. Nevertheless, the sheer fact that he had gone was in his favour. How important it was was shown by the public's reaction to the Archbishop of Canterbury, who had managed to come out with a statement that if the British Government had to use force they deserved public support. This had caused a storm of indignation which revealed only too clearly that the last thing the British public wants is the use of force or sanctions in Rhodesia. They are prepared to see us standing up for what is right but they wouldn't tolerate a war against fellow white men who are also British subjects. From this point of view Harold is right to be seen doing everything in order to prevent U.D.I. Nevertheless, it looks as though U.D.I. is coming – Smith is making this more and more insultingly clear.

However, the main item was widows' pensions. Now that we have abandoned the big all-in scheme of national superannuation, Peggy Herbison has had to postpone the new pensions and introduce short-term improvements first, i.e. earnings-related sickness and unemployment benefits; and she was pleading to be allowed an extra £7 million in order to extend the scheme to widows. After she had made her case, Douglas Houghton, her overlord, elaborately suggested that she might have got her sums wrong and urged that this should go back to the Social Services Committee. Douglas's behaviour obviously upset her. She spoke with great passion, explaining that this whole idea was something she detested. She had wanted to keep the big scheme but had been compelled to drop it by the economic Ministries, who said that only sickness and unemployment benefits were essential for the modernization of British industry, along with redundancy payments. If we were going to introduce only the short-term benefits we must surely round off the scheme by spending an extra £7 million a year on the widows.

12*

I thought she had an overwhelming case and that she was well within her ministerial rights in trying to get the extra £7 million in a supplementary estimate. I also felt sorry for her having to work under Douglas Houghton, so I spoke up very strongly. But Tony Crosland came in very quickly, saying that he couldn't see how we could allow this sort of extra expenditure. Naturally, Jack Diamond, Chief Secretary at the Treasury, said the same thing. After a long bicker we agreed that the Social Services Committee should meet again this week and make another recommendation to Cabinet on Thursday, when the final decision would be taken.

This untidy argument was at least a genuine discussion of a kind we don't have very often in our Cabinet. It arose of course out of a disagreement between Peggy and Douglas Houghton which couldn't be resolved in the Social Services Committee. In Cabinet Peggy was in a weak position because she was pre-empting money and anybody who does that makes all his other spending colleagues jealous. I was sitting in the smoking-room of the Commons after lunch when James Callaghan strolled in and said to me, 'You're a pretty awful Minister. You not only take most of the money for your Department but then you come to Cabinet and fight to get other Ministers their money too. That isn't what most people do.' It's true. They don't.

Since Parliament was resuming that afternoon I stayed in the House to see Horace King sworn in as our new Speaker. The atmosphere was pleasant because the tension had been removed by the morning announcement that Roderic Bowen had become the second of the two Deputy Speakers so that we now have one Conservative, one Labour and one Liberal in the Chair. So the Prime Minister has brought off his coup. Our majority of three has not been cut to one! I thought the performance wasn't too bad and what Horace actually said standing on the steps of the Speaker's Chair was quite moving.

There had been a great deal of opposition to Horace King in the Labour Party and it had leaked into the press. How serious it all was I really don't know. George Wigg probably used the P.M.'s name more than he should have done in an effort to keep Horace out. I was also against Horace and so was the Chief Whip; but it seemed obvious to us that since nothing could prevent him being selected it didn't pay for his own Party to be seen opposing him. Nevertheless, the damage has been done.

In the evening Anne gave a little dinner at Vincent Square for our group — Tony Benn, Marcia, Gerald Kaufman, Peter Shore and Tommy Balogh. We found complete agreement that Harold should not have gone to Rhodesia. We found that we all accepted the decision to postpone steel and had been disconcerted by Harold's attempt to reverse it. In order to keep the Party together, we all agreed that, now steel has been dropped, we must give much more emphasis to the other progressive parts of our policy, especially the modification of investment allowances to favour development areas. The one point on which we were in disagreement was over the decision to drop legislation on immigration. I strongly supported it; but there was a feeling among the others that it would be regarded as too sudden and too violent a switch.

This little group around Marcia is really quite important since she is still the most influential person in Harold's life, far more influential I should say than Tommy Balogh, and infinitely more influential than me. So it is of the greatest importance that she should not feel isolated. She is being gradually ejected from No. 10 by the Civil Service and now does most of her work across in the Commons.[1] This is all part of the battle for the attention of the Prime Minister which the Civil Service has been winning against his political friends. It was Burke Trend, for example, who went with him to Africa; none of his political friends were invited. Marcia has been fighting to get a glimpse of Cabinet papers, but she is still no nearer to achieving it; and she and Tommy cling to their place in Harold's life, well aware that they are always in danger of being thrust out.

Wednesday, October 27th

N.E.C. at ten o'clock, the first since the Blackpool Conference. The atmosphere was a good deal better, largely because we have at least agreed that a discussion of Government policy should be a part of each meeting. However, as always seems to happen, we couldn't have the discussion *that* morning because of the memorial service for the late Speaker.

This was the day of my crucial meeting with the builders and the building societies. I had to precede it by a lunch with the National Association of Property Owners at the Stafford Hotel. I was disconcerted to learn that property shares have gone up as a result of my Rent Bill.

Back from there to my Minister's room, where we had the usual business of the builders and the building societies getting round the huge table next door while I sat in solitude and waited.

The builders all sat on my right and the building societies on my left. The societies remained almost silent for an hour while the builders fired off their complaints and I reasoned quietly with them. They were ferociously hostile to any idea of collaborating with a socialist government, seething with indignation against the Land Commission and complaining about controls. They didn't really challenge the social case for raising the total number of houses built to 500,000 a year by 1968. What they objected to was the idea that they should accept a 50–50 split between the public and the private sectors. A self-imposed limitation to 250,000 a year was something, they said, they couldn't possibly accept. Gradually the building societies began to join in the discussion. I found people who had been fiercely sceptical three months ago coming in on my side and saying that, after all, building societies always have to plan the amount of money they are going to lend a year or two in advance and intrinsically there is no difficulty in discussing these plans with the Government.

[1] See Marcia Williams, *Inside No. 10* (London: Weidenfeld, 1972).

The meeting went on for nearly two hours. Finally, I said I would give them a fortnight to make up their minds since I must know hard and fast whether they were prepared to collaborate with me. At the end of it I got the impression from talking informally to Maurice Laing and to Wates, as well as to the building societies, that they are prepared to do something. They don't think we shall achieve very much but they don't want to break off the discussions. That was an improvement but it still left me in some difficulty, trying to draft a White Paper which made any sense.

I felt pretty weary and battered after those two hours when I went round to George Wigg's room for the regular Wednesday meeting of what I call the liaison committee. I am gradually changing its nature because I think its main job is to keep Transport House in touch with policy and not to interfere in the running of by-elections or the nomination of people for broadcasting as it used to under George. George said to me afterwards that he would really leave it completely to me because we shouldn't quarrel in public. I think he is right.

At seven thirty I broke the meeting off because I was due at the County Clerks' Association annual dinner, and got Molly to drive me home. After I had put on a clean shirt and rested I had a drink and then at eight o'clock — since the dinner was timed for eight — I set out for Claridge's. Molly said, 'But you can't go looking like this,' and then I suddenly realized that they would all be in tails and decorations. So I rushed back, put on a black tie and dinner-jacket and only got there at eight forty-five — I had also forgotten that the Dairy Show and the Motor Show were both on. The traffic was absolutely solid in the West End and by the time I sat down at Claridge's the dinner had started. I found myself sitting next to Kenyon, the huge, burly West Riding county clerk, who had already crossed swords with me at my first meeting with the C.C.A. He laboured the view that he didn't prepare his speeches in advance and that he was just making a few notes and he asked me some questions about myself. I said I didn't prepare my speeches either and so we both had an enormous Claridge's dinner, very good wine and moderately good eats. County clerks are important people and so are their London friends. The speeches were delivered to a resplendent collection of some 500 leading civil servants. So up gets this fellow Kenyon and moves the health of the Minister in ten minutes of extremely offensive humour. There was a great deal about busybody politicians who try to make changes and who then disappear, and something about the Minister who writes books which one doesn't bother to read. It was fairly impossible stuff and the raucous laughter which greeted his first sallies got more and more embarrassed towards the end.

Replying was quite an ordeal. I started by saying that I didn't like this kind of occasion — it wasn't my style of entertainment — and I had only accepted when Dame Evelyn had insisted: 'Minister, you have a very peculiar taste — the kind of peculiar taste which will enable you to enjoy the things that are said about you when your health is proposed.' This went down fairly well and I ended a short speech by saying that I agreed with Mr Kenyon, the average life of a Minister was not much more than three years but maybe in the course of my three years I would be the one Minister of Housing who really did fundamentally change the shape of local government in the way that we all knew it had to be changed. The county clerks shivered a bit when they heard this and said 'Hear, hear.' And that was that.

Thursday, October 28th
Ely Place, just off Holborn Circus, is a little, narrow, eighteenth-century square where they have pulled down a public house on one side and are proposing to put up a horrible modern building instead. The issue was: should one compel them instead to replace it with a replica Georgian building and so save the general shape and tradition of the square? The Department said 'No: insisting on replica Georgian isn't our job.' This, however, disregarded the fact that two replica Georgian houses on the other side of the street had been put up at great cost by order of the L.C.C. Anyway, having taken a look I let my preservationist feelings come out and gave instructions to sustain the Inspector and preserve the look and feeling of the square against the advice of the Department.

From there I just had time to get back to Downing Street for Cabinet. We hadn't any more news about Harold except that the situation was pretty grim and he was expected home on Friday so we turned to our old subject of widows' pensions.

This didn't take long because Douglas Houghton could report a decision of the Social Services Committee, taken twenty-four hours previously. When Peggy had repeated her case, once again I had immediately chipped in to say that if the money was within the limit of her estimates it was only decent to let the Minister decide for herself. Tony Crosland this time agreed and there was no one against her. So Houghton had to report against his own view and Cabinet at once agreed. I was jolly pleased. I think I have made a friend for life out of Peggy.

After that we went on to consider the Queen's Speech. It had been drafted fairly carefully but I spotted a very sinister phrase about entry into the European Common Market and said it had to go. It did. Then we had another bleat from the Home Secretary about the dropping of the Immigration Bill. But his attempt to have it put back was crushed—rather ruthlessly, I am afraid. And that is really all that happened.

Back in the Ministry after Cabinet I was amazed to hear that a Private Notice Question from John Boyd-Carpenter on the progress of my talks with the building societies and the builders had been accepted. I went straight down to the House to answer it and Question Time rushed along so fast that poor Niall MacDermot, who had Question 44 for the Treasury, wasn't there when it was reached at 3.25. Thank God I was lunching in the House and was there in plenty of time. I found myself on my feet for the first time since Parliament came back from holiday and answering Boyd-Carpenter. I was very grateful to him, actually, because I was given an opportunity to deny that I was bringing any pressure whatsoever to bear on the building societies or trying to use them for my political purposes.

Friday, October 29th
Home Affairs Committee. I was mainly interested in an item on Canvey Island. My Inspector had urged that I should turn down a request being made by a big oil company for planning permission on Canvey Island. The Dame and J.D., however, were insistent that I should overrule the Inspector in the national interest. The Foreign Office, the Commonwealth Office, the Ministry of Power, the D.E.A. and the Treasury all insisted that we couldn't afford to upset a foreign oil company. I felt it was my duty to represent the unfortunate house-owners who had left London and bought a little place in Essex and now found that their home was to be utterly ruined by this horrible erection. True, Canvey Island is a pretty awful spot which has been thoroughly ruined by unplanned building. But even when very little amenity survives, that little means more to the people who live there than all the amenity of a beautiful national park a hundred miles away. These views, I had been told by the Dame and J.D., were those of a sentimental preservationist. However, I had a stroke of luck. Just before the meeting it was revealed that the foreign company which wanted to build the refinery had decided to sell their British distribution rights to Esso on the ground that there wasn't enough market in Britain for them to worry about. This strengthened my hand against the Ministry of Power and the D.E.A., and I was able to hold the whole thing up until we could at least check whether there was an alternative site for the refinery.

Canvey Island was my special departmental interest; but what really excited the Committee that morning was a sudden proposition by the Home Secretary that we should set up a Royal Commission on Immigration. It is difficult to conceive of a sillier proposal. By setting up a Royal Commission we should simply announce our determination to postpone any action at all for years and allow a group of people to research ponderously and remain inactive, as Royal Commissions always do. Fortunately Gerald Gardiner and Bert Bowden bashed poor Frank Soskice straight away. What they did concede to him, and quite rightly, was a narrow committee on the subject of the right of appeal against deportation by an immigrant from the Commonwealth. Poor Frank had to take his defeat. He had been threatening to resign from the Cabinet; and in fact it would be a wonderful thing if with our new policy we could have had a new Home Secretary as well. Now is the time for Harold Wilson to try once again to carry his plan through of giving the job to Roy Jenkins. Whether he will do it is a very different question.

I gave Alan Bullock, the head of St Catherine's College, Oxford, a snappy lunch at the Athenaeum. He had refused the job of chairman of the Parliamentary Boundary Commission. I wanted him to be the chairman of my new Commission on Local Government. Now after only an hour he said he was interested. That was a triumph. He is the one man in England in whom I would have complete confidence.

Sunday, October 31st
On the way down in the train to Coventry this weekend I looked at the *Spectator* and found a very gratifying profile by Alan Watkins, their political correspondent. Mike Bessie, who has been staying the weekend, commented that I seemed to be standing very well in the public eye and must be one of the Government's successes. I think he is right; I am riding high – too high for comfort. It's an alarming thing how public opinion suddenly switches from saying, 'That Crossman! He's an impossible, erratic fellow. He won't last long,' to calling me a brilliant success. Certainly I shall have one solid success to my credit if I can get the Lords' amendments on the Rent Bill settled on Monday night and see the Bill an Act of Parliament. And I shall soon have rate rebates as part of my score. I have also been a success in the world of local authorities as a result of what I have been doing about boundary decisions and planning decisions. But on the housing side it is a very different picture. We have no results as yet in council-house building; and we are gravely alarmed about the effect Callaghan's deflation measures will have on the private sector. There are a tremendous number of unpredictable factors which could knock me right off my high horse as rapidly as I have been elevated to it by opinion in Fleet Street, Westminster and Whitehall. That is why I am so desperately anxious about these negotiations with the builders and the building societies. And that is why I was so relieved when I was able to read today the Dame's redraft of my White Paper. She has completely rewritten it so that the Government policy is clearly stated and we record the lack of enthusiasm shown by the builders in such a way as to show that our policy is unaffected by their opposition; we are just hoping for their co-operation. I think she may really have solved the problem of the presentation of the policy to the public. That is my first impression but I am waiting for second opinions when I go to London tomorrow.

Monday, November 1st
My mind I am afraid was almost entirely on the Lords' amendments to the Rent Bill, which were due to begin at 3.30 that afternoon, or, rather, after Harold Wilson had made his Rhodesia Statement.

Harold presented to Cabinet his report from Salisbury and his recommendation that there should be a Royal Commission. He gave us, however, four choices. Choice one: to accept Smith's view entirely – that is to say on the definition of the terms of reference of the Royal Commission. Choice two: to accept the idea of a Royal Commission but to say we disagree with Smith's terms of reference. Choice three: to accept it and have two bases for a Royal Commission, his and ours. Choice four: to reject the idea of a Royal Commission altogether—which would make U.D.I. automatic and inevitable. From the start it was clear that Frank Cousins and Barbara Castle were the only two of our colleagues who fought for accepting the inevitability of U.D.I. immediately and not doing anything whatever to try to continue to negotiate. The rest of us knew it was right to play for time and it was on this basis that we allowed Harold to make his Statement to the House on the Royal Commission.

Harold's Statement that afternoon on Rhodesia was dramatic and obviously successful.[1] I must say I fell asleep and I realized that I hadn't by any means heard all of it when it came to an end. He read it so quietly, so steadily, so boringly.

Anyway, I was concerned with the next part of the business which was the Lords' amendments to my own Bill. The debate went on from about four o'clock till about two in the morning. There were fifty amendments on the order paper of which only five mattered, most of the others being our own drafting amendments.

I will admit that I was a bit anxious as to whether I would be able to deal with all the complexities since I hadn't spent any time over the weekend re-reading the briefs, though I had glanced through the House of Lords debates. The fact is that there are whole legal areas of this Bill of which I am completely ignorant. I refused to read it through when the first draft was presented to the Department and I have not read it through since. However, I do know pretty well what it is about in practice and in a way I find it a great advantage not to understand its legal niceties and not even ever to have read it. In this debate there was virtually no fight in the Tories. They were uncomfortable about the whole business of opposing it but they had asked for extended time and therefore we had to go on till two. It was, by and large, an interminable waste of time. Anne came up before dinner—the only evening she could manage in London—and we ate in the House and then she came and sat in the Speaker's Gallery for a couple of hours; but it was too boring and she just had to go home. Looking at the amendments I admit that there were two which we could have accepted and which would have improved the Bill. But I didn't feel in the last inclined to give way to the Lords on this occasion and tactically I was prepared to have the Tories keep us all night, something I made very clear in my speeches. So the debate dragged on and on.

When it was over at two in the morning we had a fantastic little ceremony

[1] The Prime Minister gave an account of his visit to Salisbury and of his discussions with Mr Smith and other African Prime Ministers. He told the House of the proposal that a Royal Commission should be established, with the Rhodesian Chief Justice as chairman. It would seek to devise new electoral arrangements and amendments to the 1961 Constitution, so that Rhodesia could move towards independence without sacrificing the five principles safeguarding the position of the African population. The Attorney-General and Arthur Bottomley remained in Salisbury to discuss the idea.

when I moved that a committee be established to state the grounds on which we were objecting to their Lordships' amendments. Then we followed one of the Clerks into a little room where we found he had written out the five grounds on which I had resisted the amendments, though these grounds didn't have much relation to my actual grounds. I then turned to Jim MacColl and Bob Mellish and said, 'Who is in favour?' and they replied, 'Aye.' I then turned to Boyd-Carpenter and Margaret Thatcher and said, 'Who is against?' and they said, 'No.' So then I concluded the Ayes had it. Afterwards Boyd-Carpenter said, 'You know, in all my years of Government, I've never taken part in this particular ceremony.' And I replied, 'Well, you Tories don't usually reject the Lords' amendments outright, so you've never required this particular highly unusual procedure.'

Tuesday, November 2nd
A very long day entirely devoted to departmental meetings. In the evening a meeting of the strategy group over supper at No. 10. Present: Peter Shore, Tony Benn, Tommy Balogh, Marcia Williams, Gerald Kaufman, myself (as chairman) and the Prime Minister. When he came in he looked really jaded. The Rhodesia crisis has been telling on him. As soon as he flew in, after a week of activity, he was plunged into Cabinet on Monday morning and the House of Commons on Monday afternoon. Judging by the press, he has had a real success in the Commons and foxed the Tories by his proposal for the Royal Commission, even though it was pretty obvious from the word go that the Commission was a non-starter and we were merely postponing the evil day. Nevertheless, by Tuesday evening he looked tired and found it difficult to talk to us at all. Gradually he got more interested and we had a useful discussion on the line he should take in the Queen's Speech. But then his interest lapsed and he suddenly got the bright idea that because Exchange Telegraph[1] had closed down its parliamentary services, Tony Benn as P.M.G. should nationalize it.*

Wednesday, November 3rd
In the morning a P.L.P. meeting. It was supposed to be on the National Plan and I attended in order to see what the mood was. The Party is obviously critical of what it regards as appeasement on Rhodesia, but it has come to accept the Government's decision to postpone steel and immigration – and on the latter it feels it has had a great triumph. On the whole it responded well to George Brown on the Plan; and when the debate came in the House, though dull, it was quite a success for us.
    The liaison meeting at six o'clock that evening was very difficult because

---

* By next day it was clear there was nothing in the idea.
[1] Now the domestic subsidiary of Reuters. Full parliamentary coverage had always been provided by four agencies, those of *The Times*, the *Telegraph* and two independent agencies, whose correspondents co-operated so that no one agency out-scooped the others.

George Wigg made sure that it was almost exclusively concerned with the utter failure of our M.P.s to do the job, which the Tory M.P.s are prepared to do, of going out to canvass in the two current London by-elections.[1] The Tories get dozens of recruits, we get hardly any at all. Wigg's bitter complaints are perfectly justified. Where he is wrong is in believing that he or I, now that I have taken his place, can do anything ourselves. Our one chance is to make the Whips see it is *their* responsibility to get the M.P.s on the streets in collaboration with Transport House. This is the line I took throughout the meeting despite George's protests.

From there I was off to Brentford and Chiswick where I had to discuss housing with a full meeting of the Party G.M.C. Back at ten o'clock, I started to prepare for my Ministerial broadcast on the Rent Act. This broadcast has a history. Months ago George Wigg had convinced himself that whereas Tory Governments used Ministerial broadcasts for their own purposes, we neglected to exploit them. As usual he had done some homework and found that their record was sixty-one ministerials to our four. What he hadn't noticed was that in the last seven or eight years of TV these broadcasts had dwindled to almost nothing except exhortations by the P.M.G. to post early for Christmas. Nevertheless, it was true that the B.B.C. had been bloody-minded to George Brown when he wanted to do a Ministerial broadcast on the National Plan. In order to make them atone for their sins I had weeks ago put up a formal request for a Ministerial broadcast on the Rent Act once it was on the Statute Book. Ten minutes had been allotted to me on Friday, November 5th, when we expected Parliament to be prorogued; and by the early hours I had roughed out a reasonably intelligent script.

Thursday, November 4th
Another Cabinet, with Rhodesia as the first item. But there was very little to report since there was no word from Smith. All we got was an interesting episode illustrating Harold's method of handling a hot potato. On the Wednesday evening David Ennals, who is Barbara's P.P.S., and four other P.P.S.s had issued a statement laying down the conditions which a British Government should insist on for the Royal Commission. They couldn't have been drafted by anyone who had not been briefed by a Cabinet Minister, so it was obvious that David had been talking to Barbara. Tam was another of the signatories and I had a tiff with him over it, but of course he was taking a critical line not about my Department but about Barbara's. It seemed to me outrageous of Barbara to allow David to do as he did, and people said so at Cabinet. Harold Wilson walked round the subject. He was severe about David personally and said he shouldn't have done it, but he let Barbara get away with it. And I thought once again, 'He has been superb in handling Rhodesia

[1] Erith and Crayford (see p. 360) and the Cities of London and Westminster (see p. 318). In the by-election on November 4th, the latter seat was won by John Smith, Conservative, with a majority of 6,737. The Government still had a majority in the Commons of only one.

but he just doesn't like hurting a colleague and he finds it impossible to sack anybody. So Barbara gets away with gross misbehaviour and Frank Soskice with gross incompetence.'

The second item was the prices and incomes policy. We are now, as a Cabinet, faced with the most difficult problem we have ever had. What sanctions should we provide against employers who refuse to freeze their prices during the period of a submission to the Prices and Incomes Board, or who insist, for that matter, on forcing up their wages in the period of the wage freeze? Now the trouble is that once we have sanctions of this kind it means that conceivably a trade union or a trade-union leader could be punished for industrial action during the period. All the way through the development of the prices and incomes policy Frank Cousins has been against the whole idea of sanctions and has therefore been leading the opposition to the Bill. The situation in Cabinet has been very mysterious because George Brown has also made it clear that he isn't terribly keen on the legislation and that he is doing it in deference to Callaghan. Indeed, I get the impression, though it has never actually been said, that this is one of the assurances Callaghan must have given to Fowler of the American Treasury when he was in Washington, because otherwise there seems to me no reason why the Chancellor should have insisted on these sanctions being introduced into the Bill. I may not be right about this. There is one alternative explanation, namely that Callaghan himself wanted a legal wage freeze last August and that the only way George Brown avoided it was to agree this compromise on the Bill. Anyhow, the debate in Cabinet today went on and on and there was a furious row between George Brown and Frank Cousins. The more I heard of it the more worried I became, because it doesn't seem to me that we are taking in the full implications of this policy. We are really faced with an appalling dilemma. Either we have to make these penalties apply to the trade unions or – almost equally embarrassing – we make an exception of the trade unions, so that employers are liable to punishment but not trade unionists.

In the evening I held a big press conference on the Rent Act, and also finalized the text of the Ministerial broadcast so that our campaign about rents could be launched tomorrow when Parliament is prorogued. At the last moment the arrangements nearly came unstuck because we decided not to prorogue on Friday but to postpone it to Monday owing to the Rhodesian crisis. This news was brought to me in the middle of my press conference and I had to leave out any reference to the Royal Assent, and then persuade the B.B.C. to let my broadcast go out on Friday even though the Bill is not yet on the Statute Book. One can wobble the British constitution on small things as well as on big ones!

With a long Cabinet and a full day's work I didn't have much time for the script of the broadcast before I went down to Lime Grove at seven o'clock with Peter Brown. I had assumed that the B.B.C. would lay on a host of brilliant producers for me. But in fact I found myself sitting in a deserted corner of the building with one girl – absolutely no good – and I was just told to read the script aloud in that empty place. I was exhausted and I found it incredibly difficult. I struggled time after time. First of all I did it at too low a level of intensity, then I over-dramatized myself. It was only after two hours that I got it something like right when they played it back to me. It was dull and solemn and serious, I thought, but it was tolerable.

A state of emergency was announced in Rhodesia by the Minister of Justice, Lardner Burke, on November 5th and, despite a last-minute telephone call from Downing Street, on November 11th, Ian Smith declared Rhodesia unilaterally independent. The Governor, Sir Humphrey Gibbs, nevertheless proclaimed his continued loyalty to the Crown and refused to recognize the authority of Mr Smith and his Ministers. Sir Hugh Beadle, the Chief Justice, joined Sir Humphrey in Government House, which they refused to abandon.

The British Government quickly passed Orders in Council to impose economic sanctions against the rebel regime. Rhodesia was expelled from the sterling area, special exchange controls were applied and Rhodesia lost its Commonwealth preferences. All purchases of Rhodesian sugar and tobacco were banned, thus cutting 70 per cent of Rhodesia's exports to Britain. In this affair ('my Cuba') the Prime Minister's stock rose; the Conservatives, on the other hand, found themselves with an embarrassing conflict of loyalties.

Friday, November 5th
Late last night I took the train to Blackburn, met Barbara Castle next morning and had a routine official visit to the town, touring the new central development area. The only unusual thing about it was that the Member for Blackburn insisted on going round with me wherever I went and sharing my publicity. I didn't mind this very much until she sat in on my confidential meeting with the councillors. They wanted to question me about a new little Bill which I had had to introduce to deal with a minor anomaly – the compensation paid to owner-occupiers in slum-clearance areas. In previous legislation a special exception had been made for those owner-occupiers who had bought their houses between 1939 and 1955. Instead of getting the normal site value like everybody else, they were to be entitled to the full market value of the house. This special privilege was due to end in December of this year. But during the election when Harold Wilson went up to Blackburn Barbara persuaded him in an answer to a question to make an absolutely clear and unambiguous pledge to renew it although there really isn't a case for it. She had asked me to put it in the Queen's Speech, where it was obviously too small to be appropriate. Instead, I got a Private Members' Bill ready and persuaded Frank Allaun to sponsor it. But the A.M.C. decided to oppose the Bill so Frank Allaun dropped it and I couldn't get another Member to take it.

Barbara is tenacious and she insisted that it become a Government Bill in this session. Then when she saw the terms of it she thought it terrible because we didn't continue the concession intact *ad infinitum*, but proposed to taper it off as it became increasingly anomalous. I was explaining all this to the councillors when she suddenly broke in, and began to attack our draft Bill. I said rather sharply, 'But look, Barbara, you put your name to it.' She replied, 'A Cabinet Minister is still allowed personal views as a constituency Member,' and continued to denounce it. I was furious, but all I could say was that if there were complaints about the Bill in Blackburn the best way of dealing with them was to ask the Labour Member whose name is on the Bill to explain it to her constituents and give the best interpretation of it she could. This infuriated her and she walked out of the meeting and I haven't seen her since.

I tell this story because it illustrates the problems of collective responsibility. Frank Cousins has had his difficulties. For instance, he sat with his trade-union delegation at the Conference and didn't rise to cheer George Brown when he finished his speech on incomes policy. Now this week we have Barbara Castle first putting up David Ennals to express her views on Rhodesia, and then herself opposing a Bill for which she is collectively responsible. I suppose it doesn't really matter on minor things like slum-clearance compensation.

I got back by train to Birmingham at 7.30 and drove through Warwickshire, with huge Guy Fawkes bonfires all round me just petering out. We got to Prescote in time to see the end of my Ministerial broadcast. It was dull, as I feared, but I don't think it was a disaster.

Sunday, November 7th
A perfect day out on the hills behind Boddington watching the hunt career around us while we were exploring Hobbit country with Patrick. Anthony Crosland and his wife Susan arrived at 5.30 and we gave a dinner-party for them with Harry and Mary Judge from Banbury Grammar School and Richard and Ann Hartree.

My evening was spoilt by what Harry Judge had to tell me about Banbury. We had been very much hoping that his plans for a middle school for the nine to thirteen age-group, followed by a choice at thirteen, would form the basis for the reorganization of secondary education in this part of the county. However, he tells me that this plan was incompatible with the Labour Party's definition of a comprehensive school and has been scrapped, so something much more unattractive will have to take its place. Instead of our children going on to his school at Banbury, they are now likely to be sent to a comprehensive school for all the rural district council children at Bloxham. However, the headmaster and the Secretary of State got on very well, and I was impressed by Tony's proficiency in explaining his plans. But, oh dear, the more I heard him the more thankful I was that I hadn't got his job. It's an intense, narrowing job, dealing with internal problems of organization, whereas mine is a wide, exciting, expansive one. Though he talked very well Tony Crosland is only Minister of Education in order to be in the Cabinet. He still feels that his real life as a politician will begin when he moves to an economic Department, preferably the Treasury.

One small thing. I was amused to read in one of the papers today a Tory complaint that my broadcast was too political and that John Boyd-Carpenter should ask for a reply. I doubt if he'll get one.

Monday, November 8th
Much against my will I had been dragooned into making the welcoming half-hour oration at the beginning of the international town-planning week, across the river in County Hall. On Sunday night I read the brief J. D. Jones had prepared and found it terrible, so I had to spend most of this morning getting a script ready. I have now delivered half a dozen of these keynote speeches, and arranged to have them circulated to the Department as a policy guide. So they have been that much use at least. Since the State Opening of Parliament takes place tomorrow I was able to slip into the office and then catch the train to Coventry to do one of my regular ward meetings. The two previous ones had been flops; but this one at Longford had relatively a full house in the back of a pub.

Unfortunately, however, it doesn't much help the disastrous plight of the Coventry Labour Party. Its demoralization is becoming public property. We had a major scandal when they tried to sack Winnie Lakin and now the chairman of the education committee has had to resign, as well as another councillor who got into debt. The council group lost four seats last year and they only have to lose another five in order to become dependent on their block of aldermanic seats, which won't last for more than a couple of years.

We motored back to Prescote in beautiful, crisp weather.

Tuesday, November 9th
Anne wanted to go to the opening of Parliament. In nineteen years as a back-bencher this is something I have never seen because I have got a curious snobbery about not attending such state occasions. But I was rather pleased that she wanted to see it herself. And when we met Lola Hahn on the platform at Banbury we asked her to share our carriage and then gave her a lift in the black Super-Snipe, and Lola found herself passing through streets closed by the police, down the Mall, with soldiers on both sides, on the way to drop Anne at the House of Commons and me at Whitehall before Molly delivered her to her flat in Eaton Square. It was great fun giving her this little demonstration of one of the few ministerial perks I enjoy. Later on that morning the Dame and I were busy at work when there was a clatter of hooves, and we knelt on my sofa by the window and looked down at the Dragoons and almost started waving our handkerchiefs. I had never realized before how pretty the whole thing was. Then at 12.15 across to the House of Commons for the traditional meeting of the Parliamentary Labour Party to

discuss the Queen's Speech. Everything seemed to be a pure formality until suddenly convention was broken when Michael Foot asked on a point of order whether there could be a full discussion about the postponement of steel. From the chair Shinwell tried to prevaricate but Michael got his full debate conceded for Wednesday the 10th, the next morning. Then straight to the Prime Minister's room, where Cabinet considered the situation in Rhodesia.

Last week we had started the discussion of the conditions for a Royal Commission. Now after forty minutes we agreed to pledge ourselves to accept anything the Commission unanimously recommended, but only on condition that the Smith Government would pledge itself in the same way. The offer should be made in a letter to Smith.

There was just time to get back to the Ministry, where I was giving Anne a little lunch in my room, before we were back at 2.30 to hear the Queen's Speech read and Harold Lever move thanks for the Royal Address. Then Heath, witty, dry, and not very weighty, and then our Harold with his big speech. The trouble was that, as a result of Rhodesia, he had had no time to prepare it and it lasted for sixty-five minutes even though he cut out a mass of material.

Wednesday, November 10th
At ten o'clock we resumed the Cabinet discussion of Rhodesia, and at once Harold got into a long and acrid argument with Barbara Castle about the rights and wrongs of making any kind of concession to Smith on the subject of the Royal Commission. It was a bit academic since by then there was only the slimmest chance of preventing U.D.I. and it seemed to be a mere matter of hours before it was announced. However, Harold was permitted to formulate a precise offer along the lines that if we accepted a unanimous decision the Smith Government must be prepared to do the same.

After that we had to go across to the Parliamentary Party meeting which started at eleven. There I sat for an hour listening to a tremendous attack by Michael Foot and John Mendelson on the postponement of steel. They weren't really talking to their parliamentary colleagues but to the public outside, and I thought that the people who argued against them had overwhelmingly the best of the argument. Everybody said that after all we had dropped steel not on principle but merely as a question of tactics. But perhaps there was some point in those left-wing speeches, because in his effort to placate the left-wingers Harold Wilson has committed us more firmly than ever to nationalize steel in the first Session of the next Parliament if we win the general election.

At the liaison committee in the afternoon we had a report from John Silkin on the hopeless failure of Labour M.P.s to canvass in by-elections. John was able to report that he had held a meeting of the London M.P.s and forty-five people had turned up, so he has really got something moving. Not that this satisfied George Wigg, who is now extremely sore about my taking over the chair at this meeting and reversing his style of running it. When *he* discovered anything wrong he would rush in and clear it up himself. Now he would start giving orders to the agent in a by-election, and now order a book to be published by Transport House.[1] The chairman of a liaison committee just can't behave in that way. His job is to smooth things over, not to cause more blow-ups than necessary.

Thursday, November 11th
This was Rhodesia day – U.D.I. was declared. But for me it was White Paper day – I had my meeting with the builders and the building societies. The Dame had been working very hard and she gave me advance notice of the statement the builders would make on what they were likely to agree among themselves. The meeting went pretty well. The builders spent most of their time complaining about the appalling difficulty of getting land, a difficulty which is going to be accentuated by the creation of the Land Commission. This gave me my chance, and I was able to tell them that problems of this kind were best dealt with by working parties and that I was prepared to do everything possible to release land for private building. I also raised the issue of the New Towns and told them I wanted a working party to discuss how we could change the balance of house-building in them from some 80 per cent rented and 20 per cent for sale to a 50–50 balance. Gradually I worked them round; and finally I was able to say, 'Look, I'll leave it to you and my officials to fix a communiqué,' and this was issued by 11.30. Of course it was completely swamped by the big Rhodesian news and so it hardly appeared in the afternoon's papers, but this was in some ways an advantage. I had got what I really needed without too much publicity and I had the luck to get it before the afternoon's debate in the House on the Land Commission and housing.

At 10.45 I went into Cabinet and by 11.18 U.D.I. had been announced. I then listened with some interest to the preparation for the afternoon performance but of course my mind was mostly on housing; however important Rhodesia may be, if you are a departmental Minister you can't help thinking that your debate is the one that really matters. In the afternoon Harold made an extremely good Statement, and then Fred Willey got up to introduce our debate. He did it in a very hesitant speech which he explained by saying that he was ill. So I got him off to bed and had to sit through one of the most boring debates I have ever heard. It never got going and I was left to wind it up with nothing to say. I made a pleasant little speech and then I took my niece and nephew Gay and Stafford home and we heard the results of the Erith by-election on the radio. I thought it would be worse than it actually was.[1] After that I was taken to King's Cross and climbed on a train for Darlington.

In my sleeper I found myself staying awake reflecting on a day which for me had been a turning-point. Once I had got that agreement of the builders and the building societies to collaborate in my national plan for building 500,000 houses a year, the White Paper fell into line. It's not that the policy had changed; but with this agreement firm, I had something concrete to record. I am also on the way to changing the Labour Party's attitude to owner-occupation. It is a curious fact that, although the Party has been promising mortgage-holders better interest rates in the general election, there is still in most socialist minds the feeling that as a Party we stand for council houses and that private-enterprise building is something foreign to us. Now I have introduced the idea that houses to let and houses to sell must be seen as part of one big housing campaign; that we must be just as interested in the one part as in the other, and that councils must be encouraged to provide land for private-enterprise housing when they can't use it themselves. I hope it will swing the Party into a new line which will help us in the general election and also win the confidence of the builders for our national house-building campaign.

Sunday, November 14th
After routine visitations to Peterlee and Washington New Town in County Durham I got back home to Prescote to find exquisite autumn weather. I spent Saturday and Sunday here in sunshine, with hard frost at night. We seem to have saved up all the summer sunshine this year for November and the farm has been looking lovelier than I ever remember. What a difference it makes to be able to come back here to the sheer comfort of Prescote, and its beauty and rootedness, which is more and more influencing me. Is it making me more conservative? Well, in one sense being rooted is being conservative. But I don't think it is making me less adventurous in my ideas, less prepared to take risks. On the contrary I am more self-confident as the result of my married life, more ready to try radical measures even if they risk my being thrown out of my job. The radical measures which excite me are not anti-property measures in the sense that they would require us to accept the confiscation of Prescote. On the other hand I am sure Prescote has taught me a lot more about economic growth, about capital investment, about business, about tax law, than I knew before. All these things I have learnt by having responsibility here with Pritchett for these five hundred acres.

Since this has been Rhodesia week I want to put down some considered reflections about the Rhodesia crisis, since it is certainly one of the Government's turning points—at least if it isn't, Harold has judged it completely wrong. He calls it 'his Cuba'—the test of his strength and statesmanship and

---

[1] James Wellbeloved held the seat for Labour with a majority of 7,072, bringing the Government's majority in the Commons to two seats.

power to survive a really difficult situation. Certainly, he has so far survived personally with ever-growing weight and stature. This week I noticed for the first time that he seems to have spread in girth and that his photographs are taking on a more portentous, statesmanlike appearance. And if anyone should think I am laughing when I say all this, I must add that the statesmanship is getting across through his TV appearances to the general public as well as in the House of Commons. Nevertheless, his growing statesmanship hasn't made him disregard party political considerations. Indeed I think his thought has been largely dominated by the determination not to leave his flank open to Heath, and to make sure we can't be blamed for U.D.I. From outside (and even though I am in the Cabinet I am completely outside the Rhodesian crisis), it has always seemed to me that U.D.I. was inevitable. But Harold Wilson always felt so appalled by the prospect that he convinced himself that by his personal intervention he could prevent it. Only this can explain his astonishing readiness to go to any lengths in order to delay that final decision.

Looking back, I don't criticize him for this since I am sure he has gained enormously in terms of public opinion at home. On the other hand, by concentrating so much on preventing U.D.I. he has succumbed to the temptation of neglecting to prepare any strategy for facing U.D.I. when it actually came. It was almost as though he felt it criminal to consider what to do when it came because it was his duty to prevent it coming. So, whereas everything he has done to try to stop it has been quite good, I am horribly afraid he is far less well prepared to deal with it now that it *has* come.

Another strong impression I have had is of the hold that Barbara Castle has exerted upon his conscience. Barbara, who was his P.P.S. at the Board of Trade, is the left-winger closest to him, and as Minister of Overseas Development, even if her influence hasn't prevailed, her conscience has haunted him and made him uneasy and unsure of himself. All her effort throughout the crisis has been to avert any concession to the whites and to see that everything we do satisfies the blacks. Now what pleases the blacks are sanctions and Barbara objectively has been as anxious to see U.D.I. announced as the Rhodesians themselves because she felt that any alternative to it would be won at the price of appeasement. I can appreciate her attitude because it is like mine before Munich: at that time I was positively afraid that the act of appeasement would succeed in preventing war. True, she has been overruled in Cabinet – each new stalling device was proposed by Harold, opposed by her and accepted by the rest of us. But he has paid her enormous deference. If you look in Cabinet minutes you will see that every time she protested she was allowed to speak and be listened to at length. On the last day Harold Wilson said that he hadn't slept well the night before because he had been worrying about it. That is most unlike him. What he was thinking about, I am sure, were Barbara's accusations that he was sacrificing the five principles. She got under his skin in a quite extraordinary way.

Thinking about the next moves in Rhodesia, I have the uneasy feeling that not only the Prime Minister but all the Ministers concerned are taking the most appallingly orthodox, narrow-minded view of how we must now behave. I have never forgotten that first occasion when Harold Wilson laid it down as a principle that we would not use military force, and stated it in public. On that occasion I didn't dare press him very hard; but since then I have frequently tried to cross-examine him on what he is organizing, what plans he has for overthrowing the Smith regime by para-military action. I get the impression that he considers the choice for Britain to lie between conventional military action or conventional diplomatic action, and that he denies the possibility of a third course in between. This of course is ludicrous. There are only 250,000 whites in Rhodesia and we have, I presume, an S.I.S., an S.O.E. and the other organizations of para-military war. And yet I am pretty sure that Harold and his military advisers have never considered the use of black propaganda or subversive organization to put pressure on Smith.

It seems to me just as extraordinary that he never considered the possibility of sending out even a battalion to guard the Governor or to give him a bodyguard of British troops. If we had, it would have been infinitely more difficult for Smith to declare U.D.I. A month ago the Lord Chancellor said that the real trouble about U.D.I. was that it would succeed in the short run, that sanctions wouldn't prevail and that these 250,000 people would be able to cock a snook at us and at the United Nations. I thought from the start that this was true, and everything that has happened since last Thursday has confirmed my doubts. True, the Governor has not been forcibly evicted from his home; but I was interested when Mr Pritchett came in this weekend and said, 'If I'd been Prime Minister I would have put a battalion of British troops in Government House and then they couldn't have declared U.D.I.' If he can see it and I can see it, why can't Harold Wilson and George Brown see it as well? Yet I must admit that this view of mine is not accepted by any of my political friends, with the sole exception of George Wigg. Nothing more conventional, prim and proper could be conceived than this Government's reaction to what they describe as rebellion in Rhodesia. It is as though the declaration is what mattered to Harold; and once that had been made, he felt one could do nothing about it.

Tuesday, November 16th

An evening conference on Tyneside with my officials when I told them that I had finally decided to go for full county borough status for the new Greater Tyneside authority. I had of course had a good education during the day I sat in Newcastle listening to representatives of the sixteen authorities.[1] When I came back to London I had virtually decided to accept the plan for four county boroughs put up by the Commission, and impose on top of them a strong executive planning board. Then I was approached by our Chief Whip,

[1] See p. 347.

Ted Short, who is also a Newcastle M.P. He asked me to have dinner alone with him and Dan Smith, the leader of the Labour Group, and they explained to me that politically this would be disastrous, since three out of the four county boroughs would be Tory whereas a single Greater Tyneside county borough is likely to be Labour. Well, that clinched it. In this particular case what the Department wanted for administrative reasons coincided with what the Labour Party wanted for purely political reasons. So I told the Department I accepted their point of view.

Right at the end of Cabinet this morning a row suddenly blew up about army pay. I only heard the start of it because I had to leave to prepare for Questions that afternoon. But what I heard convinced me that Denis Healey's case was very strong indeed despite the fact that he was opposing George Brown and Callaghan, who for once were in agreement about a major prices and incomes issue. The issue was the so-called Grigg award, which proposed an 18 per cent increase in pay to the armed services in order to make up for the amount they have fallen behind civilian wage rates in the last two years. The Grigg award was of course the result of the abandonment of conscription. If you are going to build up a voluntary army you can only do so by paying wages comparable to what men will get in civilian life; and so it was decided to have a biennial upgrading of service pay. The only thing wrong was that it worked out this year at 18 per cent, which if it was conceded might be the end of the prices and incomes policy. Simultaneously, we received a report from Oliver Franks[1] on the pay of the higher Civil Service and this, though it isn't as dangerous as the Grigg award, still concedes far more than we should like. And now Kenneth Robinson tells us we are on the edge of a doctors' strike about their lagging earnings.

Although I was first in Questions I didn't leave much time for preparation. A few months ago I wouldn't have dreamt of taking the risk, but under Horace King Question Time is having the sting taken out of it. He tries to get some fifty or sixty Questions answered each day and to prevent supplementaries going on for too long. This increases the enormous advantage which the Minister always enjoys at Question Time. As the Warden of Nuffield points out in his book,[2] it is the easiest thing in the world to avoid answering a Question. Tuesday's experience reinforced my conviction that it is not the hostile question which should bother the Minister but the hostile letter. Whenever I have a hostile letter I do take enormous trouble about the

[1] Philosopher and administrator. During the war he served in the Ministry of Supply, and acted as Permanent Secretary 1945-6. He was British Ambassador in Washington 1948-52, and then returned to academic life. He was chairman of the Commission of Inquiry into Oxford University (a private commission) 1964-6, and of the Committee of Inquiry on the Official Secrets Act Section 2 1971-2. In 1962 he was made a life peer, and became Provost of Worcester College, Oxford.

[2] D. N. Chester and N. Bowring, Questions in Parliament (O.U.P., 1962). D. N. Chester became Warden of Nuffield College, Oxford, in 1954, and a member of Oxford City Council in 1952. He is the author of several books on central and local government. He was knighted in 1974.

answer, and I try to instil this into the Department. Because here is something in black and white which can be quoted against me if it isn't carefully phrased.

Later in the afternoon I had to receive the Local Government Boundary Commission—a delicate job because at Torquay in September I virtually announced its demise. However, the situation was eased by the fact that the chairman had suddenly fallen down dead, and I had received information that the vice-chairman intends to move to the Land Commission this year; so in fact the Commission was virtually dismantled before Torquay. Nevertheless, there are working with the Commission eighty civil servants, most of whom have high salaries. So something has got to be done; and I had the surviving members in to explain why I have flown the Torquay kite and to tell them I wasn't going to wind them up before I knew I had my new commission headed by Alan Bullock in the bag. They took it fairly well, though they didn't disguise the fact that I had upset them.

Wednesday, November 17th
I had agreed to see George Brown late in the evening. When I went into his room in the Commons he was a little flushed and he told me that he had had the most terrible three-hour row with Healey. He and Callaghan had met Denis and offered him as a compromise an unconditional immediate pay increase of 7½ per cent with everything else referred to the P.I.B. Healey had rejected this and claimed that the report by the P.I.B. should only take four weeks and the terms of reference should be far narrower than those that the D.E.A. and the Treasury suggested. He had obviously been deliberately difficult. I didn't at all want a row with George Brown and I agreed that in order to carry the army the immediate award might have to go up to 10 per cent and that the Civil Service and the doctors' claims would have to be referred to the P.I.B. at the same time. I felt gratified by George's anxiety to get me on his side—it shows that I am beginning to count a bit in Cabinet.

As the diary shows, Richard Crossman was as preoccupied by the preparation of his housing White Paper as by international events. Its provisions were tough and realistic. The building target of half a million houses by 1970 would be reached by accelerating the rate of public building (from 155,000 houses in 1964). To manage this, private building would be restrained, rising only from 218,000 to 250,000.

There was to be a change in the subsidy scheme for local authorities. The existing rate of £24 per year for each council house would be replaced by an open-ended subsidy system, equivalent to a low 4 per cent interest rate on borrowed funds. This was justified by the need to build some 3·7 million houses to replace slums, remove local shortages and provide a margin for mobility. In return, the Government would insist that councils charge realistic rents to those tenants who could afford them. The White Paper was published on November 24th.

Thursday, November 18th

Cabinet started with the first good contribution Michael Stewart has made as Foreign Secretary—a clear, dry summary of the U.N. reaction to the Rhodesia crisis. He had flown in from a brief visit to New York that morning, and he told us how inadequate the United Nations found our action. Reading between the lines you can see the difficulties which will be facing us. There is every reason to believe that the Rhodesians will be holding out successfully in six months' time, and that even the oil sanctions the U.N. are talking about will be ineffective with Portugal and South Africa neutral on the side of Rhodesia.

Other members of the Cabinet are beginning to feel my sense of disquiet. After Michael Stewart's report, James Callaghan, for example, said he thought that stronger measures should be used by us and we should try to get a quick kill. Of course this is my view, but in that case the preparations for the quick kill should have taken place *before* U.D.I. If we fail to bring Smith to heel in the next two months, Wilson will soon fall from the height of popularity. Indeed the only counterbalancing factor is the weakness of the Opposition. If, as they seem to be doing this week, the Opposition starts quarrelling fiercely about support or rejection of oil sanctions, we may not suffer too much from the problems we shall face. Anyway, for the moment things look good with the N.O.P. poll today giving Labour an 18 per cent lead.

After Michael Stewart's report we soon got back to the slanging match about army pay. Healey spoilt his own case by virtually threatening us with an army rebellion if the Cabinet didn't capitulate and grant the 18 per cent straight away before we had considered what to substitute for the Grigg method of assessment. It became only too clear that our Secretary of State for Defence is entirely in the hands of his officials and the chiefs of staff, and is being used by them as a political lawyer. It also became clear that some kind of reference to the P.I.B. was the only way of avoiding an increase so big that it would break up the whole prices and incomes policy. There came a point when Douglas Houghton said he thought that what was necessary was to ask for the Board's advice, not for a full report. Immediately Harold jumped in. He had been sitting there, nursing the meeting along and trying to help Denis to a compromise. This he saw was the chance. And so the thing got settled. I couldn't help noticing that if you are really bloody-minded, as Denis Healey was on this occasion, the P.M. feels he has to placate you. After this it was obvious, despite Jim Callaghan's protest, that the award to the higher Civil Service would also have to be submitted to the P.I.B.

By this time it was ten past twelve and I was getting anxious about my housing White Paper, which was meant to be the main item on the agenda. However, as soon as we had finished army pay Harold asked me to make a few introductory remarks. But when I began to do so he very wisely stopped me in my tracks and started to take the White Paper page by page. In the

Wilson Cabinet that is the way we always consider White Papers. Mine was quite long but he managed to get through it in eight minutes. I dealt with a few minor questions and that was that. This indicates the power a Prime Minister wields as chairman of the Cabinet. True enough, the three main issues of the White Paper had already been discussed in a Cabinet Committee: (1) the details of our new, very generous housing subsidies; (2) the negotiations with the building societies and the builders; and (3) a new philosophy of owner-occupation, which I have been rehearsing in speech after speech throughout the summer. It is a new thing for a Labour Government to admit that owner-occupation is a normal and natural way for people to live and that living in council houses is an exception to that rule. Of course we wooed the owner-occupier during the general election, but what the Party has never done before is to admit in public that if we give people favourable interest rates, in logic we have to make sure the land is available on which their houses can be built. And if we are going to take responsibility for providing the land, we must make the local authority feel as much concerned with owner-occupation as with providing rented accommodation. That is quite a shift of philosophy and that is why it is strange that we spent only eight minutes discussing the White Paper.

In the evening I had half an hour's talk over a drink with James Callaghan. This, on his suggestion, is to be a weekly affair. He knows I have now taken George Wigg's place on the liaison committee and that I am providing the link between Transport House and No. 10. So he has asked me to come along and discuss the situation with him. On this occasion the main thing he wanted to say was that there is still far too much inflation in the economy and he proposes to take another £200 million out of it by cuts in public expenditure, and possibly by increasing hire-purchase rates. He asked me whether I could think of other methods of dampening expenditure which weren't too damaging. I suspect that he really meant housing cuts but was too tactful to say so. Was it a pure accident that I was having this drink with him on Thursday when on Wednesday evening I had had a rather similar informal briefing talk with George Brown?

Friday, November 19th
I took the train to Bristol on Thursday evening. I had agreed to stay at the lord mayor's Mansion, next to the Judge's Lodgings, before making an official visit to the city. The Mansion is on Clifton Downs, an immense Victorian house one hundred years old, an almost perfect historical specimen of Victorian businessman's gothic with all the pictures and most of the furniture miraculously preserved. The lord mayor himself this year is a little Jewish trade-union organizer. He and his wife were sitting there in this huge house drinking a cup of tea before an electric fire. They were obviously enjoying it. He told me he has four changes of costume, his morning suit and top hat, his white tie and tails, his morning coat and his short jacket, and the

butler tells him how and where he should wear each of them. He insisted to me that he is just as left-wing as he ever was; but he is certainly settling in very comfortably to the pleasures of the lord mayoralty.

The Labour Party is still in power on the city council and wanted to discuss their large-scale redevelopment. There are still huge areas in the centre which need redevelopment and I had assumed they would ask for an enormous programme. So I told them that they could have a capacity programme provided they would adopt system-building, which they don't much like. They took it all quite quietly, but afterwards the leader of the Labour group and the chairman of the finance committee took me aside and told me that their real trouble was very different. They just didn't want to build any more council houses because, even with my new greatly improved subsidies, this would increase the debt on which the interest payments are so overwhelming. They have over-built and they have got too big a capital-investment programme. They would much prefer to sell off the land for owner-occupation. When I found that Bristol had already built 45,000 council houses, I said, 'Of course you needn't build any more, this suits me perfectly,' and told them to read my new White Paper. They seemed very surprised.

Sunday, November 21st
A cold, bleak day here at Prescote with snow probably coming. I shall be staying here tomorrow for the farm shoot. Ages ago I had mentioned to John Delafons that we had the shoot on November 22nd, but I never dreamt I would actually stay at Prescote for it until I noticed last week that he had been making no appointments for this Monday. I said, 'Oh no, I'll come up. We're far too busy.' He said, 'Heaven forbid, Minister. Let's keep to the plan now that we've got it.' He was obviously relieved that I was going to be away for the day. So I shall be staying on here and sending all the boxes back so that the Department can get through the work in my absence on Monday. This remark of John Delafons had made me reflect about my attitude to the Department. The other day the Dame said to me, 'You know, we have never been under such strain as we are under you.' The next day, I said to her, 'I've been wondering what you really meant. Is it my particular method of doing business or just the amount of work we have to do?' She thought it over and said she didn't find anything wrong with my methods of procedure. What made things difficult was my habit of getting too many people started on too many projects. I suspect that the Department is more than usually centralized under the Dame, so when I have a great many things going on simultaneously in housing, in local government, in planning, in legislation, and they all have to pass through her and the two Deputies, there is an appalling concentration and therefore a sense of exhaustion at the top of the Ministry. I next asked Peter Lederer what he thought was wrong and he gave a rather different answer. 'What disconcerts them', he said, 'is mainly that they are not given time enough to discuss things with you. That's what the Dame says to me.

"It would be so much better", she remarked the other day, "if we could meet the Minister for a couple of hours, but he never has time for that." ' It is true that I have cut down the time for discussions with the Ministry. But that's because there's usually not very much I can get out of a discussion with them because they haven't got the kind of minds from which I can learn very much. Indeed, I am finding on a great many subjects that what the civil servants have to contribute is rather dry, best put down on paper and not talked over. The discussions I value are those with people outside the Department, but those contacts are still resented as much as ever by the civil servants.

Arthur J. Schlesinger[1] has been over here from America and I spent an evening comparing the British and American systems. Over there the politician mans the top two echelons of his Department with experts he brings from outside. But an attempt here to have these outsiders in addition to the Private Office simply wouldn't work. The more I see of it the more I realize that the Private Office is the heart of the Ministry, the point where all my instructions and wishes go outwards and where the Department's advice concentrates on me. The Private Secretary's room outside my room is a kind of concourse, a grand vizier's waiting-room. Even the most senior civil servants, such as the Deputies, don't feel it the least undignified to stand about talking to John, asking what mood the Minister is in and discussing how to present something to him. Equally, they don't feel it undignified to listen to John presenting my ideas to them. This central point of contact between the politician and the Department must, I think, be run by a civil servant. John Delafons is superb. Personally we don't know each other much better than we did on the first day. But he is learning a lot from me, and he is dedicated and ambitious and runs the office magnificently; and he really does try to get my ideas across to the Department. Nevertheless, I have got to face it that his main job is to get across to me what the Department wants. The Private Office is the Department's way of keeping a watch on me, of making sure I run along the lines they want me to run on, of dividing my time and getting the Department's policies and attitudes brought to my notice.

Of course, it is also my medium for reaching down into the Ministry. How far down does my influence stretch? Perhaps to an Assistant Secretary level but certainly not below. I reckon I now know the Permanent Secretary, the two Deputies, the four Under-Secretaries and most of the twenty-odd Assistant Secretaries. But the vast mass of civil servants who work beneath that level hardly know me at all. I notice this when I come in in the morning and go up in the lift. Most of the people in it don't recognize me, I suppose, and there's no reason why they should. But this means that my policies are transmitted by the senior civil servants to their subordinates merely by word

[1] Son of a famous historian and himself a distinguished historian and writer. He was Professor of History at Harvard University from 1954 to 1961, when he went to Washington to serve as Special Assistant to President Kennedy. He left the White House in 1964, and since 1966 has been Schweitzer Professor of History at the City University of New York.

of mouth and very often in an unsympathetic form. We found this out recently when we had the balls-up on housing allocations; and I am now considering whether we shouldn't call a meeting of the whole housing division, including the executive officers who actually do the allocations to the local authorities. It might be a good idea to get right down to them; and perhaps the next stage in my development as a departmental Minister is precisely to extend my influence below Assistant Secretary level.

In terms of contact with the officials I am probably unusually badly off because my Ministry is run so much as a personal concern by the Dame. By the way, since she returned from holiday in September she somehow seems to have aged and to be feeling a sense of anticlimax. After all, she had all her farewell dinners and was due to retire this autumn. It was deeply gratifying for her to be asked to stay on; but I don't think she is actually enjoying it a great deal. She is certainly not working with anything like the verve with which she started introducing me to the facts of life. I don't think it's because she is anti-me now, but simply that she feels she has retired and merely come back for three or four months. Still, she knows that by doing this she has prevented Bruce Fraser becoming her successor. I think it's pretty clear now that he won't come next March because he will still have to be Permanent Secretary at the Ministry of Land and Natural Resources.

Monday, November 22nd

An absolutely perfect winter day—cloudless, brilliant, cold—for the shoot. I don't shoot but I like walking round with our guests and that is how I spent the morning. Then I came in and worked with Jennie, composing what is probably the best minute I've written since I've been a Minister. It stated the case for appointing a Royal Commission to completely reorganize local government. This is the kind of writing one simply can't do in the office. It is only if one takes half a day off that one can write something like that. By the time it was finished the sun had set and all the guests had come in and sat down to the ceremonial high tea and drinks we always provide on these occasions. Afterwards, into the drawing-room for talk over whisky before I caught the 8.50 train to London.

Tuesday, November 23rd

I'd heard by telephone on Monday that James Callaghan now felt he couldn't agree with me on two vital issues in the Rating Bill, which is due to be cleared by Legislation Committee today.[1] This was very unusual because at Legislation we are supposed only to deal with legal points—the policy is

---

[1] The two vital issues were, first, the rate threshold above which rebates should be payable (Crossman wanted this threshold to be at £5 and Callaghan wanted it at £10), and secondly, the level of income of a single person up to and including which a rate rebate should be payable (Crossman wanted this level to be at £8 and Callaghan wanted it at £7). Earlier Crossman and Callaghan had discussed these two issues and had apparently agreed to compromise on the threshold at £6 10s. Crossman insisted on keeping the upper income limit for a single person.

assumed to have been long since decided. The Lord President was extremely angry not only with the Chancellor but with me for our failure to reach agreement respectably behind the scenes. There was a pretty good row in the presence of a great many junior Ministers who were waiting to put their own Bills forward or sitting on to hear the fun after they had finished. Finally, when it was obviously not going to be resolved, Bert Bowden said, 'Couldn't the Prime Minister call a special meeting today and fix it?'

Since it was now time for Cabinet we went straight through to No. 10 and resumed discussion of all the unsettled issues of last week—earnings-related benefits and, of course, army pay. On army pay a formula had been cooked up over the weekend. George and James had basically got their way and the award was to be referred to the P.I.B. Healey threatened that if it was referred he would make things as difficult as possible by either pleading himself before the P.I.B. or ensuring that an open conflict was staged between his civil servants and those of the Treasury. I haven't said much about Healey in this diary. He has been a curiously remote, not very impressive figure, who has hardly played any role in Cabinet. Indeed, this is the first case in which he really has had to fight and it is obvious to me that in this fight he was actually concerned with his own chiefs of staff. When he talked about an Invergordon what he really meant was the danger of having his own scalp removed by those chiefs of staff.[1] And sure enough Harold Wilson told us that they had claimed their right of direct approach to him and had told him frankly how much they resented what was going on. The Prime Minister throughout helped Healey, and the final concession was his own idea.

At the end of Cabinet I stayed behind and told Harold of what had happened at the Legislation Committee. Why couldn't he call a meeting that afternoon, I asked him, and settle the thing? But no! he wasn't prepared to stand up to Callaghan on his own, so the whole thing will have to be argued out on Thursday.

In the afternoon I had a Lobby conference in order to sell my White Paper to the press. By now I was once again feeling uneasy about it. I realized it was none too original and none too complete and might be seen through as a piece of window-dressing. Nevertheless, I sold it as strongly as possible on the theme of the shift of Labour policy to owner-occupation. I then walked straight along the corridor into the House of Lords. I was the first Minister to address the Labour Peers, and I gave them roughly the talk on the housing White Paper which I had just given the Lobby. From there I went back to Vincent Square to our regular meeting with Marcia, Tommy, Wedgy and Gerald Kaufman. We are not achieving much but it may be good for us just to get together and relax and exchange ideas. Anne produced an excellent

---

[1] Snowden's 1931 emergency budget reduced the pay of all state employees by 10 per cent, but teachers and some sailors lost more than this. On September 15th the men of the Atlantic Fleet at Invergordon refused duty in protest. In the face of the 'mutiny' the Admiralty Board revised the cuts.

dinner and that does a power of good. Meanwhile, some of our back-benchers were determined to keep the House up until four o'clock in the morning on the immigration clauses of the Expiring Laws Continuance Bill. It was felt to be a matter of punctilious socialist duty that the Government should be punished in this way. I used to take a pretty active part in such operations but I suppose it's natural that I shouldn't feel so enthusiastic now.

Wednesday, November 24th
At Transport House this morning there was an astonishing scene during the N.E.C. monthly meeting. Suddenly Ian Mikardo said we had to make a decision about votes for the eighteen-year-olds; and he pointed out that if we didn't do it that very morning, the Speaker's Conference on electoral reform might have reached the item without the Labour Members having a view or having put in a paper. He therefore asked for our views. I strongly supported him and so did Tony Wedgwood Benn, and when it came to the point not a single person round the table said anything against it. So it was carried unanimously and that afternoon the news came out. Ironically enough, Harold Wilson, George Brown, James Callaghan and Michael Stewart weren't there. None of the prominent members of the Government was present, yet the N.E.C. had taken its collective decision. I don't think one can draw any conclusions from this performance except that it occasionally happens and it does the Labour Party a power of good to see the Executive really acting on its own.

The next item was another debate, this time on the modernization of the Party machine, in which Ian Mikardo and Tony Benn put forward some perfectly sensible proposals, which had been published in *Socialist Commentary*; these were turned down flat by the Executive, even the suggestion of an impartial inquiry. I missed all this because I had gone back to the Ministry to discuss with J. D. Jones a proposal to make the Chilterns a so-called 'Area of Outstanding Natural Beauty' (A.O.N.B.) which is a kind of half-way house to the status of National Park. The other day Jennie's husband, Chris,[1] had organized a delegation to me as Minister on this matter. The delegation succeeded in rousing my suspicions; and sure enough I discovered that there had been endless months of delay in ratifying the boundaries of the Chilterns A.O.N.B., the excuse being that nothing could be done until the South-East Review was published. Once I had called his bluff, J. D. Jones agreed and we went over the map; he is going to announce it as soon as possible.

After this I went to a Lobby lunch at which Edward Heath was performing for the first time as guest of honour. I was at the top table because Derek Moon, our *Coventry Evening Telegraph* political correspondent, is the chairman this year. Heath gave a pretty good performance, and I was rather

[1] On behalf of the Chiltern Society.

touched, when, after I had congratulated him, he said, without a trace of irony, 'Well, praise from you is praise one really appreciates.' What that really meant is that he is a lonely man who is having a rough time. He got himself elected in July but he hasn't yet got himself across. There is a kind of metallic professionalism about him and an artificiality in his smile which is making it very difficult for him to communicate either with the public or with his own Party.

In the evening after a meeting of the liaison committee, which is now running smoothly in the absence of George Wigg, I was off to Covent Garden. I got there too late for the overture to *Figaro* but we had an enormously enjoyable time with Jack and Frankie Donaldson, sitting in the Royal Box and having our dinner in the royal drawing-room behind the scenes. It was only marred by the fact that I had to go back to the House at eleven o'clock to see the Rhodesia Orders in Council through until one thirty in the morning. This was mildly interesting because it was the last spasm of resistance by Tory back-benchers. We were just ordered to be there by the Whips and I sat in my room working through my red boxes.

Thursday, November 25th

I had arranged an early meeting between Arnold Goodman and Sir Sydney Littlewood, the president of the London rent assessment committee. The idea was to bring them together in order to discuss the kind of people we ought to select. Littlewood is beginning to get the rent officers together, and I am beginning to see the shape which the rent assessment committees ought to take. Listening to Littlewood, I became a little anxious lest in order to make the committees respectable I had chosen a too respectable chairman. He couldn't be a much more legal kind of lawyer and the memorandum he has left with me isn't what you could call a radical document. But I have to be fair to him. It is probably a pretty good interpretation of what I meant by a fair rent, because it is fair to landlords as well as to tenants. It will disappoint some people but it carries out my intentions.

From there I moved on to the Thursday Cabinet where I now had to have a row about rate rebates because Callaghan has reneged on our compromise. Harold has refused to act on his own and the full machinery of Cabinet fixing has been put to work. Callaghan had put in his paper, I had put in my paper. Callaghan had lobbied busily behind the scenes and got Douglas Houghton on his side; and I too had done a great deal of work before we met. As so often happens we had to wait a long time. First there was a long discussion of parliamentary business, then came Peggy Herbison's wage-related benefits — again no decision reached — and then a long discussion of the bakery dispute which is causing a shortage of bread. It was after twelve o'clock when we got to local government finance and rate rebates. Callaghan made his speech, I made mine, and we reached a quite sensible settlement. Then I had to go for lunch with the Polish Ambassador while Tony Crosland put forward his proposals for a Commission on the public schools, which I had already heard discussed in the Social Services Committee.

In the afternoon I briefed the press for the Rating Bill, which I had got through Cabinet that morning and which is due to be published on Friday. Not much time. I spent two hours briefing individual journalists – *The Times*, the *Guardian*, the *Sun* and the *Mirror*. I had to do this because the Lobby, which is a pretty autocratic body, decided that they were busy enough on Thursday and hadn't time to give me a Lobby. By the way, I had been able to see in the morning press the reactions to my White Paper: not too bad despite a snooty leader in *The Times*. After briefing the journalists I briefed the housing group of the P.L.P. from six to seven and then went off to Brooks's for a dinner with J. D. Jones and Richard Llewelyn-Davies at which we discussed how to organize the new Centre for Environmental Studies. I have not mentioned in this diary that we have obtained the £1 million we wanted from Ford and the Treasury and now I have to discuss what we are to do with it and in particular who to make its chairman and director. From there to Kingsway, where I was due to be interviewed on the I.T.V. *This Week* programme by Alastair Burnet, the new editor of *The Economist*. I sat there and did my stuff and suddenly when it was over I found that I couldn't remember anything that I had said. I thought it was terrible but Anne, who watched it, said it was perfectly O.K. Exhaustion, I suppose.

From there I went back to the Ministry, where I had an hour to prepare the speech on rate rebates I was due to deliver at Plymouth next day, and then I went to Paddington and got into my sleeper. It was a characteristically full day and poor Jennie, who is due to have a baby soon, was really worn out by it and jolly glad to see the last of me.

Friday, November 26th
I stepped off at a siding in Plymouth and went off to the house on the Hoe given by Nancy Astor – a kind of Victorian-museum house – where I had a bath. The town clerk met me and we had one of our usual tours around. By mid-morning we had reached the Barbican, the old part of the town right down on the waterfront where the Mayflower jetty is. It is a lovely place but falling to pieces. What it needs is complete redevelopment as a mixed commercial/residential area for middle-class people, artists and lawyers. But no, Plymouth Council, with a solid Labour majority, require it for people on the housing list and are determined to build conventional council houses. An absolute tragedy. I had a sharp discussion with them after lunch at the top of their huge skyscraper town hall, from which there is a magnificent view. But I didn't budge them one inch.

Then I caught the train to Exeter where I was due to give a lecture to Professor Wiseman's seminar on how Cabinet government works.[1] I told

[1] H. Victor Wiseman, head of the Department of Government at the University of Exeter, and a member of the South-West Regional Planning Committee. He died suddenly in the House of Commons in 1969.

them of the modifications I was inclined to make after a year in my theory of Prime Ministerial government. Though the P.M. is certainly supreme the departmental Ministers have considerable power in their satrapies so long as they are successful. I also said that there was one Minister who had tremendous power in his own right, the Chancellor of the Exchequer, owing to the unique position of the Treasury in Whitehall. When the lecture was over I was driven over to the Judge's Lodgings in a beautiful racing Bentley. The owner was a strange man called Alderman Day, chairman of the Devon County Council. He is a wealthy ex-Liberal, who has been defeated in four by-elections – a property speculator in London and a shooting gent. down in Devon. He warned me of the trouble I was in with the county council because of my decision in June to take away from them so much rateable value in Plympton, Plymstock and Torbay.

Saturday, November 27th
Day is a solicitous host. The next morning he was up early to drive me to the station where I got on the train and found Shirley Williams and Jeremy Thorpe at breakfast after doing *Any Questions* the night before. We discussed politics all the time as politicians do when they meet accidentally. I had to listen to Jeremy and Shirley talk about the chance of our losing Hull[1] as well as Falmouth where the Labour M.P. is dying.[2] Then there were others, Shirley Williams said, such as Bob Stross,[3] who might easily pop it any moment. That shows how marginal our situation is. I was worried particularly by what they said about Hull because of the nomination which took place this week. The kitchen cabinet had wanted Guy Barnett. He was an absolutely brilliant candidate in Dorset when he won us the by-election there and he only failed by two votes to be selected for Erith, where we won comfortably. We were assuming that he would get Hull North. But no, a Catholic lecturer at Hull School of Commerce called McNamara was the constituency's choice. Perhaps this Hull constituency just likes dull members; Solomons was a very boring, elderly London Jew. Otherwise, the choice of McNamara must mean that we are quite likely to lose Hull North.*

If we do, it will be extremely awkward for us since the idea that we could last out until next October has become extremely remote. I myself have thought for some time that the only possible time for the election will be the first week of May, before we lose another thousand seats in the municipals. But now it's beginning to look as though it will have to be put before Callaghan's budget and not after it. I mentioned last week the Chancellor's

---

* I was quite wrong. McNamara was an outstandingly good candidate who developed into a very good back-bencher.
[1] Henry Solomons died on November 7th. He had gained the seat for Labour at the 1964 election with a majority of only 1,181.
[2] See p. 220.
[3] Sir Barnett Stross, Labour M.P. 1945–66 (since 1950 for Stoke-on-Trent). He was Parliamentary Secretary at the Ministry of Health 1964–5. He died in May 1967.

informal remark to me that we need another £200 million of deflationary measures. This idea has taken concrete form in a paper which is circulating, though it has not yet been circulated to me. I don't deny that these ideas are reasonable but they certainly make it difficult to fight the election *after* the budget. Harold Wilson must remember how in 1950 Attlee was forced to go to the country in February because Cripps wouldn't have the right kind of pre-election budget in April. So history may repeat itself with Harold going to the country in March for the same reason. Even if he himself were prepared to gamble on an inflationary, election-winning budget, Callaghan isn't ready to connive in that particular thing.

I had plenty of time for these gloomy thoughts before the train got to Reading and I found the official car waiting to get me back to Prescote in time for Saturday lunch. Of course Saturday as a holiday had been pretty well ruined by then, particularly as Anne was in bed with mild flu and in the evening I had to go to Coventry for a United Nations Association speech. I was expecting the Provost of the Cathedral and Edward Boyle to share the platform. But they had both called it off and I had to take the whole brunt of an endless question-time on Vietnam, Rhodesia and everything else. I felt pretty angry but spoke in a quiet way, answered as few questions as possible and got home tired.

At the U.N. Security Council in New York the Foreign Secretary staved off African demands for military intervention in Rhodesia, while at home the Prime Minister introduced further economic sanctions. By December 1st the remaining trade and financial loopholes were closed and other Governments, notably the United States and West Germany, had promised similar measures. The Conservatives gave broad support to the policy, though there were growing complaints from the right wing, led by Julian Amery.[1] On December 3rd, the Board of the Reserve Bank of Rhodesia was dismissed and a new board appointed in London. This had the effect of making Rhodesia's balances outside London legally worthless and thus undermining her economy.

Mr Smith's neighbour, President Kaunda of Zambia, asked Britain for assistance. Other impatient African leaders threatened to use Zambian airfields as bases from which to launch attacks on Rhodesia. President Kaunda was also anxious about the installations of the Kariba power station on the Rhodesian side of the Zambezi River, but Mr Wilson refused to send British troops to occupy the site and only announced that Britain would not stand idly by if Rhodesia cut off power supplies to Zambia.

Sunday, November 28th
Alan Bullock and his wife came over to lunch. I had sent him a copy of my

[1] M.P. for Preston North 1956–66 and for Brighton Pavilion 1969–70. He had been Parliamentary Under-Secretary of State and Financial Secretary at the War Office (1957–8) and at the Colonial Office (1958–60); Secretary of State for Air (1960–62), Minister of Aviation (1962–4) and Minister of Public Building and Works (June–October 1970).

minute to the P.M.[1] and was able to tell him that in reply Harold had said that there was no need to submit my proposals to a committee. They should come direct to Cabinet and I should prepare the Cabinet papers straight away. So I have now pushed my project for the drastic reform of local government to the point where it must either be approved or not approved in Cabinet. In Harold's present mood it will win approval, so we shall be able to go to the country as a Party pledged to local government reform. If I put that alongside my housing White Paper and house-building programme, my rate rebates, my Rent Act and my major reform of the rating system* I can claim that I have delivered the goods so far as the Party's election manifesto is concerned. This has been an important week in my own political life.

It has been a key week in the Government's life because the Rhodesia crisis has taken a downward turn. Until U.D.I. was declared Harold dominated the scene. There he was, struggling day by day to prevent Smith doing this terrible thing. But now it has taken place there is an awkward hiatus. The drama of the poor old Governor staying on in Government House has worn off and it is only too clear that the British Government has no plans for suppressing the rebellion. We are sitting here in London and the so-called rebels are sitting quite happily there in Salisbury. We have no means of enforcing law and order on the rebels, whereas the rebels obviously have every means of maintaining law and order in defiance of us. This week people began to ask whether this is all the Government had up its sleeve; and the answer seems to be an uncomfortable 'Yes, that's all'.

In a tiny way this new situation was brought home to me when George Wigg said to me one morning on the phone, 'By the way, about psychological warfare, have you time to talk about it and tell me who could help us?' I mentioned Hugh Carleton Greene and Sefton Delmer,[2] and George Wigg said, 'Use the scrambler.' I switched it on and then remarked, 'What the hell, George, surely you started thinking about psychological warfare before now?' George said, 'Don't get angry, Dick, but that's the situation. The Prime Minister is now beginning to wonder whether we oughtn't to use it.' I couldn't help remembering how regularly during the war the politicians only got interested in psychological warfare after military operations had stalled. When they had failed to achieve their ends by conventional means they turned to us and we always had to tell them that psychological warfare is no magic substitute for military victory. The same is true now.

Monday, November 29th

I was rung up on Sunday night and told that there was a Cabinet meeting next morning and asked if I wanted a car. But I didn't bother, caught the

---

* A gross overestimation: the Treasury watered it down.
[1] See p. 386.
[2] Like Hugh Carleton Greene, Sefton Delmer had worked with Crossman as a psychological warrior between 1941 and 1945, returning afterwards to the *Daily Express* as chief foreign affairs reporter.

train and arrived about a quarter of an hour late. They were well into the discussion about the proposal to send the R.A.F. to Zambia. I knew about it because it had been the big story in all the Sunday papers. By the time I arrived the only issue was whether we should send ground troops as well. There was some division of opinion. I heard Douglas Houghton pleading aginst reinforcement and wanting to placate the white settlers, and I heard James Callaghan wanting much stronger measures. He is concerned because the crisis is costing us a lot and might undermine confidence in the pound. The P.M. was very much in the middle. Afterwards, talking to Denis Healey, I learnt that the inner group in Cabinet which 'runs' Rhodesia has been pressing Harold for stronger action, with Healey on Callaghan's side.

In the afternoon I tried the experiment of briefing the weeklies on the Rating Bill. I think I have mentioned that the Lobby refused to discuss it with me last Thursday because they said they were too busy. As a result I had recourse to a series of private interviews and got a far better press on Friday than I otherwise would have done. So I am now trying to follow it up. I sat down with Tom Baistow of the *New Statesman* first, a cocky little Scot who seemed to like a drop of whisky and chatted in general about housing but knew very little about rates. Then I had an excellent girl from *The Economist* who really wanted to talk seriously about local government. I let her see the text of the memorandum I had sent to the Prime Minister because I wanted to curry some favour with *The Economist*. Finally I dealt with the *Observer*, but I don't know how well I got on with them.

The evening was a trying experience because I had to wait through a lot of legislation until midnight in order to handle a motion on the adjournment about slum clearance in Manchester. And after that I had to stay on for a number of miscellaneous subjects. A few weeks ago Stephen Swingler gave an interview to the *Hull Daily Mail* about the Humber bridge and poured a lot of the Ministry of Transport's official cold water upon the whole idea. This infuriated me because at Conference at Blackpool I had referred to the possibility of building a bridge and developing a marvellous New Town on the other side. At the time I had irritated my own Ministry by talking about a population of 70,000 when it should have been something like two million; I had also infuriated George Brown by poaching on his domain of economic regions. However, that is all now forgotten with the Hull by-election hanging over us and the Humber bridge the main local issue. In my new job as chairman of the liaison committee I got the Prime Minister's backing for instructing Stephen to go as far as he possibly could. So I sat there until nearly three in the morning; but all that I got was a pretty curmudgeonly statement, because that Ministry of Transport has no feeling for urban development or for the needs of crucial by-elections.

Tuesday, November 30th
At 9.45 I had to drag myself to the Legislation Committee because my

Housing Subsidies Bill was the first item on their agenda. With our completely ineffective amiable Gerald Gardiner as Lord Chancellor—he is a brilliant advocate but he is no chairman or politician—there's no hard work done
on these Bills and I got through pretty easily and then moved straight across
to Cabinet where we had still more of Rhodesia.

This time Cabinet was presented with a whole bundle of economic and
legal sanctions which included an Order to cut off the payment of personal
allowances and pensions to people living in Rhodesia. There was some
discussion between the hard-liners and the soft-liners; but it seemed to me
obvious that if we cut off the pensions of only a couple of hundred retired
civil servants we would be in trouble with the Tories in the Commons. And
we were that very afternoon. I wasn't there, but I hear that Harold lashed
back against the first really formidable Opposition attack he has faced on
Rhodesia. And later in the evening he went on the air to put over his policy.

This was the first easy day I have had in the Ministry for some weeks. I
was able to sit back, sign documents, resume an easy relationship with the
Secretary and have a long talk to John Delafons. As a result I am beginning
to see that one can work too hard in a Department and can overtax the Civil
Service as well as the Minister. With the old-fashioned, highly centralized,
hierarchical structure focusing on herself on which Dame Evelyn insists, the
Minister can easily impose an appalling strain if he starts too many enter-
prises at the same time. So I am making up a list of commandments and here
are the first three: Commandment One: be careful not to ask for research to
be done and then find that it has imposed a great deal of work for no good
purpose; Commandment Two: make sure that all the instructions I issue are
channelled properly and that the official responsible is warned in advance of
what is coming; Commandment Three: cut back those enormous briefs which
the Department provides for my official visits.

That evening Julian Snow, the very tall and bulky M.P. for Lichfield,
asked to see me.[1] He came strolling into my room in a rather insolent way,
sat himself down and informed me that, though he wasn't actually going
to vote against me on Thursday on the West Midlands Order, he would have
to warn me quite frankly that he couldn't tolerate the outrageous way I had
decided to carve up a Labour-controlled county council. (He was referring
to the Order which transforms a collection of sixteen local authorities into
four brand-new county boroughs covering the whole Black Country that I
was in great trouble about when I visited the Midlands a few weeks ago.)
What irritated me was that Julian Snow hasn't got a single Party in his own
constituency which will be affected by the Order. What he has got there—as
one of his constituents—is the chairman of the County Council, a powerful,

---

[1] A Labour M.P. since 1945, he was made a life peer in 1970, taking the title of Lord
Burntwood. He held two minor offices in the post-war Labour Government. In 1966 he
became Parliamentary Secretary at the Ministry of Aviation, moving to the Ministry of
Health in 1967, and in 1968 he became Crossman's Parliamentary Under-Secretary at the
D.H.S.S.

man called George Newman. George Wigg, who has a Black Country constituency and who has lived in Staffordshire for years, had warned me that
Mr Newman was my most formidable opponent; and I soon realized that
he had instructed Julian Snow to come and speak for him. So instead of
sloshing Julian I decided to be tactful. I told him that I had already consulted
all the M.P.s concerned, though he hadn't bothered to turn up. I told him
that Transport House was greatly in favour of the new county boroughs being
established and I think I softened him a good deal. But he has given me fair
warning that I may be in for really serious trouble on Thursday night.

So I quickly rearranged my plans. I was due to dine in Birmingham before
my official visit on Friday. I had to cancel that and arrange to catch an early
train on Friday. Next I saw Geoffrey Rhodes, who is my new P.P.S.[1] Tam
has done a long stint with me; and when I was shadowing Education he spent
a whole year on setting up supporting groups in the universities. Recently
he has felt more and more that he wanted complete freedom of expression,
so of course I let him go and chose this extremely efficient Newcastle M.P.
So I was a bit disconcerted when he coolly told me that he had an important
engagement in his constituency and would be off on Thursday night. Eventually I had to say bluntly, 'You can't go. You must stay and help me get the
Order through.' Finally, I went down to the Whips and warned them that
the trouble was on.

Dinner with our usual group, though Tommy was away in Rome. This
regular meeting is thoroughly useful because with Marcia present we get
right through to the P.M. We discussed Hull practically all the time.
Apparently the candidate has been nobbled by Transport House and is backing the January date for the by-election.

Wednesday, December 1st
Another of these confounded early Cabinet Committee meetings at 9.45.
This time it was the Social Services Committee which had had the Peggy
Herbison pension plan referred back to it. This has been going on and on and
on. The problem arises out of that fatal decision to make our reform of social
security in two parts, putting forward first a plan for short-term benefits,
unemployment, sickness, etc., and then, after a year or two, completing the
job with the national superannuation scheme. This decision was taken last
autumn under pressure from the economic Ministers, who decided that
graduated unemployment benefits plus redundancy payments were essential
for mobility of labour and essential also to deal with (what was then not a
remote possibility) mass unemployment. However, their fears have not been
substantiated, there's no unemployment now, indeed there's over-full employ-

---

[1] A member of Leeds City Council 1953–8, and head of the Business Studies Department
of Leigh Technical College, Lancashire, 1955–64. He was elected Labour and Co-operative
M.P. for East Newcastle in 1964. He became Crossman's P.P.S. in 1965, and in 1966 moved
with him to the Lord President's office, remaining his P.P.S. until 1967.

ment, so we don't really need to give this priority to short-term benefits. Nevertheless, we are committed and we are now discovering that to introduce the scheme partially brings with it appalling problems. For instance, what do you do about civil servants who already have excellent sickness schemes and who have virtually no unemployment? In finding the right answer to this question we have to be especially careful because I made such a successful denunciation of the Boyd-Carpenter graded pension as a swindle, that in Opposition the Tories have already dropped the whole plan and switched back to a belief in private pension schemes on top of a flat-rate state pension.

Peggy Herbison has produced a plan under which the civil servants would be fully integrated into the new scheme of short-term benefits. The difficulty is that they would contribute a lot more and get virtually nothing in return. And this will be proposed to them just at the time when we are turning down their wage claim to try to preserve the incomes policy. By instinct I always want to support Peggy, particularly when her overlord is snubbing her, but in this case I had a real departmental problem since I have a large number of government employees and industrial civil servants under me. Could I really impose this on them? The more I thought about it the more impossible it was.

At 5 p.m. at the E.D.C. I had to fight for my extra housing finance, essential to my target of a half a million houses by 1970. The Treasury had allowed me 5,000 houses this year and another 5,000 next. I wanted an extra 6,000 in 1966, making 16,000 altogether. When I put my case I had a surprising amount of support round the table. Then came a blank negative from Callaghan, and George Brown said, 'Well, it's not worth wasting time trying to settle it,' and then tried to settle it! I was asked whether I would be content with twelve thousand to the end of 1966; I said that was possible and went straight back to the Ministry to find out. I ran into the Dame seeing out Otto Clarke of the Treasury, who had come over to bargain with her, and she thought she could get him up to twelve thousand. But if she can't I shall have to fight it out at Cabinet next Tuesday.

Late in the evening I went down to the house of Phil Kaiser, the Minister of the American Embassy, to meet an old Washington friend of mine. The Washington friend and Phil weren't there but George Woodcock was, alone in the drawing-room. I had half an hour of fascinating discussion with him. For years I had rather begrudged George Woodcock his early refusal to be friendly with me despite—or is it because of?—the fact that I taught him for two years at New College when he got his First in P.P.E. Well, if being a Minister has done something for my status it has certainly changed George Woodcock's attitude. He now allows it to be known that he was my pupil and almost seems to be glad to see me again.

What I learnt from that half-hour was that he is giving genuine support to George Brown's prices and incomes policy. Of course he realizes its dangers and he sees that it is leading us into a number of terrible predicaments, such as playing tricks with coal prices and putting the army pay award to the P.I.B. But these things, he said to me, just have to be done, however awkward and indefensible they are, to make the policy stick. Clearly he sees it not merely in terms of an increase in his own power as the general secretary and in the power of the T.U.C. itself over the unions. He also sees it as a policy of national importance.

Thursday, December 2nd
Yet another Cabinet with Rhodesia top of the agenda – the result of the row in the House of Commons when it was announced that we were going to stop the payment of pensions to retired civil servants in Rhodesia. The P.M. obviously wanted to smooth things down and pay the pensions after all. Having an ingenious mind and sometimes also being very naive, he asked why we shouldn't pay them in Rhodesian bank notes printed in London. I thought it funny, but Callaghan got on his hind legs about forgery. I sat there wondering how the episode would be reported in the Cabinet minutes. I think I can say now that there will be no reference at all to this proposal of the Prime Minister's.[1]

After lunch at the *Observer* I went back to what I thought was going to be a routine meeting with the official body which represents the treasurers at every level of local government. I fondly imagined that all I had to do was discuss the practical problems of introducing rate rebates. But at once they revealed themselves as utterly furious with the scheme, first on the ground that it would be putting too big an administrative burden on them, and second because they thought the Government should pay for the whole thing and not merely 75 per cent. I could have sat tight and listened until the storm had blown itself out. What I did was to intervene fairly quickly and stage a great display of intellectual dialectics, perhaps as the result of having too good a lunch. There is no doubt that they were not amused and all I did was to increase their anger.

In the afternoon two leading members of the Labour Party's publicity advisory group came to see me. I had met them at a No. 10 party and found them very nice. They reported how hopeless things were at Transport House and asked me to help in putting it right. I said I couldn't intervene and tried to persuade them that perhaps their first job was to advise individual Ministers on their Departments' publicity. I have learned in the last three months the enormous difference made by the kind of skilled press relations which Peter Brown has now developed in my Ministry. Of course, if I drop a clanger that's that. But there's no doubt about it, he has been putting over my housing policy, my rent policy and my rate rebate policy with a tremendous bang. I wondered whether these two young men couldn't persuade some of my colleagues to make sure that they are as adequately served as I am.

[1] There wasn't.

This was the evening of the West Midlands Order. I had been told by the Whips to be on the front bench at 6.30 and I duly went down to the House. Actually, our debate started at 11.30 after a long, tedious argument about the coalmines. I say long and tedious, but in fact it was a desperately important debate on Fred Lee's proposals for reducing the overdraft of the National Coal Board and imposing a cut-back on coal production so severe that it may well need 2,500 new houses in the Midlands and the West Riding to provide for the coalminers who lose their jobs and have to move to other coalfields. So objectively this was a really important debate to which I should have listened with interest. But it is no good if you are a busy Minister and you are waiting for your own piece of legislation.

As an influential Black Country M.P. who was in favour of the Order, George Wigg sat loyally beside me throughout the debate. It soon became clear that if we allowed people to speak at length to the briefs they had been given by their local authorities, they wouldn't actually force a vote. In fact, we had been very lucky because the man who really would have caused trouble was John Stonehouse at Wednesbury, and he would certainly have been backed by Stephen Swingler and Harold Davies and Jennie Lee, all Staffordshire M.P.s. But all of them are in the Government and so castrated. Only John Stonehouse decided to be present and ostentatiously sat himself down on a back-bench below the gangway, giving his silent protest support to the rebels.

Friday, December 3rd
The speeches last night dragged on until 2.30 and I didn't get to bed till 3. Even then I didn't sleep much because I was afraid of over-sleeping – I had to be up at 7 in order to catch the 8.20 to Birmingham where I was due to open a new block of industrialized houses for Harry Watton. He is the kind of Labour caucus leader that I like, and after lunch I allowed him and his fellow councillors to submit me to two hours of cross-examination on the system of building controls and building licensing we are going to introduce. Characteristically enough, at the end the committee chairman who had been wildest in his wrath moved the vote of thanks and said, 'Well, we have to have a good go sometimes at sloshing our Labour Minister.' I had brought Peter Lederer and Brain (my Under-Secretary in Housing Division A) to watch the proceedings and advise me. As we were filing out I said to them, 'You sometimes complain that I am rough with your people. You can see now the treatment I have to take from my own people outside.' From there I had a two-hour drive to Huntingdon where I had to address the Parish Councils Association of the new county of Huntingdon and the Soke. I was able to talk to them as a parish council chairman because our farm at Prescote is a self-contained parish and has its own parish council. This won me a little favour, as did my reminder that in Oxfordshire our parish councils have to be consulted on all planning permissions. But it was a dull meeting, and there was

a long drive back. It was only about midnight that we got in and I really felt more tired than I had been since we took office.

Sunday, December 5th
Two days at Prescote have done me a power of good. But there has been one blow. I found a letter in my red box from Alan Bullock, who I thought I had lined up firmly as chairman of my Commission on local government. He now tells me, however, that the job is too big for him as it would mean devoting at least three years to local government and he simply can't do it. This is a great set-back because I had got my mind fixed on him as the right man, and I am pretty flabbergasted at the idea of having to find someone else.

I had deliberately chosen Brain to come with me to Birmingham and then home for the weekend because though he is one of the cleverest officials he is also one with whom I find it difficult to get contact. Here at Prescote, walking over the farm, he has found himself talking a great deal more freely. He has made me realize that what is wrong inside the Ministry is the complete separation of housing from planning. What I need is a unit in the middle of the Ministry bringing the work of these two divisions together. I felt this need more than once last week. For example, there was the problem of Basingstoke New Town centre which came up for consideration. I was told we now had to turn it down automatically because of the credit squeeze, although the population has increased 300 per cent owing to the London overspill. When I asked, 'But why turn down Basingstoke?' I was told that there are no less than four hundred local authorities in the queue for New Town development and already twenty have been turned down without my being informed. Of course I can't deal with them all personally, but what we need is a scheme of priorities under which the officials can know in what order to rank the applications. Exactly the same is true on housing allocations. Here I have had to intervene and insist that all the difficult ones should be referred to Ministers. But once again we need a clear principle on which the priorities can be ranged. And that's not all. In addition, there are the places where the authorities merely want commercial development in the town centre. That isn't my pigeon; these cases come up to Charlie Pannell, who will deal with them under his Building Control Bill.

If we are going to plan centrally and plan our spending sensibly, it seems to me that what we need is a synoptic view of all the needs – housing, commercial, education or health – of each town. That indeed was the lesson of Birmingham last Friday. I had a wonderful time going round their housing estates but the real crux came when they told me about their new estate at Chelmsley Wood, where 27,000 people will be housed and where they will want shops etc. at the same time. For this commercial development they need £2¼ million. I said that of course they were right but I couldn't get them the cash. They said, quite rightly, that they shouldn't build the houses without arranging for shops, pubs and schools at the same time. And the trouble is we haven't the central machinery to make this possible. Brain put a good idea to me yesterday evening. He said that what the Department should now do is to set up regional divisions to do the planning and the housing, and then over them we should have the central planners plotting the departmental strategy. When he said that, I saw suddenly what was wrong with my White Paper. It's a housing White Paper in which the planners were only brought in at the last moment so as to spatchcock in a couple of paras on land purchase.

Monday, December 6th
I travelled up to London last night for an early meeting on the Rent Act. It was very important to me because I was due to address all the London rent officers, gathered together by Sir Sydney Littlewood and the three vice presidents of the London rent assessment committee, on the meaning of 'fair rent'. I had had access over the weekend to the text of what had been said at the first meeting and was very disconcerted by the explanation given by the deputy chief valuer, Mr Edwards. It seemed to me to be in complete contradiction with my own exposition of fair rent during the Committee Stage. Apparently he had said that inflated land prices must be regarded as bringing supply into balance with demand and not as creating scarcity, and so could not be taken into account when fixing a fair rent. I mentioned this to Sir Sydney just before we started and then I went in and had an informal talk with the rent officers.

I think it went fairly well but I returned to the Ministry highly preoccupied. I realized that if Edwards' interpretation were established as official doctrine, the level of rents set by the rent assessment committees will be intolerably high and I shall be in appalling peril of being 'found out' by the whole Labour Party.

When I got back to the Ministry I talked to the Dame, who immediately said, 'Of course, Minister, land is an element in scarcity and one must deduct the scarcity element created by land prices from the fair rent.' 'How can we get that across?' I asked, and she replied, 'Oh, I'll talk to Sydney myself.' I then said, 'We have got to do something else as well. I admit that I have promised not to give any directives to the R.A.C.s and the rent officers. But on the other hand I have also said that all my speeches on the Rent Act, both during the Second Reading and in the Committee Report and Stages, are declarations of Government policy and can be taken as directives. What we need is to take all these statements and have them printed as a pamphlet and distributed to the rent officers. But before that we had better make sure that I did make an unequivocal statement on land values and scarcity!'*

* No one could remember that Monday whether I had made one. But the following weekend my red box contained the paste-up of all the extracts and they included one or two absolutely unequivocal statements. So these interpretations became the standards for the rent officers and rent assessment committees so long as I remained Minister.

All this took so much time that it wasn't until twelve o'clock that I was able to get down to preparing my speech for the Second Reading of the Rating Bill. Alas, it is still true that I can't rely on the Ministry, though at least on this occasion I was able to use the factual description of how rebates work; but the introduction setting the policy in its context, and the peroration, had to be done over the lunch hour. Very hurriedly, I decided my main theme: that rate rebates are merely an interim measure to prop up a bad tax which I wanted to get rid of as soon as possible. Now, I have used this argument in speech after speech and yet on this occasion I overreached myself. Because I didn't have quite enough time to prepare my speech, I said things over-vigorously and too dogmatically. It really isn't quite the thing for a Minister of Housing and Local Government to use such language about a tax which, after all, the treasurers have to go on raising. I realized as I sat down that I was in grave danger of turning the local authorities against the Minister who was pretty popular with them a few months ago.

The Council of Ministers of the Organization of African Unity announced that if Britain did not crush the rebellious regime in Rhodesia by December 15th, they would sever all relations with London. Only Ghana and Tanzania carried out this threat. To some extent the anger of black African countries was assuaged by Mr Wilson's announcement, on December 17th, of an international oil embargo chiefly designed to cut off Rhodesian supplies through the pipeline from Beira in Portuguese Mozambique. Zambia's supplies also came by the Beira route so Britain began an oil airlift for President Kaunda.

The Prime Minister was confident that oil sanctions, with no need for a naval blockade of Beira, would quickly reduce the Rhodesian economy to chaos. Mr Heath seemed to accept the oil embargo but, as he and Sir Alec wanted to resume talks with Mr Smith, they advised the Conservatives to abstain in the Commons vote. Fifty right-wing Tories, however, divided the House in protest against the extent of sanctions. More discomfiting to the leader of the Opposition was the appearance in the Government lobby of thirty-one Conservatives who supported sanctions.

Tuesday, December 7th
Judging by the morning papers I had a very good press for my speech, perhaps too good. When I got to Cabinet I found some of my colleagues remarking drily that they were interested to hear that the Government had decided to abolish rating. One of the interesting facts about the Cabinet system as it is worked by Harold Wilson is the free-wheeling which a departmental Minister is allowed to do; one gets away with anything until one falters. But one's colleagues' resentments are very real. In this case I paid the price immediately, because that very morning I was due for my tussle with the Chancellor of the Exchequer about housing subsidies.

But before we got to it Cabinet had to suffer yet another of those interminable Rhodesian discussions. On this occasion the trouble was caused by a weekend story in all the papers that Harold was preparing a peace offensive. I have no doubt he is trying to leave as many lines open to the Rhodesian Government as he possibly can; and Barbara and her friends try to cut those lines because they want not an agreement with Smith but military sanctions. So Barbara needled Harold endlessly, trying to make him say that on no account would he ever negotiate with the Smith regime; and Harold time after time wriggled out of repudiating the suggestion. That went on for an hour and a half, and it ended up with such confusion that when two Members of Cabinet, one in the House of Lords and one in the House of Commons, gave their accounts of what was happening in the afternoon they were completely inconsistent with one another.

The final discussion and decision on wage-related sickness and unemployment benefits didn't take long. Cabinet accepted the Social Services Committee recommendation and I found myself reluctantly voting against Peggy Herbison. I do hate being on the same side as the Treasury but on this occasion John Diamond was right; and, anyway, departmentally I needed to do it.

The next item was the Fairfield's Shipyard controversy. It is curious how some problem which should have been settled far away down the line suddenly comes up to Cabinet and sticks on our agenda for week after week. This Clydeside shipyard was on the edge of bankruptcy, when someone suggested the state should rescue it by going into partnership with Isaac Wolfson[1] or another great financier, each taking a 50 per cent share (I vaguely remember this idea being voiced at one of our suppers with Harold Wilson). Since then it has been taken up by George Brown and endlessly discussed at Cabinet between him, Callaghan and the Secretary of State for Scotland. So on Tuesday it was on the agenda with yet another suggestion and yet another untidy, ragged discussion.

Finally we got to my housing subsidies. I stated the case for increasing my allocation. Callaghan stated his case against giving me a single extra house, and rallied every spending Minister to his side by asserting that Housing couldn't be given any more concessions without destroying the whole PESC agreement of last July. I reminded Cabinet that it was agreed on that occasion that, if there were any slack to be taken up, the taking up should be done by housing. At once Tony Crosland chipped in, 'Why only housing? Why shouldn't schools have their share of the slack? With building licensing coming in, isn't it essential that we should look at this problem as a whole and not merely in terms of housing, which anyway has got a great deal more than its share and is pushing itself forward time and time again.' I was paying

---

[1] Chairman of The Great Universal Stores Ltd since 1946, and founder, chairman and trustee of the Wolfson Foundation, which he established in 1955 to assist the advancement of health, education and youth in the U.K. and Commonwealth. A generous benefactor to Israel and to many universities and colleges.

for my prominence, for my success and for Harold's backing behind the scenes. The Prime Minister did his best for me, arguing that in PESC we had created an instrument for controlling our expenditure but that we were now becoming the servants and not the master of our own instrument. But there was no one enthusiastically on my side except the Secretaries of State for Wales and Scotland, who of course have their own housing programmes. Willie Ross said to me afterwards that we had done as well as possible when we got the decision postponed until the end of January. Nevertheless, this was the first really big reverse I have suffered in Cabinet. It was inevitable but it was none the less unpleasant for that.

This afternoon I had my big press conference on industrialized building. We had prepared for it very carefully indeed, and Peter Brown and Peter Lederer had produced a first-rate brief. Some sixty pressmen turned up and there was a good hour's discussion. We had no luck however. Rhodesia knocked us out of the news, along with a big murder story.

From there I moved across to the House of Commons for a conference on the preservation of the coastline, one of my pet ideas which I have been working on in speech after speech around the country, against the wishes of J. D. Jones and the planning division. Despite their criticism I can't help feeling very pleased with this device for using planning permissions not to blight but to unblight areas. I was also able to announce this week that I had done the same for eight racecourses due for closure. I got them preserved as open spaces simply by writing to the local authorities warning them that if any approaches were made by developers they must be referred to me for decision. I hope it is going to be a story in one of the Sunday papers.

In the evening I had to go to the Farmers' Club. Maurice Passmore, who is a big wheat-grower near us at Prescote, is chairman of the Farmers' Club this year and persuaded me months ago to be his political guest-speaker at the annual dinner at which he presides. He said he asked me on condition that I didn't make a bloody dreary political speech as most Ministers are inclined to do when they are invited. I agreed without thinking much about it. Then to my horror I found that the engagement was pressing upon me and my job was to make a speech sandwiched between Lord Radcliffe, who is one of the most brilliant after-dinner speakers in the country,[1] and Sir Arthur Bryant, who is also pretty good at this kind of a job.[2] When I got to the Grosvenor with Anne I found twelve hundred farmers sitting in the largest and ugliest hall I have ever seen. It was one of those occasions one just has to get through.

[1] Director-General of the Ministry of Information 1941–5, and a famous barrister. He served as a Lord of Appeal in Ordinary 1949–64, and became a viscount in 1962. Chairman of many committees and commissions, of which the most celebrated are the Committee of Inquiry into the Monetary and Credit System, 1957–9; the Committee of Inquiry into Security Procedures and Practices, 1961; the Tribunal of Inquiry into the Vassall Case, 1962; and the Privy Councillors' Inquiry into the *Daily Express* and D-Notices, 1967. He was a trustee of the British Museum 1957–69, and chairman of the Board of Trustees 1963–8.

[2] Fluent and witty historian and biographer. His best-known books are probably those on the seventeenth century. He wrote the official biography of George V.

I was outclassed by Lord Radcliffe with his spontaneous charm, his ease with the microphone and his assured professional touch. Arthur Bryant, in his much more careful, deliberate way, was also a great deal better than I was. Still, I don't think they regarded me as a boring politician. Anne and I drove straight back home and relaxed over a nice cup of tea before going to bed for once in reasonable time.

Wednesday, December 8th
I had a big conference with Fred Willey and his staff on the problem of Ullswater. For years Manchester's water has been derived largely from the Lake District; and there have been terrible and legitimate complaints from the preservation pressure groups because the corporation did really ruin Thirlmere by turning that beautiful lake into the most horrible-looking reservoir. When it recently proposed to do the same in Ullswater and Windermere there was a storm of protest. Norman Birkett made the famous last speech of his life in the House of Lords and got the Bill turned down.[1] Now Manchester have come back with a new Bill which includes a much more moderate proposal, and I had my Inspector's report before me. In it he had worked out a plan for taking some of the water from Ullswater and some from Windermere, with the most elaborate series of controls to prevent the water-level sinking. A first-rate report. At first I was going to accept it virtually intact. But last week Ted Short, the Chief Whip, came to me and said that his family had lived near Ullswater for generations and that he himself was the leader of the preservation campaign. So I let him have the Inspector's report over the weekend and I got a powerful letter back yesterday saying that we must take all the water from Windermere and not a drop from Ullswater. Hence the meeting in my room with Fred Willey and his staff. My tactic was to win over the Department of Land and Natural Resources so that we could present a united front. The tactic worked: within a matter of minutes we had got them on our side and now that we are united I can face the Chief Whip.

I was pretty pleased with myself when I drove round the corner to Cowley Street to lunch with Pam Berry. There I found, as I often do, a couple of American correspondents, along with Peregrine Worsthorne,[2] Tom Driberg and Virginia Crawley and her husband Aidan.[3] Feeling thoroughly at home, I found myself explaining Harold's position, showing the Americans why he thought Rhodesia so important both in terms of *realpolitik* and in terms of the survival of the Labour Government. They asked me whether he had made

---

[1] William Norman Birkett, a famous advocate and Lord Justice of Appeal 1950–57, had been created the first Baron of Ulverston in 1958. Immediately before his death in February 1962 at the age of seventy-nine, he made a passionate and eloquent speech in the House of Lords condemning the Ministry's plans for Ullswater.

[2] Deputy editor of the *Sunday Telegraph*.

[3] Virginia Cowles, the writer and journalist, was married to Aidan Crawley, Conservative M.P. for West Derbyshire since 1962, who was also a journalist.

sufficient contingency plans and I replied that if he hadn't, he had avoided doing so because he was so determined to prevent U.D.I. They then asked me whether he wasn't relying too much on his own personal Wilsonian diplomacy. I said that there was possibly something in that; Prime Ministers are inclined to think that they can act alone. On the other hand, there is no doubt that by committing his personality so early on he has given a hostage to fortune and wasted an asset which might have been better used later in the negotiation. I also found myself stressing the tremendous pressure he is under from the Left, especially from Barbara Castle, representing Black Africa. I explained how, to some extent, she has also got the backing of others including Denis Healey and James Callaghan, each of whom, for his own reasons, would favour military measures. Finally, under pressure, I found myself saying that watching from inside I got more and more alarmed lest the position he built up for himself might be dissipated if no results are forthcoming. I didn't think he could go on playing this game from week to week, surviving by a series of diplomatic expediencies and *tours de force* on television and in the Commons; and I made it pretty clear that I, at least, would like to see an early election.

In the afternoon George Brown summoned me to an urgent meeting with Alderman Sefton, the leader of the Liverpool Labour Group. He arrived with two or three of the Liverpool M.P.s to explain to us that their housing revenue account was now in the red and we just had to give them subsidies to help them out. Our new building subsidy was no good to them because what they needed was help with the deficit on the old housing. As I listened I realized it was an absolutely outrageous demand and I couldn't even dream of baling out local authorities who had got into the red by not raising council rents fast enough or high enough. Nevertheless, I was worried because I had been warned that the Labour Group, which now runs Liverpool, is heading for something like a total disaster in the municipal elections. So the fact that I couldn't help Sefton at all on this occasion didn't make me very happy.

That night Anne and I gave the Donaldsons dinner in exchange for their splendid hospitality when they invite us to the Royal Box at Covent Garden. There we were in the Strangers' dining-room, with George Wigg sitting at the table next to us. The Donaldsons are old Gaitskellites but I think they found our company tolerable and certainly I found them extremely pleasant. She, Frankie, is the daughter of Freddie Lonsdale, the famous playwright, and is herself a remarkable writer. Her book on the Marconi scandal, which is just out, is one of the best bits of political writing I know.[1]

Thursday, December 9th

As I was chatting in the Cabinet anteroom I got a frantic telephone message from the Dame. Donald Gould, the chairman of the Council of the Building Societies Federation, had rung her up in desperation about the rumours that

[1] Frances Donaldson, *The Marconi Scandal* (London: Hart-Davis, 1962).

the Treasury was going to demand the summoning of the chairmen of eleven main building societies to tell them not to raise their interest rates. His message to the Dame was that, if the Chancellor interfered in this way, the building societies would have to break off relations with me and refuse all co-operation in my national housing plan. Could I get an assurance from the Chancellor that the rumours weren't true? I caught the Chancellor just as he was going through the door into the Cabinet room and he was huffy and snappy. I at once guessed what had happened. It had been reported to him that in our negotiations with the builders we had given an assurance about his non-intervention, which the Treasury very much resented (I hadn't given it, but Dame Evelyn had and I had thought that was O.K.). So that was that and I knew I should have a difficult time at my drink with him that evening.

This Cabinet was even drearier than Tuesday's. The Fairfield's Shipyard discussion was resumed in a somewhat embarrassed way because the whole story had appeared in the press. George Brown assured us that it was one of the trade-union members that had leaked; I suspect it had come from his own office, because they assumed that the deal had been completed. As a result of the leak the deal came unstuck and the Cabinet was left with the story once again incomplete. Nothing could be decided and yet we sat around talking for more than two hours and then turned on to another long discussion about whether or not one should have ex-officio Justices of the Peace. I got bored and went out.

At my weekly drink with Callaghan part of the talk was about Rhodesia. I was disconcerted but surprised to hear him say that more than a third of his time as Chancellor of the Exchequer was spent on the Rhodesian crisis. I am sure more than half of the Prime Minister's energies are going on the same thing. Callaghan's conversation reinforced what George Wigg has said to me more than once. The major preoccupation of the British Government now is to get the Americans on our side, because without full American backing we haven't any chance of imposing effective sanctions or defeating the Smith regime. That will take some doing. At Cabinet this morning the Foreign Secretary mentioned how completely negative the Americans have been to our first approach — rather drily reminding us that we didn't give them much help in Cuba and asking when the first British battalion would be arriving in Vietnam. No doubt Harold Wilson hopes to bring something solid back with him from his visit to Washington next week. Yet I can't believe that we are going to get an early fall of the Smith Government even by new and sharper sanctions applied with American backing. Nor are we going to avoid more and more pressure from the African states for actual military intervention, which we can't undertake partly because it will split the country from top to bottom and partly because we haven't got the troops and if we had it would be geographically impossible to put them in.

When we had finished with Rhodesia I tried to smooth the Chancellor down about the building societies. He ought to realize, I told him, that the whole of our national housing plan's future depended on my keeping good relations with them; and I added that I hoped he would never again see them without my being present. This he agreed.* Then I pointed out to him that if the societies raised their interest rates in January that ought to help him, because it would automatically ration the supply of houses for sale. If he wants a number of anti-inflationary actions why shouldn't the building societies raising their rates be part of his campaign? This he answered with one terse phrase, 'Rationing by purse'. Suddenly I saw that he was anxious to curry favour with borrowers by forbidding the building societies to raise their rates.

Then, as he always does, he turned to the present situation. He told me the balance-of-trade figures were bad again and we were not going to be out of the red by the time we had promised. There would have to be another bout of anti-inflationary measures. When they come up to Cabinet I shall again remind him of the role which building-society interest rates can play in his campaign.

The talk lasted a long time and was all a bit unfriendly. Callaghan is curiously schizophrenic about me. He regards me as able and in certain senses someone he can talk to and understand. But he also knows that departmentally I am a fearful menace to him, and he is constantly trying to organize other members of the Cabinet against me.

I went straight from No. 11 to the Wedgwood Benns' house in Holland Park, where we were having our weekly dinner with Marcia. We agreed that at our meeting with Harold next Tuesday we must concentrate on getting him to see electoral strategy in terms of dates. There were three possibilities: one, a March election before the budget; two, a May election after the budget but before the municipals; three, an October election. Marcia preferred number three. 'We haven't done enough,' she said. 'People want us to go on and deliver the goods and it is sheer defeatism to talk of a March election.' She is clearly representing the boss's view in all this. Harold isn't even considering a March election, thinks a May election improbable and wants to plan for October simply on the ground that we mustn't run away from our responsibilities. Tony Wedgwood Benn took much the same line. All Tommy and I could say was that it might be a good idea, but surely we must look at the economic troubles mounting up in front of us and weigh the chances of our being able to carry on beyond a disastrous and unpopular budget. It would be far worse to be forced into an early election by a couple of by-election defeats than to decide voluntarily to have one now.

Sunday, December 12th
I had a nice rest in the train down to Swansea on Friday where I got a lot of work done. On arrival, I went up to the university and had a gay meeting with

---

* We got it agreed later at official level, too.

the students, and then down to a school hall for a very poor public meeting. After that the Swansea city councillors entertained me to a buffet supper in one of the big hotels. Here I learnt a great deal about rate rebates. Swansea is one of the councils which have turned rate rebates down. They have done it seven times running and their treasurer detests our scheme. I simply replied that now they would be bound by law to introduce rate rebates and that would enable them to use the staff who deal with rent rebates.

I took the night train back to Paddington, got an early train down to Prescote the next morning and arrived on Saturday afternoon in time to spend the whole day helping in the preparations for the farm supper. In the evening we sat down sixteen in the hall, and went on till after midnight. This year all the ladies gathered round me to talk about the village school, where we all have our children, and discuss the headmistress. Oh dear, the complaints. 'She doesn't teach anyone in the top form'; 'She forces the children to use the italic script'; 'She doesn't concentrate enough on reading.' Actually, Anne and I think the village school pretty good: Miss Samuel is an extreme exponent of the liberal theory of having no compulsion and no competition and letting the child's personality evolve. Nevertheless, some of their complaints seem to me justified. With a new vicar coming, we may get some improvements.

Monday, December 13th
I had to go up to London on Sunday night because of a big E.D.C. meeting on industrial incentives about which Tommy had been briefing me at length. The proposal is quite simply to scrap our present system of tax allowances and replace it by a system of grants. They are all convinced that this will provide much bigger incentives to industry: instead of rewarding those who make profits by giving them tax deductions we would provide outright grants which should be available even to those who hadn't made any profits. This is a change to which Tommy, Robert Neild and the other economists attach enormous importance, and they have been pushing for it against all the weight of the Treasury and the Chancellor. Tommy had warned me on Sunday night that Callaghan was going to launch a counter-attack arguing that the grants were much too expensive. When I looked at the papers and heard the discussion in Cabinet, it did seem to me that a lot of extra money would be going out, at least £230 million extra in the first full year. I also noticed that they were tremendously regional in their effect and were of no assistance at all either to the Minister responsible for New Towns or to the M.P. for Coventry East.

So I didn't oppose the switch from tax allowances to grants; but I did point out the danger of this one-sided approach, which might really hold up development in important growth areas such as the West Midlands. My plea was listened to in silence and then I was courteously told that none of my ideas could be written into this Bill without upsetting the political applecart.

In the Labour Government there is of course a tremendous over-representation of the old development areas, the North-East, Scotland and Wales; and all those M.P.s are determined to see that their parts of the country get a bigger slice of the cake and that we don't get anything in the West Midlands or in London. I don't blame them for it; but from a national point of view, if our resources are limited and we spend them all on developing the less essential and rather backward part of the country, we may well find that we haven't allocated enough to extending the growth areas, which is vital to the Government's success. All my colleagues understood the force of my arguments. What depressed me was that no one was willing to apply them in practical politics.

At the Ministry I had an amusing meeting with Lord Macclesfield, the G.O.M. of the Oxfordshire County Council. I had long wanted to meet him because my father-in-law, old Patrick McDougall, had been his opponent throughout the 1930s in County Hall. Macclesfield has been boss of Oxfordshire for over thirty years and my father-in-law was almost the only person who dared to stand up to him and fight him week in, week out. I had summoned him because of a book by Lord Esher, my pupil at New College and now the President of the R.I.B.A., which contains the most scarifying exposure of the ineffectiveness of Oxfordshire planning for preservation of the countryside.[1] As chairman, Macclesfield has ruled that planning must be kept down and for that reason he has forbidden his chief planning officer to be, as he is almost everywhere else, a full executive officer on a level with the county architect or the county engineer or the county treasurer or the director of education. In fact, the old boy has kept planning in his pocket and in that of the members of his family he has placed on the county council. I had been warned in advance by my Department that a careful study showed Oxfordshire planning no worse in this respect than many other counties and I had therefore better be careful in using the book in evidence against the old man. However, they needn't have been afraid. I was just curious to see him! We discussed the expansion of Banbury amiably enough. Then right at the end I brought in the point about his chief planning officer and got an icy negative, to which I have since replied with a tactful letter hoping that he will change his mind.[2]

Tuesday, December 14th

At Cabinet this morning Peggy Herbison put forward the second part of her plan for reforming social security. After more than a year wasted on reflection, Douglas Houghton and she had decided that the incomes guarantee was wholly impracticable and had to be dropped. What could be put in its place? The scheme she put forward this morning was a cheap substitute, a reformed national assistance which would be sold to the public under the new name

[1] *Landscape in Distress* (London: Architectural Publications, 1965).
[2] He never did, and it wasn't till he retired some years later that the change was made.

of supplementary benefit. I am still sick at the thought of how Douglas Houghton has fragmented our major comprehensive reform and so minimized its political effect. Nevertheless, if you take it for what it is—a cheap substitute—this proposal of Peggy's is brilliantly worked out. Once again Douglas Houghton and James Callaghan got into a sinister combination trying to wreck it. Fortunately, others praised it highly and we got it through without too much delay.

In the afternoon I happened to be sitting next to Harold on the front bench while both of us were waiting for Questions. He said to me, 'If there was anything which was bound to ditch a spring election it was those press stories at the weekend.' Most of the Sunday papers had much the same story about Wilson's wish for the spring election. I had an uneasy feeling that maybe what I had been saying at Pam Berry's lunch, when Perry Worsthorne and Tom Driberg were present, had contributed to these stories. Certainly, I did make it pretty clear that in my view there should be a March election though I had stressed that Harold was against it and that the main difficulties were Rhodesia and the Callaghan budget.* Harold didn't know about the lunch but he was obviously suspicious that I had played politics over the weekend and felt that I had to be taught a lesson about this manœuvre.

However, he went on to say that the date of the Hull by-election was finally fixed, he couldn't hold out any longer and Transport House had been determined to have it at the end of January. But then he added, 'You know, of course, it's still open about the general election.' I said, 'Doesn't Hull shut out all room for manœuvre?' He said, 'No, no. It still leaves it open. Whatever happens in the by-election, we can still have a spring general election but heaven knows I really don't want one.'

In the evening our little group had arranged a supper party to have a talk with the Prime Minister. When I got to No. 10, however, I found that he had been forced to call it off because he was entertaining the Prime Minister of Nigeria. We talked about the reshuffle for which we had been waiting so long, and Marcia made a remark that revealed the real difficulty Harold faces. Frank Soskice, she told us, had already written to him saying he wasn't prepared to be stuck on the back benches and if he were removed from the Cabinet he would insist on resigning his seat and so forcing a by-election in Newport.[1] Harold does really want to remove Soskice and Tom Fraser but dare he risk two by-elections?

I was due at ten o'clock at I.T.V. in Kingsway to discuss rates with John Boyd-Carpenter. When I got there I found a very surly Douglas-Home sitting in the waiting-room with Arthur Bottomley on the other side, and a deadly silence between the two. Apparently Douglas-Home had been asked by I.T.V. to submit himself to cross-examination on Rhodesia and in particular on his

---

* I have learnt since then that it probably all came out of a little speech by du Cann, the chairman of the Tory Party, who probably got the information second-hand from the lunch.
[1] He had a majority of only 8,300 in 1964.

speech on conciliation.[1] Arthur had obviously been sent away from the Prime Minister's dinner to tail Douglas-Home and make sure that he got equal time with him. After I had done my interview I checked and found that the Chief Whip had taken Arthur virtually by the scruff of his neck and put him in a taxi and ordered him to go round and insist on being interviewed with Douglas-Home. In fact, since Arthur is no good, this made Douglas-Home look vastly superior. My housekeeper at Vincent Square, Mrs Meek, said next morning, 'You know, Mr Crossman, poor Mr Bottomley isn't quite up to it.'

Wednesday, December 15th

This morning Llewelyn-Davies came in to see me in great disturbance about our Centre for Environmental Studies. It really seems easier to get a million pounds for it than to get the right chairman and director. The Dame had been pressing for Frank Lee, the ex-head of the Board of Trade,[2] but I have insisted we won't have a sheer establishment figure. On the other hand, she has said that I can't have Llewelyn-Davies because he would get unfair advantages for his department at University College London. On this occasion I disregarded her and telegraphed Ford that Llewelyn-Davies would be chairman, whereupon the Department had put the heat on Llewelyn-Davies and he had come to ask me to find someone else!

Lunch at the annual get-together of the building-material producers, concrete, gravel, bricks, etc. – an immense collection of associations who meet four times a year and always expect a Minister to address them. I took the chance to talk about the gravel pits which have excited me ever since I saw what Hugh Dalton achieved at Corby.[3] The extraction industry needs amenity legislation in the 1970s as urgently as iron and steel needed it in the 1930s: gravel production has been leaping up at a fantastic rate and within seven or eight years there won't be any gravel and sand available for building within reach of London unless we start encroaching on very good agricultural land. And that means, of course, that we must have plans for amenity restoration in order to make this palatable.

Since I visited Corby I have met with fairly stiff resistance, not only from the Establishment Officer, who is in charge of gravel, but also unfortunately from J. D. Jones as well as from our newcomer, Miss Hope-Wallace, who turns out a pretty negative character. Finally I have got my way to some extent by a very simple device. When an urgent planning appeal was put up to me last week (there are some thirty waiting in the pipeline) I said I wouldn't deal with it until they produced a policy paper for me on the basis of which

[1] Speaking in Glasgow the previous evening, the Shadow Foreign Secretary had suggested that the time had come to negotiate with Mr Smith.

[2] Permanent Secretary at the Board of Trade 1957–9, and Joint Permanent Secretary at the Treasury from 1960 to 1962, when he became Master of Corpus Christi College, Cambridge. He died in 1972.

[3] See p. 310.

I could announce my intentions. Well, I got it just before this lunch and gave the outline to the producers. I assured them that they would be able to get the planning permissions they needed provided that they always produced a plan either for restoration or even more important for the creation of water open space. Roughly 400 acres of ugly pool are created each year. All this could be carefully lagooned into a blue belt. The speech went down all right. Now I need the legislation.

In the afternoon was the Second Reading debate on our Housing Subsidies Bill, a completely second-class affair since the fireworks were being kept for Thursday's big attack on Mulley and Healey for abolishing the Territorials. Bob Mellish started with a good, plain, ordinary speech, and a whole series of our back-benchers were enthusiastic for the Bill. John Boyd-Carpenter moved a ridiculous reasoned amendment blaming the Bill for not helping the owner-occupier. It was a routine affair. The Government is reckoned to have the upper hand and therefore there was no sense of crisis. When I wound up I remembered how unpopular I had made myself with the treasurers the week before and I took some care to placate the local authorities and to emphasize their rights in the matter of housing finance. Technically, however, I made a serious mistake which I must avoid in the future. I hadn't had much time yesterday or this morning to prepare a speech and I spoke impromptu, for the most part replying to questions. So I found myself turning my head round a great deal and that took my mouth away from the microphone, and I got an official complaint from the press gallery that they couldn't hear what I was saying or report it adequately. However, it went down well in the House with our back-benchers.

Thursday, December 16th

We began the Committee Stage of our Rating Bill this morning. I find these Standing Committees upstairs appallingly dreary. There we were with John Boyd-Carpenter getting up and saying he didn't want to meet on the Tuesday before Christmas and elaborate arguments taking place about the time-table. When this is settled we shall get down to our line-by-line discussions, and it will all be make-believe fury signifying nothing because so few of the amendments will be well-drafted or well-based. The fact is that in our system the Opposition isn't able to fight on equal terms with the Minister because it is denied the skills of the Civil Service and the Parliamentary draftsmen and has no apparatus of its own for working out sensible criticism. I would like to see a drastic improvement in parliamentary procedure for Standing Committees.

Once the Committee was safely under way I went back to Cabinet where I found my colleagues cutting back on our earlier support for ELDO, the European launcher development organization. Then came the item which interested me as a weekend farmer — broilers. Fred Peart proposed that we introduce anti-dumping legislation to stop the Danes bringing broilers into the country and so jeopardizing the healthy expansion of our own broiler industry. Douglas Jay in Cabinet Committee had opposed the Bill. As President of the Board of Trade, he admitted that Danish broilers had suddenly been dumped during the last two or three years; but he argued that this wasn't very much compared with our total broiler production. We needed good relations with the Danes; they would settle for 8,500 a year; why introduce anti-dumping legislation to get the figure down to the 6,500 demanded by the N.F.U.? Douglas made his point at inordinate length whereas Fred Peart, who is a shrewd fellow, put his case very tersely. It was clear that most of us were on Fred's side, whereupon Douglas Jay said, 'Anyway you can't legislate unless I as President of the Board of Trade say that dumping is doing material damage to agriculture and no one can say that if the difference is between 8,500 and 6,500 imports in a year.' To which I replied, 'Since the President of the Board of Trade brought this issue to Cabinet, Cabinet must decide it. If Cabinet concludes that material damage is being done, then the President will have to discover that material damage has been done.' When I said this I was thinking of Canvey Island.[1] Normally I would have decided that planning permission without consultation in favour of the unfortunate house-owners on Canvey Island and against the oil company. But the national economic interest involved was really so big that I allowed myself to be persuaded by the Dame to bring the issue to Cabinet and there I was duly overridden by the collective decision. Douglas Jay, of course, was one of the economic Ministers most insistent on having me voted down. Now he was hoist with his own petard. Cabinet simply said to him, 'No, you shan't do it.' We broke off for lunch feeling we had done a good morning's work. Cabinet government still means something—on the level of broilers or Canvey Island.

I lunched with Dunham of the Co-operative Building Society because I wanted to persuade him to help me make the building societies have a sense of responsibility about the scandals of jerry-building. The most effective way of reducing that scandal is for the building societies to agree that no house shall be given a mortgage unless there is a certificate of house-worthiness, and this was the plan which I originally adopted. However, the societies are only going to *recommend* each other to do this and that isn't enough. From what Dunham said over lunch and Potter of the Halifax told me last week, it might be possible to persuade the twenty leading building societies in council next spring to announce that, before issuing a mortgage, each of them will insist either on an N.H.B.R. certificate or another warranty of equal value. Something at least is being achieved.

In the evening in the House we had the big debate on the Territorials and it really was an exciting affair. For weeks past I have been attending the Cabinet Committee on the Bill, watching the battle between Denis Healey and poor old Frank Soskice, who was no match for this rough, rather ruthless

---

[1] See p. 366.

young man. I backed Denis Healey because my master and his in this matter had been George Wigg, who has always been in favour of cutting back the Territorials as well as civil defence. He says that both these voluntary organizations were once valuable instruments of warfare but have now degenerated into clubs using the valuable space of the barracks, training-rooms, etc., largely for social purposes. In the nuclear period what you need in defence is not Territorials sitting in England waiting for an invasion but a well-organized reserve able to go overseas at short notice. In just the same way, civil defence against nuclear war is a contradiction in terms. All we can do is to have an organization for picking up the bits afterwards. So the present Territorial Army and the present civil defence staff are useless and ought to be scrapped. The only support Soskice got in the Committee was old Charlie Pannell saying from time to time, 'You can't get rid of civil defence, Kent is still in the front line.'

There was one serious argument against Healey—that you can't afford to wind up either the Territorials or civil defence because there would be such an outcry locally. Nevertheless, he did get his way and some weeks ago it was known what we were up to.[1] This caused a tremendous outcry among the Conservatives. Many of the Tory M.P.s, including Heath himself, are colonels or lieutenant-colonels in the Territorials and all of them have ardent Party supporters who run drill halls. In fact the Territorials are largely a Conservative organization. Last week the Conservatives announced they were going to make this Thursday debate a major demonstration.

And that's just what they did. We nearly came unstuck owing to two threatened abstentions. Leslie Lever, Harold Lever's elder brother and an ex-Lord Mayor of Manchester, threatened to abstain but didn't at the last moment.[2] Richard Crawshaw, a Liverpool back-bencher,[3] however, found himself conscientiously unable to support us and it was only because the Liberals were in the Government lobby that we scraped through with a majority of one.

I was away in No. 9 Vincent Square giving a most important dinner to Bill Fiske and his wife. My job was to discuss with him how he could persuade his colleagues on the G.L.C. to reduce their minimum floor-to-ceiling height from eight feet to seven feet six inches. I know it sounds trivial but it is a matter of the very greatest importance in terms of speedy house-building in London. At dinner Lady Fiske said she had never seen the inside of the Commons so I took them round at nine o'clock and we saw the last hour of the debate and the dramatic scene at the division. Then we went back to Vincent Square and

---

[1] The White Paper was actually published on December 15th. It proposed savings of £20 million per annum by 1970 by cutting the Territorials by 70,000 men. In their place the Government would set up an Army Volunteer Reserve of 50,000 men using two recruiting systems, 'independent' units raised locally, and countryside 'sponsored' units.

[2] A solicitor, and a Manchester City Councillor since 1932, he was Lord Mayor of Manchester 1957–8. He was Labour M.P. for the Ardwick Division of Manchester 1950–70.

[3] M.P. for Toxteth, Liverpool, since 1964.

got down to the issue at stake. After a time he made it clear that if I would give him orders he would be quite happy to bring his colleagues into line.

Friday, December 17th
I spent most of the day in the High Wycombe borough and with the local R.D.C., trying to understand these small second-tier authorities and to see how their planning can be linked in a constructive way.

Saturday, December 18th
This was the day of the presentation to mark my twenty years as M.P. for Coventry East. I'd mentioned this to Maurice Edelman and found to my slight embarrassment that it hadn't been arranged for him.

When Coventry get down to it they do one proud. We were in St Mary's Hall and the rain was streaming down outside but a good hundred people had turned up. There on the dais was what was obviously a portrait covered up and beside it two other things also covered. After George Hodgkinson's longish speech came the unveiling. First a perfectly villainous portrait. Then a splendid huge cactus in a pot for Anne. And finally a really lovely piece of stoneware by Ron Morgan—Lady Godiva on her horse—which we found fitted perfectly on the table in the hall at Prescote. I made a very small speech in reply and then we had the buffet and moved upstairs for drinks in the mayor's parlour. It turned out to be a really nice ceremony.

What a book one could write about the influence the constituency exerts on the M.P. The luck of my being chosen in 1937 has kept me in Parliament with a huge cast-iron majority and with a particular kind of Party behind me which has deeply influenced by thinking, keeping me much more on the Left than I would by nature have been. And this has meant that I have not had any of the pressures that are exerted on M.P.s in marginal constituencies: I have never in my political life had to bother about appeasing industrialists or right-wing groups, churches or chapels. Coventry East would simply not have allowed me to be a right-winger, to be an anti-Bevanite, for example. On the other hand, they have given me their loyalty and their permission to be a very egocentric politician with ideas of my own; and though they have often disagreed with me they have given me pretty solid support. Since I have been a Minister I have tended to get depressed about Coventry. It's a difficult place under a Labour Government; and I am also aware of a decline in the Party and a decline in its quality on the council. Mostly it was old people who were there for the presentation; only a handful were young and proud of the part I have played in trying to modernize the Party.

The Prime Minister's decisive actions over Rhodesia had consolidated his authority but, leaving nothing to chance, he attracted further public attention at the very end of the year by a brief visit to America just before Christmas and, on his return, a Cabinet reshuffle.

In America, Mr Wilson addressed the U.N. General Assembly on Rhodesia, and discussed the economic situation and domestic politics with President Johnson. Their conversations on foreign policy included Rhodesia and the extent of Britain's Far East commitment. According to Mr Wilson, the President made no request for British troop support in Vietnam (on the Prime Minister's arrival in Washington, he had received a telegram of protest against the war from sixty-eight Labour M.P.s).

The Cabinet reshuffle was a surprise. Sir Frank Soskice left the Home Office, with the understanding that when the Parliamentary situation allowed Labour to risk a by-election he would go to the Lords. Roy Jenkins became Home Secretary and Fred Mulley replaced him at Aviation. Barbara Castle became the Minister of Transport (her predecessor, Tom Fraser, left the Cabinet altogether). Tony Greenwood became the new Minister of Overseas Development.

Sunday, December 19th

I have now had time to look at the Sunday papers and my first impression is that Harold has done something positive in Washington. But how much has he had to give in exchange? George and I have often talked over this and I rather share his view that unless we are prepared to go much further in helping the Americans in Vietnam they won't be prepared to help us in Rhodesia — and without their help we just can't down Smith. On the other hand, if Harold gives an inch on the use of British troops in Vietnam he will face a major row with his own left-wingers.

Fortunately for us the Tories have their own internal Party difficulties. Heath's position has been made much more difficult in this Rhodesian crisis by the sharp division between the constitutionalists, who really in a way support Harold Wilson, and the right-wing Tories, who believe that the Rhodesian whites should be given whole-hearted support. These right-wingers achieved a victory this week by taking over the speech proposing conciliation which Douglas-Home made in Glasgow and using it as a lever for breaking up bipartisanship. By the end of the week the Tories were split wide open.

Monday, December 20th

Harold Wilson arrived back early today and made a Statement in the House at 3.30. I got a mysterious invitation to a party in Downing Street, and when I got there after the ten o'clock division I found it was an assembly of the Transport House and No. 10 staff. Tony Wedgwood Benn and I were the only members of the Government there. I can only think I was invited as chairman of the liaison committee. There were Percy Clark and his publicity girls and Marcia and her number two and my Jennie Hall, looking very pretty and eager, and Harold himself. He was a bit exhausted — and no wonder — and as a result was showing off a bit more than I liked. But Mary was absolutely charming and easy, and it was a pleasant atmosphere with Giles and his schoolboy friends coming in to join us.

14

Harold took me back to the midnight division on the adjournment for the recess, and on the way we agreed that I should see him on Wednesday afternoon, since on Tuesday evening when our talk was due he had been invited to dinner at the Palace to discuss Prince Charles's education. By the way, talking at the party, Marcia told me that she feels less and less close to him and is being pushed aside, much like George Wigg. I agreed with her that Harold is more and more a self-contained unit, working with Burke Trend and the Civil Service and going the way of Lloyd George by casting off his radical past—if he ever had one—and becoming a national fixture with all the power in his hands.

Tuesday, December 21st
Cabinet. Harold reported on his talks with Johnson. He claimed that he had managed to get an absolute promise from the President that he would be allowed to work for peace and not send British troops to Vietnam. On the other hand, he got no more than an understanding that if we stood firm on our present position in the Far East the Americans would back the oil sanctions we were announcing that afternoon. He seems to have adopted a very lieutenant-ish posture, but possibly that is the best we can achieve in the present circumstances. What mainly struck me was his extraordinary physical vitality. On Friday he flies to Washington and from there on to Canada. On Monday he arrives back and makes a Statement in the House, and on Tuesday after Cabinet he is due to open the second day of the foreign affairs debate. All this while he is maintaining a pretty fair control of the other aspects of government.

His speech in the debate had the desired effect: it split the Tory Party and it kept the Labour Party relatively united. Indeed, when the vote came the leadership of the Tories abstained and the back benches broke in two with one section voting for oil sanctions and the other section against them.[1]

Wednesday, December 22nd
At last the reshuffle has been announced. Barbara moves to Transport, Tony Greenwood takes her place in Overseas Development and Frank Longford becomes Colonial Secretary. I heard all this for the first time at a Christmas party in Caxton House. It came to me as a tremendous surprise. I had assumed that Frank Soskice would finally be removed and wondered who would take his place. I didn't see how Harold could select Barbara, in view of her violent views on immigration, or Tony Greenwood, because of his proven incompetence. Would he give the job to Douglas Houghton for a short time and move Frank to the Duchy? What he actually decided was to give Roy Jenkins the Home Office, the job he had offered him earlier.[2] I am

---

[1] At the end of the debate on the Rhodesia Order the vote was 276 to 48 in favour of imposing sanctions.
[2] See p. 358.

sure Barbara has paid the price for her pertinacity in taking the black African point of view and in being the one member of the Cabinet prepared to prevent a settlement in Rhodesia. She was moved because he didn't want her formidable, old-fashioned, left-wing conscience there preventing him finding some kind of settlement with the Smith regime. As for her new job at Transport, I have heard from Jennie, whose husband Chris is transferring with Barbara to the new Ministry, that she realizes how much a graveyard of all political reputations Transport has become. But if there is anybody who will get us a fully integrated transport policy it is her and that makes it a good move.

I saw Harold just after the announcement and he wanted to chat with me about it. But I had so much business I had to get through that I ticked off my items for half an hour and made sure I had cleared everything before the Christmas recess.

The first item on my list was rating and how to shift the burden to taxes. I told him I had got into a dead-end because the Chancellor just hadn't the money. I therefore proposed to de-rate the domestic ratepayer. This is my own bright idea which Crocker, my Accountant-General, has accepted as a practical proposition at last. The idea is beautifully simple. If the Chancellor can only spare me £30 million a year of rate relief I am going to make sure that every penny of that £30 million relieves the domestic ratepayer; and that is going to be done by making him a special government grant which the shopkeepers and industry don't share. I got the P.M. into thoroughly good humour by telling him about this idea, which he immediately liked and regards as the sort of thing a Minister is there to invent. This time he knew it hadn't come from the Dame!

Then I popped my second question, about local government reform. Should we let the Boundary Commission do one more job by reorganizing Lancashire before we appoint the Royal Commission or should we jump to a Royal Commission straight away? He wasn't very well briefed about this and obviously hardly remembered the minute I had sent him.[1] I got the feeling that he didn't want to be pushed into a difficult decision, so I told him that if, on reflection, he wanted the Lancashire reorganization, it could go ahead even at the cost of a two-year delay in establishing the Royal Commission. I said this partly because I have got cold feet now about finding a replacement for Alan Bullock.

My third item was of course the replacement for the Dame. She is due to go in March and there is still nobody to take her place. In the car going back to the midnight vote on Monday I had tried to remind him of the agreement under which I would take Bruce Fraser if he brought with him the Ministry of Land and Natural Resources. He reacted sharply. 'A Ministry started in one Parliament is not wound up in the same Parliament,' he said. That was a pretty clear hint, so I started from there and tried to get him to think of Philip Allen. 'Oh no,' he said. 'He's booked for the Home Office – Roy Jenkins

[1] See pp. 331, 386.

insists on having him. What about Douglas Allen from D.E.A.—isn't he a possibility?' Finally I said, 'But look, one thing is surely clear. I won't take Bruce Fraser.' He was very fierce and said he had promised Bruce Fraser and I replied that Helsby had promised me and he said that it wasn't in the minute of the talk. Then he neatly turned the tables and told me that Barbara Castle was asking for a new Permanent Secretary instead of Padmore,[1] as well as a new Parliamentary Secretary, and she couldn't have both. The obvious implication was that both his closest friends were being awkward cusses. Just as I was leaving I asked him about his talk with the Queen on Charles's education. He said it had gone on for a couple of hours because it was so interesting.

Thursday, December 23rd
The Christmas feeling has been growing in Cabinet and in Whitehall all through the week. There was a tremendous sense of winding up, and I found my Ministry determined to close down on Thursday, though Christmas Eve came on Friday. I said that was impossible and they finally got me off late on Thursday evening after a solid day's work.

At Cabinet in the morning the sole item was a deadlock on leasehold enfranchisement, with Fred Willey on the one side and the Law Officers, Lord Chancellor and Minister of Housing all on the other. The lawyers were profoundly shocked by Fred's proposal that we should give every leaseholder the choice between a 99-year lease—tantamount to confiscation of the property—and an improved rent. I was shocked because this would apply not only to the private leaseholder but to the local authorities, public corporations and nationalized industries. An important issue of socialist principle was at stake here though few people seemed to bother about it. For many years the Labour Party's view on leasehold has been that it is an excellent way for public authorities to retain their basic rights while permitting owner-occupation, thus ensuring good physical planning. Right up to the election, leasehold reform, as we preached it, was limited to private property. Then at the last moment we issued a 'Speakers' Notes' to help M.P.s and candidates explain how the right to enfranchisement was extended so that public corporations and local authorities were to suffer exactly the same lot as the private landowner. As a result, during the campaign the Welsh candidates, headed by James Callaghan and James Griffiths, had promised virtual confiscation of all long leases in South Wales and the same promises had been made in Birmingham. My own view was that since this last-minute electoral bribe wasn't in the Party manifesto we could disregard it. But, as I have often noted in this diary, Harold is extraordinarily sensitive on the issue of Party

---

[1] Sir Thomas Padmore joined the Board of the Inland Revenue in 1931, and in 1934 moved to the Treasury, where he became Second Secretary in 1952. In 1962 he became Permanent Secretary at the Ministry of Transport, and on his retirement in 1968 he joined the Metrication Board.

pledges, and when I approached him privately he said, 'This is a Party pledge which has to be fulfilled.' I replied, 'The whole tradition of socialist administration of public land is against you—don't sacrifice the wise administration of our New Towns for the sake of a passage in "Speakers' Notes" in 1964.'

In Cabinet things went very badly at first. The Lord Chancellor, the Attorney-General and the Solicitor-General all denounced the proposal. Callaghan riposted that they were lawyers whose views couldn't be taken seriously. It looked as though Willey was going to win hands down when I weighed in. I was able to speak as a layman not a lawyer—perhaps the only layman there who had really mastered the issue—and I think I got across the disastrous implications for local authority planning. I insisted that if the principle was to be laid down local authorities must be exempted, but then added that to exempt them would make the Bill impossible to defend. With a great struggle I got the paper referred back to the Committee and in January we are due to start trying to find a new formula.

In the afternoon I managed to clear up the mess about housing allocations. At last we have prepared the first list of local authorities with grave housing problems which must be permitted to build up to the limit. There are 165 of them. The second job is to list the authorities which shouldn't have any priority at all. Then we can see whether we can keep public-sector housing down to 300,000 for the next two years. By the time we had finished it was getting late and I only just caught my train.

I had thought perhaps I would try a retrospect of 1965, but the trouble is that calendar years mean nothing to me as a Minister. I can't remember what I felt like a year ago and take care not to look at my diary to see what it says. I just can't look back over the whole of 1965. What I can say is that since the summer Harold Wilson has been more and more obsessed with Rhodesia and Vietnam and less and less actively concerned with the home front. But the difficulties of the prices and incomes policy have been steadily mounting and we are getting very near to breaking-point. We can't afford to let the policy fail and yet quite soon we are going to face the 18-per-cent increase of army pay which the P.I.B. will almost certainly award. Then will come a sudden forward surge of salaries and wages which in its turn will produce another round of price increases and then the pound may well be in danger. On the other hand, we are beginning to implement Government policy. Soon we shall have our option-mortgages (the scheme is now pretty well complete), our rating reforms, and Peggy Herbison's reform of national assistance and the beginning of graded benefits for unemployment and sickness.

But the immediate prospect is of course the Hull by-election. From the latest Gallup Poll it looks as though we have a reasonable chance of winning it. But even if we don't we may well carry on with the majority of one which we have got now.

Of course, this means that things are precarious. We have not only got

Hayman at Falmouth on the edge of death; I heard over Christmas that Megan Lloyd George is desperately ill with cancer and likely to die at any moment.[1] I suppose Harold calculates that if we are forced to the polls by that kind of thing we may well do better because the public will want to give us a second chance. That brings me to the Opposition. Heath as leader has not really achieved anything yet, no professionalism, no particular competence. He is rather dull and stands no comparison with Harold. But all leaders develop and it won't take long before he improves. Meanwhile the Tories are settling down to the characteristics of an Opposition, beginning to make policy statements against each other. Already a right wing is gathering around Powell, who stands for ultra free-enterprise economics, and a left wing round Iain Macleod and Boyle, who still believe in the incomes policy and national planning. As the ex-Ministers settle down on the Opposition front bench they are beginning to find memories of Government replaced by nostalgia for Government. What they miss are those red dispatch boxes and the secret contact with reality that they give. I remember how mad I got with Hugh Gaitskell when in Opposition he would sometimes say, 'That's an issue no responsible person can decide unless he can see the Cabinet papers.' Now having read Cabinet papers for a year I have more sympathy with Gaitskell and with those Tories on the Opposition front bench. Separated from his sources of information the politician feels unsure of what he knows and starts making assertions which are pure dogma. The Tories are getting these characteristics – a tremendous loss to them which strengthens our position.

---

[1] Younger daughter of Lloyd George. She was Liberal M.P. for Anglesey 1929–51, and Labour M.P. for Carmarthen 1957–66. She died in May 1966.

1966

Monday, January 3rd

We have brought the family up to Vincent Square for the first week in January, during which I was to spend half my time at the office and the other half on holiday with them. My first day's programme was upset by an unexpected telephone message on Saturday. No. 10 told me that the Liverpool M.P.s wanted another delegation about their council rents.[1] I was angry and said, 'Look here, I've seen Sefton, the leader of the group. I can't see any more delegations because there is nothing I can do. I can't change the nature of our new subsidies.' However, on Sunday I got a message from Jennie that the P.M. insisted on my seeing the delegation on Monday afternoon and would see me immediately afterwards at five o'clock.

My first job, however, was the long-appointed meeting between Jim Callaghan, myself and the building societies. The Dame and I lunched with the building societies and they were extremely keen on our working party, talked about meeting regularly once a month and were obviously mainly concerned that I should keep them out of the clutches of the Chancellor of the Exchequer. After lunch we all went round in a body to see the Chancellor. I sat beside him and he behaved quite well, though he rather alarmed the societies by asking why instead of raising their interest rates they didn't reduce their deposit rates which, in his view, would have the same effect. The fact that it would decrease the amount of money available for housing didn't seem to have occurred to him! They were a bit baffled by this; but at least he kept his faith with me and didn't give them the impression that he was going to interfere. When they filed out of the room he kept me behind and I thought he wanted to talk about domestic de-rating but he said, 'I thought you were going to discuss your personal problems with me.' So I began to ask him about the possibility of getting Douglas Allen from the D.E.A. to replace the Dame, and mentioned that Harold had thrown out the idea. After a moment or two he said, 'I hear you are going to see the P.M. this afternoon, Dick. What's it about?' I assured him it wasn't about any of those things but was about Liverpool rents.

By the time Sefton and the Liverpool M.P.s filed into my room that afternoon I had a bright idea. Why should one not ante-date the rent subsidies by a whole year, back from November 1965 to November 1964? I put this idea informally to the delegation and added, 'Anyway, I am going round to see the P.M. this evening and I'll let him know your views.'

At five o'clock I trotted round to No. 10 and reported on the grave situation in Liverpool, which of course is of the greatest interest to Harold with his constituency at Huyton. He said, 'I don't care too much about the Liverpool Council because they are doomed already. They are going to lose that election and we shall only hold four of the wards.' I said that it wasn't only in Liverpool that Labour control was threatened by the rise in council rents. I had had representations from Leicester and Birmingham and many other towns

[1] See p. 406.

14*

about exactly the same problem—the effect of interest rates in forcing up council rents and so forcing up rates as well. Then I gave Harold the idea of ante-dating. His response was immediate. 'We'll make it coincide with the rise in bank rate,' he said. Of course I had forgotten that bank rate had gone up on November 25th, 1964. 'Well,' I said, 'that's very neat, but for heaven's sake pass the idea on to Callaghan because otherwise he'll be angry that I have talked to you first about it.'

Tuesday, January 4th
Whether Harold did talk to Callaghan I shall never know but there was no doubt this morning that the M.P.s had talked to the press. Apparently immediately they left me they had gone and spilt the whole story in Fleet Street. The moment Callaghan read this he remembered what I had said the day before about seeing the Prime Minister on council rents. The fat was in the fire. Within a few minutes I had been told of the tremendous rumpus going on in the Treasury, and even Bob Mellish, who lunched with me that day, remarked. 'You shouldn't behave in that way. There must be a limit to your irresponsibility. How on earth can we run this Ministry if you change your mind in public like that?' 'Well,' I said, 'I'm not so sure I was wrong, Bob. I think you may find that we have to do something about council rents to help Sefton.' Bob, who takes the Dame and the Department very seriously, said, 'Well, Dick, I don't think you'll get any change out of that.'

Wednesday, January 5th
I saw the P.M. this evening and broached the subject of local government reform again. Harold had had time to study the Boundary Commission's proposals for Lancashire and was quite impressed by them. So once more I gave him the choice. Can I go straight ahead with the Royal Commission or should I postpone it a couple of years and reorganize Lancashire first? I also discussed my idea for domestic de-rating, which the Chancellor doesn't like at all but which is going to help us a great deal in the elections. When I had finished my agenda he asked me what I thought of the reshuffle. He remarked that it had had a wonderful press; Barbara's appointment had gone down particularly well. I agreed and said that there was also the minor advantage that she has now been removed from dealing with the Commonwealth and so he can do a deal with Smith without her conscience looking over his shoulder. He looked a bit embarrassed and said, 'I don't know about that really.' And I must report faithfully in this diary that, although I am convinced that it was an element in his mind in moving Barbara to Transport, he has convinced himself that he was determined to find somebody to provide us with the integrated transport policy which we need so badly for the election manifesto. It is clear that in his mind Barbara is a considerable election asset. She is also getting her way about officials. Harold told me that Douglas Allen, whom he had offered to me only a few days before, was now being offered to

Barbara as replacement for Padmore. He added that Otto Clarke is being moved from the Treasury to take over Aviation and he repeated that he still wants me to take Bruce Fraser.

Thursday, January 6th

When I saw the Chancellor for a drink this evening I expected a rip-roaring row. But he couldn't have been more amenable. I spoke to him very patiently about the Liverpool rents, explaining that though I had thought the whole thing utterly impossible, it was clear now that something would have to be done. I would think about it a lot more with my Department and I would present the proposals to him in a formal minute, with a copy to the P.M. This is what the Prime Minister had told him I would do and I was careful to carry out the instructions. Callaghan then said that he had really been complaining to the P.M. not about me but about his habit of seeing all the Cabinet Ministers and putting his nose into domestic affairs which were really for the Chancellor of the Exchequer. I have no doubt that one of the reasons why he was so *piano* was because he had got himself into a hell of a mess that morning. He had opened the Boat Show at Earls Court with a jolly off-politics reference, not like the usual dismal Jim, gaily saying that he hoped people would have their holidays at home to save foreign exchange – and immediately produced a tremor of nervousness about his budget intentions. He had been having to deny it all that evening, which no doubt made him more amiable to me over our drink. Nevertheless, on domestic de-rating he was still extremely difficult. I expect a lot more difficulties in the next fortnight.

Sunday, January 9th

I had a splendid expedition on Friday to the gravel pits in the West London area. The construction industries are now consuming gravel at the rate of 200 million tons a year. About half the space created can be filled in with material from demolition but at least half remains gaping holes. They showed me the water sports which were available already and I saw how hopelessly unplanned the whole amenity side was. If I could release say 20,000 acres of agricultural land for the gravel producers they would be terribly grateful. Equally I could produce a major amenity round London by imposing stringent conditions for restoration.

When I had finished with gravel I drove on to Cambridge for a conference on historic buildings, which started with dinner at Churchill College and ended after lunch on Saturday afternoon. John Betjeman and Tom Driberg were there, as well as thirty or forty other experts, and Jimmy James and J. D. Jones ran the conference brilliantly. At last we are going to be able to work out a good policy for historic towns. Our idea is to select four for pilot experiments, where we not only list individual buildings but plan the preservation of the historic core.[1] One of the four will certainly be Bath. From

---

[1] In fact, there were to be five. See p. 517.

Cambridge John Delafons motored me back to Prescote where we had a weekend of brilliant sunshine mixed with appalling snow-showers.

Monday, January 10th

I started with a meeting with Barbara at her own Ministry. I had decided to show courtesy to a junior in the Cabinet by going to see her rather than making her come across the river to see me. I had been tipped off by Richard Llewelyn-Davies that she was thinking of asking for J. D. Jones, my Deputy, to be transferred to her Ministry. I told her straight away that that was a jolly good idea and I was willing to let him go because I wanted the best co-ordination between her planning and mine. It was obvious that now she is there we are at last going to have a Minister of Transport who is really keen on planning. On reflection I think I shall ask her to help us with our Ford Foundation Centre for Environmental Studies and she could bring along Chris Foster, her new economic adviser, so that we get real joint co-operation between Housing and Transport.

Tuesday, January 11th

This morning Sir Sydney Littlewood, the president of our London rent assessment committee, came to see me at his own request. I was mildly gratified because I had been told that he and his three vice-presidents couldn't settle between them the issue I had put to them about the definition of a fair rent. Since I addressed the rent officers, the pamphlet consisting of selections from my speeches had been issued as a directive to the rent officers and the rent assessment committees. And a good thing too! Littlewood told me that the rent officers had got to work in London and were doing 800 cases a week. Of course what we haven't yet had is a decision by a rent assessment committee. I wouldn't be surprised if they kept rents at a higher level than most of my Labour supporters are expecting. But it will be a level which people will consider fair. A few outrageous rents will be brought down but most of the rents won't be greatly reduced. I have also got my assessment panels going outside London. They are already functioning in Birmingham, Newcastle and Plymouth.

Wednesday, January 12th

Unfortunately there has been a disastrous leak in the *Guardian* today: Peter Jenkins, their political correspondent, has told the whole story of how Barbara's Permanent Secretary, Padmore, is to be removed. This disclosure probably comes from a charming young economist whom Barbara has just appointed as her new Director-General of Economic Planning and who isn't experienced in the ways of Whitehall. It was already clear by this evening that the whole of the reorganization will be held up as a result.

At a Labour Party meeting at Uxbridge this evening I took the opportunity to make a declaration on our local government mortgage policy. During the July squeeze Callaghan had suddenly shut down, telling the authorities they could not spend more than the average of their spending in the previous three years. In the particular case of London, by far the biggest spender, this meant spending nothing at all. The result had been as I predicted. Houses were being left vacant and, much more important, local authorities couldn't get people out of council houses because they couldn't provide them with mortgages. Quite quietly, without telling me, some of my officials have been working out a series of concessions for particularly hard-hit classes of applicants to whom a mortgage could be given even if it meant their exceeding the top limit of money allowed them. The officials had worked out six or seven exceptions. I had heard about this for the first time up in Rochdale and I went back to the Department and praised them for an admirable modification. All I did at Uxbridge was to state these classes publicly. When they heard of this the Department was terribly alarmed and told me the Treasury would be upset if I announced these concessions publicly. I replied quite simply that if a hundred local authorities are using these special permissions I must tell the others.

Sunday, January 16th

I have had a four-day tour of the South-West. On Thursday I went off to Taunton on one of my official visits. I took Waddell, my Deputy, whom I have found difficult to get on with during the last six months because he is such a rigid, stiff civil servant who, I suspect, finds my methods unbearable. I thought it might relax the atmosphere between us if we spent three or four days together. Watching me handle a variety of local authorities, he seemed quite impressed; but our relations were just as difficult at the end of the tour as they were at the beginning. He is somebody I would dearly like to see promoted out of the Ministry.[1]

As the Minister who decided to create Torbay I was very much a guest of honour in Torquay and found myself in a magnificent suite in the Imperial Hotel – on the cliff, with pine trees and a lovely garden outside my room and a view as beautiful as anything in the Gulf of Naples. Travelling all round the crescent of the bay with the councillors, I was relieved to find that my act of faith in creating a county borough was completely justified. There is an overwhelming case for trying to end the miserable parochialism and incompetence of the three little local councils by running them into one and giving them a chance to recruit an adequate staff.

Next day I moved from the hotel suite to the house of the chairman of the Devon County Council. I had a certain amusement in letting John Day entertain me and showing that I could be on good terms with the chairman of a

---

[1] He was, in 1966, when he went back to the Home Office as Deputy Under-Secretary to take charge of the police.

council from whose territory I had excised not only Torbay but the overspill suburbs of Plymouth as well. I spent two days with him, seeing the coastline from Plymouth nearly to Seaton. Bitterly cold it was. Anne was with us and we travelled in two cars, shivering all the way. Nevertheless, I was enormously impressed by the work of the county planning officer and saw how sharp was the contrast between what is done in Devon and what is done in Cornwall for the preservation of the coastline. Devon is one of those old-fashioned, oligarchical counties dominated by 'the County'. The planners there have complete control of the coastline. When they find caravans in the wrong place they order them out and concentrate them in the lost areas so as to preserve the unspoilt areas. I learnt one lesson on this tour. Very improperly perhaps, I persuaded the planning officer to show me on the site one or two of the decisions I had already taken and one or two I was due to take in the near future. As a result of seeing on the spot the decisions I had taken, I was more aware than ever how impossible it is for me to judge them fairly when they come on appeal as bits of paper. But there is another problem. As Turnbull said to me, there is no intrinsic fairness in planning, it is *by nature* unfair. In order to decide one individual case fairly the Minister must know not only the details of that case but the whole background and above all the planning policy of the local authority. One can only see the fairness of concentrating twenty caravans in a certain combe when one knows that five other combes near by are going to be kept unspoilt. That, said Turnbull, is the only way to handle coastline preservation. When I get back to London I must see that when I take a decision I am always given the full background by the Department, and my brief must deal not only with the single case but with what the planning officers are doing in the whole area.

Leaving Day behind, I motored on to Bath to study the Buchanan Report.[1] Buchanan has now made proposals for putting a tunnel clean under the old part of the city to carry the London–Bristol road. My own officials are very much against him and my impression from the headlines was that once again he had turned out to be a hopelessly impractical idealist. But seeing the problem on the ground with Buchanan's report in one hand and the physical facts of Bath on the other, I find it overwhelmingly powerful. On the most cautious calculation of traffic requirements he conclusively proves the need both for his tunnel and for another tunnel crossing it the other way. I did my tour with the deputy planner and the deputy architect, very nice young men but a bit inadequate. When I went to their office I saw the problem of a local authority of this size. A county borough of 80,000 people simply can't hire planning and architectural staff competent to deal with the immense problems, including the traffic and economic issues, of preserving one of our most beautiful historic towns.

[1] Colin Buchanan, Professor of Transport at Imperial College, London, since 1963, and author of the celebrated report 'Traffic in Towns' (1963), had been commissioned by the Ministry of Transport to prepare a report on the traffic problems in Bath.

Tuesday, January 18th
My domestic de-rating proposals came before Cabinet. I managed to get my way—quite a triumph because the Chancellor was half-heartedly or three-quarters-heartedly against me and so was Willie Ross, representing Scotland. I tried to make Cabinet realize that if we were going to spend £25 million on shifting the balance from rates to taxation we ought to concentrate every penny on the domestic ratepayer. By doubling the amount for him we should be able to halve each year the increase in the rates which he has to face. So now, in addition to rate rebates in the immediate future, I have domestic de-rating in the medium term and also recognition in Cabinet that the complete system of local government finance will have to be overhauled as part of our local government reorganization. On this Douglas Houghton unexpectedly came to my rescue with the view that under a computerized system we could have local income tax. The P.M. supported him. I suppose this was one of my most successful Cabinets because I had once again floated an idea for which the Department gave me no support and had got it incorporated in my Bill.

In January the African and Asian nations in the Commonwealth called a conference of Commonwealth Premiers in Lagos. Mr Wilson was there when it opened on January 11th. He clashed immediately with the Prime Minister of Sierra Leone, who demanded the use of force to end the Rhodesian rebellion. Pressure was resisted and by the end of the conference a Commonwealth Sanctions Committee had been set up, with the promise of a further meeting in July if the Rhodesian regime had still not collapsed.

Between January 18th and 23rd the Chief Justice, Sir Hugh Beadle, who remained loyal to the Crown, visited London for talks but no settlement could be devised. On January 31st sanctions were tightened still further.

Mr Wilson also had talks in London with Arthur Goldberg, one of the special envoys despatched to the world's capitals by President Johnson in an effort to find a solution to the Vietnam war. The North Vietnamese leader, Ho Chi Minh, rejected the American peace initiative and the missions were abortive.

Labour left-wingers attacked the Prime Minister on two grounds, that his support for American policy was explicit and discreditable and that, as co-chairman with Russia of the 1954 Geneva Conference guaranteeing the independence of Vietnam, Britain should view American policy in a more critical fashion.

Thursday, January 20th
Cabinet. Apart from Harold Wilson's report on his return from Lagos the main business was prices and incomes. George Brown told us we were faced with the threat of a railwaymen's strike, not to mention a whole series of awkward decisions by the P.I.B. giving an 18 per cent increase to the armed forces, a parallel increase to higher civil servants and also an award to Scottish

teachers. His case was that in order to defend the incomes policy Cabinet must be prepared to slap down the railwaymen, even though they threatened industrial action. A minority, of which I was a member, argued that we as a Labour Cabinet couldn't oppose a railwaymen's strike if we were simultaneously considering conceding salary increases to higher civil servants. We were overruled. George Brown candidly admitted that he felt he couldn't in the circumstances uphold the refusal of the higher civil servants' pay award. I found this the most alarming Cabinet we have had: it probably means that when these announcements are made the incomes policy will be swept away.

Sunday, January 23rd
Alas! this is the end of a long Christmas recess. With Parliament away we Ministers have been able to get down to our Whitehall work and cope with it adequately. Looking back over the weeks, I think I can say that during this time Harold Wilson nearly decided that an early election is inevitable. Last summer he wouldn't even consider my suggestion of a snap election in early November. And when I went back to the idea again before Christmas he was equally hostile, and used the excuse of a Conservative newspaper story to slap down the idea of a pre-budget election. Now in the talks I have had with him since he returned from Lagos he seems to be moving round more and more to the feeling that things are crowding in dangerously upon us, that the prices dam is going to break and that the position he has built up in Rhodesia is strong enough to risk an election. Indeed, one of the strangest things that has happened recently is the transformation in the public attitude to Rhodesia. I still remember with what dread Harold Wilson looked forward to the proclamation of U.D.I. and with what certainty he felt it would lead the Government into a situation where the Tories might win an enormous advantage. Now every newspaper commentator is writing about the benefits accruing to the Government from Rhodesia. We are able to divert attention to Rhodesia, where we are being successful, from the home front, where we are not. Of course, this is all Harold's personal achievement. He now talks about Rhodesia as his Cuba and he has played the crisis with astonishing tactical skill. Although I have felt that he ought to have taken stronger measures, that he ought to have had some advance planning, that he oughtn't have played it by ear, that he ought to have got rid of his Commonwealth Secretary, I can't deny that he has moved step by step always in line with British opinion. First he tried to prevent U.D.I. at all costs; then he put on mild sanctions which wouldn't upset people; now he's moving forward to more serious sanctions. Each time he carries public opinion with him and creates a situation in which an unsure Tory leader has been quite unable to display any qualities of leadership.

One other impression borne in on me during the recess relates to my own position. I am now a relatively popular and successful Minister. The papers say that I am good on television and successful in getting my way in Cabinet, as well as close to the P.M. Nevertheless, I still don't play any central role in the Government. I don't read the F.O. telegrams, and in Cabinet I find myself looking out of the window at Horseguards Parade in excruciating boredom whenever Rhodesia is discussed because I am waiting for my item on local government finance. The other day I was having a drink in Nicky Kaldor's flat in Chelsea when Tommy Balogh said, 'You're getting quite unbearable, Dick. All this evening you have been trying to make out that the really important business of the Government gyrates round the Ministry of Housing and Local Government. You think the whole thing depends on that.' In a way he was making a fair criticism because I am now blinkered, narrowed and obsessed compared, for example, with Tony Crosland. He is interested in educational problems only in a secondary way: he remains an economist and his interest is still mainly in general economic issues. That is why he is a real, active Cabinet Minister, whereas I really belong with the inferior members of the Cabinet, the smaller fry.

However, there is one thing that perhaps differentiates me from them: my departmental interests do stretch a very long way. I am not only Minister of Housing. I am Minister of Local Government, and the range there is really remarkable. During this recess I have been dealing throughout with issues like the Meadow road at Oxford, the Ullswater problem and my plan for a blue belt round London, not to mention rating, council rents and local government reorganization. When I see that stretch I think it is fair to say that my Ministry is a very central Department. Indeed, this is Harold Wilson's view and he wants to make it more so. More than once when I have been trying to get a decision from him about a successor to the Dame he has said to me, 'Well, of course, I couldn't possibly promise that Land and Natural Resources should be restored to your Ministry during this Parliament. But in the next Parliament things might be different. I am thinking of a great federal central planning Ministry covering Housing and Works and Land and Natural Resources.' That naturally would interest me a great deal. That's the kind of Ministry I would like to have and that's the idea he is feeding me.

Meanwhile the struggle about my Permanent Secretary is getting more and more confused. Douglas Allen who was offered to me before Christmas was then offered to Barbara; but that is off owing to the leak in the *Guardian*. This infuriated the Permanent Secretaries and has become one of the factors in favour of an early general election. Everything is becoming more difficult for Harold and will be that much easier once he has a decent majority. Actually, there are only two Ministries which have to be settled immediately — Aviation and my own, where the retirement of the two heads has already been announced. I have been urging Harold to act only on these two and in the most limited possible way, by putting Bruce Fraser into Aviation and giving me Philip Allen and leaving everything else until after the election.

I had arranged to go up by the 7.30 on Sunday for the official meeting with Harold and Callaghan about the rents situation. Harold had asked me to come earlier to have a private talk beforehand. When he rang up I said, 'Oh, for heaven's sake, can't I make it a little later so as not to miss the whole of this weekend?' Back came the tart remark, '*I* haven't had a weekend since I was P.M.' I knew I had blotted my copybook. It is true I have my family down here and he has his family up in No. 10, so I have *some* right to try to get time with my children. But the idea that any colleague takes time off from his work shocks Harold and though when we met he said, 'Of course I understand,' I realized it had put me back in his opinion. My train was an hour late and I only got an hour with him before the meeting with the Chancellor though he had wanted a much longer talk with me.

I briefed him first about the Liverpool rents situation. When I started on the project at the beginning of January it seemed a very long shot. Now it isn't. I had seen Harold about it again last week and he said to me, 'If you are going to do anything, for God's sake make it big enough to make a real electoral difference.' I was able to say that if we really wanted to make a difference, we should ante-date the rent subsidy and pay it for all houses completed in the year up to November 20th, 1965. Then we would pay out £6 million this year to the councils and an extra £9 million in successive years and that would give them a chance of holding down the increases in rent. After discussing one or two details he told me to work it out and minute him and Callaghan, with copies to the Scottish and Welsh Secretaries of State. That minute has now been seen by all the Departments, and the Treasury has reacted by proposing its own scheme for paying the subsidy a year, or nine months, or six months in advance, so giving the authorities their cash a little earlier. But it doesn't give them a penny in the long run and it won't actually affect the level of rents. A typical Treasury scheme. We got it in time to organize our answer over the weekend. Indeed I spent a lot of today phoning the Dame, Brain and John Delafons, insisting they should get the completed draft to Paddington ready for me when I got off the train. This was all done and it was on this basis that Harold and I had our talk.

He left himself plenty of time to talk about the date of the election and for the first time he made it clear he was considering March. When I said there was a case for April, after the budget, he replied, 'But then the rate demands will already be in people's hands and that will cost us votes.' Also he was deeply concerned about council rents because 20,000 of his voters in Huyton and Kirby pay overspill rents to Liverpool City Council.

Then we went downstairs to meet Callaghan in the Cabinet room. I started by saying that the Treasury proposal meant nothing at all and Jim immediately agreed: 'We want something serious and it is not worth taking up the Treasury line.' So I put my proposals and then both Harold and Jim said, 'But your proposal involves giving money to everybody all round. Can't we have a discriminating subsidy?' I was a bit mulish and said, 'Well, we do discriminate already. The new subsidies are designed to help those people with the most houses to build and who need to build high-rise on expensive sites.' But this wouldn't do. 'Isn't there a way of giving a special subsidy for slum clearance?' Harold asked. I said that I didn't want to do that and I was even more resistant. Finally I worked out a formula which might possibly concentrate the cash on big conurbations and the meeting ended.

Monday, January 24th
The Department spent most of the day trying to find a formula agreeable to the Treasury which made sense on the subject of council rents. As soon as I got in the Dame told me that my formula was hopeless. Probably it was. She agreed with Harold that the only way to deal with the problem was in terms of slum clearance. So we settled down to try to find a way in which the extra money would go only to the big cities; and finally we got it. We would pay the subsidy on houses completed in the year up to November 1965 but only to cities whose slum clearance problem was above a certain level as defined in an extremely complicated formula.

The work was completed by six o'clock by Freddy Ward and Brain. I congratulated them on it – all the more because I knew how much they hated it. They showed their quality as civil servants by producing in twenty-four hours a solution totally against their principles. When I finally got the document into my hands I rang up Marcia and asked if I could come round with it straight away.

Having delivered the text, I went to George Weidenfeld's to dinner. Just when I was settling down to enjoy myself I had to rush back to No. 10, only to find myself waiting for Harold for more than an hour. Fortunately, I had arranged to see Gerald Kaufman because I was making the big party-political broadcast on Wednesday in reply to a sensationally successful party-political on the cost of living which Iain Macleod had done last Wednesday. Since this broadcast would take place on the eve of poll in Hull it was vital that we should have something refuting Macleod. Gerald told me that I was to divide the time with Peggy Herbison. She had been told to talk about our new earnings-related sickness and unemployment benefits; I was to deal with the cost of living and the idea was that I should launch a personal attack on Iain Macleod. I realized that that was a non-starter. When a man has made a brilliant broadcast it's an admission of defeat to try to be brilliant against him. So I decided I would deal with rates and rents and, as for mortgages, I suddenly had the idea that I might mention the subject of Nigel Lawson, the editor of the *Spectator*, who has just been given a £20,000 mortgage by the Conservative-controlled Kensington Borough Council to help him buy a house at Hyde Park Corner. After some talk, Gerald promised to do a draft for me ready for my return from Hull, where I am due to speak on Wednesday morning.

I also had a talk with Marcia. She was a bit depressed after long talks with Sara Barker about Hull, even though the reports from George Wigg were confident. What alarmed her was the prospect that the national situation would lose us votes there – the episode in the West Midlands last week, for example, where large numbers of gas workers were thrown out of their jobs because of a close-down at Tipton. Though Harold had staunchly said in the House it was the fault of the Tories, somehow it didn't redound to our credit. And there has been news each day of increases in rents and rates by local councils and of the prices and incomes policy getting out of hand. Even the success of Rhodesia had begun to wear thin.

By this time Harold had got back from his dinner and I went downstairs to see him. He looked over the paper very quickly and said it was on the right lines and then he added, 'I promise you that while you are up in Hull tomorrow I will try to clear this with James Callaghan.' It couldn't be done during the morning because there was a Cabinet and I was leaving by the 1.21 train. He then obviously wanted to relax and we talked politics for three-quarters of an hour. Once again his mind was moving towards a March election; and I realized from what he said that one of his major problems was George Brown's Bill disciplining the unions, and another that he has now got a complete reshuffle of Permanent Secretaries on his hands and it will have to be followed by a strong Cabinet reconstruction. Helsby has been told to approach the Dame and ask her to hang on until after the election, even if it's only unofficially. This will enable him to reconstruct the Ministries, including possibly reattaching Land and Natural Resources to Housing. 'Maybe', he added, 'I could get Philip Allen to head the new reconstructed Ministry after the election.' He thought that would be far easier than trying to settle it beforehand. I protested rather feebly. 'Well, surely, if the Dame is going in February, and if the Permanent Secretary at Aviation is going in February, you can limit the shuffle by sending Bruce Fraser to Aviation and giving me Philip Allen?' 'No,' I was told, 'there are other plans for Bruce Fraser. Possibly he'll get the job of Auditor-General that Compton has now and Compton will be brought back into active service.' I got back to Vincent Square about midnight.

Tuesday, January 25th
I got into the Ministry early and checked Harold's talk with the Dame. She said, yes, the offer had been made to her; Compton was due to come back, Fraser was due to take his place. So it looks as though she will be asked to hang on in my Ministry until after the election. That of course would only make sense if the election is finally timed for March. If it were at the end of April it would be difficult for the Dame to hang on as the head of my Department since she is due in Persia at the end of February.*

At Cabinet the main item was prices and incomes. This was a most extra-ordinary episode. Harold told me on the phone before breakfast that the Government had nearly been wrecked by another row between George and James. Apparently this had arisen because George Brown, after last week's

* She never got there.

Cabinet, had changed his mind. 'Might not the announcement of the higher civil servants' increase be postponed?' he was asking. 'Might the increase to the army be halved?' In any case he was no longer prepared to accept without qualification *any* of the P.I.B. reports which involved enormous sums of money that would virtually end the prices and incomes policy. So it looks as though he had now lined himself up with the minority—Ray Gunter, Barbara Castle and myself among them—who had been opposed to publishing these awards. I don't know what went on behind the scenes after Harold talked to me on the phone, but in Cabinet we had the First Secretary saying, 'I have nothing to suggest because after much to-ing and fro-ing since last Thursday, in which we have all changed our minds several times, we have come to the conclusion that we must go ahead and publish the P.I.B. reports.' After this he was duly supported by James Callaghan and duly opposed by the same minority. Then we moved to the next subject. It is on this sort of occasion that I begin to see the inadequacy of George Brown when he is at his worst.

I caught the 1.21 to Hull and found myself travelling up with George Thomson, the Minister of State at the Foreign Office, who was speaking with me, and a young man called Clark, a member of the Radical Alliance, who was speaking for Richard Gott, the anti-Vietnam war candidate. There were six candidates in all at Hull—Conservative, Liberal, Labour, Radical Alliance (Gott) and two Independents. Hull is a wonderful place to visit since there are five or six hours of physical and geographical isolation in the train. I enjoyed every moment. Transport House had done an excellent job analysing the situation there and I went up with two press releases on which I had worked very strenuously. One demonstrated that in 1965 we had built 9,000 more houses than the Tories had ever built in a single year. The second related to the proposed Humber bridge. I had had to draft this with care because Barbara had duly pledged to build it, and the sentences Harold had used in a letter to the candidate (I had written them in) were in strict accord with the statement I had made at Blackpool. That statement was valuable in Hull because it proved that we had been considering the bridge last September and that Barbara's speech wasn't a last-minute election bribe.

When I reached Hull I handed the two press releases to Percy Clark, who processed both of them, and then we had a little supper together. He was confident, but infuriated by the national press which had been spoofed by Charles Longbottom,[1] the big boss up there, who sat in the hotel drinking with the pressman while Percy had to share a bed in some shack outside the town. On the other hand, I discovered from him that we would have thirty-eight paid officials working actually in the election; and five hundred Party workers had come in during the previous weekend. So lavish was the attendance of M.P.s that every vote had been canvassed more than once and every doubtful voter as well; and Percy was certain we would get a 2,000 majority. I had a few hours looking round and at the end was convinced he

[1] Conservative M.P. for York 1959–66.

was right: the only disaster we could suffer would be from the impact of the national situation on Hull. When I left to pick up the sleeper in Leeds I was much easier in my mind.

Wednesday, January 26th

I arrived back in London at 7 a.m. fairly sure that Hull would be O.K., and got to my house to find a letter from Gerald Kaufman, who arrived at 8.30 for breakfast. Though I was a bit weary I started reading his draft television broadcast and at once realized it was unusable. Gerald had done a decent job but he had made it a defensive reply to Macleod which I thought would be fatal. Unfortunately I had a pretty busy day. Having talked to Gerald from 8.30 to 9.30 I found myself ten minutes late at the Ministry for Barbara Castle. I told her that I had been on the phone to the P.M. and he had agreed that I should make the Nigel Lawson piece the centre of my script. However this didn't assuage her anger.

I couldn't start on the script till 11 and from then till 12.30 struggled with it while the B.B.C. people and Gerald stood around waiting to get it. I then took the usual forty-five minutes to get to Lime Grove and arrived there at 1.15 to find that all the staff were off at lunch. I then had an hour and a quarter, not in the studio but in a small hutch, trying to get the script together before I had to rush back to the Commons for a Statement on the Meadow road at Oxford[1] followed by a fifty-minute press conference with Barbara by my side. There were a hundred journalists there and it went all right but it took away my time from preparing that confounded television programme.

I got back to the studio at 6.30 to find that in the interval nothing had happened. Peggy Herbison was sitting by with her script ready, resolutely refusing to make any cuts in it. She wanted exactly half the time and there was no one to say her nay. True, there was that very nice producer, Stanley Hyland, and poor Gerald Kaufman, but they weren't capable of telling Cabinet Ministers how to divide time with each other. We were due on the air for the recording at 8 and by 7.30 it was clear that my script would not be ready. I made a quick decision that we would record the first three minutes, my little introduction plus Peggy's full text, and then I would do the second half live at 9.30. It was a risk but Hyland said, 'All right, seeing it's you, we'll do it.' So we did. The recording went satisfactorily and left an hour and a half to get my script revised and on the autocue in time for the live broadcast. Of course I did it infinitely better than if it had been recorded, and it sounded really tough and hard-hitting. I got back to Vincent Square and Tam rang up and said Kathleen had seen it and was puzzled because I was so terribly tired at the beginning but very good at the end. I rang Anne, who said, 'Well, I thought you seemed a bit tired at the beginning.' Of course they had noticed the contrast between the recorded and the live sections.

[1] There was to be a completely new assessment of possible routes for a relief road through Oxford (see p. 279, n. 2). Meanwhile, in order to relieve immediate pressure, extensive redevelopment was allowed in another part of the city.

Thursday, January 27th

By the time we went into Cabinet I realized that the broadcast had been a resounding success. Mainly I think because of the nice balance between Peggy's decent, gentle, sweet style, telling the viewers about her wage-related benefits, and the rumbustious riposte I had given to the Tories. It was just the thing for the eve of poll at Hull to put spirit into our troops. So I found Cabinet that much easier, which was important because I had two major items on the agenda: a settlement of the domestic de-rating issue and my own Royal Commission on local government reform.

In the afternoon there was a vote of censure in the House, but the mood was dull because we were all waiting for the Hull result. I was getting telephoned reports from Percy Clark which supported the N.O.P.'s announcement that morning that we would have an 8 per cent lead; I thought we might well win by 2,500 to 3,000. There was tremendous suspense throughout the day. In the evening our little group met and we went round for a chat with Harold; and there in No. 10 we saw the result on television – so much better than we expected.[1] My immediate reaction was to say to myself, 'Oh dear, will Harold now give up the March election because of this good result? Will it be more difficult to get him to be sensible?' Nevertheless, it was an overwhelming victory and I felt cheered.

Sunday, January 30th

At eight o'clock on Friday morning I had to start off to Tamworth and Lichfield for an official visit. I found myself afflicted by an appalling virus flu: my inside was totally liquefied. It was very difficult to move from Lichfield to Coventry for three hours of interviews and then to totter back to Prescote. I spent the weekend recovering and in the intervals received a delegation from the Oxford Labour Party to discuss the Meadow road. I had to blackmail and bully them and say there was no alternative to what had already been decided.

One other note on the past week. Last Thursday I got the Cabinet decision in favour of my local government reform and I have been tracing its history this weekend. When I first became Minister of Housing I started with the usual ideas that were taught me, and in my very first speech I said that the one thing one couldn't possibly have was the reform of local government because no sane politician would undertake it. A few weeks later I made a rather similar speech at the Town Planning Institute saying it was obviously essential but politically something extremely difficult. Then as I travelled round the country I became more and more aware, week by week, as so often happens, that what I was told by all the local government politicians and civil servants was untrue. In sober fact the time was ripe for a total and radical reform of local government because the people in local government, the officials as well as the councillors, were aware of their own inanity and

[1] The Labour majority rose from 1,181 to 5,351, a 4½ per cent swing—the highest by-election swing for ten years.

inadequacy. And one thing which was driving this lesson home was the work of my own Local Government Boundary Commission: at vast expense to the local authorities and in hearings protracted month after month with only the lawyers benefiting, it was limited by its terms of reference to recommending only the kind of solutions which merely tinkered with the problem. Moreover, the longer I spent in studying the decisions I had to take, the more I realized that my effort to use them to make peace between county boroughs and counties was really pretty futile because the conflict was inherent in the present structure. So last September I had the idea of introducing the theme of a radical reform in my speech to the A.M.C. at Torquay and I told them that the dinosaurs would have to give way to modern animals; and I had an enormous success.[1]

It's worth remembering that local government reform is one of the things we *didn't* promise in our election manifesto. Though I had mentioned it to Harold before making my Torquay speech, I hadn't consulted my Cabinet colleagues about it. So this was a commitment for the next manifesto which I was building up completely on my own. (There was of course its second phase, the reform of local government finance, on which I have been working away, but with far less success owing to the opposition of the Treasury.)

I followed up my Torquay success with a series of speeches saying the same thing more and more strongly. Once or twice—particularly in the case of rating—there have been mild remarks in Cabinet. But I have been lucky with my colleagues, as Harold pointed out to me one evening. 'You've got nobody like Herbert Morrison or Chuter Ede[2] or Nye Bevan,' he said, 'who really is an authority on matters of local government. In this Cabinet there isn't a single person of that quality and that's why you've been getting away with murder.'

Since September I have forced the pace and carried public opinion with me, particularly in the local authorities. Indeed, the only serious opposition I have had came from my own Commission. True, they have been weakened by the death of the chairman in the summer and the retirement a few weeks later of the deputy chairman to a better-paid post in the Land Tribunal. But they could still have been dangerous and they had already insisted that they would stop their work before Christmas pending a decision in Cabinet. They were hoping to force my hand and to compel me to delay the Royal Commission for a couple of years and permit them to carry out their big reconstruction in Lancashire, along the same lines as the one I have just put through in the West Midlands. Normally, I would have taken my courage in both hands, disregarded their threats and done the thing straight away. But my difficulty in this case was that not only the Prime Minister but Barbara Castle,

---

[1] See p. 331.
[2] M.P. for Mitcham from March to November 1923, and for South Shields 1929–31 and 1935–64. He was Home Secretary 1945–51, and Leader of the House in 1951, and a member of various town and county councils for thirty years. He died in 1964.

Fred Lee and Tony Greenwood, all members of this Cabinet, are all Lancashire M.P.s liable to be nobbled by the Local Government Boundary Commission. So about three weeks ago I got Reg Wallis, our greatest expert on local government in the whole of Lancashire, to come down and dine and have a talk. He told me that acceptance of the Commission's recommendations might cost us twenty parliamentary constituencies. The next step was to make sure that this was put to Harold Wilson, so once again he came down, this time with George Eddy, Barbara's agent in Blackburn and also the leader of the Blackburn Council; and as a result of their intervention I was able to disregard the threats of the Boundary Commission, and I decided to go ahead with the Royal Commission straight away.

The next step was to get it through Cabinet. I had originally sent the big memorandum to the P.M. When he asked me to, I wrote a minute saying what the whole thing was about with a copy to George Brown which quite excited him. That was Stage I. Next came the Cabinet paper and this was prepared by the Dame. She was careful to make it an official paper, not a paper from me to my Cabinet colleagues, but a paper from her to all the relevant Departments—and then she circulated it to the Home Office, Education, Health, Transport, Scotland and Wales. So the officials got together and began to work towards an agreed official policy.

After a bit I asked the Dame how things were going, and one night I found a draft in my red box. I brought it back next morning with a whole mass of amendments. 'You can't change this,' she said to me. 'It's an agreed official paper. It's finished.' I was furious and I managed to persuade her to accept a certain number of the changes I wanted. Nevertheless, in terms of Whitehall politics she was tactically right since agreement at official level might well decide what happened in Cabinet. As a result of her work on the official committee, unanimity was achieved not only on the terms of reference but also on the crucial proposal that we should go ahead and announce the Royal Commission straight away without waiting for the Lancashire reorganization So each of the Ministers concerned received a brief telling him or her to accept my proposals without suggesting any amendment. No wonder there was virtually no discussion. True enough, Michael Stewart, who is out of the country, wrote a letter to me saying he would have liked me to go ahead and prepare the White Paper and recommend Cabinet action instead of waiting for a Royal Commission. True enough, Jim Griffiths for Wales took a similar line because there are proposals for Welsh local government reform already in the pipeline and he wants the work to continue. But apart from these two the Cabinet was effectively rigged; and this was a tactic which my Dame operates with more skill than anybody else I have ever seen.

In February there was more talk of an imminent general election but Mr Wilson still made no announcement. True, it was not an opportune moment for Labour to go to the country. America's resumption of bombing in North Vietnam after the New Year truce had stirred up disaffection among the Labour Left. On his four-day visit to Moscow on February 21st, Mr Wilson was to find the Russians critical of British support for the United States and unwilling to put pressure on the North Vietnamese Government.

At home the squeeze continued to restrict credit and consumption. In January and February exports rose and the balance of payments deficit decreased a little, but imports continued to run at a record level. There was little improvement in the reserves. The President of the Board of Trade, Douglas Jay, tightened up controls in the first week of February and the Chancellor announced changes in the control of public investment. On February 1st the Governor of the Bank of England requested the clearing banks to maintain the credit restrictions.

An escape from the endless sterling crisis seemed to be offered by entry to Europe. Britain clearly depended on the economic and financial co-operation of the E.E.C. and would derive considerable advantage from participation in its wider markets. Feeling in the Government began to move slowly in favour of entry and there was pressure from enthusiastic pro-Community advisers in the Foreign Office. Some hesitation, however, was felt by those who found de Gaulle's attitude as infuriating and puzzling as ever. He not only condemned Western policy in Vietnam and threatened partial withdrawal from NATO but among his own E.E.C. partners he seemed to put France's interests before the survival of the Community.

Monday, January 31st

I came up to London steamed up about the Cabinet paper which Michael Stewart had just circulated on de Gaulle's policies. Tommy had rung me up on Sunday and made me read it. It seemed to me a crazy paper, and was obviously the work of Con O'Neill.[1] What it argued was that we must regard General de Gaulle as the worst enemy in the world because of his wicked plan for knocking the supra-national elements out of the Common Market and for working with the Soviet Union to get an understanding over Germany's head. As I thought these were pretty sensible policies I agreed with Tommy that I would try and scotch the paper.

So the moment I got into my office I got down to dictating a caustic memo to the Foreign Secretary. This is only the second time I have done this. Last August when he circulated a paper on Germany I knocked it out in Cabinet. Now on this occasion I took good care to send copies of my memo to James Callaghan, George Brown and also to Barbara Castle. I organized the putsch on a relatively small scale because I did not want to create a Cabinet crisis, which there certainly would have been if everybody in Cabinet had been

---

[1] Deputy Under-Secretary of State at the F.C.O. 1965–72. He entered the Diplomatic Service in 1936 and during the course of his career resigned three times, in favour of military, journalistic and business pursuits. Abroad, he had served in Germany, Peking and Finland, and between 1963 and 1965 he was British Ambassador to the E.E.C. On his return to London (as Deputy Under-Secretary at the F.O.) he was regarded as a forceful proponent of European entry. He resigned, disenchanted, in 1968, but returned in 1969.

forewarned next Thursday. I was also aware that if I forced a straight vote on whether we should apply for entry to the Common Market or not, the pro-Marketeers would win. They have been pretty busy during the past weeks. I learnt from Tommy that at the beginning of December Michael Stewart had approached the P.M. urging that we should make an immediate application to enter the E.E.C. and this had only been frustrated when the P.M. point-blank refused to permit the paper to be circulated. This had already aroused the wrath of Douglas Jay and Fred Peart who approached me over Christmas. So my memorandum was written and sent off.

In the evening we had a little party in my Private Office for Jennie Hall, who is leaving because she is going to have a baby.[1] To my amazement the Dame came and made a little speech saying that the Department had always dreaded it when Ministers brought their secretaries in with them but Jennie had been splendid, she loved her dearly and she had a little present to give her. Jennie's success has been enormously important for me in my relations with the Department. Indeed, I have only really brought two people right in – Jennie and Peter Lederer – and both of them have positively helped me. Should I have introduced a lot more, like Barbara? I'm not sure.

Tuesday, February 1st
The papers are full of a Labour split. It has nicely punctured the euphoria we were all feeling as a result of the Hull by-election – which only lasted over the weekend. The trouble was a communiqué the Foreign Office issued on Monday evening announcing the full support of the Labour Government for the resumption of bombing by the Americans in Vietnam after the New Year's truce. I know as a fact that this communiqué had not been approved by Harold and I have my doubts whether it was even approved by Michael Stewart. But last night it produced a tremendous blow-up with twenty-five back-bench M.P.s sending a telegram to L.B.J.[2] So the Tories have held firm under the pressure of defeat at Hull and it is the Labour Party which has split as the result of success – if we had lost the by-election that telegram would never have been sent.

That evening for the very first time the little group was invited to dinner by Harold and I suppose you can say that this was the first occasion on which he allowed himself a kitchen cabinet. Marcia of course was there, Peter Shore, Tommy Balogh, Wedgy Benn, Gerald Kaufman. Mary and Marcia's assistant, Brenda Drew, looked after the food. Then we went down below and sat round the table and at last we felt that Harold was really treating us, his group of friends, as associates with whom he could discuss the future. We all felt it was the beginning of a completely new deal. I expect we were wrong.

In the course of the evening he said at one point, and we all waited on his

[1] She continued to work for Crossman for a few weeks longer.
[2] According to Wilson, ninety M.P.s sent a telegram to Senator Fulbright, supporting his attack on the President. See *Wilson*, p. 204.

words because he was obviously talking seriously, 'I have been reading Theodore White's book on the L.B.J./Goldwater Presidential election,[1] and it has made me think of my own role. I am not a father figure, you know, I am a doctor figure. That's what Theodore White tells me, I am a doctor figure.' We moved on to talk about how the election would be won and he said quite openly, 'You, Dick, will have to stay behind in London. You, Tony, I would like to run the television shows but as Postmaster-General you hardly can. As for me, I have got to be at No. 10 most of the time.' At this point I said, 'Well, for God's sake don't rush off to Huyton for the last five days as you did last time.' He agreed this was something that he absolutely mustn't do. We went on to discuss what kind of machinery we could have for linking Transport House and No. 10, and there was a lot of talk about Harold's relations with George and James. I told him that on the previous Thursday James had said to me that he didn't want to be Chancellor in the next Government. I had said to him, 'There is one other job you should get if you are not Chancellor and that is Leader of the House. You could be the Herbert Morrison of the Party if we return with a big majority—inspiring the back-benchers, controlling the House of Commons, planning the legislative programme.' Harold was tickled at this: it is something he really would like. But he just listened and then said to me once again, 'I want you to be a federal Minister of Housing, with Land and Natural Resources brought back and the Ministry of Works brought in. I have written a paper about it but I haven't put the part about the Ministry of Works in because otherwise I would have Charlie Pannell hanging around No. 10 every day for the next six weeks.'

It was a delightful evening and it was the first time we felt as a group that we really could do some good because he was trusting us.

Wednesday, February 2nd

It was Harold's job this morning to address the Parliamentary Party and put them right on Vietnam. He asked all the Cabinet to come and I got there on time in order to see what he was up to. This was one of the occasions when I wasn't impressed: he spoke for forty-five minutes, a long, laboured oration, pleading with the Party rather than attacking it. He went on and on saying that in all the forty days of the Christmas truce in Vietnam for which he was largely responsible he had had no thanks or consideration from the P.L.P.: they'd only barged in to criticize him when the bombing started again. As he sat down he turned to Callaghan and me, sitting behind the chairman, and remarked, 'Well, that's finished with that opposition.' But he was wrong: it hadn't finished with it. True enough, Manny Shinwell prevented any discussion; but there was a deep sense of uneasiness and I knew very well it hadn't been destroyed by Harold's speech. Indeed the mood of this meeting provided another argument for an early election.

[1] Theodore H. White, *The Making of the President, 1964* (London: Cape, 1965).

In the background but not mentioned during the meeting was of course the fact of George Brown's Prices and Incomes Bill, the anti-trade union Bill for which I can't see the need. It is a step in the process towards a legally sanctioned prices and incomes policy; and there is no doubt about it, this Bill will provide a kind of Clause 4 row inside the Party.[1] It is as silly for Harold to put it forward now as it was for Gaitskell to put forward the revision of Clause 4 when he did, and there is the added complication that we have only got a majority of three.

Thursday, February 3rd

Cabinet. When we got to item number two—as always, foreign affairs—I raised the issue of the Cabinet paper on General de Gaulle. It went pretty well. We scotched the paper and Harold had to say in winding up that he personally sympathized with much of what I wrote in my memorandum. So our manœuvre had succeeded.

Next came the Vietnam bombing. Michael Stewart said it was an 'unfortunate episode' and explained that it all arose because in the B.B.C. News one of their experts had made a statement supporting the resumption of bombing. As a result the Foreign Office spokesman was challenged by the newspapers and forced to make a statement. When he finished there was silence for quite a time. I didn't want to speak again but finally I said, 'Personally I can't accept this. I can't see why your man had to say the Government was in favour when we aren't. There is no reason why we should rush to the support of the Americans when we think they are acting in an unjustified way.' Then there came a very rough discussion which forced Harold to give full support to his Foreign Secretary. Having loosed it off, I got a message that I had to go straight across to the House of Commons because the Committee on the Rating Bill was having a division and I wasn't paired beyond 11.30. I went across to the House breathing fury against the bloody-minded John Boyd-Carpenter who throughout the previous week had been refusing to agree a time in which we could get this Rating Bill out of Committee. However, suddenly at 12.30 this morning he told me I could have it by the 17th, signed, sealed and delivered. That is only two days later than the day for which I had planned. This has suddenly been fixed up between their Chief Whip and ours. Once his bluff had been called he caved in, as the Tories now usually do, because he didn't want to be accused in the election of opposing rate rebates. No doubt our victory at Hull has also made a difference.

At 5 p.m. I was due in the Prime Minister's room in the House to discuss council-house rents. Harold and Jim had had my official paper on Monday but in between no decision had been reached. Something just had to be done. When I came into the room I found them sitting there, Callaghan looking

[1] Clause 4 of the Labour Party's Constitution pledges the nationalization of the 'commanding heights of the economy'. At the Blackpool Conference in November 1959, Hugh Gaitskell suggested that the clause should be revised to make Labour's programme more palatable to the electorate. Clause 4 was retained, but controversy continues.

droopy and tired. 'Unless we have an election it isn't politically worth while to change our subsidy laws,' he said. 'Frankly, I don't see the good of reducing council rents by about 10*d.* a week unless we need it for political reasons. If we are soldiering on and going to the country in October, it would be silly to make this change in the subsidies Bill.' I don't think Harold or I disagreed. What we both felt was that a March election would require an amendment of the Bill. But nothing was decided.

We then turned to an equally unsatisfactory discussion of mortgages. For weeks my officials and the Treasury officials have been arguing about the Ministry of Housing proposal that we should introduce an option scheme. At present income-tax payers are privileged because they get a tax remission on their mortgage repayments. But if you are a mortgagor so poor that you don't pay income tax you are very much worse off. We propose a new grant which you can only get by voluntarily abandoning the tax concession, i.e. it will only pay to accept the grant if your earnings are below the income-tax threshold. Nicky Kaldor, who advises James about tax matters, has been against me. He says what is needed is not an option scheme but a scheme which abolishes tax concessions on mortgage repayments and substitutes mortgage grants. I found this an intolerable proposal. If the Chancellor would make this his major tax reform this year and abolish all tax concessions on bank overdrafts and bank loans, as well as on mortgages, that would be fine; but to abolish them only on mortgages ... We talked round it for about an hour and I began to realize that James has been wrung dry by his year at the Treasury. As he went out Harold took me aside and said, 'I've pretty well made up my mind to go for the election, but as you saw this evening Jim's a problem. For God's sake don't tell anybody about it.'

I don't often go to the Members' dining-room these days but I ran into John Silkin and George Wigg outside the P.M.'s room and we went along the passage. There was a tremendous sense of end-of-term and a feeling that everything was being wound up.

Friday, February 4th
Up at 8.30 and off with the Dame to Southampton for an official visit. She is very fond of Jim Matthews, the Labour boss of Southampton, whom I used to know in the W.E.A. Now he is seventy-four and his chairman of housing, Mrs Coulter, is seventy-eight, the usual age, I am afraid, in Labour local authorities. Nevertheless, Southampton is a very good authority, progressive and civilized. I opened the 15,000th council house and then made the usual tour, had the usual lunch, chaired the usual talks and began to realize that these visits are falling into a dead pattern. I must be careful. Of course they are having a good effect because of the tremendous television and press play that they get. But *I* am getting less and less value out of them because I know before I get there what I shall find, what I shall see, what I shall be told. There is nothing to do but just check. That's not good enough.

Sunday, February 6th

Chequers. Poor Anne and the children were still under the weather with flu so Peter Marriott, our housekeeper's son, drove me over. Even though this time we had a map and very precise directions, Chequers was almost impossible to find. The trouble is that you must spot the tiny entrance, turn off the main road and go right round the corner before you see a single policeman, let alone the house. It is one of the most successfully secret places that I know.

This was the joint meeting of the N.E.C. and the Cabinet, which had been long awaited and which we, in the little group, were preparing for so many hours last week. It had been conceded by Harold because the Executive complained it was not being kept in proper rapport with the Government: they wanted a real chance of having it out frankly and fiercely with their political colleagues. Well, from 10.30 a.m. to 6.30 p.m. they had the chance and there wasn't a single moment in the day when anything was had out, when there was any tension, any sense of crisis. What had I expected would happen? I suppose like Harold himself I had thought back to the famous Shanklin Conference before the 1949 election,[1] which Harold had attended though I hadn't. What happened at Chequers this time was very different. We all settled down in the big room upstairs. The officers sat round a small table at one end in the bay window and the rest of us sat on lines of chairs in front of them like a schoolboy class. Physically, therefore, general discussion was difficult and it wasn't rendered any easier by the way the conference was organized. First came Harold Wilson with his general observations; then George Brown ditto; and then James Callaghan giving a long introduction to the first topic – economics. By the time he started the atmosphere was fairly somnolent and few people, I suspect, observed that he was talking in a language not very distinct from that of Lord Cromer. However, at least we were discussing the key problem, prices and incomes, the stop and the crisis. We next had a long speech from Jack Jones, whom I first met when I was adopted as prospective candidate for Coventry and he had just returned from a time with the International Brigade in Spain. Jack Jones is now a respectable number two to Frank Cousins, but he is still very left-wing and his main concern is to take Frank's place when he retires. He was playing a big role for the first time in our N.E.C. and he made a long, competent, serious speech in which he strongly opposed the statutory sanctions George Brown was demanding for his prices and incomes policy. His speech was followed by another left-wing speech from Ian Mikardo. But that was, if I remember aright, the total of the left-wing opposition on this occasion. Jack and Ian were not followed by any serious questions or threats or pressure from other members of the Executive. In fact this was all that happened before lunch.

After lunch in the somnolence of the afternoon, with the weather growing

---

[1] In February 1949 the Labour Cabinet and the N.E.C. had held a special two-day conference to discuss the draft programme, 'Labour Believes in Britain', for the next election. It was held at the Manor House Hotel at Shanklin on the Isle of Wight.

more and more beautiful outside, all we had was a series of set declarations by Ministers – punctuated by a few mild comments. The net effect of all this was a vote of confidence in the Government; and this will enable Harold Wilson and George Brown, as chairman of the Home Affairs Committee, to say to the Executive, 'You've had it, chums. We've given you your chance to complain – a whole day. You did nothing at all about it.'

I must admit that I fell asleep in the morning as well as in the afternoon. I dozed off because this was one of the most boring non-events I have ever attended. Not that my falling asleep would prove by itself that the conference was boring. I tend to fall asleep pretty often these days – even when I am reading aloud to my children, or seeing a play which interests me. I don't often fall asleep at the opera – but that's different. Whenever there is anything really interesting I still fortunately wake up.

When the meeting was over it was clear that writing the election manifesto this time would be child's play. We would describe how we took the job on after thirteen years of Tory rule, and how we now want a mandate to finish the job. And we would insert at a number of points commitments to go a bit further than individual Ministers intend. That's the job we have to do.

I had arranged to go back to London from the conference with Peter Shore, who was there as the Prime Minister's P.P.S. At lunch, however, Marcia came up to me and said she wanted us to stay behind and go up later to dine with the P.M. and discuss what had happened. So at six o'clock when the others were driving away, Peter and I stood aside along with Marcia and Gerald Kaufman. Everybody else went off, including George Brown and James Callaghan. People in the Labour Party are very suspicious and every effort was made to conceal the fact that we were staying on. We succeeded quite well until we went into the little white drawing-room where Mary sits with her family, and there we found Sara Barker and Bert Williams[1] waiting for Len Williams, who was holding the press conference with Harold Wilson. That conference unfortunately lasted one and a quarter hours. We had an awkward period sitting there together because Sara twigged very soon that we had been asked to stay behind and have a private confab with Harold.

However, finally she withdrew and after that down Harold came and said, 'There are still two journalists, old Stacpoole of Exchange Telegraph and someone else, filing their stories. After we and they have both eaten let's have them in for a cup of coffee.' Marcia said, 'If you don't take care they will record who's here tonight and who is not.' And Harold said, 'Oh yes, I must be careful about that,' and the idea fell through. Though he is the most power-ful man in the country he is still anxious lest Alice Bacon should be upset to read that Dick Crossman and Peter Shore stayed behind at Chequers to discuss things privately with the Prime Minister at a meeting from which she was excluded. This fear is still very much in his mind. So after we had had our plate of cold turkey and tongue and a glass of not very good, not very

[1] Number two in the Organization Department of Transport House.

cold beer, we moved into the long drawing-room. It was the second meeting of Harold's kitchen cabinet and it soon became clear that he wanted Peter and me to draft the election manifesto and discuss it again in a week's time at Chequers. At one point Harold sent for the full text of the speech Heath had made on Saturday, in which (as it was reported right across the front page of the *Sunday Telegraph*) he had virtually abandoned the welfare state. 'He must be nailed,' he said, and he outlined how Minister after Minister would do the job, starting off with his Minister of Housing, who was speaking at Enfield on Wednesday and who must lead off the campaign. So we went through the text of the speech and discussed exactly how the operation should be done. All through that long meeting with the N.E.C. Harold had been careful always to talk about keeping the options open, never committing himself to an early election. That night with us the commitment was completely clear. About eleven o'clock I drove off with Peter Shore and Gerald Kaufman in one car and left the P.M. to drive up in another.

Monday, February 7th
I spent most of today dealing with two clangers, one of my own making and one of the Dame's, either of which could have been disastrous. My own was a front-page headline in the *People* on Sunday stating that I was insisting on £20-a-week rents for wealthy owners of Jaguar cars living in council houses, and referring to an interview on an inside page. What had happened was that Peter Brown had arranged on Thursday an interview for the *People* in which they had asked me to define my attitude to the case for well-off tenants of council houses paying the full economic rent. I had agreed to do it but had had to cancel it because of lack of time. The correspondent had chased me down to Southampton on Friday and right in the middle of the afternoon I had been forced to give him twenty minutes. I'd talked to him in a fairly racy way and he had gone off and done me in with an extraordinary headline.

I had been rung by the *Sunday Express* on Saturday evening telling me about it and asking my reactions, and I had put them on to Peter Brown and John Delafons, who worked all Sunday and really saved my political life. Journalists from other papers were told to read the full text of the interview on the inside page and contrast it with the fantastic front-page headline and this trick worked. On Monday morning the *Telegraph*, the *Guardian*, *The Times* and the *Mail* did not swallow the *People*'s line but had stories playing it down and putting my real policy across.

Nevertheless, a good deal of embarrassing damage has been done. I have had two leading articles this morning, in the *Mirror* and the *Sun*, both wildly complimentary to the Minister who is going to soak the rich tenants in council houses. Of course, I am in favour of putting up the rents of tenants who can afford to pay and using the pool of money we collect for a decent system of rent rebates. But it is not a popular view in the Labour Party and it certainly embarrassed me to have it put into my mouth in such a vulgar form.

15

The other clanger I had to deal with related to the Packington Estate.[1] Months ago Bob Mellish came to me and complained that one of our Inspectors was recommending some nonsense about rehabilitating this part of Islington. 'We want to pull the whole bloody thing down and we are determined to develop the area for council building. Thank God we have got Islington, one of the worst Labour housing councils in London, to start doing some building, so for God's sake, don't have any nonsense about holding it up or improving the property, Dick. Turn the Inspector down.' So I took a good look at the property for myself, read the papers and realized reluctantly that the Inspector was right and we ought to rehabilitate the area. It wouldn't become as good as Canonbury but it could become a second-class Canonbury. As a result, there was a real dispute: the Dame and Bob Mellish favoured redevelopment and I and the Inspector stood for rehabilitation. Finally I refused point blank to override our Inspector. At this point the Dame said that to improve the area I should have to evict all the existing tenants from their houses and move them elsewhere. This shook me; and since I didn't want to turn it into a completely middle-class area I finally agreed a compromise letter which said that I would have one more look at rehabilitation before considering redevelopment.

As so often happens, it was this effort to reach a compromise which caused the trouble. By spatchcocking a paragraph in favour of rehabilitation into a draft decision letter arguing for redevelopment we gave the anti-developers an opportunity to reopen the issue. In the light of my letter they quite naturally demanded a second inquiry. But instead of conceding the new inquiry, the Ministry got together with the G.L.C. and the Islington Borough Council and tried to rush through a new and revised redevelopment plan. At this point the Council on Tribunals, which is there to protect the rights of the citizen, began to suspect dirty business. They summoned us to appear before them and explain what we were up to. And then the Dame and Bob Mellish made a very great mistake. Two days before we were due to appear before the Council on Tribunals they announced our new and revised redevelopment plan. Unfortunately they didn't tell me what they were up to until it was too late. Then they insisted that on Wednesday at the moment when the Council on Tribunals was publishing their attack I should make a Statement in the House. I couldn't disown the Dame and Bob Mellish publicly so I agreed.

Tuesday, February 8th
I should have been at Cabinet but I had to spend the whole morning in the Committee of the Rating Bill owing to the extraordinary behaviour of our Whips. We only have a majority of three in the House and of one on my Standing Committee. Yet one of my Labour back-benchers has been allowed to go to America to give a course of lectures so that, with two down with flu, I had to sit through all Tuesday morning to sustain the majority.

[1] See p. 324.

Wednesday, February 9th
I made my Statement on Packington at 3.30. I was pressed a bit but I got away with it. Then I went out to a public meeting in Enfield, where I found fifty people mainly concerned with a local planning dispute. But I had decided to make a big attack on Heath. As usual I had had a frantic business all that day trying to compose the speech press release. Finally I got a fairly powerful line accusing Heath of dismantling the welfare state and put it out through Transport House. After delivering it successfully I went off to John Mackie's home six miles from Enfield to have supper with him.[1] As we drove back to the House the car wireless was on and the first item in the news was Mr Heath's reaction to my Enfield speech. At first sight of the press release that afternoon he had rushed out a counter-statement calling it a pack of lies. So I'd hooked him.

Thursday, February 10th
When I looked at the press I was really pleased. I had been afraid of a lead story accusing the Minister of Housing of dirty work at Packington. Instead, he was accused by Heath of telling lies. Harold had been proved right. He had said to me, 'We won't need to bait the book, he will take it without a bait.' But even Harold when he rang me up this morning was surprised at the damage Heath had caused himself by this kind of instant politics and the help he had done me by smothering that awkward Packington story. Harold was excited beyond words. He had forgotten the railway strike,[2] forgotten Rhodesia, this was the politics he loved. His friend Dick Crossman had hooked Heath. I, however, was a good deal more doubtful because I realized that it was the railway strike which was dominating people's minds more and more. At Chequers this strike hadn't been mentioned at all and throughout Monday, Tuesday and Wednesday I had been virtually certain it couldn't take place, that somehow it would be settled. All the way through the railwaymen had been divided and Sidney Greene[3] passionately against it. I was pretty certain that at the right dramatic moment the P.M. would intervene. But the general public didn't know that and they were still afraid that the trains would stop on Monday.

Certainly when Cabinet met at ten o'clock its mind was fixed on the railway strike. George Brown told us the news that a vote had been taken by twelve to eleven to keep to starting the strike on Monday, and that this had been achieved by the Communists, who suddenly decided they wanted to break the incomes policy. It all sounded very dramatic but I still had no doubt that

---

[1] Labour M.P. for Enfield East since 1959, and joint Parliamentary Secretary at the Ministry of Agriculture 1964–70. A farmer on a large scale in Essex and Kincardineshire he was, like Crossman's other farming friend, Wilfred Cave, a supporter of land nationalization.

[2] The N.U.R. was furious at the decision to refer its pay claim to the P.I.B. and at the Board's report recommending no improvement on the employers' 3½ per cent offer. They had announced a strike from February 14th. Talks were held at Downing Street on the night of February 11th and the strike was averted.

[3] General Secretary of the N.U.R. since 1957. In 1970 he was knighted.

the strike would be settled in Downing Street. I was also clear that what George Brown deeply resented (and Ray Gunter and Barbara Castle to some extent) was that Harold was going to monopolize the credit for settling it.[1]

The next item was the Leasehold Enfranchisement Bill. On this the discussions had been going on for weeks and we had had our final meeting with Willey on Monday and agreed the deal between his Department and mine. There was only one outstanding issue. The lawyers demanded a rule that no one should be allowed to get the confiscation of site value which is implied in leasehold enfranchisement unless (a) he had lived in the house for five years, and (b) (this was the difference) he or his father had held the lease for more than twenty-one years. Willey and I were united in objecting to this.

As the discussion went on it became clear that most of my colleagues were getting nervous about whether Cabinet was not being asked to play politics *too* flagrantly. I waited until the end and then said, 'Of course, morality is on the side of the lawyers. If we are concerned with morality we should certainly introduce a 21-year limitation. But unfortunately it wasn't in the original proposal which we backed during the election. There would be an appalling shemozzle in South Wales and Birmingham if we suddenly announced an arbitrary decision to exclude anyone from the benefits of leasehold enfranchisement unless they or their father had had the lease for twenty-one years.' And I concluded by saying that I was heartily sick of the Chancellor of the Exchequer always attacking the Minister of Housing for looking at the political aspect of his proposals. I was glad that the Chancellor on this occasion saw the advantages of political expediency. There was a roar of laughter round the table because of course Jim has a Cardiff constituency and has been utterly committed to leasehold enfranchisement in its most confiscatory form. However, this speech had quite the wrong effect. It inveigled Jim into saying that he was beginning to wonder whether he shouldn't go for the Lord Chancellor's view. There was a danger of real chaos that morning until Harold rapidly put it to the vote. I threw my vote on Fred Willey's side and we won. As we left the room George Brown observed to me that practical men must chip in to save Cabinet from the liberal conscience of the lawyers.

This afternoon at 3.30 in the House was to have been the great moment, the climax of six months of work on local government reform. On Monday afternoon I had briefed all the local authorities gathered round our huge conference table in the Ministry and had got congratulations from them for promising to end local government in the form they know it. Between Monday and Thursday there had been an endless argument between No. 10 and my Ministry about the form the Statement announcing the Royal Commission should take. It was clear the Prime Minister himself would have to make it because it was about Scotland as well as England and Wales. Yet on the other hand he knew nothing about the content and wanted to hand

---

[1] 'All the Ministers concerned ... felt that I should now intervene.' *Wilson*, p. 208.

most of it over to me. To and fro went the argument and on Thursday I went down at 3.15, not sure what would happen, but instructed to sit beside him. However, as often happens on a Thursday, none of our anticipations were fulfilled. We first had a Statement from Barbara Castle on a fire which had occurred in London. Then a long Statement by George Brown on the railway strike, followed by a series of supplementaries. Then the Statement on forthcoming Business which with supplementaries took a full half-hour. It was dominated by a great argument about whether there must be a debate on a motion impugning the honour of Duncan Sandys.[1] It was after 4.30 when Harold finally got up and read aloud his piece and was asked a whole series of questions which he fended off. All the time he was trying to sit down and get me to my feet. Finally he succeeded and as I got up Barbara whispered to me, 'Cut it short, Dick. We've got the breathalyser Bill coming on.'[2] I did cut it short, partly because I had taken the precaution of spending most of the morning personally interviewing *The Times*, *Guardian* and *Economist* correspondents and then having a small, select press conference. As a result there was no criticism in the press. Drastic reform of local government is now accepted as inevitable and I can sit back and feel — well, that's that. Provided I can get Ungoed-Thomas[3] to replace Alan Bullock as chairman, with John Maud as his deputy, we shall have achieved something really pretty big, something which can improve the modernization image of the Labour Party in the general election.

One footnote to this record of a long, exhausting day. I was due to go to the Prime Minister's room in the evening at 9.30 to see if we couldn't finally get an agreement with the Chancellor on those two vital issues, mortgages and council rents. At the last moment I got a message to say that the meeting had been cancelled because of the railway strike. Nevertheless, I went along with Tommy Balogh to the anteroom and there found Marcia. She told me how they had had to cancel everything because of George Brown, who unfortunately made the final Government offer on Wednesday instead of keeping it for Harold at No. 10. Now, said Marcia, we have got nothing to do and George is throwing his weight about inside. I listened and there was the most appalling noise going on and every now and then Harold would come out with a tired look. Finally George went away and Harold emerged and said to me, 'You see, his sole concern is who gets the credit.'

---

[1] On January 31st Duncan Sandys had made a speech which some M.P.s deplored as seeming to offer comfort to the rebel regime in Rhodesia while being insulting to African Commonwealth countries.

[2] The Road Safety Bill, which had its Second Reading that afternoon, contained the controversial proposal to test whether drivers were under the influence of alcohol by taking breath samples and measuring them with a breathalyser.

[3] Sir Lynn Ungoed-Thomas. A former Labour M.P. for Llandaff and Barry 1945–50 and for North-East Leicester 1950–62, he was Solicitor-General April to October 1951. Since 1962 he had been a judge of the Chancery Division. He had served as a member of the Uthwatt Committee on Leasehold Reform in 1948 and had signed the minority report recommending leasehold enfranchisement.

Saturday, February 12th

I spent the whole of Friday on an official visit to the Warwickshire County Council and got back to Prescote that evening to find my family still down with flu, the children in bed and Anne very seedy. I spent Saturday with five boxes, struggling through my work, going for a walk, part of the while in foul weather, and then going down to the village to see the Hartrees. It's a poor life when one's family is sick; and I am off again at 9.45 tomorrow morning to Chequers to prepare for the election campaign before it is actually announced. It's been a worrying and a disappointing week for me. I have got the Packington problem on my plate and that may well get worse. I've had an anticlimax with local government reform. I have also, probably as a result of our failure to meet on Thursday night, lost option-mortgages. Heath jumped the gun and got in first. I have probably also lost my proposal for a special subsidy for councils with heavy slum-clearance problems, because that's fallen through. But these are minor affairs. I think what Harold did with the railway strike today has clinched the date of the election. With the Tories in hopeless disarray we shall have a reasonable chance if he calls an election now.

Sunday, February 13th

Peter Marriott motored me over to Chequers once again and when we got there at ten o'clock I found Peter Shore driving up in his car with Tommy Balogh by his side and Brenda, Marcia's number two, coming along in another. So the only people who stayed the night with Mary and Harold must have been Marcia and her brother. We settled down at 10.30 to work through Peter Shore's draft manifesto. He's done the first draft of all our election manifestos, first under Morgan Phillips[1] and then under the new dispensation. But each time I have been brought in to work over them, as I did at Scarborough for the last election, during my holiday. This time the skeleton he provided was pretty complete and pretty handsome. Harold was in pleasant, family form, because when he is getting near an election he suddenly can't rely on his civil servants and has to have recourse to his friends. He has recently got rid of Derek Mitchell, his Private Secretary, who bickered with Marcia[2] and I think he will probably move towards a White House concept of No. 10 if he wins this election.

When Harold left I motored to London with Peter and tried to do a little on the new draft as well as dealing with the rating White Paper, which is to explain our long Bill and which, thank God, my Ministry has at last drafted in a reasonable way.

---

[1] Born in 1902, he became Secretary of the Bargoed Labour Party in 1923; and in 1927 he joined Labour's headquarters in London as the propaganda officer. In 1941 he became Secretary of the Research Department and in 1944 General Secretary of the Labour Party. He retired in 1962 and died in January 1963. His wife Norah was made a life peer in 1964.

[2] See Marcia Williams, *Inside No. 10*.

The review of defence policy which the Secretary of State, Denis Healey, had
been working on ever since he took office in 1964 was published on February
22nd. The White Paper set an annual ceiling on defence expenditure until
1969–70 of £2,000 million at 1964 prices. The cuts of £400 million (16 per cent)
in the Estimates forecast by the previous Government were achieved by dis-
continuing several major British aircraft development projects and substituting
American planes. The cost of these would be partially offset by U.S. defence
purchases in Britain. The West German Government was again to be pressed
to meet the foreign currency costs of the British Army of the Rhine.

Back-bench Labour M.P.s were particularly upset by the proposal to appoint
a head of defence sales to promote British arms exports. Some M.P.s were also
unhappy with the decision that Britain was to maintain a military commitment
East of Suez. Aden was to be abandoned, but commitments remained to NATO,
SEATO, CENTO, and in the Persian Gulf, Gibraltar, Malta, Hong Kong,
Cyprus and Singapore. Left-wing M.P.s objected to the costs of this policy and
to the heavy dollar expenditure and the dependence on America that it implied.

So did Christopher Mayhew,[1] the Minister for the Navy, who with the First
Sea Lord, Admiral Sir David Luce, resigned on February 22nd. His principal
objection, however, was to the decision to abandon aircraft-carriers as the main
strike force of the 1970s, in favour of the shore-based F-111-A. The Royal Navy
no longer played a pre-eminent role. In the previous autumn, when TSR2 was
scrapped, the Government had hesitated to announce a decision on the F-111.
Now it seemed clear that the British aircraft industry was to lose the Government
support it had enjoyed for so long.

Monday, February 14th
Cabinet on defence. We spent the whole morning on the Defence White
Paper, and there was another two-hour session from six till eight before we
approved it.

All the talk in the newspapers was about the threat of resignation by
Christopher Mayhew and the First Sea Lord. But this wasn't a subject of
controversy in the Cabinet. The things we really argued about were the
decision to buy the American F-111 and the British role East of Suez. As
for the F-111 it soon became clear that all the details were now cut and dried,
and that the papers for the agreement with the Americans on the purchase of
the plane were awaiting signature when Healey flew off to Washington
tonight. So the whole thing was fixed. All Cabinet could do was express
opinions and influence to some extent the general tone of the White Paper
by drafting amendments. Of course, there were some Ministers like Barbara
Castle who took up postures of protest. But the rest of us felt that there
was nothing we could do and that the procedure under which we had been

---

[1] M.P. for North Norfolk 1945–50 and for Woolwich East since 1951. He was P.P.S.
to the Lord President 1945–6 and Parliamentary Under-Secretary for Foreign Affairs
1946–50. He became Minister of Defence for the Royal Navy in 1964.

excluded was not unreasonable. Fourteen of our twenty-three members of Cabinet are members of the Defence Committee. To the preparation of this White Paper these fourteen had devoted nineteen meetings and two Chequers weekends. After all this, it was natural enough that they should expect Cabinet to give formal authorization to the recommendations they had worked out.

The issue which interested me was our role East of Suez. I found myself along with Barbara and others asking questions and extracting from the P.M. a very characteristic chain of utterances. First he repeated time after time that the Americans had never made any connection between the financial support they gave us and our support for them in Vietnam. Then about ten minutes later he was saying, 'Nevertheless, don't let's fail to realize that their financial support is not unrelated to the way we behave in the Far East: any direct announcement of our withdrawal, for example, could not fail to have a profound effect on my personal relations with L.B.J. and the way the Americans treat us.' However, I got the impression that the Defence Committee want us out of Singapore in 1970 and very much hope the Australians will turn us down when we ask for a British presence there after our withdrawal from Singapore. In fact we have to wait for facts to force withdrawal on us. So, though we are not in any way committed to withdrawal, the Chiefs of Staff have been told to work on the assumption that Singapore will be untenable long before 1970 and that we shall not transfer our troops to Australia. Indeed, it is only on this assumption that we can possibly keep our defence budget within the limit the Cabinet has set—a top limit of £2,000 million. If we stay in Singapore the budget will go well over that top limit. All this is concealed from the public by the large under-spending of our Estimates this year and will go on being concealed next year when we shall be able to defer expenditure due in the four-year period which will never take place if we withdraw in time.

The Defence White Paper took nearly the whole of Monday. While it was going on I had to be away on one very important mission, to see Mr Brack of Islington. Mr Brack is a Labour councillor who has been expelled from the Islington group because he is violently opposed to the council's policy of pulling down the flats in Packington and completely redeveloping the area. Indeed, he is one of the 426 people who have formally opposed our planning decision. These were the people who were encouraged by the references to improvements which I had spatchcocked into the decision letter, and they were furious when the council, with the backing not only of the G.L.C. but of our Ministry as well, refused to wait for a second inquiry and proceeded to go ahead on an improved version of their redevelopment plan. It was at this point that these opponents appealed en bloc to the Council on Tribunals. But two days before the Council on Tribunals was due to sit and consider the matter the Ministry rushed out a new decision letter approving the redevelopment scheme and so insulted and infuriated the Council. Mr Brack had been corresponding with me for some months and I had written a whole series of replies, which fortunately read perfectly respectably, to his protests and complaints. He came to challenge me and I had a long frank talk with him and ended by saying that he could publish the correspondence if he wished but he couldn't quote what I said verbatim. What he did do was to go straight off to the *Evening Standard*, which at once published this sensational story.

As soon as Brack left I walked along the passage into the Dame's room and told her what Brack had said, adding rather angrily, 'The trouble is that when you heard about the Council on Tribunals you rushed the second letter out and infuriated the Council – without telling me anything about it.' At this she replied, 'Of course we did. We had to. If the press had got hold of it first, we should never have got our decision.' This made me very angry indeed. Here was the Dame brazening it out, saying she had to act in this way behind my back in order to get the decision taken. Outrageous! However, this was typical of the atmosphere in the Department at the moment. John Delafons and my whole Private Office were becoming difficult, partly no doubt because this is the first week when Jennie is away and I have a new secretary being worked in. But the main reason, of course, is the prospect of an election – this is the moment when civil servants begin to hedge. After all, it is their duty to do so; and even if the Dame is retiring in a few weeks and therefore not interested, she is also affected by this deep sense that the politician's authority is being undermined.

Tuesday, February 15th
Another Cabinet meeting but I had to go across to the House of Commons to deal with a crisis in the Rating Bill Committee. The Tories are making a great row about war pensioners. They had spotted that in assessing who is entitled to a rate rebate the war pension would be counted as income. This came as a great shock because in assessing income from the point of view of national assistance, or any other social service, war pensions are disregarded. And the Tories saw that this disregard of disregards was something which could be exposed as an absolute outrage, especially in a time leading up to an election. I know very well that if Boyd-Carpenter had been in charge and I had been leading the Opposition, I would have treated the Government's proposal as absolutely outrageous and blown it to smithereens. Yet when I got across to the Committee Room I found the Committee curiously quiet and waiting for me. I made a serious speech, explaining that this wasn't a social service but a tax concession which must have a wide definition of income and no means tests. To my amazement the Committee swallowed all this and not a single person on my own side attacked me. I was able to slip out and get back to the Cabinet in time to discuss broadcasting while they finished the Committee Stage of the Bill by twelve that morning.

In the afternoon Lynn Ungoed-Thomas came to see me. Now that my Royal Commission is approved, everything depends on getting the right

15*

chairman to replace Alan Bullock. I thought of Lynn, an old politician who is now a distinguished judge, and realized that he is absolutely the right man. Within a very few minutes he had told me that he is a Chancery judge and doesn't care about local government, and he couldn't possibly think of doing it; but he could recommend his friend Widgery.[1] But if I can't have Lynn I don't want a judge and so I am back where I was without a name. I suppose it will have to be postponed until after the election.

I had a lot of departmental work to do in the afternoon and it was a pretty long and exhausting day. Nevertheless, I had to go to Cambridge to a Union debate, with Boyd-Carpenter as my opponent and housing as the subject. Undergraduate debates in the Unions are less important than they were. On the other hand, it does matter whether the right Ministers go down and whether they do well. I got there expecting a great occasion but I found the Union half empty; even worse, there were five speakers before me. We started at 8.20 and I got up at 10.50, having wanted to pee for close on three hours. However, things didn't go too badly. I am used to dealing with Boyd-Carpenter and on this occasion I made a completely unprepared speech with which I rolled him up and knocked him out and made them roar with laughter. So it wasn't a waste of time.

Wednesday, February 16th
Nora and Dick David, who are going to lend us their Polzeath cottage this summer for our holiday, had invited me to stay the night in Cambridge. Just as I was about to get into the taxi taking me to my train this morning I got a telephone message from my Private Office giving me my programme for the day. This made me blow up at once. The first thing I had said to John Delafons on Monday morning was that I wanted Wednesday kept absolutely free for non-departmental work (what I had to do was to redraft the manifesto). I'd realized that it would be difficult for a Cabinet Minister to take a whole day off. What I now came to realize was that the Civil Service had made it impossible. They'd fixed a first engagement for me at 12.15 and, after that, a solid series of meetings ending with a public meeting in a West London suburb at 8 p.m. So all the time I had for redrafting the manifesto was from 10.30, when I got back to Vincent Square, until 11.45, when the car would come to fetch me. God, I blew up as I sat at home doing my tiny bit of homework on the manifesto and then rushed out to address a gang of undergraduates. After that I had the departmental meetings, and last but not least more than a hundred letters to sign. Of course my Private Office knew I was up to something with the P.M. and that means that they weren't exactly co-operative. Indeed, they were making life as difficult as possible.

[1] John Passmore Widgery was a judge of the High Court from 1961 until 1968, when he became a Lord Justice of Appeal. In 1971 he was made a life peer and became Lord Chief Justice. He was chairman of the Committee on Legal Aid in Criminal Cases 1964–5, and in February 1972 he conducted an inquiry, sitting alone, into the shootings in Londonderry in January 1972.

Thursday, February 17th

This was the day when I hoped to get a firm decision out of the Chancellor on my mortgages and new council subsidies. My office had arranged a meeting before Cabinet between him and me, with officials present. On the official level my option scheme had been accepted and Nicky Kaldor's much more ambitious scheme turned down. My officials and the Treasury were working perfectly together, and William Armstrong and the Dame were there this morning to finish the job. We made some progress before we had to go along to the Cabinet room.

Cabinet started with the Leasehold Enfranchisement Bill. We trounced the lawyers again as we had trounced them in Cabinet last Thursday, though unfortunately the drafting of the Bill was ghastly. Afterwards Fred Willey told me he had had to do the work himself because Bruce Fraser had just refused to co-operate. A jolly good thing I am not going to have *him* as my Permanent Secretary.

The other item we discussed was Tony Wedgwood Benn's plan for making the B.B.C. introduce a moderate amount of advertising as a way of helping it out of its financial difficulties. It was a sound idea but I'd feared he wouldn't get it through. Sure enough, John Fulton, who is the vice-chairman of the governors, had told Harold that they would not accept advertising of any kind on any terms whatsoever. The P.M. reported on his talks with the B.B.C.; but clearly this is something we shall have to put under the mat until after the election just as I have already put under the mat my decision on Ullswater and the Manchester water supply and a good many other awkward items as well.

That evening at five o'clock there was yet another meeting between the Chancellor, the Prime Minister and myself on housing subsidies. Outside the P.M.'s room at the House we found Christopher Mayhew sitting on the sofa waiting to have his resignation talk. After he'd gone the P.M. said to me, 'He's been coming day after day trying to talk to me about his resignation. I wish to God he would finish it quickly and let us forget him.' The meeting with the Chancellor was the result of a brief discussion at Cabinet that morning. Our aim was to help the Labour councils in the big conurbations keep their council rents down by giving them an extra slice of the new housing subsidy. The electoral importance of the housing subsidies idea was recognized by everybody, but the Cabinet was anxious to avoid reckless expense and I had been instructed to work out alternative schemes and agree them with the P.M. and the Chancellor. At our previous discussions we had all agreed that the only possible method of doing this was to allocate the money to councils with the largest slum clearance requirements. But what should the entrance level be? I had schemes costed for paying the special housing subsidy to councils with 20 per cent slum clearance, 12½ per cent and the initial 5 per cent which the Department had proposed. The Chancellor, of course, fought for 20 per cent. 'It was a pure waste of money,' he said. 'Why not give it to a very few?' I pointed out that this would exclude Birmingham, where our Labour majority was in a parlous plight. 'Heaven's alive, man,' I said, 'we are not just giving something to Sefton at Liverpool because they have mismanaged their rents. We have decided to help every city which has a major problem of slum clearance. This housing subsidy isn't just a political manœuvre, it's a good idea. It's not throwing money away.' But he wasn't convinced. Alas, he regards Housing as his greatest enemy and he finally said, 'Well, I suppose I shall have to give way.' The P.M. said, 'Yes. 12½ per cent, then.'

I just had time to get back to the Ministry, sit down and dictate a speech for the P.M. to make at Birmingham on Friday evening, when he will announce this big new concession on council subsidies. Then I got my clothes together and caught the midnight train to Liverpool.

Friday, February 18th

I spent the morning in Runcorn New Town where there is a tremendous row between the corporation and the U.D.C. because the master plan just published shows that the whole present town centre is due for demolition and will be replaced by a new one a mile away towards the centre of the area. The U.D.C. felt the usual hate and suspicion of the corporation with their brand new offices, their big salaries and their air of being the feudal masters.

In the evening I rushed into Manchester to have a talk with Reg Wallis and take a local government conference for three hours with 300 Lancashire councillors. Everything went pretty well until some Manchester councillors started complaining at my decision to impose a seven-foot six-inch ceiling height on all their council houses and so have a standard cubic space for each council room. This is the most brilliant idea Lederer has brought forward and I have already persuaded the G.L.C., thanks to Fiske, to go along with it.[1] I should have used the same tact with Manchester and kept the discussion for the informality of the dinner-table. But there is some jinx which destroys my Department's relationships with Manchester. On this occasion I caused an unholy row by jamming it down their throats in fifteen minutes. It was entirely my own fault. I should have taken the Labour councillors aside and begged their help. This is yet another trouble to be rolled under the mat until after the election.

Otherwise the meeting went pretty well and I was able to make my announcement about the new housing subsidies simultaneously with Harold Wilson's speech at Birmingham. Morale was far better than three or four months ago and they are ready for an election. When someone asked me when it was coming and I looked a bit inscrutable they roared with laughter because they felt I knew it was coming quick and I couldn't actually tell them.

[1] See p. 415.

Saturday, February 19th
Prescote. All set for the election. That was the mood at Westminster by the end of this week. In the House of Commons there comes a point when election fever is replaced by election acceptance. Whether one likes it or not, at this point the Government has committed itself to the election. I have watched Harold Wilson growing into this decision. There hasn't been a point at which he suddenly decided. He was very near it last Sunday while we were working on the manifesto. But in the course of this week it has been finally decided in the sense that it is now irreversible, and since that is the case let me make some of my hazardous predictions.

First, I predict that the date of the election will be Thursday, March 31st, and that it will be announced by Harold when he comes back from Moscow.

Secondly, let me say that Harold expects to bring something back from Russia with him, some joint initiative on Vietnam, and he may be able to link with this a Common Market initiative. He has been under tremendous pressure over the E.E.C. from Stewart and George Brown ever since last December. He has been trying to get them out of their purely anti-French position; and it looks to me as though he is right in thinking that there are reasonable chances of a new approach to Europe. As he sees it, the difficulties of staying outside Europe and surviving as an independent power are very great compared with entering on the right conditions.

Now for the Tories. I think they are going into this election beaten before they start. They are appalled by the prospect of it coming in March and they are devastated by our stream of policy statements. Of course, this is the result of their own folly. They started accusing us of breaking our pledges far too soon. We were able to reply that we couldn't do everything in the first months. But now, having held them back, we are putting out statements on practically all our policy. By the time the election gets under way we shall have either (a) actually implemented a proposal, or (b) begun the legislation, or (c) published a White Paper on the policy. There are very few promises in our programme which can't be placed in one of these three categories and that the Tories know.

Are there any snags we face? Yes, of course there are. The main trouble is that we haven't delivered the goods; the builders are not building the houses; the cost of living is still rising; the incomes policy isn't working; we haven't held back inflation; we haven't got production moving. We are going to the country now because we are facing every kind of difficulty and we anticipate that things are bound to get worse and we shall need a bigger majority with which to handle them.

Sunday, February 20th
I had to go to Birmingham for the Labour Party's annual local-government conference; I was to give the winding-up speech in the afternoon before going up to London for an urgent meeting with Harold.

I did my job, made my speech and then went off terribly late to catch the 6.05 to London. I thought I would be late for the P.M. who wanted to see me at 9 p.m. The train got in at 9.15, but when I got to Downing Street there was nothing to fuss about because he was happily back from a day's golf. I found him eating supper in the sitting-room in front of the TV with Mary and Giles, and we went down to his study to talk about mortgages. This is a terribly important election pledge but we still haven't settled the scheme. I brought Harold a note of the particular problem involved and he studied it carefully and said he would get it cleared with Callaghan next day without fail. However, I have also arranged to go and see the Chancellor early on Monday to try and sort it out.

Once business was over we sat down for another of those queer conversations I have been having with him almost every week. I pressed him very hard on the need for drastic Cabinet reorganization after the election. I wouldn't say that he took offence but I was aware that I was going a bit far. However, once again I dared to discuss the future of my Ministry. On this occasion he had a new idea. He said that Tony Part, at the Ministry of Works, was a splendid fellow.[1] I wasn't surprised because a few days ago Burke Trend mentioned his name to me, and I began to feel I should have to accept him. Then I turned to the manning of my big new federal Ministry of Housing and suggested that he should send Fred Willey to work with the Lord Chancellor and let me have Niall MacDermot as my Minister of State. 'Ah,' he said, 'Niall's only staying in Parliament another twelve months because he is marrying again.' This shows Harold's very amiable tolerance of private life. Niall has broken with his brilliant doctor wife and fallen in love with a Russian girl in Geneva. In order to marry her he is ending his political career. 'In that case,' I replied, 'I could have him for his last year and he could fight these two big Bills through for me and bring the Ministry of Land and Natural Resources back into the Ministry of Housing.' We also discussed the future of Frank Cousins. Harold said he thought the best thing was to carry him through the election and afterwards make an issue of his attitude to the national prices and incomes policy. One thing he let out to me almost in passing was that my role for the election had undergone a change. George Wigg, he said, would now be in charge of a business committee whose job would be to link Transport House and No. 10. Tom Driberg would be chairman of the election committee. I asked him what *I* was to do and he said, 'You won't be in Transport House. I want you to be the man who covers Heath all the way through and who acts as my personal adviser.'

Thursday, February 24th
I missed yet another Cabinet because I had to spend the first part of the morning briefing selected journalists on my Local Government Bill. Then I had to

[1] Sir Antony Part, Permanent Secretary at the Ministry of Public Building and Works 1965-8. He went to the Board of Trade in 1968.

do the general press release with Rayner, Crocker and Peter Brown; we must have re-drafted it at least six times. What I had to get across was that I was actually de-rating the domestic ratepayer as no previous Minister of Housing had done, helping him at the cost of the other ratepayers, the businessmen and shopkeepers. By the end of the morning I literally had to dictate the words I wanted. Peter Brown said, 'It makes no difference, Minister. You are selling such a mouldy turnip nobody will accept it. This Bill won't have any effect.'

I spent the afternoon on the front bench dealing with the Report Stage and Third Reading of the Rating Bill. After that there was a queer little adjournment debate staged by Frank Allaun, who had been my most violent critic in the Rent Bill Committee. Now, just before the election, he has come out with a sensational story about the huge decreases in rent which have been decided by the rent officers. Actually, there have been only about three hundred decisions and they include some very considerable increases. I had to make a judicious reply praising the rent officers and saying they were shaking down very well but not supporting the suggestion that all rents are going to go down. In fact, the rent assessment committees have hardly started work and hardly one rent has been finally fixed. But the great thing is that the system should be working well before the election.

Friday, February 25th
When I looked at the morning papers I was pleased with myself. I'd put Peter Brown in the wrong. Even though I hadn't done at all well on B.B.C. or I.T.V., the *Daily Telegraph* had condemned domestic de-rating on its front page as electoral bribery; it had been headlined in the *Daily Mirror*; even *The Times* gave it a huge display. What I have proved is that politics isn't just working out policies but putting them over. I have managed to give the impression that we regard rates as a foul tax and that I am really trying to relieve domestic ratepayers of part of the burden. That should help us in the election.

Yet another visit to a New Town, this time Basildon in Essex. At my morning meeting with the very militant U.D.C. I was fiercely attacked on the ground that when the corporation sells land to the U.D.C. they charge an unnecessarily high price. I said this was absurd because they must sell it at the district valuer's price; and at lunch with the corporation I raised the issue with the general manager. 'Well,' he said, 'there is something in the U.D.C.'s complaint. We do have the right to give the U.D.C. more favourable terms but your Ministry has recently forbidden it.' So I turned to the chairman, who is an ex-High Commissioner of Nigeria, and said, 'Why didn't you tell me of the Ministry's misbehaviour?' and then spent an hour and a half spelling out the proper relation between the corporation and the Minister. 'Your *officials*,' I said, 'should talk to my officials; but members of the corporation, especially the chairman, are selected by me and should communicate with me at the political level.' I realized I was talking completely against tradition – the

Dame has tied the whole New Town structure into the Ministry at official level. There ought to be a Parliamentary Secretary dealing wholly with New Towns and spending all his time with the chairman of the corporations and the chairmen of the local authorities. But at present members of the U.D.C. feel pushed aside; and as for the ordinary people at Basildon, they have no access at all. I motored back all the way through Essex, from Basildon to Banbury, and got here in streaming rain, brooding over this problem. I am always discovering great segments of the Department where my policies haven't impacted. New Towns is one of them. I must get at this section after the election.

Sunday, February 27th

What tremendous luck these last two weekends! Each time I have had a beautiful sunny walk over the farm. Yesterday afternoon with Rachel Hartree and Patrick I went to look at the two new islands that have been carved out of the Cherwell for us by the Thames Conservancy excavator. They have been straightening the winds in the river in order to get the flood water off quicker and the islands are exciting. We collected the first frog-spawn of the year.

By the end of February the Labour Government had survived for eighteen months, with a tiny majority. At this point Labour had 314 M.P.s, the Conservatives 303 and the Liberals 10. The Speaker took one seat and there were two vacancies, one at Edgbaston (a Conservative seat) and the other at Falmouth (the Labour M.P., Leslie Hayman, had died). Speculation about the date of the general election ended when the Prime Minister announced that in the following month Parliament would be dissolved and that polling day would be on March 31st.

The Chancellor, meanwhile, had prepared a Statement, to be issued on March 1st, giving the broad outlines of the budget he would introduce if Labour were re-elected. He proposed two popular tax changes, a gaming tax and some relief for mortgagors. There was to be a new national savings certificate and, in February 1971, decimal currency would be introduced. Mr Callaghan's reason for giving the electorate this unusual preview was, ostensibly, to avoid allegations that the Government were holding the general election before what would prove to be an unpopular budget.

The Chancellor was also able to announce proudly that Britain had since August 1965 repaid £318 million of short-term overseas debt and that the reserves had increased by £64 million.

Monday, February 28th

In the morning Cabinet was summoned and we formally decided the election date. Harold announced it at 6.30 in the House of Commons and he repeated the announcement on television later in the evening.

Cabinet rambled on for more than an hour before we switched over to

Callaghan's budget Statement. My main interest of course was option-mortgages, on which there had been yet another discussion between the Treasury officials and mine before Cabinet started. The Chancellor said very unpleasantly that there was no agreement yet and that anyway he wasn't prepared to put these mortgages into his budget package. They should be announced later on by me. I said very sharply this wasn't possible. The whole credit to the Government would be undermined if they were presented as a gimmick of mine. They must be part of the Chancellor's package. 'Well,' said the Chancellor, 'I can't have this forced on me in its present form.' After this bickering Harold called us to order and told us to agree this between ourselves outside before evening. If necessary he would call another Cabinet on Tuesday.

All day I had a great deal of business in the Ministry. Here's a list. (1) I had a big meeting about a new row between the Nature Conservancy and I.C.I. which will blow up when I have to take the planning decision about a new reservoir to be built high up in Teesdale.[1] (2) I had a press statement to prepare, for the announcement of my decision on the problems of Tyneside which will be made to a delegation. (3) I had to handle the announcement of our concession on housing subsidies. I had intended to do this as an amendment to the Housing Subsidies Bill but one result of a decision to call a general election is that all the House of Commons Committees automatically lapse, so I had to spend most of the afternoon preparing to launch the housing subsidies propaganda after 6.30. (4) The worst problem of all, my mortgage plan. This was something which absolutely had to be settled; and most of Monday was spent by a great number of my officials getting agreement with the Treasury. The job was pretty well done by late evening. But it had been a most exhausting day, following a weekend with very little time off. When I finished I had a drink or two with John Delafons in my own room and then went off to dinner with Mr Bailey King of the *Local Government Chronicle* at the Garrick. We started with drinks at the bar upstairs and then went down to dinner. After that I had to rush back to the division, due to take place at ten; and though it was finally called off, this didn't relieve me since I had to sit on the front bench and listen to Jim MacColl winding up on a local-government town planning order.

Tuesday, March 1st
Early this morning a very odd thing happened. I woke up with absolutely no memory of what I had done or said after meeting Bailey King. However, I took a look at Hansard and found that from the front bench I had made a

[1] The Tees Valley & Cleveland Water Board wished to construct a reservoir at Cow Green, in Upper Teesdale, to supply water for domestic and industrial consumption (particularly for the I.C.I. works and refinery). Of the many objections to the scheme, one of the most forceful came from naturalists and botanists who protested against the flooding of a valley full of rare Alpine and Arctic flora. An amended scheme was eventually given Royal Assent in March 1967.

series of interventions which were perfectly sensible but of which I had no memory at all. The last time this happened to me was on the night before I made up my big superannuation speech at the Labour Party Conference at Brighton.[1] I had been appallingly insulted and injured by Cassandra[2] and others at the *Daily Mirror* party and had drunk at lot too much and gone out to dinner with Jimmie Cameron.[3] I woke up at six the next morning not even able to remember how I got home but feeling perfectly well. The speech was totally unprepared but was a great success. It wasn't quite the same this time but still it was a strange and disconcerting feeling.

We had yet another Cabinet this morning. I didn't see much of it because I was desperately concerned now to get a really good press presentation of my mortgage scheme. Callaghan had finally agreed that the announcement of the mortgage plan should be included in his budget package and that after sitting on the front bench beside him I should then move upstairs straight away to a press conference at which I should explain how the thing really worked. This was all a bit difficult because by bad luck I was first in Questions today and had forty to answer. Nevertheless, everything went O.K. I sat beside Callaghan at 3.15 when I had answered the last of the Questions and listened to a very flat period of Prime Ministerial Questions. Then came the Chancellor's Statement. He did it magnificently with enormous parliamentary skill. He sat down to a tornado of applause from our back-benchers. I knew of course that the whole shape of his speech had been recast by the Prime Minister when he came back from Russia, and again on Monday, and I am sure the link he introduced between paying for the mortgage plan and the new tax on gambling was a typical Prime Ministerial gimmick. But that doesn't reduce Callaghan's credit. On TV in the evening he was equally superb. He is an extremely interesting example of how important image is in modern politics. He has a good public image outside Parliament, his presence in Parliament is exactly right, his personality on TV is just right and he also has a good image inside his own Department in the sense that they like him. The place where he has no reputation at all is in Cabinet where in decision-making with his colleagues he is weak and self-commiserating. But even here he has a very considerable grasp of his subject and a really remarkable power of putting it over.

After Callaghan sat down, Heath stood up—and fell straight into the trap. He must have known that after Callaghan had presented his package there would be little he could say. But he was determined to make a speech and it was a bad one. In the course of it he picked up Callaghan's admission that

---

[1] In 1957, when Crossman announced the Labour Party's new national pension scheme.

[2] William Connor, *Daily Mirror* columnist since 1935. He was knighted in 1966, and died in 1967.

[3] James Cameron, the international reporter, formerly of the *News Chronicle*. He had resigned from the *Evening Standard* when that paper attacked and libelled John Strachey, then Secretary of State for War, at the time of the Klaus Fuchs espionage case in January 1950.

our consultations with the building societies haven't started yet. On our side, in our plan, we have already consulted them, he said. I noticed that with some surprise.

When I got back to the Ministry at 4.55 the first two pages of my press release had only just been run off and at 5.15 when I was due to go into the big conference room to meet the journalists the last page was only just making its appearance. There was also a longish and extremely complex document from the Treasury which I had to master and then expound. But by the end I felt satisfied by the combination of Callaghan's presentation in the Commons and my detailed exposition to the press.

In the evening we had another of our group drafting dinners at No. 10 – this time with Terry Pitt in attendance, since I had insisted that his absence would be disastrous. We had supper and then the eight of us got to work on the manifesto round a table while Harold hovered in the background making sure that it was coming out the way he wanted it. I couldn't keep my mind on the manifesto because I was worrying about the censure debate on Packington. The Tories had arranged it for Wednesday from 3.30 till 7.00 and we had got to Tuesday evening without my having a moment in the Department to consider my reply. I had discussed it on Sunday with the P.M. and he had told me not to get the Attorney-General to speak and only to speak myself right at the end of the debate. Now it was Tuesday evening and there was no speech ready for me.

Wednesday, March 2nd
John Delafons, W. R. Cox (our new Under-Secretary in charge of planning) and I all sweated away at my Packington speech throughout the morning. By midday I had got myself a narrative typed out for the first half of the speech which I was to follow with a reply to the three main charges. I knew what they were going to be because by now I had received a letter from the Council on Tribunals in answer to mine. The three charges basically were: first, that I had been grossly discourteous to the Tribunal, second, that in my decision letter I had given the opponents of the scheme the strong impression that I would concede a second inquiry and, third, that the opponents of the scheme had been denied the right to see the second plan for redevelopment which the Department had prepared in consultation with the G.L.C. and Islington. Of course, there is a good deal in all these complaints; and J. D. Jones had the impudence to come in and say to me, 'For heaven's sake don't suggest that you didn't know, that the Dame did it behind your back and try to get out of it in that way.' I've told him more than once that of course I won't, and I won't.

The House was fairly full when Boyd-Carpenter started the indictment, which I suppose he got mainly from the insurance company and the residents' association. It was very much the speech of a prosecuting lawyer but I was relieved that there was nothing new in it. The Tories expected or pretended to expect that I would get up when he was finished and reply. They pretended to be very angry that instead I got John Silkin, Ivor Richard, and Tom Williams[1] – three of our back-bench lawyers – to make powerful speeches on my behalf arguing that in planning terms nothing whatsoever was wrong. However, they were interspersed with a series of fierce Tories accusing me of gross impropriety for insulting the Council and not allowing full consultation to the opponents. The case was pretty formidable. I had asked for forty-five minutes to reply but John Hobson, who was winding up for the Opposition, was very venomous and took eight minutes longer than he should so I found myself with only half an hour, and our Whips insisting that the vote must take place at seven o'clock if our people were all going to be there. So I made a split-second decision to scrap the whole first narrative part of the speech and found myself replying almost impromptu to the three charges. Right at the beginning I made an apology which I hadn't consciously known I was going to make. I said straight away that if I had been discourteous it was unintentional and I regretted it.

As it turned out, this apology for my discourtesy covered up the fact that I didn't give away anything on the substance of the charges. After I'd finished and the vote had taken place[2] the officials seemed pretty content and Harold remarked to me, 'You did well because you diverted attention. They wasted time on you this evening and that's the main thing during this pre-election period.' I too thought I had done well, because it would have been dangerous if I had stood firm. The truth is that I had two alternatives, either to get the headlines right across the front page 'Minister defies the Council on Tribunals' or the headline 'Minister apologizes'; and I have no doubt that of those two the 'Minister apologizes' was the best way of ending the affair.

Thursday, March 3rd

Nevertheless, I felt very unhappy when I looked at the morning papers. The *Mail, Express* and *Telegraph* all said I had apologized and gave the impression that the Minister had climbed down. On the other hand the *Guardian, The Times* and the *Sun* suggested that I hadn't been abashed but had stood firm while expressing regret for discourtesy. It wasn't too bad but it was painful; and what was even worse, looking back, was the way I had treated the three M.P.s who had spoken on my behalf. All the thanks they got for sticking up for me were two rather slick remarks about how unpleasant all the lawyers were. I had to write them grovelling letters of apology and that upset me a good deal. Still, I am prepared to claim that this was the best performance I have ever put up in the House. And it shows that my instinct isn't always too bad. I didn't do what I had been advised, I did what I instinctively wanted to do and that was to make an apology to the Tribunal without in the slightest degree passing the buck to the officials who had

[1] M.P. for Warrington since 1961.
[2] The vote was 290 to 285.

actually let me down. Very early in the debate I made it clear that I took full responsibility for everything done in my name and though I don't think anybody believed that I knew quite what was going on, this was undoubtedly the right thing to do and it worked well.

I had allocated this morning for writing my election address but I couldn't resist going to Cabinet, where the agricultural price review was being discussed. The idea that a pre-election review must be favourable to the farmers applies only to a Tory government and this is something my Mr Pritchett can't understand. There was no doubt Cabinet realized that the popular thing for us was to make the farmers attack us. This infuriated me because I think we are giving them an unfair review, and it may damage the British economy by cutting back agriculture's ability to save dollars.

Over lunch I dashed off my election address; and in the afternoon something very interesting happened. Donald Gould of the building societies' Council especially asked to see me and the Dame. When he had sat there chatting for a few minutes he drew a bit of paper out of his pocket and said, 'I'd better say what I have come to say. First of all I want to thank you for what you have done over the national housing plan — thank you personally and officially on behalf of the building societies.' Then he paused and added, 'I must say one other thing. It's about Mr Heath's speech on Monday. When he said he had consulted with the building societies in formulating his mortgage plan he cast doubt on my good faith. You have not forgotten I gave you an assurance that we would not have negotiations with the Opposition without informing you. The moment he said that, I felt I had to come and tell you this.' I asked him what Mr Heath had actually done and Gould replied, 'He asked himself to lunch and talked about the Common Market. On no occasion did he have any kind of consultation with us about his mortgage scheme.'

I shall discuss with Harold how we should make use of this during the election. It is interesting that Heath is the kind of man who can fib in this way in public and I am sure he nearly bit his tongue off for having done it when he sat down. Thinking to myself, I must admit that it is the kind of thing I could easily do — say a little bit more than is true so as to get a little bit more credit than one deserves. It's my weakness. I now know it is Heath's weakness and I am not sure we ought to use it in the campaign.[1] But it's useful to know it and have it on the record.

After Cabinet Harold had said to me that he had found me a new Permanent Secretary — Matthew Stevenson from the Ministry of Power. 'He will suit you far better than any of the others,' remarked Harold, and sure enough by the afternoon this had gone round Whitehall. The Dame told me that Helsby had been talking to her. So with a tremendous rush I arranged to have him to supper at Vincent Square since Anne is up in town. Well, he gave me the shock of my life. He looks less like a senior civil servant than anyone

[1] It was not used.

you could imagine. No mandarin he. What he looks like is an insurance representative from the Prudential. There is no doubt he is very able. Over dinner I learned that he forced his way up from being a miner's son, through the executive class to the top of the Inland Revenue. He is obviously a man of what they call first-class organizing ability, but the more he talked to us the more aware I was that in taking Steve instead of the Dame I had substituted for a fellow intellectual an absolute anti-intellectual. One thing that struck me was his characterization of Alf Robens: 70 per cent slyness, alertness and charm and 30 per cent a straight madman—almost as bad as George Brown.

I behaved as difficultly as I could because I wanted him to know the kind of Minister he had to tackle and I am sure the net result was to strengthen his tremendous inner complacency. Why have I accepted him? Because the only alternative was Tony Part, a much younger man whom I liked personally much more but who would be a greater risk for me. I have got plenty of intellectuals in the Ministry—Jones, W. R. Cox, Brain. What we need is sheer organizing ability, and in this respect Steve may serve me very well. I shall tell Harold tomorrow I am prepared to accept him.

Friday, March 4th
My official visit to Nottingham County Council (a Labour county council, but with the normal oligarchic structure and excellent civil servants) was given an unusual twist when they took me up in a helicopter to see the green belt and discuss the relations between themselves and Nottingham town. They were extremely nice and sent me home to Prescote in the helicopter. I arrived on the home pasture at 6 p.m. just before the sun set and found I had a message that I had to see the P.M. again at 9.30 on Sunday.

The Labour manifesto, Time for Decision, *asked for a mandate to continue the Government's 'radical reconstruction of our national life'. It offered planned growth of incomes (in line with productivity increases), selective investment and regional planning and a national transport plan for road and rail. Half a million houses a year were promised, and a major expansion of education and medical services. Steel nationalization was included. But there was no clear commitment to compulsory legislation on prices and incomes, or to European entry.*

Monday, March 7th
So again I had to come up on Sunday night and go to No. 10, where our group was waiting to discuss with Harold what we assumed was the final draft of the manifesto. Actually it was the penultimate draft and a copy had already been taken by Terry Pitt and Peter Shore to Transport House last Friday where it had been processed over the weekend. So any changes we made on Sunday evening would have to be amendments that Tony Wedgwood Benn or Harold or I could move at Monday morning's joint meeting with N.E.C. The evening was very pleasant and brought the work of our little

group to a close. I think one can say it was pretty useful since it made sure that the manifesto was drafted under the complete personal direction of the P.M.

I had a word with Harold about my new Permanent Secretary, Steve, and found that the announcement was due to be made on Monday afternoon, despite Thomas Balogh's cries of anguish when he heard who I had got, so it wasn't much good my discussing it. He also talked to me about Frank Cousins's future. Apparently he still expects that after the general election Cousins will retire from Parliament and return to his trade union.

At 10.30 this morning we began the mass meeting of the Cabinet and the N.E.C.; we had to sit down together and wade through the enormous 25,000-word manifesto. There had been a big inside story in some of the Sunday papers about a split over the prices and incomes policy, with George Brown insisting that the whole thing should be written into the manifesto and the trade unionists on the Executive demanding its omission. As I rather suspected when I read these stories, they were invented in order to create the split they reported. In sober fact George Brown had had the sense to agree a form of words before the meeting with Jack Jones and when we came to the crucial passage in the manifesto there was no bite in the discussion but a desperate desire to be friendly and helpful on both sides. One has to admit that in this George Brown has come off worst, in the sense that if he really wants to introduce his early warnings, his sanctions and penalties when his Bill becomes law, he will find it difficult to do so; because the Government won't be committed by this election manifesto to a prices and incomes policy with teeth. But even if this is a defeat for George I doubt if it is a victory for Cousins and the T.U.C. That would fit with what happened at the Executive this morning. So we ploughed our way through the home policy sections and at 12.30 it was clear we weren't going to get finished. I finally suggested to the chairman that he should set up a little drafting committee consisting of Tom Driberg and Terry Pitt and me and that we should go outside with the first part and finish it off. That was agreed and we worked away till 2.30, when I went back to my Ministry. As I left Transport House the manifesto was beginning to be stencilled page by page in time for the press conference at 6.

In the afternoon I had a Statement to make in the House on jerry-building. Directly afterwards I went along to Harold's room to make sure of two or three points in the final manifesto—in particular his desire to mention the reorganization of Whitehall. He has insisted on putting this in—the integration of the Commonwealth and Colonial Offices, the creation of a Ministry of Social Security and the absorption into Housing of Land and the relevant sections of Public Works. I was surprised at his insistence until I realized that this would enable him to avoid an awkward scene with the Ministers concerned. After the election he would be able to refer them to the manifesto and justify the changes in this way, instead of telling them himself.

I found him sitting with George Brown waiting for the press conference, and it didn't take long to clear up the vital passages. Then we began to discuss what he should say to the journalists. I suggested the slogan 'Work in Progress' and we all got down to knocking out as quickly as possible the statement he would make.

I had one more meeting due in the Ministry—with Michael Young, who has been appointed by Tony Crosland as the chairman of the new Social Science Research Council.[1] He had insisted on seeing me because he is furious at my decision to form the Centre for Environmental Studies and my success in getting $750,000 out of Ford. My civil servants had warned me that he would boast of his decision to make a £25,000 grant for an exercise in Glasgow University designed to test our techniques of planning. This is trespassing on my territory, and I thought he would show off about it. He duly did so. I said I was delighted that he had so much money and that he would be able to be active right across the board, including an area like planning which he knew would be covered by our own Centre. He then asked me how long the Centre would last and I told him that I had got enough money for the first five years but it would certainly be carried on for five beyond that. He said he hoped it would be integrated into the Social Science Research Council long before then. I replied that the Social Science Research Council was far too all-embracing. I hoped it would split up into its relevant parts and I was sure there would always be a centre for environmental studies and another one for economics. Altogether I found him rather irritating and succeeded in annoying him as well.

After that I went along to the Garrick and gave dinner to Christopher Sykes who wanted to talk to me about Adam von Trott, whose biography he is writing.[2] I had known Adam very well when he was a Rhodes scholar at Oxford in the 1930s. Later, he was hanged by the Nazis as one of the conspirators in the anti-Hitler plot of July 20th, 1944. It took my mind right off the subject to talk about Adam. We had a jolly good dinner and I gave Sykes some ideas, I hope.

Tuesday, March 8th
Reading the *Telegraph* over breakfast I was disconcerted to see a very curious story asserting that the building societies were deeply upset by my scheme for option-mortgages which they regarded as unworkable and which they were going to blow to smithereens next weekend. I immediately rang Donald

---

[1] He had been director of Political and Economic Planning 1941–5, secretary of the Research Department of the Labour Party 1945–51, chairman of the Consumers' Association 1956–65, of the Advisory Centre for Education since 1959 and of the National Extension College since 1962. The author of several books on education and social science (of which *The Rise of the Meritocracy* [London: Thames & Hudson, 1958] is perhaps the best known), he served as chairman of the Social Science Research Council 1965–8 and as a member of the Central Advisory Centre for Education 1963–6.

[2] *Troubled Loyalty* (London: Collins, 1968).

Gould suspecting, wrongly, that this was connected with the Heath business and that I was a victim of double-dealing. I was certain of this because I had been at tea with the building societies the day before and a number of the leading secretaries and chairmen had talked to me about our scheme. They described it as being one of brilliant simplicity, and gave no indication that anything was wrong. Donald said he would see me at 3.30.

So I went to Cabinet, where the second round about the agricultural price review was just beginning. I am the only member who knows anything about farming and I therefore agree with Fred Peart who, as Minister of Agriculture, has come to the conclusion that on the Treasury's own figures the real net income of the British farmer hasn't substantially increased over the last five years. Although production has gone up tremendously, production costs have gone up a great deal more, owing not only to wage increases but also to the increased cost of machinery. Since the prices farmers get have not been allowed to rise as fast, there has been a virtual freeze of the net income and this was aggravated by last year's price review. Coming immediately after the election we had had to cut right back on the election bribes the Tories had given the year before; and a bad price review had been matched by a disastrous year in which the weather was terrible and the crops ruined. That is the case for showing some generosity this year even though there may be no votes in it. At a previous meeting we had been told that the N.F.U. was demanding £52 million and that the Ministry was prepared at the very maximum to go up to £27 million. Cabinet, however, was feeling bloody-minded and had only authorized Fred to move from £17 million to £20 million. Fred then said he wouldn't come back to Cabinet unless there was a startling and dramatic change; for instance, if they came down somewhere near the £27 million he thought reasonable there would be some point in reconsidering the possibility of an agreed settlement.

That afternoon's meeting with the building societies was a tremendous shock for me. Donald Gould came along with the chairman of the Abbey National and with his secretary. He confirmed that the *Telegraph* story was broadly true and explained that a number of the big societies, especially the Halifax, were alarmed at the Ministry's sudden decision to switch from the option-mortgage scheme (a straightforward interest-rate reduction) they had discussed, to an annuity scheme which would be wholly disastrous administratively as well as quite impractical.[1] Donald Gould made clear that at their meeting of the Council on Friday they intended to say all this quite openly. I began to realize that once again the Dame had put me in the soup. Unfortunately it was quite true that, right at the very last moment, she and Brain

---

[1] With a building society mortgage, the effect of tax relief on interest is to give the borrower the largest tax relief in the early years and very little in the later years, when the repayments are mostly on borrowed capital. The annuity system embodied a scheme for spreading the tax relief evenly over the whole period, and the Ministry now proposed this as the optional scheme for borrowers who wished it. The annuity system would entail complicated provisions to cater for existing mortgagors.

had the bright idea that an annuity system would be more convenient to the building societies than a straight interest reduction, as well as costing us less. So just before my press conference all the examples I was giving were recalculated on the new annuity system. I had completely swallowed the assurance that this was merely a technical improvement and didn't doubt it because the Treasury man, Couzens, was just as enthusiastic as Brain.

Inside I was boiling, but I kept my temper and told Gould that I should immediately like to set up a working party to discuss the annuity system and the straight interest payment as alternatives and that I was prepared to accept whichever was practicable. Just as I was going the Abbey National man piped up and suggested that there ought to be an announcement on Friday of interest rates going up to 7 per cent since if that were combined with a Government subsidy to keep interest rates down it would suit them very well. I said I did not agree, whereupon he wished me well in the election.

By the time they left it was time for me to go to the Dame's room where she was giving a farewell cocktail party for her old favourites, the Local Government Boundary Commission. Then back to my own room where I was giving a party to celebrate the announcement of the Centre for Environmental Studies with Richard Llewelyn-Davies as chairman. Richard had only consented to this provided the Dame wrote him a letter admitting she gave the wrong advice in saying that his appointment would be inappropriate.[1]

This was the Dame's last day as Permanent Secretary and so after her little party she came in to mine and I made a little speech, and Richard made a little speech. At this point Stanley Gordon of the Ford Foundation came in and said that he hoped we were making no announcement since he hadn't cleared it with his top brass. I suppose it will work itself out all right.

I got to the House in time to hear the summing-up speeches of the defence debate, a shouting match between Enoch Powell and Denis Healey, before we got a comfortable majority of ten.

Wednesday, March 9th

This was the day of the funeral of Tom Loveday, our neighbour at Williamscot, a mile away from Prescote. I decided to go home for it because he was a wonderful old boy, and the only one of our neighbours in the country who has really been prepared to be a friend. The Department were perfectly willing to let me have the day off — one only has to say that there is a funeral to attend for them to clear the decks straight away. So I went down and lunched on the train with Anne; and Molly came down by car to take me back because I had to be at Olympia at 6.30 to visit the *Daily Mail* Ideal Home Exhibition. It was a lovely, lovely spring day. For four weeks now we have been having this warm, growth weather. But inside the church it was a

[1] See p. 412.

very dreary little burial service with no panegyric for the old boy. On the way back to London I had time just to look in at Williamscot and meet the heir, a middle-aged nephew who, because he was in America during the war, has a slight American accent. He seemed on first impression a rather strange character who is keen on getting himself an important job in a planning department. I am interested in him because I want to buy some of the fields in the two farms which adjoin ours, of which he is now the landlord.

At the Olympia dinner I had an interesting talk with Mike Randall, the editor of the *Daily Mail*. He told me that in next morning's paper the National Opinion Poll would give Labour an enormous lead. He was taking the line that the election was a disaster for the newspaper industry because of its appalling cost and because people weren't interested in it. Every column you devote to it, he told me, reduces circulation and it is not going to warm up or be anything more than a titular election because the decision has already been taken by ordinary people. I said in reply that I thought newspapers could still exert an enormous influence on campaigns. For example, if the Conservatives were to launch a strong anti-coloured-immigration and anti-trade-union line they might really start winning votes. That is the kind of difference papers can make. To this Randall replied that he couldn't possibly touch that kind of thing with a barge-pole unless, of course, he added, he were to have a directive from the proprietor.

Thursday, March 10th

I knew that something was up before Cabinet started because Callaghan cancelled an appointment with me at 9.30 in the morning. Anyway, it had been fairly obvious to any newspaper reader for the previous three days that the money market was having a dose of electionitis and heavy selling of the pound was taking place.

Directly we had settled down in our chairs Harold said that the Chancellor wanted to make a proposition. Then, in his usual ponderous way, Callaghan gave us a careful account of how the pound had come under increasing pressure and how he had discussed matters with Lord Cromer and they both now felt it was necessary as a precautionary measure to raise bank rate by 1 per cent. He was very careful after that to add that there was an alternative policy. 'We could go in with all guns blazing to blow the speculators to smithereens – a policy the Bank has adopted until now.' He thought it might work but if it didn't we would have to put up bank rate by 2 per cent instead of 1 per cent.

Even while he spoke it was obvious that there had been a disagreement. On the one side there was Callaghan and the Governor and, on the other, George Brown and Harold Wilson, who very much disliked the Governor's advice. So there followed a longish discussion, or rather, these three argued it out while the rest of us asked questions. The only question I asked was whether the Callaghan policy would mean that the building societies' Council would be entitled to raise their interest rates when they met on Friday. When I asked this there was great anger and Harold Wilson interjected, 'If they do, they must be told that it will be subjected to the Prices and Incomes Board.' Maybe. But it's not much good saying that to them and I didn't pass on the message though instructed to do so by Cabinet.

As the discussion proceeded it became clear that Callaghan's proposal was fraught with danger. Would it at the beginning of the election campaign be regarded as a sign of weakness not strength? Would it not justify the Tories making the pound sterling an issue in the campaign? When Harold began to wind up there was virtually no support left for the Chancellor apart from Douglas Houghton. The rest of us agreed that Cromer's advice should be disregarded.

The next item was Frank Cousins's personal statement about the *Daily Mirror*'s attack on him for remaining in the Cabinet while he repudiates its policies. It was, of course, intolerable that at Conference he chose to sit with his union delegation and refused to stand up for George Brown. It has been equally intolerable that in the Cabinet he has let it be known that he disagrees with the prices and incomes policy. He has been behaving in a way which, if he hadn't been Frank Cousins, would not have been permitted. But Harold Wilson hasn't got much to fear from the *Daily Mirror* attack. Under pressure Frank has got to say that he accepts responsibility for Cabinet decisions and that he has stayed a member precisely because he has not repudiated Cabinet policy and thinks, on balance, that the Government is doing a good job. He could have resigned a few months ago but he can't resign now. Harold Wilson has nursed him through his doubts to the point where he can't do us any harm.

Finally, we returned to the agricultural price review, on which Peart made a new statement. He reported that the farmers had suddenly capitulated and were now ready to reach a settlement, not at £52 million—their first bid—but at £28 million, only £1 million more than Fred thought was fair. I fancy they may have learnt their lesson and come to realize that a decision which they dispute would strengthen our position in this election. But Callaghan would not hear of any negotiation. He said they had already been given everything possible. However, Harold Wilson finally persuaded the Cabinet to allow Peart to offer them £23 million if he could get an agreed settlement at that sum. I shall be surprised if he can.

The more I reflect on this episode the more I believe that we shall have to abandon deficiency payments. It's the housewife who'll have to pay the farmers, not the taxpayer, for the simple reason that any Labour government must reduce public expenditure: to get rid of the £200 to £300 million that farm subsidies cost us would give us a margin of manœuvre in our departmental spending so that we could revise our plans on education, housing and health and set about expanding them at the rate we really require.

I had to leave Cabinet while they were starting a discussion on dock nationalization because I was due back in my own Ministry, where the news of Steve's appointment had come as something of a shock. We all agreed that we should persuade him to make his first priority the organization of the Department.

Parliament was dissolved today, and we had the first meeting of our election business committee at Transport House. The essential members are Len Williams (the General Secretary), Ray Gunter, Alice Bacon, myself and James Callaghan from the N.E.C., and such officials as are necessary. With Alice Bacon away most of the time in her constituency, Gunter, Callaghan and I will be the effective men in charge. We decided that Len should be in the chair every day and that James Callaghan should do the daily press conference, whereas I should see Harold at breakfast each morning and come straight across to Transport House for 9.30. After that I should go back to my Ministry and work there morning and afternoon, and then do evening meetings in London and the Home Counties. Only in the last week shall I go to Coventry, so my own obligations don't seem particularly heavy.

When this was settled I caught the Pullman to West Bromwich with Maurice Foley. His meeting was in the Baths and at 8 p.m. we found only 60 to 70 people in this enormous place. Fortunately they had grown to 150 or so by 8.15, making a decent, good-humoured meeting. Considering that West Bromwich is a Black Country town where immigration is the strongest issue and Maurice Foley is the Minister in charge of the integration of the Commonwealth immigrants, I felt the atmosphere was pretty good. There is no doubt that in the 1964 election the pro-Tory undertow against Labour, on the ground that we were soft on immigration, was what prevented us achieving any swing in the West Midlands. This meeting showed there was a chance of getting a swing this time. I motored home from West Bromwich, getting to Prescote at 11.30 p.m.

Friday, March 11th
I spent the whole day in Buckinghamshire selling the idea of our New Town[1] to the seven local authorities concerned, which of course include the Bucks County Council. Not unnaturally it was a useful piece of electioneering for Bob Maxwell, the local Member,[2] and I found the atmosphere fairly good. I got back to Prescote at eight o'clock at night feeling I had done a solid day's work.

---

[1] Milton Keynes.
[2] M.P. for Buckingham 1964–70. By birth a Czech, he settled in Britain after the war and founded the publishing firm of Pergamon Press in 1946, and until 1969 was its chairman. He was chairman of the Labour Party's National Fundraising Foundation 1960–69, and of the Party's working party on Science, Government and Industry. In 1970 an Inquiry was set up into the financial dealings of his company and he did not stand in the 1970 general election. In 1974 he was readopted as the Labour candidate for Buckingham, but the seat was retained by a Conservative.

Sunday, March 13th

Saturday was really a day off since I spent the whole morning at home working at my boxes and dealing with all the planning cases which Jim MacColl left behind him when he departed for his Lancashire constituency two or three days ago. I had lovely walks in the afternoon and played Monopoly with the children in the evening. Much the same today, apart from a farm walk with Pritchett in the morning. Then back by the 7.30 train to start my election routine by breakfasting with the Prime Minister at 8.45 on Monday.

Monday, March 14th

Harold rang early to say that he wouldn't be back and that I must arrange at all costs to get Ray Gunter to the press conference that morning in order to handle the Cowley affair. This is the first big event of this election campaign — the revelation of a so-called kangaroo trial by shop stewards at the B.M.C. works.[1] There is something in it, but it has been blown up enormously by the Tory press, and Heath and the rest of his colleagues have leapt upon it so that it has dominated the election for the first week. I always thought it had happened too early to really help the Tories and would conk out, and it really did conk out when Harry Urwin[2] produced an investigatory report, sober and objective, and Ray Gunter handled it at the press conference today.

In the evening I made my main TV appearance of the campaign in a long discussion with Reg Maudling and a Liberal, Professor Fogarty,[3] on social security. Maudling was obviously bored and said to me afterwards that there are no votes in that subject. I felt bored too and was aware that I had missed an opportunity, because there wasn't a spark of life in this performance. Afterwards we went downstairs for a drink and saw Heath do his party political. A bit gimmicky to begin with, but then five minutes direct to camera which I thought effective. Maudling, who I suppose is competitive, said nothing but he looked as though he thought it pretty awful.

Tuesday, March 15th

I breakfasted with the P.M. and we decided that the thing to do throughout the first week was to sustain a constant challenge to Heath and Maudling to cost their programme. In fact we are treating the Tories in Opposition just as they treated us in Opposition during the 1959 campaign. Harold observed to me over breakfast that tomorrow would be the anniversary of the day

[1] Two workers were 'tried' and fined at an unofficial union hearing. A noose was suspended over the 'court'.

[2] Secretary for the Midlands Area of the T.G.W.U. 1963–9, and since March 1969 Assistant General Secretary of the T.G.W.U. He became a member of the T.U.C. General Council in September 1969, replacing Frank Cousins.

[3] Professor of Industrial Relations at the University College of South Wales since 1951, and Professor at the Economic and Social Research Institute, Dublin, 1971–2. In 1972 he joined the Centre for Studies in Social Policy as Senior Fellow. He was Liberal candidate for Devizes in 1964 and 1966.

when Gaitskell made his fatal mistake and promised to reduce income tax. We shall smash Heath as Macmillan smashed Gaitskell by constantly asking how much his promises cost. We have costed ours, and, although it is boring, the essence of our campaign tactic is to keep to these comparative costs. Harold, of course, can be entertaining and will be. But the rest of us must be sensible, 'work in progress' politicians, a sharp contrast to a virulent, shrill Opposition. That's what we broadly agreed over breakfast. Harold was tempted to come down out of the stratosphere pretty soon and start mixing in. I begged him not to. 'You've made your decision, Harold,' I said, 'to stay out at least until the week before polling day. Don't go back on it now.'

One other thing happened at breakfast. Out of the blue Harold asked me what would be wrong with Norman Chester, the Warden of Nuffield, as the chairman of my Royal Commission. Wasn't he really the right man for the job? Doesn't he know all about it? Hasn't he got the right background? I found out that Harold knows Norman very well and I began to think seriously of having Chester after that talk.

In the afternoon Steve made his first intervention as Permanent Secretary at one of my meetings. It had been called on the subject of publications and he said he didn't want a policy meeting on that subject because it hadn't been adequately prepared for. Clearly he has been talking to John Delafons and is busily introducing some paperwork and routine into the Department, which has been run with wonderful informality by the Dame. Personally, I liked her style—it meant I could call a meeting at a few hours' notice. But it is true that she kept no records; and decisions were often taken which were never fulfilled. Steve is going to get the Department's files in order and waste no time on meetings with me when he hasn't made up his mind what is to be decided. I'm not frightened of that.

Thursday, March 17th

When I arrived for breakfast with the P.M. on Wednesday I found the staff didn't expect me and they had to give me my breakfast while he was in his bath after finishing his. He started by saying he wanted to speak about the trade unions that night. I said, 'For God's sake don't do that. Keep out of it for at least two days longer and probably the Cowley business will be dead.' Then he said that we must deal with means-testing and accuse Heath of dismantling the welfare state. There was a chance that day because Hogg had demanded that Harold and I should withdraw our total lie that Heath was going to destroy the welfare state. Harold insisted that I should go on the TV at the press conference that morning and refuse to withdraw it.

That gave me a chance of seeing what the daily conference is really like. It's a pretty boring show. Callaghan started with a longish speech and then there were some rather desultory questions and then I was allowed to make my little statement about Hogg. After that the journalists moved across Smith Square to the Tory headquarters. I suppose these press conferences do provide

some material for the evening papers, and I suppose ours are bound to be a
bit dull since we are doing the defending. Anyway, it suits the boring style
we have decided to assume.

It is obvious that the work of the Department is being slowed down. I
suppose this always happens when elections are on. The officials don't want
any issues brought up to the Minister; and with Stevenson taking over I think
it is reasonable to let him alone. I see him briefly each day and he sees Helsby
each day, discussing in particular how much of the Ministry of Works we
should take over. Should we really make ourselves the Department responsible for the construction industry as well as for all planning and housing
policy? I rather agree with him that we shouldn't try.

I did, however, point out to Steve one possible advantage. If I had this huge
federal Ministry I could have a balanced housing policy and not merely aim
to build as many houses as possible. 'Ah,' he said. 'You can have your
balance later. Let's get the houses up first.' This is the first time I saw how
quickly a Permanent Secretary adapts himself to a new Ministry and gets his
new departmental targets. Now that the legislation is almost finished, maybe
this is the kind of Permanent Secretary this Ministry will need in the next
four years.

In the evening I was due to speak in London. My first meeting was at Acton
where I found an audience of thirty or forty people. What I didn't know at the
time was that the B.B.C. ten o'clock News was there as well as a little leg-
man from the P.A. As a result, this morning the *Guardian*, the *Financial Times*
and the B.B.C. all reported that I had promised to reduce rates by half. What
I had actually said, of course, was that we would reduce by 50 per cent the
annual *rate* at which domestic rates are increasing. The fact that quite sensible
papers can print such palpable nonsense without a flicker of reaction shows
how cynical the press is becoming about politicians during an election. They
believe anything of us. When you read *The Times* election page, which consists almost entirely of taunts and counter-taunts, you can see that the press
only prints the hustings element in our speeches, which for the most part
consist of pretty objective accounts of how we run the housing subsidies,
what rent rebates are and suchlike. Then, having given this loaded account of
the politicians, the press complains that we are superficial and vulgar. It is
one of those vicious circles which we can't break out of.

I turned up late at No. 10 today because I knew the P.M. had been at a
monster meeting in Birmingham the night before with 10,000 people booing
and jostling in the hall; I had seen it all on the I.T.N. News the night before.
I found Harold lying in bed eating kippers, with one kipper skeleton thrown
on the carpet for his Siamese cat to finish. Harold sleeps in a tiny little bedroom—I suppose it was the scullery-maid's bedroom in the old days—and
there I had my breakfast with him. He looked a bit tired, having got back at
three in the morning, but he was enormously elated by the Birmingham meeting and told me with great excitement the story of how Mary had got a

scratch on her neck when something had been thrown at her. Should we give that to the press, he pondered, and finally concluded that we should. When I asked him why, he said, 'Well, you see the Tories are deliberately leaving her out of the campaign because Heath has no wife. It's a positive advantage to us that I and Mary appear together and Heath has nothing. So I would like to see her brought back into the campaign.' I said that Mary must hate it. 'Oh no,' he said. 'She liked the meeting last night a great deal.' As I was going downstairs I ran into Mary and said, 'I hear you really enjoyed last night after all?' 'Enjoyed it!' she said, with agony on her face. 'Who told you that? That man?' Her relationship with Harold is fascinating. I am sure they are deeply together but they are now pretty separate in their togetherness. It is one of those marriages which holds despite itself because each side has evolved a self-containedness within the marriage.

Harold and I had more chat this morning about the chairmanship of the Royal Commission. I tried the idea of Eric James,[1] but the P.M. said he was erratic and again strongly commended Chester. He then launched into the inside story of the agreed agricultural price review which Fred Peart had announced on Wednesday afternoon. Apparently Harold had sent for Woolley, the President of the N.F.U., and told him there was a chance of settlement. If he would come down from his £27 million, we would move up from our original £20 million. With this authority Peart and Woolley clinched it at £23 million. Callaghan, of course, thought we had given too much away, but fortunately the idiotic Tories have denounced it as a mean review and so have the Liberals. Harold saw his chance and got the Lobby together so that there could be a full story in tomorrow's papers.

At the end Harold turned to some real trouble in my own Ministry—the February housing figures. When I got hold of them I at once realized that they were sensationally down—about 35 per cent below the average of the first two months of the year. Harold leaps upon this kind of failure. Tommy Balogh has been entrusted to investigate the whole statistical position and I was instructed to report to him daily on the situation until it was cleared up. Back at the Ministry I summoned Stevenson, who straight away arranged a big meeting that afternoon. I listened to the civil servants and am still not sure how significant this fall is. Maybe it was merely a winter delay accentuated by the Treasury cut-off of local authority mortgages. Anyway, under Stevenson the Department is going to be far more methodical in studying trends.

Friday, March 18th
Harold went down to his constituency on Thursday night so I didn't see him this morning. Instead I went straight round the corner to Transport House; the results of the West Midland municipal by-elections (caused by the four

---

[1] Lord James, Vice-Chancellor of the University of York.

new county boroughs I had created) had just come in. My impression is that we are right back where we were before last March. We won four of the five councils and nearly won Wolverhampton despite the most appalling difficulties. When I remember how riven with division and defeatism the local leadership were and how half of them were against us because we were destroying their old authorities, I believe these figures are a very good result for us indeed. The fact is that the West Midlands was one of the worst Labour areas in 1964 and municipally it was right down in the dumps. This parliamentary campaign coming before the municipal campaign will have helped the councillors enormously. All this we discussed in a rather desultory meeting before I went to Luton for an official Ministerial visit.

I had hoped at Luton to give some help to our Labour candidate, Will Howie,[1] but my officials wouldn't allow me to do this bit of political work, which I thought a bit harsh. From there Anne drove me on to Hitchin and Letchworth where I did two pleasant meetings for Shirley Williams. Then we drove back to Prescote.

Saturday, March 19th
Nomination day at Coventry. We motored over in exquisite weather. Anne was in her best, I was in my best, Albert Rose and Winnie Lakin, reinstated as agent, were in their best; and the atmosphere was as though Anne and I were getting married again, with the mayor and the town clerk having a drink with us and a great sense of ease and repose. Never have I known an election as easy as this one. Labour voters like to be on the winning side and this will be something like a landslide in which we may well win seventy or eighty seats. If you ask me to make a prediction I would say we are heading for a Presidential victory of extraordinary proportions.

Sunday, March 20th
Prescote. A lovely day here, starting with a thick white fog and coming out into a cloudless blue sky and hot spring air. Steady, perfect electioneering weather. It really is getting uncannily like the autumn of 1959 when Gaitskell was fighting his valiant, hopeless campaign against Macmillan and the country had never had it so good and would have nothing said against him. All this week we have been fighting 1959 in reverse. Now it is we who are on top of the world, we who are the Government being given credit for the weather, we who are letting wages rise faster than prices. The Tories can't find a way to break through the complacent acceptance by the electorate of super-Harold. At one breakfast I caught him thinking 'You've never had it so good'. And I said, 'Well, for God's sake let's remember to draw the right conclusions and not make the mistake the Tories made. After winning this election we have got to do a drastic reorganization

---

[1] M.P. for Luton 1963–70. He was an Assistant Whip 1964–6 and a Whip 1966–8.

if we are going to hold the country through the difficult period ahead, because we are going to have a devaluation crisis. It will come after this inconceivable tide of success on which we are coasting in.' I should add that this last week has been the easiest since I became a Minister. I have had my breakfast at ease with Harold, strolled across to Transport House at 9.30, and then at 10.30 over to my Ministry for a couple of hours with very little to do. A little work in the afternoon with Jennie at Vincent Square and at most one or two election meetings each evening. What a lovely, easy, floating life it has been.

Sunday, March 27th
Only three effective days left before polling on Thursday. Today the polls agree that Labour still leads by eight points. The press, who treat elections as a sporting event, want to give the Tories a chance of winning so they make what they can of the special regional polls published in the *Guardian* and the *Birmingham Post*, which show a slight reduction in our lead. But the fact remains that Labour are still in the ascendant, the public think that everything is decided and unless something completely unpredictable happens I would still hold to my forecast that we shall have a majority of eighty.

Now for the campaign itself. It was Harold's decision from very early on that he would stay outside and above the conflict and remain the Prime Minister in Downing Street until he intervened actively on the last Saturday of the campaign and then kept on for the next four or five days. I approved of the strategy but it hasn't worked out. Every night he has spoken somewhere and so he has hogged most of the available Labour publicity. He has also been on the radio and TV every night and so the theory that he should descend as the *deus ex machina* at the end of the campaign has been completely contradicted. And the trouble is that when he speaks he puts himself on a level with Heath, neither better nor worse. And so each night we have had a snippety debate between the two of them. Despite a heavy cold, Harold is still on top. But Heath, who began terribly stiff and starchy, is beginning to catch up somewhat, and is getting something of the admiration Gaitskell got for his gallant 1959 campaign. So the Presidential descent from the stratosphere which our strategy said should take place yesterday, Saturday, just didn't happen. It was bad luck that the Grand National and the Boat Race should be held, the one at three and the other at four o'clock, on the day that Harold was doing a big meeting in the Belle Vue Stadium in Manchester. As a result, virtually nothing came through of his speech that night. Indeed, we heard more about George Brown, just back from his nationwide heroic tour (which seems to me even more Pickwickian and old-fashioned this year than ever before). But if our plan for Harold's intervention in the campaign didn't work out this was not important for the simple reason that there hasn't been any campaign. The daily strategy meetings at Transport House have been a fraud because nothing has been happening. We've been sitting round and chatting a little and then Jim Callaghan has been going down to his news conferences, which he has conducted in rather a nice way so that by now the journalists have got to like him. Of course, there were certain routine functions which had to operate, but not a single strategic decision has been taken in Transport House since the campaign started. The only test of generalship is whether you can modify your plans as the situation changes. If you win without a single modification you have hardly had to fight; and that's the case in this campaign. So it has tested neither the relationships between the Government and the Party, nor our abilities to overcome adversity. Instead, we have been coasting along; and in this Harold's personality has played a leading part. He is winning just by being himself and carrying the middle-class vote.

If the Transport House policy meetings have been futile, I have felt that my daily breakfasts with Harold have also been fairly unnecessary. And I was pretty sure that Harold felt it too when he said to me on Thursday, 'My trouble, you know, is that I never have my ideas until just after you have left and I am in my bath.' I think that's true. I have been there each day too early for him, while he was lying in bed and looking at the papers and hadn't really read them through. All he had got from me was some company but I might have been more useful to him if I had gone to see him an hour later when he was downstairs and through with reading the morning papers.

There was, however, one day when I might have changed his mind in quite an important way. It was the morning after the meeting in Slough at which a stink-bomb was flung in his eye, causing a slight injury. Walking across the Park that morning in beautiful weather it suddenly occurred to me that this was a tremendous chance. Why not keep him in bed on Thursday and Friday and make the press report that he was ill? This would create a sag in Labour morale and a sense of suspense in the whole press which would give his Saturday meeting in Manchester enormous psychological importance. When I got upstairs I put this all to him quite impressively; to which he characteristically replied, 'But suppose I don't go to Norwich today, how shall I spend the afternoon?' 'Well,' I said, 'you can govern the country.' He laughed. 'No, there are no boxes coming upstairs now in No. 10. There is no work for me. I should just sit about.' I laughed and said, 'You being you, Harold, that's something you can't do. If you really feel at a loose end this afternoon I can't stop you going to Norwich.' So off he went and made one of his best speeches.

Since the stink-bomb had grazed the white of his eye and he still had an appallingly heavy cold, he had every excuse to take a day off. But he just isn't that kind of man, nor does he calculate in that kind of a way. People think Harold a clever opportunist. But when you put to him the idea of a deliberate 24-hour withdrawal he remembers the people who will be waiting for him at Norwich and feels he can't let them down.

But if these breakfasts haven't influenced the campaign strategy they may possibly have influenced my future. On Wednesday Harold told me he had been discussing with George the possibility of his giving up the D.E.A. and becoming Deputy Prime Minister and First Secretary without Portfolio. Harold explained that George isn't a very good departmental Minister and the planning side of the D.E.A. has not been adequately developed. So it might be a good idea for somebody who isn't so personally inclined to plunge into every industrial dispute to take over direction of the prices and incomes policy. Apparently on the first occasion that this was discussed it was George who told Harold that he would like me to take his place. Now the latest is that he wants to stay where he is, but Harold has warned me that if the change does take place I must move from Housing to the D.E.A. But I have committed myself to reorganizing the Ministry and to building up the enormous central power which I hope the new federal Ministry will get, so it is disconcerting to find that all this may end. It would be promotion for me but to a far more exposed Ministry and it would mean giving up all the projects I have been working on for the past eighteen months.

One other thing that disconcerted me was the discovery that I was the last person in Whitehall to learn about my future. Weeks ago the Dame mentioned the rumour to me and I thought it was too silly to take cognizance of. Now when Harold told me I checked with Steve, who obviously thinks it is an excellent idea for him to settle into the Ministry without my presence.

Meanwhile, he is getting on with me pretty well. He has got two big jobs started. He is sorting out with Helsby the right division of function between the Ministry of Works and the Ministry of Housing. They have now agreed on quite a minor change which would leave the sponsorship of the whole construction industry to the Minister of Works. That's not what Harold intended and it is not what I should want if I stay in Housing. He's also been preparing for the Royal Commission on local government. He has seen John Maud and we have both seen Norman Chester. He prefers Maud and I, on balance, prefer Chester. I also notice that he is busy preparing his list of our members of the Commission. Here too he wants to have his way, and I know that he won't if I'm his Minister.

Apart from my talks with the Permanent Secretary very little else is on in the Ministry. But I have laid on a special investigation of the lamentable February housing figures. After five days' intensive work the Department came up with a paper so nonsensically vacuous that I refused to send it to the P.M. Now Balogh is investigating the whole set-up of housing estimates and considering ways in which we can enable ourselves to know the facts. We have also had the first meeting of the new strategy board that Steve has set up to deal with the methods of improving the local authorities' building efficiency, especially in industrialized building. Thank heavens Steve gets on with Peter Lederer.

I have also received a series of delegations, from Manchester and Coventry for example, on a new and immensely important issue. The fact is that under the Callaghan PESC policy of Treasury control we are throttling public-sector building development and thereby unwittingly facilitating the advance of the

private against the public sector. Already it is far easier for a private developer
to get a licence for redeveloping a town centre commercially than it is for a
local authority to get my permission to put up the shops themselves and so
get the profits from the property for the ratepayer. Coventry and Manchester
wanted to buy land in the centre and redevelop it as a public enterprise. But
under the PESC plan this would be increased public expenditure, which is
ruled out by the July agreement. One of the things I shall have to do if I am
still Minister of Housing after the election is to stage a battle royal against
the Chancellor and prevent this throttling down of public enterprise that
means it is hardly worth having a socialist Government.

Looking back at the election campaign I can't help feeling sorry that we
didn't have polling day last Thursday. If we had, we should have won a huge
majority because that, I reckon, was the peak of our popularity, before the
Tory attacks began to bite home. That is when people would have liked the
campaign to stop. They felt that it had gone on long enough and their growing
boredom was accentuated by the role television has played in this election.
This year both B.B.C. and I.T.V. are trying to show that they can present the
election issues better than the party political broadcasts which occur most
evenings. On every news programme, for example, you get election items—
two minutes of Wilson, two minutes of Heath, half a minute of Brown, half a
minute of Grimond. Every day on *24 Hours* you get a confrontation between
leading politicians. And in addition you have the special late-night programmes on the election put on by both commercial and public-service
television. The result has been that the election is impinging on the captive
listener day and night and boring him intensely. In the old days we thought
the party political broadcasts were the worst aspect of an election, but this
time I think they are some of the best items. If you want to get Party policy
across, you need party political broadcasts to contrast with television's own
treatment of the election, which concentrates so on personalities and leadership and gimmicks that the viewer gets a picture of bickering politicians and
no real understanding of the issues involved. And of course the newspapers
play up the same tendency in their election pages because they regard the
subject as so boring that it has to be spiced up with human interest and
politicians attacking each other.

Is this really a trivial election in which, as *The Times* and the *Mirror* have
been saying, the politician has been demeaning himself? In my view it has
been neither better nor worse than other elections. We have been trying as
usual to argue about rate and rent subsidies and, in the bigger world, about
what is wrong with the economy and how to put it right. We argue at length
on the public platform, but our arguments are presented to viewers as flashes
of a minute or two so that they only see us making a single point or answering
a heckler. It is this bitty TV treatment which gives the sense of a frivolous
election. One of the things we really ought to do when the campaign is over
is to reflect seriously on the role which television ought to play.

Labour returned to power, this time with a comfortable majority of 97 seats. The Government had 363 seats, the Conservatives 253 and the Liberals 12 (there was one Republican Labour victory and the other seat was the Speaker's). The poll, 75·8 per cent, was the lowest since 1945. This time, unlike in 1964, the issue of coloured immigration seemed to have had little effect on polling.

Though the Conservatives failed to gain a single seat and lost several distinguished former Ministers, notably Christopher Soames,[1] Julian Amery and Peter Thorneycroft, Mr Heath's conduct during the campaign had helped him to grow as a convincing leader.

Analysis of the results showed that Labour had lost some working-class votes but had attracted new middle-class support. The composition of the P.L.P. had changed, too. Of the 72 Labour M.P.s entering Parliament between 1965 and 1966, including the 1966 election, a far higher proportion had a university education and a professional background, compared with the 317 Labour M.P.s elected in 1964. The political and Parliamentary expectations of these vigorous newcomers were to give Mr Wilson some problems in the forthcoming Parliament.

Friday, April 1st

We got home at 3 a.m. Anne is still upstairs and I have given her breakfast in bed. I am in my study recording my impressions of the victory we have just scored. It has come out as I – and all the polls – anticipated. I predicted a majority of over 80 and that is what we are going to get. We have won Oxford and Cambridge, Sydney Silverman has not been defeated in Nelson and Colne despite the part he played in getting capital punishment abolished, Smethwick has been recaptured from the racialists, Gordon Walker has won at Leyton, and in Coventry we have also done pretty well. In Coventry South, which was marginal, Bill Wilson has more than doubled his majority. Maurice Edelman's majority is up to 8,000, mine up to 18,000, though the swing is concealed by the impact of the Liberal and the Communist candidates. My own campaign in Coventry East was kept down to the usual minimum. I was in the constituency for just over a week, from Thursday, March 24th, until the polls closed. That first afternoon I arrived in a blizzard and spent a couple of hours walking round Binley before two quite good meetings, one at the Bulls Head, Lower Stoke, and the other in the Golden Fleece in Longford. On Sunday I did only my traditional morning meeting outside the Wyken Pippin in a bitter, cold, driving wind. Otherwise, each day was devoted to walking the streets of a different ward and a couple of meetings

[1] Sir Christopher Soames had been M.P. for Bedford since 1950. He had held various offices, including those of Secretary of State for War (1958–60) and Minister of Agriculture (1960–64). From 1968 to 1970 he was Ambassador to France, and in 1970 he was appointed one of Britain's first Commissioners of the E.E.C.

in the evening, and Winnie Lakin didn't press us too hard. An hour and a half with the loudspeaker doing random street work every morning, a factory gate meeting at lunch-time and an hour and a half in the afternoon before the evening meetings. Of course, there has been a minimal organization in order to fold and address my election address and to distribute an illustrated leaflet at the beginning of the campaign and an election broadsheet at the end. But that's all.

On election day itself we let most of our keen Party workers go off to the marginals—to help Bill Price in Rugby[1] and Bill Wilson in Coventry South. In the constituency itself we have had virtually no committee rooms and all I did was motor round from polling station to polling station shaking hands with the council officials. As last time, I suddenly got an attack of nerves when I noticed the extraordinary quietness of the streets throughout the morning and afternoon, and observed that by seven o'clock less than half the people had voted. Yet when the polls closed our total poll in Coventry East was 77 per cent, exactly the same as last time. The 3 per cent less than the other two is probably the net effect of the complete absence of organization and knocking up. But it has made no real difference to my majority and it's pleased the workers in Rugby and Coventry South. Sitting in London I had had the impression that the campaign in the constituencies was not very real. During my week in Coventry East I have felt that it was more of a ritual than ever. Is that because I am getting old and detached and I haven't got enough energy flowing through my veins? Or is it correct that election organization today is increasingly unreal and that the public is sitting at home aloof and making up its mind without any regard to the antics of the politicians and the Party workers?

There was one point in the campaign where I began to get cold feet. That was on Sunday when I suddenly felt that the Tories were winning and people were turning against us. But then next day I went into an owner-occupier estate at Binley and my confidence was restored. I have never seen so many middle-class people in Coventry so anxious to vote for us and I'm sure this is one of the key factors in this election. The middle classes really want us to win—many of the owner-occupiers for the first time. Harold's personality has been a great help—middle class, not professional or upper class. He sees this himself. When I reported the situation on the housing estates, he said, 'Yes, they think they've got a P.M. like them.' They recognize in him a man of their own kind whom they are proud to have at No. 10; they feel they have a competent Government and will vote for it.

That is what we won on: Harold's personality and the feeling that we, a Labour Government, have been active and have helped ordinary people, and that we should be given a fair chance to show what we can do. To some extent the ineffectiveness of the Opposition, and the impression it gave of being

[1] M.P. for Rugby since 1966. P.P.S. to the Secretary of State for Education and Science 1968–70, and to Ted Short, the Deputy Leader of the Labour Party, since 1972.

divided and not really standing for anything, was a positive assistance to us. I notice all the papers have the usual build-up of the heroic leader so that, just as Gaitskell was the hero of the 1959 election, Heath may well be made the hero this time. My own view is that he fought the election unskilfully — not nearly so well as Gaitskell fought in 1959 under similar circumstances. He started with far too much bang and sprayed his bullets all over the target without any real discrimination. Also, he remained right to the end a curiously synthetic character and I doubt whether he added to his popularity during the campaign. By the way, I don't think Harold did either — though on the other hand his position was already immensely strong. Millions of lower-middle-class people voted Labour because he was someone of their class, someone to their taste, someone they had confidence in, leading the nation and acting like a statesman. Moreover, economically they felt all right. Wages have gone up faster than prices, they are prosperous, they have full employment. There is absolutely no reason why they shouldn't give us a second chance because the disaster which was hanging over us has been fended off.

This was the background issue throughout the campaign — the fight against inflation and devaluation. Heath desperately tried to warn people. He went on saying that we were going bankrupt; but of course this was completely ineffective with an electorate who felt that on this score — the responsibility for our difficulties — honours were pretty even, if not tipped against the Tories. Looking back, I see that timing was everything. If we had carried on without the election in March and gone right forward to the municipals in April and May we would have had a disastrous defeat. With rates going up and rents going up, our candidates would have been swept away. We would have had a thousand losses this year, like last year, and then there would have been no chance of going to the country in May or June. The election would have been pushed off until October and by then we might have had the most appalling crisis blowing up. So when people regard this as an *inevitable* victory, that's a very superficial judgment. It was only inevitable at this particular time, in this particular month of the year 1966. Suddenly we have got a majority of 100 and that gives a chance of stability, but heaven knows it was a very near thing. It was quite possible for Harold to have made a different decision and lost his chance in March. As it was we have given the electorate time to get to like our style and see how active we were. But they haven't had enough time to see our actions put into effect and recognize them as failures. From now on we shall never again be able to look back at the Tory thirteen years and contrast them with our eighteen months.

Sunday, April 3rd

This has been the most restful, inactive period of my life since I was made a Minister eighteen months ago. From the moment the election was announced the Ministry work began to dry up and since our victory on Friday I have had absolutely nothing to do. After I had heard the first results I went up to

16*

London with the idea of going to the Ministry and getting things moving again. However, when I got to Paddington I thought I would call round at Transport House. I got there just too late, Harold had gone off to Downing Street. But I ran into George Brown, who was looking deeply depressed because his majority had been cut in half—one of the few Ministers to suffer this ignominy. I went in and saw Sara Barker and Len Williams and Ray Gunter, and then I had to go on because I had asked my Permanent Secretary to lunch. Looking back now I see that I made a simple mistake, the kind of mistake I am capable of in my innocence. Friday was not a day to be in one's Ministry. It was the day to be in Transport House listening to the rest of the election results, hobnobbing with colleagues and using what influence there was to be used on Harold in his period of gestation. But it didn't happen and there I was in the Ministry where nothing was doing.

I took Steve out to lunch and we had a long talk about the Department. I complained bitterly that people like Crocker hate my guts, and whether I was right or not I talked very excitedly. Stevenson quieted and soothed me and talked about 'we' all the time. But more and more strongly I got the impression that he will be greatly relieved if I am moved to the D.E.A. and that that is what he and Helsby want. They want to see me moved from Housing to somewhere where my energies can be released for another eighteen months or so before I am moved elsewhere. Their view is that I don't handle civil servants well; I am far too rough with them, scare them stiff, make hasty judgments and very often scrawl rude things on paper which upsets them, especially when I haven't read the file carefully enough before scrawling. This was all put to me with considerable skill by Steve. I shall be in some difficulty settling down again if I have to stay on at Housing, as I rather think I will. Moreover, it is bound to be a new kind of life in this Department. We've done all the exciting new things, now everything depends on administrative drive and follow-through. I am always accused of being able to initiate but not to administer and there is some evidence that this is true. But I don't see myself moving to any other Department—the more I think about it, the more unlikely is it that George Brown will be willing to give up D.E.A., particularly after his election setback. But we'll have to see; until Harold makes up his mind my position is futile. I have received a note from the P.M.'s secretary which tells me I must carry on with routine business and await the Cabinet reconstruction. Of course, this has had a tremendous effect in Whitehall. John Delafons tells me that the Secretary did a little bit of hedging in preparation for the possibility of a Conservative victory during the last ten days of the campaign. I can well imagine it. But now it is over, he is preparing for the possibility of a new Minister, and meanwhile he and Helsby have been busy cutting down the takeover from the Ministry of Works to which we are committed in the manifesto.

The one thing I was allowed to do in the Department on Friday was to get on with the job of preparing for the Royal Commission on local government.

Here Steve has been busy bringing a little method into what he regards as the madness which the Dame and I have had for eighteen months as Minister and Permanent Secretary. On the whole his efficiency has been quite useful. He wants to see business and the T.U.C. represented and has made out lists of possibles. He has also made it clear that he wants to have John Maud not Norman Chester, and we have arranged that I should go up to London at 10.30 tomorrow and get John Maud and try and persuade him. John Maud is certainly a better name and will be more respectable and easier to get across. Moreover, if I am not going to be at the Ministry in two and a half years' time when the report is produced and Steve is, it's only fair for him to have the person he wants. But I wouldn't have any great hopes for a really radical report from John Maud. For that I would prefer Chester.

One other thing I did on Friday was to get in Peter Brown and begin to organize a big press conference on housing policy. Now the election is over I really must start getting houses built. I am not anxious any longer about the public sector, where the new subsidies are bound to work. I am profoundly anxious about the private sector and I must start with a bang and get things moving by launching properly the option guarantee for mortgages.

I came home on Friday with an enormous sense of anticlimax. It was as though I were in a deep trough between the waves. We won the campaign and now we are waiting. In this period one really does feel the meaning of Prime Ministerial government. Now everything depends on Harold Wilson and he has decided to have the weekend and then on Sunday night to start his discussions with George Brown about the new Cabinet. Of course, once our jobs have been reallocated we shall settle down and it will be more difficult to shake us out of them. But at this moment every single one of us is potentially movable or removable altogether. This weekend one does feel that the Prime Minister is the centre of power. I wrote in my Introduction to *The English Constitution* that the Prime Minister shares his power with the head of the Civil Service. Certainly, Helsby doesn't play that kind of role. It's Burke Trend who shares power with Harold, not the head of the Treasury. Nevertheless, this weekend it is Harold who is taking all the decisions. I talked it over yesterday with George Wigg on the phone. He told me that he wasn't going near the boss because he didn't want to seem to be pressing himself on the P.M. at this particular time. I have had the same feeling. Actually, I have not seen Harold since I left him after breakfast on the Thursday morning a week before the election and it's now ten days since I have spoken to him.

So on this Sunday I have plenty of time to reflect about our Prime Minister and ask myself what he will do with his majority of 97 now he has got it.

The first thing he's got to face is the problem of the Callaghan/Brown conflict which was with us all the way through the last Government – the struggle between the old Treasury and the new D.E.A., between the deflationists on the one side and the planners and interventionists on the other. As long as

Callaghan stays at the Treasury there will be deflation. The only way to prevent deflation is of course devaluation, which Wilson irrevocably opposes. So if he leaves things as they are, it looks as though we shall be driven into deflation and into a wage freeze at the same time. I know that some of the time Harold Wilson doesn't want this; that is why he has been talking to me about my going to the D.E.A. and running the planning and the prices and incomes policy. What he wants is to enable me to argue on equal terms with Callaghan, to stand out against his deflationism even if this ultimately means devaluation. I am sure that part of him would like to see this happen. And if George Brown allows it that is what will happen. So the only question is will George Brown allow it or will he insist on remaining in the D.E.A.? Tommy Balogh has an idea that George should be made First Secretary and Minister for all industry, taking over the modernization programme from Cousins. But from what the Prime Minister told me at my breakfasts, so far from forcing Cousins to resign he is likely to enlarge his Department for him.

Harold will see all this slightly differently. He will see reconstruction in terms of the size and balance of the Cabinet and he will be reluctant to cut out even the deadest deadwood. It is essential to remove Fred Lee, Arthur Bottomley and Tony Greenwood. But whenever I say this to him he says that they are reliable votes on the Common Market issue. Yet if he doesn't drop them, there won't be any room to promote ability. I know he would like to give Dick Marsh a job and I should like to see him promote Judith Hart — though there isn't a great galaxy of Parliamentary Secretary talent waiting for promotion. Indeed, it isn't the promotion of the young people which is the most important thing. What he most needs is to build up in Cabinet a hard inner group who will face the appalling problems of deflation and devaluation, think constructively about the Common Market, get to grips with modernization, keep the housing drive going. An inner strategy group is what he has got to form.

I've mentioned the Common Market but I don't think it's really as difficult a problem as devaluation. Harold is obsessed by the feeling that the Common Marketeers, led by Michael Stewart, Roy Jenkins and Tony Crosland, are ganging up against him. I think he exaggerates. I believe there will be far less difference in Cabinet about an approach to the Common Market; and he knows that on this issue he has in me a person who takes exactly the same line as himself. Yes to entry, but only on the right terms.

But of course the biggest issue he has to face is how to handle the Parliamentary Party. Now that we have got a majority of 97, a completely new situation arises. We Ministers will have a far more difficult time in handling the backbenchers now that they are liberated from the constraints of a tiny majority. All those Labour M.P.s who gritted their teeth and just voted with their feet and weren't allowed to speak or influence anything will be seething with life and vitality and energy and a desire to take an active part in policy-making. On all the great issues we have to resolve we shall have to carry the

Parliamentary Party with us far more intimately than ever before and that requires an entirely different style of Party management.

Moreover, the problem will be accentuated by the new intake—overwhelmingly middle class. Looking at the *Sunday Times* sample last Sunday I noticed that of fifty new Labour M.P.s only four or five are genuine trade-unionists; the rest are lawyers, scientists, teachers in technical colleges—overwhelmingly intellectuals. And they of course are the most difficult to handle in Parliament—much less reliable than the trade-unionists—and they will increase the ferment of ideas. A party of this kind can't be led into battle under the old-fashioned, military discipline of Bowden and Short. If he leaves them in charge, Harold is in for appalling trouble. But then who can he put in charge? The obvious thing would be to relieve Callaghan of the Chancellorship, replacing him with Jenkins. Callaghan as a parliamentary leader could be the Herbert Morrison of this Government. I have put this to Harold three or four times and on each occasion he has said, 'Jim is a dangerous rival. I couldn't put him there.' But he certainly does realize the need for a new kind of parliamentary leadership—it is no longer a question of merely giving orders, adding up the score of the division records and punishing those who do badly. What we need now is to organize constructive criticism on the back benches and get our back-benchers participating in policy-making with the leadership.

If Harold doesn't do this and if he doesn't get his inner Cabinet formed, what Pam Berry said to me over lunch recently may well be true. She invited me to meet Kay Graham, now proprietor of the *Washington Post*, and I had a splendid time with them. Pam told me that Heath had been saying to her that the crisis will come next November and it is then that he hopes to see the fall of the Wilson Government. Certainly as leader of the Opposition he is right to take things that way, because unless Harold changes the structure of his Cabinet and toughens up his own personal leadership there is a very great chance that this tremendous victory will dissipate itself in a few months. Looking at it from inside I see more clearly than Heath how lucky we have been. Our victory was not due to the inner strength of the Labour Party or the Government but was the result of timing—the ability to choose the right moment. There was only this one month, March 1966, which gave us an opportunity to cash in. And even though we did cash in, we didn't have all that tremendous effect. It was only a 3·1 swing, and by God a 3·1 swing can become a 4·0 counter-swing very quickly indeed.

Mr Wilson announced twenty-five changes in the Government. Two Cabinet Ministers left altogether. James Griffiths, Secretary of State for Wales, resigned on grounds of age. Richard Marsh, a thirty-eight-year-old Under-Secretary, entered the Cabinet as Minister of Power, replacing Fred Lee, who moved to the Colonial Office. Ten non-Cabinet Ministers left the Government.

In his reshuffle Mr Wilson indicated the change in Labour's attitude to the

E.E.C. When Harold Macmillan had tried to take Britain into the E.E.C. in 1962, Hugh Gaitskell, then leader of the Opposition, had attacked this as a 'betrayal of a thousand years of history'. But the Government now spoke of the advantages of membership, and the Prime Minister appointed George Thomson as Chancellor of the Duchy of Lancaster, with specific responsibility for political relations with Europe. The First Secretary, George Brown, was given general oversight of Britain's economic relations with the E.E.C. He had long supported entry and set about convincing his Cabinet colleagues of the necessity and feasibility of doing so.

Mr Heath's reconstructed Shadow Cabinet also symbolized the changing character of his Party. Duncan Sandys, who had been a Minister since 1951, retired to the back benches. Selwyn Lloyd, the former Foreign Secretary and Chancellor, Ernest Marples and John Boyd-Carpenter were replaced. All the members of the Conservative front bench team, except for Sir Alec Douglas-Home and Quintin Hogg, had entered Parliament after the war and many of them only in 1950.

Monday, April 4th

I went to London mainly in order to see John Maud and make arrangements for the Royal Commission. At breakfast I heard the B.B.C. News and the announcement that Mr Wilson was going to make no big changes because continuity was the important thing for the Government. Though this had obviously been given to a Lobby conference and then rewritten for a B.B.C. announcer, I could recognize Harold Wilson's style.

John Maud was persuadable and spent most of the day in the Ministry working away. And he made one or two good suggestions. He saw the T.U.C. list and said how dreary it was and couldn't he have Vic Feather.[1] He also said he wanted someone from education. By the time he left a great deal of progress had been made. At least we had appointed the chairman of the Commission.

In the afternoon Alan Watkins of the *Spectator* came to ask me about the composition of the new Cabinet. What I had heard on the B.B.C. that morning made it easier for me to assure him that Harold is a non-changer and that the idea of getting a substitute for George Brown was out.

Finally, in the evening I took Pen and Tommy Balogh out to the Garrick. While we were sitting at dinner a telephone call came and I took it in the foyer with the red-coated doorman around. There was the Prime Minister at the other end saying, 'I want you to stay on at your job. You've got a big collection of politicians with you, and when Land and Natural Resources is merged with your Department, you will have Arthur Skeffington in addition to Fred Willey, your Minister of State.' 'Must I have Arthur as well?' I asked. 'Yes,'

[1] A Bradford Co-op employee who joined the T.U.C. staff in 1937, Vic Feather eventually became Assistant General Secretary of the T.U.C. in 1960, and General Secretary in 1969. He was made a life peer on his retirement in 1974.

he said. 'And by the way, it will require an Act of Parliament to allow your Department the extra Minister of State.' I said, 'I can't have Fred Willey as the only Minister of State. If he gets that status Bob Mellish must be Minister of State as well. If you are going to have a special Bill for it you can create me two instead of one.' 'Right,' he said. 'You can alert Bob to the chance,' and rang off.[1] I went back to my table and resumed my conversation. Soon the doorman was back: 'He's on again.' I went back to the phone. Harold's voice, 'I'd forgotten to tell you I want you to have Kennet as well.'[2] 'Kennet!' I said. 'But what for?' 'Instead of Dick Mitchison.'[3] 'But Dick Mitchison,' I said, 'is absolutely first-rate.' A rather dry voice replied, 'He's over sixty-eight, we want young blood. You must trade him in.' I said, 'Thank you very much.' And that was that.

Tuesday, April 5th
When the full list of changes came out this morning they were even more depressing than I expected. They were so niggling—and the niggliest is the one beside me as I sit in Cabinet. I used to have Fred Lee sitting on my left, an obviously inadequate Minister of Power. Now I still have Fred Lee sitting on my left, demoted from Power to Colonies. And that's the pattern. Tony Greenwood is thrown out of Colonies but retained in the Cabinet as Minister of Overseas Development. Frank Longford is demoted still lower but is back in the Cabinet as Lord Privy Seal. Jim Callaghan and George Brown are retained and are still at loggerheads, but all the press tells me, and I believe it, that the D.E.A. is going down and the Treasury up. That means that Callaghan's powers will greatly increase. We are going to have George Brown, along with George Thomson (our new Minister for Europe), concentrating on the Common Market; and as a result Callaghan will be freer to run his deflation policy, which I suppose is Harold's only alternative to the devaluation he so absolutely opposes. Deflation combined with a moderate degree of unemployment will I presume be our economic target. All this will be done over our heads while the budget is prepared in secret. Callaghan and Wilson are now in full cahoots, with George Brown in a weak position to oppose the deflation they both want. Apart from that, Denis Healey is still very much out on a limb—rather like me. Frank Cousins is strengthened in his position, with more powers. Supposedly more powers are coming to me but even here,

---

[1] But Bob Mellish remained a Parliamentary Secretary until he succeeded Reg Prentice as Minister of Public Building and Works in August 1967.

[2] Wayland Young, 2nd Baron Kennet, served as Parliamentary Secretary at M.H.L.G. 1966–70. He became chairman of the Advisory Committee on Oil Pollution of the Sea in 1970, and was chairman of the C.P.R.E. 1971–2. A writer, perhaps he is best known for *Eros Denied* (London: Weidenfeld & Nicolson, 1965) and as the author, with his wife Elizabeth Young, of books and articles on disarmament and arms control.

[3] Richard Mitchison Q.C. had recently celebrated his seventy-sixth birthday. He had been Labour M.P. for Kettering, Northants., from 1945 until 1964, when he was made a life peer. He had served since 1964 as Parliamentary Secretary at the Ministry of Land and Natural Resources. He was married to Naomi Mitchison, the author. He died in 1970.

as I hear on the Whitehall grapevine, nothing is really going to happen – at least not immediately. The liquidation of the Ministry of Land and Natural Resources won't take place straight away and the absorption of the relevant part of the Ministry of Works will be delayed.

In the afternoon I had a routine meeting with Steve and my senior staff. I was able to assure them I was still their Minister. Most of them, I suspect, had rather looked forward to a new Minister; but they settled down bravely to their job and we went through a vast agenda on which Delafons kept full notes. Just at this point Fred Peart came into my Private Office. He wanted to ask whether I would mind if the Ordnance Survey went back to the Ministry of Agriculture. It was something I had rather wanted for myself, since I like the idea of these maps getting done in my Department. But here was my friend Fred saying 'I was a geographer at university' and complaining that Ordnance Survey shouldn't be torn from its traditional position in the Ministry of Agriculture. And as I am an easy-going, good-natured person I said yes.

So that was that and I took the two Parliamentary Secretaries to lunch at the Athenaeum where we began to divide up our jobs. Bob Mellish will remain in charge of London housing and have all responsibility for New Towns, so that we make sure that the corporations take their complement of Londoners from the housing lists and from the London council houses. Then I shall create a new local government division, and make Arthur Skeffington responsible for local government and rates. That leaves Fred Willey and Jim MacColl dealing with planning and Kennet with me on the general side.

In the evening I took Patricia Llewelyn-Davies out to dinner. Her husband had flown off to British Guiana by way of New York and she was left alone at home. I wonder if she might not become a life peer. Patricia is a darling woman. One of the few people I feel really fond of in a deep sense. She remains beautiful, young and fresh. Alas, her life is a disaster now because her husband has been made the life peer although she is the *real* politician in the family. She should have been in Parliament, but first she had a baddish seat at Wolverhampton and then she moved to Wandsworth and lost it twice and gave it up. Since then Wolverhampton has been won and Wandsworth has been won and she is still left out. At forty-five that is a terrible thing. It would be wonderful if I could find her an active job. But what job? There's nothing in my Ministry, and anyway Richard's there already. What a jam it is. All that one can do is to be nice to her and enjoy her and her children.

Wednesday, April 6th
I spent most of the day on an official visit to Stevenage and took Bob Mellish with me to indicate that in future the corporation will have to play a much more political role, in direct relationship with the politicians. The U.D.C. was quite pleased because I had put two of their members on the corporation. As for the corporation, it was sitting under its new chairman, Mrs Dennington,

11 With his wife and two children, Virginia and Patrick, at Prescote, 1964.

12 and 13 On the farm at Prescote.

14   With Patrick, feeding the penguins at Crystal Palace.

15   At Prescote with Patrick and Virginia.

16   At Cropredy country fête with John Betjeman and Neil Marten, M.P. for Banbury.

whom I had appointed from the G.L.C. She raged at me over a new way of dividing up the Ministry's subsidy to New Towns, of which she had been informed but of which I was completely ignorant. Apparently my officials and the Treasury have been deciding things behind my back again.

Back in London I held the press conference which I had decided should be my first action as the old Minister of Housing in the new Labour Government. We decided on this in the last week of the election and Peter Brown had prepared for it very carefully indeed. I started with the announcement that local-authority mortgage lending would be resumed. Then I turned to the February council-housing figures and gave the press an explanation of the deplorable facts and then some new information about our mortgage plan. After this I went into the other room and did a piece for B.B.C. television on mortgages and a special Northern piece announcing my decision on Sheffield local government boundaries.

Thursday, April 7th
A glance at the papers and I knew that Peter Brown had scored another of his tremendous successes. He knows exactly when to call a press conference, how to brief the press and how to make it a success. We managed to get a front-page story in the *Mail* and the *Telegraph*, under the headline HOME LOANS RESUMED, and a good story in *The Times* and the *Guardian*. Only the *Daily Express* did a major story on the headline CROSSMAN SHOCK – FALLING HOUSING FIGURES. In terms of news value the *Express* was quite right. It was legitimate for a Tory paper to say that the February figures were deplorable. And they could all have led with the fact that the Minister of Housing had suppressed the February figures during the election and was still trying to cover the facts up. But, apart from the *Express*, they didn't. They accepted from us what I call the establishment story: the official line put out by me and by Peter Brown was printed practically intact on their front pages. When Steve saw the press he was astonished. 'What is all this news?' he said to me. He didn't know that a Department can, with a good Press Officer, make the news it wants. At least that press conference was a sign that Peter and I haven't lost our cunning in this particular respect.

At Cabinet this morning there was a strained atmosphere. Harold started by thanking George Brown for his election tour and Jim Callaghan for his magnificent work at the daily press conferences. Then he said that this being Holy Week, we should perhaps have a little compassion for our opponents. If I had said, 'This being Holy Week, we ought to feel compassion for our enemies,' it would obviously have been a piece of atheistic irony. But when Harold, who claims to be a Methodist, says it, it only increases the puzzle of our Prime Minister.

Next, legislation. The Lord President made it clear that this would be a long session and that we would run right through for eighteen months. Then came a lengthy argument about priorities. Jim Callaghan chipped in straight away to say that we should give leasehold enfranchisement top priority and put the Land Commission second.

He has already tried to do this in the Legislation Committee and been defeated. It is extraordinary how our high-minded Chancellor of the Exchequer becomes just a Cardiff constituency Member when leasehold enfranchisement, which is a vital local problem to him, comes up. I insisted that we must get the Land Commission through first, and had my way though the pressure was extremely strong. I then pointed out that with the accession of Fred Willey and Arthur Skeffington to my Ministry in February I could at once set up a working party to get on with leasehold enfranchisement but we shouldn't expect it before the end of the long session.

It soon became clear that if leasehold enfranchisement was to be in the Queen's Speech something big would have to be omitted. At this point Harold said suddenly, 'Well, should steel be dropped?' There was an awkward silence and then Jim said that he felt steel might be moved back to the second session. Then there was another awkward silence and George Brown said, 'If we are having second thoughts on steel and re-negotiating with the manufacturers, of course it would be a good thing to postpone it.' I then said, 'Well, are we going to have those second thoughts, or is this the best Bill we have got?' To which Fred Lee, who by now was the ex-Minister for steel, observed that the Bill had been run up very quickly and we might now be able to do a better job. It looked as though a well-organized postponement lobby was going to get its way, when Dick Marsh came in with his first intervention as a Cabinet Minister. He clearly intends to be vigorous, young and dynamic. He told the Cabinet bluntly that he was going to push his Steel Bill through in the first session and at once the notion of postponement faded away.

That was another example of Harold Wilson's devious leadership. He raised the issue of postponement himself.[1] He got Jim to commit himself to it and then George Brown to half commit himself. But the moment Marsh intervened and the Cabinet swung the other way Harold closed up like an oyster. I was amused later that morning to pick up the *Daily Mail* and see he had given an exclusive interview in which he stated that the Steel Bill would be fundamentally the same as the White Paper. So he had made up his own mind but was wanting the Cabinet to defeat the postponement lobby.

But there was more to come. The legislative programme was still far too big and a tremendous effort was made to get Douglas Jay to drop one of his Bills. Poor man! Within minutes we were all agreeing that his Companies Bill was a third-rate departmental measure. Then somebody near Douglas Jay said, 'Why not drop the ombudsman Bill this session?' At this point the Prime Minister chipped in quickly. 'That would be very awkward for me. Some people here will appreciate', he said, looking at me, 'that the future of some very high civil servants depends on getting the ombudsman Bill on the

[1] But wrote later: 'I was a little surprised to be met with an attempt by a number of Senior Ministers to draw back and seek a compromise with the industry.' *Wilson*, p. 222.

Statute Book as soon as possible.' I knew very well what he was talking about. Having failed to get me to accept Bruce Fraser as my Permanent Secretary, Harold had cooked up the idea that he should become Comptroller-General in place of Compton, who should be made the first Ombudsman. Any delay in the legislation would bitch the idea. Interesting that a Prime Minister in considering our legislative strategy should be mainly preoccupied with the convenience of one of the Permanent Secretaries, or as Harold would put it, the relationships between the Government and the higher Civil Service.

Cabinet drooled on till 12.15. Then we were thrown out because the Defence Committee was there, waiting outside the door with George Wigg. As I walked out I became more and more aware of how fictitious Cabinet government really is. The big issue to be decided concerned, of course, Rhodesia and the action to be taken about the tankers which were breaking the blockade by coming through the Mozambique Channel. So at this point the Cabinet is sent out of the room and the Chiefs of Staff come in. It's the Defence Committee who manage Rhodesia. But at least that consists of half the Cabinet whereas the committee which is secretly preparing the budget consists of only Harold, George and Jim. So the two main decisions to be taken in defence and finance are lifted entirely out of the hands of the Cabinet. The rest of us are totally excluded. Am I totally excluded or is it my own fault? I must admit that as I look forward to our week's holiday in the Lake District with Tommy Balogh I feel a sense of anticlimax, or boredom with the idea of just carrying on as a departmental Minister. I have had enough of it and now I want to be a Cabinet Minister. That may mean trouble for me and also probably trouble for the Cabinet.

Monday, April 18th

I've had a lovely relaxing few days with the family at Loweswater, visiting Tommy and Pen Balogh. I spent a whole day at Ullswater with Pen, seeing what a marvellous job we have done—making sure that Manchester gets its water without too much loss to the countryside. Ullswater seems perfectly satisfactory. But Teesdale will be a different problem.

Tommy and I talked about the routine of being a Cabinet Minister. I fear that I am losing the elan that I felt at first. That may mean trouble when I return and try to put some drive into what seems more and more to be a fictitious Cabinet, where none of the real issues are discussed.

The Parliamentary Party met today at twelve o'clock for the purpose of re-electing Harold Wilson and George Brown as leader and deputy leader with seats on the N.E.C. The meeting took place in the rather carbolic atmosphere of Church House. It certainly wasn't the jubilant, thrilling occasion the Beaver Hall meeting in 1945, or even the October 1964 meeting, had been. No, there was a curious air of expectations fulfilled, which was a little disconcerting. What I noticed mainly was the treacly atmosphere of mutual self-praise in the speeches of George and James and Ray Gunter, and also the rather sinister lack of participation by the new Parliamentary Party. When the speakers talked about the new age and the great new Labour Government they were received with acquiescence at best. Indeed I felt – perhaps reading a little of my own mood into the new Members – that they weren't really any more stirred than I was. Why? Why was this election forgotten the moment it was over? Why no sense of a great leap forward? Because this was not a normal general election. All it has meant is that by shrewd timing the Wilson Government has won an increased majority and five more years. And that's why there is no sense of novelty, no excitement. We will produce the same Bills all over again. The only unknown factor is the quality of the new Members and the attitude they will have to a Government which is certainly nothing new.

Tam Dalyell, who has been around the tea-room, told me that evening that it was his impression that the Party was very disappointed by the amount of dead wood left in the Cabinet and by the fulsome formalities at Church House. So there we are, the members of the Government, just clocking in again this morning, clicking into our own places, getting down to our old routines, feeling things are very much the same as before. And there is the Party in an uneasy, expectant mood, waiting and watching.

Back at my Ministry my first job was an inquest into an appalling gaffe about Bracknell New Town. When I visited it in July I found it a very attractive, cosy little corner; but its corporation had no sense of responsibility for the London intake, and certainly what has been done doesn't justify its having a New Town status. Now during the election Bob Mellish discovered something much worse. The largest factory in the town is the Sperry Gyroscope Company's factory. Bob was told that they intend to move the whole factory from Bracknell to Brentford even though this means all the Bracknell people commuting to Brentford. It would be a deadly blow to the New Town. The news in itself was bad enough. The sinister thing was that the chairman of the corporation knew nothing about the company's intention although the Board of Trade had been informed and the local M.P.s consulted. As the inquest went on I became more and more convinced that the whole administration of the New Towns under J. D. Jones and our new woman, Miss Hope-Wallace, is wrong. Maybe Steve will help me to transfer New Towns from the planning to the housing side of the Department.

In the afternoon I had an urgent message that Donald Gould of the Building Societies Federation just had to see me. I had previously arranged that Potter of the Halifax should come to Vincent Square at 9.30 p.m., the only time we could both make it, so I asked Gould to dine with me at the Garrick first. Back in Vincent Square we sat and discussed things for hours. They were both friendly and helpful, as they always are to my face. But they made it perfectly clear that the annuity scheme[1] which the Dame and Brain

[1] See pp. 473–4.

had pulled out of the hat at the last moment just won't do. What I managed to extract from them was an idea of the things they really objected to and the kind of option-mortgage scheme they might be induced to swallow. It was obvious that they would put forward their own scheme as an alternative and only after I had turned it down could I hope to persuade them to swallow mine. My only difficulty is that I haven't got a very resolute Chancellor of the Exchequer backing me up.

Tuesday, April 19th

An awkward scene at Legislation Committee this morning about the Building Control Bill.[1] Both Reg Prentice (Charlie Pannell's successor at Public Building and Works) and I were there, neither of us knowing whether he would take the Bill because the Prime Minister has not yet decided the new relations between Housing and Public Works. At the end of this formal meeting I had a quiet talk with Prentice. I told him that if Harold really wants to make the big decision and turn my Ministry into the sponsor of the whole construction industry then I would demand a total takeover including licensing and building research. But if he isn't prepared to do that, I want minimum change. Nothing except housing statistics, historic buildings and the N.B.A. It only took us ten minutes to come to a rough agreement, and I said to Prentice, 'I will be seeing the P.M. this evening. When do you see him?' 'I'm not sure,' said the new Minister. 'I have put in a paper and he said he would see me later.'

I saw Harold late in the afternoon for ten minutes and got the whole thing fixed. He had his new number two, Michael Halls, an old friend from the Board of Trade*—quite a know-all who intervened in the conversation more than Derek Mitchell ever used to do. He was on my side and quite helpful. I started by saying that there was a choice between giving me a lot and a little and he said, 'Well, I thought at first you ought to have a lot but now I wonder whether it shouldn't be a little.' So I said, 'If it's a little, it ought to be very little,' and listed my requirements, to which he readily agreed. Having established this we can get the Order in Council prepared rapidly both for Works and for the Ministry of Land and Natural Resources; and that will help me in speeding up Fred Willey's transfer.

I had taken the precaution of bringing the March housing figures, an improvement on February but not as good as we expected. We must budget for only 210,000 starts in the private sector this year against the 250,000 predicted last summer. I told Harold that I must now put into operation the demand I made last July, and insist on taking up the slack by getting an extra 10,000 houses started in the public sector. He asked me to circulate a minute and assured me it would be put on the Cabinet agenda as soon as possible.

* He was a great success since he proved a real companion to the P.M. as well as an utterly loyal subordinate. He died suddenly in April 1970, and Sandy Isserlis took his place.
[1] The Bill was introduced by Reg Prentice on April 2nd, and given its Second Reading on May 2nd. It received the Royal Assent on August 9th, 1966.

Wednesday, April 20th

Cabinet. A very important discussion on parliamentary reform. One of the first things Harold did after the election was to minute the Lord President that in this Parliament it was essential to make a start with modernizing parliamentary institutions, and part of that start should be an experiment in 'specialist committees'.[1] Of course, for many years George Wigg and I have been lobbying for specialist committees on defence and on foreign affairs as well as on home departments; and fortunately it is one of the things which our new Members immediately demanded, to give them something to do. I am convinced it would be jolly good for Departments, which are virtually free from parliamentary criticism as Question Time is so ineffective. So I was delighted by the Prime Minister's surprisingly vigorous minute and so was Roy Jenkins, whose view coincides with mine. However, it was watered down by the Lord President who presented to the Cabinet Committee last Monday a disastrously reactionary paper, backed by the Treasury and the Scottish Department. Bert Bowden proposed that instead of specialist committees investigating Departments, they should have subjects allocated to them, such as Sunday observance or drunken driving. It is reckoned that such committees would be harmless whereas departmental committees, in the words of Niall MacDermot, who read aloud the Treasury brief at the Cabinet Committee, 'could well become lobbyists for further expenditure'. A typical Treasury reaction to a piece of parliamentary reform. In fact the reformers had a very bad time at the Committee, chaired as usual by Bert Bowden. But when he put up the majority's recommendations to Cabinet he was immediately swept aside by the Prime Minister who insisted that departmental specialist committees should be established as well. What clinched it was that three departmental Ministers, Roy and I and Tony Crosland, all individually testified that such committees could provide an astringent stimulus to our Departments by ventilating issues and exploring corners which had been covered up in the past. Dick Marsh, our bright new young Minister, was, however, blankly against it; and so was Fred Peart who obviously had listened to his powerful Permanent Secretary. However, Harold's leadership was a tonic. At last he acted strongly, and the moment he did so he got his way.

I had to rush off to Crawley New Town and so missed hearing what happened to poor Douglas Jay when he tried to get his Companies Bill reinstated in the legislative programme. But I had twice postponed my official visit, and although it rained the whole day I couldn't cancel it again. Once more I came back boiling with anger. Crawley is a New Town whose expansion has been wound up because it is said to be completed and it is now under the New Towns Commission managed by Henry Wells.[2] Yet the U.D.C. had got me

---

[1] Small committees of M.P.s taking evidence and examining witnesses on the administration of a particular department or area of legislation.

[2] Chairman of the New Towns Commission 1964–70 and chairman of the Land Commission 1967–70.

down there to tell me that they could accept another 20,000 or 30,000 Londoners on the housing list. Employers in Crawley are prepared to train unskilled labour in order to keep their factories manned yet the town's housing plans have been cut back by my miserable Department. This is something for Bob Mellish to attend to.

I had to cut short the Crawley visit to get back for the crucial Cabinet Committee on Ullswater and Teesside—both appallingly controversial. I have mentioned my problems in Ullswater already.[1] During the week we stayed with the Baloghs at Loweswater I had persuaded Pen, who is a great 'Lakeswoman', to spend a whole day at Ullswater with me. Very secretly we also got the Inspector who had drafted the report, and I convinced myself that the proposition we have put up is a really marvellous one: it makes sure that Manchester gets the water but actually improves the amenities at Ullswater and Haweswater. By insisting on purification plants well below the river we can make sure that in future the lakes which are used as reservoirs don't have to be fenced round like Thirlmere or kept very clean, so that people can boat or swim there. There is no loss of amenity whatsoever in our plan and we are actually liberating Haweswater from the present mass of restrictions. Before the election I had taken it to the Cabinet Committee and found that not only the Chief Whip was liable to cause trouble but also Fred Peart, who is Member for Workington and therefore for the Lake District. And since Harold's father-in-law was a Methodist Minister somewhere near Ullswater I expect I will get difficulties from Mary. At this post-election Cabinet Committee the opposition was still very bloody-minded and even Roy Jenkins was doubtful and unhappy, but I just had to get my way because we can't go on delaying the supply of Manchester's water and I really have done such a good job that the amenity societies will be on my side. I just got it past and I hope to goodness that it won't go to Cabinet. It oughtn't to, because I got a majority of one in the Committee and once a Committee has made a recommendation it doesn't go to Cabinet unless somebody deliberately asks for it and the Prime Minister consents. But I am still wondering if the Chief Whip will go to Harold in the hope that there is a chance of reversing the decision in Cabinet.

All that took over an hour and a half. We then got to my second major water problem, at Teesdale where we need a new reservoir high up in the mountains. There are serious objections on the ground that rare mosses which grow only where the reservoir is to go will be destroyed.[2] The case was objectively far more difficult to defend but I got it through in twenty minutes.

Since I was dining at the Guildhall that evening I had to change before rushing round to No. 10 for the formal pre-Session party at which the P.M. reads aloud the Queen's Speech to the assembled members of the Government. From there on to the Guildhall, where I had never dined before; I

[1] See p. 405.
[2] See p. 499.

found five hundred people sitting down to the first annual dinner of the chief officers of all the London boroughs. By no means a top-ranking engagement and yet Jim MacColl, Bob Mellish and I had all accepted invitations. Even worse, I was the guest of honour and due to make the main speech, of which I had not been forewarned. I was in a bad temper since I couldn't eat or drink very much before the speech. However, it didn't go too badly and I got into bed pretty tired after a full day.

Most of the measures announced in the Queen's Speech on April 21st were carried over from the previous Parliament. The Government also wished to press on with legislation to extend public control of the docks and over private building; to develop comprehensive secondary education and to introduce its new superannuation scheme, to be administered by a new Ministry of Social Security.

But this time, unlike 1964 or 1965, the Queen's Speech from the Throne explicitly mentioned the E.E.C. The Government announced that, provided that essential British and Commonwealth interests were safeguarded, they would be prepared to take Britain into the Community.

Thursday, April 21st
State Opening of Parliament. Anne brought up the children and our housekeeper, Mrs Marriott, largely because Steve had allowed us to use the Permanent Secretary's room at the Ministry, which has windows facing on to both Parliament Square and Whitehall. All the week there has been terrible weather — driving rain and storms of snow — but by some miracle the Queen got a fine, sunny morning for the state drive and the children quite liked seeing the procession. But they didn't really like it as much as we did. What excited them much more was the drive with Molly beforehand down the Mall with the soldiers on both sides and nobody else allowed to drive. They also liked a good lunch in the House of Commons.

I went into the Chamber to hear the Prime Minister, who spoke for an hour and a half. Funnily enough, however, the longer he went on the better he got, particularly during a long altercation with Heath. I went out before he had finished to keep an appointment with my Permanent Secretary. He had already infuriated me that morning when Dan Smith came to my office and accepted an invitation to serve on the Royal Commission. After he had left the room Steve said to me, 'That leaves the ninth place unfilled. The one you wanted to reserve for an educationalist. I've got the right man, the chairman of the Education Committee of Wallasey.' As it was a Tory borough I said to him at once, 'Now look, don't be silly, that's impossible.' He replied that it was all fixed and I was forced to say that I could not persuade my five Cabinet colleagues from the North-West that there wasn't a single Labour chairman of an education committee fit to serve on this Commission. But there was worse to come. As I was about to go across to the House he asked me whether I wouldn't just formally sign the Ministry's paper on the legislative programme for the next three years. 'It's an automatic thing, Minister,' he assured me. 'I've just been tidying it up for you.' I replied testily that it couldn't be a mere formality and that I had already told him twice that we must sit down to some serious policy discussion about a three-year programme for housing, local finance, planning and so on. 'It is no good telling me that a three-year legislative programme to which we commit ourselves on paper doesn't matter. I want a really good job done.' 'Sorry,' he said, 'it's got to be in by Friday morning.' This made me see red. 'And you dare to present it to me on Thursday morning?' But then I suddenly realized that he has got used to working like this with his Ministers. When he had Fred Lee at the Ministry of Power he would finalize a whole job with his staff and present the finished package to the Minister. So instead of being angry I reasoned with him. 'It would save you a lot of time, Steve,' I said, 'if you would come to me early on in a project and sit down with me and have half an hour's talk to find out what my ideas are. Then when you've discussed it informally with me, you and your officials can try it out in a draft scheme. But a three-year legislative programme is something which you can't push through without serious Ministerial participation. I am going to call a meeting of all our five politicians and get their views; and after that I will meet the staff again.' He looks pained when I say these things, but how else can I treat him in order to prevent him simply taking over his Minister? He is an obstinate man but I think he is also weak.

That evening I listened to a wonderful performance of *Rosenkavalier* at Covent Garden. Claus Moser[1] and his wife had invited me to go with them to the Royal Box and afterwards we had supper with the Marschallin and with Octavian.[2] It was the kind of evening I revel in. At the end of it I said to Claus, 'I don't want to sit in the House of Lords but I will resign my Ministry and my seat in the Commons at any time if Harold will give me this one perk, a directorship of Covent Garden which gives me the right to see an opera two or three nights every week.'

Friday, April 22nd
Again an official visit, this time to Ipswich. It has been selected, along with Northampton and Peterborough, for our experiment in doubling the size of old towns by the New Town Corporation technique. So long as the Dame was there she had kept these negotiations entirely in her own hands. I was not in the least surprised to discover that the Ipswich councillors — 25 Labour, 26 Tory and 4 Liberal, and, as East Anglians, cautious, slow and a bit dull — are by no means sold on the New Town idea. Indeed, some of them quite intelligently feel that they prefer to increase up to 50,000 by their own

[1] Professor of Social Statistics at L.S.E., he became director of the Central Statistical Office in 1967. He was a director of the Royal Opera House, and in 1973 succeeded Lord Drogheda as chairman of the Board of Directors.
[2] Sena Jurinac had sung the part of the Marschallin and Josephine Veasey that of Octavian.

town development rather than aim at 80,000 and have a New Town Corporation imposed upon them. New Towns are part of our housing programme, I thought as I went back to London. They must be put under a single administration.

Sunday, April 24th

So that was the first week of this new Parliament, and this is the Minister of Housing back in his same old job. Storm clouds are looming ahead. I am already in great difficulties with the building societies and shall have my work cut out to get them to accept my option scheme. In the last resort I shall have to impose it on them. I am also going to have a tremendous fight in Cabinet before I can force the Chancellor to let me have those extra 10,000 council houses. What I now foresee is continually increasing Treasury pressure on the public sector. Without consulting me Callaghan has decided to enormously curtail the local authorities' borrowing rights through a Public Works Loan Board. He also intends to remove the differential interest rates which bring them enormous benefits. This is all part of the anti-local-authority, anti-public-sector bias I can now expect from our Labour Chancellor. And in fighting it I shan't get as much help from George Brown or even from Harold Wilson as I used to. They are being driven to accept his point of view. I shall have to consider whether I shouldn't make some new alliances with other public-sector people like Barbara Castle and Kenneth Robinson.

Monday, April 25th

I went to see the Chancellor today about the Public Works Loan Board. I had written him a very strong letter challenging his failure to consult me before he cut back the advances available to my local authorities. There was no budget secrecy about the affair and he had put me in a terrible jam. When he half-apologized for this I pressed him and said, 'At least there must be no question of ending the differential interest rates to local authorities, as I hear you propose to do in the next twelve months. Can I have an assurance?' Well I got a kind of assurance that he wouldn't alter the differential rates except as part of a bigger change to create a new financial organization covering nationalized industries as well. That seems slightly sinister but quite sensible to me.

Then we talked about council houses. I had sent him my draft Cabinet paper demanding the 10,000 extra. He asked me to take 3,500 and in good humour, because I had checked with our housing officials, I did so.*

Tuesday, April 26th

I was sitting by Harold Wilson on the front bench when he told me that George Brown was ill in hospital and he wanted me to take his place in the

---

* I had to withdraw this agreement after the budget, since S.E.T. would discourage private builders and make the need for council houses far greater. So I banged my paper in again on the day of the budget.

last day of the debate on the Queen's Speech. This is regarded as a big occasion – the day when the Opposition moves its vote of censure. On Thursday it was to be moved by Macleod and answered by me. I didn't feel inclined to play because I would have to talk about steel and the economic situation and I felt very incapable. But there was no choice. Harold said, 'You're one of the people we have to use for general debates, not only for your Department.' So I thought that's that.

There was a big meeting of Ministers today on the future of the Aintree racecourse. This problem had blown up during the election campaign when the High Court had decided that the Liverpool Council was acting invalidly in stopping the owner, Mrs Topham, from selling it for housing. Of course, as Minister I have plenty of reserve powers for preventing this, and on Harold's and George Wigg's wish I had called in the Labour chairman of the Lancashire County Council and the chairman of the planning committee along with the Labour leaders of the Liverpool Council, and the Ministers concerned, to hold a general discussion. It soon became clear that whereas Sefton, who runs the Liverpool Labour Group, was closely connected with one of the developers, the Lancs. County Council people were all against private development and in favour of buying the racecourse outright and creating a regional sports centre. It was a very trying meeting, with the two Labour councils full of suspicion of each other, suspicions which I must say I shared by the end of the meeting.

Wednesday, April 27th
A big meeting with the building societies to try to get agreement on my option-mortgage scheme. I do agree with Steve that one of my difficulties has been the fact that the Ministry knows nothing about building societies. In fact, when I got here I discovered there wasn't one member of the staff who had any practical knowledge of how they worked. So when our annuity plan was put forward by clever Mr Brain and the Dame they did it in genuine good faith and genuine ignorance. I don't know which is worse, our ignorance of the societies or their ignorance of government. Because their alternative scheme is totally impracticable for a government. I didn't quite know what to do and I finally suggested we should set up a joint working party which should try to make their plan practicable and my plan practicable and then come back and talk to us about it.

However, my mind was on the big speech I am due to make tomorrow. I had got into my head that this would be a really big occasion and instead of preparing notes and speaking impromptu I decided to get up a full-length, written speech, which I worked away on till midnight.

Thursday, April 28th
I had to miss Cabinet, where the business was doctors' pay, and worked away at my speech all through the morning. Just when I was going to break

off for lunch I had an urgent message that the Chancellor must see me before I made the speech. So along I went and Jim said, 'I've got to tell you what's in the budget because it might make nonsense of what you are going to say today,' and he then began to tell me about S.E.T.[1] Of course, my mind was on my speech which dealt with parliamentary reform and housing figures and I couldn't relate S.E.T. to any of that. And my first reaction to S.E.T. was that in terms of farming at Prescote Manor as well as in terms of building it was absolutely unbearable. I said to him, 'Why treat farmers and the construction industry as though they were service industries when they obviously aren't?' That's about all I could think of at the time.

So I rushed back to my room and got the finished text ready and when I got down to the House all keyed up I found Macleod getting up to speak with sixty or seventy people on his side and some thirty or forty on mine. It certainly wasn't a big occasion and he understood it and made a kind of pleasant, after-dinner speech — absolutely lightweight. I was disconcerted because there was no kind of enthusiasm behind me or tension in front and the speech I had prepared was certainly too serious. However, I managed to get through it, but for me it was a disconcerting hour. Of course I must blame myself in part. As a back-bencher I never dreamed of attending the Queen's Speech debates, regarding them as the most boring occasions. Maybe this was just a normal attendance and I should have known and refused to prepare myself for a great occasion. But I did and I felt thoroughly let down.

Anne was in London and we gave my American publisher, Mike Bessie, dinner before I caught the 10.30 train to Doncaster where I was to start a three-day tour of the North-East combined with two May Day speeches.

Sunday, May 1st

Suddenly summer arrived, perfect hot weather, lovely cloudless skies, leaves rushing out from winter into summer with hardly any spring. My three-day tour has been very enjoyable; and I particularly enjoyed Scunthorpe where I started, a crude steel town but vastly nicer than Corby because these splendid people make so much of so very little. They are just the kind of authority I really enjoy visiting.

At Sunderland yesterday I had one illuminating episode. Much against my will I had been almost drafted by Tom Urwin (the local M.P. for the urban district south of Sunderland)[2] to come to his May Day celebrations and also to visit his R.D.C. He explained that they were in violent opposition to the proposal that Sunderland should mop up the whole R.D.C. I had explained to Tom that I couldn't officially visit the rural district offices unless the councillors were persuaded that my decision on this was inviolable and

---

[1] A payroll tax paid by employers. See p. 509.

[2] M.P. for Houghton-le-Spring since 1964. He was a Minister of State at the D.E.A. 1968–9; and had special responsibility for regional policy and for the Northern region 1969–70.

couldn't be revoked. Of course he gave me the assurance, but when I got there on Saturday morning it had made not the slightest difference. They all got up and denounced the decision and made me very angry indeed. Then I began the tour and found that this little R.D.C. is doing miracles and that it is a tragedy that it is being wound up. It has a completely untrained and unqualified engineer but he is building houses £500 cheaper than the houses next door in Sunderland's borough and he is doing it by making efficient use of direct labour. I was shown his houses and a great palisade some twelve feet high on the other side of them. This was the Berlin Wall which separated the Sunderland R.D.C. from the Sunderland Borough Council which was determined to mop it up. That's the spirit of collaboration in local government that you have. Sunderland R.D.C. has been a Labour authority for fifty years, they have never had a Tory elected there and there is no party politics; the authority is the private property of the local worthies and for them their council houses are household possessions they can't possibly give up to the wicked county borough next door.

From there I motored on to Newcastle to stay with the lord mayor who is the wife of a wealthy doctor, who had himself been lord mayor fifteen years ago. This lady, twenty years a councillor, is a gay, racy hostess and I had a most enjoyable evening with them before I found myself staying alone in the lord mayor's lodgings while they went home for the weekend. The weather was still baking when we set out this morning for a May Day procession which was already a mile long when we started; and it took so long that fortunately we hadn't time for a public meeting. When I caught my train I found I had to sit for five hours without anything to eat or drink. I reached London at ten o'clock.

I didn't meet anybody in those three days in the North-East who was celebrating our general-election victory. All of them had their eyes on the municipal elections. And in Newcastle the loss of one seat would lose us the majority.

The Chancellor's pre-election budget preview proved to be reliable. Contrary to speculation, there were no increases on spirit or tobacco duties, nor on motor-car licences. As he had promised, a new savings bond was issued, with an interest rate of 5½ per cent, and a betting and gaming tax introduced. Corporation tax was fixed at 40 per cent. The import surcharge, introduced in October 1964, was to end in November but British firms were to be requested to restrain their capital investment in sterling countries—Australia, New Zealand, South Africa and Eire. This move seemed to mark a formal weakening of Commonwealth trading ties.

Treasury estimates forecast an increase in Government spending from £8,456 million in 1965–6 to £9,177 million in 1966–7. Some of the extra revenue was to come from Selective Employment Tax, Mr Callaghan's one surprise. The tax, to be levied on all employees and paid by employers as an addition to the

*National Insurance stamp, was designed both to raise revenue and to encourage
the movement of labour from service to manufacturing industries. Manufacturing industries would receive a refund. The tax was expected to produce a net
gain to the Treasury of £241 million in a full year; but the year's time lag before
rebates were made would add, in 1966–7 for example, £315 million to Exchequer
revenues.*

Monday, May 2nd
At eleven o'clock we gathered to be told the budget secrets, and S.E.T. was
revealed to us. Before I went off to the North on Thursday evening I had had
time to see Steve to be educated in the disastrous effect the new tax would
have not only on agriculture but on the whole construction industry. Under
the Chancellor's plans the building industry would have a new tax piled upon
it and also be denied the new investment grants: these had been worked out
for the export industries, and were denied explicitly to construction as well
as to hotels. Steve emphasized that it was essential at the very least to extract
a promise from the Chancellor that if builders had to pay S.E.T. they would
at least be eligible for investment grants. Over the weekend he got hold of his
opposite number in the Ministry of Works and I talked on the telephone to
Reg Prentice who, because he is not a Cabinet Minister, was forbidden to
attend the meeting on Monday morning. I had to represent him. The only
other Cabinet Ministers who had advance knowledge of the secret were the
Minister of Labour and the Minister of National Insurance, whose Departments were technically required for collecting the tax but weren't affected by
its consequences. So when Callaghan started discussing this tax in Cabinet
there was bewilderment and consternation. Nobody could quite follow what
he was saying and he had the easiest time in the world. I was the only critic
there, having had time to prepare my own position. Over the weekend I
had tried to see the tax not merely as it affected housing but as it affected
economic policy. It was obvious that Callaghan was bound to have a
deflationary budget and I had assumed there would be increases in purchase
tax, spirit duty and petrol tax – it was going to be that kind of gloomy budget.
So when we heard the news this morning it was a tremendous let-down – a
relief combined with a let-down. The whole of the deflation, we heard, was
going to be carried out by introducing this single selective tax which would
produce the £300 million cut required in consumption. There was virtually
no discussion. I made my demand that the construction industry must get
its investment grants back and Callaghan hummed and hawed and said he
might give some kind of assurance in his speech if it was put to him. Fred
Peart from Agriculture was completely flabbergasted because the idea was
that the costs to farmers imposed by S.E.T. would be made good in the
agricultural price review – a proposal which showed that the Treasury simply
doesn't understand how the price review works.*

* Callaghan had to withdraw this lunatic idea as soon as the N.F.U. heard about it.

The more I thought about it the more unrealistic this budget seemed to be. Of course, technically it may help us to deflate; but what it is not going to do is create the confidence in the pound which Callaghan wants to build up. It is not going to ease our situation overseas, while at home it is going to produce an enormous increase in the cost of living. And meanwhile the trade unions are going to have an excuse for putting up wages as fast as possible. In terms of strategy I am sure Callaghan missed his opportunity. People have been waiting masochistically for something to be done to them in this budget; they expect a rise in motor-car duties and petrol and purchase tax and there will be a sense of let-down when it doesn't happen. On the other hand there is no doubt that the budget will be far less damaging in the municipal elections on Thursday week than the budget we expected. But of course by far the most important aspect of this budget is the constitutional issue. It seems to me to make an absolute mockery of Cabinet government and Cabinet responsibility to introduce S.E.T. in this way and tell none of us about it until it is too late to do anything. Barbara Castle and Fred Peart made this point in Cabinet. And I am preparing to write to Harold about it.

Wednesday, May 4th
A real little row in Cabinet this morning about steel. Dick Marsh chose to pick a quarrel by accusing George Brown and Callaghan of deliberately slowing up the work on steel nationalization because they didn't really want to push it through. He did it very stupidly, because you don't take on Callaghan and Brown at the same time. Marsh should have admitted that the problems of the so-called Hybrid Bill really do produce enormous complexities. True, Callaghan and Brown don't want the Steel Bill much this Session and don't think it is going to help us a great deal. True, even the Prime Minister said that we would need to put the Prices and Incomes Bill on at the same time as the Steel Bill so as to give the foreign bankers something which they really could believe in. The impression I got from this scrappy discussion was of the sheer burden of boring legislation with which they have loaded us this Session.

After Cabinet I went over to listen to Jim Callaghan talking to the Parliamentary Party. I had heard the budget speech in the Commons—brilliantly successful—and I had also watched the Chancellor's superb performance on TV the same evening. He handled the Parliamentary Party with just the same skill. But the oftener I heard his performance the deeper my doubts grew.

By pure coincidence I had been invited to talk to David Butler's seminar at Nuffield College in the afternoon about Cabinet Government in theory and in practice, and it was a strange sensation to try out my thoughts on this subject. I was asked nothing about the budget but David Butler did ask me why we weren't allowed to describe how Cabinet Committees work or even to say that they take place. Now this is a fair question. For instance, when I have to cancel an engagement, as I very often do, I am not allowed to say that it is due to a sudden Cabinet or Cabinet Committee meeting. That would be an intelligible and acceptable excuse. Instead, I have to talk about 'official business' because there is a rule in the Civil Service that Cabinet meetings cannot be referred to at all.

At dinner this evening I sat next to Norman Chester, who remarked rather bitterly that I had naturally chosen an Old Etonian and right-winger for the chairmanship of the Royal Commission instead of a solid Labour supporter. I couldn't tell him the reason why I had preferred Maud but I did manage to give him some satisfaction on the great issue of the Christ Church Meadow road. I had reached agreement with the city council that they should take Hugh Wilson, the Ministry architect, as consultant and we should pay 75 per cent of the expenses. That gave him some consolation.

Thursday, May 5th

I spent most of the day preparing for the Ullswater press conference tomorrow, which will be embargoed for the Friday evening and the Saturday morning papers. I should normally have made the announcement in the House. But I decided that it would be too awkward with my own Chief Whip sitting beside me and with the Tory Chief Whip, Willie Whitelaw, sitting just across the table. So instead I would do it all by press conference and get the conference over on Thursday afternoon. I think I worked harder on preparing for this conference with Peter Brown than on any other up till now. I am absolutely certain that our solution preserves all the amenities and my only doubt is whether it provides enough water for Manchester in the next ten years. I may have treated Manchester too hard.

Sunday, May 8th

I was due to spend the weekend helping my constituency Party for the municipal elections next Thursday. On Saturday I did go round Wyken and Upper Stoke appealing for support. Today it has been raining all day and I was able to stay at home.

All my mind is now concentrated on reflecting on this budget—its constitutional aspects as well as its economic consequences. I am extremely doubtful whether it will be a success. I have also been preparing this weekend for a new series of PESC meetings, and beginning the reorganization of the Department with my two Ministers of State and my three Parliamentary Secretaries—I must settle them into their jobs. In fact, I have got to buckle down to being a departmental Minister again even if it is a very big departmental Ministry.

Monday, May 9th

On the way up in the train I noticed to my surprise that I was due to go to the first meeting of the brand new Cabinet Committee on Europe. So I turned up at No. 10. After I had been sitting there for some time the P.M. threw me a little note asking whether I was really supposed to be there. I threw back a note saying, 'Yes, I had received an invitation and the papers.' He threw me back another note saying, 'Your name isn't on the list, it's awkward.' Then there was a long exchange of notes between us in which he explained that Roy Jenkins had already asked to be on the Committee and been refused and that if I were on it it would be unbalanced. However, I stuck out that first meeting and learnt a great deal. It was staggering to hear George Brown taking the bit between his teeth and announcing our collective determination to go into Europe at the moment when our official committees were advising us that there was no chance whatsoever of doing so as long as General de Gaulle was President of France, and that anyway we couldn't afford to in present circumstances because it would mean a devaluation. But despite these official estimates, Brown and Healey ever since the election have been rushing round Europe to meetings at Oslo and Bergen announcing our determination to enter the Market. It sounds to me just like a repetition of George Brown's handling of the prices and incomes policy. He is a great man at delivering big speeches in order to make big things come true. And I am afraid this technique will have the same effect here as it had on the incomes policy. Everybody is impressed at the beginning but when nothing solid comes of it a reaction sets in.

In the evening I was due to see the P.M. about the battle I was having to get historic buildings transferred from the Ministry of Works to the Ministry of Housing. However, that had been conceded before I got there and we were able to chat informally. At the end he said to me, quite offhand, 'By the way, your Mr J. D. Jones will be going as Deputy in Barbara's Department.' I knew at once he had fixed me because, of course, the Prime Minister appoints Permanent Secretaries and Deputies as well.

Tuesday, May 10th
I talked to Steve straight away about the future of J. D. Jones. I told him that the P.M., and Barbara Castle as well, had been at me and that I couldn't hold the breach. Steve, whose first reaction to the rumour was that it was impossible to let J.D. go, was already caving in. 'Anyway,' he added to me, 'Jones is miserably unhappy in the Department and he wants to go. He told me so himself.' I sent for Jones this evening and of course he denied there was anything personal in it, but under pressure it was clear that he resents the whole atmosphere of the Department since the Dame has left. It's not merely me, it's having Stevenson and five politicians on top of him. But there is no doubt I am a negative factor, and he did say to me in the course of this long interview, 'I know one has to pay a heavy price for having able Ministers and in your case we pay it.' So we've lost him and that's that.

Wednesday, May 11th
I had to make a very early visit this morning to a house in Cheyne Walk

17

which the G.L.C. wants preserved on the ground that it is one of the rare surviving examples of the art-nouveau style at the end of the last century. The owner, as usual, wants it pulled down for redevelopment. When I got there I was surrounded by representatives of the G.L.C., the builders, the contractors and the Ministry. I stalked alone through the house. Outside, it had no conceivable merit; inside, it was a total wreck with the wallpapers rotting off the walls, a staircase utterly wormeaten, and a little garden house which once may have been nice but in which all the frescoes had rotted away. Transformation into flats, which the G.L.C. recommended, would have destroyed the last trace of art nouveau. I decided to let it be scrapped.

Back in No. 10 the Prime Minister was chairing the first meeting of the Cabinet Committee on Housing which he has set up since the election. It was a very bad meeting for me because the Department's brief was utterly inadequate. The P.M. was able to show that it provided none of the detailed analysis of our failure which he required. At least on this point Steve is on my side. I was delighted last week when he said that in the Ministry of Power they had the facts about every pit in the country at their fingertips and we ought to have the facts about every local authority's building programme at our fingertips too. He is quite right. Under the Dame, intelligence and information were never organized in the Ministry. With the slump in the private sector the Prime Minister of course agrees that we must get all the building possible in the public sector. Indeed, he suggested that we should ask the local authorities to launch a campaign for building houses for sale where private industry is failing to do so. I had to warn him that that would be the end of any kind of collaboration from the private sector in my national housing plan. I went away from the Cabinet Committee with a huge long list of requirements. I was not too despondent since with Steve at the head of the Department for the first time it is possible to get these things done.

In the afternoon I had to attend a seminar laid on by J. D. Jones at which the planners were to lecture me on the conclusions they had reached from the West Midlands Review. I am beginning to find these planners slightly bogus when they get down to practical life and at one point I barged in and made it clear that I thought that what they were saying was pretty good nonsense. They were very angry with the way I treated them and Bob Mellish and Kennet said afterwards, 'You do treat your civil servants rough.' Reflecting on the meeting, I realized they were right. I wouldn't have behaved like that a year ago. Power corrupts.

Fortunately, an hour later most of them were back in my room for another meeting on planning appeals which went very differently. This is a subject I know from A to Z and I was siding with the Department against the Permanent Secretary.

Over in the House of Commons the liaison committee is now beginning to meet again regularly. It was nice seeing the old friends there, including Marcia, but the impetus of the work has suddenly gone. There we were sitting round the table and we really couldn't think of anything very urgent that needed to be done. We had won our victory; but how are we going to use it in our propaganda and in our strategy in the Commons? I don't think anyone has the vaguest idea.

I had much the same feeling when I went across to No. 10 for the party the P.M. was giving to the new M.P.s. They are indeed a puzzle. Most of them are dons and intellectuals and they are slightly to the Left. But the main characteristic they reveal is sheer detachment and lack of enthusiasm and lack of clear ideas on anything except parliamentary reform. And the strangest thing about them is that they are hardly ever in the House of Commons. Some people say that the reason is that they are just winding up their old jobs and we shall see more of them in a few months' time. I doubt it.

Thursday, May 12th

Cabinet. When we are dealing with home affairs at least we are confronted with a paper requiring a decision. But on Rhodesia, when the Cabinet gets going, the Prime Minister just sits and chats and we occasionally ask him a question and the meeting disintegrates into amiable discussion, because all the decisions are taken by the P.M. and his little group behind the scenes. I am used to this in dealing with foreign affairs but today it was the same when we turned to the seamen's strike.[1] There was nothing that any of us could say about it. There was nothing Cabinet could do. So the chit-chat went on and I walked out of the room more than ever struck by the ineffectiveness of our Cabinet. It is all right when it handles *ad hoc* problems brought up from the Departments, but when we face a big issue there is no policy discussion.

At 3.30 we had the Second Reading of the Land Commission Bill. Poor Fred Willey. The repeat of a big occasion is bound to be depressing. He had moved the Second Reading only three weeks before and now he had to do it all over again. The only difference was that he had Geoffrey Rippon against him instead of Boyd-Carpenter. I had been through the speech with Willey to ensure that he would give due emphasis to the specific direction to the Land Commission he can now give as Minister. Instead of the Commission being a leviathan, an independent public corporation, this Bill turns it into something which can be instructed to work in conformity with the programme of land purchase which the Government and the local authorities want. This is a transformation which Geoffrey Rippon didn't understand, and John Boyd-Carpenter, who I tipped off and who saw its importance, made nothing of it, I am told, when he got up.

I had to leave after Willey's speech in order to make sure that the Cabinet

---

[1] The employers had granted the seamen a 13-per-cent increase in March 1965 and now offered 5 per cent, with a 4 per cent p.a. increase in 1968 and 1972. The seamen demanded that all work over 40 hours a week should be paid at overtime rates—equivalent to a 17-per-cent increase. On May 13th the Prime Minister met forty-eight seamen's leaders at No. 10 but the efforts of Wilson and Ray Gunter could not avert the strike, which began on Monday, May 16th.

Committee on my Local Government Bill went all right. I got the rating of empty property through without difficulty and then we came to all those local-authority licences which the Department has been urged to abolish altogether. But no, with the Treasury behind it, the Department has decided not to abolish them, and the only issue was whether we should have the dog licence and how much it should be!

Next came the rating of public utilities. How much should a gas-works or a bus concern pay? I said it was an arbitrary decision and we have just got to get a political fix. And then one of the Ministers there said, 'Look, we were discussing all this a few weeks ago and stopped dead. Why do you come up now with something new?' I realized my colleagues weren't prepared for new ideas and agreed to push it back to the officials. This is the kind of thing I do now, thinking in terms of practical politics, which I wouldn't have done a few months ago when I still felt I could really reform local government finance.

In the evening I sat down with Bob Mellish and Steve and the officials to go through the P.M.'s points on the housing figures. At one point I found myself lecturing Bob on his dealings with the press and telling him on no account to try to pretend the figures are better than they are. They are bad and they are going to get worse and we shouldn't give any hostages to fortune by optimistic predictions. Bob pleaded and said that we can't just do nothing about it. Back in my room I found three journalists waiting to see me. One of them was John Beavan from the *Mirror*, which will give us a major spread on housing. And before I knew what, I was urging the builders to get on with their job in a way which I had been telling Bob was unrealistic. I only hope the article looks all right. Bob thought I did marvellously but in fact I was so tired that I hardly knew what I was doing. This went on till nine o'clock, when I went over to the House for the wind-up of the Land Commission Bill.

Friday, May 13th
I caught the 8.45 for Bath because though I was only due to make my big speech on preservation and change in the afternoon, the council had tied 23/23 the week before on the question whether or not to accept the Buchanan proposal to put a tunnel under the centre of the old town.[1] I had to try to deal with the deadlock. But first, over breakfast on the train, my big speech. I had found as usual that I had had no time to do it (with municipals yesterday I had been busy most of Tuesday on a party political TV broadcast and most of Wednesday on a radio one[2]). Thank heavens John Delafons had come to the rescue. He is the first civil servant I have found who can write me a speech. All I had to do this morning was to run through it and put in one or two

---

[1] See p. 430.
[2] Labour did badly in the borough elections, winning only 846 seats. The Conservatives made a net gain of 535 seats over Labour.

touches. We had just finished nicely when we reached Bath and I was whirled off by the town clerk, who talked to me during the tour about the inner committee of eight which I was going to face. Since my last visit there had been a municipal election and the new Labour leader, a dentist, regards himself as a great town planner and claims he has an alternative to Buchanan and so they had all voted against Buchanan's scheme, which I was down there to support.

In a week when I had been doing badly in my Department, badly in Cabinet Committee, badly with the P.M., I handled the inner group fairly well. I didn't bully or bulldoze but tried to calm them into accepting a feasibility study. Of course I made things much easier for myself by telling them that I was going to announce in my afternoon speech that Bath would be one of the five historic towns for which special studies of how to preserve the city centres would be made with the Ministry's help.[1] With the chance of getting more money by being a historic town things looked brighter to those councillors.

There were six hundred people packed into the Pump Room and appalling acoustics. Anne and her favourite aunt, May Cowper, were sitting right underneath me and they found it a pretty good show. We finished at five o'clock and went out to dinner on a lovely evening at the Vineyards, outside Bath. Much too expensive but very enjoyable.

So I ended the week with one job well done. But managing to deal with the problems of the historic centre of Bath is not going to help me to survive as Minister of Housing. It is the housing figures which will be the test for me and they are very bad indeed. We are going very badly this year and nothing I do or say will stop it. Of course, I can reorganize the public sector, which in the long run will make for efficient building and good housing figures. But it is the private sector that matters. Here it is the Chancellor's policies which decide the number of houses built, not mine. As long as he introduces S.E.T., makes a concession to the farmers and refuses one to the construction industry, I am going to be the fall guy and take the kicks.

Sunday, May 15th
The drive back from Bath across the Cotswolds is lovely, and even lovelier on the kind of early summer day we had yesterday. Unfortunately, the day was ruined because that evening when Pam Berry and the Hartrees came to dinner, Anne suddenly at the end of dinner felt sick and giddy and disappeared. When she had been away for some time I went upstairs and found her collapsed on her bed unable to move. I got Dr Long and he found nothing organically wrong. He's been back again today and thinks it is something to do with the labyrinth of her ears and she ought to stay quiet. What she needs is our Whitsun holiday and I am only slightly anxious now whether the flight will upset her eardrums.

[1] The others were Chester, Chichester, King's Lynn and York.

This has been an important, sobering week in my life. I have been thinking about the whole theory of budget confidentiality and whether a reformed PESC could play a part in opening it up. I have had no success there. When I sent a note about this to the Cabinet Office I got a formal acknowledgment and Harold hasn't spoken to me about it. As for PESC, Steve has done a little letter to George Brown watering down all my complaints. The truth is that I can't force the pace in Cabinet or in my relations with Harold because the first, gay phase of Ministerial elation is over. I have thrown all the balls into the air and now I have got to catch them all as they come down and already two of them have fallen wide. I have not only got bad housing figures. I am in trouble with the rent assessment committees. We have now had the first score of decisions by Sydney Littlewood and his colleagues in London. In most cases they have increased the reduced rents fixed by the rent officers and this is bound to encourage a great many more landlords to apply. It has also not unnaturally alarmed our Labour back-benchers, headed by Frank Allaun, who never liked the idea of the fair rent anyway. While I was at Bath on Friday they had a fine time assaulting poor Jim MacColl; and the people there weren't only left-wingers – there was also Ivor Richard, a very powerful right-wing London lawyer who carries a great deal of weight. They were banging and crashing and saying the whole Rent Act had broken down. Undoubtedly one of the troubles is the dominating position of the lawyers and surveyors on all these rent assessment committees. I have tried to prevent it but in some areas I have failed because I find it extraordinarily difficult to recruit efficient, outstanding lay men and women who can talk on equal terms with the lawyers and surveyors.

The other ball which is falling wide is of course the housing programme. It now looks as though we shan't reach 400,000 this year and the reason is Jim Callaghan's financial policy. The high interest rates, his new selective employment tax and the whole business of controls and licensing – everything has conspired to make the private-housing sector suspicious of the Labour Government and to destroy their confidence in me. True, in the public sector I have been able to fix up the figure for starts of new council houses but there are grave limitations in the capacities of the councils to expand their programmes very quickly. However, at least the responsibility really is mine. If we fail it's my fault. Whereas on the private sector I am not really in charge. And if we fail, as we are failing now, and the Prime Minister gets excited and demands an inquiry, I am the Minister who takes the kick.

Also, we are in real trouble in the Department. I have lost the Dame and got this fellow Steve, who is an extraordinary mixture of civility and stubbornness, of drive and bureaucratic obstruction, of energy and unimaginativeness. And I am afraid the Department finds the combination of Steve and Crossman infinitely worse than the combination of the Dame and Crossman. Then I have also lost Waddell to the Home Office, and J. D. Jones is due to go to Transport. Steve never misses an opportunity of telling me how I demoralize the Department by my behaviour and how exhausting I am. For some time I didn't believe him but I am very conscious after this week of taking it for granted that I have the right to be bloody-minded and have tantrums and pull people to pieces. I have got to be careful that I am not falling a victim to the disease of Ministeritis, becoming corrupted by power.

Monday, May 16th
Directly I got to Paddington this morning I was whirled off to the Crystal Palace to see the Industrial Building Exhibition. I went there mainly because I wanted to hold a press conference on industrialized building as a preliminary to my defence in the censure debate on our housing and building policies on Thursday. I think this little plan succeeded. Certainly, one shouldn't hold things back for one's speech in a debate, one should put them out in advance because people like hearing facts again and recognizing them. As for the exhibition, which I saw with Peter Lederer, it was a dull show because all the people with really good schemes were already at work with the local authorities and didn't bother to come. The only stands there were for people who hadn't been able to sell a scheme or were just struggling.

That afternoon I had the first of our joint Ministry of Housing/Ministry of Transport committees. Once Barbara had become Minister I was very anxious to use our personal friendship in order to achieve genuine joint planning between the two Ministries. First, I wanted us to compare our commitments in the next five years; and second, to have a longer-term study done by the planners in both Ministries; and third, of course, I wanted her backing for a town and country planning Bill next session.

The Transport people were all very cagey indeed but I did manage to bring Barbara along a little. Of course I didn't bring her the whole way. She insisted on a working party to decide how to do the job. I managed to narrow this discussion down to the two or three issues I wanted. But Barbara is not giving me anything for nothing.

Then down to Oxford to speak to the Oxford Democratic Socialists. Oh dear, oh dear, how things change. In the heyday of the University Labour Club one was met at the station, taken up for a fine drink and a good dinner at the Union and then taken to the Union Hall, which would be full to the doors for a really big show. Now the University Socialists are split into a right wing and a left wing, and I had the virtuous little right wing to talk to. I found myself addressing about a hundred people on a hot summer evening in that little Regent's College Hall in a back street.

Afterwards I went down to Univ.[1] to talk over with John Maud the arrangements for the Statement on the Royal Commission which is due next week. I thought I had got the membership finally fixed when we received a ferocious letter from the A.M.C. complaining that although the county councils were represented formally by a county councillor as well as by Jack

[1] University College.

Longland, education officer for Derbyshire County,[1] there was neither an official nor a councillor's representative from the county boroughs. They complained that no one could say that Dan Smith was a pukka A.M.C. man. When I read the letter I thought the objection absolutely sound and I had to act quickly. The A.M.C. were asking for Barbara Brooke, the wife of Henry Brooke and a peeress in her own right. That seemed to me a danger since we might have two prima donnas on the Committee with Dame Evelyn and Lady Brooke, so I asked John Maud if he would support Francis Hill,[2] who is fortunately a Tory and will balance Reg Wallis. I got consent, in the nick of time.

Tuesday, May 17th
I had to get back to London by an early train in order to be in time for Legislation Committee as the Local Government Bill was first on the agenda. This is a hell of a Bill and my life has not been made easier by having as my chief adviser Crocker, our Accountant-General, who is as clever as he is obstructive and difficult, and as parliamentary counsel a very senior, very distinguished man who is neurotic and terribly slow. All my hopes of a great reform of local government finance have been baulked: this is an officials' Bill! Sitting in the train to Paddington I briefed myself on it but I couldn't really grasp what many of the clauses meant. However, that didn't matter because the only thing discussed at the Committee was dog licences. It was clear how few of my colleagues have any notion of what this Bill is about, even where it vitally affects their Departments. Barbara Castle clearly didn't know her highway clauses, and Tony Crosland didn't seem to realize what he was signing away when he agreed to dispense with his special education grant.[3]

At the Ministry I found Duncan Sandys waiting for me. He'd rung up saying that he had got first place in the ballot for Private Members' Bills and did we have available a nice Bill about keeping the countryside clean. Duncan is an odd mixture—a passionate European, a hard-headed Tory, but also a founder of the Civic Trust. I told the officials that they should tell him for heaven's sake that we wanted a new Bill on historic buildings and preservation of town centres. It was a good moment to talk to him about it because of the scandalous news of a man who had bought a beautiful, listed

---

[1] Sir Jack Longland (as he became when he retired in 1970) had been the director of education for Derbyshire since 1949. He served on many other committees, commissions and councils, including the Sports Council (since 1966) and the Countryside Commission (since 1969).

[2] Sir Francis Hill, a solicitor and chairman of the A.M.C., had been Conservative candidate for Lincoln in 1950.

[3] Hitherto local authorities had received their share of the General Grant and various additional grants, including one for educational services, calculated on a separate, special basis. In introducing a single rate-support grant, for which local authorities would be assessed according to a complicated formula weighted to take account of such services as hospitals, schools and bowling-greens, the Local Government Bill benefited the less wealthy areas, but also gave the Treasury greater control over local authority expenditure.

manor house near Solihull in order to pull it down. This has brought into the open the obvious fact that we have no deterrent to preserve listed buildings. He liked the idea and agreed to put the Bill forward early in July when he was back from Independence Day celebrations in British Guiana—provided of course I cleared it through the Cabinet Committee.

Early on in our talk Duncan had said how interested he was in my concept of townscapes as against the listing of individual buildings, and I said that that was marvellous and we would make a point of getting that into the Bill. At this point the official who represented the division said, 'I'm sorry, Minister, that isn't possible. We shall have to limit ourselves to individual listed buildings in this Bill.' Duncan Sandys at once got huffy and said in that case he wouldn't be interested. And I said, 'This Private Bill will be a great opportunity to test the ideas the Department itself has been pressing on me for more than a year.'

In the afternoon Steve and I finished off the job of reorganizing the work of the Department. We also had to consider the shape of the Department after the new elements are transferred from Land and Natural Resources along with their army of politicians. Of course, Steve has had his way in most things. He's left the Ministry of Land and Natural Resources as a kind of ghetto whereas I wanted to break it up and integrate its separate divisions, to have countryside for instance as part of planning. But no, he said it was too difficult to do it now. As for dividing the politicians, I've got Willey and MacColl doing planning, Mellish doing housing and New Towns, Skeffington doing local government and countryside and Kennet doing historic buildings. I hope it works out all right. The great thing is to get the decision now, before the recess, so that they can sort themselves out while I am away.

When this was done I caught the train to Torquay to speak to the gravel interests who were having their annual beano at the magnificent Imperial Hotel. I gave them my usual address on the problems of amenity and gravel pits and the notion of surrounding London with a blue belt of linked lakes, in addition to the green belt. I still haven't got it over in the press despite making the speech half a dozen times. But the really important thing about going to Torquay was that it gave me the chance of a long private talk with Littlewood, who is legal adviser to the gravel merchants. On the way down in the train I read a report on the first fair-rent cases—there are now thirty of them. What impressed me in reading them was their sheer objective competence. They are attempts to ensure that in assessing a fair rent for a house, you disregard altogether the needs of the landlord and the needs of the tenant as people and study the house as a fact, measure its size, its location, its state of repair. And it is on these objective points that you assess the rent, deducting scarcity. So I am not surprised about the row in the House on Friday, when Littlewood sat in the box hearing himself abused. Littlewood seemed to be disturbed not by the Labour Party but by the Council on Tribunals where I am due to make an appearance this week. They have turned down what he specifically asked for, the appointment of 'referencers', clerks who aren't fully trained valuers, who will bring back to the R.A.C.s the objective facts about each house in standardized form. Littlewood knows that the Council has the support of Gerald Gardiner, our Lord Chancellor, in rejecting this. But he revealed to me that he had appointed his valuers and lawyers to the committees on the understanding that they wouldn't have to go out and do the visiting themselves since this would double the time taken on each case. I suggested that there was one person who would have seen every house and that was the rent officer; why shouldn't he appear before the R.A.C.? Littlewood replied that this would upset the rent officers a great deal. They wouldn't like to be cross-examined by the R.A.C. and made to look fools in public.

Wednesday, May 18th

I caught the 1 a.m. sleeper at Newton Abbot last night because I wanted to start preparing my speech for the vote of censure early. As usually happens, I didn't get very much time for it; today was the day when Callaghan and I were due to meet the building societies for our long-postponed meeting about the rate of interest. I have always held that the building societies have got to fix a rate of interest which enables them to compete with the local authorities, for example, who may be borrowing money at 7½ per cent. If their offer is worse than the prevailing rate they go out of business and the whole private sector of house-building collapses for lack of funds. This is a point at which the Treasury officials and mine, particularly my new Permanent Secretary, see eye to eye. And I agree with them against Callaghan, who hates high interest rates and likes to put the blame for them on somebody else. The rest of us all felt that this whole meeting with the building societies was going to be a waste of time. It was obvious that whatever we said they are going to put the rate of interest up and all we can do is to refer the issue to the Prices and Incomes Board.

I thought I should see Callaghan before the meeting so I went along the corridor at 12.30, after preparing my case in our own Ministry. I found him as difficult as ever and as unwilling to admit that house-building was stopping. He was also unwilling to see the issue referred to the Prices and Incomes Board. 'I shan't get a recommendation in my favour,' he said. 'No,' I replied, 'you won't get that, but whoever thought you would? What we want is to get this out of the way.' But he didn't see it in that light.

At the meeting in the afternoon Callaghan went on and on and on. Finally I said, 'It's fairly clear these gentlemen have come with their minds made up, Chancellor.' But even then Callaghan continued to plead with them and said, 'Can't we put this to a joint meeting of our officials and postpone the decision till they report?' At this they withdrew to consider their attitude. I knew exactly what their reply would be. However, I had time to rush back to my office and see Littlewood, who was waiting for me, before they returned.

They duly said that they were going to put their interest rates up. Then Callaghan finally announced that we would refer it to the P.I.B. I whispered to him, 'Make it ex post facto. Let them take their decision first and do it afterwards. Otherwise we shall be in trouble with George Brown.' How right I was. The moment we had made our decision, George was telephoning to say that on no account must the building societies be allowed to put up their interest rates until after we had received the P.I.B. report. In fact, of course, though they had decided already to raise the rate from 6¾ per cent to 7¼ per cent, it would take three months to implement this decision. It seemed absurd for George Brown to be intervening in this way. Once again one sees how constrictive this prices and incomes policy is. What a price we have to pay for it although it is now in ruins and not working at all.

In the evening we had a meeting of the liaison committee, now reconstituted. I am still in the chair and it consists of the same people and it still provides the only link between Transport House and No. 10 and the Whips' Office. Before the election we were in tremendous form, knowing just what we had to do. Now that victory is ours and we have four years of Government ahead, we are afflicted with an extraordinary lassitude. Finally I said to them that we ought after the recess to spend an evening together trying to think out the strategy of the Party because nobody else is doing it. They all felt pleased and that was the decision.

Thursday, May 19th

I woke up early because I was worried about my speech this afternoon in answer to Geoffrey Rippon moving the vote of censure, the Opposition's biggest debate of the week. I had assumed earlier that I would just do the wind-up at the end of the debate and let our new Minister of Works, Reg Prentice, start. But when I heard that Geoffrey Rippon was opening and remembered the trouble I had had with the censure debate last time, I came to the conclusion that I must reply to him direct. This was clinched when Ted Heath made a great blast against me over the weekend, quite clearly indicating their line of attack since it was followed by nearly all the Sunday papers. When I got to work at 6 a.m. I found that Freddie Ward had provided a pretty good reply to Heath's attack and my invaluable John Delafons had done the big piece on the Land Commission for the end. So the speech was pretty well on. I worked hard at it all through breakfast.

As a result I arrived late at Cabinet. They had already had some talk about Gibraltar[1] and Rhodesia and had begun a long debate on the seamen's strike.

[1] Throughout 1966 Spain complained that Britain was invading Spanish airspace and violating neutral territory at the frontier. Following a recommendation of the U.N. General Assembly in December 1965, talks between Britain and Spain were held at Ministerial level in London on May 18th and 20th, and were to continue in July, September and October. The links between Britain and Gibraltar were strengthened in the coming winter by visits from the Secretary of State for the Colonies to the Rock and by the Governor of the Rock to London. The matter was eventually referred to the International Court at The Hague for adjudication.

When I got there Ray Gunter was saying that he had assumed that there would be no kind of Government intervention before the middle of next week, but now it might come earlier. Whereupon somebody asked, why, if we were going to be firm and were committed to breaking the seamen's strike, there could be a suggestion of our intervening so quickly? When challenged, Gunter was suitably obscure and I began to suspect that he and the P.M. were trying to get some sort of implicit Cabinet approval for an earlier action to achieve a settlement.

If I am right, they didn't get much change out of the Cabinet this morning. Obviously it is formally committed to breaking the strike in the way we didn't break the doctors', the judges' and the civil servants' strikes. Of course nobody in the Cabinet likes this, but we know it's a fact. We listen to George Brown telling us to resist to the death. We listen to James Callaghan telling us to resist to the death, although it would cost us a small fortune in foreign exchange. Only Dick Marsh disagreed and said that he thought the strike was no issue to fight on, since the men had a very strong case. But after he had finished no one gave him very much support. Altogether, we had one of our untidy, desultory conversations in the course of which we found ourselves drifting into even more implacable opposition to the men. We are committed to fighting this strike, although it may go on all through the summer, although it may involve the docks and although there may be clashes between the dockers and the armed services. Even worse, we are committed to it although in the general public mind and even more in the minds of our back-benchers it seems outrageous for a Labour government to quarrel with the seamen and defeat them after all those lavish increases to professional people. Sitting there and listening I couldn't help asking myself whether we had ever had any choice in that matter. The answer is that Cabinet control was, to put it mildly, not very effective. Yet the issue was submitted to Cabinet and Cabinet felt that there was no alternative but to back George Brown and his prices and incomes policy. If it hadn't been for that the Cabinet would have been for standing aside and letting the ship-owners do what they always wanted to do. We have got to be clear with ourselves that it is we, the Labour Cabinet, who have prevented the ship-owners from surrendering to the seamen, simply because a surrender would have made nonsense of the $3\frac{1}{2}$-per-cent norm and given the men too big an increase. We are paying a very high price for George Brown and his policies.

I had to get back to my speech, and I left the Cabinet rejecting yet another appeal by Callaghan for postponement of steel nationalization. I wasn't too sorry to be absent since I had an uncomfortable feeling that Cabinet is drifting into a position of inflexible opposition to the dictates of common sense. It would have been common sense to negotiate with the steel magnates and get four-fifths of what we want without the appalling political complexities of a nationalization Bill. But apparently we can't risk it in terms of our back-benchers and, incidentally, in terms of our new Minister of Power, who is determined to show that he is more virile than poor old Fred Lee. So Fred Lee's bad Bill will be pushed through by the vigour of Dick Marsh.

Now for the debate. There was virtually nobody there when it started, about forty-five people on each side. The mood was a little less flaccid than during the Queen's Speech debate but not that much. Geoffrey Rippon is a ponderous fellow and his attack wasn't very effective. In my reply I deliberately provoked a tremendous lot of interruptions. I hadn't written into my text the claim that the Tories were telling lies but when I said it they gave me the kind of atmosphere in which I feel comfortable. By and large I did a good job. With housing figures as bad as ours it is quite an achievement not to lose a debate.

By the time I sat down, Alderman Griffin, the new Conservative leader of Birmingham, was waiting in my room upstairs. He had come to pay his compliments to the Minister, and started by smoothly telling me that he had found the housing revenue account empty. I knew that! Alderman Watton had deliberately left nothing in the larder in order to force these Tories into putting rents up and getting all the odium for it. Alderman Griffin asked me if I would let them sell the council houses and so put the revenue account in the black. I said he must put this on paper as a formal request.

Meanwhile, in the Commons Charlie Pannell, now on the back benches, had launched an all-out attack on S.E.T., pleading on behalf of the construction industry. His speech was extremely useful to Reg and me. In his winding up Reg didn't rebuke Charlie but thanked him. Altogether the day wasn't too bad for us.[1]

Friday, May 20th
I had asked Duncan Sandys to come in again, the day before he went out to British Guiana, in order to firm things up about his Private Members' Bill. The Department had done its homework and so had I. I was able to tell him that the Cabinet Committee had given its consent to the main outlines of his Bill. I was also able to tell him that I was still determined to make sure the Bill dealt with townscapes – that is groups of buildings – and not merely with individual listed buildings, although the Department had obstinately drafted my policy paper for the H.A.C. excluding this concept. When I said all this, Miss Williams, who is the number two in historic buildings, was enormously excited. She could hardly believe her ears and felt for the first time that something really was going to happen. No doubt this was partly due to the fact that the control of historic buildings was unified under me a few days ago as a result of the Department taking over one section of the Ministry of Works. But largely I think she had the feeling that her Minister was battling, and had fought down the resistance of her superiors. It had taken me nearly two years to do it.

[1] The vote was 327 to 230, a sizeable majority for the Government.

In the afternoon after a hard grind at the Ministry I was off by train to Llandudno where I was the main speaker at the annual meeting of the Welsh Council of Labour. It was delicious to be on the train for that lengthy, leisurely journey and I met the new young Member for Conway, who had won his election entirely in terms of leasehold reform.[1] He clearly hadn't expected to be in Parliament and we had a most interesting talk.

In the evening I had to address the conference rally, two-thirds full, the same old faces and a pretty routine show. After supper I had a private chat with Cledwyn Hughes, who has replaced Jim Griffiths as Secretary of State for Wales. I took the chance of asking him about Rhodesia, since he had been at the Commonwealth Office before. I said I simply didn't understand why no serious contingency plans had been prepared before U.D.I. Cledwyn confirmed George Wigg up to the hilt. He said that no preparations were made before U.D.I. because it was felt to be defeatist to imagine that U.D.I. would ever be declared. After the declaration, according to him, there had been continual turmoil and disagreement behind the scenes. He talked vaguely about much stronger measures which would cost a million pounds and which had been turned down by Callaghan on grounds of cost. I always suspected this, though the ground would be not only cost but also respectability. I asked him why we hadn't done anything to organize underground opposition, black propaganda, subversive activity. Cledwyn said he had tried to press all these things but had been defeated by the mixture of responsibility and priggishness which motivated politicians and officials.

Saturday, May 21st
Without a press release to worry about I gave the Welsh Council a serious lecture on modernization of our institutions, Parliament, local government and the Party. The press were there, but not a line was printed about my speech. I didn't mind. I caught the train at 12.55 and changed at Crewe, and all the way down was able to work on my red boxes so that I haven't had too much to do this Sunday, the last before we leave our children for our fortnight in Crete.

Monday, May 23rd
Over to Coventry football ground first thing in the morning. I had to stand in for Harold Wilson who, at an earlier match between Huddersfield and Coventry, promised to visit the football team and the manager, Jimmy Hill. Of course he can't get there so I had to go instead. I had never visited the ground before or seen a football match there but I found Jimmy Hill a nice person, and we had lunch together.

[1] Ednyfed Hudson Davies had won the seat on a 5·5 per cent swing from Peter Thomas, a former Conservative Minister of State, who had had a 3,500 majority in 1964. In 1970 the Conservatives won Conway back again.

At the Ministry that afternoon I found waiting for me the trust deed of our new Centre for Environmental Studies – the million-pound show I got out of the Treasury and Ford. After long arguments we have at last got an excellent group of Trustees under the chairmanship of Richard Llewelyn-Davies.

Tuesday, May 24th

At the end of Question Time Harold Wilson made the formal announcement about the terms of reference and membership of the Royal Commission on Local Government.[1] I sat beside him and every time he sat down he checked over with me and I briefed him on the answers to the supplementaries. It was a tricky job for him to answer these questions and he did it superbly. Listening to him, I saw one of his best qualities, a really elegant ability to be imprecise, to steer a non-committal hedging course and to say things which are not definitely wrong but aren't quite right in order to avoid any commitment. Afterwards I went back to the Ministry and briefed the press with John Maud.

In the evening I had to go on I.T.V. to debate the housing figures with Geoffrey Rippon. It was really a repeat of the Commons debate the previous week. Fortunately, he was too much the lawyer, too bloody pleased with himself and always referring to what he did when he was Minister of Works. I was able to get away with it. But this won't last for ever. Unless we can improve our housing figures I am going to have an increasingly rough time throughout this year.

Wednesday, May 25th

Despite the seamen's strike the quality press gave our Royal Commission quite a good display. But the popular press didn't even mention it and the weeklies – the *Spectator*, the *New Statesman* – will certainly leave it out, as they have always done. But this is the most important piece of modernization the Labour Government has launched. I have got further and faster on the reform of local government than anyone has thought possible.

At the N.E.C. in the morning at Transport House George Brown gave a report on Europe. I will quote my notes in full because this seems to me an important meeting. George Brown said, 'If I am asked when in fact in terms of present probabilities we could get into Europe, the answer would be "Never". But the question isn't about our getting into this Europe. The issue is whether we should get into a new transformed organization or stay outside it.' Then he listed quite fairly the main difficulties. Firstly, we would be outside Europe until General de Gaulle was out of the way. Secondly, the crisis with France about NATO had to be resolved or got over.[2] Thirdly, we had to

[1] He also announced the establishment of the Royal Commission on Local Government in Scotland, with Lord Wheatley as chairman.
[2] In March 1966 General de Gaulle had announced that France would cease to be a member of NATO and would withdraw her forces and facilities by the end of July.

get our own economic situation under control. As of today entry to Europe would require devaluation. The fact that we are coasting along without any expansion of the economy makes entry impossible. Having listed the obstacles very clearly, he then added, 'Still, it's a good thing to make friendly noises.' If he'd said this publicly it would have been thought a complete about-turn from what he has been saying in his journeys round Europe. But it is true to George Brown's character. He regards propaganda as a substitute for action. All his life is salesmanship and he seldom waits for any solid achievement before beginning to boast of it. I think this is what has happened in the case of Europe. George Brown wants to get in and he also thinks that the less chance of getting in we have the more we must shout about it to fill in the vacuum.

In the afternoon I had my long-delayed meeting with the Council on Tribunals. I have recorded in this diary the vote of censure which I underwent as a result of Dame Evelyn's determination to push the second Packington redevelopment plan through in defiance of the Council.[1] Well, I was finally due to meet them and went into a little room off Trafalgar Square which I found crowded with people, mostly lawyers. I had decided with my officials before the meeting that I would just mention the Packington issue and then discuss the future. But the Council was determined to argue about Packington. It seemed totally unaware of the difference between telling a Minister what his decision should be and warning him afterwards that he was wrong and shouldn't repeat it. *Post facto* advice is something the Council can and should give. It is quite different from interfering halfway through a process of Ministerial decision-taking, which is what they had done in the case of Packington. I said that although I didn't want to be discourteous, I ought to make it clear that if they made a habit of intervening *in medias res* I should have to disregard them altogether. To my surprise this came as a considerable shock to them and they seemed to regard it as quite a blow that a Minister should take this line. However, we went on to discuss our future Bill on planning and I am pretty sure I mended in part at last this particular fence in a way which was impossible as long as Dame Evelyn was there.

In the evening we had a farewell party for Peter Lederer and a welcoming party for Kenneth Wood who is taking his place. Peter has been a most successful importation, not because he is a dynamic influence but because he has fitted himself in very quietly and gets on with the civil servants as well as with the local authorities. I have chosen in his place a much bigger man — Kenneth Wood, who has built up Concrete Limited, a firm which makes high-rise blocks of flats. He is just what I need for my second outside expert in the Ministry. Nevertheless, I am eternally grateful to Peter for breaking the ice and making the idea of someone from the construction industry coming into the Ministry acceptable to the civil servants. Kenneth Wood couldn't possibly have been my first experiment.

[1] See p. 467.

As the seamen's strike built up, the Government assumed powers to control the ports, dock labour and food prices and to regulate shipping, dock and other transport services. A State of Emergency had been declared on May 23rd. On June 8th Lord Pearson's Committee of Inquiry made an interim report, proposing a 40-hour week within two years, and as a first stage a reduction from 56 to 48 hours within a year. The report also recommended a percentage rise in earnings slightly higher than the 5 per cent and 4 per cent offered by the employers. It severely criticized the National Union of Seamen, who rejected the report immediately.

Thursday, May 26th

Early in the morning the Polish Ambassador came to ask me to visit Poland this autumn. I have said I will spend a week studying Polish planning and building development. Then came the last Cabinet before the Whitsun recess. We had our usual little address from the Prime Minister about the seamen's strike but this time Dick Marsh intervened. He asked what the devil the strike was about and said how unpopular it was and how much damage we were suffering. James Callaghan replied that maybe it was doing damage but that to stop it now would damage the pound even more. Then everyone else chipped in that we couldn't possibly give way and must fight it out. Of course this is the line Harold Wilson had taken in his TV and wireless Ministerial broadcasts earlier in the week.

Then a curious thing happened. Ray Gunter made a report and then added that though there wasn't any promise of anything happening there was some chance of a contact being established earlier than he had expected. At this point people pricked up their ears and asked what the reasons were. Ray said that there was reason to think that some contact would be made by the seamen. At once Cabinet became suspicious that some kind of deal was contemplated, which upset James Callaghan and also upset George Brown, whose incomes policy is at stake. Gunter, who is a cunning devil, wouldn't have dreamt of saying a word of this if he hadn't been put up to it by Harold. I am still pretty sure that Harold was hoping to get some approval from Cabinet for an approach to the seamen. But he didn't get it. Ray Gunter made it perfectly clear that we could have a settlement at any time, since the owners were ready to put up the cash: it was the Government that was preventing the settlement because of the prices and incomes policy. Ray's intervention produced great unease. The people who were talking about fighting it out and the impossibility of giving way were uneasily aware that standing firm was also going to ruin us. It struck me as a very similar situation to the one we got into over Rhodesia: despite all the high talk about forcing the Rhodesians to give way there seems to be no sign of any weakening in Salisbury. We are given encouraging reports at every Cabinet meeting yet we have drifted into a deadlock which is costing us a tremendous lot in our balance of trade. On both the Rhodesian crisis and the seamen's strike the

P.M. has taken personal control and played them by ear from moment to moment. He has never worked out a strategy for winning in Rhodesia and I don't think before the seamen's strike started it had ever occurred to him to plan how he would win it.

Next we turned to ELDO, the European launcher development programme, which we inherited from the Tories together with that awful Concorde. Concorde is costing us hundreds of millions and we have been trying to get rid of it, but we are failing on legal grounds. This makes us all the more determined to cut back ELDO. We pay 47 per cent of the cost of ELDO against the French and Germans together paying the rest. It is this which made us decide to scrap it nine months ago. In fact the Cabinet keeps deciding to cut it back. Now it has been raised again by the Foreign Secretary, this time on the ground that we can't afford to alienate Europe. After Michael Stewart had made his case Denis Healey repeated that ELDO was of absolutely no value to the Ministry of Defence. This was confirmed by Frank Cousins as Minister of Technology. He admitted that it was no good to them whatsoever and added that it is only in terms of our relations with Europe that we must consider it. Could we really afford to upset our friends? Back came the Chancellor of the Exchequer 100 per cent for saving the money, supported of course by Jack Diamond. But then Tony Crosland intervened. He said that he had been against wasting money on ELDO but he didn't see how we could launch the positive approach to Europe which the Cabinet had authorized George Brown to undertake and at the same time walk out of ELDO. It was for this reason that he, Tony Crosland, had changed his mind. Roy Jenkins took the same line. I immediately followed him and said that I didn't know anything about a new Cabinet line on Europe. I gathered that our line was exactly the same as it had been before the election. As for our E.E.C. soundings requiring us to go on paying for ELDO—if that were true, it only strengthened my opposition. At this point George Brown said that it was quite untrue that we needed the ELDO payments in order to support the E.E.C. probing. He would like to go on with the probings but cut the ELDO payments. Harold Wilson sat on the fence, waited, weighed it up and said it was all very finely balanced. Finally, Fred Mulley was instructed to go back to Geneva and tell them we've decided to close our subscription.

In the afternoon I had a meeting with the Manchester City Council. Usually, whatever I have touched in Manchester has got me into a row with the Labour group. It was a relief to have a satisfactory meeting at which I could talk to them about the Ullswater decision and thank them for accepting my solution of the problem. I had really taken a lot of trouble with that decision and the result had been a wonderful press in Lancashire and the Lake District, even among the amenity interests which had been passionately opposed to the whole idea of Manchester's water supply being taken from the Lakes. They have now come round to the idea that on the whole we are not only protecting the amenities but positively improving them. So there has been a complete change of view. So much so that Willie Whitelaw (the Tory Chief Whip, who is Member for Penrith) came up to me in the lobby a day or two ago and said he had been converted and wouldn't oppose me if there was a debate. Indeed, he would like to speak in it. With this news I went back to our Chief Whip, Ted Short (whose father lives near Ullswater), and told him I had a chance of getting it through the House of Commons and weakening the Lords' opposition. But our Chief Whip didn't prove as progressive as the Tory Chief Whip. However, I have split them and that's the main thing. All this I had to report to Manchester. I added that since I had refused them a lot of the water they were expecting to get from the Lakes, I must take responsibility for obtaining further supplies either from the Ribble or from the Morecambe Bay project.

My last meeting that day was a full-scale Ministry conference on historic buildings. Kennet is really splendidly energetic. Though he peeves me a little by his desire to take everything over, I am delighted that he is that sort of person. He is going to run the historic buildings as hard as he possibly can and he is going to be helped by Duncan Sandys' Bill as well as by the decision to get working parties going on my five selected towns. That was a good meeting to have before I went off to Crete.

Nevertheless, I am leaving for my holiday with a pretty gloomy prospect ahead. Not only is there no likelihood of any solution either to the seamen's strike or to Rhodesia but, even more serious, the S.E.T. budget, which seemed to those who thought it out such a brilliant idea, has not worked out. Indeed, it has gone off at half-cock and done a great deal of damage because it hasn't really produced a sense of confidence amongst the overseas bankers. I haven't asked Tommy much about the pound but it hasn't been going too well. I think we are moving now towards another Government crisis.

The pound was certainly not sturdy. Gold and dollar reserves fell by £38 million in May and on June 11th and 12th a meeting of central bankers in Basle agreed to review international support for sterling. Existing credits were due to expire in the summer and the foreign bankers were believed to be ready to support the pound with some $1,000 million.

On April 25th, Lord Cromer, the Governor of the Bank, who had worked valiantly to secure international backing for the pound in the 1964 and 1965 crises, had announced his retirement. The Labour Party had felt temperamentally unsympathetic to one whom they saw as a typical City traditionalist and they were to be far happier with his successor, Leslie O'Brien, the Deputy Governor, who had risen through the Bank's hierarchy from the bottom to the top.

Sunday, June 12th

Back from our holiday in Crete. I must admit that this fortnight was a total vacuum in my life. We had a real honeymoon holiday, most of the time on

Minos beach in a little house of our own, bathing, sunning ourselves, tootling round in a Volkswagen which Helga Greene's villainous friend Johnnie in Heraklion had rented to us. We had just the kind of holiday that I enjoy, permitting ourselves little outings, little climbs, but not really serious expeditions, not really serious climbs, the kind of pretences which are complete relaxation for me. Anne just likes doing nothing: I like pretending to be doing something. We both like eating Greek food, mostly tomatoes soaked in olive oil and fresh red mullet. During the whole of that fortnight I never once pined for my work or felt anxious to go back. I never heard the wireless news, or read an English paper or indeed any paper. I never even wanted to. Seldom have I felt so utterly and satisfactorily cut off.

We got back to London airport at four o'clock on Friday afternoon and at once there was the usual muddle. Molly had been sent to the V.I.P. lounge but they expected me in an hour later than our actual arrival. So I stood about for half an hour trying to find her. After that we drove off to Prescote and on the way I opened *The Times*, the *Guardian* and the *Telegraph* and I found that nothing had happened to change the situation. The seamen's strike is factor no. 1. It's still going on and the only thing that has changed as a result is the reputation of Harold Wilson and the Government. That has been on the downgrade—and so incidentally has the reputation of the Minister of Housing. The lastest housing figures are very bad indeed and the rent assessment committees are getting even more unpopular in London. I think I can remember aright what I felt before the election and what I predicted. If my memory is correct it's happening roughly as I foresaw. We won terribly easily, coasting to victory. So we were really unprepared to deal with all the problems which would afflict us. We are a Government pledged to an expansion of the economy—and expansion refuses to come though we are well into our second year.

Of course there has been full employment—over-full. Of course there have been soaring wages, and prices not rising as fast as wages. Hence the lack of public indignation. But the job we set ourselves of modernizing the economy, expanding it rapidly and thereby earning the money for the expansion of the social services, is just not being done.

Factor no. 2 is the pound. It is still in difficulties. There are difficulties too about the balance of payments. Figures are now coming out that show that we won't be in balance by the end of 1966 or anything like. Indeed, when we take off the 15-per-cent surcharge on imports next autumn we are bound to have another major crisis. Very soon it will dawn on people that this Labour Government hasn't mastered the situation, hasn't solved the balance of payments, hasn't made the national prices and incomes policy work, hasn't got a housing drive really going. We have achieved very little indeed and the people are only content because there is still over-full employment.

The third factor we shall face is the growing disillusionment of our own back-benchers. This Government had dramatic successes when it only had a majority of three. Now it has a majority of a hundred, it has relaxed its efforts; and as a result it has created a sense of impatience and disillusionment among the new intake of able, vigorous, intelligent, but politically naive M.P.s. Quite legitimately many of them are beginning to feel that this is not a socialist Government, not even a leftist Government, but just any old Government teetering along and carrying out its election programme in a rather uninspired way.

And that brings me to factor no. 4. It's coming home to me more and more that the programme we started with is really irrelevant. The Land Commission? I am trying to make it relevant so that it can do something useful in providing land for private-enterprise builders during the next five years. But frankly we don't need the cumbrous machinery of a Land Commission. It will cause nothing but disillusionment when it is on the Statute Book. Nationalization of steel? We don't need it and it won't make much difference to our position. Even our big social security measures are disappointing. All we have got is Peggy Herbison's little social security Bill, by which we change the name of the National Assistance Board and don't do much more. We have had to scrap the incomes guarantee and we have had to postpone national superannuation, so that on the social service side too there is disappointment. And our national prices and incomes policy? That's the biggest disappointment; and it's obvious why, when we look at the seamen's strike. How can any new young M.P. feel enthusiasm for an incomes policy under which we conceded to the judges, the higher civil servants and the doctors increases of salary far beyond the 3-per-cent norm and then decided that we can't permit the employers to settle the strike even when they are willing to do so? It is we who have stood out, and no wonder our back-benchers are turning against us.

But factor no. 5 is the main thing they dislike — not home policy, but foreign policy. Here there is a curious similarity with the situation when I was a back-bencher in the Keep Left Group of 1946–7. The same kind of Left is growing up in our Parliamentary Labour Party. They feel that we are under the heel of the Americans and that we are carrying out a Bevinite policy but from a far weaker position than we had in 1945. These new back-benchers are beginning to say 'No' to an East of Suez policy which is costing us £250 million a year; and they are strengthened in their resolve by the fact that the confrontation between Malaya and Indonesia, which was the ostensible excuse for keeping troops out there, has now eased off and peace is breaking out.

That's the impression I get as a result of reading the papers while I sit here at Prescote sweltering in a heat-wave and enjoying the children. Actually the heat-wave has broken into thundery weather and I have done nothing since Friday except work through eight red boxes and play with the children, who were splendidly happy in our absence thanks to Laurie upstairs. She has turned out a perfect nanny without the disadvantage of our old professional nanny.

Monday, June 13th

My first day back and here I am once again in the reserved compartment in the train from Banbury to London. The stationmaster now knows his routine and is even willing to carry my briefcase as we move on to the platform. Thank heavens I see Edward Courage coming from Edgcote and I pick up Harry Judge, our local headmaster, now on the Public Schools Commission, and also Neil Marten our local M.P.[1] It makes me unpopular on the line to have a whole reserved compartment and for once it is nearly full. At Paddington there is John Delafons waiting for me on the platform and we get into the back of the car together and Neil Marten gets into the front and I start filling John in and he starts making notes before we get to the office, because we have got a lot to do before the P.M.'s Cabinet Committee on Housing at 11.30. I get Steve and the others to brief me but while I am waiting for them I take a look at the Private Office and see how it has been running in my absence. The whole second floor of the Ministry has now been taken over by one Minister, four Parliamentary Secretaries and three or four P.P.S.s. John Delafons is in charge of the whole show at official level; and it seems as though the sorting of the correspondence each of us should get has been cleared up in my absence as well as the decision on which papers come straight to me and which go to officials first.

With a Ministry this size it is very much easier to remain the kind of Minister who doesn't play much of a role in Cabinet. It keeps my reading of Cabinet papers down. For example, I don't often look at the Foreign Office telegrams unless Tommy or George Wigg rings me up over breakfast and mentions something. I don't really look at Ministry of Education or Social Security matters, and when Tommy the other day told me I was on the Prices and Incomes Cabinet Committee I had to check before I was sure that I am not on it. My only top-level Committees are the E.D.C. and the H.A.C. I refused to attend the Emergency Committee on the seamen's strike because I get bored sitting there under Jenkins, doing nothing. I think it has been a great mistake not to get myself made a member of the Social Services Committee but that's that. As for wider Cabinet affairs, I thought by luck I was going to be a member of the Committee on Europe but, as I related in this diary, it was all a mistake[2] and now, though I asked and Jenkins asked to be put on it, it hasn't happened because Harold wants 'balance'. Certainly, in terms of his method of running the Cabinet it's much easier to have departmentally minded Ministers who stay departmental. He doesn't want to see me expanding beyond housing except when he asks me to do so. He is much happier having all his relations with Ministers bilateral, no inner cabinet, no general discussion. And since he is happy, I am settling down again and it is going

[1] Conservative M.P. for Banbury since 1959. P.P.S. to the President of the Board of Trade 1960–62, and Parliamentary Secretary at the Ministry of Aviation 1962–4. A leading Conservative anti-Marketeer.

[2] See pp. 512–13.

to be difficult to change unless there comes a crisis where cliques and cabals are formed.

Now for the Cabinet Housing Committee. I had hoped it would be a practical committee with officials and experts present. For example, I would have liked to bring Bob Mellish, who does London housing, and Stevenson and Brain and Ken Wood. But no, it is the standard type of Cabinet Committee with only Ministers and Cabinet officials present. Harold takes the chair and, besides myself, has nominated Reg Prentice, Willie Ross and Cledwyn Hughes, plus the Chancellor of the Exchequer and the First Secretary.

In view of what happened before I had to be very fully briefed by Stevenson and Brain. When they had finished the job, Steve warned me that the Chancellor was going to raise the question of the total scale of the housing programme and propose that we should abandon the target of 500,000 a year by 1969–70. I said, 'Well, I'll at least have the support of D.E.A.,' and Brain replied, 'I'm not sure you will, Minister. I think you'll find the First Secretary is now on the Chancellor's side and will be asking particularly about the rate of renewal.' 'Renewal of what?' I said. 'They will be arguing that the number of new houses you need to build depends upon the number of houses you demolish. If you don't accelerate the rate of demolition you won't need 250,000 council houses a year.'

I couldn't quite believe this but I should have known that the Civil Service grapevine is nearly always correct. This is exactly what happened at the meeting. With Harold in the chair I had to follow the agenda we'd put up and so we started with a long discussion of our statistics, in which I reported on the improvements we were introducing. In view of the Ministry's total inability to make any assessment of the development of the housing situation, Cairncross[1] and Balogh had been asked to submit a long, 25-page paper. I was able to show that there was nothing in it which I hadn't learnt from my officials and that prediction in this field is bound to be based on far too many unknown factors to make accuracy possible. As a statistician Harold was extremely reluctant to accept this and I had to agree to accept a Professor Marian Bowley as a personal adviser.[2]

Item no. 2 was the paper in which I argued the case for increasing this year's approvals by 7,500, bringing the total up to 160,000. I showed that this was justified by the sag in the number of starts in the private sector. We had expected it to go up to 240,000 but starts were now hanging round about 210,000 and we had to fill in the vacuum with council housing. The Chancellor and I had agreed on an extra 3,500 for this year but I was now concerned with next year and that was why I made the further demand.

The moment I had finished Callaghan and Brown began their argument that

[1] Sir Alec Cairncross was head of the Government Economic Service 1964–9. In 1969 he became Master of St Peter's College, Oxford.

[2] Professor of Economics at University College, London, and herself the daughter of a distinguished economist. Her appointment was about to be settled when Crossman left M.H.L.G. and the matter was dropped.

we might well be over-committed on housing. The National Plan was having to be revised and since we had only achieved a 2 per cent increase, not the $3\frac{1}{2}$ per cent predicted, it was obvious that something had to go in public expenditure. At this point Callaghan brought up the point about the rate of renewal which Brain had mentioned. Forewarned, I was able to reply that even to keep pace with the minimal demolitions resulting from slum clearance and road building we had to build 150,000 new houses a year. Harold then raised his old question about how many working-class houses private enterprise was demolishing in order to replace them with luxury flats. And once again I couldn't provide hard enough figures, though I knew that this was a relatively minor point. Then he said that I had referred to the difficulties in which small builders found themselves, but what about the big builders, what were the figures about them? And of course I didn't have two sets of figures, one for big builders and one for small builders, and was made to feel inadequate for that reason.

Then came my pitched battle with James Callaghan, during which George Brown opted out and Harold Wilson also stood aside. I said that we were being blamed for the falling housing figures already; if I wasn't given the 7,500 quickly we would face a major crisis in 1967. Callaghan replied, 'How do you know? My confident belief is that the private sector will start building suddenly this autumn and we shall find ourselves with far too many houses started.' 'Then', I said, 'I should have to apply the regulator to the public sector. I give you my word that if the private sector suddenly gets going I will curb the public sector next autumn or the following spring.' Callaghan replied, 'I know the Minister of Housing well enough to tell you that he will get out of doing that when the time comes.' I then showed a great deal of moral indignation but of course what he said was true. I wouldn't dream of ever cutting back public housing, and I was having the row which every effective Housing Minister has with his Chancellor. It has been going on since 1945. Nye Bevan fought it, Macmillan fought it, and now I'm fighting it. Chancellors are bound to consider housing inflationary and try to throttle us. Housing Ministers are bound to be regarded as hoggers getting more than their share. But unless we hog we are defeated by the alliance of the Chancellor and the other social service Ministers. The fact that I have now got a reputation in Cabinet as a bully and a thug is really to my credit. A Minister who did less than that would be squeezed and pounded into subjection.

I finally ended by saying that this Committee had been established not to scale the housing programme down but to discuss how to get our houses built, on the assumption that we must reach a figure of 500,000 by 1969. 'Of course,' I said, 'if the Cabinet decides to scale that figure down, it is a very different matter. But you gentlemen are not entitled to come to this meeting and design a new, reduced housing programme or even to discuss whether the programme should be cut.' On this I got support, at last, from the Prime Minister. He and George Brown both accepted my formula. But then as a last desperate effort Callaghan suddenly brought up the 7,000 miners' houses which the Minister of Power has ordered us to build in Yorkshire and the East Midlands. 'I can't agree to the Minister of Housing getting both 7,000 miners' houses and the 7,500 increase in the general housing target.' I blew up. 'Those miners' houses aren't part of the housing campaign,' I said. 'They are what Robens[1] and the Minister of Power insist on in order to move the miners from the inefficient areas to the efficient areas. They are nothing to do with my housing programme.' At this point the meeting broke off and we are resuming it next week.

I spent the rest of the day in the Ministry preparing my speech for the Second Reading of the Local Government Bill. By eleven o'clock at night I got it finished with the help of a first-rate brief by the Accountant-General and his officials.

The Prime Minister prepared to announce a thorough inquiry into the whole structure and organization of the shipping industry. On June 17th he was to meet the seamen's executive for a 3½-hour meeting at Downing Street. There were now 838 ships idle in the docks.

Tuesday, June 14th
Cabinet. For the first time Harold Wilson deliberately tried to make each of us commit ourselves on our attitude to the seamen's strike. We weren't in a very happy mood for the experiment because the meeting started with a reference by the P.M. to the investigations into the ELDO leak. I reported in this diary how, just before the Whitsun holiday, Cabinet had for the fourth time decided to cancel our subscription. However, even before Fred Mulley could arrive at the meeting in Geneva there was a leak of our intention to withdraw and an outburst of complaint throughout Europe. As a result, while I was away in Crete, the Cabinet was successfully bulldozed into letting Fred Mulley go back and try to get a big cut in our subscription. It was an ignominious climb-down. But as usual Harold seemed more interested in the leak than in the substance of the issue.

When we got to the seamen's strike we were told that the T.U.C. had a proposal from the seamen which they would like us to consider although it went well beyond the terms of the report produced by the Pearson Court of Inquiry which had just been published. So the issue was, should the Cabinet stand firm and say 'Not a penny beyond the Pearson proposals' because these are not the basis for negotiation but a firm offer? Or should we let the T.U.C. find a solution which made further concessions to the union? George Brown and James Callaghan immediately said that we mustn't go an inch beyond

---

[1] Alfred Robens had been an USDAW official 1935–45 and a Manchester City councillor 1942–5. He was Labour M.P. for Northumberland 1945–50 and for Blyth 1950–60. From April to October 1951 he was Minister of Labour and National Service. In 1961 he accepted, from the Conservative Prime Minister, a life peerage and the chairmanship of the National Coal Board, a position he held until 1971.

Pearson and then each member of the Cabinet was asked to commit himself to support this tough line. There was obvious reluctance to do so. Dick Marsh, never exactly enthusiastic for fighting the strike, said that since Cabinet had committed itself as far as this it had to carry on. Roy Jenkins took the same line. Only two people stood out really firmly, Frank Cousins and Barbara Castle. Barbara made the very sensible, simple point that it would be crazy to find ourselves in open conflict with the T.U.C. I was one of the last to speak because I had remained silent throughout the long debate. When it came to my turn I said that my major preoccupation was that we must avoid finding ourselves fighting the seamen against the protests of the T.U.C. This seemed to me an appalling prospect because we should then quite certainly have more than half the other trade unions on the seamen's side and we should be fighting a civil war against them.

Maybe we three influenced the Cabinet slightly on its tactics in dealing with the T.U.C. But the fact is that Harold is out to smash the seamen's union. It is this which makes us so unhappy as a Cabinet in our relationship with our back-benchers. We are trying to smash the seamen although we have just given huge concessions to the doctors, the judges and the higher civil servants. It is an ironical interpretation of a socialist incomes policy.

I spent the rest of the day on the Second Reading of the Local Government Bill. It was after four o'clock when we started because first the House had to listen to a long Statement by the P.M. on the strike and a long and disastrous Statement from the Chancellor on the monthly trade figures. It is a very important Bill for anyone who understands local government expenditure but there were only a handful of people in the House and there weren't enough Labour Members wanting to get up for us to match the Tory speakers man for man. This indicates the malaise of this new Parliamentary Party. At least twenty of the new Members were people with wide experience of local government, absolutely capable of speaking on this Bill. That they didn't may partly be owing to my failure to send Geoffrey Rhodes round the tea-room to stir them up in the previous forty-eight hours.

In the evening we had a little supper in Vincent Square for the old gang. There were Tony Wedgwood Benn, Peter Shore, Gerald Kaufman, Tommy Balogh and Jennie and myself—Marcia couldn't come. I felt very disconsolate because I had been appalled by the atmosphere of the P.M.'s Housing Committee on Monday. On reflection it was quite clear to me that they were now going to scale down the National Plan and the Chancellor would get his deflation and a degree of unemployment, which would mean that housing was bound to be cut. I was equally depressed by our getting ourselves into this ridiculous fight with the seamen for the sake of a prices and incomes policy which had fallen to pieces before the strike began. I suppose I said all this too freely in view of the presence of Gerald and Tommy—who of course report to the P.M. and sometimes do it slightly maliciously. They urged me to take a more active part in Cabinet meetings. I said that if I move outside my brief I get out of bounds and I should only find myself opposing the prices and incomes policy along with Frank Cousins. Or possibly I should be saying, 'If you're going to deflate, deflate and get through the period of unemployment and face realities.' However, having let myself go I went back to the House for the concluding speeches and the vote on my Bill.

The left wing of the P.L.P. objected, obsessionally, to British support for the United States in the Vietnam war, to the level of defence spending and to the Government's continued commitment to an East of Suez presence. These criticisms were voiced on June 15th at a meeting of the P.L.P. to debate a motion calling for 'a decisive reduction' in East of Suez commitments, to enable defence expenditure to be cut to £1,750 million (at 1964 prices).

The left-wing protest was joined by right-wing supporters of European entry, who wanted withdrawal from the Far East. The Prime Minister based his reply on the need for Britain to keep bases to carry out her peace-keeping role in Asia and Africa and on her responsibilities to the United Nations. Actions in Zambia and at Beira were given as examples. The Government was supported by 225 votes to 54.

Wednesday, June 15th
Before the big debate in Committee Room 14, where the P.M. was going to meet his critics in the Parliamentary Party, I had a little meeting with Professor Bowley, the economist Harold insisted on. Tommy brought her over to see me and she turned out to be a trim, sleek, good-looking, white-haired lady, obviously very distinguished. Steve, who was there to look at her, wondered how she was going to fit in as my personal adviser. There would be some advantage having a person in my office reading Cabinet papers. I was not sure she would do, but I said I would consider her because with Harold as my boss I must be careful to show a proper respect for statisticians.[1]

Since we had been instructed to attend by the Chief Whip, I went across to the Commons in good time to get a seat on the platform. It was a good thing I did so because otherwise I would have missed an extraordinary incident. Woodrow Wyatt got up and made a long statement about his having been hauled before the liaison committee on the ground that he had leaked an account of the previous Party meeting in his *Daily Mirror* article. He then proceeded to annihilate the platform by reading aloud the counter-leaks which had been given out by poor Gerald Kaufman. With all the points of order which followed, this took so long that Manny Shinwell had a good excuse for limiting speeches to five minutes and then letting the Prime Minister wind

[1] As a former university lecturer in Economics and between 1943 and 1944 the Director of Economics and Statistics at the Ministry of Fuel and Power, the Prime Minister was notoriously contemptuous of (Conservative) statistical illiteracy. In 1970 he became President of the Royal Statistical Society.

up. When I saw the thickness of the Prime Minister's manuscript I knew we were in for fifty minutes and was worried at the idea that all that Mayhew and Joel Barnett[1] and the other chief speakers had from the floor was a miserable five minutes each. They could not make much use of it and there was a good deal of ill-feeling when Harold replied.

He started by pointing out the strange alliance between Christopher Mayhew and Woodrow Wyatt on the right[2] with the traditional left-wingers and then went on to make his usual Bevinite speech. His theme was that though he was prepared to withdraw and reduce the number of troops East of Suez he would never deny Britain the role of a world power. He also asserted once again that there's no kind of understanding between him and Johnson about Malaya and Vietnam. But most of his audience realized that there was no understanding because there was no need of one: the President could reckon on Harold Wilson. While he was talking, Jim came in and sat beside me on the other side from Fred Peart. Throughout the speech he whispered to me how totally he disagreed and told me that he thought Denis Healey holds much the same view as he does and that George Brown wasn't enthusiastic. East of Suez is solely the P.M.'s line—the P.M. with George Wigg's backing. Undoubtedly, it's all a fantastic illusion. How can anyone build up Britain now as a great power East of Suez when we can't even maintain the sterling area and some of our leaders are having the idea of creeping inside Europe in order to escape from our independence outside? Of course, it was done with very great skill, but I was sure when Harold sat down that if I hadn't been a Minister I wouldn't have held up my hand in the vote when it was taken.

I talked afterwards with Geoffrey Rhodes and said to him that if I hadn't been on the platform I would have abstained. He said to me (you could have knocked me over with a feather—Geoffrey Rhodes, the most careerist young right-winger), 'I did abstain after that speech. I couldn't possibly have supported it.' Though the speech may have a good effect on public opinion outside Westminster, I am sure that inside the Parliamentary Party it will have done nothing to heal the rift. If the Left can disentangle itself from the Woodrow Wyatts and the Mayhews, it can grow really strong, because this policy is based on pure wish-fulfilment. Harold is now trying to be a kind of British de Gaulle but, unlike the General, at the same time he wants to nestle under the shadow of the U.S.A. and restore Ernest Bevin's concept of the special relationship.

I gave lunch to Lord Antrim, the head of the National Trust, whom I wanted to persuade to work with me on the preservation of the coastline. It's ridiculous, I told him, for the Trust to buy all the land safeguarded already by the planning controls of local authorities. It should concentrate on grey

[1] An accountant, he had been Labour M.P. for the Heywood Division of Lancashire since 1964.
[2] Mayhew was upset about defence policy and Wyatt about steel nationalization.

areas under bad local authorities, which are not safeguarded. I think I made some impression but he is obviously deeply suspicious.

I had to get across the river to the Ministry of Transport by 2.30 because Barbara and I were having a big meeting with all the representatives of the interests concerned with Humberside planning and the Humber bridge. It was a sweltery, thundery afternoon; and it was one of those examples of a meeting which is an absolute waste of time. Everybody made the right speeches, we made the right replies – no decisions were taken. There are a great many non-events taking place in Whitehall every day. One of the jobs of a Minister is to reduce their number to the very minimum.

At the Ministry in the afternoon Ullswater was once again on the agenda and for a very curious reason. I had convinced the amenity interests that I was really in earnest about conservation by promising drastically to amend the Manchester Water Bill. Up comes a paper from Mr Street, our divisional head, which had succeeded in amending the Bill by implication and to the least possible extent. Indeed, it looked exactly the same. I had to explain that it must look as different as possible and he must ostentatiously spatchcock the changes into the old text as though I had really made hay of it. There are some times when a Minister really has a job to do because a civil servant can't see what the right procedure is. In the end I think Mr Street realized that we must not only amend the Bill effectively but be seen to be amending it.

By this time Sydney Littlewood, Pilcher, Donnison and our Rent Act staff were all waiting for me. My own people had been deeply upset by Frank Allaun's attack on the way the Act was being interpreted in the rent assessment committees. On the other hand, Littlewood seemed blithely unaware of the damage his speech to the National Association of Property Owners had done when he had remarked that Labour M.P.s didn't know their own Act. I still believe that Littlewood is interpreting the Act rightly. The trouble is that he is pompous and in the rent assessment committee he is turning what we meant to be an informal factual inquiry into a forensic process on which he pontificates like a judge. However, I managed to persuade him to go down to Tower Hamlets and have a big case this weekend where he would really reduce some of the rents at the bottom of the scale.

Having given a dinner to Hans Habe, the German novelist who used to work as the head of American leaflet-writing with me during the war, I caught the train at King's Cross for a three-day visit to Yorkshire and Lincolnshire.

Saturday, June 18th
I spent my first day in Lincolnshire studying Humberside planning and my second day in Lincoln town, from whence I went on to Leeds where I spent the evening with Karl Cohen at one of his typical Jewish suppers. Afterwards, in came people from all the big construction firms, Wimpey, Parkinson, etc. What a power Karl Cohen as chairman of the Leeds housing committee

holds over these big contractors. If he wasn't a strictly honourable man, which he is, he could be so easily corrupted, because he is personally disposing of millions of pounds'-worth of contracts and this is particularly open to corruption now that 70 per cent of his building is industrialized.

I caught the train back to Banbury in time to give George Hodgkinson dinner. I'd had a furious row with Steve during the week when I discovered that the knight on the M.H.L.G. list was not to be George Hodgkinson but Charles Barratt, the town clerk. I had put George Hodgkinson forward as my very first choice but in the end under pressure I had agreed to have Barratt put in as second best. Of course they saw their chance and preferred Barratt. That was the last act the Dame committed as Permanent Secretary.

Sunday, June 19th
While I have been away the P.M. has intervened in the seamen's strike but has failed to settle it. Now it is a straight fight and the balance of payments is getting rapidly worse. We are drifting on to the rocks and another July crisis is almost certain.

Monday, June 20th
The first meeting of the new Cabinet Committee on Environmental Planning, which Harold Wilson has set up in order to bring together George Brown, Barbara Castle and myself in the organization of physical planning. When the idea was first ventilated Steve was very much against it. He told me it was dangerous poppycock and that the only aim was to enable D.E.A. to take over control of physical planning from me. I told him that there was a great deal to commend the idea and that if I had been in charge of D.E.A. I would have done just the same. Nevertheless, I didn't want to allocate staff to a new unit which would plan in the abstract. What I wanted to see was an integrated unit getting down to preparing for the planning of Humberside, a job which can't be done by my Ministry or Barbara's Ministry or George's Ministry in isolation. In this spirit I had a meeting with George Brown; and I was upset that John Delafons interpreted the minutes as giving a clear victory to D.E.A. Well, today I proved myself right. I got it agreed that Humberside should now take priority over everything else and that the new integrated unit should be a practical operations unit and not work in the stratosphere. Richard Marsh was very cynical and worldly-wise and suggested that it was natural gas which was giving Humberside priority. I wasn't too upset. Natural gas is a useful argument to add to the other arguments for building the bridge and getting on with the New Town.

So I am pleased; but I am also quite clear that anything I get done about Humberside won't affect me as a Minister or indeed us as a Government. There can't be a house built there until long after the next general election. Even if I cut back by years the time taken to designate the area and get the New Town machinery moving, it will be at least three years before we can hope to see anything on the ground. What we shall do as a Government is to make the infrastructure for a New Town to be built by our successors.

The other interesting meeting today was with members of the Basingstoke development group. The town development at this wonderfully ugly little Hampshire town is being run jointly by a very good county council, the G.L.C., which is also very capable, and, of course, the U.D.C. It is probably the most successful scheme outside Swindon. I had been down to see it and I found the first housing there very dreary—lines of cantonments. Then I had a first warning last January that the architect of the Basingstoke Group had a wonderful new idea called 'Popley II'—an ambitious scheme for five-storey blocks of maisonettes. It is an extremely ingenious architectural device which provides decks for the top maisonettes so that there can be families on the fifth storey. There would be no private gardens but rather better public and open space. The Department pointed out that to do this would cost at least £150 a house more than our costing yardstick allowed. Moreover, Womersley had persuaded Southampton to do a small experiment of 120 houses in this style of building. Now, before that had been finished, he was trying to get loan sanction for 8,000 houses to be built at Basingstoke during 1967. I had begun to realize that largely as a result of accepting the Parker Morris standards, council housing is already becoming dangerously expensive. I felt here was an opportunity to set an example by refusing to allow the Basingstoke Group to exceed our Ministry cost yardstick by such a huge amount. So there was the delegation, headed by Steel, the chairman of the Development Group, and Womersley, on one side of the big conference table when I came in from my room. At once they pummelled, bullied and tried to blackmail me into conceding the agreement, mainly on the ground that they had carried things right the way forward and already got all the tenders and contracts out. With the full support of Stevenson, who sees the need for economy, and also of Peter Lederer, though he has now left the Department, I turned them down flat. I said I knew I was doing this terribly late in the day but I had to make an example of one scheme and I had selected Basingstoke because the architecture was good. If we allowed this one, all the other much worse architects would say that they would have the right to go beyond Parker Morris standards and to exceed the Ministry yardstick. I added I would never again permit our Ministry people to let a scheme get this far without exerting our sanction.

When I had finished I realized that I now had the theme for my big speech on Friday to the Urban District Councils Association and I said to John, 'Here's another chore for you.' John Delafons has developed into much more than a Private Secretary. He is now writing a large part of my speeches. I wasn't in the least surprised when I found Steve saying to me this week that I must appreciate that he will soon get promotion and I can't have him much longer.

I gave dinner in the House to a strange developer who had taken columns of space in *The Times* and other papers to advertise his dislike of delayed planning permissions. What was odd was that when we came to examine his cases we found that they really weren't cases of serious Ministerial obstruction. During dinner I became quite clear that what he really wanted was that he and other developers should get inside the Ministry. Perhaps he had heard about my talks with Hyams. There is something in the idea of getting one of the developers closer to us for consultation.

Tuesday, June 21st

Cabinet. The interesting question was how, individually and collectively, we would react to Harold's cool and deliberate Statement to the House yesterday that he knew the names of the active communists who had been responsible for starting the seamen's strike.[1] This had caused consternation on the Labour back benches, but Harold showed no kind of repentance. Instead, he went round the table and forced each of us to define our position. Frank Cousins, Barbara Castle and I were all pretty critical of him, and on this occasion we had rather more support from people like Fred Lee. The Cabinet in fact was fairly balanced and his position is not too strong.

Next we had a desultory discussion on the Channel Tunnel and the fact that we can't build it unless we hand it over to private enterprise. Frank Cousins raised a furious protest—if ever there was a case for public enterprise this was it. Barbara pointed out that the French, in 50-per-cent collaboration, don't want to burden their public economy with the capital cost. I supported Barbara pretty strongly, though with a different argument: it really would be insane to insist on the cost being met out of public funds since it would simply mean there would be less for housing and schools. It was strange to find myself on the same side as the Chancellor.

At about twelve o'clock we came to the main issue—prices and incomes. The question was what George Brown would say next day to the Parliamentary Party, where we thought there would be very strong opposition to his reintroducing the Bill (which fell when the general election was announced). He told us that a great deal had been done to make it less offensive and in particular to reduce the risks of imprisonment. Moreover, it might never come into operation; but he demanded complete Cabinet backing for the policy as represented in the Bill.

This started off an excited Cabinet discussion. Frank Cousins, as always, said the whole thing was complete poppycock and this time he would have to make a real stand. Barbara launched the idea of a policy with two different levels of award—a two-norm policy; and Callaghan wanted a complete freeze—a nil-norm—for the next twelve months. Barbara then said we ought to cut our Ministerial salaries and at this point Ministers began to drift away. It was an occasion when Harold's leadership was a bit shaken because we

[1] The Prime Minister alleged that hidden forces, 'a tightly knit group of politically motivated men', were working to prolong the seamen's strike.

were coming into the open with our anxieties about the whole economic situation. Right at the end I said that a prices and incomes policy was not an adequate substitute for a socialist alternative to the old-fashioned deflation with unemployment into which we were drifting. It was the measures with which he proposed to stop that drift that I wanted to see. I didn't mind them being linked with an incomes policy but what I didn't want was to see us using an incomes policy alone. The P.M. was rather shirty and said he would have a discussion on productivity on July 5th. He had to make the concession when people like Tony Crosland were telling him not to drift into another July crisis like last year. He must also have realized that the reason for all this disturbance was the failure of his S.E.T. budget. We are only just starting on the Finance Bill but already we are having to consider measures to prop up a budget policy which has proved inadequate.

In the evening I went across to No. 10 for a liaison committee supper which Harold was due to attend. This was the meeting we had decided upon before I went on holiday. Ron Brown, George Brown's brother,[1] had said he would do a strategy paper from the Parliamentary side, and Terry Pitt was to do one from the Transport House point of view. By the beginning of the week I found that this was having the strangest repercussions. As soon as Len Williams and Sara Barker at Transport House heard about the strategy discussion they wanted it stopped. Then Ted Short heard what one of his Whips was up to and wanted it stopped from his side. And then George Brown heard what his younger brother was up to and began to ask why he had been left out. So everyone got into action to stop our little group from having a meeting to discuss Party strategy – and when, as he told me, George Wigg was rung up and accused of running the meeting he was able to say he'd had nothing to do with it.

So when I went across to No. 10 at 7.30 there were Terry and all the rest of them sitting downstairs rather sheepishly over their drinks. Ron Brown rushed up to me with the paper he hadn't typed and asked me to read it, and I said, 'Oh, there aren't any papers this evening. I've told your brother there's nothing much on.' Then Terry Pitt took me outside and said it was quite right to meet like this but there was tremendous feeling at Transport House.

So we hung around and talked until Harold came; and then after a little supper we moved into the drawing-room. To my amazement we settled down to a perfectly sensible discussion. I told Harold we were worried about exactly what we were to do, what we were aiming at now, what our short-term and long-term objectives were. Then he skilfully got each person to say what he or she felt to be wrong (Terry Pitt was quite good) and we did have a coherent discussion about the nature of the crisis inside the Parliamentary Party and in the Party outside Westminster. Harold seemed to leave us with the single,

---

[1] M.P. for Shoreditch and Finsbury since 1964. He was Assistant Government Whip 1966–7.

clear, practical conclusion that we must concentrate on preparing for Party Conference. He also revealed that Barbara and Tony Greenwood had suggested to him that this year they shouldn't stand for the Executive, whereupon Callaghan and Tony Wedgwood Benn had said that they would certainly stand. I suppose Barbara and Tony are scared of being knocked off because being in Cabinet they will be associated with Harold Wilson's anti-communist line on the seamen's strike.

I got home at 11.45 and started on my red box. Tam had to stay for the Finance Bill at the House until four in the morning.

Wednesday, June 22nd
I went to Vincent Square to lunch with Anne and Jennie in order to tidy up my office and set up Jennie in her new job as the archivist who manages my diary. The arrangements with the publishers are nearly completed and it was very nice for a change to be doing a little work, having a little life, apart from the Ministry.

In the afternoon Barbara presented her draft Transport White Paper to the E.D.C. I had had a look at it when I was at Humberside and had got the impression that she was rushing it forward much too soon. Now it is clear that it incorporates far too much of the original Tom Fraser White Paper which we rejected and far too little of Christopher Foster's new approaches. Getting real changes into Ministerial policy takes quite a long time. I think her determination to rush it into print is a disaster because it is most of it pretty second-hand stuff. But I did what I could to help her, partly for old-times' sake and partly for tactical reasons. I want to get real integrated planning between myself and Transport.

In the evening I addressed the annual dinner of the Institute of Sewage Purification at the Metropole Hotel at Brighton under the chairmanship of the mayor, a very handsome woman. I had agreed to do this a year before on the clear understanding that I would use the opportunity to denounce the scandal of Brighton's antiquated sewage arrangements and to announce action by the Ministry to compel seaside resorts either to have adequate screening plus long enough pipes into the sea to stop the stuff coming back or, alternatively, to have it processed in very expensive plants inland. John Delafons and I had worked out a jolly good speech and I delivered it with great verve, just managing to get away with it by introducing a joke about the Brighton outfall being listed as an ancient monument. I also released the astonishing fact that most of the french letters in the Brighton filth after being taken out to sea get swept up on the beach at Rottingdean a few miles away. It was curious that only one paper, the *Sun*, even mentioned that I had spoken. As for what was really a sensational news story, nobody carried it. Instead, every one of them carried a story that I had let Mellish represent me at the annual lunch of the N.H.B.R.C. as though I had funked making a speech on the occasion. It only shows you what luck is in public relations.

Thursday, June 23rd

Cabinet. We started with the seamen's strike. There was a lot of detailed discussion of the work of the strike emergency committee; but the important fact was that the atmosphere is now slightly better and the strike is almost certainly coming to an end since the seamen are prepared for some kind of settlement.

So we resumed Tuesday's discussion of prices and incomes. Right at the beginning Frank Cousins made a melodramatic remark. 'You ought to remember', he said to Harold, 'that the Minister of Technology is first for Questions on the day after the Second Reading of the Prices and Incomes Bill. He ought to be warned of this, you know.' This was Frank's way of telling us that he was going to resign on the day the Bill was debated. James Callaghan pleaded with him and then Harold said that he was impressed by Frank's brilliantly successful ideas and vigorous policies and that he had also received some instructive suggestions about productivity increases. Why couldn't we consider all these? Harold will certainly do everything to keep Frank. He has loaded him with new jobs, expanded his Ministry and given him two first-rate young Parliamentary Secretaries, Peter Shore and Edmund Dell.[1] But can he keep him now? After that, Barbara Castle fired off and really made a very good speech on a socialist prices and incomes policy. She behaved as I should really behave, she was a Cabinet Minister playing that role. Her main theme was the two norms under which we would try to use the incomes policy to improve the lot of the lower-paid worker while holding down the higher salaries. She also urged the introduction of a national minimum wage and the application of the policy on dividends as well as wages.

In our weekly lunch with the Parliamentary Secretaries we discussed an item which illustrates the working of Whitehall pretty well. Weeks ago Denis Howell complained to me that as Minister of Sport he was sick of the sabotage he was getting from my Ministry, which prevented him getting a clear definition of what sport is and how it should be run. I looked into it and found that we were being fairly obstructive, so said to Steve that he should let D.E.S. deal with sport and not cling on to our bits and pieces in the Department. As a result, a paper came up to me saying that the officials of both Departments had discussed my instruction and as a result they recommended that the whole of sport should be transferred from D.E.S. to Housing. So that's what happens when a Minister tries to be generous. You offer to give up to a colleague some little bits and pieces and you are presented on a plate with the whole thing.

After lunch I went back to my room for the meeting with Mr Pearson, the new president of the National Federation of Building Trades Employers, and Mr Grafton, the director-general, whom I had seen before with the old

---

[1] A former history lecturer and I.C.I. executive, elected in 1964 as M.P. for Birkenhead.

president, Kirby Laing. This was the most extraordinary meeting. But let me explain. On Monday morning Peter Brown showed me an outrageous statement which had been issued on Saturday by the builders and which had provoked another leading article in the *Sunday Express* saying that the building programme was collapsing because of the prejudice I was displaying against owner-occupation. I was furious, and that day I issued a statement challenging the president of the N.F.B.T.E. to meet me on television and make this charge to my face. What I didn't know when I issued the statement was that Kirby Laing had now been replaced by a brand-new little man from Durham who was terrified by the challenge and was trying to get out of it. We had a long talk this afternoon and for some reason we hit it off. I told him straight away that he might like to know that those councils employing direct labour and building new houses in competition with private enterprise would have to pay S.E.T. on the employees engaged on new housing. On maintenance, on the other hand, the local authority as the owner of the houses would claim the right to be reimbursed. 'My God, that will make a difference,' said Mr Pearson. When he got up to go I asked him about the broadcast, and he told me he couldn't possibly do it. With a tremendous effort I persuaded him to appear with me on *Panorama* on Monday—Peter Brown had, during the week, got a whole twenty minutes. I said, 'I have challenged you, Mr Pearson, but if you don't want it to be a challenge let's go on the air and show that we are working together and that neither of us has any prejudice against the other. I want a change of atmosphere.' And then Mr Pearson said, 'Well, I don't want a political dogfight.' Have I achieved anything? Well, we'll see on Monday.

In the evening, with Peter's help, I started mending my fences with the press, which has been giving me a thoroughly bad time since I got back from Crete. I briefed Anthony Shrimsley of the *Sunday Mirror* and Nora Beloff of the *Observer* as fully as I possibly could on what I am going to say on Friday, including an account of the option-mortgage—Steve and I have virtually worked out the details of what is really a brilliant scheme. I also lunched Jimmy Margach at the Ecu de France, and told him we were going to help the private builders cope with S.E.T., and all about the option-mortgage. So I hope we shall have a relatively friendly press this weekend as a lead-up to the *Panorama* show on Monday, which is really tremendously important for me.

Meanwhile, all through the day John Delafons had been working away at the text of my speech for the U.D.C.s in Blackpool on Friday. We decided, and Steve liked the idea, that it was to be a cost-conscious speech. Kenneth Wood threw in all his own excellent ideas and I decided to make a big thing of the Basingstoke situation (without of course quoting the name Basingstoke) and say I wasn't going to go on allowing local authorities to waste money on standards higher than Parker Morris. Then, after announcing the direct labour concession to the builders, I would end with a tough statement on rent rebate policies for the councils, as well as on the councillors' code of conduct. By the end of the day the Secretary was so excited about the speech that he wanted to circulate it to the Department. I really had only a minor responsibility for shaping it. The job was done by John Delafons.

I had had to cancel all my engagements except the Cabinet Committee on Procedure which has been discussing the new specialist committees and other ideas for modernizing Parliament. It's got into a terrible rut; but we discussed a possible time-table for two morning sessions a week. I am rather hoping this will work because it might at least give the impression that we are modernizing Parliament. Meanwhile, the House of Lords has stolen a march on us by agreeing to have a TV experiment. It's quite clear they are determined to use every kind of publicity in order to keep themselves alive when they know they are threatened by the Labour Government. As for the specialist committees to investigate Departments, the plan, which I like so much, has got bogged down because there are so many people in Whitehall opposing it and briefing their Ministers to oppose. So the reform of Parliament has already lost the drive the P.M. gave it during the election campaign.

I just had time to get back to Vincent Square, pack a bag and catch the sleeper to Preston.

On June 28th the Prime Minister substantiated his charges of hard-core militancy in the seamen's union by naming eight communists, some within the union. He accused them of using the strike to sabotage the Government's prices and incomes policy. While some critics questioned the Prime Minister's use of Parliamentary privilege in this way, it nevertheless seemed that his statement had some effect on the union.

But July brought more troubles. The publication of the Steel Bill on July 1st was to lead to further internal Party quarrels. On July 7th the Government again came under fire from its own back-benchers in a debate on the Vietnam war. The debate had been conceded after 113 Labour M.P.s had signed a Commons motion calling on the Government to dissociate itself completely from United States policy in Vietnam.

Gold and dollar reserves had dropped again in June and on July 5th sterling was to fall to its lowest point ($2·78\frac{11}{16}$) for twenty months.

Sunday, June 26th

On Friday morning I got out of the train at Preston into driving rain; and when the car reached Blackpool I had never seen such a storm coming in from the sea. Lying in my bath in the hotel I had a relaxed feeling that all I needed to prepare was the beginning of my speech before I got on to what John Delafons had drafted and sent out in an admirable press release. So I put together all the extra bits they wanted me to do about the councillors' code of honour, representation on the Royal Commission, pay of councillors, etc. There were 3,000 people there in the Winter Gardens, not as full as for a

Labour Party Conference but a very big occasion, and I got pretty good coverage in the Saturday morning papers as well as in the provincial evenings. But the newsiest item, my concession to the builders, wasn't mentioned by anyone. A good thing too because it left something for Jimmy Margach in the *Sunday Times*.

After lunch with the executive, Lord Grimston, who I remember as chairman of Committees in the House of Commons, motored me all the way back to Coventry in his Jaguar. There I had my surgery before coming home to find Connie Bessie, the wife of Mike Bessie, my American publisher, who has been left by him and who brought her two adopted children to stay. Michael and Jill Foot had been utterly exhausted by them after a few weeks; we were utterly exhausted after one weekend. American children are exciting but ours are a bit of a relief after them.

Looking back over a very long week I realize how bad it was for the Government – and also for me personally, although there are chances of my staging a comeback. It all starts from last Monday with Harold Wilson's phenomenal attack on the communists in the seamen's union. It was a deliberate act, rather like his speech on East of Suez with which most of the Cabinet disagreed. It has put the Parliamentary Party into an even more difficult mood. They have refused to accept the report of the liaison committee on their bicker with Woodrow Wyatt and they are looking forward to a new clash with Harold on foreign policy. But it is not only the Parliamentary Party – Fleet Street is geared up to a campaign against the Government, and the weeklies like the *Spectator*, *New Statesman* and *Tribune* are joining in; so that there is virtual press unanimity about the failures of Wilson's leadership and also of his individual Ministers. As I say, I had a fairly bad week. Denis Healey had an even worse one. There was an appalling incident in the House when he was caught out about our attempt to pay for the new American planes with offset purchases. I think the S.E.T. debate on Thursday was pretty disastrous, too, despite the nonchalant style in which Jim defended it as a good tax. Everybody I know feels it was a gimmick which will prove a disaster to us all.

M. Pompidou, the French Premier, was due to visit London for two days on July 6th. Some hoped that this would improve Anglo–French relations, damaged in 1963 by General de Gaulle's veto on Britain's entry to the E.E.C. and injured still further by differences over defence and foreign policy. But the remarks of the Defence Secretary, Denis Healey, shortly before the visit, did not augur well. The Minister had referred to the General as 'a bad ally in NATO and a bad partner in Europe'. He apologized in Parliament on June 7th.

The only concrete outcome of M. Pompidou's visit was a decision by the two Governments to proceed with building a Channel Tunnel. The French Premier's reminder that before joining the Common Market France herself had undergone a devaluation and a severe wage freeze was not pleasant to British ears.

Tuesday, June 28th

I travelled up to London on Monday extremely pleased that I had prepared myself so carefully for the crucial meeting of the Cabinet Housing Committee in No. 10. I had extracted a first-rate brief from my Ministry and also got a first-rate Sunday press. We were due to start at 11.30 but a Rhodesia meeting dragged on. When I finally went into the room I found the P.M. looking harassed and George Brown and James Callaghan pretty sullen. Before I could sit down the P.M. said, 'I wonder whether it is worth having these meetings with the kind of leaks we saw in the Sunday press,' and George Brown added, 'This whole option-mortgage scheme is in the *Financial Times* this morning. I don't know whether we can really carry on with this Committee in this situation.' This took my breath away because, of course, I had organized the interviews with Jimmy Margach and Anthony Shrimsley and Nora Beloff, and thought they had done a first-rate job. I hadn't seen the *Financial Times*, which had got a detailed account of the option-mortgage scheme. But there again I had instructed Peter Brown to let them have all the information they asked for because there is no security on the option-mortgage scheme and I wanted the papers to know that we were on the edge of agreement. So after they'd gone on for two or three minutes I said quite sharply, 'There is no question of a leak, this was done on my instructions by the Department. Let's get down to business.' We did so in a thoroughly bad atmosphere and it soon became clear that I was going to have the usual resistance from the Chancellor and not much help from George Brown. The case I put in my paper was that since the private sector was now sagging badly Cabinet must make good its promise to let the public sector take up the slack. I had also inserted two proposals which would help owner-occupiers – the relaxation of restriction on local authority mortgages and assistance in bridging finance for builders. When I asked about the second, the Chancellor replied, 'Bridging finance? I've made housing bottom priority and that's where it stays. As for local government mortgages, there can't be any more money this year.' 'Well,' I said, 'if that is so, the private sector can't recover. And in that case, Chancellor, you've give away my case for putting up the figures for public-sector building.'

If this didn't endear me to him it did to all the other members of the Committee. But then they are all housing ministers – the Secretary of State for Scotland, the Secretary of State for Wales, the Minister of Works and Bob Mellish. I only lost on one thing: the Prime Minister ruled that the 7,000 miners' houses must be reckoned next year as part of the public sector.[1]

Though I had won, I came away from the meeting a bit shaken by Harold's outburst about leaks. I had no doubt of the explanation. Two or three months ago Nora Beloff wrote a couple of articles about the P.M. which contained a certain amount of gossip she had collected from the P.M.'s colleagues, and

[1] See p. 537.

two quite friendly stories clearly came from me. The P.M. had taken deep umbrage at these articles, cut her off from access to No. 10 and told Cabinet that she must be denied interviews by any of us. Now right across the bottom of the *Observer* front page last Sunday was a Beloff story on housing. Of course, if he had read it carefully he would have seen it was an official hand-out which Peter Brown was perfectly entitled to give. But he just objected to my having gone near her and felt that this proved that I was the person who had provided all the gossip for her stories last December.

If I left it, this could work out dangerously. There was only one thing to do. I wrote the P.M. a very strong minute and sent it across to Marcia Williams by hand to make sure copies didn't go to Callaghan and Brown. On the other hand I knew that once it had got into the Downing Street machine everybody in No. 10 would know that I had written him a strong minute asking for an apology for what I thought was an outrageous comment.

All that day I was looking forward to my meeting with Mr Pearson on *Panorama*. I assumed that he would be allowed to put a whole series of questions to me about option-mortgages and land, and I would answer them simply and frankly. So I briefed myself very carefully for this. But it isn't what happened. As soon as I got there I suspected that Robin Day, who was in the chair, was determined to have a row. He wasn't going to tolerate what he thought was collusion (he had read in the Sunday papers about Mr Pearson and myself). What the B.B.C. wanted was good entertainment and that required a row either between me and Mr Pearson or between Robin Day and me or between Mr Pearson and Robin Day. Before we went on I said, 'For God's sake, Robin, don't have a row with the poor president. He's terrified out of his wits.' So Robin started on me but that didn't go particularly well since I knew my facts. Quite soon he got tired of it and turned on poor little Mr Pearson and asked him whether he personally agreed with the attacks on me. This put him into a tail-spin and he talked on and on and became an unmitigated bore and we really achieved nothing. The more I think of this incident the more outrageous it seems. Robin Day wasn't in the least concerned to let the public know about the issue between me and the builders. He was just concerned with what he calls 'good broadcasting'.

I went from Lime Grove to the House where I had agreed to reply to the half-hour adjournment debate on my Ullswater scheme. Alas! I had said I would take it myself before I realized that it would come at the end of a session of the Finance Bill and so not at ten o'clock but at the end of an all-night sitting. When I did realize this I tried to pass the buck back to the Parliamentary Secretaries, but they of course had got themselves paired. So I went back to my room and got a bit of sleep, went down at midnight to see how things were going and again at five in the morning and each time had a good talk with our back-benchers in the tea-room. Finally at 7.30 Alf Morris[1]

---

[1] Labour M.P. for Manchester (Wythenshawe) since 1964.

and Mr Jopling, the Tory Cumberland M.P.,[1] made their points and I was so tired that I misread the clock and took six minutes for my reply instead of the fifteen to which I was entitled. Nevertheless, I had done my duty and incidentally acquired a lot of goodwill among the back-benchers. 'Dick Crossman was about the place,' they said. 'Wonderful to see him staying up for an adjournment debate.' Little did they know ...

Having stayed up all night I decided to go to Cabinet and let Harold react to my minute about the leaks. I listened to the usual chit-chat about the seamen's strike and Rhodesia and then there was a really interesting discussion on the draft White Paper dealing with the House of Lords. The issue was whether we should simply cut the powers of the Lords or also change their composition. Frank Longford wanted to change composition. This is something on which I have differed with Frank for ages and I was relieved to find that practically everybody round the table, headed by George Brown, was also against dealing with composition. Winding up, the P.M. said to Frank wryly that any attempt to change the composition would be bound to cause trouble in the Party. He was quite right. Once you consider such a proceeding you get into the conflict between those who want two chambers and those who who want unicameral government, as I do. I said quite bluntly that the best way to get unicameral government in this country was to have two chambers officially but to have the second one so discredited by its composition that it was no threat at all, i.e. to cut the Lords' powers but otherwise leave it composed of hereditary peers and just enough life peers to keep it going. Frank Longford called me utterly cynical and destructive and added, 'What would happen if the Minister of Housing ever found himself Leader of the House of Lords?' To which Harold Wilson replied, 'Well, he's not going to be in the Lords for a very long time. I can tell you that, my dear Frank.' After which Cabinet broke up and he took me aside and gave me his apology, though he said he wouldn't put it into writing.

In the afternoon there were important doings in the House of Commons. I got there very sleepy to answer Questions and after I had finished I sat in a half-doze while Harold Wilson had a brilliant passage of arms with Heath. It arose because on Monday we had had a bad day, with Denis Healey apologizing for insulting General de Gaulle and Callaghan apologizing for rewriting Hansard in a very minor way. Now in came Heath with a fresh attack on the P.M., once again about General de Gaulle. Harold annihilated him by showing that if Healey had been fairly rude to de Gaulle, Heath had been even ruder in the past. No sympathy for Heath. A professional politician is tempted to rub salt in the wounds but if he tries that trick he ought to anticipate what he will get in return. I went out after that, leaving Harold to make his Statement naming the men responsible for the seamen's strike, which he had discussed in Cabinet that morning. I didn't want to hear it.

[1] Michael Jopling, in fact Conservative M.P. for Westmorland since 1964. In 1971 he became an Assistant Government Whip.

In the evening I talked to Tam Dalyell at length about this whole naming affair. We both feel it is an example of Wiggery-pokery.[1] George Wigg has been busy on this for weeks, organizing the counter-security against the trade-union communists, collecting the whole story into his hands, trying to get it into the press and, when he couldn't, selling it to the P.M. instead. This has been George's biggest success since the Profumo affair.[2] Neither he nor the P.M. pretended it was necessary in order to finish the strike. What they wanted was to use the strike to discomfit the communists, not only in the seamen's union but in other unions as well. But would it after all prevent the ending of the strike? Tam and I just couldn't believe the strikers could be so abject, that after this attack had taken place they would call it a day. Then we went back to Vincent Square and switched on the television. There on *24 Hours* were six of the nine men he had named being questioned by Robin Day. It was a tremendously effective cross-examination which showed them up not only as formidable communists but as obviously guilty men. Yet I still wondered whether it was possible for the strike to be called off.

Wednesday, June 29th

I spent the day at Peterborough clearing up another of the New Town entanglements Dame Evelyn left behind. The idea of using the New Town technique to double the size of old towns had been worked out by the Dame under Keith Joseph. Under me she still kept it all in her own hands and told me she had left everything signed, sealed and delivered. A few weeks ago I went to Ipswich only to find that it wasn't by any means signed and sealed. Now I had to go to Peterborough because open conflict had broken out between the town council, which wanted to accept our consultant's report, and the county council, which had put forward a counter-plan. A morning on the ground showed me what had happened. The county of course wanted to put all the Londoners to the north-west of the town, whereas our consultant proposed to put them to the south-west where the gentry live in beautiful country. It was just the problem we have at Banbury. We Banbury farmers are trying to keep Londoners out of our part and push them into the other side. Influential county people were trying to do the same thing in Northants. It was a perfect day and I had a wonderful time seeing the country as well as some of the ancient monuments, stately homes and churches in which it abounds. As I was going round the cathedral there was a great service going on for the patron, St Peter, and a Canon was being inducted. I went into the cathedral behind the chief warden, who said, 'Hello, is that Dick Crossman? Spencer Leeson used to talk to me about you when he was

---

[1] George Wigg carrying out his part as special investigator on security matters.

[2] In the summer of 1963 there were rumours that John Profumo, the Secretary of State for War, was associating with a call-girl, Christine Keeler. George Wigg assembled evidence that there was a security risk and the subsequent scandal assisted the decline of the Conservative administration. See *Wigg*, pp. 263–90.

Bishop.[1] What are you doing here?' I said I was the Minister of Housing and he replied, 'You've come for no good purpose. You've come to create a New Town and double my rates.'

As we motored back to London I switched on the wireless and heard that the strike had been called off. So Harold Wilson had won yet another of his 'extra' victories. It was good enough to get the strike settled without giving anything away; it was even better to get it called off on the day after having denounced the communists in the union and challenged them to do their worst.

In the evening I dined with John Silkin in the House. It was a quiet evening, with the Finance Bill still teetering along in the Chamber. But despite Harold's tremendous victory, Silkin and I found a sense of discomfort in the Members' dining-room. The P.M.'s operation had been too McCarthyite for the taste of our new back-benchers; the naming of names had been gratuitous and unnecessary. Even though it was a great triumph, none of us sitting round the big table that evening really liked it.

Thursday, June 30th

This was the day for my big Cabinet battle on housing. But first we had to discuss compensation for steel owners (much less generous than last time) and then endure a long argument about the Parliamentary situation. Once again the Lord President and the Chief Whip have tried to pack far too much into the Session and we are already being pushed into the second week of August.

I was next on the agenda; and this was one of the few times I spoke in Cabinet from full notes. In addition to the case I knew by heart, I released a document which Steve had brought to my attention on Monday. It was the text of the Governor of the Bank of England's directive to banks on lending. It stated categorically that whereas exports were to be given priority, the construction industry was to get none at all; in particular council building, including council-house building, was not to be given priority. I was able to add this evidence to a description of how the Chancellor had cut back local-authority spending on mortgages and refused to assist the builders with bridging finance. In that case, I said, he must permit us to use public-sector building to make up for the sag.

The moment I had finished speaking Callaghan said that he would talk quite briefly because he had to go out to see the German Ambassador. Poor man, he had been up all night once again, dealing with his bloody S.E.T., and he was exhausted and bad-tempered, and maybe he had calculated that if he left the room he would thereby be able to stop Cabinet taking a decision. He put his case very clearly. Whatever the strength of my arguments for an immediate increase, he asked Cabinet to remember that I was demanding it a fortnight before his own proposals were to be submitted to Cabinet

[1] The Reverend Canon Spencer Leeson had been Bishop of Peterborough 1949-61.

for cutting back public expenditure as a whole. All he asked now was for housing to be considered along with other demands. If this wasn't done, the whole PESC exercise would fall to the ground. He concluded with the threat, 'If you concede this £31 million to the Ministry of Housing I shall take it away from the other spending authorities.' And with that he stalked out of the room.

Before anybody else could weigh in, the Prime Minister backed me to the full. He confirmed that last July Cabinet had cut back the housing programme for 1965 and for 1966 on the express understanding that if there were a sag in the private sector I could compensate in the public sector. Unless this were done, the whole programme would be in jeopardy. At once Tony Crosland and Barbara Castle jumped in to urge that the decision should be postponed until after PESC. I replied that I had been postponing it for seven months, ever since last December when the Chancellor predicted that the private-sector building would go up to 235,000. His predictions had proved wrong and mine had proved right. The figure for 1966 is 210,000, 20,000 short of his own prediction, and I must ask for that number of council houses. At last George Brown came in, more or less on my side. He even admitted there was truth in the complaint I was putting forward, with Tommy Balogh's help, about the intolerable nature of the PESC exercise, and concluded that if I were to get my way, the cost of the extra houses must not be taken from some other social service. And that is how it was finally minuted in the absence of the Chancellor and against the protests of Barbara and Tony. I was to get my extra £31 million but they were not to be taken off anybody else's estimates.

So I got my way—with the help of the P.M. and at the cost of creating a great deal of resentment. The rest of Cabinet complain that the Housing Committee is packed with housing Ministers, and James Callaghan is protesting that no other spending Department is permitted the licence I get. Everybody really feels that we should have waited for the PESC exercise. I know that's how I would have felt if any other Minister has got away with it.

Cabinet wasn't by any means over. We now turned to discuss Concorde. I had to listen to that miserable little Mulley proposing once again that since the Attorney-General could find no loophole we should commit ourselves to it. I said this was absolutely mad and I would rather cancel the whole thing. Others joined in and said that it would be absurd to imagine that General de Gaulle could sue us for £120 million—or indeed, win his case if he did. It was also pointed out that if only we had held out for ten days longer in October 1964 the French would have given way. This Concorde commitment has been one of our major disasters and I was so disgusted that I walked out. I gather that after I left Cabinet agreed, in return for a substantial reduction in our contribution to Concorde, to remain a member of ELDO although we had four times decided to get out of it. If we got clean out of ELDO *and* cancelled Concorde, *that* would be the right atmosphere in which to discuss our relations with the European Community.

The P.M. also asked Cabinet to approve the Foreign Office press release issued the day before regretting the American decision to bomb Hanoi. We did so unenthusiastically because few of us, I think, felt it was more than a posture. We knew perfectly well that as soon as he got across the Atlantic and talked to Johnson, Harold would indicate to the President that there was nothing in what he had said or done which made his loyalty to the Vietnam policy less profound. Harold made a Statement of the recorded Cabinet decision to the House in the afternoon.[1] The back-benchers obviously shared our doubts, and a storm broke out. Strange to think that this humiliating rupture with his back-benchers took place less than forty-eight hours after the P.M.'s success over the seamen's strike. The demands for a debate went on for forty-five minutes.

The amended Prices and Incomes Bill was eventually published on July 4th. It gave the Government power to require wage, price or dividend increases to be submitted to the statutory Prices and Incomes Board. It would impose a delay of up to four months on any settlement but, as yet, sanctions were moral rather than penal.

On July 3rd the Minister of Technology, Frank Cousins, resigned. He had argued for voluntary co-operation between both sides of industry instead of an incomes policy.

The Postmaster-General, Anthony Wedgwood Benn, took Frank Cousins's place and the Chief Whip, Edward Short, succeeded Mr Benn. The Deputy Chief Whip, John Silkin, became Chief Whip. The full impact of the changes in the Whips' Office only became apparent some months later.

Sunday, July 3rd
Tommy Balogh rang up this morning to ask whether I had seen Foreign Office Guidance Cable 188. I said I would look for it in my red box. I could do so because I had actually asked John Delafons only last week to select some of the Government's key cables and submit them in the weekend box. So I went through the box and there it was, spelling out the line which all our embassies in Europe should take on British entry to the Common Market. True, it was strictly in accordance with the speech George Thomson had delivered to the Council of Europe. But what sense does this make when all the incoming official telegrams tell us there is no possible chance of our getting into Europe? I sat down this afternoon and tried to think it out. I'm sure now that we are drifting on to the rocks. I was nearly sure in March before the election; but now gold reserves are pouring out of the country again and the Callaghan budget has obviously failed to inspire confidence. Very soon we shall be faced with the choice between devaluation or intensive deflation. I suppose to some of my colleagues the idea of escaping from this terrible choice into the Common Market is attractive because once we are members

[1] See *Wilson*, pp. 247-8.

the blame for the deflation, the blame for the suffering, could be put not on this British Government but on conditions inside the E.E.C. That was really the reason why Macmillan suddenly became an enthusiastic Marketeer as soon as he got to No. 10, and I suspect much the same pressures are now working on Harold Wilson. Of course, he is far more reluctant than Macmillan to commit himself positively to the E.E.C. But though he personally is being pretty cagey about it, he is letting other people commit themselves because of his awareness that this Government is unable to master the crisis into which it is drifting.

But the big news in all the papers this weekend is, of course, Frank Cousins's resignation, which has finally been announced. He has managed to do it in the most clumsy way. Having announced his resignation, he rushed round to the T.G.W.U. in Smith Square and spent five hours with them working out what he was to do. After which he made a statement that he had decided to go back to being General Secretary of the union and that his salary had been increased. He added that he might as well stay in Parliament to oppose the Prices and Incomes Bill.

As a matter of fact the Committee Stage won't start till November and the Bill probably won't be on the Statute Book until March of next year so he'll stay quite a long time. Moreover, as all the Sunday papers are saying, he has probably committed a breach of privilege by announcing that he will work for his union while a Member and pay his Parliamentary salary back. He has also got into a bit of a mess with his constituency party. He was foisted on them, but they now like him very much as a good Member and a nice man. Just when they have got used to him, they certainly don't want another by-election! Moreover, being a left-wing Party they support his opposition to the Prices and Incomes Bill, and have unanimously told him that they want him to remain their M.P. even while he is General Secretary of the T.G.W.U. This puts him in a difficult position. If he stays on there will be no sense on the Left of the Parliamentary Party that a great leader has descended from Cabinet on to the back benches. In fact, he is much less dangerous to the Government in the House of Commons than if he goes outside and thrashes about like a great whale in industrial waters.

From what I can see, this Cousins crisis, if it is a crisis, is the kind which Harold is fully capable of overcoming. The resignation could not have come at a less inconvenient time for Harold Wilson. The only danger of it lies in our relations with the Conference where Frank—if he were let loose—could stir up the Left. This is something which Barbara Castle noticed. Directly she heard the news she rang me up (I was down at Slough on an official visit) and asked whether I was still thinking of not standing for the N.E.C. this year. That *had* been my idea, particularly since I had heard that she and Tony Greenwood were thinking of doing the same thing. Barbara said to me straight away on the phone that Frank's resignation made all this impossible. Marcia Williams, as I now hear, takes the same view; so I can assume that when I ask Harold's advice he will be against it. This is a big change for me, since as recently as last Saturday my mind was made up. It was the day of our Cropredy Country Fair and Albert Rose and Betty Healey were over with a lot of Coventry supporters. I discussed the idea very fully with them. They agreed that if I wanted to go this was a good year since nobody could say I was a coward being chased off by fear of defeat. If I resign this year people will know it is because I want to make room on the N.E.C. for younger people. They said that they would put this to the executive of the Coventry East constituency Party and that when I heard their advice I could make up my mind. However, I am pretty sure now that the decision must be 'not this year'.

Monday, July 4th

My first job when I got to London was to get down my minute to the Foreign Secretary on the Common Market. I have learnt the trick of this kind of minute during the last two years. One must write it very carefully in an informal style, halfway between talking and writing. Then one must be sure about the people who get copies. I first thought I would send it to all the Cabinet, but then I realized that that would be a declaration of war. In the end I sent copies to the P.M., the First Secretary, the Chancellor, the Minister of Agriculture (because he is an anti-Common Marketeer on the Europe Committee), and privately to Barbara and George as well as Tommy, who had already been rebuked by the P.M. for putting me up to it.

At twelve o'clock I had a big conference on countryside policy. This is something the old Ministry of Housing used to do. It was then lost when the Ministry of Land and Natural Resources was established, deservedly lost because it had been neglected under the Dame. It has now been brought back along with Willey and Skeffington and Richard Chilver, the new Deputy Secretary in charge. The difficulty is that Willey and Skeffington had rushed out a White Paper on this subject last March in time for the election and there was absolutely no new thinking in it. They now wanted to go ahead and produce a Bill based on the White Paper. I had come to the conclusion that we really mustn't put forward legislation on the countryside without a lot of rethinking and a really radical policy. My tactic at the meeting was to show that a whole number of important issues had been shirked and that they would all have to be seriously considered before we were ready for legislation. Fortunately I was just about able to do this. Then I announced that we would have a Churchill College conference next autumn at which we would prepare a policy. I hope by this method to have pushed off the danger of a miserable little departmental countryside Bill being rushed forward by the officials.

In the afternoon I had a meeting of our national housing-plan working-party – builders, insurance people and building societies – on land acquisition. It developed into a tremendous confrontation on the issue of the Land Commission, with the builders strenuously maintaining that it was a tremendous obstacle to new building. When I recaptured Willey's Ministry I was horrified to discover that the Land Commission had already been established, with fourteen regional headquarters and thousands of staff. Their main job will be to raise the betterment levy, which of course could have been collected far more cheaply by the Treasury as part of capital gains. The only part of the Land Commission's work which affects the builders is its land purchase and land sale policy. As the meeting went on I became more and more uneasily aware, from my own personal knowledge, that the builders' case is indeed extremely powerful. As the Land Commission created by Fred Willey begins to operate, there could be a genuine freeze-up for six months or even for a year after the appointed day. Nevertheless, my job was to allay the suspicions of the builders and I think I made a little progress. Lord Goodman has promised to set up one of his evening parties for me with his old friend the developer Hyams, and I have arranged for Norman Wates and Kenneth Wood to come for the discussion of how a Land Commission can avoid the danger of degenerating into an obstructive Government Department.

In the afternoon I had to tackle a planning crisis which I had detected over the weekend. I had been told by Bob Mellish that he and Fred Willey were in agreement that we ought to let several hundred acres of land inside the green belt in the Lea Valley, north of London, go for housing. In order to do so I should have to overrule my Inspector, who has recommended against the development. On Sunday I looked at the documents and rather reluctantly agreed. This afternoon John Delafons brought in the draft decision order and asked me to approve the press release, which was attached. I took one glance at it and knew that I had got another Hartley on my hands.[1] Once again the decision letter was drafted so as to make it appear that I had over-ridden my own officials without adequate reason. Indeed, in this case all sorts of opinions had been written into the letter I was to sign about the violation of the green belt. The drafting was in fact as near objective sabotage by a civil servant as was humanly possible. I wrote one stinking minute to Willey and another to the official concerned, pointing out how disastrous this kind of sloppy work is. If you are to override the Inspector on an amenity issue and get away with it, everything depends on the presentation of your case. After this I had Willey in, showed him how near we were to disaster, and begged him to take an active part in the drafting of policy decisions. He is a theoretical left-winger as well as a lawyer, and his P.P.S., Joyce Butler,[2] is even further to the Left, but he is inclined to accept what his civil servants give him. I must persuade him that I really want him as my right-hand man on planning. I have already given him an important job on a Dartmoor reservoir, about which we are in difficulties because of its coming just after Ullswater. I told him to do it himself and I think he will, provided the directive comes clearly from me. He is in some ways rather like Jim MacColl—able and clever but reluctant to take decisions himself.

[1] See p. 115.
[2] M.P. for Wood Green since 1955.

In the evening I had dinner with John Mackintosh[1] and Tommy, a real academic dinner because John, the author of *Cabinet Government*[2] and the inventor of the theory of Prime Ministerial government, wanted to discuss with me how things were working out. I gave him a lot of material and then I took Tommy home to discuss my minute on the Common Market. I have already had a good response from Douglas Jay and Fred Peart.

Tuesday, July 5th
In the morning I went to the Standing Committee on the Local Government Bill. Fortunately for me, Geoffrey Rippon, who has taken Boyd-Carpenter's place in leading the Opposition, is idle as hell. He would be prepared to pair with me for every single sitting and leave the work to Temple, the Chester M.P.,[3] who is a kind of professional representative of the local government associations. My job is to go there whenever the Whips feel that my presence would move the Committee on a bit faster. Oh dear, the whole procedure of a Standing Committee is insane. What is the sense of starting at the beginning and working line by line through each clause when in many cases there is no one there who understands what they mean? If we had a Select Committee at which I could be cross-examined on the main policy and the Committee could get down to discussing the controversial issues, that would be far more constructive. Under the present system there is no genuine committee work, just formal speech-making mostly from written briefs. All the Opposition can do is to read aloud the briefs they get from the city or county treasurers and I then read back to them the brief I get from my Department. Talk about Parliamentary reform. This is an area where it is really needed.

In the afternoon I went and sat on the front bench quite deliberately to give support to Leo Abse, who was moving his ten-minute Bill on homosexual reform in order to prove there is a majority in favour of changing the law.[4] The Lords have now twice passed this particular Private Members' Bill,[5] and we can only get it through the Commons by showing that the Members want it so much that any reasonable Government must provide the time. I found myself sitting between Harold Wilson, who had just been answering Questions, and Roy Jenkins. All our other colleagues stayed away. The vote was two to one in favour of reform.

After this I saw Sir John Newsom, of the Newsom Report,[6] and asked him

---

[1] M.P. for Berwick and East Lothian since 1966.

[2] His book was in fact called *The British Cabinet* (London: Methuen, 1968).

[3] John Temple, M.P. for Chester since 1956, was vice-president of the Association of Municipal Corporations and the Rural District Councils' Association.

[4] M.P. for Pontypool since 1958. A solicitor, he sponsored several other successful Private Members' Bills on such subjects as divorce, family planning, legitimacy and widows' damages.

[5] The Earl of Arran had persisted with this measure. See his article in *Encounter*, March 1972.

[6] As Chairman and Vice-Chairman of the Central Advisory Council on Education, he had produced the report on secondary education, *Half Our Future* (H.M.S.O., 1963).

to become chairman of the Harlow New Town Corporation in place of old Richard Costain. Newsom's firm, Longman the publishers, have moved there, and he lives there as well. The Department didn't want him and indeed told me he wouldn't accept. But I had no difficulty in persuading him to take it and I have also persuaded my old pal Peggy Jay, Douglas's wife, to be the woman on the New Town Corporation in place of one of Dame Evelyn's minions, who has retired.

In the evening I went to see the first night of *The Magic Flute*, once again as the guest of Claus Moser and his wife in the Royal Box at Covent Garden. Anne tells me I fell asleep in the first act. This question of falling asleep is now getting serious. I am fifty-seven, or is it fifty-eight, and I sometimes think that I fall asleep after eating and drinking too much. But this wasn't true at Covent Garden because I had eaten and drunk nothing. After the decent meal between the acts I didn't fall asleep. Certainly, I find myself falling asleep on the front bench next door to the P.M. when he is making a long Statement, and I didn't hear very much of his speech last week when I went in to listen to him winding up. Indeed, Douglas Houghton and I were quietly snoozing next door to each other. The fact is one goes to sleep when one's interest is not really alerted. Usually sitting on a crowded front bench while a speech goes on at the dispatch box is the most boring process I can imagine.

Wednesday, July 6th

I was due to spend the day on the Thames Conservators' launch watching them do their annual inspection and was surprised when the new Chief Whip, John Silkin, told me that Harold required every Minister to be at the P.L.P. meeting at one o'clock to vote on the resolution of confidence in him over the Statement on the U.S. bombing of Hanoi. Since I am allowed to be absent from the vote of censure this evening, it looks as though a P.L.P. decision is considered more important than a major debate in the House.[1] I turned up in plenty of time to get a seat and saw Callaghan come in, pursed and pensive; he fell asleep beside me. He is in one of his gloomy moods because of the sterling crisis. The actual show was pretty flat. Sydney Silverman killed the debate right at the start by moving the motion—it demanded a new policy in Vietnam—in a very, very long speech. His motion was really a vote of no confidence. After him the left-wingers were subdued since they were trying to show that they weren't splitting the Party. They were really completely answered by Raymond Fletcher, a left-winger from the Tribune group.[2] He reminded the Party that Harold Wilson was due to go to Washington to see President Johnson on July 28th. Would it really strengthen his hand if the Party were at this moment to pass a resolution demanding total repudiation

[1] Iain Macleod moved a vote of censure against the Chairman of Ways and Means for curtailing discussion of various clauses of the Finance Bill by accepting a Motion for Closure on June 29th. The Motion was, however, withdrawn.
[2] M.P. for Ilkeston since 1964. A journalist and a member of the T.G.W.U.

of American policy in Vietnam? At the end Harold Wilson read aloud a fairly solid speech which ended with a nasty phrase about the left wing cheering Heath and a vague threat of a general election. Then Manny Shinwell got up and asked Sydney Silverman to withdraw his motion and Sydney Silverman characteristically refused. This lost him at least half his supporters. He would have done far better to withdraw; by not doing so he strengthened Harold's hand.

After that I was motored down to Chertsey Lock where the Thames Conservators were due to pick me up. It was a nice sunny afternoon, but what a racket this inspection is. These old boys with their yachting caps—all the county council magnates—spend four days each year doing nothing but sitting on this huge launch, eating solid slabs of pork pie and bread and butter and blackcurrant jam and strawberries and cream, and drinking whisky. Perhaps it's all right for one day, but I have never been submitted to such intensive lobbying. I was lobbied by the Hampshire County Council man on the new Buchanan Report on Southampton. I was lobbied about Bletchley New Town by the Bucks County Council man. I was lobbied by the Wiltshire County Council man on the expansion of Swindon. What an extraordinary collection of political issues one has to handle as Minister of Housing. Which makes it even more difficult to forgive the behaviour of those civil servants who don't provide the Minister before he goes on this kind of a trip with a brief on his hosts or keep him in the political picture about them.

That evening I was giving a dinner party to the Polish parliamentary delegation. It took place at the Admiralty and was the first time the newly redecorated rooms had been used for hospitality. It was also literally the first occasion when I had taken any part in the work of the Inter-Parliamentary Union. I think it went fairly well and laid the foundations for my trip to Poland next October.*

Thursday, July 7th
At Cabinet we started with yet another discussion of the parliamentary time-table and were threatened with having to go on till August 10th. The Finance Bill is at last off the Floor, but it is to be followed by the S.E.T. Bill which may well consume ten days in Committee if the Opposition want. I suppose it will have to be guillotined.

Then came my moment on foreign affairs. Michael Stewart said he had nothing to report, whereupon I chipped in, although my Private Office had pleaded with me against doing so. However, though Harold tried to freeze me off, I held on tenaciously and brought into the open the contradiction between the speeches of George Thomson and George Brown and the assurances given to us in private that there is really no prospect of our getting into the Common Market. I got some support from Fred Peart. But Douglas

* It was cancelled in July on the orders of the Prime Minister as a result of the July crisis.

Jay was in Moscow opening the British Fair, and Barbara Castle was too tactful to join in. (She doesn't want to side with me just now because I am an important rival for money—Housing versus Transport.) Nevertheless, I think I made sure that we shall have a serious discussion of Europe at the end of this month when the official reports are ready.

Then the P.M. had to explain this morning's leak in the *Daily Herald* and the *Morning Star* about his forthcoming visit to the Trade Fair in Moscow; it had completely bitched his plans for winding up in the House that evening with a dramatic announcement. He was very nettled because he foresaw the debate would now end in a complete anticlimax.

The last item was Barbara Castle's Transport White Paper, an enormous document which she has pushed and bullied through the E.D.C. I don't know whether it is an appalling disaster or a really impressive performance. My White Paper on Housing failed because it was too short. She may be right that if you want to impress people you must make things unreadably long. There was very little discussion of its substance. What people were mostly concerned about was whether the publication of the White Paper would ensure that she got parliamentary time in the next session for a Transport Bill. This was raised first by Tony Crosland, and when I supported him everybody laughed at me and said, 'What are *you* grumbling about?' However, we were given a solemn assurance that the publication of the White Paper didn't commit the Cabinet to a Transport Bill in the next Session. That assurance means nothing. Barbara has got her way and her big Bill will be the major measure of the second Session of this Parliament.[1]

In the afternoon I had a meeting with all the London rent officers. When I came through the back door from my room into the huge conference room I found it packed. However, it turned out to be a very informal meeting and I got the impression that the rent officers are much more worried and much more upset about the behaviour of the rent assessment committees than Littlewood had given me to imagine. Nearly all those who spoke felt that the R.A.C.s were wrong to refuse to visit the house whose rent they are fixing and to rely on the report of the so-called 'referencer'. They all urged that the R.A.C.s should spend at least ten minutes inside every flat before coming to a decision. I promised to put this to Sir Sydney Littlewood and then added that there was an alternative. Couldn't the rent officer attend the R.A.C. and describe what he had seen? The overwhelming majority said they didn't want that. But they obviously have their own differences: some of them are trying to work out semi-mathematical formulae for rent fixing; some believe there should be no mathematical formula; some obviously feel that their job is simply to keep rents down. I mustn't be too complacent about the working of the Act, but I did find this was a very fine body of men and I only hope they won't find their work made impossible by the arbitrary decisions taken over their heads by the R.A.C.s.

[1] It was introduced in October 1967.

That evening there was a big reception in Lancaster House for Monsieur Pompidou. I never even saw him. I found myself talking to Tony Crosland's wife, Susan Barnes, which was very nice indeed. From there I went back to the House and found it difficult to keep awake during Harold Wilson's speech winding up the Vietnam debate. It was (as expected) a flop and the thirty-one left-wingers, whom he had hoped to impress by announcing his Moscow visit, did abstain.[1]

From there I caught the train to Bradford.

Friday, July 8th

Bradford. An old Yorkshire city with a tremendous Labour tradition but a bit in a rut. However, there is a new chairman of housing who has got a great big housing programme going. But alas, the planning is poor, the architecture dull, the city architect obviously not up to it. What can one do about it? Not much. At twelve o'clock, after three hours' intensive sightseeing, I held the press conference which was the main object of my visit to Bradford. I repeated the second half of my Blackpool speech and made it clear that I am really serious about making councils introduce rent-rebate schemes. This is the second prong of my propaganda strategy. Cost-consciousness in building council housing on the one side, cost-consciousness in introducing rent-rebate schemes on the other.

By getting myself whirled to Manchester in the mayor's car I caught a train which got me home to Prescote at 8.45 for a decent weekend, though I found a tremendous collection of red boxes waiting for me.

Saturday, July 9th

The most awkward problem which came out of my red box today concerned the doubling of Northampton. Once again, as with Peterborough, I discover that the job which the Dame promised me she had done before she left has come unstuck. Northampton borough is up in arms because they say they weren't consulted before the publication of our draft report designating the New Town area. I also found that the county is opposed to the direction in which we plan the expansion. I shall have to go down to Northampton; and meanwhile I must write a minute to Miss Hope-Wallace at least as formidable as the one I wrote this week to the planners and the politicians about the mess-up over the Lea Valley.

Here I might add one thought. When I came to the Ministry I found minute-writing extremely difficult. I had written articles before but had done all my business by word of mouth. I started writing minutes in longhand but the officials found it illegible. As I get used to the job, I am taking to dictating my minutes. I am increasingly impressed by the importance of minuting: if I merely say things to officials or ring them up they can forget to pass my message on; but the typed minute, dictated and signed by me, has got to be passed

[1] The vote was 331 to 230.

on. So I tend now to spend more and more time writing notes for my minutes in longhand from which I dictate a draft to be finalized in the Private Office.

Sunday, July 10th

Reading the morning papers, I see that people are beginning to realize how Cousins's resignation has produced quite an important Cabinet reshuffle. The fact which most of the correspondents missed at first is that Harold has used the opportunity to make John Silkin his Chief Whip. I am told that this has saved me from being moved to the Ministry of Technology. When I ran into George Brown in the Chamber he assured me that this would have happened had not Harold been determined to appoint a new Chief Whip. Since he couldn't possibly make Ted Short Minister of Housing he had to liberate a minor Ministry, and so he moved Tony Wedgwood Benn to Technology in order to make Short Postmaster-General. These stories are never absolutely true but there may be a good deal in this. Certainly, both Tommy and Marcia have wanted to have me put in Technology and the fact that I was quite a vigorous Shadow Minister of Science would have made the move quite sensible. It would also have fulfilled Harold's pledge to give me a big Ministry which is bound to be right at the centre of things.

However, Crossman didn't become MinTech because the Prime Minister realized he very much needed a new Chief Whip. This is something which some of us had been urging for a long time. Bert Bowden and Ted Short were quite capable of managing a majority of three but this new Parliamentary Party with a majority of a hundred is obviously quite beyond them. I welcome the change, but by doing it this way Harold has made sure that all the big changes in the Post Office that Tony was preparing—breaking it up into three nationalized corporations, altering its whole future relationship with the B.B.C. and I.T.V.—will collapse when Ted Short takes charge. We shall watch and see, but I predict all Tony's plans will perish.*

What will Tony be like as MinTech? Up till now he has shown no great administrative grasp and the maximum power of alienating people and so not getting his way. Maybe this is because he was outside the Cabinet. That's what he felt. Now he is going to be a very senior, central Minister, who if he wants can be one of the leading figures in an inner Cabinet.

Monday, July 11th

I spent the whole morning trying to get the water division of the Ministry, which has been virtually on its own for ten years, responsive to political directive. When I first got here I couldn't stand water and wanted to give it away to the Minister of Land and Natural Resources. Now I see the organization of water and drainage and sewage as a great technological service in which a degree of nationalization can really take place.

In the evening I ate in the Members' dining-room, something I don't very

* A false prophecy.

often do, with Eric Heffer, one of our left-wingers from Liverpool, Ben Whitaker, the left-wing M.P. from Hampstead,[1] Tom Driberg and Hugh Jenkins.[2] I got their gossip. They seemed entirely obsessed with Vietnam and unaware of the economic crisis into which we were drifting. Another interesting thing I learnt in the dining-room and in the smoking-room was that none of these left-wingers feel that Ted Short had been a bad Chief Whip. On the contrary they were surprised at his going and assumed that he'd wanted promotion to a Ministry. Moreover, none of them felt John Silkin would be an improvement. Yet I am convinced that John was a very good appointment, since the Prime Minister will now hear from him a number of the things which he ought to have heard but hadn't been hearing over the last eighteen months.

Throughout the first half of July sterling was feeble. On July 12th the Chancellor announced that banks would not be allowed to provide loans to assist industry to meet the cost of S.E.T. payments and on July 14th bank rate was raised from 6 to 7 per cent.

The City had not been reassured by the Iron and Steel Bill, which reduced the promised level of compensation to shareholders. The publication of the Industrial Reorganization Bill did not improve matters. This established an Industrial Reconstruction Corporation (I.R.C.) to assist private industry by encouraging mergers or providing extra capital. Its chairman was to be Sir Frank Kearton, chairman of Courtaulds.

On July 15th there was heavy selling of sterling. But none the less Mr Wilson set off on July 16th for a three-day visit to Moscow, to discuss Anglo–Soviet trade with Mr Kosygin. Although it was reported that the Cabinet would not discuss deflationary measures until the Prime Minister's return on July 19th, naturally Westminster and Whitehall hummed with rumours.

Tuesday, July 12th
This was the day for the long-announced Cabinet discussion on productivity. All the papers previously circulated were desultory and of no interest. Moreover, at the last moment the Chancellor circulated a sensational Top Secret document. This admitted he had based his budget on the expectation that he could hold consumption until S.E.T. started working in September and that this expectation had been proved wrong; that is why he would need to cut back public-sector expenditure by at least £500 million.

The meeting only really got going when Tony Crosland said that whatever happened he didn't want a repetition of the July 1965 crisis. He didn't want to see us once again combating inflation by cutting public expenditure. I

[1] M.P. for Hampstead 1966–70. P.P.S. to the Minister of Overseas Development 1966, at Housing and Local Government 1966–7, and Parliamentary Secretary at O.D.M. 1969–70. Since 1971 he has been director of the Minority Rights Group.
[2] M.P. for Putney since 1964. He was Assistant Secretary to the British Actors' Equity Association 1950–57, and their Assistant General Secretary until 1964. He was a member of the L.C.C. 1958–65.

chipped in and said to the Chancellor, 'We came into office as socialists and the essence of a socialist policy is a shift from private to public expenditure. The public sector is not too big now—it's far too small. There can be no question of a cut-back.' At this point the Chancellor woke up and said that he must tell Cabinet frankly that he didn't know how we were going to get out of the mess. We had totally failed to reach our objectives, we were drifting into devaluation in the worst possible conditions and he didn't know how he could retain his position as Chancellor. This set everyone round the table arguing either for or against another July cut in public expenditure. I think everyone who spoke, with the exception of Dick Marsh, was against the Chancellor. And that is about as far as Cabinet got.

In the evening I had to go to Downing Street for a party Harold was giving for the Transport House staff. There I learnt from Douglas Jay that the reason why Cabinet had been so inconclusive was that the Chancellor and the First Secretary had failed to agree on the cuts. The Chancellor insisted the package should include a £100 million cut in overseas spending whereas the First Secretary said that this was unacceptable if it involved any change of policy.

Wednesday, July 13th
Official visit to Nottingham. The Department is very proud of the briefs it gives me for each town I visit—enormous bundles of pages about planning and housing and administration. I have tried patiently to teach them that the vital facts I need are first and foremost the political situation and the background story of the councillors I am likely to meet. Supplying information of this sort doesn't come naturally to them. At Nottingham today I gave a press conference in the presence of the Conservative leader of the Opposition all about rent rebates, and I complained that with 35,000 council houses Nottingham gave no rent rebates at all. It was only just as I was leaving that I learnt that the Nottingham Labour Party had won its majority on the council by attacking as inegalitarian the whole scheme of giving rent rebates rather than setting lower rents.

On the way back to London I had an interesting talk with Pugh, who is head of Planning, and Jimmy James, who is our chief geographer and professional planner. At the time when J. D. Jones put in his resignation, Jimmy announced that he wanted to go to the U.N. as his last fling before he retired. I was furious at first but finally I let him go and see for himself. A good thing too, because after a few days in New York he came back, aware he wouldn't have got the job. He was the wrong colour—they wanted a non-white official! Now he is back as an enthusiastic supporter of mine. Pugh is a very different kettle of fish. Cold, thin, ambitious, in the Ministry of Transport originally, he was then seconded to the planning division of M.H.L.G., and is now Under-Secretary in charge of Planning. We all agreed how anxious we had been about Steve and how relieved we are now to find he is a very good organizer and works well with our officials. That brought us to discuss the relation of Ministers to officials, and Pugh said, 'Most people in the Department think that what you have been doing for the last two years has been good for them but nobody would say they liked it very much.' And he added, 'You have gone into every cranny in the Department and made them all look at their methods and change them. But the trouble is that you've made them look over their shoulders as well. Take Planning—we have really slowed up now because we are not quite sure what the Minister will be up to next. Until you came, no Minister bothered about individual planning decisions but once you started doing so people became anxious, and feel lost because they don't know how to please the Minister.' We spent the rest of the journey discussing how to improve and hurry up the administration of planning decisions.

As I got to Vincent Square for the meeting of our kitchen cabinet I couldn't help asking myself why I should be worrying about this when the whole existence of the Cabinet was hanging suspended. However, though the Cabinet might possibly break up and we might have a '31, I don't believe we shall.[1] With our majority we can recover from anything provided the Cabinet doesn't split. I am not expecting to cease to be a Cabinet Minister, though I might cease to be Minister of Housing. I hope this won't happen because I want to operate from this Ministry where at last I am getting a grip and understanding the full length and breadth of the work and also learning how to impose my will without infuriating people or wearing them out or destroying their morale. This is something which as a Minister I really have to learn.

Tommy, Peter Shore, Tony Benn and Judith were at the meeting of our little group at Vincent Square; and we discussed the crisis that was coming and the line that Tony and I should take in Cabinet. We agreed that if cuts of £250 million were required on the home front they should be made by using the regulator and not by cutting public expenditure. We also considered the reimposition of import controls, restoration of the surcharge, etc. As for wages and prices, we should try to get a two-norm system so as to stop wage increases at the higher levels.

Thursday, July 14th
As soon as we got to Cabinet Harold made a long statement making it perfectly clear that there had been disagreement between Callaghan and Brown and that a holding Statement would be required in the afternoon. Meanwhile our main job would be to work out our new policy in the fortnight before August 7th. The Statement would come just after the announcement of the increased bank rate and must include the announcement that there would be a £100 million cut in overseas expenditure. Everybody was critical. Roy

[1] In 1931 the Labour Party split when Ramsay MacDonald formed a National Government at a time of acute financial crisis.

Jenkins wanted in addition to this cut a specific commitment to a wage and prices freeze. Dick Marsh said that would be fine if anybody knew what a wage and prices freeze really meant and whether it was practical. Barbara wanted the cut in foreign expenditure even though it would include overseas development, whereas Tony Greenwood was fighting against it. But the big confrontation came between the Chancellor and the Foreign Secretary, who obviously hadn't been consulted until the night before. Michael Stewart said he couldn't possibly cut £100 millions without either withdrawing totally from Germany or totally from East of Suez. Clearly this couldn't be done as a sudden emergency plan for helping the balance of payments. On the whole he got his way and it was clear that Harold's Statement would not be specific on the subject of overseas cuts.

During the Statement Jim sat beside me on the front bench. He was back in serene form and turned to me and solemnly said, 'We achieved great things this morning; we prevented the purely deflationary package we are all fighting to avoid.' In fact, of course, the interaction of Callaghan's pure deflation and Brown's pure anti-deflation has produced a disastrous dilemma which the P.M.'s Statement did nothing to resolve.

In the prices and incomes debate in the evening one of my predictions came badly unstuck. Frank Cousins proved himself in parliamentary terms not a blundering fool but a potential left-wing leader. Of course, to read, his speech is impenetrably obscure but he has personality and it came across. The Tories helped him because they wanted him to succeed. But so did a lot of our own side. The question now is whether the new package, when we bring it out, will be able to rally the Left, or whether we shall be in open conflict not only with the Tories but with our own Party.

Sunday, July 17th
When I got home from an official visit to Lancashire I found I was being rung up by almost every Sunday columnist. This is partly because since Thursday's Cabinet the newspapers have been full of startling inside stories. The *Sun* has told us how Harold Wilson saved the country from really savage deflation. The *Guardian* gave us a long statement on Mr Callaghan's views on cuts in overseas spending. It is clear that these leaks haven't come from Cabinet because the rest of us had no idea what is going on between the big three. Nevertheless, the columnists ring us up to ask us our views, all the more so in my case because I gave a press conference on Friday at which I said that I knew the private sector of building would suffer even worse as the result of the crisis but that I was hoping that council house completions wouldn't be affected this year. This got a lot of publicity on Saturday and the *Daily Telegraph* tried to make out that Barbara and I were opposing any kind of cuts. Harold Wilson had sent me a message via Tommy that I must stress the unity of the Cabinet in everything I said and this is what I did in fact do. I saw a lot of Tommy last week and he gave me some useful briefing. It is now

pretty clear that ever since we won the election this could have happened to the pound. Yet no contingency plan of any kind has been prepared and our big three were caught completely unawares when the pound suddenly became unstuck.

This has damaged us in the public eye because it has helped to create the image of Harold Wilson just opportunizing from expedient to expedient; and hopping off to Moscow this weekend seems a palpable political gimmick.[1] Tommy tells me the crisis is now so serious that the full Statement will have to be made on Tuesday of next week if we are to prevent a devaluation. Personally, I sincerely hope we shall devalue, come what may, because looking back I am sure the basic mistake Harold made was trying to save the pound. If he had got off the pound right at the beginning he could really have given Britain a new start.

Now the question is, can we get that new start twenty months after the Government came into power? Of course we have a majority of a hundred, of course the Cabinet has a good deal of experience. But are we doomed to a bout of deflation such as the Treasury wanted to force through last Tuesday? Here I think we have to consider how we can persuade Harold to get a policy group around him to consider the Government's strategy. I have been sitting outside, as a departmental Minister. So have Tony Wedgwood Benn, now at Technology, and Barbara at Transport. We all felt last Wednesday that we must now say to him, 'Look we've let you run things on your own and they are all coming unstuck. We must now have some strategic long-term planning.'

I have also got to say the same things about the relationship between the Government and Transport House. There is no question now of my resigning from the Executive. After Frank Cousins's resignation I have got to stick by Harold and try to see him through. I was struck that Albert Rose and Betty Healey, good left-wingers, rang me up and said that Coventry East wouldn't let me stand down in the present crisis, because if I did the wrong person, Sydney Silverman for instance, might take my place. So that's out of the way and instead of resigning I shall now take a far more positive role in the relations between the Government and the Party.

I must add one last word to get things in perspective. I've been talking a great deal about Harold's failures and my disillusionment with his gimmickry. I must say that it was a tremendous shock last night when I saw his face during his interview on TV just before he left London Airport for Moscow and heard the bitter remarks of the B.B.C. correspondent on his arrival. There is no doubt Harold is going through a terrible time, though the N.O.P. poll published on Thursday showed us with a $16\frac{1}{2}$ per cent lead and Harold right up and Heath right down. We must never forget that. But we haven't got too much time before the Gallup Poll shows us collapsing. We had a dramatic

[1] 'The British press … , worked up about the economic crisis, regarded my visit as a purposeless and irrelevant interlude.' *Wilson*, p. 255.

by-election this week in which we lost Carmarthen to a Welsh Nationalist.[1]
That was due partly to special Welsh conditions but also to the deepseated
malaise which set in immediately after the election and which was confirmed
by the disastrous S.E.T. budget and, since then, by the fact that Harold
Wilson, who showed himself a master of the art of surviving with a majority
of three, has shown himself quite unable to use the powers he has obtained
by his majority of one hundred. He hasn't yet settled down to a real job of
work based on a real strategy, and that is what we have got to see if we can
make him do next week.

Monday, July 18th
Since the PESC meeting was starting at 9.30 on Monday I went to London by
the Sunday night train and looked in on Tommy Balogh, because I wanted
his briefing. At that time I didn't know that the whole weekend had been
devoted to a struggle between George Brown and Callaghan — Callaghan
wanting cuts and deflation, and George Brown fighting against them and
moving more and more into support for the floating pound. I also didn't know
that this support had been also forthcoming from nearly all the economic
advisers, including Neild, Balogh and Kaldor. Tommy had to be discreet,
but he didn't oppose me when I started by telling him that what worried me
was the memory of Tony Crosland's remark during the July squeeze last year,
that we must never again make sacrifices of public-sector spending for parity.
From that I went on to argue that we must go for the floating pound, otherwise we should have another package of cuts in six months' time and another
and another, and what was the point of that? The more we talked the more
my mind was made up and I went to bed that night with the clear conviction
that when Harold came back from Moscow my job was to put the case in
Cabinet in favour of seizing the full possibilities of the floating pound.

This morning before PESC I went into my office and gave John Delafons
instructions to make appointments for me that evening with Tony Crosland,
Roy Jenkins and Barbara Castle. I would see them separately in their rooms
at the House of Commons during the debates on the Selective Employment
Payments Bill when we had all got to be present. To my surprise each of them
jumped at the chance of a private talk. This was the first time that I have ever
tried to organize a cabal in the Cabinet, or, to put it more modestly, to discuss
with a group of colleagues in advance the line we should take on a big issue
of policy.[2]

The PESC meeting has become our regular July exercise. Its job is to keep
the growth of public-sector expenditure in line with the growth of the
economy. This year it had been found that although the rate of economic

---

[1] In the by-election caused by the death of Lady Megan Lloyd George, a 9,000 Labour
majority was converted to a 2,400 majority for Gwynfor Evans, the Plaid Cymru candidate.
[2] But 'there was no plot, no conspiracy, no cabal, no organization. There was a great deal
of concern and a lot of loose talk.' *Wilson*, p. 256.

growth had declined, the growth of Government expenditure had jumped from 4½ per cent, the level at which we wanted to keep it, to something like 10 per cent. As part of our regular process of Government, therefore, there had to be something of a cut-back. What was clear to me was that it was useless to attempt this regular annual cut-back until we had seen the crisis measures which were being prepared behind our backs. It took most of my colleagues a full hour before they grasped that official Whitehall was busy quietly working out a precise package of cuts for announcement on Wednesday while we as Ministers were sitting round the table blithely discussing the remote possibility of retrenchment. When they realized, everybody was infuriated. I had remarked right at the beginning of the meeting that it ought to be cancelled, which peeved the Chancellor. By the end there wasn't much doubt that that was the general view of everyone there.

After it was over I went up to George Brown and said that I must talk to him straight away. He said, 'Come round quietly to my office.' On my way I looked into my own Ministry and checked on the situation with Delafons. It didn't take me long to confirm that my Permanent Secretary, without being allowed to talk to me, had been instructed on Sunday to work out the cuts he could agree to on behalf of my Ministry. In his case it wasn't too bad because he was told that housing would be omitted and he would have to make cuts only in the rest of local government expenditure. But he had got down to the job and had agreed on my behalf, without consulting me, to a £34 million cut in miscellaneous local government expenditure – town-hall building, town-centre development, bathing-pools, etc. It was already clear that over the weekend the centralized mandarin machine had once again been put to work, working out a desperate programme without Cabinet knowing about it. The total – £500 million – would be achieved partly by cuts in personal consumption, using the regulator, partly by cuts in the public-sector and nationalized industries and partly by cuts in overseas expenditure. I was sad that Steve, though he knows me pretty well by now, didn't feel able to ring me up and bring me in.

Armed with this information I went along to George Brown and told him straight away that I was in favour of the floating pound, and that I was going to see Roy Jenkins, Tony Crosland and Barbara Castle that evening to discuss it with each of them separately. He said this was also his view; but he emphasized that he wasn't going to take part in any kind of conspiracy, and indeed the whole tone of what he said that morning was very careful. He had been fighting with Harold while he was in Moscow, using telegrams and messages carried across by Burke Trend. Indeed, Harold had issued a statement saying that Ministers could resign if they liked but they would have to take it or leave it. Yes, he had been tempted to resign and talked a lot about it. But there was no question of that now. He would go all out for persuading Harold, when he got back, to float the pound. Obviously there were strained relations between him and Harold, but equally obviously George Brown at

this stage was prepared to have a try in Cabinet on Tuesday. In preparation
for the battle he filled me in about the size of the cut the Treasury was
demanding and the amount he would be prepared to take. He also told me
that, as the result of last week's Cabinet, Harold had decided that the public-
sector programme, housing, hospitals and schools, should not be cut. Altogether it was a sensible, coherent talk. When I left I promised that in my talks
with Barbara, Roy and Tony I would not mention my talk with him.

Barbara was the first Minister I saw that evening. We had a talk in her room
and she told me straight away that she was seeing George Brown later. She
expressed herself entirely willing to commit herself to the floating pound.
After that I had a quick dinner with Nicholas Davenport. When I asked him
what would be the sensible thing for me to advocate, he said, 'The sensible
thing would be to have a floating pound, but you can't get that through your
Cabinet because it is not a view held seriously by any of the people who
matter.' After dinner Roy came to see me. We were going through one of
those terrible long summer nights in the Commons – it was the debate on the
guillotine on the S.E.T. Bill. Roy immediately said he was in favour of
floating the pound and would speak in favour of it, though he made it clear
that he would make no offer to resign. He said he had talked it over with
Tony Crosland, who shared his view. He had just been dining with George
Brown, he observed, who seemed to be in a hysterical, resigning mood. I then
asked Roy about the European background to this affair. You know, I said,
how Harold is working against you, telling us anti-Europeans that anyone
who wants to devalue the pound is trying to do so as a practical way into
Europe. 'Tell me, Roy,' I said, 'what have the two things really got to do
with each other?' And he said, 'Plenty, of course. I mean we will have to do
something about sterling in order to enter Europe. This might mean devaluation; but in my view a floating pound gives a certain freedom of action, either
to enter Europe or to do anything else, and what we are trying to regain this
week is freedom of action. If we go on as we are, we remain prisoners of the
situation and prisoners of our own weakness.'

After this I went back to George Brown, as I had promised. I found him
worked up into a passion and plunged into one of his most maudlin, self-
commiserating moods. He at once told me there was no chance whatsoever
of Harold Wilson agreeing because he was now bound personally and
irrevocably to President Johnson and had ceased to be a free agent. That was
why he, George Brown, knew he would have to resign. I argued for fighting
it out in Cabinet as he had suggested only that morning, and George replied
there wasn't any chance whatsoever. Just as I was getting up to go, George
Brown said to me, 'Look, would you support me if Harold had to resign?'
I said, 'Certainly not.' And he said, 'Well, Barbara said the same thing to
me. Of course, you two are bound to Harold, that's why you can't do any
good.' I didn't know how seriously to take this, but he certainly implied that
there were other people prepared to go with him to the last resort; and Harold

had to be replaced in order to float the pound. Maybe it was one of those things George Brown says late at night. But certainly it was something which would get back to Harold on the grape-vine.

I left him very late, knowing that although he had impressed on me the need for absolute security, he had been talking in much the same kind of way to Barbara, Roy and Tony Crosland. The last person I saw was Tony Benn, who also agreed to take the same line. So the numbers had been mounting up that day.[1] We had Roy, Tony Crosland, Tony Benn, Barbara Castle and myself all firmly committed to opposing a new package of cuts except as a preparation for floating off the pound. Moreover during the course of the talks it had become clearer and clearer to me that the scale of the package required to float the pound was not very different from that required to save it. So the issue is not what package of cuts we should have but what should be the strategy behind the cuts, what would make it worth imposing them.

Tuesday, July 19th
Early in the morning I was rung up by George Wigg who said to me, 'There are times when loyalty is all-important. What matters now is that when Harold comes back you support him.' And he added, 'You know, I have good sources. I know what everybody is doing.' I said, 'Thank you very much, that's all right.' That was useful because it showed me what the Wilson line was going to be: a demand for loyalty and toughness – take the package and be damned. Wilson was going to be Napoleonic.

I cleared the whole morning for work with my Permanent Secretary on the Ministry's cuts. We'd expected that the papers would have come round by then. In fact, they didn't arrive until two o'clock in the afternoon and when they were opened they consisted of a rather flaccid set of hypothetical calculations. Excluded from the papers was any statement of the total amount of the package – it was deliberately being hidden from Cabinet members. I just had to try to tot it up with my Permanent Secretary.

When Steve and I had done what we could with our departmental estimates, I rang each of my colleagues to discuss the line we should take. It was agreed that at Cabinet George Brown should hold back. There should be no talk of resignation, and I should start the attack. After this I rang up Bill Nield, an old friend of mine who is now a senior official in the Cabinet Office, and said I must see the P.M. at all costs when he got back. I had begun to realize that, since I had really organized all this, I must in fairness see Harold and warn him of what we were up to. At first I was told that it was impossible. Then Bill Nield said I could see him after Questions. That suited me because I happened to be first for Questions that day and had to spend lunch-time with the Parliamentary Secretaries preparing for a rather awkward bunch on

[1] 'Seminars were taking place all over the Palace of Westminster: Dick Crossman in the tea-room was instructing the young, and George Brown … was also involved, principally with junior ministers. But there was no organized movement.' *Wilson*, p. 257.

housing which had to be answered before the package was known. Harold came in and sat beside me and then at 3.15 he answered his Questions pretty well and we withdrew to his room. I started off straight away: 'Look here, some of us have been thinking very carefully and we just can't take another package without any kind of assurance that it won't end in another crisis.' I told him that I personally was in favour of floating the pound, but what I had come to discuss was the procedure in Cabinet that day. We wanted a discussion on devaluation before we considered the cuts. Since the packages for floating off the pound and for staying on the pound would not be so very dissimilar, that was all the more reason why we must get the strategy clear first before we came to the cuts.

Harold immediately gave way on this and gave me the assurance I asked for. I then told him that I had been talking to a number of colleagues and we all wanted to argue the case for floating. Harold replied that it was a matter of time-tabling. 'I'm not adamant against devaluation, but we shall have to get the pound stabilized first so that we can float from strength not from weakness.' And he began to outline a plan (of which Tommy had informed me the night before) for strengthening the pound now, getting import controls in the autumn and floating off in the spring.

It was the first time I had led, not a Cabinet revolt, but Cabinet resistance to the personal government he has been conducting. The talk went fairly well. I stayed with him half an hour, listening most of the time and chatting with him a little bit at the end. Then I went back to the Ministry to get my Cabinet papers and looked at the officials' document for twenty minutes and realized how thin it was.

Cabinet started at five o'clock with a very long statement by Harold. As I had agreed with George Brown and the others I came in second. I said that, frankly, the package as Harold had outlined it was the 1965 package, only rather more so. I wanted to consider the possibility of a package based on a properly worked-out strategy and linked to an announcement of a floating pound. I believed that this kind of policy would have much more chance of getting public support and also economic growth. Immediately I had finished, Roy Jenkins came in quietly saying he fully supported me. Tony Crosland said much the same. Up to this point the Chancellor remained silent, and even now the first person to support the P.M.'s package was Douglas Houghton, who represented the lowest common denominator of common sense. Perhaps we should be forced off the pound, he observed, but we mustn't *decide* to float the pound since this would betray our obligations and shock the British people. As the debate went on it became clear that all the people concerned with foreign affairs were for the Prime Minister – the Colonial Secretary, the Commonwealth Secretary, for example – and so were Fred Peart and Willie Ross.

Harold had intended to stop the meeting at seven thirty and start it again at nine next morning. But by seven thirty we'd scarcely finished the stage where each person round the table stated his point of view. So it was decided to go on till nine and start work on the draft statement next day.

This put me in a fix because I had not cancelled the important dinner to discuss the Land Commission that Arnold Goodman had arranged. So I slipped out at eight o'clock just when Barbara was making a dramatic statement about the merits of devaluation. I thought she was making a mistake, because she was playing into the hands of those who say that devaluation isn't a wonderful formula which would save the pound without hurting anybody. And that's true. But the main thing about this Cabinet was that the issue had been put to the P.M. and by nine o'clock he had been forced to make some important concessions. First, he had conceded that there could be no question of just sticking to parity. If we got through this crisis, we would have to work out a strategy; and if the level of unemployment was to rise markedly above 2 per cent (480,000), then he would consider devaluation. This was an assurance he gave across the table to George Brown.[1] And second, he had assured us that the whole issue of the various methods of devaluing the pound, whether by floating or moving to another fixed rate, would be considered by a special Cabinet Committee. This he conceded in answer to Richard Marsh, who was supporting the Chancellor but who also saw the need for a proper, considered Cabinet assessment of a contingency plan.

In the Statement on July 20th the Prime Minister announced the imposition of six months' standstill on all wage, salary and dividend increases, to be followed by a further six months' severe restraint. Price increases were to be frozen for twelve months. The House was told that the Government planned to strengthen the Prices and Incomes Bill to give the freeze statutory authority.

The White Paper was published on July 29th and the proposals were tabled as new clauses to be added to the Prices and Incomes Bill. This device caused anger in Parliament.

The voluntary principle was retained in the new Part IV of the Bill but there was also a compulsory element. In the case of a deliberate breach of the standstill, an Order in Council could be laid before Parliament, to impose penalties of up to £500. In Cabinet, the argument over compulsory powers continued.

Wednesday, July 20th

As we came into Cabinet George Brown said to me, 'You still think I am right not to resign?' 'Certainly,' I said, 'there is no question at all.' 'Good,' he answered, and throughout that meeting he was perfectly all right. He wasn't very enthusiastic but he took the lead in the detailed discussion of a prices and incomes freeze. I still regarded this as a theatrical device, an attempt to make the voluntary system look stronger and I didn't pay much attention when George Brown spelt it all out in detail. I noticed, however, that he insisted on going to tell the T.U.C. and the C.B.I. about it at 2.30.

[1] 'There was virtually no pressure for devaluation to a fixed, lower parity.' *Wilson*, p. 257.

19

After that we went back to the old problem of the cuts. There were special papers on such items as building controls and the regulator, and also on overseas expenditure. The Foreign Secretary had only agreed to a £100 million cut if there was no change of policy. I regard this as the most dangerous policy of all. By continuing to sustain all our commitments but cutting our costs, we shall weaken ourselves and make our foreign policy totally ineffective. There was no concession on East of Suez, no concession on reducing the troops in Germany and yet there was an agreement to a big cut. As for the public sector, all we were really doing was slowing up growth in various areas. Of the £34 million cut Steve had conceded on Sunday I offered to accept £26 million and got away with it. It meant very little more than that certain local authorities would take a year longer on various building projects, particularly town-centre development.

Throughout the whole of this Harold was his dreary, competent self, tiddling with the figures. George Brown was sulking on the other side of the table. The Chancellor was talking big about getting tough with Germany. And Cabinet was a desultory affair. Nothing had been adequately prepared. Nothing had been thought out properly. We were fixing things once again, horribly inefficiently, at the last moment.

At one o'clock it was over and Harold got down to drafting the Statement. I rushed back just in time to see the Huntingdon County Council, who had been waiting for me. Then I had a little lunch with Jennie and Helga Greene to discuss a contract for my diary and my memoirs. Then I had to sit on the front bench to see how Harold fared.

Just imagine it. He had had a gruelling Moscow visit with all these crisis messages coming across while he spent hours sweating round the State Fair. Then he had flown back on Tuesday straight into this crisis and, as one of his secretaries said to me, he had had a 21-hour day. Now, on Wednesday, he had had a 4-hour Cabinet, then 2 hours to get the Statement ready, and then at 3.30 he had to be on the front bench in order to make it. Moreover, he had to make it in the absence of George Brown, and already by then he knew that George was in one of his moods. No wonder he sounded jaded and tired and his replies to supplementaries were verbose. It was a fairly poor Statement and he didn't make the best of it. If it had any virtue, it was that in it he saved our social priorities and avoided deflation across the board. What the Statement gave us was a selective deflation, intensifying controls but saving the key programmes, industrial building, hospitals, schools and houses.[1] So it wasn't a complete Selwyn Lloyd 'stop'. I suppose it was partly in order to impress the bankers that he put it over with a strong emphasis on what was being saved. But it was a sad performance and on this occasion I thought Heath did considerably better.

Later in the afternoon I had a lot of things to do in the Ministry and sweated away there completely unaware of the hoo-ha about George Brown,

[1] See *Wilson*, pp. 258–60.

who had resigned. I had been rung up in the morning to ask whether I would go on television after the P.M.'s broadcast that night and discuss it with Macleod and Grimond. So as well as dealing with departmental worries I had been mugging up the cuts all day and had then gone across to the liaison committee to get myself properly briefed for dealing with all the questions likely to be asked on television. I had also been ringing up Downing Street for bits of briefing, but nobody bothered to tell me about George because they thought I knew that as soon as he walked out of the Cabinet he had shot through the cameras, round the corner to the D.E.A. and announced his refusal to see the T.U.C. and C.B.I. at 2.30. Marcia told me later in the evening that they hadn't taken his letter of resignation too seriously because they had a file of his resignation letters.[1] But apparently on this occasion it was flashed on to the news, so all evening George Brown was going to Downing Street, talking to the Chief Whip, being photographed outside.

While all this was going on, Anne and I were dining with Lord Kennet and his charming wife in their lovely house in Bayswater. It was a most enjoyable dinner since they are some of the nicest new people we have met. From there I rushed to the Television Centre; the news about George was being splashed around and I found myself the first Cabinet Minister to react to it. I said quite genuinely that it was a surprise to me, and added that nobody else in Cabinet was thinking of resigning. I then got through the session quite creditably, defending the Government without disaster.

After that I went back to the Kennets and we talked late about the situation.[2] We discussed whether Harold should have accepted the resignation, and my first, instantaneous reaction was to feel that he had muffed it and to think what Attlee would have done in similar circumstances. He would have been short and sharp—'Goodbye, George. O.K. You must know your own mind. Out.' Attlee would never have argued for an afternoon and evening with his number two after his resignation and then let him return. But as a leader Harold remains a kind, easy-going man and I think also he must have known that a Brown resignation might have finally pushed us off the pound.

When I got back to Vincent Square very late there was Tam Dalyell to tell me about the mood in the Commons, the catastrophic affect of the Brown resignation and the scenes with Bill Rodgers, his Parliamentary Secretary, rushing about, round-robin in hand, getting M.P.s' signatures praying George Brown to stay, and building up his ego. The more I heard about it the more disastrous I thought it was.

Thursday, July 21st
Cabinet this morning had been called to deal with the Concorde problem and to hear a report from Harold about his discussion of this with Monsieur

---

[1] See *Wilson*, pp. 257–8.
[2] After talking to the Prime Minister, the Lord President and George Wigg, that evening, George Brown decided to stay at the D.E.A. and accept full Cabinet responsibility.

Pompidou on his visit to London. I got there five minutes early and looked round the anteroom to see George Brown standing in a corner talking to Barbara Castle. The other people standing about looked pretty disgusted and upset. Nobody said anything.

Once round the table we had a long discussion about parliamentary business, which was dragging into August. Then the P.M. made some remarks about our holidays abroad and tourist allowances and then he said, 'Now overseas business.' Throughout the quarter of an hour we had been discussing parliamentary business I had been screwing myself up to be the unpleasant bastard who would raise the problem of George Brown. It was obvious that if I didn't do so, nobody else would, but that once the issue *was* raised, the P.M. and George would have to say something. So I pulled myself together, screwed up my courage and I said, 'Before we move to overseas business I think we would like to hear, Prime Minister, something from you about the events of which we have only read an account in the newspapers this morning.' At this point somebody else muttered the word 'resignation' and at once the P.M. said George hadn't resigned because the Queen hadn't been informed. He had only sent a letter. George Brown indignantly said it was a matter between him and the P.M., and Harold also tried to argue that it was something which Cabinet had no right to discuss. To which I replied that we might have no right but a public resignation, even if withdrawn, undermined the whole Cabinet policy and we did have the right to discuss this. I then repeated my demand that we should have a Cabinet Committee to control economic strategy. The P.M. replied that this was difficult because of secrecy: no Cabinet Committee could, for instance, discuss devaluation. I replied that there was a Defence Committee which worked in secret, and an economic strategy committee could have the same kind of structure. The P.M. reluctantly agreed. Then somebody raised wider objections about the whole issue of secret committees, and even the question of budget secrecy was brought in. Again the P.M. defended himself by counter-charges about leaks. This exasperated Cabinet because 99 per cent of the so-called leaks come from No. 10 or from the D.E.A. or from the Treasury. With the Prime Minister, George and Jim leaking about each other there is no good blaming the rest of us. Yet the Big Three believe that everything they tell the press is 'guidance' and anything ordinary members of the Cabinet say to the press is a 'leak', and this demoralizes all of us.

We went on to discuss Concorde; and Harold admitted that he had got nothing out of the talks with the French Prime Minister. So we would have to go on with the confounded plane.

The morning hadn't been wasted. What we had established as a result of that discussion of George's resignation was: (i) that the Cabinet must now consider the alternative methods of dealing with the pound; and (ii) that we were going to have a discussion on economic strategy and Europe. Both these were conceded under pressure which I had started. I didn't see Harold again on Thursday. All I received was a message from No. 10 that the Committee meeting he had called on housing had been cancelled and the Minister of Housing would have to wait a long time for a decision.

In the evening we were due to have a meeting of our little group. It was cancelled because Tommy Balogh had been forbidden by Harold to attend, and anyway Marcia had not been at the last meetings. With Marcia out, Tommy terrified, me out of favour and Harold retiring into his shell, I guess the group will cease to exist. That's sad.

Friday, July 22nd

I had to go to Northampton to sort out another of the muddles I had inherited from the Dame as a result of her decision to enlarge old towns by a New Town technique. I found the situation worse than I expected since both the county and the town were opposed to the consultants' plans. I used my morning press conference to play up quite deliberately the savage cuts imposed on local government expenditure, saying I was glad to accept them provided I could preserve the expanded housing programme. I didn't know it but at the same moment Barbara was giving a press conference saying that there were no cuts in the roads programme. It only shows the difference between our propaganda techniques. I thought it was positively good publicity to emphasize the size of our cuts on the building of new town halls and swimming-baths because people expect that of the Government in a crisis. Then I could emphasize how we had preserved the housing programme.

Sunday, July 24th

Another week behind us and certainly the crisis has deepened. We have had during this week the destruction of the Wilson myth in the public eye and, even more, in my own private eye. It's amazing how his luck ran up to a certain point and suddenly stopped. I could name that point – the day he went down to the House of Commons and listed the nine communists in the seamen's union and pulled off the end of the strike next morning. That was the apex of his luck. But he was never able to cash in on it because of the Vietnam bombing Statement two days later. This also spoilt the effect of the announcement of his Russian visit. What is more, after he had briefed the weekend press that nothing was wrong with the economy, suddenly the crisis hit him and he left for Moscow with the crisis on top of him. Since then catastrophe after catastrophe, culminating in the tragi-comic incident of George Brown's semi-resignation this week.

I suppose it is the most dramatic decline any modern P.M. has suffered. More sudden than Macmillan's, which started with the July massacre of one-third of his Cabinet.[1] The first result is reflected in the N.O.P. poll which

[1] On July 13th, 1962, seven Ministers (the Lord Chancellor, the Chancellor of the Exchequer, the Secretary of State for Scotland, the Ministers of Defence, Education and Housing, and the Minister without Portfolio) were sacked from the Cabinet. On July 16th there were nine further resignations.

showed a slump from a $16\frac{1}{2}$ per cent lead to a $7\frac{1}{2}$ per cent lead in one week. It's also reflected in the revival of the Tory Party. On the telly even Heath looks much more like a leader these days.

I try and reflect on why all this hit us. Harold, of course, is anxious to say that the seamen's strike was the cause of the trouble, and it is true that the strike was a great blow. But one has to go right back to the S.E.T. budget, which was the first absolutely fatal mistake. Instead of doing what we expected him to do and imposing the austerity budget we are now getting in July, he and Callaghan avoided unpopularity (and helped to win the municipals) by introducing the gimmickry of S.E.T. The fact that the new tax would only operate as a 'deflater' from September left five months of the year in which the price and wage inflation could run wild. That is what has really got out of control.

And together with the Wilson myth, the three-man regime has gone for a burton. Up till now our economic policy has been run by the system of having two Ministries permanently at loggerheads, the Treasury and the D.E.A., with the Treasury gradually gaining mastery over the D.E.A. but sufficient tension remaining between them to cancel out both Departments' policies. Our big economic decisions have been made by Harold's arbitration between the Chancellor and the First Secretary. This system, which looked pretty crazy anyway, came completely unstuck this summer when it was revealed that there is no contingency planning of any kind at all.

What is really wrong — and Tommy has said this all along — is that we have no real instrument of central decision-taking for the home front. In the case of foreign policy and defence, the Defence Committee, on which the Chiefs of Staff at least are present, is a central instrument which has worked for thirty years and gets some coherent decisions taken. When defence problems come up there may be wrong decisions, but at least decisions and contingency plans are made. Nothing of this sort exists to deal with the economy. (Here Harold's proclivity for opportunism completely coincides with Whitehall's desire to prevent a coherent decision-taking body being imposed upon it.) In its absence the P.M. has run the Government Prime Ministerially, arbitrating between George Brown and Callaghan, and in every other field retaining the right of final decision and, in this particular crisis, working direct with the Permanent Secretaries behind the backs of their Ministers. As for his own personal decisions, they've taken in consultation with a very small inner private circle. In the first place there is the real inner group, the real kitchen Cabinet — that is Marcia Williams, Gerald Kaufman, Peter Shore. And in addition there are three independent personalities — George Wigg, Tommy Balogh and, last but not least, Burke Trend, the one really powerful force in this entourage.

This week we have had the beginnings of a collective Cabinet reaction against this Prime Ministerial method. The odd thing is that I, who wrote the Introduction to Bagehot, am now busily trying to reassert collective

Cabinet authority because I see how disastrous it is to allow Cabinet government to decline into mere Prime Ministerial government. It's better to get back to something much more like Cabinet responsibility; just as it is better to get back to effective Cabinet responsibility to Parliament, and the reassertion of parliamentary control over government – one of those bright ideas Harold announced during the election campaign and at the beginning of the Session but which has got entirely lost since then.

I think it is true after this week nobody in Cabinet will ever again believe that this triumvirate can safely be left in charge. If I achieved anything it was by asserting the right of Cabinet to take part in the making of economic strategy so that Harold conceded that we must be given that right. If we really have achieved an economic strategy committee parallel to the Defence Committee, it could produce a complete change in the relationship between the P.M., the First Secretary and the Chancellor on the one side and the rest of the Cabinet on the other. We shall have to wait and see whether this has been achieved, however, when Harold returns from his two days in Washington at the end of next week.

One last word about my own position. This week I have emerged inside Cabinet as a counter-force round which people were grouped. By this I have done myself no good in the P.M.'s eyes, and as I haven't switched my loyalty to George Brown I may have done myself harm with him as well. So now I am unpopular with Harold and George, as well as hated by Callaghan, and that is both a dangerous and an exposed position. Because I am a heavyweight Minister and because I am alone, I am liable to destruction.

Here's where my private life makes such an enormous difference. There is Anne, who came up this week for that lovely dinner with the Kennets. Fortunately, she is delighted at the prospect that I may be able to retire and have my life prolonged, as it probably would be by retiring now and writing my book at home. Anne wants that with her whole heart. And I have a home to retire to and enough money as well. This gives me an inner detachment, an ability to face resignation which I think none of my colleagues have at all. Roy Jenkins, Tony Crosland, Tony Benn are all young ambitious men with a whole life of politics in front of them. I am now fifty-seven, nearly fifty-eight, and I shall only fight one more election. I have only got – if things go as I want – three or four more years as Cabinet Minister before I retire. And if that three or four years is cut down and I retire a few years earlier I have enough on this tape to write the kind of book that I want.

This gives me a certain strength but it doesn't affect my loneliness. There's no one in Cabinet who I can claim is a real personal friend except Barbara. Roy Jenkins and Tony Crosland are people I like, but they are not real friends. Fred Peart I get on with as a professional colleague but I wouldn't dream of knowing him outside, or for that matter Michael Stewart, Willie Ross, Fred Lee, Cledwyn Hughes or Richard Marsh. My relations with George Wigg are strained now because he is in charge of security for the P.M. in the Party and he requires absolute loyalty from everyone. We have got to be either for or against Harold Wilson and since I am criticizing Harold I am now classified by George as against. Of course, I still have Thomas Balogh as a friend, but he's apprehensive of seeing or telling me much in my new exposed position. As for the rest of the Parliamentary Labour Party, Tam Dalyell is the person I know best and I can talk to and trust him completely. He is a kind of Sancho Panza to the Don Quixote of this diary.

Really, of course, Harold is nearer to me as a person than anybody else I have mentioned. But Harold is very much separated from me now, first by his position and second by his suspicion that anyone who stands up to him is intriguing against him, maybe wanting power. He certainly always suspects Jim Callaghan of seeking to replace him, and he must be aware that last week George Brown was talking about a coup against him in the last resort. And I suppose that now I have reared my head he is beginning to think the same about me.

Having committed myself, I have got to go on fighting. My next step must be to insist that the officials will sit along with Ministers on the economic strategy committee as they do in the Defence Committee. I must also insist on the new Committee to discuss Europe and the new committee to discuss methods of devaluation getting going straight away. Indeed, I have got to pin Harold down on all this before we break up on August 10th or 11th for the recess.

Monday, July 25th
I had been invited to lunch at *The Economist* by the editor, Alastair Burnet. When I went into the Ministry that morning Peter Brown said to me, 'For heaven's sake, no contact with journalists this week. I don't want any kind of suggestion of leaking from our Ministry during this crisis where you are being so active.' I had looked with some anxiety at the Sunday papers and duly found in both the *Observer* and the *Sunday Times* a round by round account of what happened in the Cabinet rebellion. But both accounts centred on the melodramatics of Harold and George and Callaghan and there wasn't a trace of the actual debate which took place. I was greatly relieved because it meant that Roy, Barbara, Wedgy Benn, Tony Crosland and I were keeping faith with each other in not saying a word to the press.

I would normally have cancelled the *Economist* lunch on Peter's advice. I didn't because I felt I ought to go and be tough with them about the housing policy. At the lunch, when we'd given the housing subsidies, rate rebates, option-mortgages and the cuts a good going over, I deliberately moved to the constitutional aspects of the crisis on the ground that I had written the Introduction to Bagehot, and I sold them at length the idea of an economic strategy committee parallel to the Defence Committee. I also mentioned this to Ian Waller[1] and Arthur Gavshon[2] later in the day but I don't expect any

---

[1] Political correspondent of the *Sunday Telegraph*.
[2] A.P. foreign and diplomatic correspondent in London.

one of them even to refer to it in anything he writes. What I think of immense importance isn't accepted as such even by well-informed journalists looking on from outside.*

The Party meeting in the evening was, by agreement, limited to questions and answers. It was not particularly full and there was no particular tension, despite all the alarms and excursions worked up in the weekend press. Indeed, nothing really happened except to George Brown. Coming in late, he found nowhere to sit on the platform and put himself down on a chair just below it. After the meeting he said, 'You see, Harold didn't have the decency to get anybody to stand up and give me room.' I am sure the truth is that Harold didn't know that George had come in, and anyway we would all have offered George Brown a seat, but he wants to feel injured. I should add that Harold is equally injured by the damage George Brown has done to him and the relations between the two are worse than ever. (George Wigg on the phone this morning told me that he was spending nearly all his time now behaving like a Christian full of brotherly love, and trying to sustain and keep George Brown since we can't afford to lose him at this particular time.) But apart from George feeling injured, nothing really happened. The P.M. was, as always, extremely competent, and on this occasion happened to be precise. Pressed about the level of unemployment, he gave the explicit assurance that it wouldn't rise above 2 per cent. The economy was over-inflated now, we needed to take some of the heat out and to drive a little of the employment out of it. This would be a good thing since it would put people into useful instead of candy-floss production. When he said this I whispered to Fred Peart by my side, 'My God, if that was recorded and played back to the Zurich bankers there would be a devaluation tomorrow.' But he went further and assured the meeting that if we ever got into difficulties we could always reflate: 'I tell you we have powers of reflation now. Why, Dick here beside me can take up the phone the minute I ask him and put another £10 million-worth of houses into the production line.'

This is not only dangerous but quite untrue. If the P.M. had reflected for a moment he would know that I can't pick up the phone and put houses into the production line. Public-sector housing is a very slow and laborious process which we can't switch on and off at will. In fact, there is nearly a two-year gap between the decision to increase public-sector housing and the first completed houses. I want to hurry this up, but it is characteristic of this side of the P.M. that he has such a natural instinct for making the best of the things to his audience. So, talking off the record to the Labour Party, he was able to give the comrades the feeling that it is all going to be painless and that nothing is really wrong. I will bet you when he talks to the bankers off the record and President Johnson he gives a very different impression. He is never actually untruthful but he does blur it all the time.

When I got home late that night Tam told me that a number of left-wingers

* I was quite right. None of them mentioned it.

19*

had been furious because Manny Shinwell had refused a discussion after the questions. They felt that subjects which should have been brought out in the open had been evaded by the P.M. I think there is something in this because forty-seven of our people have tabled a vote of censure on the Government package in preparation for the debate starting tomorrow.[1]

Tuesday, July 26th

I spent the whole morning grappling with the Department on the issue of how to finance New Town housing. Long before the Dame left I had pointed out how unsatisfactory it was that the rents of the houses built for the new-comers by the corporation of a New Town are always much higher than the rents of the houses built for the old residents by the local authority, the U.D.C. It is equally troublesome that nobody in the New Town understands the basis on which the rents of corporation houses are fixed. I have argued that it is time we brought the corporation housing-revenue account into line with the U.D.C. housing-revenue account, so that we could really judge between the two and make sure that there is sufficient reason for the difference between the rent levels being so large. Before I had solved this problem a new one was on my plate. I discovered that my officials, without telling me, had gone to the Treasury and proposed to recast the special New Town housing subsidy so that the older New Towns would help the newer New Towns to keep their rent levels down. There was a great deal of injustice in the idea, and I realized it was also politically impossible since it would upset the older towns and widen the gap between their corporation and U.D.C. rents. I discovered at Harlow, for example, that they are now letting three-bedroom houses to married, childless couples because nobody with three children can afford the £6 or £7 a week. So I had to stop this scheme and also to rule that the housing subsidy for New Towns should be exactly the same as for town developments undertaken without the help of the Ministry, like, say, the development at Basingstoke.

After the meeting I was pleased when my Private Office told me of friend Pugh's complaint. He had said that the Minister now seems to know as much about these subjects as the officials do, and as he travels round the country and has so much more contact with the local authorities and the New Town people he gets the edge over officials in our discussions. It's true that I am just beginning to feel that on a few subjects I am on top of the Department and can take the decisions: in housing, in certain parts of planning, in New Towns and on local government boundaries I am now an effective Minister. It is also true that in huge areas of finance, administration and planning I am still really out of my depth.

In the afternoon I deliberately sat on the front bench, even though I knew my Questions would not be reached. I wanted a quarter of an hour's talk with

[1] The motion condemned the Government's policy and demanded an immediate review of the position of sterling as a national currency.

Harold and I have come to learn that he is a tremendous front-bench talker—
and so am I. There we sat together, and I said to him, 'Yesterday's Party
meeting went pretty well. You pretty well floored the opposition.' 'Yes,' he
said. And then he added, 'Anyway, you don't realize that I am not so unpopular as everybody thinks. I was in Liverpool last weekend and I went to
the Cavern, where the Beatles first played, to be present at its reopening and
the whole place stood and cheered me. Each time I go down Downing Street
now more people cheer me than ever before. It's quite untrue that the people
are against me, it's only these journalists and Parliament. If we could pack
Parliament off each year on July 1st, we could run the country properly
because those fellows opposite are no good whatsoever.' He chatted away
almost without ceasing and I began to wonder if he was talking just to keep
up his pecker. Had he really lost his nerve inside or was it that he had drawn
a thick skin round himself? Or has he—as I tend to believe—a deep natural
survival instinct which enables him to deceive himself as a protection against
collapse? Because he really had a terrible press this last weekend. All those
speeches he made when he was leader of the Opposition and in his first year
as Prime Minister denouncing the Selwyn Lloyd 'stop–go' were chickens
coming home to roost in the columns of the press. Of course, it's true that
we are not doing the same as Selwyn Lloyd. Ours is a controlled, selective
deflation. But this is something Harold failed to put over last week and as a
result he has been battered and smashed over the weekend. Moreover, all
this row with George Brown hasn't exactly helped him.

I was back in my Ministry doing some routine work when Kenneth
Robinson walked in. He had obviously come to take soundings, and he
explained to me the problem with the doctors into which George Brown had
shoved him. Payment for the very generous award for the doctors had been
fixed for April 1st. But owing to the Ministry of Health's failure to get the
arrangements perfected, the date had been postponed and George Brown is
now arguing that for that reason the payment must be postponed for the
duration of the freeze. I said that I suspected that what George Brown really
was facing was the fact that if the doctors were at once to become an exception
you can say goodbye to any gas worker or any other industrial worker taking
the wage freeze seriously. Nevertheless, I saw that Kenneth had a serious
case and that he wasn't talking nonsense when he mentioned the possibility
of resigning if he couldn't get his way.[1] We discussed the whole freeze and I
became more and more aware of how neglectful I had been in disregarding
its importance, and in sending MacColl to represent me on the departmental
committee where the details are being worked out. But what really brought
me up against my danger was the other item on Ken's agenda, the jam they
are in in the Borough of Camden, where he lives, where the district auditor
is threatening that if the council doesn't put up the rents he will have them

[1] The council of the B.M.A. agreed to defer the award for six months with a limited
amount of backdating once it could be implemented.

surcharged. The more I talked to him the more I realized what a mistake I had made in the Party meeting the night before. We had been sitting there while Harold was answering questions when suddenly one turned up about rents and Harold looked down to me and said, 'You do the answer to that one, Dick.' All I had seen had been the draft White Paper and so, almost without thinking, I replied that council rents would have to be excluded from the freeze because they could only be kept down by putting up the rates. I said this off the cuff, remembering it was in my brief from the Department. Nevertheless, I noticed from the reaction of several of my friends among the back-benchers that I had gone off the rails, since you can't impose a freeze of wages if councils are allowed to increase their rents. I was really grateful to Ken Robinson for finally making me realize this.

In the evening I dined with Gerald Kaufman because I felt it was time I patched up my relations with Downing Street. Afterwards I strolled round to Cowley Street where I found Pam and Michael Berry sitting at home; and we looked at the Rab Butler television show together as she had suggested to me at lunch the week before. Butler had done five hours' recorded conversation with Kenneth Harris mainly on why he had failed to become leader,[1] and this had been cut to one hour with Butler being permitted the right to help in the editing. I sat in front of it for an hour and I am afraid for a lot of the time I dozed because it was so flat. Though he is Master of Trinity and completely retired from politics, he still feels it is his job as a member of the team to obscure the issues and 'say the correct thing'. I doubt if I shall do the same in his position.

Afterwards Pam and Michael asked me about the situation. I was very discreet but I did compare Harold Wilson and Macmillan as two Prime Ministers confronted with not dissimilar problems, and I argued that Harold was no worse than his predecessor. I added that I didn't much like being a Cabinet Minister under Prime Ministerial government but I suspected it was something that Cabinet Ministers had been suffering under ever since Churchill's war Cabinet in 1940.

Wednesday, July 27th

To Transport House at ten o'clock for the meeting of the N.E.C. It turned out to be far the most important discussion we have had since 1964. We'd soon finished with formal business and got down to a talk about the freeze and the package. Almost before we knew it, Jack Jones* had launched out into a tremendous attack in which he made it clear that his union would try to ensure that the entire T.U.C. opposed the whole policy tooth and nail. He was saying all this before he knew the enormous extra powers George Brown

---

* As Frank Cousins's number two in the T.G.W.U., he served on our N.E.C. at this time, while Frank, like other top trade-union leaders, occupied a place on the General Council of the T.U.C.

[1] Of the Conservative Party in 1963. See his *The Art of the Possible* (London: Hamish Hamilton, 1971), and Harold Macmillan, *The End of the Day* (London: Macmillan, 1973).

was taking in the new Part IV clauses. When Jack Jones had finished, Chapple, the E.T.U. ex-communist,[1] chipped in and said, 'If only one of the big unions opts out of a voluntary wage freeze, the rest are sooner or later forced to come into line. What you are asking us to do is to stand by you in a policy which we can't afford to support if only a minority determines to bust it.' And this theme of his was repeated by all the other trade unionists present. I don't think I quite realized at the time that Chapple was really arguing that the Government should take compulsory powers. If that happens, the right-wing unions who would like to support the Government can give the excuse that they can't afford to break the law.

Afterwards at my Ministry I received a delegation from the Camden Council who, following up Robinson's visit of yesterday, had come to ask me what they should do if the district auditor surcharged them. I told them that I thought when the White Paper was published it would authorize them to delay putting up the rents for the duration of the freeze. I am delighted to find that behind my back Bob Mellish has been taking the same line because he realized that I had been wrong in my reply at the Party meeting. He and MacColl have been drafting a clause for the White Paper which will authorize local authorities to hold down rents as far as possible and instruct them in any case not to put them up without consultation with the Minister.

In the evening I went across to the Commons, because I had been asked by our Labour Party housing committee to discuss their dissatisfaction with my rent assessment committees. This has been a growing worry during the past weeks. The gap is steadily becoming wider and wider between the inter-pretation of fair rents laid down by Sydney Littlewood at the top level and that of the rent officers, who are much more sympathetic to the tenants. Fortunately, that morning I had had a meeting with Littlewood and he had caved in to the rent officers' main demand that in future the rent assessment committees should inspect the dwellings and make up their own minds instead of sending a so-called 'referencer' to do the practical work for them. Of course, it really had been outrageous of Littlewood to suggest this idea of the R.A.C.s sitting on their judgment seats and never getting out to visit the flats and houses. However, he has agreed, and I was able to tell this to the com-mittee in the House and also to say that the surveyors have now agreed that just as there are poor men's lawyers so there will be poor men's surveyors whom tenants can go to for free advice before they go to the rent officer. So I met my colleagues on one or two of the issues they had raised. But I knew that at the back of their minds was the feeling that Sydney Littlewood is a pretty reactionary solicitor, much more reactionary than any of the rent officers. Indeed, last weekend Girling, the chief rent officer for Westminster,

[1] Frank Chapple was the E.T.U. Assistant General Secretary from 1963 until September 1966, when he became General Secretary. He had been a member of the Communist Party, but had left it at the time of the Russian invasion of Hungary in 1956. In 1958 there had been court proceedings into the affairs of the E.T.U. and a communist group was found guilty of ballot-rigging and expelled from the union.

had come out in an almost open attack on Sir Sydney. I shall be in great
trouble unless I can fairly rapidly get a definition of fair rent which will heal
the gap.

By the time I had finished with this committee the big two-day censure
debate which had started on Tuesday afternoon was getting towards its end.
The P.M. had started the second day with a crashingly boring speech,[1] but
he got away with it because although Heath's speech was brilliant, the only
person with any constructive ideas had been Maudling. Now came the final
wind-up and I went in to hear Macleod answered by Brown. Macleod was
short and quite clever, naming the three guilty men, Wilson, Brown and
Callaghan. Then George got up and it was one of those evenings ... I have
seen it happen before now. He was overwrought, overtired, and he spoke so
slowly that he incited the Tories to interrupt him.[2] Nevertheless, he was
wonderfully received by our own side since he had been basking in a weekend
press and warmed by the round-robin and had stolen all the limelight.[3] I
knew he would get away with it but the speech was disastrous in the sense that
it produced huge headlines in the *Daily Express* about the collapse of George
Brown. This just wasn't true. He hadn't been drunk; he had been overwrought.
But he has enough character and personality to get over it.

Thursday, July 28th
One of the disconcerting features of the recent crisis has been the Cabinet
Secretariat's habit of suppressing whole sections of the minutes on the ground
that they are too secret to circulate. But this morning they didn't feel like that.
The section on prices and incomes was reported at enormous length and most
of what we all said has been very adequately summarized. Of course, this
means that the Cabinet Secretariat regards the whole subject as fraught with
danger and was careful to record the arguments of the opponents. Cabinet
minutes are highly political and the way they are written has enormous effect.
By eliminating whole sections from the discussion and reporting other sections
in full the Secretariat can greatly affect the way a decision is interpreted in
Whitehall. In this case, when I was looking round, I caught the eye of one of
the minute-takers. He put his hand to his throat as though George Brown
was cutting his, and afterwards said to me, 'He may want to commit suicide
but why should he drag you all down with him?'

All this excitement was caused by the text of the new Part IV of the Bill
which George Brown presented to us on Thursday morning. His four new
clauses were put forward as the logical result of the decision reached by
Cabinet in the previous week. But they also conferred an immense *new* power
on the Government. Now, when the Bill had been passed and Parliament had
gone away, an Order could be laid which automatically brought the new

---

[1] 'It was a hard-hitting speech.' *Wilson*, p. 262.
[2] Wilson describes it as 'the Tory benches at their traditional post-prandial worst'.
Wilson, p. 262.
[3] The Government defeated the Opposition by 325 to 246 votes.

Part IV into force, giving complete economic dictatorial powers to George Brown and the D.E.A. As the discussion went on it gradually dawned on more and more of us that it would be impossible to get this through Congress or through the Labour Party Conference and anyway why should we in Cabinet accept it? Whenever this question was put to George Brown he replied, 'This is what you instructed me to do. If you want the wage freeze to have effective sanctions behind it, this is the way you have to proceed.' But, as more and more of us began to say, when we talked about this last week there was no suggestion of this kind of economic dictatorship. Harold said, no, it had been perfectly clear, and he sent for Hansard. But for once I was right. The public statement had been very mild, saying that the Government was still determined to rely on the voluntary principle and that though we were going to introduce some reserve powers these must be kept well in the background. Even so, the effect of the reserve powers suggested was nothing like as extensive as the reserve powers of the new Part IV. After a couple of hours we had really boiled the problem down to two questions, on which we voted. The first vote was taken on a proposal by Tony Crosland, that the new punitive powers should not apply on the wages and incomes side but only to prices. I voted for this along with seven others, including Fred Lee and Barbara Castle. Roy Jenkins was not with us on this one. He joined the Foreign Secretary, the Defence people and Fred Peart and of course the Chancellor of the Exchequer and George Brown. The second vote took place on a proposal of mine. I had asked whether it would be possible to bring Part IV into force during the recess. George Brown said that since everybody knew the voluntary system wouldn't work, he would give it just a fortnight and then clap the Order on. I said this was intolerable; and moved an amendment instructing George to write into the Bill an express commitment that Part IV could only be introduced by an Affirmative Resolution, requiring the assent of Parliament to a 28-day Order which would lapse after that period unless renewed. This means that if the Order is laid in the recess Parliament will have to be recalled. The amendment was carried. It was a considerable victory since it will now be far more difficult to implement Part IV.

I must record one minor incident of this strange Cabinet which should not be forgotten. There were towards the end a whole series of secondary issues, such as how to deal with wage claims which had been announced a few days before July 20th or where the date of the payment, as with the doctors, was before July 20th. On all these issues votes were taken and Harold wrote down the score. At one point it came to 10–9. Willie Ross switched his vote and it came to a tie, and Harold said, 'What shall I do, it's a tie?' I said *sotto voce*, 'Be a Prime Minister,' and Richard Marsh giggled. But Harold repeated plaintively, 'What shall I do, it's a tie?' He is a very strange man.

This incident also reveals something about Cabinet government. The Prime Minister has suddenly become weak and the Ministers with big Departments, like George Brown and Callaghan, are now stronger than he is. So he must try to square them and the whole Cabinet on every minor issue. Sometimes he is tossed about like a cork on the water.

I had to leave Cabinet before all the detailed decisions were taken because I was off to Southampton where a helicopter was waiting to take me for a view of the planning problems of Southampton, Portsmouth and Hampshire County Council. I stayed the night at Winchester as the guest of the county council and had one of those racy dinners where they provide such excellent hospitality and I really enjoy myself. Back at the Wessex, looking out over the cathedral, I began to reflect on the Cabinet conclusions and to think that I ought to write to Harold or at least to warn him that although I voted for making Part IV require the recall of Parliament, I would actually oppose it if the Order were ever brought into force. My aim would be at all costs to prevent the Order being laid. While I was thinking about this Roy Jenkins came on the phone to discuss with me the problem of the Birmingham rents. I tried him out on the whole idea. He took a rather different view. He thought we should examine the whole administrative structure and be sure of how exactly it would be enforced before making up our minds on tactics. I agreed with him about the undesirability of my writing a letter in any way threatening resignation or trying to force Harold's hand. But it is something I shall have to talk to Harold about.

Friday, July 29th

It was most beautiful weather for my Hampshire tour. In the morning I was due to open some new housing at Romsey with Lord Mountbatten and I thought I would make a statement which should get into all the papers about my opposition to the element of compulsion and the need to retain the voluntary principle in the Prices and Incomes Bill. So I worked out a little thing about housing and then tacked on to it the following sentences:

> I now turn to the matter of compulsion. You have heard a lot about the powers the Government are determined to take. I will just say this to you. Personally, I feel there is a terrible danger here. Of course governments have to take powers in reserve but they should only be taken for the express purpose of making the voluntary system work. If they are taken for any other reason, that is quite wrong, and if, when taken, they have to be used, then the Government should recognize it has failed to make the voluntary system work, in which we believe.

On the way to Romsey I rehearsed those sentences in the car. When I got there I found I was addressing thirty or forty of Lord Louis's retainers in a tiny village hall. However, the press were there and I got the sentence out successfully and waited throughout the day for the B.B.C. wireless news. Not a word about it.* It is always an anticlimax when one screws oneself up to say the big thing and the big thing doesn't appear.

* And not a word in Saturday's press, either.

I spent the rest of the day with the three big shots of the Hampshire County Council, touring the New Forest and studying the problems of the coastline. It was delightful weather and delightful company. Another person accompanying us in the afternoon was the young Lord Porchester who I had heard of from Denis Howell as very helpful in all the problems of sport. He turned out to be an extremely pleasant person.

Anne was due to meet me with the car at the Wessex at six and drive me back over one of my favourite roads—from Winchester, over the downs to Newbury, Oxford and on to Banbury. When Lord Porchester heard we were going that way he said, 'Why don't you come and dine with me at our little house outside Newbury?' I accepted straight away and off we drove independently in our two cars. We found ourselves by eight o'clock driving up to a delicious miniature Trianon built near the big house and looking out on its own lake. It was one of the most perfect places I have seen in the whole world and I fell in love with it at sight. Sitting on exquisite furniture at dinner over exquisite food and drink and looking out on a jewelled evening I had the kind of feeling of aesthetic excitement which hasn't been with me for many years. And maybe the food and drink were too good—I got into one of my furious intellectual rows with Lord Porchester about monarchy. Reflecting now, I can't think it was very polite to my host since I knew quite well he is one of the Queen's most intimate friends. However, I took it on myself to explain the Bagehot theory of monarchy as part of the dignified element in the constitution, and to dilate on the snobbery of the people who love the monarch and the dreary role both of the monarchy and of the court.

I thanked God I was Minister of Housing and didn't have to mix with the court. He said, 'The Queen is one of my greatest personal friends, and I am a tremendous admirer.' In a way that put me in my place but I said, 'Well, maybe! But she finds me boring and I find her boring and I think it is a great relief that I don't have to see her.' The argument got quite hot at one time; and then the heat cooled out of our conversation and we parted on perfectly pleasant terms with one another. We were back at Prescote before midnight and I found I had forgotten about the great declaration I had made at Romsey which simply hadn't come into existence!

Sunday, July 31st

Back with the Sunday papers to read and back in the crisis. I see now that last week I was still treating the prices and incomes policy as a gimmick, something I never really believed in, something which really couldn't be made serious. It is this which made me so astonished and appalled at Thursday's Cabinet, when the full meaning of Part IV was revealed to us. It transforms a harmless Bill into a measure giving powers of economic dictatorship to the Government and in particular to George Brown. Under Part IV he can penalize any employer or trade union that raises prices or raises wages, he can make every strike illegal and he can gaol any trade-unionist who stands against his policy. This is economic dictatorship.

But how far was this announcement on Thursday a new and completely unexpected departure? I had better admit that, in Cabinet, when I had got my way about discussing devaluation and the setting up of the economic strategy committee I didn't really listen to the part on incomes and prices and I only woke up at the last moment to the significance of council rents. Nevertheless, I am certainly not the only person who was utterly surprised on Thursday. When the T.U.C. were shown Part IV they were absolutely flabbergasted, and so was the C.B.I. and so were most of my Cabinet colleagues. But the Government's economic planners, including Tommy Balogh, weren't surprised. Talking to Tommy this morning, I realize that it is a repetition of the S.E.T. affair. Once again he was in on the secret, thinks it perfectly practicable and is strongly in favour of it. My own view is that it is impracticable, not for economic but for political reasons. If you make all strikes illegal you will have trade unionists going to gaol; and anyway, we can never get this approved by Congress or by our own Conference in October as a proper thing to do. What infuriates me was that we were presented with a *fait accompli* on Thursday and I am still busily engaged in trying to limit and confine the danger. I rang up Harold this morning at Chequers where he is resting, back from the U.S.A., and I am seeing him at 10.30 tonight.

Meanwhile, I must record a big change in Harold's personal position. Luck was running against him till the end of the week; now it seems suddenly to have turned. I would guess he has had quite a good trip and a real success with President Johnson. But it is also a tremendous help for him that we won the World Cup on Saturday.[1] That may well mean that his luck, which deserted him after he had dealt with the seamen's strike, has really turned now. When I told Anne over lunch today that the World Cup could be a decisive factor in strengthening sterling she couldn't believe it. But I am sure it is. It was a tremendous, gallant fight that England won. Our men showed real guts and the bankers, I suspect, will be influenced by this, and the position of the Government correspondingly strengthened.

I set out for London by the 9 p.m. train. It was five minutes early at Banbury but as it approached London it went slower and slower and finally only got in at 10.40; and I got to No. 10 in pouring rain after 11 p.m. I rushed upstairs and there was Harold in the flat waiting to take me into the little drawing-room. I remembered that I hadn't been there more than once since the election. But here we were, settling down, and I was aware that he was aware that I hadn't come just for a pleasant chat and that his job was to fend me off from saying what I wanted to say. He started straight away with a long story about how the whole devaluation discussion in Cabinet had been a set

[1] Harold Wilson had flown to Washington on the 28th, held his talks with the President on the 29th on further dollar support for the pound, and returned—via Ottawa—in time to see the World Cup Final at Wembley. See *Wilson*, pp. 264–6.

piece—a trap set by the pro-Europeans. He described how he had told Barbara that they had taken her for a ride, and how she had indignantly denied this.

Having discredited the Europeans—he described Roy Jenkins as a dangerous, conspiratorial type—he turned back to James Callaghan and spent the next twenty minutes telling me how inert he was and how he, Harold, had to rescue him time after time, and finally how he had now become a secret European convert, a danger to the cause of all of us who, like Harold, were not prepared to go into Europe except very much on the right terms.

I then said that surely there was not much to be alarmed about in all this after his visit to L.B.J. 'No,' he said, 'that's perfectly true. What I have fixed with L.B.J. is enough to make de Gaulle foam at the mouth. We needn't really worry now about any possibilities of going into Europe.' Harold then began to talk about his Washington mission, which had been pretty fully described in the Sunday press, and the astonishing panegyric L.B.J. had given when toasting him at lunch.[1] I said, 'I suppose L.B.J.'s speech was all written out before.' And Harold said, yes, he thought that most of it was, 'but the passage about Dunkirk did seem to be an impromptu.' He added that it had rather embarrassed him and he thought that Peregrine Worsthorne was a bit unfair in his article to talk as though this had given him any pleasure.

From time to time during the course of his monologue I said that I really must talk about my worries about Part IV and finally I got out—all in one sentence—that I was really shocked by the absence of any strategic Cabinet control of economic affairs. 'Ah,' said Harold, 'I know you have made that point. You've made it to Burke Trend. Well, I can assure you that this committee you have asked for, corresponding to the Defence Committee, will be set up with nine Ministers on it.' I then said, 'Couldn't we have officials there as well, like the Chiefs of Staff?' And Harold replied, 'The Chiefs of Staff aren't always at the Defence Committee, and anyway we can't have Tommy there' (Harold always knows what you are really talking about) 'because though he is a marvellous adviser he is no good at committees.' He then added, 'Don't lay too much hope on this strategic committee. You've insisted on it and I can promise you that you are actually going to get it. But don't have too high hopes of it.'

Then I said that what worried me at this week's Cabinet was the fact that this absolutely revolutionary proposal for economic dictatorship was presented to us as a *fait accompli*. It was just as bad as the treatment of the Cabinet over the S.E.T. budget. And Harold replied, 'If you think you were upset and surprised by it, so were we all. You ought to know that George Brown originally intended to push Part IV through without reference to

[1] Proposing the Prime Minister's health, the President spoke of ' ... the nation that has given us the tongue of a Shakespeare, the faith of a Milton, and the courage of a Churchill ... ' and now 'a leader whose own enterprise and courage will show the way'. The passage is quoted in *Wilson*, pp. 264–5.

Cabinet at all. It was only I who said it must go to Cabinet. And how right you were, my dear Dick, to insist that it can only be made operative by an Affirmative Resolution. That idea of yours made the whole difference. I entirely agreed with you on that.' So he placated me and I found it very difficult to say what I had intended to say—that he couldn't rely on me not to resign if the attempt was made to lay the Order. I did get as far as saying that the powers were absolutely unworkable, to which he replied, 'Maybe I agree with you, but we may be able to keep the voluntary system and never bring the Order into effect.' To which I said, 'But look, what I am saying to you is that if it were brought into effect I would do everything I could to stop it and get as many other members of Cabinet to work with me as possible.' At this point he said very quietly, 'Never organize a cave in Cabinet, Dick. That's a great mistake.' And then he went on with the conversation. I was aware that now I had made my point things would never be quite the same between us again. But I admired him for the way he just dropped in that remark and then went on with our talk. It gyrated mostly round James Callaghan's ineffectiveness and his monomaniac belief that he could some day replace Harold and possibly be Prime Minister of a national government. All this Harold spelt out to me as well as his problems with George who, though loyal and charming, was so erratic and difficult. Throughout all this talk about colleagues I tried to insist on the need for collective Cabinet responsibility. But of course my insistence sounded at the time as though I was merely asking for a more important position for myself and I was very much aware that to Harold's ear all I was doing was asking a price for my loyalty. I fear I have made a poor account of this conversation which started at 11 and ended at 12.45. Then he took me downstairs and I got into my car in driving rain, went back to Vincent Square and worked at my box for some time.

Monday, August 1st

I have already described in this diary how I was caught unprepared at the Party meeting by a question about council rents and said they wouldn't be frozen. Over the weekend I was made to realize that this position was totally untenable. Now that we were contemplating a total freeze of all prices and wages, council rents stuck out like a sore thumb. After all, as Minister of Housing, I already control all private landlord rents under the Rent Act. If gas workers and municipal bus drivers, who are the kind of people who live in council houses, get large rent increases, then the whole freeze will break down.

This was brought home to me yesterday morning by Alderman Griffin, the Conservative leader who took over Birmingham after the defeat of Harry Watton in the municipal elections. He rang me up at Prescote and said he wanted to consult me about whether Birmingham rents could go up next day. He explained that Monday was the last day of the statutory month's notice which had been given to all Birmingham municipal tenants before the new rent increases came in. These had been occasioned by the deliberate decision of Harry Watton in the last months of Labour rule to leave the housing-revenue till empty and throw on the Tories the odium of increasing the rents. Griffin therefore had an overwhelming case for raising the rents, since the housing-revenue account will be nearly £2 million in the red in March of next year. All this he explained to me on the phone and I couldn't deny that he had a powerful case. Nevertheless, I told him that morning that if he asked me the direct question whether they could go up my direct reply was, 'No, you certainly can't do that on Monday morning.' I wasn't sure what he was going to do, but I invited him to see me in London next day.

I had luck this morning because the P.M. had fixed a Housing Cabinet Committee at 11 — an hour before the Birmingham delegation was due to arrive. I went round to No. 10 at 10.45 because he wanted to discuss the possibility of the Huyton Council in his constituency being given permission to build a large office block, for their own use under present conditions but for selling as ordinary offices if local government boundaries should be altered. My Department, I learnt that morning, had told me to tell the P.M. that the squeeze would make this impossible in the immediate future. After this Harold remarked, 'I have been talking to George Brown about your anxieties of last night and I can assure you that we are absolutely clear that there will have to be a debate in Parliament before the Order is laid.' Then the other members of the Committee came into the room. George Brown had sent Austen Albu,[1] but the Chancellor himself was there, and Willie Ross for Scotland and Bob Mellish and myself, and I was allowed to fix the agenda. I started with something I had been trying to get out of the Chancellor for weeks, a firm commitment that the option-mortgage scheme was still on despite the freeze, that it would be included in our Housing Subsidies Bill next Session, and that the moment the Bill was through the scheme would come into effect. For weeks the Chancellor has been trying to announce its abandonment or indefinite postponement. But now I was able to get it through.

I then raised the question of council rents and explained how the Birmingham deputation would be waiting for me in the Ministry. Could I tell them that as part of our total freeze we should be insisting that councils for the first six months postpone all rent increases since they so profoundly affect the cost of living? Callaghan immediately said, 'Don't put too much stress on that, because after all what we want is not a price freeze but price increases so as to cut back consumption. We don't want anything which stops that.' I replied rather peevishly, 'Whose directive are we carrying out? I have just been told that we are to have a wages *and* a prices freeze and that the control of prices is just as important as the control of wages.' Harold looked across the table appealingly as if to say 'Don't argue with him, he doesn't matter.'

[1] M.P. for Edmonton since 1948. He was Minister of State at the D.E.A. 1965–7.

And so the argument went to and fro, and finally I got from Harold a clear directive to persuade the Birmingham delegation that morning to call a special council meeting and postpone the rent increases for six months.

Back in the Ministry I sat down with Alderman Griffin and asked him to go ahead and tell his story. This he proceeded to do at great length, outlining the whole long history of what he called Labour's 'turpitude' in postponing the necessary rent increases. Finally I broke in and said, 'Look, Alderman, I know you have an excellent rent rebate scheme. I also know you have got a very strong case for raising rents at once. But however strong that case is, I am going to put it to you that in the national crisis we have got to have a complete wages and prices stop and Birmingham City Council must play its part. What you do in your tremendous city can influence the whole country, and if it were known that you had decided to freeze rents at the cost of nearly half a million pounds to the ratepayer you would be striking a blow for Britain. If you won't do this, don't blame me if you are held responsible for the voluntary prices and incomes policy collapsing.' The Alderman and his friends looked very uncomfortable and sparred with me, and finally I said, 'Why not have some lunch and come back at 2.30 and then we will decide what to tell the press?' Then I went across to the House of Commons for a quick lunch and at 2.30 the Alderman came back, furious (I am told) by the way he had been fixed by this socialist Minister of Housing but knowing that he couldn't risk defying the Government on this issue and losing his own Tory support by being made to seem unpatriotic. So that was that.

After that I had a long series of television interviews, one for the B.B.C., two for I.T.V., and a radio interview for the B.B.C., and also I had to deal with the press. I spent the rest of the day engaged, excited, invigorated by what I was doing and by the notion that I was getting on with things.

Sanctions had not yet caused the collapse of the illegal Rhodesian regime, although by June it had only sold 35–40 per cent of the 1965 tobacco crop. At this point, the official estimate of the cost of sanctions to Britain was about £10 million.

Informal talks between British and Rhodesian officials had been held in London from May 9th to 20th and in Salisbury from June 2nd to July 5th without result. In his Commons Statement on July 5th, Mr Wilson hinted at more determined action but he was still unwilling to resort to force. The Conservatives were also becoming impatient with the Government's policy, but their objection was that it was unrealistic to demand that the Smith regime abandon their illegal independence before constitutional negotiations could be held. In this stalemate, Mr Wilson announced on August 8th a further round of official talks.

Tuesday, August 2nd
At Cabinet there was a lot of business held over from the previous week, in

particular Rhodesia. Before we got to that, however, we had quite a long discussion of the Prices and Incomes Bill. George Brown was away that morning in the Standing Committee, where he is working virtually day and night to get the Bill pushed through with its new clauses. That didn't deter me from saying that part of our reason for Part IV being made dependent on an Affirmative Resolution was to emphasize that we regarded it as giving us merely reserve powers to strengthen the voluntary principle. At this point the Chancellor said that he didn't believe that at all; he wanted the compulsory powers put into effect before we broke up for the recess. He was supported in this by Douglas Houghton, speaking on behalf of the civil servants. He thought it would be intolerable if the Government compelled public employees to come into line while relying on mere persuasion in the private sector. That is why he wanted Part IV as soon as possible. Gradually the whole Cabinet joined in and I think most of them thought that for tactical reasons it would be sensible to postpone Part IV until after the T.U.C. Congress and after our Conference in September.

Then we turned to Rhodesia. For months and months we have been told by Harold that the Smith regime was collapsing and we are becoming more cynical about it. On this occasion Judith Hart, who is a very bright number two at the Commonwealth Office, put forward a paper in which she argued for large-scale assistance to Zambia to try to stiffen their resistance and enable them to cut off Rhodesian exports. She admitted it would cost £8 million extra in foreign currency. At this point Frank Longford wondered whether we should go on spending all this money as now there was no chance of overthrowing the Smith regime. This question was strongly backed up by Dick Marsh who said that he thought the whole sanctions affair was nonsense and he wasn't sure we wouldn't be driven to the use of force. And then he turned and rebuked the P.M. for the absence of any collective Cabinet action. So even on this Rhodesian issue Harold's authority is sadly undermined.

In the afternoon I had to make a speech to assembled builders at the R.I.B.A. All the press were there, hoping to have a wonderful story about Crossman mauled by the builders in a great verbal fracas. But over the weekend John Delafons had once again done a wonderful job of work on my speech. All I had to do was to link his draft to some ad lib polemics about what the builders' President was likely to say, and I was able to deliver it with a bang. The builders who came to curse went away praising us to some extent. At five o'clock I rushed back to the Ministry for another series of meetings and television and radio interviews and once again I felt exhilarated that I was really on the job, and in the public gaze again as an energetic Minister.

In the evening I had dinner with Richard Llewelyn-Davies, back from a holiday in Crete, and Jock Campbell of Booker Brothers,[1] who I badly and unnecessarily upset last week. He wanted to make a speech about housing

[1] Created Lord Campbell of Eskan in 1966. As chairman of the Statesman and Nation Publishing Company he was to play an important part in Crossman's later career.

and when he asked me to help I behaved to him, in his own words, 'like a headmaster caning a small boy'. So I thought I had better make my apologies over dinner while Richard was telling me about the New Town at Swindon. However, what we really talked about was the crisis and the sense of disintegration which all of us felt. I am very moody just now, elated at one point and depressed at another, and I used that dinner-party to relieve my own inner feelings, which must have been fairly depressing for them. No doubt other Ministers do the same to their friends; and as a result there is an awareness in Fleet Street that many members of the Cabinet detest Part IV and hate the whole idea of gaoling trade-union members as much as the left wing of the Parliamentary Party. But these doubts are only shared with a tiny number of people in Fleet Street and Whitehall. I am sure the rest of the public is pretty well in favour of what the Government is doing. They think the country is in a bad state and the big freeze is proof that the Government is facing up to the difficulties.

Wednesday, August 3rd

I had a splendid morning back with my old interest of national superannuation. I have now become a member of the Social Services Committee in which Peggy Herbison, the Minister, is trying to make our scheme relevant to the conditions of 1966. Apart from the chairman, Douglas Houghton, I was the only Cabinet Minister there. The rest were non-Cabinet Ministers, like Kenneth Robinson, or Parliamentary Secretaries. What a relief it was to discuss in a fairly technical and professional way how to superimpose national superannuation on the present chaos of private and public pensions. Here at last we were tackling something we really knew something about!

After that I was due to motor out to Gospel Oak, a curious little village in the middle of Camden next to the railway-line from Broad Street, where you see gigantic tower blocks going up all round you among little artisan houses built in 1820 or 1830, very poor in quality, no damp courses, no modern conveniences. Yet certain developers will pay £12,000 for these little houses in order to turn them into immensely profitable luxury accommodation.

I remarked the other day that the only definition of a slum which makes any sense is 'a building which nobody thinks worth improving'. In London at least if people spent enough thousands of pounds on any building, however bad, it can be improved and made profitable. This has started at Gospel Oak so that the houses almost alternate, this one a slum, the one next to it luxury accommodation. Peggy Duff, who was once the organizer of C.N.D. and is now the chairman of the Camden Planning Committee, gave me a splendid insight into the problem. Then I came back to lunch – on his suggestion – with Richard Marsh.

In Cabinet he and I are the two who have been most insisting on collective Cabinet responsibility. But we are also the two who are on the whole most pro-Harold and anti-George, at least in this most recent crisis. At lunch today his main point was that we must keep contact with the trade unions. Why for instance didn't I keep contact with Jack Jones and George Woodcock, the one a friend from Coventry, the other a friend from Oxford? Why didn't we all mend our fences and realize that we can't afford to be isolated from the trade unions? He's right, we ought to do this. But he didn't seem to have any other very clear ideas. One thing he did tell me over lunch was that there was no doubt that George Brown and Jim Callaghan were both opposed to the introduction of the Steel Bill, saying that at this point it was premature and awkward. Moreover, each of them had independently tried to negotiate with the Iron and Steel Confederation, each cancelling the other's negotiations out. I must say I don't quite believe this, but the picture of George trying to do this has its own humour.

After lunch I sat on the front bench especially in order to hear George Brown make his comeback. I hadn't taken his disaster on the previous Wednesday too seriously and sure enough, after Heath had made another quite obvious attack on the Government, George made a well-delivered, competent reply that fully restored him in popular estimation. I had just been talking to Dick Marsh about George but this afternoon I had to admit that though his relations with Harold are appalling there is still something immensely valuable about him. One must never underestimate Brother George, particularly not his ability to get a grip on the real situation when he is in good form.

I had agreed to dine with Barbara Castle, who was full of the idea that she and I must stick together, along with Peter Shore and Tony Benn, and that in particular I must promise never to resign without consulting her and vice versa. This of course I agreed. And then we came to a most interesting discussion about our two Departments. She told me that immediately she had moved into Transport she made a point of getting hold of all the relevant trade unionists and talking to them, and she found she was the first Minister to do so. Dear me, this is something I have never done in the Ministry of Housing. I never asked NALGO[1] to come near me. How right Barbara is. How important it is that in this respect I should follow her example.

As for Part IV of the Bill, she doesn't share my feelings about it and she obviously thinks it is going to work. That's the difference between us. For Barbara, if it works it's O.K. Also, she is obviously deeply influenced by Harold's story about how she was taken for a ride by the pro-Europeans. She is shaken by this and will take far greater care in future. She said Harold hadn't forgiven her for siding with me about the floating pound. He had never trusted me quite as much as he trusted her but now she was out of favour. I said that it would come all right and she mustn't worry too much. But she obviously does worry.

After dinner we went in for the end of the big debate on the Prices and

[1] The main white-collar trade union dealing with local authority staff.

Incomes Bill, and heard Herbert Bowden orating away.[1] Then we saw some twenty-seven of our back-benchers abstaining and Manny Shinwell, who was standing close to us behind the Speaker's chair, said, 'That won't be the last time they'll do that. We must impose discipline.' I then went through the Chamber to the inner lobby where I don't often go these days. John Silkin was surrounded by journalists trying to make him commit himself about what he would do. In another corner George Wigg was shouting about discipline and I have no doubt there will be a crisis early next week. I don't think it will break the Party up because the twenty-seven are now regarded as unrepentant and in that sense the separate left wing has now become an accomplished fact.

Thursday, August 4th

Lying in bed, I began to wonder how I could get Harold really firmly committed to the strategic economic committee. Then the news came on and I heard how he dined sixteen bankers in Downing Street the previous night and assured them not only that devaluation was out of the question but that the floating pound was just as bad as devaluation. It struck me that these assurances to the bankers must be tested. Were they a front to conceal from the outside world the quite different assurances he had given us in Cabinet, namely that if unemployment were to rise above 2 per cent then devaluation must become a serious possibility? I walked across the park to No. 10 determined to find a device to smoke him out about this.

But in the Cabinet room the first thing we got was a long discussion, under Parliamentary business, of the rebel votes the night before. It was John Silkin's first test as Chief Whip and I thought he behaved extremely well. He said that there was strong pressure from the constituency rank and file as well as from the Party to have these people punished and the Whip withdrawn. But if he drummed twenty-seven people out of the Parliamentary Party he was merely creating a new party on the Left which would have its own parliamentary rights, its own representation on all committees, its own share of spokesmen on the floor, which is exactly what they wanted. He said that in his view some carpeting and disciplining might be needed, but before the recess he didn't want to go further than rebukes. He wanted to play out this Session, get Parliament sent on holiday and then deal with the rebels after the Party Conference when we came back in October.

One or two people piped up to say that this might be John's view but there was a very strong contrary view expressed by George Brown, Manny Shinwell and the liaison committee, who wanted immediate action against the rebels. I then came in and said, 'Why give them their martyrs' haloes so that they can go to Conference and get volleys of cheers which everyone will see on the

---

[1] Mr Heath had moved a motion demanding that the Committee Stage of the Bill be continued in a Standing Committee of the Whole House. The Government carried the division by 277 to 225.

television? That would be disastrous. We must concentrate everything on winning at Congress and at the Conference. When we've got an endorsement for our policy, then we can consider what to do with the rebels.' And I added, 'Do remember they have some right on their side when they point out that the line they are now taking is the line Harold Wilson and George Brown were preaching last March before the election. Part IV is unprecedented and has no kind of support in the Party manifesto or in any previous statement of Party policy. Play it cool', I concluded, 'until we have got our mandate from Conference.'

I found myself speaking absolutely in tune with John Silkin and we got our way. But my mind was really on the P.M. and the bankers, and after a little bit of overseas business I chipped in to ask if Harold had anything to tell us about that dinner other than what we had heard on the wireless in the morning. There were smiles round the Cabinet table but Harold took it quite calmly and gave us an interesting chat about what the bankers were doing and saying. Then the Chancellor chimed in and said it was all very encouraging but what terrified him was all the talk about devaluation, and he urged Cabinet on no account to let the talk spread; we must stop all kind of leaks. This gave me a chance for a second intervention and I said that of course there must be no talk of devaluation but I hoped the P.M. hadn't forgotten that some of us only supported his present policy on the clear understanding (i) that devaluation was still on the *tapis* if unemployment rose above 2 per cent, and (ii) that we should prepare contingency plans for preventing another crisis and for overcoming our difficulties. On both these points we had had explicit assurances and I should like to know if he had anything else to tell us. Harold immediately renewed his assurances. There would be a strategic committee on a par with the Defence Committee to consider economic strategy and he must be given time to set it up. Then came a long discussion on what the committee should do. There was a great deal of talk about such subjects as international liquidity and Harold dazzled us all with his economic theory and then assured us that papers were being prepared on all the various alternative methods of devaluation and they would be ready for discussion by the new committee in September.

That part of the discussion lasted forty-five minutes and at one point Harold again mentioned the danger of leaks. At this Tony Crosland barged in and said, 'Of course we don't mind that kind of thing being said by the Prime Minister, but we all know that most of the information goes to the press either from No. 10 or from the environs of the D.E.A.' There was an awkward silence and I think this has cost Tony dear in his relations with Harold. Still, he had the courage to say it. This is the fourth Cabinet running in which he has played an active part, talking not just as a departmental Minister but as somebody who understands economics and who rates himself equal with the P.M., George Brown and James Callaghan, somebody who has forced his way into their stratosphere.

In the evening I dined with the Chief Whip at the Ecu de France before catching the midnight train to Cornwall for a weekend with my family, who have gone on to Polzeath. In the course of that dinner he made one remark I couldn't help noticing. He told me I mustn't run away back to Cornwall on the following Thursday without a word with him. I caught the train feeling he knew something about my future. Is there a Cabinet reshuffle in the offing?

Friday, August 5th

I reached Devonport at 7.15 this morning to be met by Kim Foster, chairman of the Cornwall County Council, in his big Rolls Royce. He whirled me to his lovely house across the Tamar Bridge where I had a bath and then breakfasted with his plump, nice Gertrude. They are a very pleasant couple indeed. Gertrude drove us on down into Truro where I had an excellent meeting with the council on the twin subjects of how to control the coastline and how to deal with the pollution caused by the china clay industry.

While I was still in the middle of the meeting messages began to come streaming in from my Private Office saying I must at all costs ring London before my news conference. When I got on to John Delafons he told me there was an unholy confusion about mortgages. George Brown had been demanding that mortgages should be frozen compulsorily and I had told him this was impossible. Next he had asked me to apply to mortgages the treatment I had applied to council rents. Couldn't I browbeat the building societies voluntarily to freeze the mortgage rates? Callaghan and I had written a longish minute explaining that this really was impossible since they had decided to put the mortgage rate up as long ago as last March and all the notices had already gone out to the societies giving October 1st as the date of the rise. George Brown, however, was apparently still not content with this and was asking me to prevent them putting the rates up until we received the Prices and Incomes Board report on the building societies. Confusion in the press was arising because of what George was saying in conducting the Committee Stage of the Prices and Incomes Bill. I was a bit worried when I went in to see the journalists at my press conference. But they wanted to discuss china clay and Cornish planning and couldn't have cared less about mortgages and I began to think it rather an unimportant subject when Kim motored me across to Polzeath and I found Dick David's house, where we were staying, looking pleasant in a brilliant, sunshiny afternoon.

In the evening Patrick and I had a splendid walk round Pentire Head.

Saturday, August 6th

Today, however, the mortgage affair began to boom. It boomed all through the day and I began to hear on the wireless how the Government was paralysed by indecision. In the afternoon Peter Brown rang to fill me in on the row between George and Callaghan and how Harold couldn't fix it. So I rang Harold at No. 10 and asked him why we couldn't just announce that the three of us would get together on Monday and decide the mortgage policy, to which Harold replied that he wasn't sure that he could get the other two together to reach any agreement on Monday.

Monday, August 8th

The Sunday papers were full of the story and I had a number of telephone talks with Peter Brown before I caught the night train from Bodmin Road. I got to Paddington at 7.15 this morning to find that the hot water had been turned off and I couldn't have a bath at Vincent Square.

I had hoped to have a quick meeting under Harold's leadership in order to fix this idiotic problem of mortgages. It seemed obvious that I should meet George Brown to the extent of asking the building societies not to raise their mortgage rates until the P.I.B. had reported and then making sure the P.I.B. gave us their report by early October. This is exactly what we did in fact finally agree on, but first I had to square my Permanent Secretary, who thought I was giving far too much to George and that I should stand firm on the original statement Callaghan and I had made. I found this terribly negative and when we got into our meeting finally, shortly after twelve, we settled it along the lines I have described.

In the afternoon I saw the building societies and got their agreement that I should make a Statement in the House to that effect next day. After that I had to see George Brown about the Centre for Environmental Studies. I had promised Richard Llewelyn-Davies the headquarters would be in London. George Brown was insisting on Edinburgh. After we had disagreed in quite a friendly way, he asked me to stay behind in his room and told me that he would be out of the D.E.A. within a few days and he was glad because he had been doing that job far too long. Then he went on to say how much he appreciated my behaviour on the day before the devaluation Cabinet. I had been honest with him, unlike some other people he could mention. 'Whatever happens,' he said, 'don't do anything without telling me. I gather you want to make it as difficult as possible to introduce Part IV. I don't agree with you but I am not so far away from your position. Keep in touch with me. I trust you, you trust me, I support Harold and so do you.' That was George at about four o'clock.

On August 10th the Prime Minister rearranged the Cabinet. George Brown left the D.E.A. to become Foreign Secretary, as he had long desired. Michael Stewart, whom he replaced, went to the D.E.A. Arthur Bottomley moved to the Ministry of Overseas Development, and his place at the Commonwealth Relations Office was taken by Herbert Bowden. Anthony Greenwood, Minister of Overseas Development, became Minister of Housing. And Richard Crossman found himself Lord President of the Council and Leader of the House.

Wednesday, August 10th

Throughout Tuesday little indications were becoming stronger and stronger that a Cabinet reshuffle was in the offing. I got a tremendous final hint at 3.30. It was Prime Minister's Question Time and Harold had been doing some not very effective sparring about Gibraltar. Then he made a brilliant come-back on Suez, roundly announcing there was a *prima facie* case against Selwyn Lloyd on the charge of collusion;[1] and he started preparing the way for a Select Committee of Inquiry. After this I answered a Private Notice Question on mortgages and cleared the whole confusion up in a perfectly competent way. When I sat down, Harold turned to me and asked me whether I was still going to stand for the Executive. I said that I was and then I thanked him for putting off the Cabinet on Wednesday (today), because it meant I could get away to Cornwall early on Thursday morning. 'Oh, don't get off early that morning,' he replied. 'I shall need you here. But don't tell anybody because it might give the wrong impression.' Then he added, 'You could go by the Thursday night train. We'll have finished everything by then.' Out of the Chamber I mentioned this to John Silkin and said, 'This seems to link up with what you were saying to me last Thursday night.' 'I can't tell you,' he replied. 'I'm sworn to secrecy; but it's something that gives me enormous pleasure because it means you and I will be working together.' It was then that I began to ask myself whether Harold could possibly be planning to make me Lord President and Leader of the House, the only job which would involve working closely with John Silkin. With that thought in mind, I went back to the Department and sent for my Permanent Secretary. Not unexpectedly, when I told him what I thought he seemed to be rather pleased, because it is what he has been telling me. He added that I had probably done my best work in the Ministry and he had had enough yeast in the Department to last him a long time; now he wants as my successor somebody to consolidate the work which I had set in train and which would last them for five or six years.

That afternoon and evening the Report Stage of the Prices and Incomes Bill was taking place on the Floor of the House with divisions all the time. I had dinner with Callaghan in the Members' dining-room and from that meal I mainly remember the impression of the strength of his feeling against Harold as somebody he couldn't personally trust. His main object was obviously to win me over as a supporter. I doubt if he got much change from me. What the talk emphasized for me was how he combines smallness with ambition. He certainly feels himself the heir apparent – or is it the young pretender?

---

[1] Discussion of possible British endorsement of American policy in Vietnam had revived interest in the Conservative Cabinet's role in the 1956 Suez venture. Some M.P.s had been pressing for an inquiry into the Anglo–French–Israeli Treaty of October 1956, when Selwyn Lloyd had been Foreign Secretary. It was alleged that the then Prime Minister, Anthony Eden, and the Foreign Secretary had engaged in collusive action with the French without informing or consulting the Cabinet. Harold Wilson was replying to a question on the Treaty.

I spent all that night up till five in the morning in the House of Commons acting as good lobby fodder and heard George Brown make a magnificent speech. Harold told me later that it was good mainly because he then knew that he was going to be Foreign Secretary.[1]

Wednesday, August 10th
By the time Cabinet met at 11.45 I knew that the appointments would be announced that night, that we had to be at Buckingham Palace on Thursday morning to be sworn in, and that we were also to have our first meeting of the new Economic Strategy Committee. Meanwhile, I started the morning at the Social Services Committee, working on the new pensions scheme, and thinking about my future. The Cabinet went in a perfectly normal way. The Chancellor made it clear that, despite the cuts already announced, he wanted the PESC exercise to be carried through, cutting back all departmental estimates from $11\frac{1}{2}$ to $4\frac{1}{2}$ per cent. I said we couldn't consider that request unless we knew what the total deflation packet was. How much will consumption be cut by last week's package? How much will S.E.T. cut consumption when it comes into force in October? Harold replied by at last giving his priorities for expenditure. Number one, expenditure designed to increase industrial productivity, number two, our three public works programmes – housing, education and hospitals; number three, social security and social services; number four, individual consumption. What we can't commit ourselves to are expanded programmes of pensions, which blow up consumption. If we'd thought of it, added Harold, we would never have abolished prescription charges, but in those days we were young and inexperienced. Instead, we would have cut back school meals, which cost us £120 million.

At 1 p.m. Harold said goodbye to the Cabinet for the summer recess and then I went back and had lunch with Silkin in the Members' dining-room. I was working quietly in my office with Steve when I heard the P.M. wanted to see me at 4.15. I had time to go to the liaison committee, where I couldn't say a damn thing because they weren't supposed to know that I was to be Lord President, and then I talked to Jennie and Marcia and said I was very depressed, disappointed and scared by the new job. I was all the more scared because I had just heard that I would have to make the speech for the Government in the debate on the adjournment for the summer recess.

I hate the idea of giving up the Department where I have just got firm control and where I adore all the various activities, which stretch from planning, through housing, through New Towns, and which enabled me to go all over the country and visit places I want to visit and master techniques which I haven't previously understood. I have got to leave the Department and that knowledge will be wasted. I have got to have a job without any Department

[1] See *Wilson*, pp. 272–3, for his reasons for the changes.

at all and be just a member of the Government and a politician. It is deeply depressing.

I saw Harold punctually at 4.15 and he at once made the offer I expected. I admitted to him that I wasn't surprised by it and at once said it was a tremendous loss to me, mainly because it was a loss of power. How often had he told me that a Department is a tremendous source of strength to a Cabinet Minister? He replied, 'Yes, but look. This is a job where I really need you.' I replied, 'Because it means working with you, Harold, I shan't really mind it.' In fact I gave way straight away and didn't resist all the time I was talking to him until I asked him who was my successor. When he told me it was Tony Greenwood I was really shocked and said I would have much preferred Bert Bowden. But he replied that Bert had to be selected as Commonwealth Secretary and when he had told the Queen she had said how delighted she was that that kind of non-political man was in the job. He took tremendous trouble to emphasize the importance of my new job. I was to be a completely different kind of Lord President. The substitution of John Silkin for Ted Short had been the first part of a major change which replaces two bureaucrats with two politicians. We should be in the key positions of Party power and we should form the link with Transport House. That is why, he explained, he had asked me on the front bench whether I was still going to stand for the Executive; he wants to feel that as Lord President I could do the job of linking Transport House and No. 10. He was very much aware of the criticism that Attlee's Government lost contact with the Party and he wants me to do the job of organizing and making sure that the rank and file feel themselves linked with the leadership. In addition, I would lead the House and work as hard as possible for parliamentary reform. And in the House I would be a political Lord President, the C.O. of the Parliamentary army, with John Silkin as my Chief of Staff, leading the Party, taking part in all the major debates, winding-up—indeed, behaving in this 1966 Parliament much as Herbert Morrison behaved when he was Leader of the House between 1945 and 1950.

As for Cabinet, I should be on every Cabinet Committee, including the new Economic Strategy Committee and the Rhodesia Committee and, if I wished, the Defence Committee as well. All this was said, I think, to make me realize that I would be elevated to a completely new level, the top level. And he said that we should be running things a bit differently now, more like an inner Cabinet of which I should be a member.

He asked me to come back at 6, when the time for the announcement would be fixed. This I did and he then told me there would be some delay in the timing of the news release because of George Brown. He added that George was very angry because he, Harold, had forgotten to tell him about my appointment as Lord President and Greenwood's taking my place. I wasn't very clear whether it was my appointment or the fact that he hadn't been consulted which had enraged George. He also made it clear that in all the discussions one of his major preoccupations had been to fox Mr Callaghan. The only person who was not going to get any change, he remarked, is the person who has gone to William Davis of the *Guardian* and got him to write about his wish to be given the Foreign Office.

I couldn't help remembering the time when I had suggested to Harold that Callaghan was the right man to be Leader of the House and he had told me that he couldn't trust him there because he would be a threat to his own future. It looks as though he has selected me for this key job as the only person who *hasn't* got political ambitions against him. I then asked him about the other changes and he told me George Brown was delighted to be at the Foreign Office and Michael Stewart also seemed pleased, though he was sorry to lose it. But mainly it was Harold himself who was enormously exhilarated and openly claiming that he had now got his friends about him. By this time George Wigg, Marcia and John Silkin were there and I was part of the menage. And Harold said, 'What I have done this time is to surround myself with friends and isolate Callaghan. When people see the result of what I have done they will realize he has been defeated. Only he doesn't realize it yet.'

At this moment Callaghan came in for a further talk, and we retired. I dined quietly in the Members' dining-room and then went upstairs to do my last boxes for the Department. I sat quietly up there until Jennie came in and brought with her Sir Godfrey Agnew from the Privy Council Office.[1] He had rung me up at 5 and I had snubbed him, saying that nothing had been announced. However, along he came at 9 p.m. By this time I was utterly depressed about my loss of a Department and told him I was the last person who one could expect to be given this job with all the mumbo-jumbo of the Privy Council and seeing the Queen, and I made it clear that I wanted never to attend anything which required a white tie, etc., etc. I may have overdone things a little but I found him a jackass. He then rehearsed me for my interview at the Palace at 2.15 the next day.

Not long afterwards the division bell sounded and I knew the announcement had been made and went down into the lobby where I was due to meet Barbara Castle. I was just going to speak to her when Harold Wilson breezed up and said, 'Meet your new Lord President.' She was absolutely flabbergasted and couldn't believe it for three or four minutes. There she stood chatting with Harold while I stood beside them and found my colleagues pretty well disconcerted. They were astonished that Harold had upped me into the stratosphere, but I think they also allowed themselves to wonder whether I hadn't run away from the Ministry of Housing because I felt the problems were getting beyond me. Anyway, there weren't many congratulations from them that evening. Indeed the only person I talked to who really

---

[1] Sir Godfrey Agnew had entered the Privy Council Office as Senior Clerk in 1946 and since 1953 had been Clerk to the Privy Council. Since 1972 he has also been a Deputy-Secretary at the Cabinet Office.

enjoyed my promotion was Tam. He was supposed to be on holiday and had flown back from a boat in order to find out what was happening to me! And I think he wasn't saying anything untrue when he told me that a large number of back-benchers were fairly pleased by this particular appointment.

Thursday, August 11th

A look at the morning papers gave me a sense of my real importance. First reactions were entirely in terms of George Brown becoming Foreign Secretary. Only Ian Trethowan of the B.B.C. said mine was a fascinating, mysterious appointment. What this really showed was how dim the office had become under Herbert Bowden. After all, when Butler and Herbert Morrison were Lord President and Leader of the House it was a really big political appointment. Under Herbert Bowden it had dwindled into a bureaucratic job.

I had agreed when Harold spoke to me that I would take over from Herbert the job of replying to the debate on the adjournment for the summer recess, which was due to start at 3.30 and go on till people exhausted themselves at seven or so. At this point I would have to reply. Harold wondered whether I could fit it in but I said I must duck myself in the water as soon as I possibly could. So in the course of the morning I was served up with a kind of a brief on whatever possible things I might have to reply to. I had a few moments to look at it before I went into the Department where I had meant to spend the morning. I had to be out and at the Palace by 2.15 and I knew that by then Tony Greenwood would want to be taking over. I saw a few people, then I agreed with Delafons that I should give drinks at 1 p.m. and that he would gather the clans. Off I then went to the first meeting of my famous Cabinet Committee on Economic Strategy. Oh dear, it is a panjandrum committee – the Prime Minister, First Secretary, Foreign Secretary, the Minister of Defence, the Minister of Labour for some reason, myself. Of course, none of the people who really wanted to be on it – Tony Crosland, Roy Jenkins, Barbara. It's just the top people, sitting around without briefing and without officials. Without a Department I shall certainly need an economist to help brief me as well as a Chief of Staff.

I'm afraid my little party was a formality. I made the Secretary make a speech, and I made a little speech in which I said I had never been happier in all my life but I knew a lot of people would be relieved when I had gone. And indeed the Secretary said so too. However, I finally said that John Delafons had given us the finest Private Office in Whitehall, which was a nice farewell before I left for the Palace at 2.15.

I really hadn't the courage to tell Molly that I find her driving impossibly slow so I took her and my old Super-Snipe with me to the Palace. I got there to find George Brown waiting, not exactly in an enthusiastic mood and I didn't improve it when I said to him that I had heard from Harold that he wasn't pleased at my appointment. What he disliked was that I who was once, as Minister of Housing, bottom of the pecking order must now go in first to see the Queen and then introduce the others to receive their Seals of Office. Even more ironically, I couldn't help remembering as I went in alone how a fortnight ago I had told Lord Porchester over dinner how I detested the mumbo-jumbo of the monarchy and he had said that the Queen was his best friend. So I wasn't in the least surprised when the Queen began the conversation by saying, 'Ah, Lord Porchester was telling me about you.' And I said, 'Well, I never expected this.' It was very clever of her to mention it straight away and let it be known that Lord Porchester had passed on my remarks – and I found it was perfectly simple and straightforward to get on with her. Indeed, she puts one at ease immediately and we were able to chat about other things fairly happily. And then in the actual reception George Brown took over and was as familiar and cosy with her – 'my dear' and such nonsense – as anyone could possibly be.

I went back to the Ministry after that and lunched for the last time in the little room with Arthur, the janitor in charge, while Tony Greenwood was being photographed at my desk with his new publicity officer, Jack Cooper. Cooper's presence was fortunate for me since it enabled me to persuade Peter Brown to come with me to the Lord President's Office. I mightn't have got Peter if Tony hadn't arrived with Jack Cooper as his press man.*

After lunch I just had time to take a glance at the Lord President's office, the really palatial room with its beautiful decorations and furniture and wonderful view of the Horseguards Parade, and to get the indelible impression that these are not working offices but the formal offices of a Minister whose job is a formality.

I was on the front bench at 3.30, sitting next to Harold who chatted with me to put me at my ease. The debate started with a very witty, funny and amusing speech by Mr Heath which included an attack on me. Then came the usual back-bench speeches. I had asked Michael Foot to speak and also a number of back-benchers interested in parliamentary reform, and they all did their stint. When 7 p.m. came near there were still six or seven people on each side getting up but I knew the House wanted to adjourn and I got to the dispatch box, steadied myself and made the right kind of speech, informal, skating over the subjects, and was thought to have made a pretty good start when I sat down at the right time and the vote was over.[1]

I had a quiet dinner with John Silkin and Bert Bowden, who was very sad at leaving but delighted that at last he has got a Department. At 10 I went back to Vincent Square where I had lent my house to Geoffrey Rhodes (he is now my P.P.S., not Tam, though it is surprising to think so). I packed my clothes for the night sleeper to Cornwall and that was the end of Thursday, the day of my shift-round.

---

* But I hadn't really got him.
[1] It was carried by 141 votes to 90.

Wednesday, August 24th

The last day of my Cornish holiday before going up to London to become Lord President. The weather has been splendid. The first day I spent looking at the china clay industry with Dalton, the head of it, who met me at the station and took me over. I wrote a pretty thorough letter to Tony Greenwood, which will be found in the file, describing what I would have done about Cornish planning decisions. It made me sad writing it because this is the kind of job I like. I have worked terribly hard these twenty-two months. I have got to know all the leading personalities in the local authorities, in the building societies and in the building industry. I have got interested in their plans and visited them all. Now all this knowledge, these personal acquaintances, this lovely departmental detail, goes by the board. I am cut off, wrenched out of it, and in that sense all the effort was wasted. I suppose that is the thing which disconcerted me most when I tried to explain it to Harold when he offered me the job. 'Come, come,' he said, 'you would have to leave it anyway, why fuss about it?' He just couldn't understand that I adored being a departmental Minister and found it an ideal life. And maybe I found that particular Department ideal. Because Housing isn't a specialist Department; it's full of variety and practical decisions which stretch over the whole life of England. Wherever you go in England there is something to do with housing or local government or planning, and therefore wherever I went I could be interested. All this holiday in Cornwall I have been aware that Cornish planning and Cornish housing and Cornish local government boundaries were once my province and are now no longer.

The more I have reflected during this holiday on my promotion the more depressed I have become. In fact there has only been one cheerful feature and that was the press reaction on the Sunday after my appointment. Directly the adjournment debate was over I went straight to a press conference I had arranged with the Chief Whip. It was with the Sunday press and it was the first time that a Lord President had talked to them for a year or two. People like Jimmy Margach were quite excited. I told them what I thought my job was going to be and I got really excited in telling it. As a result the press response on Sunday was very big indeed. They got the idea that my job was to make the leadership of the House political again in the sense that it had been under Herbert Morrison and Butler. Of course there were sardonic comments as well. There were the *Express* and the *Sketch* saying that I had run away from Housing because I was a failure. But this doesn't really make sense since I have been not merely transferred to a parallel Department, say Education, but catapulted into the stratosphere. If I am deprived of the strength which a Department provides for an ambitious politician at least I am now in a position of great political power.

So that Sunday's press did give me pleasure. And then on the following Tuesday I had down from the Lord President's Private Office a girl to do my dictation and write my thank-you letters to people in the Ministry of Housing.

A Miss Janet Gates turned up, extraordinarily beautiful but also to my great surprise a competent stenographer.* I dictated to her the letters to people in the Ministry that John Delafons had suggested I should write to.

We had a marvellous time for the rest of our stay in Polzeath. We left on Saturday and spent a long weekend at Dulverton on Exmoor in a splendid hotel run by Wilfred Cave's daughter. There I spent a whole day with the Forestry Commission studying their problems and in particular the conflict between the economic needs of forestry as an extractive industry and its amenity needs in terms of planning.

Before I forget all about it I want to add some reflections on the real motivation of the Cabinet reshuffle of which I am a victim, and then survey my twenty-two months at the Ministry and what I achieved and what lessons I drew.

First the reshuffle. I am pretty sure that until the end of July there was no intention to have one. Indeed, I am inclined to think, as a result of what Harold said to me on August 11th, that what put the idea into his head was mainly George Brown's behaviour.[1] This had made it impossible for George to stay at the D.E.A. And he had also indicated at times that once he had served Harold loyally at D.E.A., he would like a turn at the Foreign Office. Theoretically there were two possibilities for George, the Treasury and the Foreign Office. But there were two reasons why the Treasury was out. In the first place, George had revealed himself as in favour of devaluation and opposed to any kind of deflation. This move was therefore unacceptable to Harold. In the second place, moving Callaghan would have upset the pound. He had to be kept there for the time being. On the other hand, Harold's fury with James Callaghan was also a major motivation. The cause of that fury was the interview he gave to William Davis in which his wish to become Foreign Secretary was revealed. This really alarmed Harold and made him think that James Callaghan was getting dangerous thoughts and regarding himself as the heir apparent. So he had to be taught a lesson; and since he couldn't be moved, the best way of doing that was not only to make George Brown Foreign Secretary but to complete the sense of drastic change by moving Herbert Bowden from Lord President of the Council and Leader of the House and making me take his place.

But why did he choose me? Partly no doubt because of my own behaviour during the July crisis, when for the first time I took the lead as a departmental Minister in challenging his authority. Inside the stratosphere I would be less dangerous than if I remained a powerful departmental Minister outside. But also this change was the completion of a plan which he had had in store ever since March. I discussed with him countless times the need for changing Bowden and Short, and I had put forward Callaghan and Brown as two possibilities for the new Lord President. He had dismissed the idea of

* Now Janet Newman. She went with me first to D.H.S.S. and then to the *New Statesman* before leaving to have a baby.
[1] See *Wilson*, p. 272.

Callaghan always by saying that it was too dangerous a position for such an ambitious man. After the election he had used the resignation of Frank Cousins to put John Silkin in Short's place. Now he used the second crisis to replace Bowden with a new kind of Leader of the House. His eye fell on me partly because Marcia and George Wigg would strongly support the idea, partly because of his view that Dick Crossman is always good at starting things off.[1] I had twenty-two months at Housing, and I had pushed all the policy changes through. Now was the time to associate me with the new move for parliamentary reform.

Now for my impressions of the Ministry and of the Civil Service. The main conviction I had when I got there was that the Civil Service would be profoundly resistant to outside pressure. Was that true? I think it was. I found throughout an intense dislike of bringing people in, whether they are politicians or experts. There is, for example, a determination to freeze out your Parliamentary Secretary and even more your P.P.S. Unless you lay down that your Parliamentary Secretary will receive a certain paper he will automatically not receive it. You have to remember each time to say 'Has Bob Mellish had it?', 'Has Bob Mellish been asked to the meeting?'. So too with bringing in outside experts. I broke into the Department very early on when I showed Arnold Goodman the draft of the little anti-eviction Bill and on his advice insisted that something had to be done. The Dame threatened to resign when she had heard what had been done but Arnold was right and from then on he was accepted along with such members of the Milner Holland Committee as Pilcher and Donnison, with whom I was able to work out the fair-rent clause. With regard to housing, I had luck with Peter Lederer, a personal friend of mine who was also the brightest man in the firm of Richard Costain, and himself a friend of the Dame. But to get two or three people into a Ministry isn't a major breakthrough by any means and as long as the Dame was there I had tremendous difficulties even in building up an economic intelligence inside the Department. When I got there the number of established statisticians on the payroll was three, and Penrise was the only one actually there. The Dame had hired him three months before. Apart from that, there was no kind of intelligence or method of adequately assessing month by month the number of houses being built. When I tried to get change I met nothing but resistance. Since Steve has arrived there has been a marked improvement in all this.

Nevertheless, I should say that in general I have found profound resistance in the Civil Service to a Minister who brings in outside advisers and experts, and profound resistance to interference by anybody with direct access to the Minister. What they like is sole Ministerial responsibility because they are convinced that under this system the amount of outside influence exerted is minimal.

[1] See *Wilson*, p. 273: 'I wanted to see a little play given to the inventiveness and iconoclasm of Dick Crossman.'

Question two. How efficient did I find the Civil Service? The answer, I am afraid, is that in the Ministry of Housing they were far less efficient and reliable and far more unpredictable than I expected. This is largely due to under-staffing, most of all in the planning division. Here I found when I arrived that eight or nine months was accepted as a reasonable time for a planning appeal to wait in the Ministry before a decision. There was an extraordinary sense of timelessness in that division. There was also a great sense of timelessness in my Private Office when I first got there with regard to correspondence. After months I got the letters written personally to me treated reasonably efficiently. As for planning appeals, I had arranged by the end of my time that the head of the division must be responsible for selecting for special treatment those which are likely to come to the Minister and for giving them priority. In return I had to agree not to interfere with the progress of the run-of-the-mill appeals through the factory.

But the trouble is not only shortage of staff but also their constant change. It is difficult for me to assess how much this is the fault of Harold Wilson, through his tremendous shake-up of Ministries in Whitehall. But there is no doubt about it that while I was at Housing everybody was changing round all the time and as a result no one official knew very much. During my time at the Ministry I lost my Permanent Secretary and both her Deputies and at the lower level there was a constant shifting around so that nobody seemed to be doing the same job for more than six months on end. By the end, in fact, I often knew more than the official in charge in a division.

Another factor was sheer incompetence. Ministers have got to get used to the idea that they themselves have to be on the look-out for gross mistakes, particularly relating to publicity. We worked out an excellent plan for Ullswater and then, when the official drafted the Order, he did it so as to underplay the changes we were introducing. If I had let that go out, the whole process would have failed and the amenity societies would have been against us. I found a whole series of examples where I caught officials out in incompetence and inaccuracy. Steve always told me that this was my fault: I put too much pressure on the Ministry and that was the reason it was working badly. To some extent the Dame tried to give the same excuse. I swallowed it at the time but now I am not so sure. I suspect there is a great deal of second-rate material among the administrators today. The ordinary Assistant Secretary without his files is completely impotent because he doesn't know very much about his job.

And then there is the influence of the Treasury. One cannot overestimate this. All the civil servants I worked with were imbued with a prior loyalty to the Treasury and felt it necessary to spy on me and report all my doings to the Treasury, whether I wanted them kept private or not. There was nothing I could do, no order I could give, which wasn't at once known to the Treasury, because my staff were all trained to check with the Treasury and let it know in advance exactly what each of them was doing. When this Treasury system is reinforced by PESC, you get a staggering centralized control which is being in no way counteracted by the existence of the D.E.A.

No doubt this is explained in the case of ambitious young men and women by the fact that the Treasury is the prime source of promotion. Without Treasury support they can't get on. But there are other senior people, like my Accountant-General, who just feel the Treasury is their natural boss; and whereas the Treasury and the head of the Civil Service are permanent, the Minister changes once every three years on average. Why should they worry about giving any particular loyalty to me?

Loyalty to the Treasury is greatly reinforced by the system of official committees, which neither Tommy Balogh nor I knew anything about before we got into Whitehall. Yet it is the key to the control by the Civil Service over the politicians. The Minister is not merely subject to control by his own Department seeking to make him work according to their departmental policies, there is also a wider network of Whitehall control exerted through these official committees. In the Cabinet Committees the Ministers may sit down together, each with his departmental brief, and discuss policy. But then they leave it to the official committee both to prepare the briefs and to carry out the policies when they have laid them down.

Now for personalities and, in particular, my Permanent Secretary. I came into a very unusual situation. When I got to the Ministry I was the sixth Minister Dame Evelyn had served under as Permanent Secretary. Her life in one Ministry was far longer than that of any other Permanent Secretary. She was sixty-one, on the edge of retirement, and quite unique in Whitehall, not merely because she was a woman but because of her long-sustained connection with a single subject, town and country planning and local government, through a whole series of Ministry reconstructions. So life with her was not typical. She had quite unusual good qualities, and quite unusual bad qualities as well. Her good ones were first and foremost her immense hard work and her patriotism and loyalty to the state. She really felt that it was the duty of the civil servant to be a public servant, serving the community. So she was convinced that any civil servant must put the interests of the country before those of his or her own Department. She was always allowing her staff to be raided because she recognized that national requirements should be given priority over, say, town planning considerations. In addition to having this tremendous sense of loyalty, she had drive and was a hard, slogging worker and a superb drafter of minutes. Indeed, this was probably her most superlative skill. She could draft me a minute to the Prime Minister or to anybody else which said what needed to be said in the straightest possible way, and she was pretty good at knowing the kind of way in which I would say it. Also, as the result of her ten years she had an incredible knowledge of local government personalities – their strengths and their weaknesses – as well as of the whole planning machinery of Whitehall. Moreover, as she had had her term in the Treasury she had the proper background for carrying weight in the councils of Whitehall and in particular in the weekly meetings of Permanent Secretaries, which play such an important role.

Her weakness was her waywardness and her recklessness. I had been warned by Harold that it was the Minister who had to caution the Permanent Secretary against irresponsibility and not vice versa and this I very soon found out was a wise warning with the Dame. She could also be terribly indiscreet. She is a great gossiper with her fellow civil servants and terribly unfair in her personal prejudices about people. The Department was run as her personal domain and that is why it was badly run and badly organized. It was under-staffed at the top, not just because of her high-mindedness but because she couldn't tolerate really able people around her and had to have Deputies who would serve her purposes. In addition, she had this streak of recklessness and sometimes sheer carelessness. There was the moment when she got me into a vote of censure by the gross contempt with which she treated the Council on Tribunals without consulting me. I found her equally reckless in her handling of the mortgage scheme. We had spent months working out the details of an extremely ingenious scheme with the Treasury and had discussed it with the building societies. Then on almost the last day of her term of office she and Brain had the bright idea between them of substituting a process of calculating an annuity method of tax relief for borrowers over a period of time for a straight interest-rate reduction method. This was spatch-cocked in at the last moment so that the scheme poor Callaghan announced in March was immediately denounced by the building societies as totally impracticable. The fault belonged to Dame Evelyn.

I found this again in the case of the project she had developed for doubling the size of Ipswich, Peterborough and Northampton by use of the New Towns machinery. This was a wonderful idea but a complicated and difficult thing to carry out in practice, and I asked her to work out a policy paper on it. I also insisted that as a politician I should deal with the politicians among the elected councillors and our officials should deal with their officials. She refused to sanction either of these ideas, took the bit between her teeth and fixed up each of the cities in her own style. Alas, she made the most reckless assurances in each place: for example, that Ipswich and Northampton county boroughs would be allowed to extend their own boundaries to cover the areas of the New Towns. And she did all this without consulting me. A few weeks after she had left I found that she had already negotiated with the Treasury a complicated reorganization of housing subsidies for New Towns which I found completely intolerable the moment I saw it.

With my predecessors I think she had a comparatively easy time, apart from Harold Macmillan and possibly Duncan Sandys. To me she always recognized the quality of Macmillan and applauded him for bringing in Percy Mills and getting things done the way he wanted. But Macmillan never took a great interest either in local government or in planning. Indeed, I think I was the first Minister who showed a passionate interest in both these aspects of

20*

the Ministry and also in the science of town planning. The fact that I did so disconcerted her a great deal.

The contrast since Steve took over is remarkable. The whole Department is now being reshaped by the new Permanent Secretary and by Under-Secretaries like Pugh and Brain. There has been a tremendous change in the whole organization and Steve is making it a more conventional type of Whitehall machine.

Apart from the Permanent Secretary, the other main feature of the Ministry from my point of view was the Private Office. Before I arrived I had not appreciated its importance. By the time I left there were some sixty people there to help the Minister and his four political colleagues. Under George Moseley it was a good solid Rover of a Private Office, under John Delafons it was a Rolls Royce. He was the man I selected myself, having seen him at work at one or two meetings. Under him the Private Office provided the machine I needed for controlling the Department, as well as help with writing my speeches. I had ten to twelve meetings a day. They were not all meetings with formal delegations; half of them at least were meetings inside the Department with officials brought in to discuss policy decisions with me and help me to take them. Under John's management I was able to get my Ministerial correspondence in decent order and to write more letters than any previous Minister and to make more reasoned replies on all aspects of the Department's work. I started by trying to reply adequately to M.P.s' letters but by the end I had expanded letter-writing and was answering a great many letters from the general public. I think I succeeded in improving the style of the answers, though they began to fall back by the end of my time and I was finally compelled to get Geoffrey Rhodes to come in and help in the drafting, particularly of letters to constituency Labour Parties, which no official could do.

From my experience I am sure it would be worth a Minister's while to include in his Private Office one person with some experience of political parties and, if possible, the press, who would be responsible for letter-writing to friendly people inside one's own party and also for speech-drafting, because one can't reckon on having a John Delafons as one's Private Secretary. But in saying this I have to remember that when a Minister signs any number of letters every night it makes an enormous burden of extra work for the Ministry, because every letter to whose answer the Minister gives his signature must be dealt with not by a lowly official but by at least an Assistant Secretary if not an Under-Secretary. So every time a Minister decides to sign more letters he is in fact imposing throughout the Department a fresh burden of work on the higher range of officials, where the burden is already far too heavy. This is something I found one couldn't alter. I tried once or twice early on to get hold of the executive officer or the principal who had done the original draft and discuss it direct with him. But it wouldn't work. A Minister can't go down below the Assistant Secretary level. So that severely limits the number of letters a Minister can sign without making life in the Department impossible.

In addition to my Private Office I had by the end of my term a superb press office, organized by Peter Brown. He had worked for Macmillan and found him a great boss; and, like the Dame, he had worked for every Minister of Housing since then. I must confess he is not an easy man. He's a bit of a snob, but he knows a good Minister when he sees one and he worked for me like a navvy every weekend and that made more difference than I can say. He wasn't much good at the drafting of press releases or decision letters; that is something I could do better than he could. What he was superb at was keeping me both alerted and under control, keeping things sweet in Whitehall, organizing press conferences, and above all seeing that wherever I went the press were always there. Then he would chase them to make sure I got a good press. Thank God he is coming with me to my new job, though God knows what he is going to do in the Lord President's Office.

Now for some generalizations about the work of the Department. First of all, legislation. If the Ministry of Housing is anything to go by, the Civil Service always recognizes that an incoming Government will have its election manifesto ready for fulfilment, and they will want to help each Minister fulfil his part of it. They will do it partly because they want to get their Department's share of the legislative programme that year. But they will recognize that the legislation has got to be in line with the views of the Minister and of the Party. In my case they knew there would have to be a rent Act and, *de facto*, they would have to repeal the Tory Rent Act. They also knew there would have to be a new Bill dealing with local government finance and a new housing subsidies Bill as well. I have already described the role my outsiders played in working out our rents policy. Though the Dame said she had never been more insulted, I proved I was right to bring my experts in because I produced the kind of Rent Act which she realized was not mere doctrinaire socialism and which she finally admitted was genuinely better than anything the Department would have dared to put up before I arrived. In fact, she realized that this Rent Act, which was relatively fair to the landlords, was the kind of legislation only a socialist Minister could produce. So she became an enthusiastic supporter and when we came to setting up the organization for rent assessment committees and rent officers (where, by the way, she was also peculiarly difficult) she took responsibility for a lot of the manning and got a decent salary scale from the Treasury. Departmentally, in fact, I had a very easy time.

On housing subsidies, however, things were much more difficult because the Department, I soon discovered, had its own policy. It wanted to introduce a measure which would redress the grave injustices between local authorities caused by the piecemeal introduction since the 1920s of successive subsidies. The Department's plan was to capitalize all the existing subsidies, going right back to the 1920s, and also to persuade the Minister to do this in a way which would move rents up towards the 'economic' level. I had to tell the Secretary quite early on that this was not our Labour Party policy; we were firmly committed to a new subsidy which brought the burden of interest paid by local authorities on new houses down to 4 per cent. It was four months before the Department abandoned its own policy. It was many more months before they actually agreed to carry out our policy and put it into practice. Once they knew they had to do this, they carried it out pretty faithfully.

On local government finance I had a far easier time, because most of the policy was departmental policy. However, I insisted on having two Bills — a short Bill before the 1966 election, introducing rate rebates, and a long Bill after the election, which I planned as a drastic reform of local government finance. The short Bill I duly got through before the election and it was a winner for me, but on the long Bill I had in the end to leave the Department the victor. I had the idea that we could abolish rating by substituting for it a more progressive local tax. The Department, and in particular the Accountant-General, disliked this because they knew the Treasury was passionately opposed to it. In the end they won; most of the second Bill was departmental policy which I virtually handed over to Jim MacColl.

Finally, what about mortgages? Once it was clear I was determined to put our pledge into practice, the Department was extremely resourceful and Brain and the Dame thought up the ingenious idea of the option-mortgage. I was deeply grateful to her, as well as for her relationship with Donald Gould, and though I myself worked up the idea of a national housing plan the Department carried it out pretty faithfully once they saw it had a chance of success.

Of course, when I look at legislation I can't leave out the Land Commission Bill. Now in this case, as on leasehold reform, the Dame detested the whole idea. On both these Bills she used the Ministerial committee to fight a running departmental battle against them. I think she behaved extremely badly over the Land Commission Bill, using me to try and sabotage, or emasculate, it when I hadn't enough knowledge of my job to stand up to her. Looking back I can see that in principle she was right. The Land Commission as presented in the Labour Party manifesto was a futile thing. The Cabinet should have dropped the whole idea once we got a view of it, and achieved the same end by changing the planning law and the laws of compensation on compulsory purchase. But once the new Ministry of Land and Natural Resources had been created, it was obvious that its Bills were bound to be put through and the Dame and I should not have opposed them. The moment Stevenson took over he made me realize how vital it was not to fight the idea of the Land Commission but to shape it to the needs of the Ministry of Housing. This is something I started doing only after the Dame had left; but perhaps this change was the result not of a change of Permanent Secretary but of a change in the situation. As long as the Land Commission and leasehold enfranchisement belonged to an independent Ministry, our Department, whoever was Permanent Secretary, would fight them tooth and nail. As soon as the little Ministry returned to us and we had departmental responsibility for both Bills our attitude was bound to change and we would make the best of each of them.

So I can conclude this section by saying that a Minister who wants to act through legislation can rely on his Department being quite helpful, even if he brings in outside advisers. Of course, the Department would be even happier to put through its own Bills. In my case there was one Bill, the Planning Bill, created by P.A.G. That's the Bill I adopted and I have no doubt we shall see it put through by my successor. But it isn't a Labour Party Bill. It is the kind of Bill which any government will pass in due course.[1]

What about administrative control of the Department? I took practically no part in appointments. True enough, I kept the Dame as my Permanent Secretary longer than the Prime Minister wanted, and then, greatly to his perturbation, put a veto on Bruce Fraser succeeding her. Nevertheless, even Harold Wilson has got to admit that Stevenson, who was finally given me, was a great deal more suitable than Bruce Fraser. Apart from my Permanent Secretary, however, I had virtually nothing to say about any appointments. When it was decided that J. D. Jones had to go to the Ministry of Transport to help Barbara, I at first tried to insist that he should only go as Permanent Secretary. But I lost and he went as a Deputy. I would have lost Jimmy James to the U.N. if he hadn't himself wished to come back. I lost Waddell to the Home Office by mutual agreement. I can only claim that I played some role in the appointment of the Permanent Secretary to succeed Evelyn Sharp. Down below I had no influence at all.

Then how did I achieve any control of the Department? I concentrated at the beginning almost entirely on the large Rent Bill. I spent months on end breathing the Rent Bill in with my daily life and learning all the parts of Whitehall that had any relation to it. That brought me in touch with only a tiny part of the Department, which wasn't a very good thing. But gradually, willy-nilly, I was being dragged into control of local government and planning. Local government was Miss Fox's division, and because I really cared about local government boundaries and understood their political importance I took personal control from a very early stage. Come what may, no decision would be taken about a local government boundary without the parliamentary repercussions being fully considered and without my trying to shield the Labour position. I started by protecting Bert Bowden's position in Leicester, and then I dealt with Nottingham and Middlesbrough in the same way. All the way through I think I managed to combine a sound local government policy with an extremely shrewd defence of Labour's parliamentary interests. This gave me my first effective control in the Department over a particular division, which I think fairly well shocked Miss Fox and her colleagues.

It was as a result of this that I achieved one of my few big successes. I got

[1] It became law as the Town and Country Planning Act 1968.

the Royal Commission on Local Government through, by going down to
Torquay and addressing the A.M.C. during the August holiday in a speech
the Dame would never have allowed me to make if she had been there. Indeed,
I think I can claim that it was my policy of personal intervention in the
decisions of the Local Government Boundary Commission which changed the
whole situation. By taking complete charge of all the decisions which had
piled up on Keith Joseph's desk I succeeded in breaking the assumption that
all a Minister could do was to sit by, watching the cold war between the
expanding boroughs and the county councils over the green belt. In my
speeches I began to break down the simple notion of the urban area on the
one side and the county area on the other and to build up the idea of the city
region, the urban area with the rural area attached to it for planning purposes.
I launched this idea and simultaneously I denounced the present county
boroughs and county councils as dinosaurs belonging to a prehistoric age
and got a standing ovation for the denunciation.

The next division of the Ministry which forced me to attend to it was planning. My attention started with the Hartley case. Letting me go ahead and
override my Inspector without any warning of the consequences was rough
on a new and innocent Minister. What made it even rougher was that J. D.
Jones let me put out a decision letter in which the whole case for rejecting the
appeal was argued at length and my decision apparently just arbitrarily
imposed upon it. However, the blow-up was pretty useful. It taught me that
I should never again send a junior like Jim MacColl to go and see a case on
the ground. After this, despite the protests of the Department, I visited the
crucial areas myself, incognito, and made up my own mind on the spot. I
was told this would prejudice my findings and put me into a sea of trouble.
But the Department soon found they couldn't sustain this objection. I talked
to people vitally concerned, visited the trouble spots and did all the things
the Department said were grossly improper. None of this rebounded on me
in any way. I learnt my lesson from Hartley, and I think, marginally, the
decision was right. But of course it was the wrong one for me to make at that
particular stage in my career and without fully explaining it. It took me two
months to repair the damage by a carefully prepared press conference at
which I announced my decisions about Chelmsley Wood at Birmingham and
Stennington at Sheffield. This gave me an opportunity to define my whole
attitude to the problem of reconciling the preservation of the green belt with
the provision of the requisite areas for new housing. I also learnt one important lesson—never to trust the Department's attitude to the Minister in such
critical decisions. Right at the end I had a very similar case to Hartley in the
Lea Valley. Bob Mellish was quite right that I ought to override the Inspector
and allow 180 acres of grassland in the green belt to be built over. When I
looked at the press release, however, I found that it attributed to me in the
letter stating my decision the remark that though this was completely against
my green-belt policy I had to allow it. Once again the officials who were

drafting for me in the Department were determined to emphasize that I was overriding my Inspector out of pure arbitrary wilfulness. The man who tried to do this to me was an extremely severe and extremely good-looking civil servant, who on other occasions tried to trip me up and expose me for abusing my judicial position. Of course the real truth is that all this talk about judicial attitudes to planning procedure is moonshine. There isn't any planning law, it's all planning lore, planning mythology. Planning inquiries aren't and shouldn't be legal inquiries. They are *ad hoc* information inquiries which have been turned into pseudo-legal inquiries, just as decisions have been turned into pseudo-judicial decisions based on a mass of lore.

I took a number of other important decisions — about water at Ullswater, about mineral extraction, about gravel pits, about china clay, and about pollution — as in the case of Woburn, where I scrapped the whole inquiry. By and large I found that nearly all my technical advisers were passionately in favour of the producer and against the amenity lobby. This was particularly true of the Alkali Inspectorate. In all these areas a Minister who actually read the documents and made his own decision was keenly resented. But I found I was making headway in establishing new precedents and new principles. This was possible because in the case of planning, as in the case of local government boundary decisions, the Inspectors being the Minister's Inspectors and the final decisions being the Minister's decisions, the law is flexible and can actually be changed. Inspectors are human and they will pay great attention to what a Minister decides for himself. I found that if I wrote the decision letters myself and expounded my own principles with the greatest care this did have an immediate effect on the decision the Inspectors themselves were carrying out at the time. Maybe this is what the Department didn't like.

One of the areas in which I took a particular interest was historic buildings. When the 1966 election was won and I got my way, I insisted that there should be a new allocation of functions in the Ministry of Works and I got the whole of the listing of historic buildings and the subsidies transferred and centralized in the Department. This kind of work was utterly despised by Dame Evelyn. She regarded it as pure sentimentalism and called it 'preservationism', a word of abuse. She who counted herself a modern iconoclast took the extremely — yes, I will say it — illiterate view that there was a clear-cut conflict between 'modern' planning and 'reactionary' preservation. During my time as Minister, in speech after speech, I tried to break down this false dichotomy and to establish a new and sensible relationship between planning and preservation.

In doing this I found the actual division which deals with historic buildings extremely rigid and difficult. One of them expressed to me a passion for Duncan Sandys and showed himself an extreme political conservative as well. Although I was the first Minister to show a genuine enthusiasm for their subject they continuously resented my interference and tried to defeat me whenever they could. On one occasion, when I tried to get the Karl Marx

Library in Clerkenwell listed as an historic building, the vote of the officials present turned me down. Altogether my relations with them were very hostile, in contrast to my relations with the R.I.B.A. and the architects which got more and more friendly. (I got a letter from Lord Esher the other day saying that in their considered view I was the best Minister they had ever had.)

By the time I left I had got a long way towards solving the problem of preserving the coastline. I had achieved a real change in the Ministry's attitude, and I think I had begun to persuade the National Trust, with its Operation Neptune, to be more sensible in its buying policy. I hadn't got nearly as far either on gravel-pits or on china clay. But here too I was trying to work on the precedent of Hugh Dalton's astonishing success with open-cast iron mining at Corby. Not only did he get co-operation between the mining firm and the local authority, but his scheme for a levy to finance a reclamation programme prevented the landscape from being utterly despoiled. It seemed to me that this principle could now be applied to gravel-pits and also to china clay. I might have got a similar result in the brick-making industry too.

As for water, I had one success, at Ullswater. But I was convinced that we needed a lot more research and I was just about to insist on more money being spent on obtaining the necessary information in time. At present all decisions about water supply are taken at the very last moment. You are told by your officials that if you don't take the decision within two months there will be no water in Manchester in three years' time, or in North Devon. They can only tell you this because the ways of estimating water resources are utterly inadequate. With the Water Resources Board established,[1] I was convinced that real progress could be made if we could develop new techniques for assessing the flow of rivers and so getting the decisions taken with a clear knowledge of the alternatives available.

But there was one problem in planning which I completely failed to deal with. Wasn't there something wrong with the whole way in which appeals were presented to the Minister? Was it right to permit such a complete absence of alternatives? The usual appeal is presented in the form: is this proposal right or wrong? But another way of presenting it would be: is this proposal preferable to methods b, c and d, when one considers them all together? I saw this difference most grotesquely in the case of Stansted airport. We had a special inquiry on Stansted which lasted fifty or sixty days at enormous cost. The results were practically useless because the Inspector was not allowed to consider whether we needed a third London airport or whether Stansted was preferable to Sheppey in Kent. I would hope that my successor will face this problem firmly.

I now turn to the housing programme – the ostensible reason why I was

[1] It was established in 1964 under the terms of the 1963 Water Resources Act. Before that, responsibility for water resources lay with the River Boards established by the 1951 Central Water Advisory Committee.

sent to the Ministry. After I had dealt with rent control I concentrated on housing subsidies, and I obtained from Callaghan at an early period of relaxed optimism a far more generous subsidies deal than he would have dreamt of agreeing to later on.

But what about getting the houses built? Here I very largely relied on Bob Mellish, a splendid, tough, faithful man, but sometimes unable to stand up to the Department. There is an interesting comparison between him and MacColl. Mellish was far the better politician, a first-rate sergeant-major, hard-working and able to take decisions. But when it came to paperwork he tended to be in the hands of his officials. Whatever they gave him to sign, he signed. Whatever paper they told him was departmental policy, was his policy. Jim MacColl on the other hand was a man of congenital indecision. He really understood the subject from A to Z, housing, rents, planning, he had a wonderful detailed knowledge. So he was a man who was absolutely superb in the Committee Stage of a Bill. But when it came to making administrative decision or impressing the Department he was hopeless. Faced with him, the Dame was merciless. She gave him the reputation of indecisiveness and equivocation, a reputation he never lost, so that when Fred Willey came into the Department Jim remained number two. On the other hand he completely took over the legislative side of the Local Government Bill, so that I only spent two hours on the Committee Stage in the House of Commons. My opposite number, Rippon, wasn't there at all.

I did give Mellish one job straight away. When I came to the Department there was absolutely no kind of organization for progress-chasing on housing. The Minister just seemed to assist the local authorities to do what they wanted, helping their own architects along, inspecting them, approving design – but with no sense of driving energy at all. So I set about getting a real drive going in London, and gave Mellish power to visit every borough in the whole G.L.C. area to work out a new expanded programme for London. This he did; but within six months we found that it meant very little because the authorities, having doubled their targets, had achievements lower than the year before. This indicated the need for a quite different relationship between the Ministry and the local authorities. The basis for the new relationship was the recognition that most local authorities don't want to build houses, and, if they do, are grossly incompetent and drive any contractor crazy by the arbitrary methods of their committees and their sullenness and incompetence.

To get the drive going we therefore had to select the right local authorities and train them for the job. I can take credit for one major thing, the institution of priorities in this regard. The Ministry told me this was quite impossible. I wouldn't survive the announcement that certain authorities would have far more than their fair share and other authorities less. This went on for months until I said, 'We are just going to list the authorities in the greater conurbations and we are going to give this 130 an unlimited authority to build up to capacity, even if it absorbs 60 or 70 per cent of the total allocation. The rest will be spread very thin among the other authorities.' This was a bold decision which took some selling. The Department was against it but I had it written into the White Paper, and it was being carried out when I left.

Of course there were difficulties. We soon found that some of the 130 select authorities were not using up their allocation and we had some very nice re-allocations to do in order to make sure that our total didn't fall down. It meant, for example, that authorities we had cut back in the South-East region would at the last minute get an increase in approvals. We were always fiddling round with approvals and this was awkward since they all had to be calculated within the calendar year. One difficulty here was the split between us and the Ministry of Works which controlled the N.B.A., the organization which was designed to be a progress-chaser for the local authorities but which never for a moment did this job. When I got it transferred to our control I found it didn't do any better. My experiment with Peter Lederer was far more successful. He chose as his successor Ken Wood of Concrete Limited, a much bigger man, who was doing extremely well when I was moved from the Ministry.

The other problem I had to solve was the relationship between the private and the public sectors. Here again I can take some credit for modest achievement. I did set up the national housing plan. Although the builders started by being bloody-minded and went on attacking me in the most violent ways, behind the scenes they were gradually getting used to my methods. At the last big conference I had with them I submitted myself to questions for an hour and a half and came off practically unscathed. There was no newspaper story in it and that was the proof of my success.

Nevertheless, the fact remains that the man who controls the number of houses produced by the private sector is not the Minister of Housing but the Chancellor of the Exchequer. The private sector was booming when we took over, but the sudden increase of interest rates followed by the imposition of S.E.T. damaged it terribly. The fact is we nearly knocked the private sector out. Not unnaturally there was a continuous struggle between the Chancellor and myself. We fought about the private sector, where his interest rates and mortgage policy were ruinous. We fought about the public sector, where he was always ordering me to impose cuts for the sake of our foreign trade balance. I succeeded in saving the public sector from the cuts he wanted to impose. As for the private sector, I was well on the way to persuading the builders and the building societies to believe that I really believed in owner-occupation. Indeed, I hope I laid the foundations for a completely new relationship between the Ministry of Housing, the building societies and the builders. But I am pretty sure myself that the next stage we should go for is the establishment of a national housing corporation for mortgage finance, with which we could replace the effete, old-fashioned building society.

Now let me try to balance up my success and failure. The first failure undoubtedly relates to the rent assessment committees. I didn't succeed in controlling the appointments. The Dame sold me Sydney Littlewood who may develop into a major problem – forensic, self-important, difficult. And I allowed her virtually to take over the manning of the R.A.C.s. Nevertheless, I am still prepared to say that it is a good Act which has taken private rents out of politics. But it is going to present my successors with a good many problems when they come to decide at what stage to bring controlled rents into regulation.

On local government reform I got the Royal Commission launched with a due sense of urgency and I hope it is going to report in the two years necessary. Reform of local government finance? Well I got rate rebates and not much else.

Housing? We would have done better if I had had more political experience. It took me fifteen months before I realized what was wrong. With knowledge we could have had a much more concentrated housing drive. In relation to the private sector I went as far as a Minister of Housing with the backing of the Prime Minister could. But I just had the facts against me.

In planning I think the Land Commission was a thoroughly bad mark against me. I should have seen much earlier what the Dame was up to and made sure far earlier that the Land Commission was going to be useful to the Ministry of Housing in the purchase of land. As for the rest of planning, I may have spent too much time on individual cases, but as with local government boundary decisions I enjoyed particular cases and learnt so much from them. In the end I was capable of making a number of policy speeches at the T.P.I. and the A.M.C. which put the Ministry on the map.

Looking at the Ministry now, it is clear that practically every division was affected by me in the end. I managed to spread my influence and this was done very largely by my ability to read fast. Of course the Private Office at first tried to flood me. But the more they gave me the more I digested, and they soon discovered that the more I digested the more I interfered.

One very great difficulty for a Minister is in handling the Department's hierarchical organization. For instance, the Dame preferred me to talk only to her; and often no notes would be taken, so that she only remembered selected parts of our discussions. I soon learnt from John Delafons that my success depended essentially on keeping a note of every meeting. Each night I would go through the notes in my box, checking that each point was covered. The follow-up, the implementation of any policy decision, is the essence of a Minister's success. Departments are delighted to sit about at meetings with Ministers, agreeing or disagreeing, but taking no further action. But in my Private Office John Delafons and his assistant were extremely quick at making notes and ensuring that decisions were taken on this basis. And on all this Steve was reorganizing the whole attitude of the Department and enabling me to move along.

But there's no doubt about it, a lot of people heaved a sigh of relief when

I went. It wasn't because they were idle or conservative. The main reason was perhaps because I bullied them and made a fool of them in front of others, quite often their subordinates. I *was* unpleasant and difficult and brutal in meetings and that didn't sweeten relations. But also they didn't like this new pressure, relentlessly applied through the Private Office, to carry out the decisions we had reached. Many also felt that I was unfair because I didn't give them time enough to state their case before I interrupted. This was mainly because I had read the whole case beforehand and thought it a waste of time to hear it stated again. And because my mind works quicker than most people's minds. Nevertheless.

I turn finally to the biggest question of all – the relationship of a departmental Minister to Parliament. How effectively does Parliament control him? How careful must he be in his dealings with Parliament? The answer quite simply is that there is no effective parliamentary control. All this time I never felt in any way alarmed by a parliamentary threat, even when we had a majority of only three. Of course, things are different when one is a Minister. One enters the House of Commons by a different way. I drive in the car into Speaker's Yard, I go by the policeman and up in the lift and in at the back to answer a Question or make a speech at the time I want. I don't have to sit about and wait. And when I am there I have my Private Secretary in the box. It's a Rolls Royce way of being a Member of Parliament, all the wheels are oiled especially for you and your life is made extremely easy. The whole of our Parliament is geared not to help back-benchers criticize Ministers but to help Ministers overcome back-benchers.

Can I remember a time when I was seriously upset? Well, there was a vote of censure by Heath in the first summer of 1965 and there was a vote of censure on Packington, both of which I greatly enjoyed. I can't remember a single moment in the course of legislation when I felt the faintest degree of alarm or embarrassment and I can't remember a Question Time, either, when I had any anxiety. And that's not good. Life is too easy for Ministers in our Parliament. Take Question Time. Now that Questions have been speeded up, the last anxiety has been removed. At the beginning, naturally, I was nervous and took the most tremendous trouble on Tuesdays when I was due to answer Questions. I used to go through them with my officials and make sure that there were proper draft answers to Supplementaries. But gradually as I grew confident I have done less and less of this. Of course I look through them beforehand now, but particularly with fifty Questions to be answered in one afternoon there are only one or two Supplementaries where there is anything to be alarmed about; and in the last resort a Minister can always refuse to answer. What I have confirmed is the view of the Warden of Nuffield that the letter is a much more important and formidable threat to a Minister than the Question in Parliament.[1] If a letter is sent to me by an M.P. or an ex-Minister, I have to take great care because I have to answer it in writing

[1] Chester and Bowring, *Questions in Parliament*.

and make a considered reply which could be published in the press. So in my view letters are a greater check on the Executive than Questions.

What about legislation? On the Rating Bill and the Local Government Bill there was virtually no parliamentary control. These were specialist Bills and the Opposition got nothing out of them. On the large Rent Bill there was rather more genuine discussion. As a result of Opposition pressure I was able to make a number of improvements in the Bill which I wanted and which I had been told by the Department or the parliamentary draftsmen were quite impossible. Nevertheless, I agree with those who say that the Committee Stage as managed at present is an intolerable waste of time. The Opposition only have a limited number of objections to make and they pour them all out on the early clauses, and then they get tired and give in on the later clauses and schedules which, though they may be very important, are rushed through without any proper attention.

Of course, I was spoilt by having Jim MacColl. As a result of his presence I never bothered to read any of the Bills I got through. I glanced at them and I read the briefs about them and I also knew the policies from the White Papers and therefore I knew exactly how the briefs and the White Papers corresponded with the clauses of the Bills. But I never bothered to understand the actual clauses, nor did many Members, not even the spokesman for the Opposition. Both sides worked off written briefs to an astonishing extent.

I wonder whether the whole procedure of Standing Committee isn't too formalized today, with Government and Opposition facing each other and debating line by line on amendment. Wouldn't it be possible for the Minister to sit down informally and put the major principles of the Bill for the Committee to discuss? There must be a whole number of Bills on which you ought to be able to get a pooling of minds, which doesn't occur with the Standing Committee procedure in Parliament. I tried to help the Government Members by having a meeting once a week of my own back-benchers to discuss the Bill; it worked very well on the Rent Act but not on the others. I suppose the objection is that you can't do this if the Opposition are really to oppose. But quite frankly, Standing Committee is also intolerable for the Government Members—it is a terrible chore to sit there and listen to the eternal prosying of an Opposition that is usually so badly briefed that it is unable to sustain any long or detailed criticism of a Bill, and even if the Government Members know something about it they have to sit there saying nothing because discussion prolongs the time and the Government's only concern is getting things through as fast as possible.

Therefore Governments are able to get away with murder in a Bill. Where rating was concerned, I suddenly decided that I wasn't going to introduce the penal clauses detailing the penalties the National Assistance Board could impose in the case of people double-claiming from the Board and from the city treasurer. After the Chequers meeting and a word with Willie Ross and Peggy Herbison I just left these things out. Now this really alarmed my

Accountant-General and the Treasury, and of course the Treasury got hold of my Accountant-General and they tried to put the fear of God into me. I wasn't unduly alarmed and said there was plenty of time to run it; we'll see if anything goes wrong. Nothing of course did go wrong—the clauses were quietly inserted into the National Insurance Bill last summer, putting in what was required, and the crisis, the first I could remember about there being something seriously wrong with a Bill, disappeared.

Of course, you do get the most astonishing mistakes surviving in a Bill, like our leaving the words 'substantial difference' in the definition of a fair rent. None of us noticed the word 'substantial', which in the context was meant to be 'non-substantial'. That kind of thing goes through despite every effort. Naturally the parliamentary draftsmen play an absolutely key role. We get the instructions ready for them in the office and the key thing is for those instructions to be translated into the legal lingo of the Bill. Here you are absolutely at the mercy of the draftsman who just says he can or he can't do it. And very often he says he can't at the beginning and he can at the end.

I learnt to be more and more sceptical about that particular objection, but in terms of general parliamentary control of legislation I don't think myself that all those hours and hours Parliament spends on the improvement of a Bill justify, in terms of influence, the waste of time. That's my considered conclusion. I'm clear that if I really want to make parliamentary control effective we must have specialist committees able to study the detailed working of Departments. I'm more than ever convinced that Tony Crosland, Roy Jenkins and I were right in saying that we would welcome this for our particular Departments. One of my aims is to try and get this through the House of Commons at the beginning of next Session.

Apart from that, what about general control through adjournments, through policy debates, the general sense that the Minister is being kept on his toes? Well, I had my share of votes of censure, and of attempts to stir people up about housing. Gradually Mellish and I asserted a mastery over the House as Housing Ministers. I must say we had damn little success and we were fighting on a terribly bad wicket in the sense that we weren't keeping our pledges, we weren't getting the houses built. And yet we managed to get away with it. It was amazing how little protest was effectively made. Indeed, the only serious problem I had to deal with was discontent with the rent assessment committees and this was, entirely, discontent among a small number of Labour M.P.s I care about, left-wing people whom I'd had on the Standing Committee—Eric Heffer, for instance, Frank Allaun, Julius Silverman, Lena Jeger. All alarmed because the R.A.C.s weren't lowering rents as much as they desired.

But this isn't something about which parliamentary pressure was very great. Indeed, I was absolutely safe here because the Tories were delighted to see the landlords better off than they'd expected, and weren't going to attack me. No, this was simply an internal *Party* matter and will come up again at

Conference. So over this, my most serious protest, where I had to go once or twice to the Party group and discuss it with them, it was with the Parliamentary Party that my relations were certainly being affected. Here we come to the next point: the relationship of the Government with the Party in Parliament. This is quite different; it involves the Party meetings, the back-benchers, it is where your P.P.S., your walking into the tea-room, has an effect — and here I was fairly good. Better than most Ministers, but I think most Ministers have been miserably deficient and have been allowed to be so because of the failings of the Leader of the House.

The Whips were quite good at adding up the votes and keeping a majority of three going because there was nothing but discipline required. But with a majority of one hundred Ted Short failed to establish the right relationship with the back-benchers. One of my first jobs as Leader of the House is to tactfully persuade Ministers, if I can, to take far more trouble with back-benchers, to groom them, consult and have contact with them, and in this way to make the Parliamentary group a success. Because the key to the Government's success is its relationship with its own rank and file; and I have no doubt that it was Harold's recognition of this that brought me my present job. We have an entirely new situation, with a difficult, fractious and disturbed Parliamentary Party, subjected to great pressures from outside and worried about what we are doing, about prices and incomes and the failure of the Government. I've got to see them through and this will mean seeing that in so far as their views are intelligent and constructive they impinge on the Government.

Looking back, I think I can say that Bob and I were probably better than most Ministers. As Minister of Housing I had relatively a good House; the Tories thought the policy a failure but they knew I was quite a good Minister, and I had quite a good relationship with the Party. Well, that's how I see my life today. I've already got out of the worst period of homesickness for Housing and Local Government but I shan't ever lose it altogether. I shall always miss this. Really what I would most like to do is to get out of this new job and back into the Department.

Summer has really come with splendid weather, but our Cornish holiday is over. Now we go up to London for the last few days of August to have some family expeditions — to Hampton Court and the cinema. Harold is due back from the Scillies on Sunday night and politics is coming back to life. I shall go and have my first talk to him on Tuesday and then I must get down to reading the official papers on Rhodesia, to preparing the new concordat on Party discipline and settling into my new job.

Members of the Cabinet 1964–66

October 18th, 1964

Prime Minister	Harold Wilson
First Secretary at D.E.A.	George Brown
Lord President of the Council and Leader of the House of Commons	Herbert Bowden
Lord Chancellor	Gerald Gardiner
Lord Privy Seal and Leader of the House of Lords	Frank Longford
Chancellor of the Exchequer	James Callaghan
Foreign Office	Patrick Gordon Walker
Home Office	Frank Soskice
Agriculture, Fisheries and Food	Fred Peart
Colonial Office	Anthony Greenwood
Commonwealth Relations Office	Arthur Bottomley
Defence	Denis Healey
Education and Science	Michael Stewart
Housing and Local Government	Richard Crossman
Labour	Ray Gunter
Chancellor of the Duchy of Lancaster	Douglas Houghton
Overseas Development	Barbara Castle
Power	Fred Lee
Scottish Office	William Ross
Technology	Frank Cousins
Board of Trade	Douglas Jay
Transport	Tom Fraser
Welsh Office	James Griffiths

Changes on January 22nd, 1965

Foreign Office	Michael Stewart
Education	Anthony Crosland

Patrick Gordon Walker left the Government.

Changes on December 23rd, 1965

Lord Privy Seal	Frank Soskice
Home Office	Roy Jenkins
Colonial Office and Leader of the House of Lords	Frank Longford
Overseas Development	Anthony Greenwood
Transport	Barbara Castle

Tom Fraser left the Government.

Changes on April 6th, 1966

Lord Privy Seal and Leader of the House of Lords	Frank Longford
Colonial Office	Fred Lee
Power	Richard Marsh
Welsh Office	Cledwyn Hughes
Chancellor of the Duchy of Lancaster	George Thomson
Minister without Portfolio	Douglas Houghton

James Griffiths and Frank Soskice left the Government.

Change on July 4th, 1966

Technology	Anthony Wedgwood Benn

Frank Cousins left the Government.

Changes on August 6th–11th, 1966

First Secretary at D.E.A.	Michael Stewart
Lord President of the Council and Leader of the House of Commons	Richard Crossman
Foreign Office	George Brown
Commonwealth Relations Office	Herbert Bowden
Housing and Local Government	Anthony Greenwood
Overseas Development	Arthur Bottomley

Biographical Notes

ALLEN, Douglas. Sir Douglas Allen (K.C.B. 1967) entered the Board of Trade in 1939 and, apart from a year in the Cabinet Office (1947) and two years at the Ministry of Health (1958–60) had spent his life in the Treasury, where he became Third Secretary in 1962. He was Deputy Under-Secretary of State at the D.E.A. 1964–6, and Permanent Under-Secretary 1966–8. Since 1968 he has been Permanent Secretary to the Treasury.

ALLEN, Philip. Sir Philip Allen (K.C.B. 1964) entered the Home Office in 1934. He was Deputy Secretary at M.H.L.G. 1955–60, and then returned to the Home Office to serve as Deputy Under-Secretary of State until 1962. He was Second Secretary to the Treasury 1963–6, and from 1966 until his retirement in 1972 Permanent Under-Secretary at the Home Office.

ARMSTRONG, William. Sir William Armstrong (K.C.B. 1963) entered the Board of Education in 1938 and served as Private Secretary to the Secretary of the War Cabinet 1943–6. He was Principal Private Secretary to successive Chancellors of the Exchequer 1949–53, and spent the greater part of his career in the Treasury, becoming its Joint Permanent Secretary in 1962. Since 1968 he has been official Head of the Home Civil Service and the Permanent Secretary of the Civil Service Department.

BACON, Alice. Labour M.P. for Leeds from 1945 to 1970, when she became a Life Peer. A member of Labour's N.E.C. since 1941. She was Minister of State at the Home Office from 1964 to 1967, when she moved to the D.E.S. where she remained until 1970.

BALOGH, Thomas. A Fellow of Balliol College, Oxford, Lord Balogh served as Economic Adviser to the Cabinet from October 1964 until 1967. He was made a Life Peer in 1968 when he returned to Oxford.

BARKER, Sara. Dame Sara Barker (D.B.E. 1970) was Women's Organizer of the Yorkshire Labour Party from 1942 to 1952, when she became Assistant National Agent to the Labour Party. She was National Agent 1962–9, with her headquarters in Transport House.

BARBER, Anthony. Conservative M.P. for Doncaster 1951–64 and for Altrincham since February 1965. He served as P.P.S. to the Under-Secretary of State for Air 1952–5, and in the Whips' Office 1955–8; in 1958 he became P.P.S. to Harold Macmillan. He was Economic Secretary to the Treasury 1959–62, and its Financial Secretary 1962–3. He was Minister of Health 1963–4. On the Conservatives' return to Government in 1970 he became Chancellor of the Duchy of Lancaster, and on Iain Macleod's death in July 1970, he succeeded him as Chancellor of the Exchequer.

BENN, Anthony Wedgwood. Labour M.P. for Bristol South-East 1950–60. In 1960 he succeeded to his father's viscountcy, a title he eventually disclaimed after successfully pressing for the Peerage Act of 1963. He was re-elected, for the second time, as M.P. for Bristol in August 1963. He was Postmaster-General 1964–6, and Minister of Technology 1966–70.

BERRY, Pamela. Daughter of the Earl of Birkenhead, and wife of Michael Berry, now Lord Hartwell, chairman and editor-in-chief of the *Daily Telegraph* and the *Sunday Telegraph*. She has been president of the Incorporated Society of London Fashion Designers since 1952.

BOTTOMLEY, Arthur. Labour M.P. for Rochester and Chatham 1945–59, and for Middlesbrough since 1962. He had been a Parliamentary Under-Secretary for the Dominions 1946–7 and Secretary for Overseas Trade 1947–51 in the post-war Labour Government. He was Secretary of State for Commonwealth Affairs 1964–6 and Minister of Overseas Development 1966–7.

BOWDEN, Herbert. Labour M.P. for Leicester from 1945 until 1967, when he entered the House of Lords as Lord Aylestone. He had served as P.P.S. to the Postmaster-General 1947–9 and in the Whips' Office 1949–51 in the post-war Labour Government; and as an Opposition Whip, and eventually as Opposition Chief Whip, between 1951 and 1964. He was Lord President and Leader of the House 1964–6 and Secretary of State for Commonwealth Affairs 1966–7. From 1967 until 1973 he was chairman of the Independent Television Authority.

BOYD-CARPENTER, John. Conservative M.P. for Kingston-upon-Thames 1945–72. In 1972 he became a Life Peer. He had been Financial Secretary to the Treasury 1951–4, Minister of Transport and Civil Aviation 1954–5, Minister of Pensions 1955–62 and Chief Secretary to the Treasury 1962–4. He acted as chief Opposition spokesman on Housing, Local Government and Land 1964–6, and also served as chairman of the Public Accounts Committee 1964–70. In 1972 he became chairman of the Civil Aviation Authority.

BROOKE, Barbara. A member of the Hampstead Borough Council 1948–65, and served in the North-West Metropolitan Regional Hospital Board 1954–66. She was chairman of the Executive Committee of the Queen's Institute of District Nursing 1961–71. In 1964 she became a Life Peer, taking the title of Lady Brooke of Ystradfellte. She is married to Henry Brooke.

BROOKE, Henry. Conservative M.P. for West Lewisham 1938–45 and for Hampstead 1950–66. He had been Financial Secretary to the Treasury 1956–7, Minister of Housing and Local Government 1957–61, Chief Secretary to the Treasury 1961–2 and Home Secretary 1962–4. He became a Life Peer in 1966, taking the title Lord Brooke of Cumnor.

BROWN, George. Labour M.P. for Belper, 1945–70; in 1970 he became a Life Peer, taking the title of Lord George-Brown. He had served as P.P.S. to the Minister of Labour and then to the Chancellor of the Exchequer in 1947, and as Parliamentary Secretary at the Ministry of Agriculture 1947–1951 and at the Ministry of Works in 1951. In 1963 he was an unsuccessful candidate for the leadership of the Labour Party. In 1964 he became First Secretary and Secretary of State at the D.E.A.; in 1966 he became Foreign

Secretary. After his resignation in 1968 he remained deputy leader of the Labour Party for a short time.

BROWN, Peter. The most able Press officer in Whitehall, according to Crossman, whom he joined in 1964.

BULLOCK, Alan. Master of St Catherine's College, Oxford, since 1960. He was chairman of the National Advisory Council on the Training and Supply of Teachers 1963–5 and of the Schools Council 1966–9, and a member of the Arts Council of Great Britain 1961–4, and of the Organizing Committee for the British Library since 1971. Among his publications are *Hitler: A Study in Tyranny* (London: Odhams Press, 1952) and *The Life and Times of Ernest Bevin* (London: Heinemann, Vol. I, 1960; Vol. II, 1967). He was Vice-Chancellor of Oxford University 1969–73.

BUTLER, R. A. B. Conservative M.P. for Saffron Walden from 1929 until 1965, when he became a Life Peer. He held various offices in the pre-war Conservative Governments and was a notable Minister of Education 1941–1945. After the war his offices included that of Chancellor of the Exchequer (1951–5), Leader of the House (1955–61), Home Secretary (1957–62), First Secretary of State (August 1962–October 1963), and he acted as Deputy Prime Minister and Foreign Secretary 1963–4. He did not, as many expected, succeed Harold Macmillan as Prime Minister in 1963. Since 1965 he has been Master of Trinity College, Cambridge.

CALLAGHAN, James. Labour M.P. for Cardiff since 1945, and a member of the Labour Party N.E.C. 1957–67; in 1967 he became Treasurer of the Labour Party. Consultant to the Police Federation 1955–64. He had been Parliamentary Secretary at the Ministry of Transport 1947–50 and at the Admiralty 1950–51 in the post-war Labour Government. In 1964 he became Chancellor of the Exchequer, becoming Home Secretary in 1967, a post he held until 1970.

CASTLE, Barbara. Labour M.P. for Blackburn since 1945, and a member of the Labour Party N.E.C. since 1950. She had been chairman of the Labour Party 1958–9. In 1964 she became Minister of Overseas Development, and in 1965 Minister of Transport, an office she held until 1968, when she became First Secretary of State and Secretary of State at the newly created Department of Employment and Productivity. She served there until Labour's defeat in 1970.

CLARK, Percy. He became Publications Officer of the Labour Party in 1947, and in 1957 Regional Publicity Director. He was Deputy Director of Information 1960–70, and has been Director of Information since 1970.

CLARKE, (Richard) Otto. Sir Richard Clarke (K.C.B. 1964) served in the Ministries of Information, Economic Warfare, and Supply and Production 1939–45. In 1945 he went to the Treasury, remaining there until 1966. In that year he became Permanent Secretary at the Ministry of Aviation, and then at the Ministry of Technology, where he served until his retirement in 1970.

COHEN, Andrew. Sir Andrew Cohen (K.C.M.G. 1952) had been Governor of Uganda 1952–7, and Director-General of the Department of Technical Co-operation 1961–4. He became Barbara Castle's first Permanent Secretary at the Ministry of Overseas Development. He died in June 1968.

COMPTON, Edmund. Sir Edmund Compton (K.C.B. 1965) joined the Civil Service in 1929 and spent the greater part of his career in the Treasury, becoming Third Secretary in 1949. From 1958 until 1966 he served as Comptroller and Auditor-General, the senior official with responsibility for auditing all departmental accounts. In 1967 he became the first Parliamentary Commissioner for Administration (Ombudsman), serving until 1971, in which year he was also Parliamentary Commissioner for Northern Ireland. Since 1971 he has been chairman of the Local Government Boundary Commission.

COUSINS, Frank. A member of the General Council of the T.U.C. and General Secretary of the T.G.W.U. 1956–69, he obtained leave of absence from his union to become M.P. for Nuneaton in January 1965 in order to serve in the Cabinet as Minister of Technology. He returned to the T.G.W.U. in December 1966. He served as chairman of the Community Relations Commission 1968–70.

COUZENS, Kenneth. He joined the Inland Revenue in 1949, moving to the Treasury in 1951, where he remained until 1968. After two years in the Civil Service Department he returned to the Treasury as an Under-Secretary in 1970.

CROSLAND, Anthony. Labour M.P. for South Gloucestershire 1950–55 and for Grimsby since 1959. Minister of State for Economic Affairs 1964–5, Secretary of State for Education and Science 1965–7, President of the Board of Trade 1967–9, and then Secretary of State for Local Government and Regional Planning until 1970. He is the author of various books on the theory of socialism, notably *The Future of Socialism* (London: Cape, 1956) and *Socialism Now* (London: Cape, 1974).

DALYELL, Tam. Labour M.P. for West Lothian since 1962. He was the Crossmans' lodger at Vincent Square. He had worked with Crossman when he was Shadow Minister of Education and Science, and served as his P.P.S. 1964–70 with only one short interval. He was a member of the House of Commons Select Committee on Science and Technology 1967–9.

DELAFONS, John. He was a Principal in the Ministry of Housing and Local Government/Ministry of Transport Joint Urban Planning Unit 1962–4. In 1965 he became Crossman's Private Secretary, in charge of the Private Office at the Ministry of Housing and Local Government. Since 1972 he has been Under-Secretary and Director of Personnel Management at the Department of the Environment.

DIAMOND, John. A practising chartered accountant. A Manchester M.P. 1945–51, he represented Gloucester from 1957 until 1970, when he was made a Life Peer. He was Chief Secretary to the Treasury for the whole of the 1964–70 Labour Government, and a full Cabinet Minister after 1968.

DONNELLY, Desmond. Labour M.P. for Pembroke 1950–70. He resigned the Labour Whip on the issue of defence policy East of Suez in 1968, and between 1968 and 1970 he acted as an Independent. In 1971 he joined the Conservative Party, but was unable to find a seat. He was political correspondent for the *News of the World* 1968–70.

DONNISON, David. Professor of Social Administration at L.S.E. 1961–9, and chairman of the Commission of Inquiry into the Public Schools 1968–70. Since 1969 he has been Director of the Centre for Environmental Studies.

DOUGLAS-HOME, Alec. Conservative M.P. for Lanark from 1931 to 1951, when he succeeded his father, the 13th Earl of Home. He had held various offices before and after the war, and had been Leader of the House of Lords 1957–60 and Foreign Secretary 1960–63. In October 1963 he disclaimed his peerage and was thus enabled to become Prime Minister (being elected M.P. for Kinross and West Perthshire in November 1963). His ministry was brief, and from October 1964 to July 1965 he was leader of the Opposition. When the Conservatives returned to government in 1970 he returned to the Foreign Office as Secretary of State.

DRIBERG, Tom. Labour M.P. for Maldon 1942–55 and for Barking since 1959. He had been on the editorial staff of the *Daily Express* 1928–43, and was the first editor of the 'William Hickey' column; and as a journalist and broadcaster he contributed to many newspapers and periodicals.

DU CANN, Edward. Conservative M.P. for Taunton since 1956. He was Economic Secretary to the Treasury 1962–3, Minister of State at the Board of Trade 1963–4 and chairman of the Conservative Party Organization 1965–7. Since 1971 he has been chairman of the House of Commons Select Committee on Public Expenditure.

DUNNETT, James. Sir James Dunnett (K.C.B. 1960) entered the Air Ministry in 1936. In 1945 he transferred to the Ministry of Civil Aviation where he remained until 1951. He served at the Ministry of Supply 1951–3, and from 1953 at the Ministry of Transport, becoming Permanent Secretary in 1959. He was Permanent Secretary at the Ministry of Labour 1962–6, and since 1966 has been Permanent Secretary at the Ministry of Defence.

EDELMAN, Maurice. Labour M.P. for Coventry North since 1950. Author of several political novels, of which the best known are probably *Who Goes Home* (London: Hamish Hamilton, 1953) and *Disraeli in Love* (London: Collins, 1972).

FOLEY, Maurice. Labour M.P. for West Bromwich since 1963, and a trade unionist. He was a Parliamentary Under-Secretary at the D.E.A. from 1964 to 1966, when he moved to the Home Office. In 1967 he went to the Ministry of Defence and eventually to the Foreign and Commonwealth Office, where he served until Labour's defeat in 1970.

FOOT, Michael. Labour M.P. for Ebbw Vale since November 1960; he had represented Devonport between 1945 and 1950. A member of the Tribune Group, he was editor of that paper 1948–52 and 1955–60. Author of the biography *Aneurin Bevan* (Vol. 1, 1897–1945, London: MacGibbon & Kee, 1962; Vol. 2, 1945–1960, London: Davis-Poynter, 1973).

FOWLER, Henry. American civil servant. He became Counsel to the Tennessee Valley Authority in 1934; from 1938 he spent the greater part of his career working on economic affairs. He was Secretary of the U.S. Treasury from 1965 until 1969, when he returned to private banking and finance.

FRASER, Bruce. Sir Bruce Fraser (K.C.B. 1961) joined the Scottish Office in 1933; in 1936 he transferred to the Treasury, where he remained until 1960, becoming Third Secretary in 1956. He was Deputy Secretary at the Ministry of Aviation January–April 1960; Permanent Secretary at the Ministry of Health 1960–64; and Joint Permanent Under-Secretary at the Department of Education 1964–5. He became Permanent Secretary at the Ministry of Land and Natural Resources in 1965, and in 1966 became Comptroller and Auditor-General, an office he held until his retirement in 1971.

FRASER, Tom. Labour M.P. for the Hamilton Division of Lanarkshire 1943–67. Joint Parliamentary Under-Secretary at the Scottish Office 1945–51 and Minister of Transport 1964–5. He was a member of the Royal Commission on Local Government in Scotland 1966–9 and of the Highlands and Islands Development Board 1967–70. After leaving the House of Commons in 1967, he became chairman of the North of Scotland Hydro-Electric Board.

GARDINER, Gerald. Lord Gardiner was called to the Bar in 1925 and took silk in 1948. He had long been interested in sweeping reform of the law and in the establishment of a Law Commission. In 1963 he became a Life Peer, and in 1964 Lord Chancellor, holding that office until 1970. Since 1973 he has been Chancellor of the Open University.

GOODMAN, Arnold. Lord Goodman (Life Peer 1965) was the senior partner of Goodman, Derrick & Co., Solicitors, and since 1967 has been chairman of the Observer Trust. He was chairman of the Arts Council of Great Britain 1965–72; and since 1972 he has been a director of the Royal Opera House, Covent Garden, and president of the Theatres Advisory Council.

GORDON WALKER, Patrick. Labour M.P. for Smethwick 1945–50 and for Leyton since 1966. He had been Herbert Morrison's P.P.S. in 1946, and had served as Parliamentary Under-Secretary of State at the Commonwealth Relations Office 1947–50 and as Secretary of State 1950–51. In October 1964 he became Foreign Secretary but was obliged to relinquish that office in January 1965, when he failed to win a by-election at Leyton. In 1967 he became Minister without Portfolio and, from 1967 to 1968, Secretary of State for Education and Science.

GREENWOOD, Anthony. Labour M.P. for Heywood and Radcliffe 1946–50, and for Rossendale from 1950 until he became a Life Peer in 1970. He was a member of the National Executive Committee of the Labour Party 1954–70. He was Secretary of State for Colonial Affairs 1964–5, Minister for Overseas Development 1965–6 and Minister of Housing and Local Government 1966–70. Since 1970 he has been chairman of the Commonwealth Development Corporation.

GRIFFITHS, Jim. Trade union organizer and Miners' Agent since 1916, he represented Llanelly from 1936 to 1970. He was a member of the National Executive Council of the Labour Party 1939–59, and had been Minister of National Insurance 1945–50 and Secretary of State for the Colonies 1950–51. In 1964 he became Secretary of State for Wales, an office he held until 1966.

GRIMOND, Joseph. Liberal M.P. for Orkney and Shetland since 1950 and Leader of the Parliamentary Liberal Party 1956–67.

HALL, Chris. A journalist, he joined the Ministry of Overseas Development in 1965 as public relations adviser to the Minister. From there he transferred to the Ministry of Transport, where he became Chief Information Officer. In 1969 he went to the Ramblers' Association as General Secretary. He is married to Jennie Hall.

HALL, Jennie. She had been Crossman's indispensable personal secretary since 1962; in 1964 she joined his Private Office at the Ministry of Housing and Local Government where she remained until 1966. In 1973 she returned to a full-time career and joined the Private Office of the leader of the Opposition, Harold Wilson.

HART, Judith. Labour M.P. for Lanark since 1959 and a member of the National Executive Council of the Labour Party since 1969. She was Joint Parliamentary Under-Secretary of State for Scotland 1964–6, Minister of State at the Commonwealth Office 1966–7 and Minister of Social Security 1967–8. She became a Cabinet Minister in 1968, as Paymaster-General, and from 1969 to 1970 served as Minister of Overseas Development.

HEALEY, Denis. Labour M.P. for Leeds since 1952, and from 1945 to 1952 Secretary of the International Department of the Labour Party. He was Secretary of State for Defence 1964–70.

HEATH, Edward. Conservative M.P. for Bexley since 1950. From February 1951 to October 1959 he served in the Whips' Office, becoming Government Chief Whip in December 1955. He was Minister of Labour 1959–60, and Lord Privy Seal with Foreign Office responsibilities, which included the direction of the British attempt to join the E.E.C., 1960–63. He was Secretary of State for Industry and Trade 1963–4. He was elected leader of the Conservative Party in 1965 and led the Opposition until 1970, when he became Prime Minister.

HELSBY, Laurence Norman. Sir Laurence Helsby (K.B.E. 1955) joined the Treasury in 1946 and, after serving as Principal Private Secretary to Attlee (1947–50), went to the Ministry of Food as Deputy Secretary (1950–54) and then to the Civil Service Commission (1954–9). He was Permanent Secretary at the Ministry of Labour from 1959 to 1962 and Joint Permanent Secretary to the Treasury and Head of the Home Civil Service 1963–8. On his retirement in 1968 he received a Life Peerage.

HERBISON, Peggy. Labour M.P. for North Lanark 1945–70 and Joint Parliamentary Secretary at the Scottish Office 1950–51. Minister of Pensions and National Insurance 1964–6 and Minister of Social Security 1966–7. From 1970 to 1971 she was Lord High Commissioner to the General Assembly of the Church of Scotland.

HOGG, Quintin (now Hailsham of St Marylebone). Conservative M.P. for Oxford City 1938–50, when he succeeded to his father's Viscountcy. He was Joint Parliamentary Under-Secretary for Air 1945, First Lord of the Admiralty 1956–7 and Minister of Education 1957. From 1960 to 1963 he was Leader of the House of Lords and held various offices, including that of Secretary of State for Education and Science (April to October 1964). From September 1957 to October 1959 he was chairman of the Conservative Party Organization. In 1963 he disclaimed his peerage and stood, unsuccessfully, as a candidate for the leadership of his Party. He was elected M.P. for St Marylebone and represented that constituency from 1963 until he became Lord Chancellor and a Life Peer in 1970.

HOLLAND, Sir (Edward) Milner. A barrister, he took silk in 1948. From 1958 to 1962 he was a member of the Council on Tribunals, and in 1963 was appointed chairman of the Survey into Rented Housing in London. He died in November 1969.

HOUGHTON, Douglas. Labour M.P. for Sowerby, Yorkshire, since 1949. An L.C.C. Alderman from 1947 to 1949, he became widely known as a broadcaster in the B.B.C.'s *Can I help you?* programme 1941–64. He was chairman of the Public Accounts Committee from 1963 to 1964 when he became Chancellor of the Duchy of Lancaster. In 1966 he moved to become Minister without Portfolio and in 1967 he left the Cabinet and replaced Emanuel Shinwell as chairman of the Parliamentary Labour Party, serving until the general election of June 1970. He resumed the office in November 1970.

HUGHES, Cledwyn. Labour M.P. for Anglesey since 1951. He was Minister of State for Commonwealth Relations 1964–6, Secretary of State for Wales 1966–8 and Minister of Agriculture 1968–70.

JAMES, John Richings. He joined the Ministry of Town and Country Planning in 1946, becoming Deputy Chief Planner in the Ministry (now the Ministry of Housing and Local Government) in 1958 and Chief Planner in 1961. He held this post until 1967 when he moved to the University of Sheffield as Professor of Town and Regional Planning. Since 1970 he has been Pro-Vice-Chancellor of that University.

JAY, Douglas. A former civil servant (1941–6), he has been Labour M.P. for North Battersea since July 1946. He was Economic Secretary to the

Treasury 1947–50 and Financial Secretary to the Treasury 1950–51. He was President of the Board of Trade 1964–7.

JENKINS, Roy. Labour M.P. for Central Southwark from 1948 to 1950 and, since 1950, for Stechford, Birmingham. He was Minister of Aviation 1964–5, Home Secretary 1965–7 and Chancellor of the Exchequer 1967–1970. From 1970 to 1972 he was deputy leader of the Labour Party. An author and journalist, his biographies include those of *Sir Charles Dilke* (London: Collins, 1958) and *Asquith* (London: Collins, 1964).

JONES, James Duncan. He joined the Ministry of Town and Country Planning in 1946 and served there and in the Ministry of Housing and Local Government until 1966, becoming Deputy Secretary in 1963. In 1966 he moved to the Ministry of Transport as Deputy Secretary, and in 1970 became Secretary of Local Government and Development in the newly-created Department of the Environment, moving to the position of Permanent Secretary of that Department in 1972. Since 1970 he has been Visiting Professor in Environmental Studies at University College London. He was knighted in 1972.

JOSEPH, Sir Keith. Conservative M.P. for Leeds North-East since February 1956. He served as P.P.S. to the Parliamentary Under-Secretary of State at the Commonwealth Relations Office (1957–9), and as Parliamentary Secretary at the Ministry of Housing and Local Government (1959–61) and Minister of State at the Board of Trade (1961–2). He was Crossman's predecessor at the Ministry of Housing and Local Government, holding that office from 1962 to 1964. In 1970 he became Secretary of State for Social Services at the Department of Health and Social Security. He succeeded to his father's baronetcy in 1944.

KALDOR, Nicholas. Fellow of King's College, Cambridge, since 1949, Reader in Economics, University of Cambridge, 1964–5 and Professor of Economics since 1966. Economic adviser to many foreign governments and Special Adviser to the Chancellor of the Exchequer, 1964–8.

KAUFMAN, Gerald. He was Assistant General Secretary of the Fabian Society 1954–5, and a member of the political staff of the *Daily Mirror* 1955–64. Between 1964 and 1965 he was the political correspondent of the *New Statesman* and in 1965 he moved closer to the Prime Minister as Party Press Liaison Officer. He held this post until 1970, when he was elected M.P. for Ardwick, Manchester.

KING, Dr Horace. Labour M.P. for Southampton from 1950 to 1970. He was chairman of Ways & Means and Deputy Speaker from 1964 to 1965, when he was elected Speaker of the House of Commons. In 1971 he became a Life Peer, with the title of Lord Maybray-King, and he now acts as a Deputy Speaker of the House of Lords.

LEE, Fred. Labour M.P. for Hulme (Manchester) from 1945 to 1950 and since 1950 for Newton, Lancashire. He had been P.P.S. to the Chancellor of the Exchequer and, from 1950 to 1951, Parliamentary Secretary at the

Ministry of Labour. He was Minister of Power 1964, Secretary of State for the Colonies 1966, and Chancellor of the Duchy of Lancaster 1967–9.

LEE, Jennie. Widow of Aneurin Bevan, and herself an M.P. representing North Lanark 1929–31 and Cannock 1945–70. She was a member of the National Executive Council of the Labour Party 1958–70. She was Parliamentary Secretary at the Ministry of Public Building and Works 1964–5 and Parliamentary Under-Secretary at the Department of Education and Science 1965–7. She became Minister of State at that Department in 1967 and held office until 1970 when she took a Life Peerage and the title of Baroness Lee of Asheridge.

LEVER, Harold. M.P. for Manchester Exchange 1945–50 and for Manchester, Cheetham, since 1950. He became Joint Parliamentary Under-Secretary, Department of Economic Affairs, in 1967, Financial Secretary to the Treasury in September 1967 and Paymaster-General in 1969. Since 1970 he has been chairman of the Public Accounts Committee.

LITTLEWOOD, Sir Sydney. A solicitor, he was chairman of the Legal Aid Committee of the Law Society 1946–52 and president of the Law Society 1959–60. He had been legal member of the Town Planning Institute since 1956. He was president of the London Rent Assessment Panel from 1965 until his death in September 1967.

LLEWELYN-DAVIES, Richard. Senior partner of the architectural firm of Llewelyn-Davies, Weeks, Forestier-Walker & Bor, and chairman of the Centre for Environmental Studies since 1967. From 1960 to 1969 he was Professor of Architecture at University College, London, and since 1969 has been Professor of Urban Planning. He became a Life Peer in 1963.

LLEWELYN-DAVIES, Patricia. Married to Richard Llewelyn-Davies. A former civil servant and secretary to Philip Noel-Baker, M.P., she had three times stood unsuccessfully for Parliament. She was director of the African Educational Trust 1960–69 and chairman of the Board of Governors of the Hospital for Sick Children in Great Ormond Street 1967–9. She became a Life Peer, as Baroness Llewelyn-Davies of Hastoe, in 1967, and in 1973 was elected Opposition Chief Whip in the House of Lords.

LLOYD, Selwyn. Conservative M.P. for Wirral, Cheshire, since 1945. He was a Minister of State at the Foreign Office 1951–4, Minister of Supply October 1954–April 1955, Minister of Defence April–December 1955, Foreign Secretary 1955–60 and Chancellor of the Exchequer 1960–62. He was Lord Privy Seal and Leader of the House of Commons 1963–4, and was elected Speaker of the House of Commons in 1970.

LONGFORD, Frank. An unsuccessful Labour candidate for Oxford City in the 1938 by-election, he was created Baron Pakenham in 1945. He was a Parliamentary Under-Secretary of State at the War Office 1946–7, Chancellor of the Duchy of Lancaster 1947–8, Minister of Civil Aviation 1948–51 and First Lord of the Admiralty May–October 1951. In 1964 he became Lord Privy Seal, in 1965 Secretary of State for the Colonies and in 1966

Lord Privy Seal once more, an office he held until 1968. From 1964 to 1968 he was Leader of the House of Lords. On the death of his brother in 1961 he succeeded to the Earldom of Longford, as the seventh Earl.

MACCOLL, James. A member of the L.C.C. since 1936 and mayor of Paddington 1947–9. He had been Labour M.P. for Widnes since 1950 and became Joint Parliamentary Secretary, Ministry of Housing and Local Government, in 1964, remaining there until 1969. He died in 1972.

MACDOUGALL, Sir Donald. A wartime civil servant, in the Statistical Branch, from 1939 to 1945, he returned to academic life at Wadham College, Oxford, in 1945 and remained there until 1950. In 1951 he became Chief Adviser in the Prime Minister's Statistical Branch and since then has held various influential offices, including those of Economic Director of N.E.D.C. (1962–4), Director-General at the Department of Economic Affairs (1964–8) and, since 1969, Chief Economic Adviser to the Treasury and Head of the Government Economic Service.

MACLEOD, Iain. Conservative M.P. for Enfield from 1950 until his sudden death in July 1970. He joined the Conservative Party Research Department in 1948. He was Minister of Health 1952–5, Minister of Labour 1955–9, Secretary of State for the Colonies 1959–61 and Chancellor of the Duchy of Lancaster and Leader of the House of Commons 1961–3. From 1961 to 1963 he was Joint Chairman and Chairman of the Conservative Party Organization, and when the Conservatives returned to Government in 1970 he became Chancellor of the Exchequer for one month.

MARSH, Richard. Labour M.P. for Greenwich 1959–71. He was Parliamentary Secretary at the Ministry of Labour 1964–5 and at the Ministry of Technology 1965–6, Minister of Power 1966–8 and Minister of Transport from 1968 until his resignation in 1969. Since 1971 he has been chairman of British Rail.

MAUD, Sir John. During the war he had served at the Ministries of Food and of Reconstruction, and in 1945 he became Permanent Secretary at the Ministry of Education. He was Permanent Secretary at the Ministry of Fuel and Power 1952–9, and British Ambassador to South Africa 1961–3 and High Commissioner for Basutoland, Bechuanaland Protectorate and Swaziland 1959–63. He was chairman of the Local Government Management Committee 1964–7, and chairman of the Royal Commission on Local Government in England 1966–9. In 1967 he became a Life Peer, with the title of Lord Redcliffe-Maud. In 1973 he became the chairman of a committee of inquiry into local government financial practices and procedures. He has been Master of University College, Oxford, since 1963.

MAUDLING, Reginald. Conservative M.P. for Barnet since 1950. He was Parliamentary Secretary to the Minister of Civil Aviation 1952, Economic Secretary to the Treasury 1955–7, Paymaster-General 1957–9, President of the Board of Trade 1959–61, Secretary of State for the Colonies 1961–2 and Chancellor of the Exchequer 1962–4. He was an unsuccessful candidate for the leadership of the Conservative Party in 1965. He became Home Secretary in 1970 but resigned that office in July 1972 when the Director of Public Prosecutions undertook an investigation into the affairs of the bankrupt, Mr John Poulson. Although this did not relate to Mr Maudling, he explained in a letter to the Prime Minister that he considered it would be inappropriate for him, as Police Authority for the Metropolis, to continue to hold this office, in view of the fact that his name had been mentioned at the hearing.

MOSELEY, George. Crossman's Private Secretary at the Ministry of Housing and Local Government from 1964 until 1966. In 1973 he was an Under-Secretary in the Urban Planning and Transport Division of the Department of the Environment.

NEILD, Robert. He had served on the Fabian executive for several years, and between 1958 and 1964 was deputy director of the National Institute for Economic and Social Research. A former temporary civil servant, he was brought in as an economic adviser to the Treasury in 1964. In 1967 he left to become the director of the International Peace Research Institute in Stockholm, and since 1971 has been Professor of Economics at the University of Cambridge.

NIELD, William. Sir William Nield (K.C.B. 1968) entered the Ministry of Food in 1946 and, apart from two years in the Treasury (1946–9) remained at the Ministry of Agriculture, Fisheries and Food until 1964. He then joined the Department of Economic Affairs and became its Permanent Under-Secretary of State in 1968. From 1966 to 1968 he was a Deputy Secretary in the Cabinet Office, where he returned as Permanent Secretary in 1969. In 1972 he became Permanent Secretary at the Northern Ireland Office. He is now a director of Rolls-Royce (1971) Ltd.

PAGET, Reginald. Labour M.P. for Northampton since 1945. A barrister and an advocate of the abolition of capital punishment.

PANNELL, Charles. A member of the Amalgamated Engineering Union since 1918, and M.P. for Leeds West since 1949. He became Minister of Public Buildings and Works in 1964, an office he held until 1966.

PEART, Fred. Labour M.P. for Workington, Cumberland, since 1945. A schoolmaster, he had been P.P.S. to the Minister of Agriculture in the post-war Labour Cabinets and from 1964 to 1968 was himself Minister of Agriculture. From 1968 to 1970 he was Leader of the House of Commons and Lord President of the Council.

PILCHER, Charles Dennis. Senior partner in a firm of Chartered Surveyors. A member of Hemel Hempstead Development Corporation 1949–56 and of Bracknell Development Corporation 1956–71. He was the vice-president of the London Rent Assessment Panel from 1966 to 1970 and since 1971 has been chairman of the New Towns Commission.

PITT, Terry. He joined Transport House in 1962 and worked on the development of Labour's science policy, helping Crossman with the preparation of the document 'Labour and the Science Revolution' which Harold Wilson moved in his famous speech at the 1963 Scarborough Conference. He became Head of the Research Department in January 1965, when Peter Shore went into Parliament.

PONSFORD, Brian. Crossman's Assistant Private Secretary at the Ministry of Housing and Local Government from 1964 until 1966. In 1973 he was a Principal in the Property Services Agency, dealing with Civil Service Accommodation.

POWELL, Enoch. Conservative M.P. for Wolverhampton since 1950. He was Parliamentary Secretary at the Ministry of Housing and Local Government 1955–7, Financial Secretary to the Treasury 1957–8 and Minister of Health 1960–63.

PRENTICE, Reginald. Labour M.P. for East Ham (North) since 1957. He became a Minister of State at the Department of Education and Science in October 1964 and Minister of Public Building and Works in 1966. From 1967 to 1969 he was Minister of Overseas Development.

RIPPON, Geoffrey. A former mayor of Surbiton (1951–2) and a member of the L.C.C. (1952–61), he was Conservative M.P. for Norwich South 1955–1964 and for Hexham since 1966. He was Minister of Public Building and Works 1962–4. In 1970 he was made Minister of Technology but soon moved to become Chancellor of the Duchy of Lancaster, with responsibility for negotiating Britain's entry into the E.E.C. In November 1972 he became Secretary of State for the Environment.

ROBINSON, Kenneth. Labour M.P. for St Pancras 1949–70. He served in the Whips' Office 1950–54. He was Minister of Health 1964–8 and Minister for Planning and Land, Ministry of Housing and Local Government 1968–9. On leaving Parliament he joined the British Steel Corporation.

ROLL, Eric. Sir Eric Roll (K.C.M.G. 1962) joined the Ministry of Food in 1946 and in 1959 became its Deputy Secretary, having in the meantime spent some years at the Treasury and on various international bodies. He was Deputy Leader of the U.K. delegation for negotiations with the E.E.C. 1961–3 and Head of the U.K. Treasury Delegation in Washington 1963–4. He served as Permanent Under-Secretary at the Department of Economic Affairs 1964–6, when he retired to a career in business and banking.

ROSS, William. Labour M.P. for the Kilmarnock Division of Ayr since 1946. He became Secretary of State for Scotland in 1964 and held that office for the whole life of the Labour Government.

SANDYS, Duncan. Conservative M.P. for Lambeth 1943–5 and for Streatham since 1950. He was Minister of Supply 1951–4, Minister of Housing and Local Government 1954–7, Minister of Defence 1957–9, Minister of Aviation 1959–60, Secretary of State for Commonwealth Relations 1960–64 and for the Colonies 1962–4.

SHARP, Evelyn. Dame Evelyn Sharp (D.B.E. 1948) entered the Home Civil Service in 1926 and spent the greater part of her career at the Ministry of

Housing and Local Government. She served as Permanent Secretary 1955–1966, when she became a Life Peer.

SHINWELL, Emanuel. Labour M.P. for Linlithgow 1922–4 and 1928–31, and for Durham (Seaham, and later, Easington Divisions) 1935–70. He had held various offices in earlier Labour Governments, including those of Minister of Fuel and Power (1945–7) and Minister of Defence (1950–51). He was chairman of the Parliamentary Labour Party from October 1964 until his resignation in 1967. In 1970 he became a Life Peer.

SHORE, Peter. Labour M.P. for Stepney since 1964. He had been head of the Research Department of the Labour Party from 1959 until 1964 and was influential in Party councils. He was P.P.S. to the Prime Minister 1965–6, Joint Parliamentary Private Secretary at the Ministry of Technology 1966–7 and at the Department of Economic Affairs 1967. He was Secretary of State for Economic Affairs 1967–9, Minister without Portfolio 1969–70 and Deputy Leader of the House of Commons 1969.

SHORT, Edward. Labour M.P. for Newcastle-upon-Tyne Central since 1951. He served in the Opposition Whips' Office 1955–64. He was Government Chief Whip 1964–6, Postmaster-General 1966–8 and Secretary of State for Education and Science 1968–70. Since 1972 he has been deputy leader of the Labour Party.

SILKIN, John. Labour M.P. for Deptford since 1963. He was a Government Whip 1964–6, Deputy Chief Whip April–July 1966, and Chief Whip 1966–1969. From 1969 to 1970 he was Minister of Public Building and Works.

SKEFFINGTON, Arthur. Labour M.P. for Hayes and Harlington 1953–72. Joint Parliamentary Secretary at the Ministry of Land and Natural Resources 1964–7, and at the Ministry of Housing and Local Government 1967–70. He was an early Fabian and had held office in the wartime coalition Government and the post-war Labour Government. He died in 1972.

SMITH, Ian. Prime Minister of Rhodesia from April 1964 until November 1965, when the unilateral declaration of independence was made and he became Leader of the rebel Rhodesia Front regime.

SOSKICE, Frank. Labour M.P. for Birkenhead East 1945–50, Neepsend, Sheffield, 1950–55 and Newport, Monmouthshire, 1956–66. A barrister, he took silk in 1945. He was Solicitor-General 1945–51, Attorney-General April–October 1951. He was Home Secretary 1964–5 and Lord Privy Seal 1965–6. He became a Life Peer in 1966, taking the title of Lord Stow Hill.

STEVENSON, Matthew. Sir Matthew Stevenson (K.C.B. 1966) was an Under-Secretary at the Treasury 1955–61; he joined the Ministry of Power in 1961 and became its Permanent Secretary in 1965. He was Permanent Secretary at the Ministry of Housing and Local Government 1966–70. Since 1970 he has been deputy chairman of the Mersey Docks and Harbour Board and, since 1971, a member of the British Steel Corporation.

STEWART, Michael. Labour M.P. for Fulham since 1945. He had held various offices in the post-war Labour Governments, and was Shadow Minister of Housing while Labour was in Opposition. He was Secretary of State for Education and Science 1964–5, Foreign Secretary 1965–6, First Secretary at the Department of Economic Affairs 1966–7. He returned to the Foreign Secretaryship in 1968 and held that office until the 1970 general election.

STONEHOUSE, John. Labour and Co-operative M.P. for Wednesbury since 1957. Director of the London Co-operative Society 1956–62, and its President 1962–4. He was Parliamentary Secretary at the Ministry of Aviation 1964–6, Parliamentary Under-Secretary of State for the Colonies 1966–7 and Minister of State at the Ministry of Technology 1967–8. He became Postmaster-General in 1968 and Minister of Posts and Tele-communications in 1969.

THATCHER, Margaret. Conservative M.P. for Finchley since 1959. She was Joint Parliamentary Secretary at the Ministry of Pensions and National Insurance 1961–4, and was to become Secretary of State for Education and Science in 1970.

THOMSON, George. Labour M.P. for Dundee 1952–72. He was a Minister of State at the Foreign Office 1964–7, Secretary of State at the Commonwealth Office 1967–8, Minister without Portfolio 1968–9 and Chancellor of the Duchy of Lancaster, with responsibility for negotiations with the E.E.C., 1969–70. He was Shadow Minister of Defence after the 1970 general election until in 1972 he accepted Edward Heath's offer of appointment as one of Britain's two Commissioners to the E.E.C. in Brussels.

THORPE, Jeremy. Liberal M.P. for North Devon since 1959. He succeeded Jo Grimond as leader of the Liberal Party in 1967.

TITMUSS, Richard. Professor of Social Administration at the London School of Economics from 1950 until his death in 1973, and the author of numerous books and articles. He was deputy chairman of the Supplementary Benefits Commission 1968–73.

TREND, Burke. Sir Burke Trend (K.C.B. 1962) joined the Civil Service in 1936 and spent the greater part of his career in the Treasury, becoming Second Secretary in 1960. He was Deputy Secretary of the Cabinet 1956–9 and Secretary of the Cabinet 1963–73. He became Rector of Lincoln College, Oxford, in 1973, and a Life Peer in 1974.

WADDELL, James. He joined the Civil Service in 1940 and spent the greater part of his career at the Ministry of Housing and Local Government, becoming Deputy Secretary in 1963. He became Deputy Under-Secretary at the Home Office in 1966 and Deputy Secretary in 1973.

WARD, Frederick. Crossman's Assistant Private Secretary from 1966 to 1968. An Under-Secretary at the Department of the Environment (formerly Ministry of Housing and Local Government) since 1968.

WHITELAW, William. Conservative M.P. for Penrith, Cumberland, since 1955. He was P.P.S. to the Chancellor of the Exchequer 1957–8 and served in the Whips' Office 1959–62 and as Parliamentary Secretary at the Ministry of Labour 1962–4. He was Opposition Chief Whip 1964–70. He was Lord President of the Council and Leader of the House of Commons 1970–72 and Secretary of State for Northern Ireland 1972–4. In 1974 he was made a Companion of Honour for his services in Northern Ireland, and he became Secretary of State at the Department of Employment.

WIGG, George. Labour M.P. for Dudley 1945–67. He was Shinwell's P.P.S. in the post-war Labour Government and an Opposition Whip 1951–4. He was Paymaster-General 1964–7. He took a Life Peerage in 1967 and became chairman of the Horserace Betting Levy Board (1967–72).

WILLEY, Fred. Labour M.P. for Sunderland since 1945. He was P.P.S. to Chuter Ede at the Home Office 1946–50 and Parliamentary Secretary at the Ministry of Food 1950–51. In 1964 he became Minister of Land and Natural Resources; in 1967 his office was transferred to that of Minister of State at the Ministry of Housing and Local Government.

WILLIAMS, Leonard. An official of the National Union of Railwaymen and of the Labour Party since 1920. He was the Party's National Agent 1951–9 and its General Secretary 1962–8. Knighted in 1968, he became Governor-General of Mauritius in the same year.

WILLIAMS, Marcia. The Prime Minister's personal secretary and confidante, who has given her own account of the Labour Government in *Inside No. 10* (London: Weidenfeld and Nicolson, 1972).

WILLIAMS, Shirley. Labour M.P. for Hitchin since 1964. She was P.P.S. to the Minister of Health 1964–6, and Parliamentary Secretary at the Ministry of Labour 1966–7, Minister of State at the Department of Education and Science 1967–9 and at the Home Office 1969–70. She was Opposition spokesman on Social Services 1970–71 and on Home Affairs since 1971.

WILSON, Harold. Labour M.P. for the Ormskirk Division of Lancashire 1945–50 and for Huyton since 1950. He joined the Civil Service in 1943 as an economist and statistician. From October 1947 until his resignation in April 1951 he was President of the Board of Trade. From 1959 to 1963 he was chairman of the Public Accounts Committee. He was chairman of the National Executive Council of the Labour Party 1961–2 and in 1963 he succeeded Hugh Gaitskell as leader of the Party. When Labour won the 1964 general election he became Prime Minister and First Lord of the Treasury; after 1970 he continued to lead the party in Opposition. He published *A Personal Record* of the 1964–70 Labour Government in 1971 (London: Michael Joseph).

WYATT, Woodrow. Labour M.P. for Aston (Birmingham) 1945–55 and for Bosworth (Leicestershire) 1955–70. He was Parliamentary Under-Secretary and Financial Secretary at the War Office May–October 1961. A journalist and director of several companies, including printing companies.

Abbreviations Used in the Text

A.E.U.	Amalgamated Engineering Union
A.F.H.Q.	Allied Forces Headquarters
A.M.C.	Association of Municipal Councils
A.O.N.B.	Area of Outstanding Natural Beauty
B.M.C.	British Motor Corporation
C.B.I.	Confederation of British Industry
C.C.A.	County Councils Association
CENTO	Central Treaty Organization
C.P.O.	Compulsory Purchase Order
C.P.R.E.	Council for the Protection of Rural England
C.R.O.	Commonwealth Relations Office
D.E.A.	Department of Economic Affairs
D.E.S.	Department of Education and Science
D.H.S.S.	Department of Health & Social Security
D.S.I.R.	Department of Scientific and Industrial Research
E.D.C.	Economic Development Committee
EFTA	European Free Trade Association
ELDO	European Launcher Development Organization
F.O.	Foreign Office
G.L.C.	Greater London Council
G.M.C.	General Management Committee
H.A.C.	Home Affairs Committee
I.C.I.	Imperial Chemical Industries
I.L.E.A.	Inner London Education Authority
I.M.F.	International Monetary Fund
L.C.C.	London County Council
M.H.L.G.	Ministry of Housing and Local Government
M.L.F.	Multilateral Force
NALGO	National Association of Local Government Officers
NATO	North Atlantic Treaty Organization
N.B.A.	National Building Agency
N.E.C.	National Executive Committee
N.E.D.C.	National Economic Development Council
N.F.B.T.E.	National Federation of Building Trade Employers

N.F.U.	National Farmers' Union
N.H.B.R.C.	National House Builders' Registration Council
N.I.E.S.R.	National Institute of Economic and Statistical Research
N.O.P.	National Opinion Polls
N.R.D.C.	National Research and Development Council
N.U.A.W.	National Union of Agricultural Workers
N.U.R.	National Union of Railwaymen
N.U.T.	National Union of Teachers
O.D.M.	Ministry of Overseas Development
P.A.	Press Association
P.A.G.	Planning Advisory Group
PESC	Public Expenditure Survey Committee
P.I.B.	Prices and Incomes Board
P.L.P.	Parliamentary Labour Party
P.P.S.	Parliamentary Private Secretary
Q.C.	Queen's Counsel
R.A.C.	Rent Assessment Committee
R.A.G.	Research Advisory Group
R.D.C.	Rural District Council
R.I.B.A.	Royal Institute of British Architects
SEATO	South-East Asia Treaty Organization
S.E.T.	Selective Employment Tax
SHAEF	Supreme Headquarters Allied Expeditionary Forces
S.I.S.	Secret Information Service
S.O.E.	Special Operations Executive
T.G.W.U.	Transport and General Workers' Union
T.U.C.	Trade Union Congress
T.C.P.A.	Town and Country Planning Association
T.L.S.	The Times Literary Supplement
T.P.I.	Town Planning Institute
U.D.C.	Urban District Council
U.D.I.	Unilateral Declaration of Independence
U.G.C.	University Grants Committee
USDAW	Union of Shop, Distributive and Allied Workers
W.E.A.	Workers' Educational Association
W.V.S.	Women's Voluntary Service

Index

22

273; and selection of Banbury candidate, 279–80; and Douglas-Home's resignation, 285; and housing finance, 301–2, 317, 397, 403; and thirty-year rule, 303–4; and coal prices, 304–5, 344, 352; and rent assessment committees, 309, 346, 518, 564, 589; and open-cast mining, 310–11; and Sept. 1965 Special Cabinet, 315–16; and Party relations, 315–16; and liaison committee, 315–16, 326, 330–31, 346, 354, 364, 375–6, 389, 514–15; and positive economic policies, 317–21; and propaganda policy, 324; and housing residence qualification, 327; and A.M.C. conference, 331; and housing allocations, 332 and n, 333, 350, 421; opens Balderhead Dam, 344; and Rhodesia, 344, 349, 355–6, 361, 375–6, 378–9, 599; and housing White Papers, (Oct. 1965) 345, 360, 367, (Nov. 1965) 375–7, 381–3, 387, 401, 564; and Banbury development issue, 350; and amenities at Bladon, 353; and Town Planning Association speech, 353; and legislative programme, 357–8, 498, 505, 511; and County Clerks' Association dinner, 364–5; and planning permission on Canvey Island, 366, 414; public popularity of, 367, 432; and strategy group, 369, 387, 396, 408, 443–4, 538, 581; and prices and incomes policy, 371, 421; and State Opening of Parliament, 374–5; and armed services pay award, 380–82; and sanctions applied to Rhodesia, 382, 392, 395, 398, 406–7; and Rating Bill, 386 and n, 389–90, 394, 620, 629; and Royal Commission on Local Government, 386, 400, 419, 439, 441, 453, 457, 479, 481, 494, 527; and votes for 18-year-olds, 388; and Rhodesia Orders in Council, 389; makes U.N. Association speech at Coventry, 392; achievements of, 393; and Government's weakness over Rhodesia, 393–4; and Nov. 1965 West Midlands Order, 396, 399; and social security benefits, 396–7; and interpretation of the Rent Act, 401, 428, 521; and Second Reading of Rating Bill, 402; and Ullswater preservation, 405, 503, 512,

530–31, 541, 624; and Liverpool housing, 406, 425–7, 433–4; and industrial incentives, 409–10; and planning in Oxfordshire, 410; and Housing Subsidies Bill, 413; and abolition of Territorial Army, 413–15; and Committee Stage of Rating Bill, 413, 445, 450, 457; and G.L.C. house-building, 415; and Dec. 1965 Wilson's Washington visit, 417; and Dec. 1965 Cabinet reshuffle, 418–19, 426; and Local Government Bill, 419, 431, 439–40, 462–3, 515–16, 520 and n, 537, 538–9, 561, 620, 629; and local authority mortgages, 429; and tour of South-West, 429, 454; departmental range of, 433; and Hull by-election, 437–9, 439n; and council-house rents, 445–6, 449, 587–9, 596–8; and option-mortgages, 446, 454, 459, 465–6, 472–4, 491, 507, 620; and Feb. 1966 meeting between N.E.C. and Cabinet, 447–8; and 1966 election manifesto, 449, 454; and Packington Estate, 450–51, 454, 456–7; and Leasehold Enfranchisement Bill, 452, 459; and rating White Paper (Local Government Bill), 454; and defence, 455–6; speaks at Cambridge Union debate, 458; and 1966 election preparations, 461–2, 469–71, 477–8, 480, 482–4; and Report Stage and Third Reading of Rating Bill, 463; and censure debate on Packington, 467–8, 528; and bank rate, 475–6; and election business committee, 477; and housing statistics, 481, 485, 497, 501, 516, 527; and public-sector development, 485–486; and 1966 general election results, 487–90; and 1966 possible Cabinet, 492–5; on holiday, 499, 521–2; and parliamentary reform, 502, 549, 553; and Aintree racecourse, 507; and April 1966 Queen's Speech debate, 507–8; and 1966 budget, 509–10; and S.E.T., 509–10; and Cabinet Committee on Europe, 512–13; and Cabinet Committee on Housing, 514, 535–6, 538, 551, 597; and May 1966 censure debate on housing, 519, 523; and 1966 seamen's strike, 524, 529–30, 537–8, 544, 554; and Government's reputation, 532–3; and Humber